P9-BZC-943

LOVE, SEX,
and MARRIAGE

through the ages

A royal wedding of the late medieval period. (Original print, Bibliothèque Arsenal)

LOVE, SEX,
and MARRIAGE

through the ages

BERNARD I. MURSTEIN

foreword by

WILLIAM M. KEPHART

℔

Springer Publishing Company

New York

Library of Congress Cataloging in Publication Data

Murstein, Bernard I
  Love, sex, and marriage through the ages.

Bibliography: p.
1. Marriage—History. 2. Sex. 3. Love.
I. Title.
HQ503.M85   301.42'09   73-92201
ISBN 0-8261-1460-1

The credits on page 639 constitute an extension
of this copyright page.

à Nellicent

une femme vraiment extraordinaire

Contents

Foreword

"Marriage and morality," writes Dr. Murstein, "once seemed as cut and dried as a package of aged Bull Durham tobacco." He goes on to say that times have changed. He could have added—with little fear of contradiction—that books on marriage and morality have changed too. His own volume is a striking example.

It used to be that works dealing with the history of marriage would include a half-dozen or so standard sources: Howard, Lecky, Calhoun, Goodsell, Morgan, Zimmerman. It was not that these standard sources were "wrong" (though I suspect that in some respects they were), for history is, ultimately, a matter of interpretation. The difficulty was that these sources were selective rather than eclectic.

The same was true of the older anthropological approach to marriage, as exemplified by such writers as Westermarck, Bachofen, Maine, Briffault, McLennan, and Lewis Henry Morgan. These writers tended to marshal evidence to support a specific point of view; hence it was inevitable that they would disagree with one another on major issues.

The upshot was that a great number of derivative books on marriage—using the above works as primary sources—also came to be written from a rather restricted point of view.

Only within the last few years has the perspective been enlarged. On a cross-cultural basis, new journals have appeared—such as the *Journal of Comparative Family Studies* and the *International Journal of Sociology of the Family*. On the historical scene, several new monographs dealing with marriage have been published and one journal—*The Family in Historical Perspective*—is now firmly established.

In the present volume Dr. Murstein has followed the new broad-gauge approach to love, sex, and marriage, but he has gone far beyond any of his contemporaries. In fact, as the thousand-odd footnotes will attest, the scope of his book is enormous. Moreover, he has given us a genuinely original work. Homer, Euripides, Socrates, Ovid, Augustus, Jesus, Paul, Aquinas, Chaucer, Dante, Boccaccio, Luther, Shakespeare, Rousseau, Milton, Ellis, Freud. Biologists, sociologists, psychologists, historians, politicians, psychiatrists. Poets, novelists, playwrights. Public figures and private citizens. In no other book on the subject has such rich and varied source material been employed.

Dr. Murstein's writings on the current psychosociological scene are, of course, well known. As a matter of fact, in the all-important sector of mate-selection, he is probably America's principal theoretician. To his theoretical contributions he now adds the present work, which may turn out to be the most definitive volume on the history of love and marriage ever undertaken.

One final word. Authors write for many reasons: prestige, money, compulsion, a desire to influence others. Every so often, however, a writer is moved for a different reason: he has a genuine enjoyment of his subject matter and wants to share the enjoyment with others. My intuition tells me that this was Dr. Murstein's reason. Whatever the motive, both family students and family scholars are in his debt.

William M. Kephart

Acknowledgments

A book of this scope and size could scarcely have been written without the aid of a considerable number of persons. Fortunately, aid was forthcoming from colleagues and friends in such diverse disciplines as history, sociology, psychology, English, French, Italian, German, Russian, Chinese, Asian studies, government, and religion. I cannot recall them all and regret if any have been inadvertently omitted.

For reading large segments of the manuscript I am indebted to Otello Desiderato, Jerold Heiss, and Nelly K. Murstein. Specific chapters or groups of chapters were read by Thomas M. Ammirati, Richard D. Birdsall, Andrea Lee Buff, Cecile M. Davit, Eleanor and Marijan Despalatovic, Marian E. Doro, Daniel Dudek, Lloyd Eastman, Robley J. Evans, Shirley Feldman-Summers, Lilian M. Greene, Thomas R. H. Havens, C. T. Hu, Sande Jason, Peter Juviler, Eleanore B. Luckey, Betty M. Morrison, Joanne and Robert Proctor, James Purvis, Doreen Quinn, Regina D. Roth, and Denise and Matthew Shafner.

For helpful information and material I should like to thank Charles J. Chu, Alice E. Johnson, John R. MacKinnon, Helen F. Mulvey, Vance Packard, Mason T. Record, Dorothy S. Riley, Gordon P. Wiles, George J. Willauer, Jr., James H. Williston, Susan M. Woody, and J. Melvin Woody.

Professor William M. Kephart graciously consented to write the Foreword. That he patiently waited a year or two beyond the promised date of the manuscript and then responded punctually to our request to send in the Foreword in a very short time earned him a double measure of gratitude.

The entire Connecticut College library staff gave inestimable assistance. While space limitations prevent naming them all, I should be remiss in not mentioning Helen K. Aitner and Eleanor H. Geisheimer, whose aid was invaluable in connection with borrowing and purchasing books and articles used to write the book. Janet Shackford and Marjorie F. Cheatham were so eager to be of service as to win my vote as "the librarians I'd like most to borrow a book from."

The typing was done by a goodly number of persons, including Ceclia Hagen, June Hughes, Fay Bomberg, Karen K. Daniels, Nancy Kriscenski, Betty M. Morrison, S. Danielle Murstein, Doreen Quinn, and Deborah Spiegel. Library, xeroxing, and typing costs were met unstintingly by annual grants from the Connecticut College Faculty Research Fund, for which I am most appreciative.

Ursula Springer somehow found time from her duties as president of Springer Publishing Company and a college professor to read the entire manuscript and offer countless helpful suggestions.

Last, but surely not least, I am indebted to my wife, Nelly K. Murstein, for her cooperation throughout the near-decade of research and writing. By far the most severe critic of my chapters, she was the least critical regarding the inconveniences surrounding the gradual construction of this book; and all this despite her own heavy responsibilities as chairman of a college department and mother. I have tried to convey some measure of my gratitude and esteem by dedicating the book to her.

LOVE, SEX,
and MARRIAGE

through the ages

I

Introduction

This book tells the story of people's involvement—from Biblical days to our times—in the most intimate aspects of their lives: love, sex, and marriage. It is intended for a wide audience, including the intelligent layman, students, and scholars from various disciplines relating to the family.

Our life styles have drastically changed in the past half-century. Mores and beliefs that once formed our attitudes toward love, sex, and marriage are no longer adequate. Science and technology, new economic patterns, and the diminishing influence of religion have brought greater opportunities, mobility, challenges, and problems. A candid, often radical, reappraisal is under way—by individuals, couples, and social institutions.

In the reshaping of our concepts and attitudes on love, sex, and marriage, there is minimal guidance by church, government, school, or community conventions. These institutions have voluntarily diminished their spheres of influence or involuntarily suffered a decline in power. The net result is that in an era where everyone "does his own thing," choice of a domestic life style is increasingly becoming a matter of individual preference.

Marriage and morality once seemed as cut and dried as a package of aged Bull Durham tobacco. In his youth a man slept with a "bad" woman, or visited a prostitute, or masturbated, or, in a few cases, remained virginal and continent. He eventually married a "good" woman and "disappeared from circulation," although in reality he might engage in clandestine adultery. The options for a woman were narrower: she was expected to be virginal at marriage and faithful thereafter.

Today's new life styles are bewildering in their diversity. Indeed, to many young adults the only variation beyond the pale of acceptance is the time-honored clandestine adultery—unacceptable because of its basis of deceit and breakdown in communication. A large number of college students are practicing cohabitation, either on or off campus, as a gratifying alternative to traditional dormitory living. Other variations in living styles—open-ended marriage, group marriage, swinging, and homosexual marriage—though less popular, do not want for staunch advocates.

As to the desirability of premarital chastity, psychotherapists report an ever-increasing number of young clients who are not concerned about "naughty sexual dreams" but rather about why they can't adjust readily to a life of casual sex so prevalent among their peers. It may come as a shock to some readers, but a recent survey of Cornell undergraduates indicated that 90 percent of the women had engaged in premarital sex by the end of their senior year, whereas the figure for men was a paltry 80 percent.[1]

The drastic changes in attitude and behavior regarding sex and marriage styles have been accompanied by a questioning of the viability of the institution of marriage itself. In an era dominated by technology, mobility, anomie, and the loss of moral absolutism, many people feel that the traditional concepts of marriage are as outdated as bustles and pantaloons.

The Women's Liberation Movement, in its goal to end the legal and social discrimination against women, has also attacked traditional marriage as an exploitive relationship, one in which women are consigned to the role of exploitee or, at best, "junior partner." One radical wing of the movement staged a sit-in at a city marriage license bureau, raising the slogan, "Marriage is slavery."[2]

It has been argued that the greatest evil of marriage is that it leads to a family, and that relationships based on blood ties, accidents of birth as it were, tend to have a stultifying effect on interpersonal development and "self-actualization." A contemporary writer cheerfully envisages "the death of the family—that system which, as its social obligation, obscurely filters out most of our experience and then deprives our acts of any genuine and generous spontaneity."[3] Presumably, in a society based on ascribed rather than lineal relationships, an individual will not inherit a full complement of parents and siblings to whom he will be irrevocably attached until adulthood. Instead, he will choose associates whom he perceives as conducive to his personal growth.

Even the traditional argument that marriage is still the preferred means of populating the earth seems to have lost much of its force. Never has the earth seemed less in need of added population. Ecologists are alarmed that Malthus' prediction is soon to be realized, with the number of new mouths to feed far outstripping the world's food supply.

It can also be argued that many other previous functions of marriage, such as education, protection, and economic security, have disappeared or been weakened and that marriage is therefore outdated and should be replaced by a living arrangement more suited to the times. On the other hand, we hear the argument that marriage has not lost its functions but in fact suffers from a surfeit of functions,[4] that is, it has assumed many more functions of an emotional nature. In the more stable and structured society of the past, with its rigid sex rules, married partners were externally oriented and did not have to rely on each other for emotional gratifications that could readily be obtained from friends and relatives. Today's industrial societies, however, are the antitheses of stability and permanence; highly mobile and changing, they force a couple to turn to each other for functions otherwise served by the extrafamilial societal network.

While the concept of love as the primary determinant of marital choice is today accepted as obvious, this was not always the case. A few hundred years ago, love was considered to be independent of, if not antithetical to, marital choice. In the nineteenth century, most spouses were satisfied to be polite to each other and socially compatible, while frequently leading separate lives. Today, vis-à-vis each other, married persons are assuming the roles of lover, therapist, friend, sports partner, and colleague, to name a few. Will marriage survive such demanding expectations? Is marriage obsolete and doomed to inevitable decline, or will it surmount these challenges, as it has managed to do throughout the ages?

It would be foolish to attempt simplistic answers, but at the very least our understanding will be enhanced by examining the historic roots of present-day thinking on the concepts of love, sex, and marriage. How did we arrive at our contemporary mores and regulations? And what projections for the future can we make on the basis of past and present theories, attitudes, and practices?

The dusty files of history show that much which seems at first glance to be novel has many an antecedent. Western sexual mores have their roots among the ancient Hebrews and the early Christians. Some understanding of the purpose and operation of these mores within the context of their origin should lend understanding as to why their viability is being severely questioned. Over the centuries the perception of sex changed from that of a natural function to that of being filthy and guilt-provoking; today we are witnessing an unprecedented return to the former concept.

The communes of the 1960s and 1970s, as another example, were anticipated by hundreds of communes in the United States a century ago. And in 1963, Betty Friedan's *The Feminine Mystique* ostensibly signaled the onset of women's liberation, a movement for parity within the sacrosanct confines of the "man's world." Yet this was no sudden upsurge, for Mary Wollstonecraft's *Vindication of the Rights of Women,* issued in 1792, should be credited with initiating the modern woman's rights movement. In fact, the movement can even be traced back to the ancient Greek and Roman epochs.

Detection of the historical roots and antecedents of our present modes in love, sex, and marriage is the main purpose of this book and has been a major criterion in the selection of its content. A second aim of the study is to provide a sourcebook of information. Several thousand works—both primary and secondary sources—have been combed for data on attitudes and practices regarding love, sex, and marriage, past and present. Nevertheless, in comparison to the wealth of material on the subject, they constitute only a small sample.

My method has been to choose a representative sample of work from all possible sources covering a given period—anything that would aid in describing the attitudes, customs, regulations, and problems regarding marriage. To determine when the sample was sufficiently adequate to describe the period of time in question, I depended on "convergence"—that is, when additional sources seemed to be uncovering very little in the way of new insights and were reiterating earlier materials, I went on to the next time period. In the final chapter, I have attempted to integrate the totality of material and to draw some succinct generalizations.

My principle has been to let the data speak for themselves rather than to advocate a pet theory. By way of contrast, for example, Carle C. Zimmerman[5] devoted an entire volume to an attempt to interpret the history of the family as an endless cycle of three family types. Civilizations, in his view, begin with the "trustee" family, reach their apogee under the "domestic" family, and decline under the "atomistic" one.

In my opinion, shared by others,[6] the faults of such a method outweigh its virtues. The attempt to compress all the data on the family so that they serve a single point leads to the temptation to utilize data which fit the hypothesis while ignoring other data which reject it. Moreover, history becomes little more than a projective technique, a set of inkblots on which the author sees only the interpretation he wants to see while bypassing other explanations. Nevertheless, the approach I have chosen is not directionless. For each of the societies considered, an attempt is made not only to describe marriage customs and regulations but to focus on the society's concept of marriage, the respective roles to be played by men and women in it, and the problems involved in fulfilling these roles.

OUTLINE OF THE BOOK

We start in chapter 2 with a review of theories on the origin of marriage. We then consider the forms of marriage and the validity of the different explanations of the near-universal incest taboo, and close with a survey of the many methods used throughout the world to choose a spouse. Chapter 2, in short, serves as background for an analysis of various societies in subsequent chapters.

Chapter 3 deals with the Old Testament Hebrews, who provided some of the basic ethical roots on which Western concepts of marriage are founded. Chapter 4 assesses the Greeks, in Homer's day and in the Golden Age of Athens and Sparta, as well as the psychological and sociological significance of homosexuality in Greek society.

The effect of empire-building on the Roman family, as it moved from a patriarchal system to an almost anarchical one, is examined in chapter 5. The failure of the Emperor Augustus to stem the tide is heightened by the dissoluteness of his own daughter and granddaughter.

The early Christian period, the New Testament's philosophy on sex and marriage, and the views of such Church fathers as Augustine and Tertullian are the subject matter of chapter 6. "The Middle Ages: The Church and Marriage," chapter 7, discusses two battles: between Church and state as to who will regulate marriage, and within the Church as to whether priests should marry. We shall also read the mathematical formula by which the great ecclesiastical philosopher, St. Thomas Aquinas, concluded that virginity was exactly 3.33 times as virtuous as marriage.

In chapter 8, "Marriage among the Medieval Laity," the love affair of the millennium, that of Abélard and Héloïse, is described, as is the more powerful role presaged for women in Chaucer's "Wife of Bath." "Courtly love," and the songs and poems of the troubadours and Italian and German love poets (chapter 9), provide evidence of the changing marital role of highborn women in the thirteenth and fourteenth centuries.

Chapter 10, "The Renaissance and the Reformation: 1500-1615," which introduces us to the views of Rabelais, Montaigne, Shakespeare, Luther, and Calvin on marriage, also describes how Henry VIII's domestic trials and tribulations affected the history of England. "The Age of Reason and Licentiousness: 1615-1789" (chapter 11) shows the weakening of theological influence on marriage. We see the first serious attempts to change England's marriage laws in order to accommodate the growing demand for individual freedom in choosing or shedding a marital partner. This search for freedom is illustrated through the personal lives and writings of such notables as Charles II, Milton, Pepys, Boswell, Johnson, and Rousseau.

"Romantics and Victorians: 1789-1918" (chapter 12) examines romanticism and the subsequent life style typical of the bourgeoisie: "Victorianism." The activities of the Marquis de Sade and of Leopold Sacher-Masoch (whose names engendered the terms "sadism" and "masochism") are discussed in the light of the strong concern with sex in that period. The leading nineteenth-century writer of sex manuals, Sir William Acton, assures us that the normal woman is insensitive to sex and the man who has intercourse three times a week is doomed to an early demise. Chapter 13, "Havelock Ellis and Sigmund Freud: Philosophers of Sex," covers the lives and theories of the two prominent sex experts of the early twentieth century.

In chapter 14 we cross the ocean to "American Marriage: From the Colonies to the Civil War," where we consider the varying conceptions of marriage brought to America by diverse European groups—from the Puritans of New England to the Cavaliers of the South. We also investigate the love life of a great American leader of the period, Benjamin Franklin, and examine his views of the purposes and functions of marriage, often misunderstood by later writers such as D. H. Lawrence.[7] In chapter 15, extensive coverage is given to the numerous marriage experiments in the United States that marked the nineteenth century: the Anarchists, the Oneida community, and the Mormons, among others.

In chapter 16, "The Dawn of Women's Liberation and American Marriage: 1865-1918," we meet one of the first "free love" advocates, presidential aspirant Victoria Woodhull, alias "Mrs. Satan." We note also the bitter struggle over women's rights and easy divorce that marked the emergence of the "new" woman.

In chapter 17, "Marriage and Love in Contemporary America," we see the onset of the American phenomenon of "dating." Various theories accounting for marital choice are described, including my own theory. Also described is the research into the relationship between marital happiness and number of years married, as well as the status of the married woman today. Chapter 18 deals with the sex explosion in the U.S.A. and traces the impact of Freud and World War I on American sex attitudes and habits, including the findings of such sex researchers as Terman, Kinsey, Masters and Johnson, and others.

Chapters 19 through 22 concern themselves with four societies which have recently undergone profound changes in marriage structures or are in the process of rapid change. Prerevolutionary Russia is compared with the Soviet Union (chapter 19). The tribal agricultural family life of the black African states of twenty and thirty years ago is compared with present-day black African marriage, reflecting the impact of urbanization and industrialization (chapter 20). Finally, both pre- and post-World War II China and Japan are described (chapters 21 and 22).

Utopian marriages, both old and new, are the subject matter of chapter 23. Our coverage ranges from Plato's *Republic* to Robert Rimmer's *Harrad Experiment*. We also examine varying theories of marriage, including those of "doomsday prophets," "functionalists," and "idealists." In chapter 24 we consider modern alternatives and variations in marriage: unmarried cohabitation, group marriage, polygamy, "swinger" marriages, and "gay" marriages. Last, in chapter 25, we scan the major historical trends of love, sex, and marriage, as well as current trends, and close with some predictions about the forms of future marriage.

THE USE OF SOURCES

A book as broad in scope as the present volume presented a problem as to choice of sources. The courageous reader who consults the roughly one thousand cited sources will find that they are more varied than the nationalities once represented in the Austro-Hungarian Empire. They might be classified as primary, secondary, and tertiary; or, more descriptively, as historical-documentary, historical-narrative, biographical, autobiographical, literary, correspondence, empirical studies, legendary, and scriptural.

One factor influencing the use of other than primary sources was the vast scope of the book and the mortality of the author. To have relied exclusively on primary sources would have consumed several lifetimes more than the nine years actually spent on the book.

For some time periods, objectively verifiable descriptions of marriage are quite scarce or sketchy. Moreover, the flavor of interaction between man and wife cannot generally be gleaned from ancient tomes on church and civil law. I have not hesitated, therefore, to use literary sources—novels, poetry, and legends—

which provide much more than a description of the customs and laws of the period. They reflect the value systems of the social strata depicted, as well as their needs, aspirations, and frustrations—factors not readily discernible in laws or customs.

The use of literary, revelational, and legendary sources is more or less inversely proportional to our distance from the period. In dealing with the ancient Hebrews, for example, much reliance is placed on the Bible. For the ancient Greeks, a mixture of legend and reports by contemporary observers of the period and by historians has been utilized. Starting with the Romans, written observations and commentaries became more common, and the period from the Renaissance on is fairly well documented.

Novels are not without value even in the modern period. I have made special use of the utopian novel as a guide to understanding the underlying tensions of societies and as a portent of future change in marital traditions. B. F. Skinner's *Walden II,* for example, was published shortly after the end of World War II, when there were only a few unpublicized communes in the country. Despite its technical shortcomings as a novel, *Walden II* captured the spirit of those disappointed with the contemporary style of life who were searching for something different. Today, there are a considerable number of communes, including several called Walden.

For the current era, there is a marked change in the range and quantity of source material. Since 1930, a multitude of empirical, quantitative studies relating to love, sex, and marriage has appeared in various psychological, sociological, anthropological, and historical journals, and I have not hesitated to use these sources.

In a book covering so much territory and time, generalizations are inevitable. While it is understandable that exceptions could be raised to almost every general statement I have made, a discussion of such exceptions would add considerably to an already voluminous text.

A more serious problem is that the recording of history is by and large not democratic: various economic classes are not represented in proportion to their size, or even given equal weight regardless of size. In general, leaders and the influential and affluent are the subject of historiography, while the "unremarkable" poor go unrecorded. From time to time I have attempted to say a few words about lower-class marriage, but little is known about these marriages, and few writers of the past have deemed them worthy of discussion. This is scarcely surprising, for, until recently, most writers on marriage have been men from the upper or middle class, and many of them have compounded their class bias with a sexist one. For this reason the hostility of many women toward men, however regrettable, may be more easily understood within the perspective of history.

To the prejudices and limitations of past historians I must add my own. Since it was inconceivable to describe marriage in every major culture across time, I have contented myself with a sampling of cultures and time periods for which my language skills (English and French) and the available sources would be most adequate. Not surprisingly, therefore, the book relies heavily on American, British, and French sources in that order. Where works written in English or translated into it were available—as in contemporary materials about the Soviet Union, Africa, China, and Japan—I have had the temerity to deal with marriage in these countries. For more distant historical times this was generally not possible.

When you finish the book, I do not know if you will agree with Heinrich Heine that "the music at a wedding procession always reminds me of the music of soldiers going into battle" or if, like Alfred Tennyson, you will avow that at least some "marriages are made in heaven." Sydney Smith's characterization is probably more accurate: "Marriage resembles a pair of shears, so joined that they cannot be separated, often moving in opposite directions, yet always punishing anyone who comes between them."

REFERENCES

1. E. D. Macklin, W. Jennis, and D. Meyer, "Preliminary survey of study on heterosexual cohabitation among unmarried college students," Cornell University, 1972.
2. S. Brownmiller, *Sisterhood Is Powerful.*
3. D. Cooper, *The Death of the Family,* p. 4.
4. W. G. Bennis and P. Slater, *The Temporary Society.*
5. C. C. Zimmerman, *Family and Civilization.*
6. G. R. Leslie, *The Family in Social Context.*
7. D. H. Lawrence, *Benjamin Franklin.*

2
The Evolution and
Classification of Marriage

The definition of marriage we shall use in this book is "a socially legitimate sexual union, begun with a public announcement and undertaken with some idea of permanence; it is assumed with a more or less explicit marriage contract, which spells out reciprocal rights and obligations between spouses, and between the spouses and their future children."[1]

There are relationships that some might consider to be marriages which do not contain all these elements. Among the Nayar of India, for example, there was no direct public announcement or any ideas of permanence in sexual relationships. Marriage contracts in Israeli kibbutzim (self-contained collective settlements) have varied with the arrangements of the couples: couples who wished to "marry" usually bypassed a public wedding ceremony; they simply applied for a common room. When the woman became pregnant, they were legally married by Israeli law. Recently, however, there has been a trend toward large public ceremonies.[2] Children are raised in communal nurseries and spend most of their time there, except for daily late-afternoon visits with their parents to ensure continuous family interaction. With respect to our definition of marriage, the explicitness of the kibbutz marriage contract is somewhat hazy since it can rest on an understanding between only two people. Further, the responsibilities of parents and children toward each other are not spelled out apart from visitation rights.

The fact that the above-mentioned relationships do not fit our definition too well points to the existence of a broad panoply of male-female relationships and demonstrates that marriage is not as clear-cut a relationship as might appear at first sight. Moreover, it is not universal, for a number of exceptions, such as those we have sketched, are found among thousands of contemporary societies. Our definition probably applies to more than 99 percent of the world's population, and since man is given to countless innovations—both in interpersonal relationships and in technology—a definition that seems to cover so many societies can be deemed adequate. We shall therefore move on to a consideration of how marriage came into being.

THE ORIGIN OF MARRIAGE

Marriage was a firmly established institution when recorded history began a few thousand years ago, and we can only speculate on its origins. When anthropological evidence from the primitive societies began to be systematically collected during the nineteenth century, several schools of thought developed with regard to these origins. The four main theories may be classified as follows: original promiscuity, matriarchy, monogamy, and patriarchy.

Sexual Promiscuity and the Matriarchy

The sexual promiscuity theory holds that, in the distant past, men and women cohabited with whomever they pleased. Ancient Greek and Roman writers have described the promiscuous customs of African and Asian tribes; in more recent times, the Nayar and the Todas apparently practiced promiscuity. In the main, however, the promiscuity theory was elaborated deductively by researchers who considered it a necessary precursor to more developed forms. According to McLennan, Morgan, Engels, Bachofen, and Briffault, the sequence was from promiscuity to group marriage (in which a group of brothers and sisters lived communally), and then to matriarchy.

In *Das Mutterrecht* (Mother-Right), Bachofen[3] tried to explain logically why matriarchy preceded patriarchy. His materials, consisting mostly of ancient myths and the meager anthropological data available in the 1850s, suggested that women had rebelled against promiscuity and then established the marriage relationship, which they then dominated. In the myth of the Amazons, Bachofen saw the establishment of the gynocracy: women headed the family, children took their names from the mother's family, and inheritance descended through women. There came a time, however, when the men rose up and by dint of superior physical strength smashed the matriarchy. By the time of the early Romans a fully established patriarchy was in evidence.

Turning to the societies extant in his day, Bachofen could find few grounds for the belief that patriliny was ever succeeded by matriliny, but many patrilineal societies seemed to contain vestiges of earlier matrilineal cultures. Further, common sense suggested that the association between mother and child was a physical necessity, whereas that of the father and child in early "nomadic" days must have been relatively trivial. The socialist thinkers Engels[4] and Briffault[5] were in full accord with this schema: they saw the triumph of patriarchy over matriarchy as the commencement of the exploitation of women by men.

Attacks on both the promiscuity and matriarchy positions were not long in coming. No study of primitive tribes or of well-documented ancient societies revealed any evidence of promiscuity as a substitute for marriage. Additionally, as the anthropological evidence increased, it became clear that many tribes traced descent by kinship structure rather than by biological birth. The pater, or husband, assumed charge over all children borne by his wife even if he was not the genitor. Another blow to the theory of promiscuity was provided by Westermarck, the Finnish sociologist,[6] who pointed out that prostitutes tended to be relatively infertile; hence the promiscuous would disappear because they underreproduced themselves. Evolution thus gallantly sprang to the defense of the "moral."

The proponents of group marriage, including Morgan[7] and Engels, fared little better. No evidence of any stable society with group marriage could be found, no matter how primitive. The alleged occurrences turned out to be the result of misunderstandings about the significance of events. If Eskimos exchanged wives, for example, it was only under special circumstances. An Eskimo might need to take a long trip, but his wife might be pregnant or nursing a child.[8] He could take the wife of a willing neighbor and, in turn, the neighbor could reciprocate later and take the first man's wife on a trip. These specialized exchanges apparently demonstrate the principle of reciprocity and masculine dominance more than group marriage.

Supporters of the matriarchy theory also found little cheer in the newer anthropological research. The argument that the pater, and not the genitor, was the key figure in tracing patrilineal descent weakened the matriarchal cause as much as it did that of group marriage. Further, Murdock's careful study[9] of 250 societies revealed that several modes of descent were found at different levels of culture, including patriarchal societies that preceded matriarchal ones. According to the matriarchal argument, only the matriarchal society, representing the earlier stage of development, should have been found in primitive preagricultural cultures.

Monogamy

Edward Westermarck[10] and Herbert Spencer[11] championed the idea that monogamy, far from being a derivative of earlier stages, had existed from the beginning of the human race. They believed that man, like the gorilla, must have originally formed single monogamous families which then gradually became larger groupings.

Turning to the emerging science of zoology, Westermarck noted that in many species the male and female remain together after mating until the birth of their offspring. In man, where the infant is unable to minimally care for himself until at least the age of ten, the necessity for parents to stay together would be even stronger. He reasoned, therefore, that an instinctual process accounts for this tendency; and since nowhere do parents desert their young except under unusual conditions, it followed that the principle of natural selection was involved.

According to Westermarck, masculine sexual "jealousy" with respect to access to females—a trait found in many species besides man—must also be a selective factor supporting pair marriage. Furthermore, the primitive tribes' emphasis on premarital chastity must be an instinctual derivation of the pairing instinct, which served the purpose of guarding the pubescent for future pairing. Last, the presence of an equal number of men and women ensured the greater probability that each would find a mate under a monogamous system rather than under a polygamous one.

Desmond Morris, the noted zoologist, also supported the notion of a pairing instinct.[12] In his view, early man, possessing only meager physical strength and crude hunting tools, could survive only by hunting in bands. If only the strongest men kept all the women, the much-needed aid of the somewhat weaker men would not be readily given. Hence each man had to be assured of his woman, and in that way, by selection, those bands favoring pairing would tend to be most effective in the fight for survival.

Despite these arguments, the monogamist position has not wanted for critics. The argument that monogamy is a biological evolvement is difficult to reconcile with Murdock's classification of societies, in which 193 were characterized by polygyny as opposed to only 43 by monogamy.

The same data tend to refute the significance of a one-to-one male-female ratio since this ratio does not seem to inhibit the formation of polygynous societies. Likewise, the concept of "instinct" has found little favor among behaviorist-oriented social scientists. Certainly, no such pairing instinct has ever been demonstrated in the case of man, whose complex central nervous system requires little aid from fixed instinctual responses. In protest fasts and in self-immolation, man has demonstrated no difficulty in ignoring survival instincts when he so desires. It would seem strange, therefore, if he were in the grip of so relatively subtle an instinct as pairing. As to the argument that premarital chastity was symbolic of adherence to pairing, Murdock reported that 70 percent of his societies countenanced premarital sexuality.

Even the primates seemed to turn on Westermarck: more complete evidence indicated that chimpanzees, gorillas, and baboons were not monogamous after all. Though the females might have a favorite stud, they often took sex where they could find it, not blushing even at incest. Briffault gleefully countered that Westermarck had in vain tried to detect elements of Christian morality among apes.[13]

Patriarchy

As far back as 1861, Maine[14] stated that the concepts of matriarchy and private property were irreconcilable, that the matriarchy had never existed, and that the patriarchal state had been prevalent since time immemorial.

Sigmund Freud developed a more imaginative patriarchally oriented theory.[15,16] He posited that in antiquity there existed primal hordes, each headed by a powerful father who kept all the sexually interesting females for himself and drove away his sexually mature sons. But the sons, not to be denied, united, slew, and ate the father. This cannibalistic act had a long precedent in the history of man, where eating a brave animal or adversary was said to enable the consumer to partake of the heroic qualities that the victim had possessed in life. Thus, in eating the father, the sons identified with him. But they were also ambivalent toward him—loving and admiring him for his strength, yet hating him for his power and for his possession of the women. With his death, however, certain guilt feelings ensued. In addition, open competition threatened to break out for possession of the women, with no one of the brothers proving capable of replacing the father. Accordingly, to head off the collapse of their new unity, they developed a taboo of incest to prevent access to the coveted mothers and sisters. This taboo may also have been strengthened by homosexual relationships during the years of powerlessness under the father.

The persistent need to come to terms with their guilt led the sons to search for women outside the immediate environment (law of exogamy) and also to erect a totemic system under which they substituted an animal for the father. They also made amends by proscribing the killing of this animal. It was held that the animal, if properly treated, would confer benefits on the group by providing ample game and crops. During this period, too, in the absence of central power emanating from any single male, a gynocracy was established.

In time, however, the still-unsatisfied longing for the father led to the humanizing of the totems. Both male and female deities appeared.* The presence of the latter is rather weakly explained by Freud as a partial compensation for the gradual transition of the tribe from a matriarchy to a patriarchy. The animals, "no longer high on the totem pole," became mere sacrifices to the powerful gods. At first there was a bevy of gods, all vaguely owing allegiance to a paternal supergod. Gradually, however, the supergod became the sole god to whom all earthly inhabitants owed allegiance.

At the same time, new patriarchs emerged; they bore little resemblance to the former patriarch, for they continued to observe taboos against murder and incest. Eventually, strong patriarchs evolved into chieftains, lords, and kings. The pariarchal system had been transformed into the state, and the primal father had won out because power once again rested in the "father" of the state.

Freud's theory accords with the position of the family in Western Europe as understood during his lifetime. Although it did not agree with all observed societies (e.g., the matriarchal Hopi Indians), a Freudian would doubtless have explained away the anomaly by stating that their evolution was not yet

---

*It is interesting to speculate why matriarchal deities should have appeared prior to the patriarchal ones. In Freud's day, leading theorists like Bachofen and Morgan asserted this on the basis of rather flimsy evidence, and Freud presumably adapted his theory to current sociological belief. Fromm, in *The Art of Loving,* offers a rationale: based on the nature of the mother-child relationship, mother-love may be viewed as all-protective and, most important, *unconditional.* Father-love, he believes, is based on making demands and establishing principles and laws. Father loves those who fulfill the requirements demanded of them. His love is conditional, and is unequally distributed among the offspring in accordance with their ability to fulfill their tasks. At first, the general nomadic character of living, wherein property and material wealth played a small role, was most conducive to the support of an all-giving maternal deity. The rise of property, with its complexities of maintenance, defense, and inheritance, led not only to a patriarchal family but to the projection of a patriarchal deity in place of a matriarchal one. There is, however, no empirical evidence to support any of these conjectures.

complete. More trenchant criticism came from A. L. Kroeber, who considered the theory illogical because the necessity of searching for brides outside the family should have dispersed the family instead of uniting it, as Freud claimed.[17]

Franz Boas questioned whether ethnic phenomena were the simple expression of psychological laws. The content of totemism showed striking differences in various regions of the world. Could such diversity really stem from the same psychological source?[18]

Bronislaw Malinowski asked for more specifics. Was culture present when the slaying took place? If it preceded culture, as Freud implied, how was the guilt transmitted without benefit of a racial unconscious?* Further, he found it hard to believe that a group of young men would voluntarily accept years of sexual deprivation and participate in the group while awaiting the courage to slay the father. He concluded: "It is easy to perceive that the primitive horde has been equipped with all the bias, maladjustments and ill tempers of a middle-class European family and then let loose in a prehistoric jungle to run riot in a most attractive but fantastic hypothesis."[19]

In reviewing the differing concepts on the origin of the family, it must be concluded that there are difficulties in each of them. In addition, the assumption that primitive societies are latter-day representations of earlier family types is highly questionable. "Primitive" societies have gained their appellation on the basis of level of technology; but with respect to kinship protocol, some are far more complex and detailed than the more technologically advanced Western societies. The truth of the matter is that we do not know with even a modest degree of certitude how the family actually got started. We shall, perhaps do better to study the kinds of family for which there is documentation.

FORMS OF MARRIAGE

The forms of marriage may be categorized under three headings: group marriage, polygamy, and monogamy.

Group Marriage

The most tenuous form of marriage is group marriage: several men and women live together, each having sexual access to the others. There seems little indication of this practice having been permanently established anywhere. Rather, it appears to have been an expediency stemming from local conditions or a temporary phenomenon during the transition to other forms of marriage. The Todas, for example, once practiced female infanticide prior to the influence

---

*Freud pondered this criticism a long time and finally, years later, in *Moses and Monotheism,* added the racial unconscious.

of the British in India. The modal marriage was polyandry (several men, often brothers, married to one woman). When the British discouraged infanticide, the burgeoning female population necessitated an adjustment, with the result that occasionally a group of brothers would add wives to the one already shared.[20]

It is not difficult to see why group marriage has not made much headway. It offers no greater variety of females to whet the masculine sexual appetite than does polygyny, but it has the drawback of prohibiting exclusive access. Because incest taboos are practiced by the vast majority of tribes, the number of eligible spouses would be drastically cut even though a male offspring's "sister" might not be biologically related to him at all.

Finally, the difficulty of assigning property rights to individuals under such a system would be formidable. In short, group marriage offers nothing that other forms of marriage could not match, yet it possesses handicaps that are peculiarly its own.

Polygamy

The form of marriage involving multiple spouses of one sex with one member of another sex is called polygamy. We shall first consider the case of polyandry. This form, though rare, has been definitely documented among several groups, including the Todas, Tibetans, Marquesans, Karaites, and Jats. It is often associated with severe economic hardship and with the attendant practice of female infanticide. In certain cases, as among Tibetans and Jats, two or more brothers are married to one wife. Among the Jats, if the father is not sufficiently wealthy to provide a single wife for each son, he secures one for the eldest son and she is expected to—and usually does— accommodate the other brothers. There is apparently little jealousy, and to avoid confusion, when a brother enters the wife's room, he leaves his shoes or hat at the door to serve notice that she is "occupied."

The fact that there is only one wife for several husbands might lead to the assumption that the woman's position was enhanced. This was rare. The Todas, for example, thought so little of women that female infants were alleged to have been put into buffalo pens to be trampled to death.[21] Moreover, the wife did not have her choice of husband-brothers; she had to accept all of them.

Apart from the question of economics, there is little to commend the practice of polyandry in comparison with other forms. It provides no exclusivity of partner and, in societies in which the number of females increased due to male wartime casualties, polyandry would leave many women unmarried. Further, the ascription of paternity would be difficult. The Todas solved this problem by having a meeting in which a brother, usually the eldest, was chosen to "give the bow": by presenting the wife with a ceremonial bow of twigs and grass, he assumed official paternity. All in all, however, this form of marriage has not been popular and is today nearing extinction.

Polygyny. The practice of one husband having two or more wives is called polygyny, often confused with the more general term for multiple marriage—polygamy. The term "sororate" is used where the choice of extra wives is restricted to the sisters of the first wife.

Although more societies practice polygyny than monogamy, the former are much smaller in total population than the latter; moreover, even in a polygynous society, the majority of its members are monogamous. Polygyny has quite a few advantages. Where women outnumbered men, it assured that all women would marry and have the opportunity to bear children—a vital consideration for societies in constant need of warriors and labor. For the woman, overburdened with pregnancies, backbreaking toil in the fields, and a lack of companionship in the home, there were manifold benefits: relief from successive pregnancies, a longer time to nurse her child, someone with whom to share the domestic chores, and companionship.

The husband also benefited: as the men of Angola expressed it, men are "not able to eat always of the same dish."[22] In addition to sexual variety, the taboos of sexual abstinence during the wife's menstruation, pregnancy, and postnatal care could be obviated by turning to another wife. In addition, a man's many wives and children not only furnished a cheap source of labor but represented a mark of status in terms of wealth and potency. Finally, since the strong and the intelligent were most likely to attain the wealth to support more than one wife, from a eugenic point of view the best strains of society tended to be reproduced.

Because of these advantages, it has sometimes been suggested that polygyny should be adopted in Western society. It is one thing, however, to be born into a polygynous society and quite another to attempt a transition from monogamy to polygyny. To share a husband in a polygynous society, where women occupy a subordinate position, may be a blessing to some women. In Western society, which emphasizes equal rights and centers on the companionship marriage, such a move would invoke hostility and jealousy.

There are other disadvantages. The cost of maintaining multiple wives is sufficiently high that most men have only one spouse. Some societies require that each wife be kept in a separate household; and where matrilocal residence is in effect, the husband is in the analogous position of the circuit preacher in America, riding from wife to wife as from congregation to congregation. Further, it is not always easy to manage a number of women. As Linton has wisely said, "Either his wives cannot agree or they agree too well. In the first case he is subjected to multiple conflicting pressures which leave him no peace. In the second, the wives and children tend to form a closed group from which he is largely excluded."[23]

The most serious criticism against polygyny, however, is that it is predicated on unequal rights and is incompatible with the increasing worldwide emphasis on sharing and companionship between husband and wife. What is more, interpersonal closeness, so necessary to this kind of relationship, could surely not flourish on the basis of a husband's weekly or monthly visits.

Finally, it has recently been empirically demonstrated, in an analysis of 500 societies, that monogamy is associated with complexity of society.[24] Since the world is moving in the direction of ever greater complexity, the practice of monogamy should continue to increase, to the detriment of polygyny.

Monogamy

The only form of marriage universally accepted in any society is monogamy. Polyandry has been associated with hard economic times, polygyny with an agricultural economy, and monogamy with industrialization. The advantages of monogamy are easy to see. Imagine the difficulty of a man with 27 wives moving his family and possessions from one abode to the next! A more or less equal sex ratio assures that almost every man who wants a spouse can have one, and this is almost as true for women. It costs less to support one woman than several, and competition among wives is eliminated. While sexual diversity is also eliminated —or, more correctly, reduced (recourse to a mistress or prostitute may still be possible)—for the man there is still a maximum of sexual gratification with a minimum of economic expenditure. Children enjoy the undivided attention and care of *both parents,* contrary to other forms of marriage. The problem of the transmission of inheritance rights and property is far smoother than in any other form of marriage. Most important of all, the emotional and companionate interaction consistent with the concept of sexual equality is easier to achieve.

That is not to say that monogamous societies are problem-free: extramarital affairs, a high divorce rate, boredom, and satiation point up some negative aspects. Moreover, so much is expected of the partner that the effect of marital disintegration due to death or divorce may lead to intense emotional isolation. A possible buffer is parental support—provided they are alive, reside close enough, and are willing and able to act in this capacity. How much of this support the individual may call upon in an emergency may be clarified by distinguishing between nuclear and extended (consanguineal) families.

NUCLEAR AND EXTENDED FAMILIES

The nuclear family consists of a tightly knit group: a husband, a wife, and children. The extended family consists of a diffuse group of blood relatives and may comprise several nuclear families. The father, mother, and unmarried children represent one conjugal family; the married son, wife, and their children, another. The totality, including aunts, uncles, cousins, all stemming from a common ancestor, constitute the extended group.

Prior to the twentieth century the extended family played a much more important role in an individual's life than it does today. When a man married, he often brought his wife to his father's residence (patrilocal) or went to live at the residence of his wife's mother's kin (matrilocal).

Marriage did not affect an individual's primary allegiance to his family. In Euripides' *Electra,* for example, it is Electra's father and mother, not her husband, who are the key factors in her life. Antigone sacrificed herself not for her husband, but for her brother. And in the Chinese family of not too long ago, the son owed his primary allegiance to his parents, not to his wife.

Marriage in the extended family tended to be an arrangement between families, not between individuals, and little attention was given to the sexual and romantic notions of the bride and groom. Consider, for example, the following conversation in an account of French life several hundred years ago: "Father," said the son of the president of Dijon's parliament, "is it true that you intend to marry me to Mademoiselle X?" "Son," replied his father, "mind your own business!"[25]

Property was a paramount concern of the extended family. It remained in the family, and the death of the father or mother did not usually result in its division. In the wealthy extended family, whose members often lived in the same house or nearby, and where the family occasionally numbered 20, 30, 40, and more, the individual and his emotional needs were not crucial. This tended to minimize the involvement of the marital partners in each other, for the extended group could meet every need except sex—and sex for the wealthy man could be satisfied readily enough through a concubine rather than a spouse. As a consequence, the marital relationship had little intrinsic meaning and was largely stabilized through external pressure.

Despite these limitations on individuality, the consanguineal family still possessed certain advantages over the nuclear one. In case of personal tragedy, its members were less dependent emotionally on each other and were better able to bear the bereavement. At the same time, the diffuse support of the entire group was available to the mourner. The family was also likely to provide some kind of work for its members. The elderly were venerated and not regarded as burdens, as was often the case in the nuclear-centered home. Divorce was rare because a network of two families was involved rather than merely two individuals.

Granted that the nuclear family is fragile from a structural point of view, it is, nevertheless, increasingly replacing the extended family in importance throughout the world. One reason is the rising tide of individualism, with its emphasis on each person's right to actualize his own abilities to the fullest rather than sacrifice them "for the good of the family." Obviously, the nuclear family is more able to support this principle than the extended family. Moreover, in the past, the forcing of each individual into an extended family role doubtless provoked strain, but so long as certain benefits accrued to him he might tolerate some discomfort. But, today, the services of the extended family cannot often compensate for the strains it imposes. Thus, the emphasis on physical mobility in the twentieth century, as well as the rapidity with which individuals in the United States change jobs, has caused a rapid breakdown in strong extended family communication and influence.

In the past, the force of social ostracism in small village communities guaranteed some degree of compliance to family tradition: here and there, in very old rural settlements, one still feels the strength of the extended family; also, among the very wealthy, for whom the preservation of social standing, tradition, and lineal descent is a major concern, the extended group still survives. But in the anonymity of contemporary urban life, social visibility is greatly diminished. For the most part, therefore, the nuclear family is supplanting the extended one.

The foregoing discussion is not intended to suggest that the influence of the extended family and, particularly, of the family of origin, is nil. A study of the interaction between the nuclear family and the family of origin in the United States has shown that a considerable amount of financial and personal services are still tendered by the members of each of these families to each other.[26] However, there is little doubt that the formal requirement for these services has greatly lessened and that the influence of the family of origin on its married offspring rests mainly on the quality of the personal relationships.

Having briefly differentiated nuclear and extended families, we shall now examine some of the regulations concerning marriage. Since regulations vary from culture to culture, we shall focus on some that are found in almost all societies: the incest taboo and the laws of endogamy and exogamy.

INCEST TABOO

In its narrowest sense, incest taboo may be defined as "the prohibition of sexual intercourse between the members of the same family who are not married to each other."[27] In a broader sense, Murdock defines it as the prohibition of intercourse "if its participants are related to one another by a real, assumed, or artificial bond of kinship which is culturally regarded as a bar to sex relations."[28] This distinction has been made because the factors accounting for the first definition are not the same or of equal importance as those accounting for the broader definition.

Murdock, in his survey of 250 societies,[29] could not find a single instance in which sexual relations or marriage were generally sanctioned between unmarried members of a family. There were special circumstances when such inhibitions were lifted: the Incas and some Hawaiian kings allowed brother-sister marriage, and the Azande of Africa even permitted father-daughter marriage for a high chief.

More recently, however, there have been suggestions that brother-sister and, to a lesser degree, father-daughter incest have also been countenanced for commoners. Some ancient Iranian and Greek writings suggest that incest was at one time permitted for the general Iranian population,[30] and evidence has been found in Egyptian marriage records that brother-sister marriage was not a rarity among Egyptian commoners during the Roman rule of Egypt.[31] The primary motivation for such marriage apparently lay in the estate laws, which permitted women to inherit property. To preserve the integrity of the estate, therefore, a brother could marry his sister. These rare exceptions do not preclude the conclusion that the incest taboo in the family is practically universal.

Numerous arguments are advanced to account for the incest taboo in the immediate family: instinctual horror, familiarity, genetics, psychoanalytic theory, role disruption, social reciprocity, life expectancy, and learned avoidance.

Instinctual Horror

Hobhouse and his associates[32] believed that each individual instinctively possesses a natural horror of incest. This view, however, does not accord with the cases of incest that come to the attention of most clinical workers. Moreover, psychotherapists have indicated that a solid minority of persons have at one time or another entertained *thoughts* of incest even if they did not put these thoughts into action. We may conclude that there is no firm evidence for the theory of instinctual horror.

Familiarity

Westermarck[33] championed the view that inbreeding has deleterious biological effects on survival. The result among inbred survivors was an innate instinctual revulsion for sex relations with someone with whom they lived closely; the savage mind, as he saw it, was unable to differentiate between biology and propinquity as causes of harmful inbreeding effects.

It is true that habituation often dulls interest. In a study of rats, for example, it was found that males raised apart from certain female rats showed a greater ability to ejaculate when eventually paired with these rats, as compared to when they were paired with rats with whom they were raised.[34] However, the need for variety is not necessarily equivalent to an aversion to one's housemate. The evidence with humans indicates that familiarity more often leads to friendship, and even to marriage, rather than to aversion.

Several hundred years ago, it was customary for European families to arrange marriages and to send a child, when only a few years old, to live with his prospective in-laws. Among the Angmagsalik Eskimos, marriage is also permitted among children who are raised together.[35] Further, individuals reared together are generally bound to have similar values and attitudes. Countless studies on marital choice indicate that individuals marrying tend to be very similar on these variables. Many studies indicate that most individuals will not travel far in search of a spouse: the average person marries someone who lives less than a mile away. Clearly, the propinquity factor as well as value similarity should make housemates quite attractive to each other. The "aversion to similarity" hypothesis, therefore, is without support.

Genetics

The theory of genetic influence on the formation of the incest taboo has had a cyclical history. Westermarck, among others, argued that inbreeding has a harmful effect on progeny, citing a multitude of observations and comments to support this thesis.[36] The first half of the twentieth century saw this viewpoint in eclipse. It was argued that inbreeding simply accented the genetic qualities in the family and thus had an equal probability of being either good or bad. If these qualities were good, inbreeding would assure a superbly healthy race; if they were bad, we had the notorious examples of such crime-prone families as the Jukes in the United States. This line of reasoning appears even as late as 1966 in a standard sociological text on marriage.[37]

It was also argued that even if the effects of inbreeding had been deleterious, they must have been subtle and often delayed, and hence beyond the comprehension of primitive man. Recent evidence, however, has suggested that these views are in error.

First, it must be noted that the supposition that any mutation in gene characteristics has a 50-50 chance of being benign is wrong. The environment, whether cultural or physical, poses specific criteria for the organism to cope with. Organisms that cannot cope with them quickly disappear. Those that remain will themselves undergo mutation from time to time. Since mutations are assumed to be randomly distributed, it is highly unlikely that any given mutation will chance to be adaptive to the environment. Certainly, successful mutations do evolve, but usually at a cost of countless failures before the random arrival of the successful mutation. Where a species can sacrifice trillions of its members without being extinguished, as with bacteria, this is scarcely a problem. In the case of man, with his longer life span and slow reproduction rate, it is quite another matter.

Inbreeding has the effect of raising the homozygosity of resulting offspring and, in approximately twenty generations of parent-child or brother-sister inbreeding, one approaches the asymptote for homozygosity (at each locus all alleles, either of a pair of alternative Mendelian characteristics, are identical).[38] The significance of this fact is that any change in the environment will act against a population that is rigidly incapable of varied biological response to such changes. Genetic variability—the species' way of coping with environmental change—would be drastically curtailed, and fearsome maladaptive consequences would ensue.

Another advantage of heterozygosity over homozygosity is its masking action over lethal recessive genes.[39] Since any new mutation has a high probability of being maladaptive, the emergence of a new mutation through the mating of recessive alleles with recessive alleles is harmful for a species. But this eventuality is much more probable for inbreeding than for exogamous breeding, where the recessives are more likely to be kept in check by the presence of dominant genes.

Another consideration is that polygenes (groups of genes) have been selected over time for their mutual and interactive effects. This genetic homeostasis, however, is disrupted by inbreeding and also results in a loss of adaptation to the environment.[40] As one writer concluded, nature abhors not only a vacuum but also a homozygote.[41]

A great deal of recent animal research indicates that hybrids, as compared with inbreds, have larger litters and greater longevity, and are more resistant to disease.[42] Further, when performance tests are given to adult mice,[43, 44] crossbreeding has a strong buffering effect against noxious stimuli experienced in infancy.

Although the presence of the incest taboo makes it much harder to establish evidence with regard to mankind, data from studies in the United States, France, and Japan are consistent with animal results.[45] Specifically, such diseases and conditions as phenylketonuria, amaurotic idiocy, and albinism show a higher incidence among the consanguineous.

In a study among the Japanese, the offspring of 2,300 consanguineous marriages were compared with those of more than 2,000 nonconsanguineous ones, with possible contaminating influences (such as socioeconomic status) being controlled.[46] While nuclear incest is not represented in the sample, there was nevertheless clear evidence that, regarding fetal deaths, first-year deaths, age of walking and talking, physical stature, neuromuscular functioning, IQ, physical defects, and visual and physical acuity, less pathology was found for nonconsanguineous families.

In a more potent test of consanguinity,[47] the participants in 18 nuclear incest matings (12 brother-sister, 6 father-daughter) were matched with 18 control couples for age, weight, stature, intelligence, and socioeconomic status. After six months, only 7 of the 18 incest cases were found to be nonpathological and fit for adoption. Of the remaining 11, 5 had already died, 2 were mentally retarded and subject to seizures, one had a bilateral cleft palate, and 3 were of borderline intelligence (IQ about 70). The nonconsanguineous children showed only one major physical defect and no deaths, institutionalizations, or severe mental retardation; also, 15 children were ready for adoption.

A review of the evidence strongly supports the conclusion that incest taboos must have a biological basis. While the factor of biological selection does not necessarily presuppose conscious awareness of the consequences of inbreeding in primitive man, we must question the conclusions of earlier writers who sneered at the possibility that primitive man could be aware of the effects of inbreeding. The last study cited shows that dramatic results may be seen in one generation. And when one examines the myths of many cultures, there are many recorded instances of incest being followed by grotesque or malformed births. It seems probable that these myths were in part based on actual observation.

Psychoanalytic Theory

The orthodox psychoanalytic position is that both boys and girls fixate initially on the mother as the primary source of satisfaction. The girl, however, finds her mother to be, like herself, a "castrated" male, so she turns toward the father for her symbolic penis. The result is that the boy and girl develop a sexual attraction toward the opposite sex parent.[48]

The demands of reality check these tendencies, and the child is forced to repress these desires. Since repression does not lead to the disappearance of the unconscious pressure experienced, an unconscious mechanism must be resorted to in order for the individual to be at peace with himself. This mechanism is "reaction-formation," whereby the individual violently opposes the incest he unconsciously desires by tabooing any access to nuclear family women. The origin of this taboo (as conceived by Freud) within the "primal horde" has already been discussed.

The crux of the psychoanalytic argument is that where there is a near-universal taboo, there must be a near-universal desire. But we have noted that it is doubtful that incestuous wishes are universally experienced. Also, many parent-child relationships do not manifest the emotional intensity that is necessarily the residue of a taboo. A Freudian might retort that conscious acceptance of incestuous wishes would be minimal because of the factor of repression. Nevertheless, to argue that a phenomenon exists but that it is, practically speaking, beyond empirical confirmation is to make acceptance a matter of faith rather than of evidence. We shall, therefore, attempt to pick up the thread of the family-disruption hypothesis from a nonanalytical framework.

Role Disruption

Although other animals often function as a group, man's survival and technological progress depend even more on his ability to work cooperatively with others. In the view of Talcott Parsons, the roles assigned to individuals become increasingly specialized as society progresses. Since the family as a group also involves specialized roles, if incest were permitted, the execution of roles would become exceedingly difficult.[49]

Consider the case of father-daughter marriage. A resulting son would be a half-brother of his mother, his grandmother's stepson, his mother's brother's half-brother, and not only his father's child but his grandson as well! Note the problems of identity and exercise of authority: should he act toward his mother as a son or as a half-brother; should the uncle be treated as an uncle or as a half-brother?

Although somewhat less confusing to describe, the confounding of the brother-sister role with that of husband-wife is also inimical to family functioning. The two roles are not identical, for each involves different responsibilities and interests. Further, if the brother and sister were to marry and then divorce, could they readily revert to their original relationship?

Another factor to consider is that the suppression of the sexuality of a mature animal is no simple matter. In the infrahuman world this is no problem. The young are usually self-sufficient and separate from their parents before they are ready to mate. Infrahuman species have so evolved that the more promiscuous are more apt to wander far afield and are thus less likely to come upon a member of the nuclear family and mate with him. Animals which form permanent groups—geese, for example—experience an asexual imprinting that inhibits them from mating with members of the group.

The preparation of a human for independent existence—a slow process—is not completed by adolescence. How is the youth to be kept in the family until he is economically and socially ready to establish his own family? Today he can direct his energies outside the family to some extent, but we can assume that extrafamilial contacts were not so readily available in earlier times. Further, the factors of propinquity and similar values and attitudes would have turned him back toward the family in search of a sexual partner. In that case, to prevent competition for mates and to maintain family unity, a taboo would need to be imposed.

Some data on a role-incompatibility hypothesis have been presented by Wolf.[50] He compared the marriages of a sample of traditional, parent-arranged marriages on the island of Taiwan with an alternate form in which the child is sent at a very young age to the family of his future spouse and raised with the spouse, but the marriage is not consummated until after puberty. Wolf found a greater frequency of extramarital involvement among the participants in these alternate forms of marriage than among the traditional kind. He concluded that the role of brother and sister is inimical to that of sexual lovers.

His study suffers from the fact that a causal relationship cannot be demonstrated between being raised together and extramaritality. The indifference to the spouse, based on observation and interview, seems true enough, but it may have stemmed from resentment at being forced into a marriage as a child without having any say in the matter. Even in a parent-arranged marriage of the ordinary type, the nubile youth, as compared to the child, would probably exercise more influence on his parents' choice through his greater status as a result of age. In the absence of a demonstrated cause-effect relationship, therefore, there are any number of tenable explanations for Wolf's findings.

The argument of role disruption, in sum, has a certain logic; but in order for it to have been important, one must assume that incest actually took place, that it proved eventually to be disruptive and was banned. Most theorists have not made this assumption; yet if it is not made, it becomes difficult to counter the argument that family roles merely adapted themselves to the already existing taboo. Otherwise, to claim that the taboo furthers family unity is tantamount to concluding that mankind grew noses in order to support eyeglasses. Also, family disruption does not seem to have the emotional impact necessary to have instilled the notion of horror and disgust so often associated with incest. I conclude, therefore, that while role disruption may have had an auxiliary importance when tacked onto the biological dangers of incest, it is doubtful that it alone could account for the taboo.

Social Reciprocity

Claude Lévi-Strauss[51] and others[52] have devised a rather imaginative approach to the incest taboo: it is not an attempt to suppress a desire, but rather to make the individual conform to a norm that is vital to group functioning—the norm of reciprocity. Reciprocity, it would seem, is one of the key organizing factors in society.

Within this framework, the prohibition of incest is simply one of the most meaningful ways of honoring the rule of reciprocity by giving up a most valued property—woman.

The value of reciprocity, according to Lévi-Strauss,[53] must have been learned by experience. In the distant past, a family might by chance have contained many desirable women. Other members of the group, despite the availability of less attractive women, must have complained about the unavailability of choicer specimens. In a climate of mounting social tensions, the reciprocity principle must have again served to reestablish a more equilibrated state of affairs. Even though a man may have grudgingly yielded a daughter or sister, he received someone else's in exchange—and he could see the advantage of such an act. In time, the custom became institutionalized as marriage.

The principle of reciprocity seems to make a great deal of sense when it is used to explain many interpersonal transactions. But it fails to clarify why almost every society that ever existed has adopted an incest taboo. After all, reciprocity could be achieved in countless ways. Why should a positive interaction be the objective of a restriction of incest? Modern behavior theory suggests that the inhibition of a desired response does not permanently remove it from the response repertoire; it merely delays its occurrence.

Life Expectancy

Slater advocates a "life expectancy" theory; he suggests that, in prehistoric society, children did not mate with their parents because by the time the former were sexually capable, their parents had either died or were too old and feeble to perform. Eventually, life expectancy changed, but by then the institution of nuclear exogamy was firmly established and "it was functionally impossible to change the institutions that had become enmeshed with it."[54]

It should be noted that we do not know the life expectancy or sexual capacity of ancient man. It seems likely, however, from our knowledge of the increase in life expectancy over the past two centuries, that ancient man's short life expectancy was derived from his vulnerability to infant and childhood diseases rather than to those of adulthood. In any event, Slater's theory does not account for the horror often felt about incestuous behavior, nor for the taboo against brother-sister marriage.

Learned Avoidance

Learning theory plays the key role in Fox's explanation of incest taboo:

> The intensity of heterosexual attraction between co-socialized children after puberty is inversely proportionate to the intensity of heterosexual activity between them before puberty. . . .
> Mutual stimulation during play (tickling, wrestling, exploring, soothing, stroking—all tactile interaction) between brother and sister leads to heightened sexual excitement, which, while nearing climax, cannot be (or rather is not) consummated by a successful act of coitus. The frustration engendered by the lack of tumescence will lead to anger and aggression and the episode will end in pain and tears. This, if repeated often enough, should act as an effective negative reinforcement. Thus, when sexual maturity is reached, each will try to avoid sexual approaches to or from the object of painful sexual experience. Hence one will find "positive aversion" to the sex act between these two actors. In the case of separation during sexual immaturity, there will have been no chance for this conditioned aversion to develop, and yet the other will remain as a stimulus object at the approach and onset of puberty. Thus, the other will provide an object of temptation which the actor has perhaps learned *consciously* to avoid, but to which avoidance has not been unconsciously conditioned.[55]

This fanciful thesis does not accord with the data and biological facts on incest behavior. First, Kinsey has shown that preadolescent orgasm is possible; hence there would be no reason for a certain number of children engaged in coital play not to receive "positive reinforcement." Second, the anthropological data referred to earlier indicate that children raised together can marry without difficulty. Next, Bagley cites evidence that children who indulge in incest will sometimes continue such activity into postadolescence.[56] In addition, the occurrence of sororate and levirate unions is contrary to the theory where there has been childhood interaction prior to the marriage, and the presence of a strong taboo suggests that incestuous desires must be present. To the extent that learned avoidance is a factor, therefore, it must reside in the roles taught to children which effectively *preclude* the serious search for sibling coitus.

Conclusions on Incest Taboos

As might be expected, in the absence of data, there are many speculations about the origin of incest taboos. Most explanations have treated incest as if it were a unitary phenomenon, and have generally avoided the difficulty of explaining why some nuclear family pairings have been more apt to violate the taboo than others.

A helpful classification of incest, based on a review of actual published cases, has been presented by Bagley. These include accidental or disorganized incest (e.g., in crowded, disorganized postwar Germany), pathological incest (where one or both participants are mentally retarded or psychotic), object fixation (e.g., on young girls), psychopathic incest (where no apparent reason for incest exists), and functional incest.

> The essential features [of functional incest] seem to be: 1) a patriarchal family structure; 2) either an isolated rural family or an "introverted" family; 3) a father who is often, though not always, of low economic status; 4) in every case, a wife unable or unwilling to fulfill either her household or sex roles, or both; 5) in every case, the family's relations with the community are poor, or the community is non-existent; 6) in every case, the wife, if she is alive, gives her tacit or open consent to the incestuous union (which is usually father-daughter); 7) the union appears to have the moral approval of the whole family; and 8) the family usually operates smoothly as a functional unit over an extended period of time, the daughter seemingly very happy in the "wife" role—although her long-term adjustment is uncertain if the incest is commenced in the postadolescent phase.[57]

All but the last of these categories is clearly maladjustive. The final category, however, illustrates that no one has an instinctive horror of incest. It must be learned—either by experience (genetic malformation), by role disruption, or by incorporation of the mores of the parents and/or society.

These mores do not condemn incest equally among all possible pairings. The greatest frequency of incest should be found when the most powerful status figure makes advances on the least powerful person. Men occupy a higher status in most societies than women, particularly prepubescent or pubescent girls. Not surprisingly, the most frequently reported cases are of father-daughter incest. No doubt this figure is also enhanced by the possibility that men are more likely to experience interest in sex independent of the quality of the interpersonal relationship.

Mother-son incest should be most rare because, traditionally, a women's sexual being was the property of her husband, and a mother would not develop a fulfilling role relationship with her son that was conducive to sexuality. Brother-sister incest should be relatively facilitated because of the greater opportunities available to siblings, but it might also suffer from excessive habituation (more so than father-daughter incest, where the father was out of the house much of the time) and from the lack of status of both parties. Hence it should occupy an intermediate position in frequency.

In sum, the origin of the incest taboo was probably a function of the observance of the consequences of failure to implement the taboo (with resulting physical malformation of the neonate) and also of role disruption within the family. Individually or in tandem, these factors may be presumed to have been operative in nearly all societies. It also appears logical that if no desire for incest had been present, it would not have been necessary to establish a taboo.

Currently, with the prevalence of contraceptive information, the genetic factor is probably not very influential; however, role disruption still serves as a deterrent, as does the learned belief that incest is "indecent." Adherence to the taboo is also facilitated by the increasing ease of obtaining sexual partners outside the family in the event of spouse disinterest or incapacity.

EXOGAMY, OR NONNUCLEAR INCEST TABOOS

The close bond between the nuclear incest taboo and exogamy is apparent. If the individual could not seek a mate within the family, specific rules had to be formulated as to how far beyond the family he was compelled to go. Exogamous rules, however, have been posited to exist independently of the incest taboo. Emile Durkheim, the French sociologist, has suggested that exogamy stemmed from the primitive fear of menstrual blood.[58] The deflowering of a bride was believed to offend the tribal totem because the supreme totemic being was said to reside in blood; hence no man of the totemic clan might trespass on the spot where the sacred blood fell. Since the totem's power did not extend beyond the tribe's population, however, one might marry an outsider with impunity.

Wilhelm Wundt, the father of psychology, held that exogamy was the cause of incest taboos, not vice versa.[59] McLennan, a Scotsman, believed that exogamy stemmed from bride capture due to a preponderance of men in early tribes.[60] According to Herbert Spencer, the ability to capture a bride became such a mark of prestige that to marry within the tribe became synonymous with a lack of masculinity.[61] To Köhler,[62] exogamy was a diplomatic measure for uniting tribes, whereas Lang[63] viewed it as stemming from the custom of driving the younger brother out of the house in times of shortage, thereby forcing him to secure a wife outside the family.

It is not difficult to demonstrate that no single theory is sufficient to account for the presence of exogamous rules. Contrary to McLennan's view, a shortage of women is found in few tribes. Further, in some societies the husband goes to live with the bride's family. If anyone is "stolen," therefore, it is the husband, not the bride. Spencer's view does not take cognizance of the fact that not all tribes can be conquerors. If one tribe takes women from another tribe with some frequency, the other tribe is forced to look for a still punier tribe. Eventually, however, the one tribe that could not capture another tribe's women would end up endogamous rather than exogamous. Köhler's view not only supposes a natural warlike state but also fails to account for taboos against nonmarital sexual unions within tribes. Lang's theory offers no explanation as to why both elder and younger members of the family are forced to pursue exogamous marriage.

Studies of actual primitive practices do not clarify matters. The taboos outside the nuclear family do not coincide with the proximity of biological relationship.[64] Some societies prohibit the marriages of first cousins; others encourage them. In still others, certain cross-cousin marriages are permitted, whereas others are eschewed. Taboos may extend to adoptive, affinal, or ceremonial relatives who are wholly outside the pale of blood relationship.

It does not seem likely, as was the case with the nuclear taboo, that one or two explanatory principles can account for the myriad variations of nonnuclear taboo. Rather, it would seem that any one of many reasons suffices to explain them. In our earlier discussion, we noted that first-cousin marriages yielded significant but not overly dramatic evidence of genetically damaged offspring. Some groups, but hardly all, may have developed taboos by concluding that if nuclear incest showed a high probability of breeding deformed offspring, first-cousin marriages might also contain some danger. Having once involved the necessity of looking elsewhere for a spouse, this exogamous tendency might be further rewarded by the fact that, in accordance with the reciprocity principle, peaceful relations between groups were promoted.

In some cases, the need to cement family ties might be of key importance to the family; thus, in some matrilineal societies a young man would be expected to marry his maternal uncle's daughter. Since the young man was in line to inherit from his uncle, the latter could simultaneously provide this inheritance and ensure his daughter's security through the marriage. We thereby conclude that the genetic factor plays a small role, if any, in exogamy rules.

Just as societies have rules about whom their members may not marry, they also have rules regarding whom their citizens *must* marry. The limitations may be narrow or extensive; the rules may be formal and institutionalized, or informal and indirect. In contemporary American society, for example, there are no restrictions against religious intermarriage and only a few rapidly disappearing laws regarding racial intermixture. Despite this, we find only a small amount of racial mixing. In addition, religious intermarriage, although it is steadily increasing, is not very high.

Endogamous rules are instituted to keep unwanted people from entering the family or tribe or, by maintaining the group's cohesiveness, to deter any of its members from straying from the fold. Generally, the more stratified the society, the more important it is to maintain endogamous rules. The German Nazis, for example, made marriage to a non-Aryan (Jew, Gypsy, etc.) a severe infraction of the law. Most societies maintain a high degree of endogamy within classes without resorting to legal stipulations. The wealthy generally fraternize only with the wealthy: their children are sent to exclusive schools so that they can meet the offspring of their peers.

MATE SELECTION METHODS

Having discussed the rules and customs of who may or may not marry, let us consider the methods of selecting a marriage partner.

Bride Capture

This method was once believed to be the earliest means of obtaining a bride; the tradition of the groom carrying the bride over the threshold is said to be a vestige of this ancient custom. Several African tribes practice a formalized capture ritual. The future bridegroom surreptitiously observes the house of the bride-to-be in order to determine where she sleeps. His presence is noticed, but not officially. He may then come by in the evening and make off with the obviously willing bride while a family posse takes up the chase, deliberately maintaining a respectful distance.

While this ritual has been interpreted as drawing its inspiration from earlier days when the capture was in earnest, many other interpretations are possible. One could say, for example, that the pursuit dramatizes the family's loss of a household member. Certainly, there is little historical evidence to indicate that bride capture was ever a flourishing activity. True, in cases of conflict, victors often took the women of the losers; but the motives were usually economic or sexual, and the women became either slaves or concubines.

Bride Exchange

In a few societies, the economic loss suffered by a family when a woman leaves to become a bride is compensated by the exchange of a suitable female (often the sister of the groom). The Arab village of Artas, for example, has a saying: "Take thou my sister and give me thy sister."[65] As we have seen, Lévi-Strauss believes this method to have been the inspiration for the incest taboo.

Bride Price

In some societies, a bride price is paid to her father by the groom or by his father. The setting of a price does not necessarily mean that the woman is regarded as a mere chattel. Stipulated rights and privileges are a part of the transaction, and the amount paid is one indication of the status of the bride.

The price is frequently looked upon as compensation to the father for the loss of an economically productive member of his household. In other cases, the bride price has a ceremonial significance and is paid to the father for the care he exercised in rearing his daughter—for example, in preserving her virginity (the fee is sometimes called the "virgin price").

The money also helps to ensure that the wife will be treated humanely by the husband. If she is forced to leave her husband's house because of his cruelty or because he divorces her, he forfeits the bride price. On the other hand, if there is any untoward action on her part or if she should prove barren, the husband may ask for a whole or partial refund on a pro rata basis.

Dowry

Among the nobility of many ancient societies, the custom arose of presenting a dowry with the daughter. It is probable that the importance of the dowry increased as the economic value of woman declined. In some cases this dowry in goods or money became the property of the husband. Later on, however, it often assumed a special status whereby the husband might partake of all or part of it while he lived, but the remainder reverted to his wife if he died. In the event of divorce, where the responsibility was not clearly the wife's, the dowry often returned with her to her former home.

Bride Service

In societies where economic development had not progressed far and money was quite scarce, or where the bridegroom was a poor man, the custom of bride service might supplement or replace the bride price. In return for (or prior to obtaining) his bride, the groom would perform services of a personal or utilitarian nature for his father-in-law. Perhaps the most famous case is that of Jacob, who labored seven years for Laban in order to win Rachel.

Love

It is sometimes made to appear that love was invented by the courtly troubadours of the late eleventh century and became the basis of marriage in seventeenth-century novels. Actually, we can speculate that love, if by that term we mean a powerful emotional passion accompanied by idealization, has existed much longer. However, it seems not to have played a significant role in marital choice because it posed a distinct threat to the existing kinship bonds that defined one's place in society. Marriage, more than today, was a consanguineal affair, not a matter to be trusted to foolish, impetuous youths. Parents reasoned that love, if not blind, was sufficiently myopic to ensure that their offspring, when left to themselves, would rarely pair off in accordance with their parents' wishes. As Goode says, "Kinfolk or immediate family can disregard the question of who marries whom, only if a marriage is not seen as a link between kin lines, only if no property, power, lineage honor, totemic relationships, and the like are believed to flow from the kin lines through the spouses to their offspring."[66]

But we have seen that society was indeed based on kinship lines and that, accordingly, it was incumbent upon society—through its agents, the parents—to control this dangerous passion. There were several means of doing this. I have already referred to endogamous prescriptions limiting the field of eligibles. Another method was to isolate young people from potential mates, psychologically or physically. The former might be achieved by child betrothals, whereby infant children were pledged to each other by the parents. The latter might be achieved by sequestering young ladies under the care of duennas, or female guardians. Later on, in Europe, the convent proved a good protective device to assure the innocence and naiveté of the young lady. This pattern lasted well into the seventeenth century and expired only when kinship patterns could no longer supply the individual with enough benefits to compensate for the restrictions.

To understand the changes that brought this about, the next chapters will examine the expectations regarding marriage in a selected number of societies, starting with the ancient Hebrews.

REFERENCES

1. W. N. Stephens, *The Family in Cross-Cultural Perspective,* p. 5.
2. M. Gerson, *Women in the Kibbutz.*
3. J. J. Bachofen, *Das Mutterrecht.*
4. F. Engels, *The Origin of the Family, Private Property and the State.*
5. R. Briffault, *The Mothers.*
6. E. Westermarck, *The History of Human Marriage.*
7. L. H. Morgan, *Ancient Society.*
8. H. R. Hays, *From Ape to Angel.*
9. G. P. Murdock, *Social Structure.*
10. E. Westermarck, *The Future of Marriage.*
11. H. Spencer, *Principles of Sociology.*
12. D. Morris, *The Naked Ape.*
13. R. Briffault, op. cit.
14. H. J. S. Maine, *Ancient Law.*
15. S. Freud, *Totem and Taboo.*
16. S. Freud, *Moses and Monotheism.*
17. H. R. Hays, op. cit.
18. Ibid.
19. Ibid., p. 224.
20. W. M. Kephart, *The Family, Society and the Individual.*
21. S. A. Queen, R. W. Habenstein, and J. B. Adams, *The Family in Various Cultures.*
22. W. Durant, *The Story of Civilization,* p. 40.

23. R. Linton, "The natural history of the family."
24. M. Osmond, "Toward monogamy."
25. N. Epton, *Love and the French.*
26. M. Sussman, "The isolated nuclear family: fact or fiction?"
27. B. Farber, *Family: Organization and Interaction.*
28. G. P. Murdock, op. cit., p. 261.
29. Ibid.
30. J. S. Slotkin, "On a possible lack of incest regulations in old Iran."
31. R. Middleton, "Brother-sister and father-daughter marriage in ancient Egypt."
32. L. T. Hobhouse, G. C. Wheeler, and M. Ginsberg, *The Material Culture and Social Institutions of the Simpler Peoples.*
33. E. Westermarck, op. cit.
34. J. Kagan and F. Beach, "Effect of early experience on mating behavior in male rats."
35. P. D. Bardis, "Family forms and variations historically considered."
36. E. Westermarck, *The History of Human Marriage.*
37. W. F. Kenkel, *The Family in Perspective.*
38. G. Lindzey, "Some remarks concerning incest, the incest taboo, and psychoanalytic theory."
39. D. Aberle et al., "The incest taboo and the mating pattern of animals."
40. I. M. Lerner, *Genetic Homeostasis.*
41. I. I. Gottesman, "Personality and natural selection."
42. G. Lindzey, op. cit.
43. H. Winston, "Influence of genotype and infantile trauma on adult learning in the mouse."
44. H. Winston, "Heterosis and learning in the mouse."
45. L. Sanghui, *Inbreeding in India.*
46. W. J. Schull and J. V. Neel, *The Effects of Inbreeding on Japanese Children.*
47. M. S. Adams and J. V. Neel, *Children of Incest.*
48. J. C. Flugel, *The Psychoanalytic Study of the Family.*
49. T. Parsons, "The incest taboo in relation to social structures."
50. A. P. Wolf, "Childhood association, sexual attraction and the incest taboo."
51. C. Lévi-Strauss, "Reciprocity, the essence of social life."
52. R. Fortune, Incest.
53. C. Lévi-Strauss, op. cit., p. 28.
54. M. K. Slater, "Ecological factors in the origin of incest," p. 1058.
55. J. R. Fox, "Sibling incest," pp. 132-133.
56. C. Bagley, "Incest behavior and incest taboo."
57. Ibid., pp. 509-510.
58. E. Durkheim, "La prohibition de l'inceste et ses origines."
59. W. Wundt, *Elements of Folk Psychology.*
60. J. F. McLennan, *Studies in Ancient History.*
61. Spencer, op. cit.
62. J. Köhler, "Indisches Ehe- und Familienrecht."
63. A. Lang, *Social Origins.*
64. J. Goody, "A comparative approach to incest and adultery."
65. R. H. Lowie, *Social Organization.*
66. W. J. Goode, "The theoretical importance of love," p. 42.

3
Hebrew Marriage in the Old Testament

Any investigation of marital practices among the Hebrews must depend heavily on the Bible as a source of information. Unfortunately, from a historical point of view, the Bible is not entirely suitable as a chronicle of ancient days. Compiled by a series of editors, its accounts of different epochs from various sources are sometimes welded together into a single time period. The book of Genesis, for example, has three sources ranging from 850 to 400 b.c.[1] The condensing of chronicles from three disparate sources to reflect one consistent viewpoint makes it difficult to pinpoint events with any degree of certainty. To this must be added the difficulty of knowing to which classes the customs described apply and whether they represent the ideal, the atypical event, or everyday behavior. If we add the fact that the Bible has undergone numerous translations and editings, it is little wonder that it leaves much to be desired for use as a chronicle of the times. Yet, despite all its limitations, it remains our chief source of information about the ancient Hebrews.

PRE-BIBLICAL SEMITIC MARRIAGE

The earliest form of marriage among the nomadic Semitic clans is believed to have been the *sadiga* type, whereby the women remained with the clan at an oasis and were visited by husbands of other wandering clans.[2] A regular visitor was considered a *beena;* an irregular one was a *mota.*[3]

One writer has pictured the ancient Semitic wife as more emancipated than modern woman: "In many ways free of restraint; often the head of her family, if not of her clan; usually leaving her maidenhood behind by one or more acts of free love; contracting marriages at will as fancy dictated, but each of which was of short duration; cherished as the mother of her children and the perpetuator of her family; performing the drudgery of nomadic life, but mingling in, even when she did not direct, the counsels of her uncles, brothers, and sons."[4]

Although there is little evidence in the Bible of woman's high status, there are

34

some traces of a matrilineal culture in early biblical documents, indicating that the mother gave her name to children more frequently than did the father (this trend is reversed in the later chronicles).[5]

Abraham married his half-sister Sarah, the marriage being permitted only because they had different *mothers,* whereas siblings with different fathers but the same mother were not permitted to marry. Likewise, Tamar pleaded with her half-brother Amnon not to rape her because the king "will not withhold me from thee,"[6] suggesting that King David would permit them to marry since they had different mothers. Finally, matrilocal residence occurs in the case of Samson, who married a Philistine woman from Timnah and stayed with her family.

Be that as it may, by the nineteenth century b.c., when the Bible reports that Abraham and Lot parted to pursue separate grazing grounds in their nomadic existence, the Hebrew family type was clearly patriarchal in nature. The patriarch completely ruled his household of single daughters, sons (single or married), and their families. He could choose wives for his sons, sell his daughters into slavery, and set aside any religious vows made by his daughter or wife.

MARRIAGE REGULATIONS

Every man and woman was expected to marry at an early age, even priests. The importance of children, repeatedly stressed in the Bible, was undoubtedly due to high infant mortality, ceaseless wars, and the rigors of an ever-mobile people. Marriage took place shortly after puberty for both men and women,[7] and most widowers and widows who had not reached menopause usually remarried.

Endogamy and Exogamy

The Hebrews generally favored endogamous marriages: Abraham married a half-sister; his brother Nahor married a niece; Isaac, Esau, and Jacob married cousins; and Amram, the father of Moses, wed his aunt. Marriage with foreigners (usually women) took place from time to time. Judah and Simeon took Canaanite wives, Joseph espoused an Egyptian, Esau married a Hivite, and Moses was wed to both a Midianite and a Cushite.

The plaint of Samson's parents seems to have been the forerunner of the modern Jewish parent's plea: "Are there no Jewish girls around that you have to marry a Gentile?" In King James English they ask, "Is there never a woman among the daughters of thy brethren, or among all my people, that thou goest to take a wife of the uncircumcised Philistines?"[8]

Intermarriage during this period can be understood in the light of the fact that the tribes of Israel were not very united and, therefore, not very much less strange to each other than they were to neighboring Gentile tribes. Unification and the days of glory under David and Solomon, however, did not change this policy much. David, otherwise most virtuous, slept with Bathsheba, the wife of a Hittite, and then married her after arranging to send her husband into the thick of battle where he was sure to die.[9] Solomon, the son of David, married many "strange women," including Hittites who had earlier been interdicted by Moses.[10]

Royal violations of laws that are strictly applied to the common people did not originate with the Hebrews. However, there is another possibility that may account for the disparity between Moses' interdiction against intermarriage and the actual practice of the Hebrews. Although Moses lived in the fifteenth century b.c., the book of Deuteronomy, which quotes his words, is generally believed to have been written 800 years later, during a period marked by the decline of Hebrew power. The struggles with invading foreign powers and the competition with heathen religious cults resulted in renewed cries for avoidance of marriage with Gentiles. Thus, the writers of Deuteronomy may have slanted Moses' words to explain why Yahweh had seemingly turned against the Hebrews.

The fall of Jerusalem and the Babylonian exile seemed to reinforce this belief. The prophet Ezra commanded that not only should future intermarriage be banned but that all "strange" wives of the Hebrews should be put away.

Rules of Consanguinity

We have noted that because of a desire for endogamy, relatives were not only not forbidden to marry but were encouraged to do so. This policy continued during the entire period of the Old Testament, but some changes were made to reflect changing social conditions. Abraham, for example, married his paternal half-sister, presumably during a matrilineal or transitional period. However, the nomadic Hebrews eventually settled and became an agricultural people with a patriarchal culture, and restrictions were eventually placed on maternal half-sister marriages.

Perhaps to promote intrafamily harmony, permission was not renewed for maternal half-sister marriages. Among nonnuclear family relatives, increasing freedom was given in at least one case for maternal relatives to marry, since these blood ties now counted as less significant than in the earlier maternal period; as a result, marriage to the wife of the mother's brother was permitted, but not to the wife of the father's brother.

Marriage of Priests

As interpreters of Yahweh's wishes to the people, the priests were expected to conduct themselves in a more pious and virtuous manner than their flocks. Accordingly, greater restrictions were placed on their choice of a bride: they could marry neither a divorcee nor a widow (except that of another priest), and only a virgin.

If an ordinary man's wife was captured in war or by bandits, it was assumed that the wife had had intercourse with strangers (apparently with justification in those rough times), either voluntarily or involuntarily. If the wife could *prove* that this was not the case or that she had been raped, she could return to her husband. For the priest, however, the slightest suspicion of his wife's defilement was horrible to contemplate: consequently, if she returned, she was automatically "put away" by her husband.

MARRIAGE CUSTOMS

The choice of spouse was generally made by the parents, with the father's role predominating. The children's veto right could be exercised only by strong-willed individuals like Esau and Samson. That women also exercised this veto power is suggested in Abraham's message to his servant to search out a spouse for his son Isaac from among Abraham's landsmen: "And if the woman will not be willing to follow thee, then thou shalt be clear from this my oath."[11]

Bride Price

The father, having selected a bride for his son, paid the bride price, or *mohar,* generally consisting of 50 shekels of silver. There were alternate forms of payment. Jacob, for example, was too poor, and in lieu of the traditional *mohar* he contracted to work for his beloved Rachel's father, Laban, for seven years. Unfortunately, the wily Laban, true to another ancient custom of marrying off the oldest daughter first, slipped the veiled Leah into Jacob's tent. After the consummation, there were no marital refunds, and Jacob had to toil yet another seven years for Rachel. Happily, because Jacob loved her, his earlier seven years had "seemed unto him but a few days."[12] One may presume that the second seven years passed almost as quickly.

The question might be asked: What do you give as a *mohar* to the man who has everything? When David requested the hand of Michal from King Saul, the monarch had no need of the petty sum of 50 shekels. He did, however—perhaps as a function of his incipient schizophrenia—have a strong desire for David's death, and requested "not any dowry, but an hundred foreskins of the Philistines, to be avenged of the king's enemies."[13] Despite Saul's hopes of seeing his prospective son-in-law slain in battle, the victorious David delivered twice his required "pounds of flesh" to his king.

The dowry, a gift by the bride's father for the bride to take with her, seems to have had less significance. It is mentioned occasionally in the Bible—e.g., when we learn of the gift of handmaidens to Sarah, Rebekah, Leah, and Rachel.

With the acceptance of the *mohar,* the couple was considered betrothed, a state that was legally binding. The next step was the departure of the bride from her father's household and the move to the home of the groom. If the groom's family was wealthy, an extensive celebration was held at their home. If his family was poor, he would simply lead her to his tent to consummate the marriage.[14] When evidence of the bride's virginity (i.e., a bloodstained cloth presented by the bride's parents to the elders of the city) was forthcoming, the bride became a recognized member of the married women's community.

The importance invested in the marital state and in producing an heir is seen in the fact that all married men were exempt from military service during their first year of marriage. The major importance of producing an heir, however, is more readily seen in the levirate.

Levirate

The term levirate referred originally to the obligatory marriage of a man to his brother's widow. Its purposes were manifold. Most decisive was the belief that immortality rested in the continuation of the family line. Accordingly, if a man died without an heir, remarriage of the widow was imperative if her husband's "name be not put out of Israel."[15] The sin of Onan, the levir of Tamar, was not, as is sometimes mistakenly interpreted, that he merely "spilled his seed on the ground." Rather, by refusing to allow Tamar to conceive, he undoubtedly hoped to acquire his brother's property for himself, and for this avarice he was slain by the Lord.

A second, later reason for the levirate was to ensure the preservation of the family property by having the brother assume responsibility for the widow and her lands. Otherwise, her position would have been extremely hazardous, as is seen in the fact that Ruth and Naomi were on the brink of starvation until Boaz, a distant relative, married Ruth in a quasi-levirate act. Last, the levirate allowed for the continuance of ties with the husband's family after his death.

In time, the custom evolved so that it no longer applied where the brother lived at a great distance from the widow. It also became permissible to reduce the duties of the levir if the brother disliked the widow or if he simply preferred to tend his own fields. The prescribed action under such circumstances was as follows:

> And if the man like not to take his brother's wife, then let his brother's wife go up to the gate unto the elders, and say, My husband's brother refuseth to raise up unto his brother a name in Israel, he will not perform the duty of my husband's brother. Then the elders of his city shall call him, and speak unto him: and if he stand to it, and say, I like not to take her; then shall his brother's wife come unto him in the presence of the elders, and loose his shoe from off his foot, and spit in his face, and shall answer and say, So shall it be done unto that man that will not build up his brother's house.[16]

The presence of the shoe here refers to the fact that, symbolically, he who wore shoes on the land possessed the land and, by loosening his shoe, the widow denied him the charge of caring for her lands.

Subsequently the books of Leviticus and Numbers sometimes ignored the levirate, while at other times distinctly forbidding it, as in the dictum, "if a man shall take his brother's wife, it is an unclean thing: he hath uncovered his brother's nakedness; they shall be childless."[17]

A reasonable explanation for the variations in the levirate custom is found in the changing sociological conditions covered in the Old Testament. At first the patriarch completely ruled the family holdings, which included the wife as property. When the oldest brother died, the next oldest succeeded to the family herds and other holdings.

In the changeover to an agricultural economy, the family became smaller and, upon the father's death, the estate first went to the eldest son, but was later distributed among all sons. Under these conditions the religious incentive to "raise up seed to the brother" persisted, but the economic motivation declined. For one thing, since the property was divided among the living sons, no property was attached to the widow of a deceased son. In addition, by the time of the writing of Deuteronomy, women had acquired a measure of legal independence.[18] The invocation of the levirate, therefore, declined greatly with the breakdown of the patriarchal family. It was not officially rescinded until 1869, when the Rabbinical Conference at Philadelphia declared the practice to have lost its meaning and to be no longer binding.[19]

Polygyny and Concubinage

Polygyny was acceptable but not universally practiced among the early Hebrews, due to the rigors of nomadic life and the cost of plural wives. Many of the original leaders of the Hebrew nation had only one spouse: Adam, Noah, Lot, Isaac, Joseph, and Job.

The primary factor in plural marriages was rarely lust. Abraham, for example, was asked by his spouse Sarah to "go in unto my maid; it may be that I may obtain children by her."[20] Jacob, desiring only Rachel, had to take her older sister before being allowed to marry her.

After the Hebrews settled in Palestine and turned to a pastoral-agricultural life, however, polygyny became more economically feasible. Also, the influence of the avidly polygynous Canaanites, who lived nearby, may have stimulated interest in this marriage form. By the time of the monarchy, in any event, the indulgence in polygyny for sensual rather than procreative reasons can scarcely be doubted. Solomon, for example, with 700 wives and 300 concubines, could hardly have been seeking an heir!

The rights of all wives were equal, as is stated in various places in the Bible, and as might be expected from the generally equal social status of the wives.

Next below them in status were the concubines, free women who usually came either as war booty or from the families of less affluent Hebrews. The latter could buy back their daughter if she did not satisfy her master. If the husband tired of her, he could resell her, but not to a foreign master. If he kept her and took other wives, he still had to maintain her in a proper state.

Captive women, usually only virgins, also possessed clear legal rights despite the circumstances that brought them to their masters. They were not to be "touched" for a month while they mourned their father and mother. If they later proved displeasing to their lord, he could still not sell them once they were elevated to the status of concubine.

The slave-wife's social status often did not differ from that of the concubine; legally, however, the former was free, unlike the latter. At the bottom of the hierarchy was the female slave; she lacked both the social status of the slave-wife and the legal status of the concubine. It was rare for Hebrew women to be slaves, and the Bible urges that they be treated as hirelings. In any event, the law required that Hebrew male and female slaves be set free after six years of service.

Despite this legal protection, the biblical description of the outrage against the Levite's concubine, and the clear discrimination against Hagar, the handmaiden of Sarah and concubine of Abraham, makes it clear that the concubine's and slave woman's lots were hardly enviable. With the passage of time, however, the initially strong monogamous disposition of the Hebrews, as evidenced in the counsel that husband and wife "shall be one flesh,"[21] gradually asserted itself and monogamy became increasingly more the rule, until the complete disappearance of polygyny among Jews in the Middle Ages.

THE DOUBLE STANDARD

A strong devaluation of women is expressed in the words of Yahweh in the book of Genesis: "I will greatly multiply thy sorrow and thy conception: in sorrow thou shalt bring forth children; and thy desire shall be to thy husband, and he shall rule over thee."[22] The Bible also refers to men as the "sons of God," whereas women are only "the daughters of men." Again and again, the trespasses of the Israelites in worshiping other gods are symbolically referred to as "the daughters of Jerusalem playing the harlot." Elsewhere, the preacher looking for worthy persons complains: "one man among a thousand have I found; but a woman among all these have I not found."[23] Further, a woman became unclean after bearing a son and needed 33 days in which to purify herself. If, however, she had a daughter, the requisite period was 66 days.[24]

The inferior position of women is illustrated much more dramatically in other incidents. When Lot is visited by two angels, the wicked men of Sodom, unaware that they are angels, cry out for Lot to send the two men out for some homosexual sport. Lot pleads with the mob and, instead, ungallantly offers his two virgin daughters.[25] A similar situation occurs in Gibeah, where a group of rowdies espies a Levite in town and ask his host to send him out. After all entreaty fails, the Levite finally pushes out his concubine. She is violated so repeatedly and harshly that she staggers back at dawn only to fall dead at the door.[26] That the security of a guest in the Mideast was and remains sacred does not explain the fact that *women* are inevitably offered to the mob rather than the male host himself or the male servants.

ATTITUDES TOWARD SEX

The early Hebrews displayed a strong, earthy interest in sex, as evidenced in the sensual Song of Solomon. Indeed, the genitalia of a man were so sacred that when Abraham sent his servant on a mission to seek a Hebraic wife for his son Isaac, he asked him to put his hand under his (Abraham's) "thigh" (euphemism for genitals) and swear to God that he would not lead his son to marry a Gentile.[27]

Further testimony of the inviolateness of the male genitals is furnished in Deuteronomy 25:11-12: if two men fight, and the wife of one, in order to aid her husband, grabs the genitals of the other, she is to have her hand cut off. But the rules governing sexual relations between the sexes were a bit more complicated and detailed.

Fornication

The Old Testament gives no indication that fornication (sex between unmarried persons) is evil,[28] but a number of circumstances would seem to have made this practice rare. For one thing, the Hebrews married quite young. For another, until late in Biblical times, a woman was a man's property: either the property of her husband or, if unmarried, the property of her father. No man could trespass on the property of another without paying a penalty; thus, if a man seduced or raped an unbetrothed woman, he had to marry her and give her father 50 silver shekels. Moreover, because of his sin, he could never divorce her. If her father declined to marry his daughter to the seducer, the seducer had to "pay money according to the dowry of virgins."[29]

If a man found that his wife was not a virgin on their wedding night, he could make a public complaint, saying:

> I took this woman, and when I came to her, I found her not a maid: then shall the father of the damsel, and her mother, take and bring forth the tokens of the damsel's virginity unto the elders of the city in the gate: and the damsel's father shall say unto the elders, I gave my daughter unto this man to wife and he hateth her; and, lo, he hath given occasions of speech against her, saying, I found not thy daughter a maid; and yet these are the tokens of my daughter's virginity. And they shall spread the cloth before the elders of the city. And the elders of that city shall take that man and

chastise him; and they shall amerce him in an hundred shekels of silver, and give them unto the father of the damsel, because he hath brought up an evil name upon a virgin of Israel: and she shall be his wife; he may not put her away all his days. But if this thing be true, and the tokens of virginity be not found for the damsel: then they shall bring out the damsel to the door of her father's house, and the men of her city shall stone her with stones that she die: because she hath wrought folly in Israel, to play the whore in her father's house. . . .[30]

Adultery

In the legal sense, only women were punished for *adultery,* but male adulterers could be severely punished for *violating another man's property.* If a man had intercourse *in the city* with a betrothed or married woman, both were to be stoned to death. If the act took place in the *country,* however, only the man was put to death. It was reasoned that if the woman had, in fact, been raped in the country, she might have screamed and no one would have heard her; thus she was given the benefit of the doubt. In the city rape was considered impossible without her consent, for if she had screamed, aid would have been forthcoming and the rape prevented; hence the death penalty was justified.

If the woman was not a free person (wife or concubine) but a slave, punishment was less severe. The girl received a *scourging,* while the man *gave a ram to the priest* to be offered up in a sacrifice as atonement for his minor peccadillos.[31]

A jealous man who considered himself unlucky enough not to have caught his spouse *flagrante delicto* could still bring matters to a head. He brought an *ephah* (a little more than one-tenth of a bushel) of barley meal to the priest as an offering of jealousy. The priest put the offering in the woman's hand and uncovered her head. Then he took some dust from the tabernacle and put it into an earthen jar containing very bitter holy water that she must drink. If she was innocent, no harm would result; but if she was guilty of adultery, her belly would swell and her thigh rot. At this point the priest took the offering of barley meal from the woman, waved it around, and then offered and burned a handful of it on the altar. If time passed and the woman fell ill in accordance with the curse, her guilt was confirmed. If nothing happened, she was not only declared innocent, but assured that she would very likely conceive shortly.[32] Doubtless this often came to pass when her husband, relieved of his fear of jealousy, would most likely "go unto his wife" at a greater-than-average rate.

Prostitution

The Old Testament offers frequent examples of disdain for harlotry when it compares the sacrilegious behavior of the Hebrews to "playing the harlot" and "going awhoring after false gods." Prostitution, nevertheless, was accepted as a fact of life, especially for the poor who might not be able to afford a wife, a concubine, or a slave. The strong language used against the harlotry of Israel's neighbors is directed more against the religious prostitution in which they indulged rather than against sexuality per se. Such behavior was opprobrious for its religious blasphemy and for its threat of drawing converts from the ranks of Yahweh. This fear is symbolically realized when Yahweh commands the prophet Hosea to marry a prostitute because Israel herself "hath committed great whoredom, departing from the Lord."[33]

Divorce

In early Biblical times divorce was executed by the man simply telling the wife to leave.[34] At other times, the cessation of cohabitation for whatever reason was taken as evidence of divorce and the occasion for remarriage, as in the case of Samson and the woman of Timnah and that of David and Michal. At a later date a formal procedure came to be adopted, as noted in Deuteronomy: "When a man hath taken a wife, and married her, and it come to pass that she find no favour in his eyes, because he hath found some uncleanness in her: then let him write her a bill of divorcement, and give it in her hand, and send her out of his house."[35]

The question of what constitutes "uncleanness" proved a ticklish one, and the argument raged for many centuries. Eventually, much later, two schools arose: the adherents of Rabbi Hillel argued for a "loose interpretation"—almost anything seriously unpleasing about the wife constituted "uncleanness." But the followers of Rabbi Shammai interpreted the term as adultery.

Technically, the only way a woman could obtain a "divorce" was to catch her husband in an adulterous act with another man's wife, as attested by two or three witnesses. In that case, since he was put to death, she became less a divorcee than a widow. If a marriage produced no children, it was presumed to be the woman's fault and she could be divorced.

In case of divorce, a father was invariably given custody of his male children, but girls could remain with the mother if both parties agreed.[36] So long as polygyny was possible, economic means permitting, it was more likely the husband would take another wife or concubine rather than divorce his wife, for Yahweh frowned upon divorce even though he permitted it.[37] To further inhibit divorce, no divorced persons were allowed to remarry each other; aside from this restriction, the parties were free to marry whomever they wished.

Despite divorce laws biased in favor of men, women were not wholly without protection. As noted earlier, a bride falsely accused of unchastity prior to marriage could never be divorced by her husband *if* she chose to live with him. Moreover, we learn in Exodus (21:7-11) that a woman servant (concubine), once betrothed to her master, could not be sold to a foreign land. In addition, if she became betrothed to her master's son, she must be accorded the status of a daughter. Finally, if the master took another wife, he was not permitted to

diminish his concubine's "food, raiment and her duty of marriage. . . ."[38] If he
failed in these responsibilities, she was free to depart. It appears probable,
therefore, that what obtained for a low-status concubine must have surely
existed for a full-fledged wife, and that these circumstances provided the wife
with an indirect means of divorce.

The Model Wife and Husband

The model wife is portrayed in the Book of Proverbs:

> Who can find a virtuous woman? for her price is far above rubies. The
> heart of her husband doth safely trust in her, so that he shall have no need
> of spoil. She will do him good and not evil all the days of her life. She
> seeketh wool, and flax, and worketh willingly with her hands. She is like
> the merchants' ships; she bringeth her food from afar. She riseth also while
> it is yet night, and giveth meat to her household, and a portion to her
> maidens. She considereth a field, and buyeth it: with the fruit of her hands
> she planteth a vineyard. She girdeth her loins with strength, and
> strengtheneth her arms. She perceiveth that her merchandise is good: her
> candle goeth not out by night. She layeth her hands to the spindle, and her
> hands hold the distaff. She stretcheth out her hand to the poor; yea, she
> reacheth forth her hands to the needy. She is not afraid of the snow for her
> household: for all her household are clothed with scarlet. She maketh
> herself coverings of tapestry; her clothing is silk and purple. Her husband is
> known in the gates, when he sitteth among the elders of the land. She
> maketh fine linen, and selleth it; and delivereth girdles unto the merchant.
> Strength and honour are her clothing; and she shall rejoice in time to
> come. She openeth her mouth with wisdom; and in her tongue is the law
> of kindness.[39]

Concerning expectations and desires of Hebrew women with regard to a
husband, the *men* who wrote the Bible tell us nothing. A kind husband and,
above all, an unsuspicious one must have been a boon in a situation where
women held a subordinate role and could be divorced easily or be stoned to
death for inability to produce "proof" of virginity. Since it is well known that
the hymen may be lost as a result of many activities (without actual loss of
virginity), and since hymenal bleeding itself is quite variable, the ability to
convince a husband of one's virginity through verbal means might well have been
a matter of life and death.

CONCLUSIONS

Marriage was of fundamental importance to the Hebrews, and there is ample
evidence of the companionate but subserviant role played by women in
marriage. The fact that on rare occasions some women—such as Sarah, the only

woman accorded the honor of being buried in the caves of Machpelah, and Deborah, the renowned prophetess—could achieve distinguished reputations speaks for some freedom of expression for the Biblical woman.

Actually, discrimination against women was primarily based on rules prescribing their sexual conduct, a crucial factor in a society concerned with family lineage. Since a man's offspring, by his wives or otherwise, were as a rule acknowledged by him and could inherit land except under unusual circumstances, it was not necessary for men to control their own sexual expression. The woman, as a sexual being, was essentially her husband's property. In her nonsexual functions, however, she enjoyed considerable freedom. The Hebrew culture, therefore, represents a forward step in the rights of women when compared, for example, to the traditional Chinese pattern.

REFERENCES

1. R. Smith, "Hebrew, Greco-Roman, and early Christian family patterns."
2. D. Mace, *Hebrew Marriage.*
3. J. Morgenstern, *Rites of Birth, Marriage, Death, and Kindred Occasions Among the Semites.*
4. G. A. Barton, *A Sketch of Semitic Origins,* pp. 58-59.
5. E. B. Cross, *The Hebrew Family.*
6. II Samuel 13:13. (All references in this chapter are to the King James Version of the Bible.)
7. R. H. Kennett, *Ancient Hebrew Social Life and Custom.*
8. Judges 14:3.
9. II Samuel 11.
10. Deuteronomy 7:1-3.
11. Genesis 24:8.
12. Genesis 29:20.
13. I Samuel 18:25.
14. R. Patai, *Sex and Family in the Bible and the Middle East.*
15. Deuteronomy 25:6.
16. Deuteronomy 25:7-9.
17. Leviticus 20:21.
18. L. M. Epstein, *Marriage Laws in the Bible and the Talmud.*
19. M. Mielziner, *The Jewish Law of Marriage and Divorce in Ancient and Modern Times.*
20. Genesis 16:2.
21. Genesis 2:24.
22. Genesis 3:16.
23. Ecclesiastes 7:28.
24. Leviticus 12:5.
25. Genesis 19:1-8.
26. Judges 19.
27. Genesis 24:2-4.
28. L. M. Epstein, *Sex Laws and Customs in Judaism.*

29. Exodus 22:17.
30. Deuteronomy 22:14-21.
31. Leviticus 19:20-21.
32. Numbers 5:11-28.
33. Hosea 1:2.
34. W. G. Cole, *Sex and Love in the Bible.*
35. Deuteronomy 24:1.
36. D. Mace, op. cit.
37. Malachi 2:16.
38. Exodus 21:10.
39. Proverbs 31:10-26.

4

Marriage among the Greeks

"He's married, I tell you!" says a character in one forgotten play. "What's that you say?" replies the other. "He's really married?—but I just left him alive and well."[1] This misogamistic attitude was far from atypical among the upper classes in Greece's Golden Age in the fifth century b.c. How it came to be that way is the subject matter of this chapter.

HOMERIC GREECE

Much of our knowledge about the Greece of antiquity (approximately 1200-750 b.c.) stems from the *Iliad* and the *Odyssey,* traditionally attributed to Homer. His works concern themselves with the Trojan War (1194 b.c.) and its aftermath, and depict the customs of the Greece of his day (eighth century b.c.) integrated with a description of earlier events associated with the war with Troy.

It was a period of frequent wars in which Greek society was relatively unstratified, comprising mostly freemen and few slaves. As is true of many primitive cultures where a daughter is a highly valued economic commodity, marriage in Homer's Greece required a bride price to be paid by the groom to her father. On occasion, since strength and courage were essential traits in that warring, unsettled age, the father might hold contests to screen out physically weak or fainthearted suitors.

Although polygyny had been part of the traditions of the past, by the time of the Trojan wars the Greek kings had only one wife but enjoyed varying numbers of concubines. Priam of Troy, it is true, is reported to have had more than 60 offspring, but he was a monarch of Eastern custom and not a Greek.

In a society composed largely of self-sufficient family units,[2] the formality of the marriage ceremony and the legality of offspring were not major considerations. Marriage tended to be de facto: those who lived together were considered married, and the distinction between wife and concubine was a fine one. Under the circumstances, the bastard was not the victim of discrimination, the good right arm of a "natural" son being valued more than his pedigree; thus, when Helen bore Menelaus no sons, he obtained one via a slave concubine, and this son was fully entitled to inherit his father's crown.[3]

47

The position of woman was subservient to that of man: she had no say in the choice of marital partner; she was a purchase and, as chattel, could be traded or lent. Whereas she was expected to be as faithful as was the noble Penelope, the husband, as typified by Odysseus, engaged in numerous affairs. She was permitted to leave the house only if attended by maids, but she played an important role in rearing the children, preparing food, and supervising the household. Most important, her valued role was recognized by her spouse and, despite barrenness and even adultery (as in the case of Helen), her husband rarely divorced her.

The nature of the relationship is well illustrated in the *Odyssey*. After countless trials and tribulations, Odysseus returns twenty years after his departure. Having performed "their bed-rites in the old fashion," he and Penelope are depicted as a model of easy communication between husband and wife: "After the first thrill of love has passed, the pair began to exchange histories for mutual entertainment, the fairest of women telling what she had put up with in the house, watching the suitors' greedy swarming, and the multitudinous sheep and cattle they slew for the sake of her, and all the broached jars of wine; while heaven-born Odysseus told of every hurt he had done to others and the woes he himself had suffered, detailing thing by thing; and eagerly she heard him, slumber never weighing down her eyelids until all was told."[4]

The *Iliad*[5] and *Odyssey*[6] reveal a comradeship between husband and wife that undoubtedly stemmed from a clearly defined, valued role for both sexes. Both books make clear, nonetheless, that the woman's position was inferior. Telemachus, the son of Odysseus, dismisses his mother when he wishes to call an assembly. When Menelaus takes Helen back as his wife after the fall of Troy, her inferior status is reflected. Despite her beauty, such an act would not have been possible in the Greece of Pericles, some years later, when the shame of being deceived would have necessitated at least a divorce.

Helen, for her part, expresses an attitude toward infidelity more typical of later Greek thinking. She does not love Paris. Her mind is, in fact, moved much more by the noble Hector. Yet Paris is too handsome to resist, and despite her lack of respect for his character, she lusts for his body. This sharply drawn division of sexuality and love of the soul (Aphrodite *Pandemos* as opposed to Aphrodite *Urania*) was to characterize Greek thinking in future years.

Hesiod, the eighth-century writer, saw marriage as unfortunately necessary to preserve the race and to rely on for support in old age. But he had no doubt that women were more useful for work than as marital partners. In *Works and Days,* he advised, "First of all get yourself an ox for plowing, and a woman for work, —not to marry— one who can plow with the oxen."[7]

In sum, Homeric Greece depicted a period of expansion in which the Greeks rapidly changed from a rough-hewn culture of hardworking freemen to an era of upper-class refinement and leisure made possible by the acquisition of slaves. The Homeric woman, despite her inferior position vis-à-vis her husband, exerted a considerable influence on the family by virtue of her solid economic contribution to the household.

ATHENS AND GREECE'S "GOLDEN AGE"

The Family

As we move into the period between the sixth and the beginning of the fourth century b.c., information on Athenian marriages becomes more plentiful. The father was the most powerful figure in the family, and each male child, as a potential father, was accorded special status from birth. Finances permitting, boys learned to read and write, and acquired what formal knowledge was available at one of the philosophic schools.

A father had the right to expose a newborn child to the elements so that it would die. He could also choose his children's spouses without consulting them. His children owed him the filial piety due a god.[8] With the influx of slaves, he could devote himself wholly to the games, to preparation for war, and to philosophical discourse with Socrates or other leading scholars. In the main, he avoided manual labor.

Woman, contrariwise, suffered a progressive erosion of her rights after Homeric days. She had never had any kind of formal education, but in Homer's time had been highly skilled at such household arts as grinding grain, carding wool, spinning, weaving, and embroidering. She rarely sewed, for few clothes had seams, and she did little cooking because this was a male prerogative. But she worked hard, since there were few and primitive household utensils, just feeding and clothing her family. With the burgeoning supply of slaves, who outnumbered Athenian citizens by 25 or 30 to 1, there was little need for the Athenian citizeness to sully her hands in work. All she had to do was supervise the servants and bear children. Reduced to a combination head servant and broodmare, she became the victim of the Eastern habit of secluding women, a custom that presumably originated in the last migrations from the Near East to Ionia and thence to Attica.[9]

As a result of her new status, she could not go out into the streets unless veiled, and then only for festivals, special purchases, religious occasions, and to the tragedies but not the comedies.[10,11] Otherwise, she was shut up in her apartments and could not even be seen at a window. When her husband had guests, she could not dine with them as in earlier days, nor could she go from one apartment to another without permission. It was considered good breeding for men not to speak of their wives outside of their house. Thucydides observed that the use of the name of an honorable woman, like her person, should be restricted to her home.[12]

The laws, however, restricted much more than the wife's person. They told her that she had to wear simple, heavy clothing that hung properly. Failure to comply meant payment of a fine.[13] She was not allowed to make contracts, incur more than petty debts, or even bring a legal suit of any kind. The lawgiver Solon stated that anything done under the influence of a woman was without legal standing.

Her role in childbirth was viewed by Aristotle[14] as only that of a carrier for man's precious seed. She was also inferior to men in that she contained less "vital" heat, which meant that, unlike men, she could not produce semen, but only an inferior concoction—menstrual blood. The implication, therefore, was that her inferiority was genetic and not susceptible to environmental modification.

If her husband died, she could not inherit his property and was at the mercy of the son or nearest male relative.[15] If she had brought a substantial dowry, she could stay on because to send her back to her kinsmen meant returning the dowry. Without the support of a dowry, she had few prospects. In fact, testimony to her insignificance is found in two legal speeches in which the orators went to great lengths to prove that the women in their cases actually *had existed* rather than being merely legal inventions.[16]

In sum, the wife was respected if she performed her duties as supervisor of the household staff, and she was loved by her young children. To her husband, however, such an uneducated partner must have been uninteresting, and the thought of marriage scarcely excited him; as a result, heavy societal pressure was often required to induce men to marry. This lack of stimulation is quite evident in Xenophon's *Oeconomicus:* Socrates asks his friend Critobulus about his wife, "Is there any one with whom you talk less than you do your wife?" The friend replies, "There are few or none, I confess."[17]

The likelihood that a husband would love his wife was considered so remote that when Xenophon has Socrates mention in the *Symposium* that Niceratus was in love with his wife, the implication is that his power of love was so great that he could love *anyone*.[18] Nevertheless, hundreds of years later, the poet Palladas mirrored the classical Greek view when he observed that the wedded man's joyous days are restricted to two: "the day he takes his bride to bed and the day he lays her in her grave."[19]

There were, of course, exceptions to this attitude toward women. Socrates believed that women were not inferior to men, but that they needed more physical strength and energy of mind. His own wife, Xanthippe, fulfilled this requirement well. A termagant who went beyond verbal abuse, she occasionally lit into him tooth and nail and drenched him with water as well. An incredulous Athenian once asked him why he put up with such a virago. Tongue in cheek, Socrates replied, "Since I wish to converse and associate with mankind, I chose this wife, well knowing that if I could learn to endure her, I should easily bear the society of all other people."[20] Perhaps Socrates was drawn to her because her free spirit was so unusual, and even attractive, in comparison with the dull, robot-like mien of the typical Athenian housewife.

His pupil Plato went so far as to allow a few women in his school, but they were foreigners. Plato's successor, Aristotle, said that marriage should not be merely a species-propagating alliance, but a relationship involving reciprocal affection and tenderness.[21] However, in his *Nichomachean Ethics*[22] he reasoned that an inferior being (woman) should love a superior being (man) rather than vice versa, so as to counterbalance their natural gifts. Happily, he found this balance suitably achieved in marriage.

The ideal wife, as conceived by Xenophon in his *Oeconomicus,* sounds little more appealing than the viragos described by the misogynists. In the book, Ischomachus, a mature Greek who has married a young girl—not quite fifteen—tells Socrates how he chose and trained her. The choice on both sides was devoid of romance; it was made by reviewing the possibilities and choosing the best on the market. The marriage goal of husband and wife, apart from producing offspring, is described by Ischomachus as assuring "that their possessions shall be in the best condition possible, and that as much as possible shall be added . . . by fair and honorable means."[23]

All the virtues that Ischomachus has inculcated in his spouse involve the management of material resources: industry, thriftiness, docility, and orderliness. These are the qualities of a good head servant, but as Ischomachus shrewdly notes, his wife is more valuable than a servant. The latter guards his master's property as part of his job without any real involvement. The wife, however, "gains most by the preservation of the goods and loses most by their destruction, [and therefore] is the one who is bound to take most care of them."[24]

This, then, is the ideal marriage: the man works out of doors and adds daily to his material stores, which are delivered to his indoor partner; she supervises the servants and slaves to ensure that every last ounce of value is extracted from the raw materials entrusted to her care. There is no mention of emotional interaction between husband and wife.

The feeling against marriage in post-Homeric days became so great that Solon considered, but did not pass, a law making marriage compulsory. By Pericles' time, however, legal pressure was necessary, and legislation was enacted restricting the occupations of orator and general to married men only.

Little is known about how women felt about this state of affairs, since few women could write and male writers did not concern themselves with this question. There is reason to believe, however, that in many cases marriage meant no more to women than an externally imposed duty; hence, their main ties rested with their family of origin. Sophocles' Antigone, in her self-sacrifice for her brother, explains that brothers are irreplaceable but husbands are not. Herodotus, in his *History,* relates that King Darius of Persia took a woman's husband and brother captive in a conspiracy against the crown. Taking pity on the weeping wife, he allowed her to choose one prisoner who would be freed. She chose her brother.[25]

Not all Greeks were insensitive to the vast injustice done to women. The playwright Euripides had an ambivalent attitude toward them but was aware of the unhappy role into which women were forced. In *Medea,* his eponymous heroine reflected the pathos experienced by most Athenian wives:

> Surely, of creatures that have life and wit,
> We women are of all unhappiest,
> Who, first, must buy, as buys the highest bidder,
> A husband—nay, we do but win for our lives
> A master! Deeper depth of wrong is this.
> Here too is dire risk—will the lord we gain
> Be evil or good? Divorce?—'tis infamy
> To us: we may not even reject a suitor! . . .
>
> But we, say they, live an unperilled life
> At home, while they do battle with the spear—
> Unreasoning fools! Thrice would I under shield
> Stand, rather than bear childbirth-peril once.[26]

The terrible Peloponnesian wars, which decimated the population in conjunction with the declining birthrate, thrust a somewhat more active role on women. In Aristophanes' plays we already see women portrayed in a more favorable light. The Athenian and Spartan women in *Lysistrata* deny their husbands sexual intercourse until they sign a peace treaty. In *Ecclesiazusae,* they take over the parliament in Greece, with beneficial results for all.

It was during the same period of Athenean decline that Plato wrote his Utopian treatises, *Republic* and *Laws.* Plato was no doubt sickened by the fratricidal wars between the city-states and by the intracity strife in Athens between the oligarchs and democrats. He wrote of a time when individual selfishness would be cast aside and the preservation of the state would be of primary concern.

In the *Republic,* Plato depicts a state in which wives and children are to be held in common, "and no parent is to know his own child, nor any child his parent."[27] He did not advocate licentiousness, for pairings were to be arranged by the rulers; rather, he favored the idea that, in not knowing which children belonged to whom, adults would consider all children "my children" and children would regard all adult men and women as "my fathers" and "my mothers." Because loyalty to one's family usually takes precedence over loyalty to strangers, the state would comprise a populace strongly committed to each other. In the *Laws,* written years after the *Republic,* Plato abandons the idea of women and children in common, but not that of sacrifice for the good of the state. Since the state requires citizens to man its armies and serve in the government, anyone who failed to marry was shirking his duty and should be fined. The purpose of sex was to produce healthy citizens, and breeding was to be undertaken on a eugenic basis. Apart from procreation, sex would not be encouraged.

Marriage vows would be strictly honored, and adultery punished. The basis for marriage in the *Republic* was a homogamy of "natures" with respect to interests and personality. In the *Laws* there was more concern with temperament and socioeconomic status. The desire was to have a "well-mingled cup" that avoided extremes; hence the rich were to marry the poor, the quick the slow, and the powerful the nonpowerful.

For those without children divorce would be simple, "for their mutual benefit."[28] In other cases the disputants would appoint ten citizens to render judgment. The women among these judges would enter the house and by admonition or threat make the couple resolve their problems. If they failed, their male counterparts would try. If they failed, the names of the recalcitrant parties would be brought before the people, who would then socially ostracize them and prohibit them from participating in religious festivals.[29]

An unusual feature of this Utopia was the high place reserved for women. Considering the low status of women in the Athenian culture of Plato's time, it is noteworthy that he called for equal education for both sexes. While acknowledging that women were somewhat inferior to men, he maintained that they possessed basically the same nature and should share equally in the maintenance of the state except for physically strenuous tasks. In sum, the key motif regarding marriage in Plato's Utopia was that "every man shall follow, not after the marriage which was most pleasing to himself, but after that which is most beneficial to the state."[30]

It was, however, too late in the world of reality. In crushing woman's spirit and demeaning the importance of family life, Athenian men had sealed their own doom. The general disintegration of family life had gone too far. The gymnasia became rendezvous for homosexual encounters as much as for exercise. In desperation, bigamy was permitted during the Peloponnesian wars for procreative purposes, but to no avail. As the dwindling populations of the city-states battled each other, their puny numbers were smashed by the barbarians from the north and the Roman legions of the west.

Marriage Regulations and Customs

No Greek could have more than one legal wife, although he could have as many concubines as his wealth allowed. That the importance of family ties had not completely disappeared is indicated by the fact that cousins, as well as half-siblings, were allowed to marry.

Proud of their rights and privileges, the Athenians decided not to permit marriage between a citizen and a noncitizen. Pericles, who was instrumental in passing this law, lived to regret it when he fell in love with Aspasia, a stimulating courtesan. Though he was the head of the state and had put away his wife and lived openly with his mistress, he could not legally make her his wife.

Fathers arranged a marriage with an eye to the dowry (at least one-tenth of the bride's father's estate), but also with a concern for the similarity of social class of the principals. Once the father had arranged the best possible marriage, the betrothal and signing of the contract took place in the girl's home before witnesses, but often without the bride and groom. Some days later, a feast was held in her house. Any month except May could be chosen, but the time of a crescent moon was considered especially auspicious. Before coming to the bride's home, the prospective groom, usually in his thirties, and the bride-to-be, usually in her early teens, underwent ceremonial purifying baths. The disparity in ages is explained by one of Euripides' characters as follows: "To mate a youth with a young wife is ill, for a man's strength endures while the bloom of beauty quickly leaves the woman's form."[31]

Religious services were conducted by the girl's father, who fulfilled here the priestly office of making sacrifice to the gods. The connubial pair were crowned with wreaths and their houses garlanded. In addition to her gay and festal clothing, the bride wore a long veil. She had shortly before cut off her tresses and dedicated her maiden girdle and her toys to Artemis or another god.

At the banquet, the newly married couple ate sesame cakes to insure fertility. Upon their departure, they were showered with dates, figs, nuts, little coins, and sweetmeats—as a portent of prosperity. As they left, old shoes were hurled after them to ward off the evil eye.

The procession to the groom's house was led by torches; the bridal chariot, in which the couple and the best man sat, followed. Accompanying the procession were musicians playing flutes and harps and singing joyfully, "Hymen, Hymen, Ho." In Boeotia, upon the arrival of the procession, the axle of the carriage was burned, signifying the irreversibility of marriage.[32]

At the groom's house, a mock battle between bride and groom ensued, with the groom demonstrating his supremacy by carrying her over the threshold. After other ceremonies and libations, the weary couple finally ascended to the bridal chamber while the guests chanted epithalamia urging the groom to be strong in his manhood. Outside the chamber, a burly friend of the groom stood ceremonial guard. In the chamber the groom unveiled the bride (whose face he had conceivably never seen before) and presented her with a gift. Shortly thereafter, if all went well, the bridegroom announced to the jolly crowd outside his door that the marriage had indeed been consummated, and the revelers retreated down the stairs.

Concubinage

Considering the insignificant role allotted to the Greek wife, it should come as no surprise that Greek husbands created an elaborate hierarchy of mistresses to fill the void. "We have courtesans for the sake of pleasure," said Demosthenes, "concubines for the daily health of our bodies and wives to bear us lawful offspring and be the faithful guardians of our homes."[33]

Prostitution, in fact, was recognized as indispensable for the preservation of the honor of secluded virginal maidens, since men did not customarily marry before thirty. However, the married man who wanted a sexually stimulating companion also contributed to the maintenance of the "oldest profession." Since prostitution was heavily taxed, it became an integral part of Grecian life. In fact, that is why prostitutes were not permitted to leave the country. Solon, the lawgiver, was highly praised for simultaneously draining the libido of men while stuffing the coffers of the treasury.

At the bottom rung of the prostitutional hierarchy were the *pornae,* run-of-the-mill strumpets. They worked for meager wages in brothels whose identity was proudly proclaimed by a red priapus planted near the door. These women had no social rights, nor could they make any demands on their children for support. To distinguish themselves from others, they were required to wear a special ornate costume and dye their hair with saffron. The *auletrides,* or flute players, were a higher class and were often rented out to feasts to entertain and, after enough had been drunk, to share the beds of the guests. At the top of the profession were the *hetaerae* (intimate female friends). Many of them were neither slaves nor lower-class women, as was true of the other prostitutes, but Athenian citizens. To become a high-class courtesan was actually one of the few occupations open to a woman at this time. Unlike her married sister, she was sexually exciting, better educated, well groomed, charming, and steeped in all the social graces. She usually lived in her own home and could have multiple lovers or be "faithful" to one man. Intellectuals as well as lovers gathered in her salon to pass the time agreeably. Indeed, the poet Philetaerus remarked that there were many shrines to the *hetaerae,* but in all of Greece there was not one dedicated to the Greek wife.[34]

Some of the more desirable *hetaerae* became wealthy. Phryne, sculpted by Praxiteles as the perfect model for Aphrodite, once offered to rebuild the wall surrounding Thebes if it bore the motto "Destroyed by Alexander; restored by Phryne the courtesan."[35] This same lady was once defended by an orator against a charge of impiety. Seeing that the judges remained cold to his oratory, he wisely ceased talking, approached his client, and tore open her bodice to bare a splendid bosom. The judges could not believe that the heart of this wondrous woman could be less perfect than her bust and speedily acquitted her.

Aspasia, the concubine of Pericles, was known as the uncrowned Queen of Athens and succeeded in having her child recognized as a free citizen although she herself could not attain this state. Courtesans were, in fact, legally distinguished from wives only by virtue of the fact that they came with no dowry and sometimes were not citizens.

Despite the zest for life that the *hetaerae* brought to their male companions in Athens, they did not fill the emotional void in men's lives very successfully. The odds against succeeding in this kind of life in a misogamistic empire were great, and few *hetaerae* could be considered in a class with Aspasia. Moreover, the precariousness of their position ensured that only those who were tough and financially adept could succeed for any length of time. Knowing that the continuance of their income could scarcely extend beyond the duration of their beauty and that for obvious reasons they were disliked by the wives, the *hetaerae* sought to earn as much as they could within a few years. This brought many complaints about their rapaciousness, avarice, and commercial outlook. Since few men could support a *hetaera* by themselves, the competition between various lovers worsened the situation. As the Hellenistic period began, the emerging status of women, in addition to the always tenuous position of the *hetaerae,* conjoined to presage the decrease and near-disappearance of this group as an important factor in Athens.

HOMOSEXUALITY

The same suppressive attitudes toward women which spawned the *hetaerae* also gave birth to another phenomenon, homosexuality, whose rise and decline roughly paralleled that of the *hetaerae.* Homosexuality can scarcely have been unknown in Homeric days. Its minor role, however, is attested by the dearth of references to it in the literature of this period, as compared to the era that followed.

Homer's description of the relationship between Achilles and Patroclus bears no overt sexual connotations, but in the fifth century b.c., Aeschylus, in his *Myrmidons,*[36] describes Achilles mourning Patroclus' "lustrous thighs."

Today, ancient Greek society has the connotation of a homosexual society, and the term "Greek love" is often employed as a euphemism to describe this practice. I shall attempt to show, however, that homosexuality in ancient Greece was in many respects quite different from twentieth-century homosexuality.

We do not know the specific causes of homosexuality. Many consider it a learned phenomenon; others see it as biologically induced; and of course there is the possibility that both factors interact to produce it. One thing is certain: homosexuality is found in every country in the world and among most, if not all, of the members of the animal kingdom.[37]

In ancient Greece the maladjustive implications of homosexuality for men were largely absent. The incidence of homosexuality was proportionately larger than that which exists in our society, although even among the very wealthy it was never more than a minor phenomenon. Psychologically, it was not characterized by the inability to respond to the opposite sex. Most homosexuals were bisexual. Alcibiades indulged in countless homosexual and heterosexual affairs, including an adulterous episode with the Queen of Sparta. Such individuals generally fulfilled their biological duties and married, however reluctantly, in order to raise offspring for the continuity of the state.

From the social point of view, the situation among Americans and ancient Athenians differs greatly. The American man has the opportunity to marry a woman who, despite discrimination against her, is frequently his equal in education, intelligence, and emotional maturity. The Athenian man had to marry a cloistered girl, often much younger than himself, less experienced in the ways of life, and probably foisted on him by his father. What could he have had in common with such a creature? The only individuals with the money and freedom of movement, as well as education, to attract adolescent Greek youths were wealthy older Greek men. Homosexuality, in short, was in no small measure a direct consequence of the vilification of the Grecian wife.

In the homosexual relationship, the youths played the passive role. The typical age range was from 12 to 20; the older male was usually somewhat below 40. Many relationships ceased when the youth grew a beard.

All the typical behavior of adolescent heterosexual love in modern society is found in the description of Grecian homosexuality. In Plato's *Lysis* we encounter Hippothales, whom Socrates immediately perceives as a lover.

Questioning him as to the name of his loved one, he finds him too modest and shy to speak, but a friend tells all: "Indeed Socrates, he has literally deafened us, and stopped our ears with praises of Lysis; and if he is a little intoxicated, there is every likelihood that we may have our sleep murdered with a cry of Lysis . . . when he drenches us with his poems and other compositions . . . his manner of singing them to his love; he has a voice that is truly appalling . . . and now . . . behold, he is blushing."[38]

It is important to note that the homosexual relationship implied something much more than a carnal experience. The word "pederasty" stems from the Greek *paiderasteia*, meaning "love of boys." Today, the term signifies simply sexual inversion. To the Greeks, however, the term referred to both bodily pleasures and a kind of pure, passionate love.[39] The lover was to embody a fusion of the two loves, teach and inspire his beloved to become the most worthy of men. As Marrou says: "homosexuality contributed to the formation of the moral ideal which underlies the whole practice of Greek education. The desire in the older lover to assert himself in the presence of the younger, to dazzle him, and the reciprocal desire of the latter to appear worthy of his senior's affection, necessarily reinforced in both persons that spirit of all mankind."[40]

This philosophy helps to explain the seeming paradox that there were laws against homosexuality from the time of Solon in the sixth century b.c. However, as Aeschines' speech *Against Timarchus*[41] indicates, the laws against homosexuality focused on the selling of young boys to men of licentious character more than on homosexuality per se. Thus humiliated, a boy did not have to provide food and lodging for his aged father. Likewise, a male prostitute could not serve in any public function or even express his opinion publicly.

The ideal of masculinity, however, was typified by the teacher whose sexual longing for procreation was transformed into the education of beautiful adolescent boys. It was considered natural that an educated masculine man would want to create a copy of himself in his student, whereas a baser person would simply procreate with a woman in the ordinary biological manner.

A key to the fact that Greek homosexuality was primarily based on depreciation of women is found in their disgust at the "Scythian disease," named after the Scythian kings who allegedly went about in women's clothes and painted and rouged their faces.[42] Even the man who energetically wooed women was regarded as effeminate, since only an effeminate person would want to spend time with such inferior creatures.[43]

In fact, the issue of dominance-submission was more important than the choice of sexual object. Anal intercourse and ventral-dorsal intercourse were highly popular because the individual offering his buttocks was signaling his or her submissiveness to the more powerful male who mounted him or her. A woman of any age or occupation was regarded as inferior to a man and as a suitable "mountee"; but among male couples the mounted was generally either younger or in an inferior servile status to the mounter.

Some of the greatest literary figures of the age were active pederasts, including Sophocles and Aeschylus. Socrates, about whom we find no evidence of physical relationships with youths, clearly loved some of them intensely.

We must note additionally that several other aspects of Greek life contributed to homosexuality. The gymnasia, where physically splendid youths exercised in the nude, must certainly have aroused the sexual drives of many onlookers who could not obtain such stimulation from their wives. Moreover, since the Greeks believed that every beautiful body contained a beautiful soul, these handsome youths appeared that much more attractive. Xenophon, in his *Symposium,* describes the profound effect of the beautiful youth Autolycus when he made his appearance at a banquet: "Just as the sudden glow of a light at night draws all eyes to itself, so now the beauty of Autolycus compelled every one to look at him. And again, there was not one of the onlookers who did not feel his soul strangely stirred by the boy; some of them grew quieter than before, others even assumed some kind of pose."[44]

Last, the segregation of the sexes, especially in Sparta, resulted in the containment of youths and older men in military camps for long periods of time. Many homosexual bonds were formed there and proved to be of immense military value, for homosexual pairs fought like demons to be worthy of each other. The Spartans had a special corps of homosexual pairs; the "sacred band" of Thebes fell into this category.

Homosexuality received a tremendous boost in popularity when the tyrannicidal lovers, Harmodius and Aristogiton, slew Hipparchus, brother of the tyrant of Athens, who had made advances to the youth Harmodius. Their heroism was attributed to the strong bonds created by their homosexual relationship. Similarly, Cleomachus, an ally of the Chalcidians, displayed great bravery in the presence of his beloved. When he died, after routing a superior hostile cavalry, many Chalcidians, impressed by his feat, adopted homosexual practices.

Female homosexuality was not unknown, though once again we have little information because male authors wrote mostly about men. Aristophanes, in Plato's *Symposium,* states that some women have "darlings" who are also women. The clearest indication of female homosexual feeling, however, comes from Sappho, who ran a school for girls on the Aeolian isle of Lesbos. Though she was a widow and had a child, expressions of burning love for her pupils appear in fragments of her poetry. Although the term for female homosexuality, "lesbianism," is derived from the alleged activities at the school, we have no proof, as in the case of Socrates, that her feelings were expressed physically.

It may appear contradictory, after our description of the Athenian woman's inferior status, to note that Sappho was so revered in the ancient world that she earned the epithet "tenth muse."[45] Her case cautions against overgeneralizing about women's position in Athens as compared to other Grecian states. The Ionians (including Athens) exhibited a much more negative attitude toward women than the Dorians or Aeolians. Sappho possessed other advantages: in being of the Lesbian nobility, she had an above-average education and enjoyed both wealth and freedom from a husband's supervision (her husband had died when she was rather young). She was, in addition, a dynamic and unusually gifted person, as judged from her poetry. All these factors combined to make her the most famous poetess in the Grecian world, but she was surely an anomaly among Grecian women of the period.

MARRIAGE PROBLEMS

Adultery and Divorce

While the Athenian man could legally divorce his wife for any cause, only two were socially acceptable: adultery and barrenness. If his wife was caught in the act of being unfaithful, the law allowed the husband the privilege of killing the culprit in *flagrante delicto.* Otherwise, he might content himself with beating up the usurper or, if physically unequal to the task, sending a beefy servant to do the job. The monetary-minded husband could simply accept an indemnity. In any event, he had to divorce his wife if he could prove his charge, or else he would face the loss of his civil rights. To continue living with an infamous wife was considered a total disgrace. One can imagine, however, that a husband who had received a handsome dowry would evince greater charity toward his spouse in this regard than would a husband with custody over a mediocre stipend, since in all divorces the dowry left the household together with the banished wife.

Furthermore, the adulteress could not henceforth attend the public sacrifices. If she did, passersby were allowed to manhandle her in any way short of homicide.[46]

In the case of a husband's impotence, the wife could not divorce him, but the nearest male relative was called in to serve as a proxy, with the child remaining in the husband's family. Adultery on the part of the husband also was not a matter for the divorce courts. The wife could obtain a divorce only if she demonstrated to the archon's (magistrate's) satisfaction that her husband's actions, whether cruel, adulterous, etc., were endangering the safety and security of the family. This law was rarely enforced, if the case of Alcibiades is any example. This notorious rake led such a life of debauchery that his spouse, Hipparete, finally went to court to divorce him. Alcibiades and his cohorts, however, zoomed into the court, took hold of the startled Hipparete, and carried her off. Apparently, no one protested since the courts were primarily interested in the preservation of marriage. In actuality, therefore, a wife could divorce her husband under most circumstances only if he gave his consent.

SPARTA

The lot of the Spartan wife was much better than that of her Athenian counterpart. As a girl, although she remained at home while her brother went to training camp, she was involved in vigorous athletic endeavors to strengthen her physically and to make her eventual motherhood easier. She wore a tunic that ended well above her knees, but on festive occasions, such as dances and processions, she went naked. Such affairs were conducted with modesty despite the nudity of the participants, but the sight of these damsels was considered to be a strong incentive to marriage.[47]

Boys who had not been killed at birth because of physical weaknesses were brought up at home until the age of seven. They then attended a sort of military school run by the state, usually living in barracks until the age of thirty. In general, the young men became involved in close relationships with older men, often of a homosexual nature. Because they had access to many women, prostitution was rare. Marriage occurred at around thirty for men and twenty for women.[48]

Marriage

Celibacy was considered a crime, and bachelors had no franchise. They were not even permitted to watch the processions of nude maidens and men. According to Plutarch, bachelors were compelled to march *au naturel* in public, even in the middle of winter, singing songs to signify that they were receiving just recompense for their boorish ways. Recalcitrant bachelors might even be set upon in the streets by crowds of angry women. Married persons without children were only slightly less reviled. One youth refused to give his seat to a famous commander, explaining, "You have no child to give place to me, when I am old."[49]

The best description of the marriage day is given by Plutarch:

> The bridegroom carried off the bride by violence. . . . Then the woman who had the direction of the wedding cut the bride's hair close to the skin, dressed her in men's clothes, laid her upon a mattress and left her in the dark. The bridegroom, neither oppressed with wine nor enervated with luxury, but perfectly sober as having always supped at the common table, went in privately, untied her girdle and carried her to another bed. Having stayed there a short time, he modestly retired to his usual apartment to sleep with the other young men. He observed the same conduct

afterwards, spending the day with his companions and reposing himself with them in the night, nor even visiting his bride but with great caution and apprehensions of being discovered by the rest of the family. The bride at the same time exerted all her art to contrive convenient opportunities for their private meetings. And this they did not for a short time only, but some of them even had children before they had an interview with their wives in the daytime. This kind of commerce not only exercised their temperance and chastity, but kept their bodies fruitful and the first ardor of their love fresh and unabated, for, as they were not satiated like those that are always with their wives, there still was room for unextinguished desire.[50]

If the usual marriage arrangements failed, several men and women were pushed into a pitch-black room to pick their mates in the dark. This method was not considered any blinder than love.

Lycurgus, the dictator of Sparta, was greatly concerned about improving the breed of Spartans. Since one mated only the best farm animals, why not do the same for humans? Hence, wives with less than prepossessing husbands were encouraged to mate with more promising specimens.

A Spartan woman, unlike an Athenian, could walk with her husband on the street and also inherit land. By the time of Aristotle, some two-fifths of the land in Sparta was owned by women, owing to the high male deathrate.

In sum, it would appear that the quasi-communistic nature of Spartan society served to provide the Spartan woman with a more equal (though not completely equal) status in relation to her husband than was true of the Athenian wife.

CONCLUSIONS

Mention the Golden Age of Greece and immediately there comes to mind a splendor that dazzled the world—a splendor not of shining gold or glittering jewels that some despot gathered about him to reflect his glory, but of the spirit that gave us such concepts as democracy and philosophy. Two thousand years later, when the Europeans spoke of "Renaissance," they had in mind this beauty of spirit and art that served as their model. Yet for all this greatness of mind and spirit, there was also shallowness. To be sure, the great philosophers spoke of good and evil, but it never crossed their minds that the abject conditions of the Grecian slaves might have some relevance to this topic. Nor did they realize that, in the Grecian woman, they had in their midst an exploited sex that they might have educated and enjoyed as an equal being. In the end, their wars and misogyny combined to decimate their little states by causing a sharp decline in the birthrate and population, and they soon fell under foreign sway. All this, of course, was not novel to Greece and was soon to recur in Rome. What was paradoxical, perhaps, was that the Golden Age of Greece was golden for men only. For the Grecian wife it was more akin to the "dark ages."

REFERENCES

1. M. M. Hunt, *The Natural History of Love*, p. 26.
2. C. Seltman, *Women in Antiquity*.
3. W. K. Lacy, *The Family in Classical Greece*.
4. Homer, *The Odyssey*, p. 312.
5. Homer, *The Iliad*.
6. Homer, *The Odyssey*.
7. E. Westermarck, *The History of Human Marriage*, Vol. 2.
8. Hesiod/*Hesiod*/ p. 67.
9. W. Durant, *The Life of Greece*.
10. F. W. Cornish, *The Wife in Ancient Greece*.
11. R. Flacelière, *Love in Ancient Greece*.
12. Thucydides, *The History of the Peloponnesian War*.
13. E. Saltus, *Historia Amoris*.
14. Aristotle, *The Works of Aristotle*.
15. A. G. Keller, *Homeric Society*.
16. W. K. Lacy, op. cit.
17. Xenophon, *Memorabilia and Oeconomicus*.
18. Xenophon, *Symposium*.
19. M. M. Hunt, op. cit., p. 26.
20. Ibid., p. 26.
21. Aristotle, op. cit.
22. Ibid.
23. Xenophon, *Memorabilia and Oeconomicus*, p. 419.
24. Ibid., p. 445.
25. Herodotus, *The History of Herodotus*.
26. Euripides, "A Greek woman's protest."
27. Aristophanes, *The Plays of Aristophanes*.
28. Plato, *Plato*, p. 360.
29. Ibid., p. 712.
30. Ibid., p. 707.
31. W. Durant, op. cit.
32. P. Bardis, "Family forms and variations historically considered."
33. W. Smith, *Dictionary of Greek and Roman Antiquities*, p. 349.
34. M. M. Hunt, op. cit.
35. Ibid., p. 38.
36. Aeschylus, *Myrmidons* (referred to in Flacelière, op. cit.).
37. C. S. Ford and F. A. Beach, *Patterns of Sexual Behavior*.
38. Plato, "Lysis, or friendship," p. 14.
39. Plato, *Plato*.
40. R. Flacelière, op. cit., p. 87.
41. Aeschines, *The Speeches of Aeschines*.
42. D. Day, *The Evolution of Love*.
43. S. Lilar, *Aspects of Love in Western Society*.
44. Xenophon, *Symposium*, pp. 383-385.
45. A. Weigall, *Sappho of Lesbos*.

46. H. Licht, *Sexual Life in Ancient Greece.*
47. Plutarch, "Life stories of men who shaped history," in *Plutarch's Lives.*
48. W. Durant, op. cit.
49. Plutarch, op. cit., p. 22.
50. Ibid., pp. 22-23.

5
Roman Marriage

There have been few more powerful figures than the early Roman patriarch. His authority, as it existed before the fifth century b.c., has made such an impression on the modern mind that the term used to describe his patriarchal power, *patria potestas,* is one of the better-known Latin phrases in the English language. This power derived from his role as chief protector of the family name; he decided whom his children could marry, and he could kill or sell members of his family into slavery. He was not likely, however, to use such power without the support of other members of the *gens,* or family tribe, who, in their advisory role, served as a brake in the event of extreme actions on his part.

The patriarch was the chief representative and high priest in the worship of the family ancestors; within the nuclear family, only he could enter into legal contracts and purchase, own, or sell property. His wife's dowry was completely under his power, and he could control all her actions because she was legally a perpetual minor.

When a child was born, he could acknowledge it as legally his own by holding it in his arms, or he could repudiate it and condemn it to death by exposure. Since his children had no legal status, their possessions or acquisitions were legally his, but he could permit them to treat these belongings as their own. If his wife committed a crime, she was given into his hands for judgment and punishment; he might be compelled to pay a fine or, if he saw fit, he might simply turn her over to the injured party for disposal. In the words of the Censor Cato, "The husband is the judge of his wife. If she has committed a fault he punishes her; if she has drunk wine, he condemns her; if she has been guilty of adultery he kills her."[1] At his death, his wife could neither inherit nor transmit property, which was passed down through the *agnates,* persons descended through the male line.[2]

Despite his status, we find that he had no disinclination to soil his hands in manual labor, as was true of Greek men. For one thing, the economy was rather crude, the farms were small, and there were as yet few slaves. Work was not only admired, but absolutely necessary. The plow came to be the symbol of virtue, and the prototype of the Roman hero was Cincinnatus, who, when trouble knocked at the state's door, was usually found plowing in his beloved field. With a sigh he would lay down his plow to check the forces of villainy and then return happily to his plowshare.

We might imagine that the wife's lot was a piteous one under such a despot, but her actual condition is not fairly described by her legal position. The complete acceptance of the father's status may have made it unnecessary for him to resort to his more fearful legal prerogatives. Further, the strong functional and vital role of the Roman wife would make it unlikely that a man would destroy such an important cog in the family machine without due cause.

The wife worked hard, like all farm wives: she produced children, managed the rustic household, and spun wool. Unlike the Grecian wife, she was not restricted to her apartments. She was free to attend banquets, to be seen by nonfamily members, and to venture forth from the house to enjoy the spectacles and theater—always, of course, with her husband's permission and with an escort. The bridal bed was proudly displayed in the *atrium* (main room) as a token of the value and honor of married life, and when a Roman mother walked in the streets clad in her *stola maternalis* (married woman's gown), men made way for her as befitted the honor due a Roman matron.[3]

THE LATER ROMAN FAMILY

As the state grew, the power of the husband was absorbed by the state and declined, while that of the wife increased. The first two Punic Wars (265-241 b.c., 218-211 b.c.) served as catalysts for this transformation. Since the husbands were away during much of the prime "fighting weather," in spring and summer, the wives who had to run the farms and homes brought pressure on the Senate to modify the legal restrictions against them.

Increasingly, women now entered marriage without *manus* (the property the wife brought to the marriage remained under her father's control rather than her husband's). Women now also became eligible to inherit property, and as a plethora of slaves and tribute poured into Rome, many women became independently wealthy. Among the upper classes, marriage became a diabolical struggle for wealth and power.

Sulla, the dictator of Rome, wished to attach the rising star of Pompey to his banner by having the famous young general marry his stepdaughter, Aemilia. The fact that his daughter was already married and quite pregnant, and that Pompei himself was married, proved no deterrent. He told his daughter to divorce her spouse, and Pompei, who was very ambitious, did likewise.

Women also profited from their new freedom under the early empire. Clodia, wife of a high Roman official, exhibited such tradition-shattering behavior as accompanying her male friends without benefit of a chaperone, hailing friends on the street, and even kissing them instead of lowering her eyes and crouching, as was prescribed for a Roman woman.

A major step in women's independence came when they were allowed to retain their dowry even when divorced for infidelity.[4] Yet their overall position was not sound; women could become very wealthy but still possess no political rights. Slaves had long taken care of most farming in the now extensive estates, and few professions were open to women, though many upper-class women had received adequate schooling for the times.

Aside from marrying a wealthy political figure, the chief profession with prestige was that of vestal virgin. The six keepers of the holy fires had to take a vow of virginity for 30 years, after which they were free to live any life they chose.[5] Unlike other women, they could make a will in the lifetime of their father, as well as freely administer their affairs without a guardian.

In view of the impediments to any kind of meaningful activity, it is scarcely surprising that many wealthy women turned to adultery as a means of expressing their individuality. In turn, this influenced many men to feel that women's freedom was responsible for the decaying morality. Pliny the Elder insinuated that some consuls bore striking resemblances to the gladiators they watched.[6] Juvenal complained that these "selfish, shrewish, adulterous [creatures were] substituting lapdogs for children, going in for athletics, [and] worse yet, for literature."[7] The elder Cato intoned, "All men rule over women, we Romans rule over all men, and our wives rule over us."[8] The new god was wealth, leading Juvenal to note, "She bought her husband for a million sesterces—that is the price at which he calls her chaste."[9]

As the institution of marriage disintegrated among the upper classes, the birthrate declined—children seemed more bother than they were worth, a luxury now appropriate only for the poor. Seneca, in fact, comforted a bereaved mother whose son had died by saying that "childlessness gives more power than it takes away."[10] Indeed, packs of avaricious bounty hunters gathered around the childless elderly, like buzzards circling a carcass-to-be. No task was too menial, no wish too trivial, for these obsequious ghouls to fulfill in the hope of coming into a legacy when the will was opened. Martial, speaking of the suitor Gemellus hovering over a sickly widow, observed, "He begs, he beseeches, he makes splendid gifts, and yet there is no creature in the world that is uglier than she. Where the charm then? She has a bad cough."[11]

The aged and the celibate were aware of the motivations of their "suitors" and played along with them, compensating them in expectations rather than in gold while graciously accepting gifts, favors, and attention. The sycophants often had real cause to weep when their "benefactors" died, for when the will was read, they discovered that they had acquired only wisdom in the ways of man—not cash.

Needless to say, there were many happy marriages in Rome; and if fewer paeans of praise have survived, it is because complaining is cathartic whereas satisfaction is best enjoyed, not verbalized. There are, however, numerous recorded examples of marital felicity and devotion. Octavia, the wife of Marc

Antony and sister of Augustus, remained faithful to her husband, raising his children with great care while he wallowed in the fleshpots of Egypt. Pliny entreated his young wife Calpurnia to write once and even twice a day so that he need not worry over her. Arria, when her husband was ordered to die by Emperor Claudius, plunged the dagger into her chest and handed it to her spouse, saying, *Paete, non dolet*—"It does not hurt, Paetus." An imperial slave (*dispensator*) said of his wife: "She was the patron-saint of my home, my hope and my life. Her wishes were mine; her dislikes mine. None of her secret thoughts was concealed from me. She was a busy spinner, economical, but generous to her husband. She did not delight in eating, save with me. She was a good counsellor, prudent and noble."[12]

It is probable that the lower classes did not experience the disintegration of marriage that the wealthy did; after all, they were far too concerned with their daily sustenance to indulge in the luxury of adultery. But this must remain a speculation, since the poor left little in the way of written documentation.

MARRIAGE REGULATIONS

Marriage was a personal, civil affair and required no religious or governmental sanction. Before the appearance of the Twelve Tablets of Law (451 b.c.), however, the father's consent was required, and custom forbade marriage between blood relatives (*cognati*) within the sixth degree.[13] This provided an interesting contrast to the Greeks, where cousins and occasionally half-brothers and sisters could marry. The difference probably lay in the greater closeness of the Roman family; unlike the Greeks, sons remained in the father's house after marriage, with cousins on the father's side being brought up as brothers and sisters.[14] These restrictions gradually weakened, and by the time of the Second Punic War cousins could marry. Later, even marriage between an uncle and a niece was reluctantly recognized under a decree of the Senate, inspired by Emperor Claudius' desire for his niece Agrippina.

Ancient tradition held that all persons should marry, but the failure of this custom eventually led to the imposition of a tax on bachelors in 413 b.c. The minimum age of marriage for girls was 12; for boys, 14. Boys could not marry until their father permitted them to don the costume of manhood, the *toga virilis,* at about the age of 16. The Romans were strictly monogamous, inclusive of concubines, so that officially a man could not have both a wife and a concubine simultaneously, although he could have either with approbation.

Types of Marriage

Unlike the Greeks, the Romans had no elaborate hierarchy of courtesans. Instead, most of these were incorporated as subtypes within the institution of marriage:

Marriage *justum:* marriage between persons of the same social class who were Roman citizens. The children would also be full-fledged Roman citizens. If a citizen married a noncitizen who, however, possessed the *jus conubii* (franchise to marry a Roman), the marriage was still considered a *matrimonium justum* and the children acquired the father's status.

Marriage *non justum:* legally acceptable concubinage involving a citizen and a spouse of inferior social rank (e.g., a patrician and a plebeian). The children of such marriages had no legal claim to the titles or possessions of the parent of higher social status.

Marriage without *manus* (power of husband over the wife): the wife remained under the authority of her father or his family, and she retained whatever property they gave her.

Marriage with *manus:* only those married in *matrimonium justum* were eligible for marriage with *manus.* The husband exercised autocratic power over his wife in a similar manner to that of the father over the son. In fact, his wife was legally considered a daughter (*filiae loco*). The husband acquired all property possessed by the wife at marriage, the right to such holdings as she might subsequently acquire by gift or labor, and even the right to sell her if he so desired. Nevertheless, this fact did not put her in the status of a slave, for she still retained her personal rights and her position as a married woman; her labor, however, was at the disposition of the new owner. The wife in *manus* shared in her husband's estate at his death, but not in her father's.

There were three kinds of marriages with *manus.*

Confarreatio. The patrician almost invariably married within this form. The name is derived from the grain used to make the cake of spelt (*farreus panis*) employed in the religious rites of the ceremony. The ceremony occurred in the bridegroom's house and, as a religious observance, included a sacrifice to Jupiter Farreus. The *pontifex maximus* (head priest) and ten witnesses, perhaps symbolic of the ten guardians of Rome, were required to be present.[15] After the ceremony a sheep was sacrificed on the family altar and the couple sat side by side on the skin, symbolizing their oneness. The couple ate the blessed cake of spelt and, after prayers, the ceremony ended and was followed by a banquet.

Coemptio. A sort of poor man's *confarreatio,* this marriage was purely secular and was most common among plebeians. The preliminaries, depending upon the wealth of the principals, might be similar to the *confarreatio.* However, perhaps as a vestige of a long-forgotten "bride price" era, the heart of the ceremony consisted of the ceremonial sale of the bride in the presence of five adult Roman witnesses. A solitary coin placed in the balance signalized the transfer of parental authority over the bride to the groom or to his house.

Usus. This third form of *manus* marriage was essentially a marriage de facto, involving no ceremony at all, and was most common among plebeians. If a man and woman cohabited continuously for a period of one year, the man gained full power over his spouse; but if she left the home for three days in succession during the year, she was not considered to be married.

Other forms of marriage included the *contubernium,* a quasi-marriage among slaves who legally could not marry. A free woman marrying a slave acquired his status, but a bondswoman did not lower the status of a patrician in becoming his concubine.

The *concubinatus* involved cohabitation between two unmarried free individuals or between a free man and a woman servant. This relationship constituted no marriage; the concubine neither brought a dowry nor achieved the rank of her husband, and her children were not legally recognized as relatives of the father.[16] Last, the term *stuprum*[17] was reserved for illicit intercourse, the children of such congress being without any legal status.

There were more specific regulations for various professional and familial roles. A widow's remarriage, for example, while not strictly forbidden, was looked upon as an insult to her former spouse. At first the military were forbidden to marry. Even if they had married before entry into the service, their wives subsequently found themselves relegated to the status of concubines. These restrictions were eventually removed, however, during the realm of Septimus Severus (a.d. 193-211).[18]

The law forbade marriage between Romans and barbarians, between senators and freedwomen, and between a patroness and her freed slave. Further, freemen could not wed women of tarnished reputation, and senators could not even wed the offspring of parents of "ill repute." Though *matrimonium,* in this case, was forbidden for these distinguished gentlemen, the law, sensitive to the biological realities of life, did not forbid the state of *concubinatus.*

Changes in the Regulations

By the middle of the fifth century b.c., marriage involving *manus* had become exceedingly rare. As the government's control over its citizenry became more powerful and superseded that of the father's role in the family, his sons, daughters, and wife gained additional freedom. As a reward for their efforts in the Punic Wars, sons could henceforth retain property gained in military endeavors without falling under the sway of their fathers. Later, the father's punitive power over the son was limited to moderate forms of punishment, and for serious offenses the son had to be released to the ordinary tribunals to stand trial.

Despite these changes—as some maintain, because of them—the moral fiber of the nation seemed to weaken daily, and the birthrate fell. The Emperor Augustus determined that only strong measures could bring a return to the hallowed days. In 19 b.c. he was instrumental in putting through the Senate a series of laws designed to aid marriage and the production of children so desperately needed to man the Roman legions. The *Lex Julia* and the succeeding *Lex Papia Poppea*[19,20] related to marriage in the following ways:

(a) *Concerning celibates (men over 25 and women over 20)*. Marriage was obligatory for men under 60 and women under 50. Celibates could not inherit from nonrelatives unless they married within 60 days after their benefactor's death, nor could spinsters inherit after reaching the age of 50. Celibates could not attend festivals or games. Bequests contingent upon the legatee's maintaining his celibacy were void. Women owning more than 20,000 sesterces paid a 1 percent annual tax until married.

(b) *Concerning those whose marriage had been terminated*. Widows and divorcees had to marry within six months of their divorce or their husband's death, or they could not partake of his estate (this period was later extended). Women could reclaim their dowry after divorce, except for portions deducted for compensation for financial damage to the husband, for misconduct, and for maintenance of children.

(c) *Concerning who could marry whom*. Men of the senatorial class could not marry a freedwoman, actress, or prostitute; conversely, no actor or freedman could marry such a man's daughter.

(d) *Concerning the advantages of having children*. Women with more than 20,000 sesterces had their tax reduced after marriage. The tax continued to decrease with the arrival of every child, terminating with the birth of the third. Of two consuls, the one with the greater number of children had precedence over the other. In office appointments, the individual with the most children was favored. A mother of three children or more could wear a special garment, be free of legal "tutelage" of her husband, and inherit directly from these children. A freedman could pass along portions of his estate to his children rather than to his former patron, in proportion to the number of children the freedman had. On the other hand, if the former owner was a woman, she could still inherit from the freedman to the extent that she produced her own brood. Under certain conditions, husband and wife could not inherit from each other, or they could inherit only a small fraction of the total estate, if their marriage had borne no issue. The usual biases favoring the man were still in effect, however; a man need have only one child to escape the penalty of noninheritance; a woman had to have three children; and a freedwoman, four.

Effects of the Laws

Conservatives complained bitterly about these laws, saying that the "three-children" clauses gave women too much freedom. Male celibates rationalized their status on the grounds that the extravagance, imperiousness, and untrustworthiness of the new Roman woman made her a poor risk as a wife. Childless men complained that in these uncertain times they favored the abortionist, else they

Adam and Eve expelled from Paradise. (Bronze relief from a door of San Zeno in Verona, Italy).

might find themselves the father of an "Ethiopian."[21] A less strong ruler than Augustus might well have been toppled by such popular unrest.

It is difficult to assess the full effect of this legislation. True, the number of Roman citizens increased from 4,063,000 in 28 b.c. to 4,937,000 by the time of Augustus' death in 14 a.d. Would this have happened anyhow? How many of these citizens were enfranchised barbarians? We do not know. It is also true that some of the nobility confessed that they had married and sired children only to achieve their high status. However, while it is possible that the laws may temporarily have halted the falling birthrate, the attempt to inculcate the spirit of the laws never succeeded. For example, when it proved impractical to determine at the games who was or was not a bachelor, this law was quickly repealed. Further, a scandal occurred when Emperor Tiberius had to dismiss a Roman quaestor who had married two days before the lots for office were drawn (in order to fulfill the requirement that candidates for public office be married) and had then divorced his wife a day after his election.

Some had children for the purpose of tax cuts, and then officially "emancipated" them to roam the streets. After a while, even the physical act of procreation was no longer necessary to obtain the privileges attendant on having three children: emperors granted this status to favored individuals who were not even married!

The law allowed women to retain their dowry after divorce so that they could attract suitors, remarry, and bear children. However, the lucrativeness of the dowry served as a wife's weapon against her husband. Juvenal pityingly predicted to a husband, "No present will you ever make if your wife forbids; nothing will you ever sell if she objects; nothing will you buy without her consent."[22]

During Hadrian's reign (117-138 a.d.), after she bore three children, a woman gained the right to inherit from each of them intestate.[23] Marcus Aurelius, in 178 a.d., promulgated a law that the mother's children, whether sons or daughters, took precedence over other male relatives as heirs to her estate.[24] Hadrian went so far as to state that women had to give their free consent in marriage and that they could also manage their own property and purse with the aid of a legal guardian. By the end of the second century, women were free of all compulsory "tutelage" after the age of 25.[25]

In some cases the wife received a kind of dowry from the husband, a *donatio*. A portion of his estate was set aside for his bride although it remained formally under his control. In the event of his financial insolvency, however, the *donatio* could not be attached by his creditors.

The consent of both fathers was still required for a valid union, but marriage by *confarreatio* was practiced in only a few patrician families, and *usus* became increasingly popular. Women favored this type of marriage because by absenting themselves from home at least three nights per year, they retained control of their property.

The improvement in married women's rights is best seen in the shifting control of the dowry. Originally, the dowry had remained in the possession of the husband in a *manus* marriage, not only for the duration of the marriage but also after its termination. After the *Lex Julia* of 18 b.c., however, he could not alienate or mortgage any Italian property. Much later, under Justinian (527-565 a.d.), he could not do so with any dotal land even if he had his wife's consent. Before Justinian, the husband maintained a semigrip on the dowry through managerial privileges; later, however, if the marriage broke up, he had to answer for the entire original value unless he could prove that the wife's conduct had caused the marital schism.

Emperor Justinian used the prerogative of changing the law to fit his own needs. When he wished to marry the courtesan Theodora, he was first forced to make her his concubine, for the law expressly forbade a man of high rank to marry a woman of ill repute, of servile origin, or of the theatrical profession. Theodora, unhappily, qualified for all three categories. Justinian, however, managed to get a law passed that offered "glorious repentance" to those who had earlier prostituted their persons to the theater.[26]

It is apparent that the laws merely followed the weakening of psychological and emotional marriage ties. As marriage became more and more a political and economic contract, wealthy fathers would not risk losing control of any dotal sums they might grant their daughters, and, accordingly, marriage contracts stipulated that the marriages were without *manus*. If the husband, then, could not touch the wife's dowry, she could no longer inherit from him. The concept of marriage as an uneasy and limited alliance now settled upon the wary participants.

MARRIAGE CUSTOMS

Throughout the Roman period, children could be betrothed by their fathers while quite young—the age of seven was considered the onset of "reason." Although there is some dispute about whether these contracts were legally binding,[27,28] their social importance is attested to by the fact that the relatives gathered to witness the breaking of the *stipula,* the straw, as a token of agreement between the families.

The events preceding and following the ceremony included many ritualistic acts which usually had the purpose of warding off the evil eye, predisposing the couple toward fertility and prosperity, and symbolizing their unity.

A typical wealthy marriage might occur at any time except during the *dies parentales* (February 13-21), the *kalends* (first of the month), the *ides* (13th or 15th of the month, varying with the month), the *nones* (the ninth day before the *ides*), and the entire month of May and the first half of June, all of which were considered most unlucky for nuptials. The actual date would be settled by a sacrifice and a reading of the entrails.

A ceremony would take place in the *atrium*—the central half of the house; gifts were exchanged and a ring was placed by the groom on the third finger of the bride's left hand. The groom was probably between 16 and 20; the bride was not much above the age of puberty. The early Romans believed that virginity was essential in a bride, and the best way to ensure this state was to marry the pubertal girl off as quickly as possible after the initial menses.

The evening before the wedding, the bride dedicated her girlhood garments and ornaments to the *Lares,* the ancestral spirits of her father's house, who protected and guarded the home. On her wedding day she wore a long one-piece tunic; around her waist was a woolen sash tied in the "knot of Hercules," which the husband would untie at the time of consummation. Her hair was parted with a spear point to commemorate the ancient rape of the Sabine women. Over her face she wore a red veil to protect her against the evil eye. The red may also have symbolized the bride's virginity or her successful defloration, for the nuptial bed was covered with red cloth.[29]

At the ceremony in the bride's house, the *pronuba,* a matron who had been married only once, placed the bride's hands into the hands of the groom. Presumably this was a token of earlier forms of marriage, which had always been *in manus* (in hand), according to which the bride was in the power and under the protection of the groom. (This ceremony survived Roman marriage and later became part of the ceremony between a feudal vassal and his lord.) A sacrifice was made, the bride and groom walked around the altar in clockwise fashion, and a cake of *far* (a grain) was offered to Jupiter Farreus.

A mock fight ensued: the bride was ritualistically torn from her mother's arms, again perhaps symbolizing the rape of the Sabine women, and the procession set out for the groom's home. One of the torches was of whitehorn, for the express purpose of keeping the ubiquitous evil eye at arm's length. Singing, flute playing, and general carousing characterized the general festive mood. The bride and groom wore floral wreaths, and symbols of feminine industry, the distaff and spindle, were carried after her.[30]

Along the way, the procession halted; the bride, who had brought three *asses* (Roman coins) with her, now offered one to the gods of the crossroads for good luck and another to her husband as a symbol of her dowry. She later laid a third coin on the hearth as a propitious offering to his household gods. In the course of the procession, the groom scattered nuts through the crowd as a symbol of fertility and prosperity.

On arriving at his residence, the bride anointed the doorposts with fat and oil, and hung bands of wool around them, perhaps as signs of plenty and industry, respectively. The groom then carried the bride over the threshold and she delivered a carefully rehearsed "Where thou art Lord, I am Lady."[31] The significance of being carried over the threshold may have stemmed from the belief, prevalent among many cultures, that the threshold is haunted by spirits or is somehow very dangerous.

At this point, only the invited guests continued on into the house. In the *atrium,* the husband offered his wife fire and water as protection against witchcraft. The bride lit a fire in the hearth and recited a prayer. The festivities continued for some time, highlighted by each guest eating a laurel cake. Finally, the bride and groom were led by the *pronuba* into the marriage chamber, and the marriage was consummated while the guests stood outside.

SEX

The reputation of the Romans for sensuality is understandable when we compare them with the Athenians, who preceded them, and the Christians, who followed them. Athenians were hardly ascetic. However, apart from selected courtesans, they never permitted the average women to develop into a worthy object of passion. Seclusion and lack of education do not inspire the development of intelligence and personality, and the greatest "sex symbols" of history, when studied carefully, are usually revealed to have been exciting as much for their intelligence and personality as for their curves.

That the Romans appear sensual in comparison to the Christians is hardly startling. Roman religion, unlike that of the Christians (whom we shall describe in succeeding chapters), did not denigrate sex or the body. Sex was viewed as a natural and interesting experience which the gods endorsed strongly. Hence, the task of the god Virginiensis was to loosen the bride's girdle, Subigus saw to it that the bride yielded, and Prema held her down while the man penetrated.[32]

Sex was no less accepted in everyday life. The great god of fertility, Priapus, was much esteemed. Cakes were baked in the shape of male and female genital organs, and children wore amulets of phalli as good-luck charms.

The Roman poets Catullus, Ovid, Propertius, Tibullus, Plautus, and Lucretius wrote much about love, but they stressed the joys of sex more than those of mental excitement. Lucretius, however, although he had nothing against sex, deplored the madness it engendered. He described the sexual act dispassionately, as if he were watching the mating of fruit flies: "They greedily clasp each other's body and suck each other's lips and breathe in, pressing meanwhile teeth on each other's mouth; all in vain, since they can rub nothing off nor enter and pass each with his whole body into the other's body."[33]

Ovid, in his major works *Loves* and *The Art of Love,* gives advice on how to woo and make love. There is little talk of emotional involvement, but much on how to plan the strategy of seducing an enticing woman. The would-be lover must be attentive to his lady, but it is not the lady's character that is important, as the following excerpt from *The Art of Love* makes clear:

> If Dust be on her Lap, or Graine of Sand,
> Brush both away with your officious Hand,
> If none be there, yet brush that nothing thence.
> And still to touch her lap make some Pretence.
> Touch anything of hers; and if her Train
> Sweep on the Ground, let it not sweep in vain;

> But gently take it up, and wipe it clean:
> And while you wipe it, with observing Eyes,
> Who knows but you may see her naked thighs![34]

It should not be thought that the sensuousness of the Romans led to a great incidence of adultery. For citizens (a minority of the population), the ease of divorce made it more desirable for the politically ambitious to divorce and then marry their lover. The kind of women of whom Ovid speaks, therefore, came mainly from three sources: slaves, freedwomen, and wealthy widows or divorcees. The last-named, as independent women, had little to gain from marriage, which entailed the loss of legal rights.

Prostitution

The flowering of prostitution seems to have occurred during imperial times. The squeezing of the small farmers off their lands into the metropolis of Rome, the influence of wealth, the influx of foreigners, and the growth of a slave class that supplied bodies—all these factors hastened the development of the "oldest profession." The ubiquity of prostitution was attested to by its variety—a type for every taste and pocketbook.

The average working prostitute, a *meretrix*, registered with the magistrate and paid a yearly tax of something like a full day's earnings, for which she received a modicum of police protection. The brothel keeper could employ slaves as prostitutes. In that case, the girls had nothing to say about whether they liked their work, and they had to give their earnings to the keeper. Other prostitutes, freedwomen but probably not citizens, rented cubicles and kept their earnings for themselves.

The lowest group was the *prostibulae*, who were not registered on the rolls and who often used the pavement to service their clients. Many of these women waited in the archways underneath public edifices, such as theaters and circuses. Some plays were erotically stimulating, and when the theater goers emerged they would encounter the waiting prostitutes. Spectators at the Coliseum, excited by the display of blood and death in the arena, also found a ready outlet for their aroused senses. These sub-stadium arches were so much frequented that the Latin word for a series of arches, *fornix*, has lent us the word "fornication."[35]

Some of the most colorful types were the *lupae*, the "she-wolves," who frequented parks and emitted wolf-like howls to attract their clients. The *busturiae* were professional mourners who doubled as prostitutes, often using the graveyard as a convenient site for their trade. Another very low type was the *quadrantaria*, who took on all comers for a quarter of a paltry Roman coin (as).

The upper classes of prostitutes were courtesans, actresses, flute players, and artists. They lived in comfortable villas, selected their lovers, and were "kept" instead of receiving a straight fee for their services.

Some writers have described Julia, the daughter of Augustus, and the Empress Messalina, the wife of Claudius, as such nymphomaniacs that they engaged in prostitution to supplement their adulterous affairs. Messalina, who is alleged to have serviced no less than 25 men a night, is depicted by Juvenal as she reluctantly shuts her cell:

> Still raging with the fever of desire,
> Her veins all turgid, and her blood all fire,
> Exhausted, but unsatisfied, she sought
> Her home, and to the Emperor's pillow brought
> Cheeks rank with sweat, limbs drench'd with poisonous dews,
> The steam of lamps, and odour of stews![36]

That these ladies were adulterous can scarcely be questioned. That they accepted anyone, no matter how ugly or filthy, seems most unlikely because they mixed with the cream of Roman society. This doubt is further reinforced by the fact that the highly respectable Roman historian, Tacitus, mentions no such incidents.[37]

Despite their acceptance, prostitutes were not held in high repute by the state. This derived not so much from disapproval of their sexual behavior as from their low social status, since almost all were slaves, foreigners, or freedwomen. Anyone who frequented them habitually, therefore, might be looked upon suspiciously—why would a Roman citizen become emotionally involved with a person of such low status? It is in that sense that we can understand the story related about Cato the Elder: Observing a youth coming out of a bordello, he said, "Good," doubtless thinking that the draining of libido in this harmless manner might be keeping the youth from "grinding some husband's private mill." But when he later discovered that the youth was becoming a habitué of the place, he told him in no uncertain terms, "When I said, 'Good,' I did not mean that you should make this place your home."[38]

In order to guarantee that prostitutes did not mix with Roman citizens, the state forbade them to marry citizens. A pimp, however, could marry a female citizen with impunity.

Appearance was highly associated with status in ancient Rome; therefore, to distinguish the harlot from her higher-status married sisters, prostitutes were forbidden to wear the *stola* and were required to wear the *toga* normally worn by men. They were also forbidden to wear shoes, but not sandals; purple, the color of honor, was proscribed; and they could not wear their hair in fillets, a mark of maidenly virtue.[39]

Homosexuality

Homosexuality was neither esteemed nor rejected by Romans, but there is little question of its pervasiveness. Gibbon tells us that of the first 15 emperors of

Rome, only Claudius seems to have been untainted by the "odious vice."[40] And, unlike Greece, there was no rejection of women by the majority of those who engaged in homosexuality. The wealthy Roman man pursued a catholic taste in sex and was more apt to be bisexual than homosexual.

As a youth, Julius Caesar bore the sobriquet "Queen of Bithynia" because of his relations with the king of that nation. Yet he also had four wives and countless adulterous affairs, earning the title of "the husband of every woman and the wife of every man."[41]

In sum, whether the Romans were as perverse as the Christians of that epoch claimed depends on one's value system. During the Christian Emperor Justinian's reign in the sixth century a.d., pederasty met with "painful death" by the amputation of the sinful instrument, or the insertion of sharp reeds into the pores and tubes of most exquisite sensibility.[42]

MARRIAGE PROBLEMS

The old Roman matron was the prototype of womanly honor. Lucretia, when raped by Tarquinius, earned a virtuous death by impaling herself rather than presenting her "soiled" person to her spouse. But as individual freedom increased for both sexes and as new views regarding sexual freedom and the permanence of marriage developed, adultery became a problem of some concern.

Adultery

Concubinage did not flourish as a safety valve for marriage because Roman law did not allow a man both a wife and a concubine—he had to choose one or the other. Further, marriages were still based on financial or political considerations rather than on personal preferences. These factors, combined with the seemingly ingrained human need for sexual variety, predisposed the marriage partners toward sexual infidelity. Adultery was more popular in Rome than in Greece because the Roman matron, with her superior education and experience, was a more exciting person than her Grecian counterpart. Moreover, from the point of view of practicality, unlike her Athenian sister, she was not shut up in her apartments, and hence was more available.

Naturally, there are always problems for those with the urge for illegal sexual union. Since secrecy was required, daytime rendezvous invited identification. On the other hand, nighttime excursions were risky because traveling without a retinue was an invitation to robbery or worse. Perhaps, then, the lady's home? Horace rejected this possibility, preferring a medium-priced strumpet. In her presence, he had no fears that "a husband may rush back from the country, the door burst open, the dog bark, the house ring . . . with the din and clatter of his knocking; that the woman, white as a sheet, will leap away, the maid in league with her cry out in terror, she fearing for her limbs, her guilty mistress for her dowry, and I for myself. With clothes dishevelled and bare of foot, I must run off, dreading disaster in purse or person or at least repute."[43] Ovid was more adventuresome (in his writing, at least). He preferred to cultivate the husband's friendship before seducing the wife: "Be polite to her husband. . . . If you play at dice and by chance you win the crown, disclaim the honor for his benefit. Take off your laurel wreath and place it smilingly upon his head. Dismiss all notions regarding his inferiority. See that he is invariably served before you; say nothing to him that might be unpleasant. . . . Drink a toast to your mistress and a toast to him who shares her bed. It is your privilege to curse him under your breath."[44]

The law defined adultery as sexual intercourse with another man's wife; intercourse between a married man and a single woman did not fall under this rubric. The wife, in any event, could not punish the husband, as Cato the Censor clearly indicated: "If you were to catch your wife in adultery, you would kill her with impunity without trial; but if she were to catch you, she would not dare to lay a finger upon you, and indeed she has no right."[45]

In practice, however, there is no evidence that any extensive killing was done. Instead, fines were usually levied; in 285 b.c. a temple was built to Venus from the fines paid by adulteresses! The male lover too could be fined. A number of witnesses were needed, and the wronged husband was permitted to retain the culprit in his home for 20 hours until they could be obtained.[46] Some men failed to survive the wrath of an irate husband, and were killed.

Augustus' program for marital reform also contained provisions to crack down on growing marital infidelity. Under the provisions of the *Lex Julia de Adulteriis,* the father still retained the right, if he chose to exercise it, of immediately killing an adulterous daughter and her paramour if he caught them in the act. A husband might act in similar manner if he caught his wife and her paramour in his own home. If he discovered the adultery afterward, however, or if he did not wish to commit murder, he had 60 days to bring her to court. In the event that he failed to report her, her father was required to file a legal complaint. If he was loath to act, any citizen might report her. Failure to report a wife left the husband open to prosecution as a pander.[47]

Because moral degeneracy had made the most serious inroads among the nobility, and because they were exemplars whose customs the plebeians followed, penalties for adultery were made much stiffer for the former. At the same time, Augustus wisely declined to exercise the death penalty for adulterers because the birthrate was already at a precariously low level. Instead, the adulteress faced banishment for life, payment of a third of her fortune and half her dowry as a fine, and the loss of the privilege of remarrying. The husband who connived at his wife's adultery incurred the same penalty, but the wife still could not bring her husband to account for his own adulterous behavior or for consorting with certified prostitutes. As noted above, he could be apprehended by others, in which case he was compelled to return his wife's entire dowry, suffer the loss of half his property, and face banishment to a distant island.[48]

Augustus had a daughter by an earlier marriage, Julia by name, who turned out to be the bane of his existence. He brought her up strictly, perhaps too strictly, and, like children from whom so much is expected, she had the option of becoming either a superconformist or a rebel. She chose the latter course. Her first husband, Marcellus, succumbed after two years without leaving an heir. Augustus, craving a grandson, put pressure on his friend and general, the 42-year-old Agrippa, to divorce his wife and marry Julia, which he did. Rumors began to spread that Julia was engaging in adultery, despite the fact that the five children she bore Agrippa resembled him. Her explanation, according to the rumor, was logical and unusually forthright: *"Numquam nisi nave plena tollo vertorum,"* which translates to something like "I never take on a passenger until the boat is full."

Agrippa died, and Augustus pressured Tiberius, the son of his wife Livia by a former marriage, to divorce his pregnant wife and marry Julia. Tiberius, a dour Stoic, was less than thrilled at the idea, but both he and Julia had no choice, and the move at least brought him closer to the throne. Tiberius' continuous absence on military campaigns gave Julia the opportunity to resume her sexual escapades. Her husband, although he disobeyed the *Lex Julia de Adulteriis* by discreetly not revealing her infidelity, fumed inwardly. At first he sought to avoid any scandal that might threaten his position and his possible succession to the throne. Finally, because of Julia's nocturnal caterwauling or because of jealousy of the favored position of Julia's children by Agrippa, or simply because of a weariness of life, Tiberius left on a self-imposed exile to Rhodes, allegedly to study philosophy.

Julia was an aging 38; each new gray hair added to her frenzy to seize another day of pleasure before the imminent reckoning. Finally, somebody talked. Shocked, Augustus wrote out an indictment, and in a fit of masochism had the Senate read it aloud. One lover was forced to make an end of himself, the others were banished, and Julia was exiled to Pandateria, a bleak and rocky island off the Campian coast.[49]

Her friends, as well as Tiberius himself, eventually asked Augustus to rescind the exile, but he would do no more than send her to the more comfortable city of Rhegium, where she died 16 years later. Often generous to his vanquished foes, Augustus could not give up his role of impartiality for his own child and leaned over backward in refusing to pardon her. To those who spoke on her behalf, he noted sourly, "May you, too, be blessed with daughters and wives like her."[50] But the mocking gods had not yet finished with this austere old man. He soon received word that Julia's daughter, his grandchild Julia, was taking up where her mother had left off, perhaps inspired by her friend Ovid's verse. The 70-year-old monarch shipped her to an isle in the Adriatic, and Ovid, whom he regarded as a degenerate viper, was sent to Tomi in the Black Sea. Ovid protested that he knew nothing about young Julia's adventures and that his verse was never intended to be more than a lark and had no relationship to his chaste life—but to no avail. The adulterous behavior of Augustus' family, which the law failed to inhibit, characterized the population as a whole. Adultery has proved refractory to legal proscription throughout history.

Divorce

The first statement about divorce is attributed to the legendary founder Romulus: a wife could not leave her husband, but he could leave her for (1) poisoning the children, (2) counterfeiting his keys, (3) drinking wine, or (4) committing adultery. If he repudiated her on other grounds, he had to give one-half of his estate to her and the other half to the goddess Ceres. He also had to atone by sacrificing to the gods of the dead.[51]

Under the various forms of marriage in *manus,* a wife could be divorced but could not herself initiate a divorce action. The patrician marriage of *confarreatio,* however, required a special ceremony of *diffareatio.* All the guests present at the marriage were invited back, and the husband and wife, in the presence of witnesses, rejected the sacred cake proferred by the priest. The social stigma attached to this type of divorce made it extremely rare. The *coemptio* marriage was dissolved by the *remancipatio,* whereby the husband symbolically resold the wife back to her father. Marriage by *usus,* which involved no ceremony to start with, required none to terminate it. The husband simply made the wife leave his house.

In case of a divorce action, if the husband was in the right as his family and friends saw it, he kept the wife's dowry. If he had no official reason for initiating a divorce, the family counsel would try to dissuade him because of the social stigma. If he persisted, he was expected to return the wife's dowry by a freedman messenger or by mail, with the message *"Tuas res tibi habeto"* ("Keep your property for yourself").[52]

In the case of marriage without *manus,* divorce could be obtained by either party or by mutual agreement. By the act of *repudium,* one spouse notified the other, by message, of his intention to dissolve the marriage. The father of the husband in a marriage with *manus,* as well as the father of the wife in a marriage without *manus,* also had the privilege of dissolving the marriage.

The first officially noted divorce was that of Spurius Carrilus Ruga, who divorced his spouse in 231 b.c. for barrenness. With the increase in marriage without *manus,* however, and with the growing ability of a wife married in *manus* to repudiate her spouse, the rate of divorce rose rapidly. The same political and economic motives that induced people to marry at a later age made it expedient for the socially mobile to divorce mates who could no longer advance their interests. As individual freedom increased, divorce for incompatibility was eventually permitted. Plutarch describes a situation in which a man was chided by his friends for his divorce: his wife was chaste, attractive, and had borne him children. "Holding out his shoe, [he] asked them, whether it was not new and well made. 'Yet,' added he, 'none of you can tell where it pinches me.' "[53]

Many of the best-known ladies of Cicero's time had been married more than once. Ovid and Pliny the Younger chalked up three marriages each. Caesar had four, as did Antony, who imitated him in his taste for women; Sulla and Pompey were a bit more fickle, with five wives each.

Augustus, although himself a thrice-married man, sought to curb the injustice and moral laxity associated with unofficial divorces. He thought that publicity, as in the days when the family council was convened, would deter those who sought divorce without just cause. Accordingly, he passed a law that seven Roman citizens above pubertal age had to be present when the *repudium* was tendered and that divorced persons could not remarry for 18 months.

Nevertheless, the divorce rate continued unabated. Less than 100 years later, Seneca remarked that women of rank counted their years by their husbands, and Tertullian, still more cynically, observed that divorce was the result of marriage. But the laws remained on the books until 500 years later, when Justinian, a Christian emperor, drastically overhauled them.

THE DECLINE OF ROME

There is no reason to conclude, as the Roman Christians did, that growing moral degeneracy and a decline in the birthrate caused the collapse of the Roman Empire. Its disintegration stemmed from a number of factors, and probably would have occurred even if the Romans had led model family lives and procreated with the fecundity of rabbits.

Although Rome was extremely wealthy, its fortunes were concentrated in the hands of a few families. The majority of the inhabitants, who had been pushed off their farms to make way for vast feudal-like plantations, had migrated to the cities and lived off the dole. Slaves constituted 80 percent of the population and, not surprisingly, were so inefficient that they could scarcely supply enough to feed the rest of the population, which did little work. In time, the Roman provinces began to produce their own products rather than depend on Rome. As foreign markets shrank, the home market could not expand to fill the void because the majority of the Roman populace had little purchasing power.[54]

Strong leaders might have reversed the situation, and from time to time Rome did produce leaders of strength and vision. Unfortunately, they rarely lasted long enough to effect any permanent reforms. In the third century a.d., 37 men were crowned emperor within the space of 35 years! Assassination was the chief mode of changing rulers, although not a few perished in battle. To these internal misfortunes we should add such external considerations as the population growth among the barbarians, the vast westward migration of the Huns, and the increasing military sophistication of the invading tribes.

In the face of these difficulties, the dispossessed city hordes lacked the motivation and manpower to sacrifice themselves for the state. Marcus Aurelius could find few men willing to serve in the army for the required 20 years. To avoid military service, some men amputated a part of their thumbs to make it impossible to wield a sword or javelin. In desperation, Aurelius enrolled criminals and gladiators and hired foreign tribes as mercenaries.

At the same time, the family was also disintegrating. Marriage had never been a sacrament, and although Roman women possessed more rights than Greek women, they were never politically or educationally equal to men. As a result, religion and companionship between spouses were not sufficient to keep the couple together once the economic tie became enfeebled—as occurred when the dispossessed peasants flocked to the city and lived off the dole.

Additionally, the decline of the birthrate may have acted as a catalyst of the decline of the family. Although there are numerous references to childless monarchs, it is not certain that their infecundity, perhaps influenced by inbreeding, was typical of the entire population. The role of abortion is also unknown. What does seem clear is that a loss of responsibility and involvement seems to have developed—vis-à-vis both the state and family members. In the corrupt atmosphere, people expected to receive and few cared to give.

Attempts to return to a simpler mode of life had been made as far back as 215 b.c., during the Carthaginean Wars, with the institution of the Oppian Law. The law forbade women to use gold, varicolored dresses, or chariots. With the defeat of Hannibal in 202 b.c., women demanded the repeal of the law, and it was terminated in 195 b.c. Still convinced that ostentation leads to decay, Cato the Censor noted the growing rate of childlessness, celibacy, and divorce. Acknowledging that wives were as difficult to live with as without, he asked men to marry and propagate for the good of the state. Sometime afterward, Julius Caesar prohibited the sale of exotic meats and forbade persons below a certain age and rank to appear in public in litters and bedecked in jewels and purple robes.

Augustus, as we have seen, succeeded in getting numerous laws passed to strengthen the family, but was no more successful than his predecessors. Mere fiat could not suffice when the motivation for sacrifice and discipline had vanished. Quintilian, the brilliant orator and professor, got to the heart of the matter in a penetrating commentary:

> Would that we ourselves did not corrupt the morals of our children! We enervate their very infancy with luxuries. . . . What luxury will he not covet in his manhood, who crawls about on purple! We form the palate of children before we form their pronunciation. They grow up in sedan chairs; if they touch the ground, they hang by the hands of attendants supporting them on each side. We are delighted if they utter anything immodest. Expressions which would not be tolerated even from the effeminate youths of Alexandria we hear from them with a smile and a kiss. Nor is this wonderful; we have taught them; they have heard such language from ourselves. They see our mistresses, our male objects of affection; every dining-room rings with impure songs; things shameful to be told are objects of sight. From such practices springs habit; and

afterward nature. The unfortunate children learn these vices before they know that they are vices; and hence, rendered effeminate and luxurious, they do not imbibe immorality from schools, but carry it themselves into schools.[55]

As Rome slowly crumbled, a new concept of marriage and family was about to emerge from the moral corruption of the empire. The gods were dying, but the legions of Christ were blossoming in the midst of adversity, and it is to their story that we turn next.

REFERENCES

1. H. N. Couch, "Woman in early Roman law," p. 46.
2. E. Gibbon, *The Decline and Fall of the Roman Empire.*
3. W. Goodsell, *A History of Marriage and the Family.*
4. J. P. V. D. Balsdon, *Roman Women.*
5. Ibid.
6. W. S. Davis, *The Influence of Wealth in Imperial Rome.*
7. W. Durant, *Caesar and Christ,* p. 438.
8. W. Goodsell, op. cit., p. 135.
9. W. S. Davis, op. cit., p. 292.
10. L. Friedlander, *Roman Life and Manners under the Early Empire.*
11. W. S. Davis, op. cit., p. 290.
12. L. Friedlander, "Marriage customs in Ancient Rome," p. 101.
13. S. A. Queen, R. W. Habenstein, and J. B. Adams, *The Family in Various Cultures.*
14. E. Westermarck, *The History of Human Marriage.*
15. W. F. Kenkel, *The Family in Perspective.*
16. *Encyclopedia Britannica,* "Roman marriage."
17. C. C. Zimmerman, *Family and Civilization.*
18. E. Westermarck, op. cit.
19. C. C. Zimmerman, op. cit.
20. W. Durant, op. cit.
21. Ibid.
22. J. Carcopino, *Daily Life in Ancient Rome,* p. 98.
23. S. de Beauvoir, *The Second Sex.*
24. J. Carcopino, op. cit.
25. W. Durant, op. cit.
26. E. Gibbon, op. cit.
27. W. Durant, op. cit.
28. E. Westermarck, op. cit.
29. Ibid.
30. P. D. Bardis, "Family forms and variations historically considered."
31. Ibid., p. 435.
32. O. Kiefer, *Sexual Life in Ancient Rome.*
33. Lucretius, *On the Nature of Things,* p. 58.
34. E. R. Pike, *Love in Ancient Rome,* p. 61.

35. E. R. Pike, op. cit., p. 208.
36. Ibid., p. 150.
37. Tacitus, *The Annals and the Histories.*
38. J. P. V. D. Balsdon, op. cit., p. 226.
39. E. R. Pike, op. cit.
40. E. Gibbon, op. cit.
41. W. Durant, op. cit., p. 168.
42. E. R. Pike, op. cit., p. 249.
43. Horace, *Satires, Epistles, and Ars Poetica,* p. 29.
44. Ovid, *The Art of Love,* pp. 33-34.
45. H. N. Couch, op. cit., p. 46.
46. P. D. Bardis, op. cit.
47. C. C. Zimmerman, op. cit.
48. W. Durant, op. cit.
49. Ibid.
50. M. M. Hunt, *The Natural History of Love,* p. 75.
51. Plutarch, *The Lives of the Noble Grecians and Romans.*
52. P. D. Bardis, op. cit., p. 439.
53. Plutarch, op. cit., p. 215.
54. F. Müller-Lyer, *The Family.*
55. W. Goodsell, op. cit., pp. 151-152.

6
Early Christian Views on Marriage and Sex

JESUS AND THE DAWN OF CHRISTIANITY

The Biblical Hebrews considered marriage a divine ordinance: wedlock should impose a strong moral obligation not only to beget children but to satisfy sexual needs. Virginity was important only before marriage, and the continuance of such a state beyond youth was a blasphemous frustration of divine will.

All this changed with the onset of Christianity: virginity became exalted, marriage lost favor, polygamy was abolished, and sexual relations were condemned except for procreation. Chastity, once considered important only for women, was now equally vital for both sexes, and marriage was invested with a sacramental, symbolic significance. To understand this change, let us examine the *Zeitgeist* when Christ appeared on the scene.

The increasing emphasis on sensuality and on the material aspects of life in Rome was well under way. But there was also a strong countertrend. From the Neoplatonists and Stoics came a disdain for the material aspects of life. The Essenes, a sect that existed before and after Jesus, practiced asceticism and, perhaps, celibacy; they lived in monastic communities and supported themselves solely by manual labor. The reign of Alexander the Great, despite its brevity, accelerated the fusion of Eastern and Western philosophy which, in turn, led to Gnosticism. This movement, an amalgam of heterodox occult Judaism, Babylonian astrology, and Iranian dualism, derived its name from the Greek word *gnosis*—knowledge.

The Gnostic sects tended to believe in a dualism of God and the world. The former was spiritual; the latter, physical. The physical universe is ruled by Archons (rulers), whose leader is the Demiurge. The Archons, each ruling a sphere, aim to enslave man and to prevent the passage of his spirit toward the light (God) after death. Within each soul is the spirit, or *pneuma*, a divine spark that fell into the world from God. The Archons, in fact, created man for the express purpose of preventing the return of the divine spark.

A pneumatic morality requires rejection of the world and of all mundane ties, since these are not the products of God but of the Demiurge. This was done by tampering with the normative habit patterns of the Archons. Most people ate at set intervals, cohabited regularly, and wore standard raiment. The Gnostic, however, fasted, flaggelated himself, and practiced celibacy, not only rejecting the mores of the inferior universe but lashing out at the rules prescribed by Archons.[1]

Although the Church formally treated Gnosticism as a Christian heresy, it had a considerable influence on the thinking of its religious leaders from the second century on. It was the direct precursor of asceticism, whose ideas were to strike at the heart of the marital relationship.

Paradoxical as it may seem, Christ's views, as described in the New Testament (King James Version), are rather "un-Christian," if the statements of subsequent spokesmen such as Paul, Tertullian, Jerome, and Augustine are accepted as defining the Christian viewpoint. He appears to have been a virgin, for he is so referred to by others, and there is no record of a wife or lover in his life. Yet there is no evidence that he held virginity to be especially superior to marriage; his view was that some are called to virginity and others to marriage.[2] Jesus condemned adultery, but he exhibited compassion when he saved an adulteress' life, saying to those who were prepared to kill her, "He that is without sin among you, let him first cast a stone at her."[3] When no man stoned her, he told her, "Neither do I condemn thee: go, and sin no more."[4]

His attitude toward the family might best be described as indifferent. The New Testament is replete with his statements in praise of the Father (God), but not of his nominal father, Joseph. On one occasion, while talking to the people, he learned that his mother and brothers were outside and wished to speak to him. But he left them waiting outside, saying to the messenger: " 'Who is my mother? and who are my brethren?' And he stretched forth his hand toward his disciples, and said, 'Behold my mother and my brethren! For whosoever shall do the will of my Father which is in heaven, the same is my brother, and sister, and mother.' "[5]

On another occasion he met with a follower who made a request before leaving: "Lord, suffer me first to go and bury my father. Jesus said unto him, Let the dead bury their dead; but go thou and preach the kingdom of God. And another also said, Lord, I will follow thee; but let me first go bid them farewell, which are at home at my house. And Jesus said unto him, No man, having put his hand to the plow, and looking back, is fit for the kingdom of God."[6]

Clearly Jesus had a mission, and earthly entanglements relating to families could only interfere with God's work. One sees, in his teaching, a deemphasis of the physical and a disapproval of the sensual, but they are combined with tolerance for "weakness of the flesh"—a tolerance that was not so apparent in his followers.

EARLY CHRISTIAN LEADERS AND THEIR VIEWS
ON SEX, MARRIAGE, AND THE FAMILY

Paul, a former persecutor of Christians and not one of the original apostles, had to exert himself inordinately to rise to a position of leadership among the followers of Christ. He did this with the proverbial zeal of the proselyte, touring the Mediterranean cities until his death was ordered by Nero. His epistles reveal the superb missionary: fearless, forceful, and articulate. On the subject of marriage, however, he was somewhat patronizing: "For I would that all men were even as I myself. But every man hath his proper gift of God, one after this manner, and another after that. I say therefore to the unmarried and widows, It is good for them if they abide even as I. But if they cannot contain, let them marry: for it is better to marry than to burn."[7]

But "better" is a relative term, whereas "good" has more of the flavor of the absolute. The presbyter Tertullian, some 150 years later, pointed out that it is better to lose one eye than two, but that neither alternative is good.[8] Conclusion: it is best to neither marry nor burn.

Paul ostensibly states that marriage is honorable, and that if a man gives his daughter in marriage he does well; but, Paul adds, "He that giveth her not in marriage doeth better."[9] Similarly, St. Augustine observed that, whereas in the next life the unmarried would beam like emblazoned stars in the firmament, the married would be more akin to the less brilliant heavenly bodies.[10]

While Paul might today be perceived as strongly misogynistic, such an appraisal would fail to consider adequately the context in which he wrote. The epistles to the Corinthians, for example, were not intended as polemical treatises on his philosophy of life, but as answers to specific questions raised by the latter. Various licentious practices in Greece were threatening the viability of the Christian movement. On the other hand, certain Gnostic sects were violently opposed to marriage in any sense. Despite an evident personal bias against women, Paul acknowledged that God called some to wedlock, but the better person was chosen for celibacy.

Hardly an arch-conservative, Paul can best be described as a middle-of-the-roader in the Christian movement of his time. He threaded his way between the naturalism of his Jewish heritage (which he could neither completely accept nor reject) and the pessimistic dualism of Gnosticism which, despite its appeal of sexual abstinence, seemed too impractical as a realistic program for the masses. Marriage could save the highly sexed from burning, as well as offer minimal respectability, in that it symbolized the marriage of Christ and the Church.

Among the most prominent of the early Christians in the second to fifth centuries were Augustine, Tertullian, and Jerome. Each had tasted the delights of the flesh, and each had never basically accepted his experience. Their writings reflect the struggle between their gonads and their guilt.

Of the three, Augustine seems to have most successfully resolved his conflict.

Born of a pagan father and Christian mother, he believed that his youth "boiled over in fornications." But the examples for which he chooses to castigate himself indicate that he suffered more from an overly suppressive super-ego than from a psychopathic personality. His misdeeds included stealing pears on one occasion (even though he was not hungry) and being sexually promiscuous.[11] Elsewhere, however, he says that he liked to exaggerate his misdeeds in order to gain the approbation of his peers, an admission that is supported by the fact that the allegedly promiscuous youth had a concubine to whom he was faithful for 15 years.

His *Confessions* record the quest for meaning that led him through Manichaeism, Skepticism, and Neoplatonism to his final Christian faith. All along the route, the specter of venality haunted and mocked his spiritual aspirations. He realized that he could be at peace with himself only by renouncing his sexual impulses, but he had become so habituated to sex that for years he could make no progress; hence his almost neurotic but meaningful prayer, "Give me chastity and continency, only not yet."[12]

In his thirtieth year he settled in Italy with his mother who, seeing that he leaned toward Christianity, decided that marriage would contribute to his moral stability. A marriage was arranged, and his concubine was dispatched to Africa to smooth the nuptial road. The poor concubine, who was never named by Augustine, did not complain bitterly, as well she might have, but swore eternal fidelity. Augustine mentions that "my heart which clave to her was torn and wounded and bleeding."[13] Despite these protestations, he apparently acted rather feebly in the matter, and was little more than his mother's pawn.

Since his bride-to-be was under age and he had to wait two years for the marriage, he took another mistress—after all, he was the victim of habit. But his salvation, unknown to him, was close at hand. Hearing of the conversion of a well-known Roman rhetorician, Victorinus, he had a distinguished example to emulate. A fellow African, Pontitianus, then described to him the joys of monastic life. Augustine retired to a garden in a state of turmoil—his attachment to earthly pleasures seemed to contradict all the joys of continence—and he heard a voice saying, "Take up and read."[14] Picking up a volume of St. Paul, he found: "not in rioting and drunkenness, not in chambering and wantonness, not in strife and envying; but put ye on the Lord Jesus Christ, and make not provision for the flesh, to fulfil the lusts thereof."[15] Immediately he understood, and all the darkness of doubt vanished.

Augustine's conversion resulted in a decision against both marriage and coitus. The combined effects of his age and of the Christian environment lowered his sex drive and enabled him finally to adopt a behavioral pattern consistent with his beliefs. His subsequent writings showed the effects of his personal experiences and solution. Because he had had a fairly satisfactory sex life, he could perhaps not bring himself to agree with the Manichaean sect, which considered coitus as the product of the Demiurge and, therefore, an unmitigated evil. His continuing inability to accept his sexual behavior, however, ensured that he could not endorse the position of the Pelagians, namely, that sexuality was good and unaffected by the fall from Paradise. Sexuality, he believed, was a gift of God, necessary for procreation and not inherently corrupt; but concupiscence was a sin. In accordance with this philosophy, he proceeded to reinterpret history.

What would Eden have been like had not Eve tempted Adam? How would they have populated the earth without stooping to carnal passion? The answer lay in man's will, which before his fall was a tower of strength, and now, alas, was somewhat enfeebled. Yet some vestiges remained, for: "There are persons who can move their ears, either one at a time, or both together. There are some who, without moving the head, can bring the hair down upon the forehead, and move the whole scalp backwards and forewards at pleasure. . . . Some have such command of their bowels, that they can break wind continuously at pleasure, so as to produce the effect of singing."[16]

He concluded, therefore, that man had lost this absolute control over his body because of his sin in eating the forbidden fruit. It would surely have been no problem for God to have created him so that what now moved only by lust would have initially been fully at the command of the will. In those benevolent times: ". . . husband and wife embraced in the marital act not goaded on by the heat and prickings of voluptuous desire, but rather in peace of soul and with integrity of body. . . . Hence, as now we know, a virgin is not physically changed by the menstrual flow, so in those days the wife could receive into the womb her husband's seed without rupture of the hymen; for indeed, the semen could flow in through the same ducts that bear out the menstrual discharge."[17]

Augustine believed marriage to be good even in his day, because although pregnancy might be a by-product of lust, married persons having sexual congress committed only venal sins as compared to the graver sins of fornication and adultery. While condemning fornication between the unmarried, he held that those who join in coitus, but preserve their mutual fidelity and faithfully rear the issue of their relations, are in truth married even though they have not obtained legal sanction. Thus he happily rationalized the memory of his relationship with his concubine as common-law marriage and not debauchery.

Tertullian, however, would not even concede that marriage was a bad means (sexual relations) to a good end (children). The Lord had prophesied, "Woe to them that are with child and that give suck."[18] "Who are so fortunate, then as those without children?" "At the first sound of the angel's trumpet they will leap forth lightly, easily able to endure any distress or persecution, with none of the heaving baggage of marriage in their wombs or at their breasts."[19]

As for marriage itself, "Marriage and fornication are different only because laws appear to make them so; they are not intrinsically different, but only in the degree of their illegitimacy. For what is it that all men and women do in both marriage and fornication? They have sexual relations, of course. . . ."[20]

Tertullian, who was married, referred to his wife in his writings as his "dearest companion in the service of the Lord." But he also congratulated the man who became a widower, saying, "Your debtor days are over. O happy man!"[21]

Chrysostom, the brilliant orator and exegete of the Church, sought to restrain his friend from marrying by appealing to his love of the sanitary. Even if his girl friend was beautiful, nevertheless, "The groundwork of . . . corporal beauty is . . . phlegm, and blood, and humor, and bile, and the fluid of masticated food. . . . When you see a rag with any of these things on it, such as phlegm or spittle, you cannot bear to touch it with even the tips of your fingers, nay you cannot even endure looking at it; and yet you are in a flutter of excitement about the storehouse and depository of these things?"[22]

Martin of Tours was somewhat kinder in his evaluation of marriage. By way of analogy, he saw virginity as an ungrazed field, marriage as a pasture cropped by cattle, and fornication as a field uprooted by swine.[23]

Was there, then, nothing positive that could really be said for marriage except that it was better than roasting in the fires of damnation? Not exactly! St. Jerome, who had a lifelong preoccupation with virginity, said, "I praise marriage, praise wedlock, but I do so because they produce virgins for me."[24]

MARRIAGE OF THE CLERGY

The ideal of celibacy was based on the example of Jesus and Paul, the role of the priesthood in some Greek sects, the reaction to the loose life in Rome, and the Biblical belief that the world was coming to an end and that only virgins would ascend to heaven. In the early days of Christianity there was no official policy, and some leading Christian clergymen married, including Peter and Tertullian. But gradually the policy of making oneself a "eunuch for the kingdom of heaven's sake"[25] took hold. This maxim was undoubtedly intended as an allegory, but it is paradoxical that the man most renowned for his allegorical interpretations of the Scriptures, Origen, should have interpreted this phrase literally and castrated himself.

Many Church fathers, however, considered emasculation a coward's way of dealing with temptation. Great men, and great women too, prove themselves by rising to the occasion. The matador can be a hero only when he faces a brave bull, not a timid cow. The good Fathers, therefore, indulged in the practice of *syneisaktism,* a spiritual marriage with virgins, or *agapetae* (spiritual lovers), who came to reside in the monasteries as "brides of the soul." Theoretically, this entailed the coexistence of the sexes in strict continence, though they might share the same house, room, or even bed. Some men with a low testosterone level may have emerged unscathed from the flames; but in many cases a vindictive nature took its toll, and the woman exchanged her spiritual role for the more earthly one of housekeeper and mistress. The men, as Jerome put it, suffered "their feet to sink beneath them."

In a converse form of *syneisaktism,* wealthy young unmarried women or widows invited clerics or monks to share their homes in chastity. The man's role alternated between house steward, chaplain, spiritual lover, and occasional sexual partner. Even in its nonsexual aspects, Jerome's description of these clerics is far from spiritual: "They pretend to be plunged in sorrow and protract long periods of fasting by means of furtive snacks at night . . . there are others who are ambitious of obtaining the priesthood . . . that they may be able to visit women more freely. All they care about is dress: if they are well perfumed, if their shoes are not baggy because of a loose fold of leather. Their locks show traces of the curling iron, their fingers gleam with rings, and they take little mincing steps so that the wet street may not bespatter their feet. When you see such men, look upon them as bridegrooms rather than clergymen."[26]

The more prudent villages in many locales would sometimes insist that the priest take a concubine to ensure the fidelity of the wives of the parishioners. Indeed, by the tenth century an Italian bishop sadly declared that in the event he were to "enforce the canons against unchaste people administering ecclesiastical rites, no one would be left in the Church except the boys; and if he were to observe the canons against bastards these also must be excluded."[27]

Pope Siricius, in the year 385, tried to put celibacy on the books as a requirement for clergymen, but heavy opposition and violation of this edict eventually resulted in the Trullian Council of 680, which decreed that members of lower orders might marry. It was only at the Lateran Council of 1215 that the celibacy requirement for the priesthood was officially adopted.

ASCETICISM AND THE ATTITUDE TOWARD THE BODY

The years preceding the fall of Rome were marked by poverty, unemployment, civil wars, plagues, increased pillaging by the barbarians, declining commerce, and a breakdown in family unity. The Christians found an explanation for these terrible times: the sensuality of the wealthy Romans had provoked God. In addition, the persecution of Christians had provided the martyrdom so necessary for a religion seeking to emphasize the meaninglessness of the material world. Though persecution ended with the ascension of the Christian Emperor Constantine, more masochistic individuals, however, now sought self-imposed martyrdom. The idea was hardly novel, for the Christians were echoing the Essenes, Stoics, Neoplatonists, and Gnostics who had earlier practiced indifference to or renunciation of the material world.

Asceticism was a fierce attack on the body and its sensual appetites. Baths were shunned; filth became a virtue. St. Simon the Sylite, bound with ropes caked with filth, became the ideal when he tenderly picked up the maggots that fell from his festering side and said, "Eat what God hath given you." Lice were euphemistically referred to as "pearls of God," and Jerome said that a full-grown virgin should never bathe and, in fact, should be ashamed to see her own nakedness. Both food and baths were on his list of dangerous aphrodisiacs. The ideal was to eat just enough to keep from starving, but not so much as to sate oneself. A full stomach or hot food generated lust. "I think that nothing so inflames the body and titillates the organs of generation as undigested food, and convulsive belching."[28] On that account, one should not starve oneself either. To do so was to invite lust by eating a great deal afterward. Slowly to starve, to incur all manner of gastric distress—that was the happy corollary of piety, for each painful spasm promised spiritual salvation.

St. Abraham, a man of great beauty, of whom it was said that "his face reflected the purity of his soul," did not wash his face or his feet for 50 years after his conversion. The virgin Silvia, however, felt it not too sacrilegious to wash only the tips of her fingers.[29] Surely the stench of sanctity must have been stupefying.

THE ATTITUDE TOWARD SEX

Constantly preoccupied with repressing biological urges—which returned periodically, as such urges are bound to do—the early Christians projected the responsibility for sexual visions and temptations onto the devil.

The nights were most difficult, for with sleep came lustful dreams. Nuns and other decent Christian women often angrily protested that the incubus, a fallen angel, had visited them and forced them to commit indecent acts. St. Jerome, iron-willed though he might be, confessed to seeing visions of dancing maidens and feeling the hot fires of lust pervade his parched flesh as he lay fasting in the desert.

The devil did not cease his pursuit of man even to the latter's dying breath. A priest, having parted from his wife 40 years earlier to pursue a life of celibacy, lay dying. His wife hastened to keep vigil over the bed she had not shared for so long. Seeing her spouse in an inanimate condition, she bent over him to determine whether he still breathed, whereupon the good saint gathered his fading energy and gasped, "Get thee away, woman: a little fire is yet left, away with the straw."[30]

In truth, even the dead were not considered sexually impotent. One Church edict directed that a male corpse was not to be buried next to a female one until the latter was safely decomposed.[31] The attempt to repress sex actually led to constant preoccupation with it. If victory meant eternal vigilance, was it not a pyrrhic victory?

THE ROLE OF WOMEN

Jesus had little to say about women. His disciple Paul was more expressive on this subject, remarking that man was not made for woman, "but the woman for the man."[32] Consequently he advised women: "Submit yourselves unto your own husbands, as unto the Lord. For the husband is the head of the wife, even as Christ is the head of the church. . . . In like manner also, that woman adorn themselves in modest apparel, with shamefacedness and sobriety; not with braided hair or gold, or pearls, or costly array. . . . Let the woman learn in silence with all subjection.[33]

Some Church officials considered women worse than an inferior being. Tertullian's judgment was that: "*You* are the devil's gateway: *you* are the first deserter of the divine law: On account of (you) . . . even the Son of God had to die."[34]

Even the hair of these temptresses of the devil was feared: it was considered so seductive that angels could be distracted by it during the service. Moreover, since demons most readily entered women with long hair, all women were required to cover their heads in church. The nadir of women's status may have been achieved in the year 585, when the Council of Macon, debating whether women truly had souls, concluded that they did—by one vote![35]

Occasionally we hear a kind word for women, as when Paul enjoined husbands to love their wives[36] and Clement of Alexandria pointed out that the "God of both is one."[37] What was implied, however, was that inferiors should be loved and cared for despite their inferiority. Clement preached, "Women are [permitted] to philosophize equally with men, though the men are preferable at everything, unless they have become effeminate."[38]

In the early days of Christianity, the participation of women at religious meetings was eagerly welcomed.[39] When the assemblies became more organized and bishops and priests were elected, women were held in less favor. A woman could hold the minor office of deaconess in the Church hierarchy, but she could not receive the sacrament.

In sum, most Church leaders saw women as weak, frail, slow-witted, simple, unstable, deceptive, and not the kind of person to be trusted with public affairs.[40] God loved men best because he created a woman from Adam's rib, the woman being of man and *for* him. Finally, the fall from Eden was not Adam's fault for eating the apple (the Christian fathers were not existentialists), but Eve's—she gave it to him! Even though men should have good reason to resent womankind, the Christian way was not to resent an inferior but to take care of her. And so it followed, according to Augustine, that "they who care for the rest rule . . . and they who are cared for obey."[41] True enough, men should rule not from a sense of power but from love and mercy. Whatever their motives, however, men ruled!

After Roman times, the status of women advanced in some respects but deteriorated in others. The advances were indirect, and not primarily intended to improve the life of women. In practicing monogamy exclusively, for example, the Christians went no further than the Greeks. In preventing the coexistence of a wife and concubine, they did no more than the Romans. However, in declaring marriage indissoluble, in addition to the aforementioned restrictions, they strengthened the position of women by severely limiting the freedom of men.

Women were, of course, also prevented from shedding their spouses, but since this privilege had heretofore been largely a male function, mutual restriction was considered a gain for women.

Finally, male adultery was for the first time officially condemned as much as female adultery. Again, however, the motivating force was not to grant equal sexual rights to both sexes, but to inhibit carnality on the part of both.

THE WONDERS OF VIRGINITY

Jesus was a virgin, as were John the Baptist and, presumably, Paul. Jesus was also believed to have been born of a virgin—a notion that is inconceivable to the average man. Initially, Jesus' divine conception served only to demonstrate his supernatural status. In time, however, ordinary conception by comparison came to connote a polluted act.

In Revelation, we learn that the exalted, who are the company of the Lamb (Jesus), number 144,000. Each of the exalted has one characteristic in common: "These are they which were not defiled with women; for they are virgins."[42]

Virgins were thought to possess supernatural powers, including the ability to foresee the future, and their powers extended even to the animal kingdom. When a lion, closing in on Thecla, mysteriously divined that she was a virgin, he meekly licked her feet.

Though they were hardly Freudians, Christian leaders realized that the energy available when sexual needs are impeded and libidinal drive is channeled into other regions could be put to practical use. Thus Paul pointed out the crucial difference between a virgin and a wife: "The unmarried woman careth for the things of the Lord, that she may be holy both in body and in spirit; but she that is married careth for the things of the world, how she may please her husband."[43]

It should be noted, however, that sexuality was considered incompatible with virginity only when it led to physical intercourse. Indeed, the language used to describe the relationship of virgins with Christ is replete with sexual symbolism. Jerome tells how Christ (the Bridegroom) was always with them (the virgins): "When sleep comes upon you, he will come behind the wall and he will put his hand through the opening and will touch your body. You will arise, trembling, and will say: I languish with love. And again you will hear his reply: My sister, my spouse, is a garden enclosed; a garden enclosed, a fountain sealed up."[44]

To safeguard herself from earthly lovers, a virgin should commence training for her high station in early childhood; consequently, Jerome praises mothers who dress their daughters in dark clothes and do not allow them to wear fancy trinkets around their necks. In his letter to the young virgin Eustochium, he cautions her to avoid the company of married women, for why should "the bride of God make haste to call on the wife of a mortal man? Know that you are better than they."[45]

There are no reports on how the virgins fared under such a regime. Doubtless, many were torn between the satisfactions of marriage and the glories and tortures of virginity. Eustochium herself, supported by her strongly religious mother Paula and by Jerome, seems to have functioned adequately as a secretary to Jerome in the Bethlehem monastery.[46] Other virgins who had been officially "married to Christ" did valuable social work: they visited Christians in prison, tended the ill, and administered relief to the needy. Their high spiritual status not only served as recompense for the absence of motherhood and family life, but it offered them the chance of a "career" to which married women had no access.

Not all priests, however, were enamored of the cult of the virgin. Helvidius stated that the mother of Jesus did not remain a virgin, thus demonstrating that marriage and celibacy had equal value. Jovinian maintained that God did not distinguish between virgins, wives, and widows on the basis of their marital or virginal state. Vigilantius saw a wedded clergy as greatly to be desired. Each of these men was denounced by the Popes and by the virginophile Jerome. Strangely, their views were throttled, whereas the writings of Jerome maintained the myth of the virgin until the twentieth century.

EARLY CHURCH MARRIAGE REGULATIONS AND CUSTOMS

At first, marriage was viewed as a civil and private affair, which followed Roman civil law with one notable exception. Under Pope Calixtus (218-222), the marriage of free women to men of servile rank received full recognition. The measure seems to have been one of expediency, since free women outnumbered free men among the Christians and it had been impossible to marry within one's rank and still do so "within the Lord."

The Church also emphasized the necessity for free consent of the partners, but there was wide latitude in interpreting the free-consent clause. Tertullian held that no marriage was valid without the consent of the father, whereas the bishop of Symrna, seeking to extend Church power, proposed that the bishop's consent should be obtained.

The Church, as in Roman custom, maintained the traditions of separate betrothal and wedding ceremonies. The betrothal consisted of an exchange of consent before witnesses, the gift of a ring from the man to the woman, the drawing up of a matrimonial contract, and the delivery of the agreed-upon dowry. Sober celebrations were permissible, but the bacchanals, drinking, obscene performances, and "blue" hymenal songs characteristic of Greek and Roman weddings were prohibited.

Marriage Prohibitions

There were three main impediments to marriage: consanguinity, affinity, and spiritual affinity.[47] Although the Romans had relaxed the prohibitions against marriage between relatives and even first cousins could marry, the Christian emperors tightened the restrictions. Theodosius I prohibited marriage between first cousins on pain of death or burning. According to the Council of Agde of a.d. 506, any known degree of consanguinity was considered an impediment. This measure proved too restrictive, and Pope Gregory I (540-604) declared the seventh degree of relationship to be the closest relationship permissible in marriage. The degree is counted by considering the process of generation from one collateral to the common ancestor and then adding that number to the number of steps from the common ancestor to the second collateral; thus, brothers are related in the second degree, an uncle and nephew in the third degree. A seventh-degree restriction meant that no one could marry anyone related more closely than a third cousin.

The prohibition of the marriage of affines (people related by marriage) seems to have been based on Christ's phrase, with reference to husband and wife, that "the twain shall be one flesh." All the relatives of the husband and wife were thus considered to have entered into some mysterious relationship through the marriage of the pair. Any degree of affinity was a reason to prevent a marriage, according to the Council of Agde.

Spiritual affinity referred to the relationship said to exist at a child's baptism between his godfather and godmother, and the godchild and his relatives. The net result of these restrictions was to accelerate Church influence on marriage, since intensive ecclesiastical investigations were often necessary before the judgment by officials could be rendered as to who could marry whom.

Other important legislation involved the repeal of the Lex Julia et Papia Poppaea, in a.d. 320, by the Emperor Constantine. These laws, in effect since the reign of Augustus, had penalized the unmarried and the childless, both socially and financially. In an age when asceticism was beginning to make headway, however, these laws had become anachronistic. The *patria potestas* was also essentially eliminated, and the remaining powers were essentially those possessed by most parents today.[48]

The impetus for these legal changes does not seem to have come primarily from Christian doctrine. The general tone of the pagan philosophers of Greece and Rome in previous centuries, as well as the Roman legislation, had increasingly favored amending some harsh laws and freeing the individual from the bonds of his family. Now, the Church proposed to substitute itself for Roman law as the regulator of individual behavior. It could do this through its influence on the Christian emperors and, consequently, on civil legislation. Commencing with the reign of Constantine, the Church also established its own quasi-legal jurisdiction over problems relating to marriage.

Regulation of Sexual Intercourse

The early Fathers were presented with a paradox. While virginity was the most exalted state, the Church approved of marriage, and marriage was on its way to becoming a sacrament. Yet the very process of producing virgins often involved lust and sensuality. Surely, in sanctifying marriage, the Church was not condoning lust. Perhaps the best way to make this distinction clear was to regulate sexual congress so as to clearly categorize it as an inferior by-product of marriage.

In *The Instructor,* written in the third century, the presbyter Clement of Alexandria told married people that the daytime should be devoted to prayer and to reading religious tomes. Accordingly, a couple might lie with each other only after supper.[49] This permission was not intended as a license for coitus, for the act could remain without sin only if voluptuousness were eliminated and control and restraint maintained.

Jerome went much further: a man should not love his wife with passion, but with judgment. In fact, he who loved his wife too ardently was no more than an adulterer.[50] The fourth Council of Carthage, in 398, pronounced that out of reverence for the benediction, newlyweds should abstain from sexual union for the first night. Happily, however, by paying a moderate fee, a dispensation could be obtained to permit cohabitation even on the first night.[51]

Such regulations can scarcely have had a salubrious effect on marital relations. What is more, they contained contradictory elements. On the one hand, passion was evil and the body a foul cesspool. Yet out of this morass came life, virginity, and all the saints.

Mixed Marriage

The Church at first permitted the marriage of Christians to nonbelievers in the hope that the latter might be converted. Paul did not favor such marriages; but once such a marriage was a *fait accompli,* he argued that the Christian spouse could not leave or "put away" the nonbeliever—with one exception: "But if the unbelieving depart, let him depart. A brother or a sister is not under bondage in such cases: but God hath called us to peace."[52]

Tertullian, 150 years later, came out strongly against mixed marriage, pointing out that the New Testament condones a marriage with a heathen only where both were originally heathens and one subsequently became a Christian. The Bible thus refers to "he that *hath* a wife that believeth not," not to "he that *taketh* a wife that believeth not."

Some people opposed intermarriage because of their belief in the mysterious unity of Christ and the Church. Since Christians were "the limbs of Christ," it was felt that marriage between a Christian and a heretic was a species of adultery or fornication. But civil law did not impose any restrictions on intermarriage until the advent of the Christian emperors.

By the fourth century, the Church felt strong enough to halt officially the still prevalent intermarriage with non-Christians. Because it could make few inroads with the Jews, who continued to practice their own religion despite increasing pressure, the Church was particularly vindictive toward them.

The Council of Elvira, in 305, stated that henceforth Christians giving their daughters in marriage to either Jews or heretics would suffer excommunication for five years. Shortly thereafter, Constantine the Great made Christian-Jewish marriages illegal, and in 388 a Roman law declared persons contracting such marriages to be living in a state of adultery.[53]

Polygyny and Concubinage

The Christians regarded monogamy as the only acceptable form of marriage. Augustine excused the prophets for practicing polygyny and concubinage on the grounds that their sole motivation was not lust, but propagation. Now, however, he saw the world as amply stocked, and a world that would soon meet its Maker did not need multiple wives. He opposed polyandry for any period, because it did not enhance fecundity and would confuse tracing the family line when the father's identity would be uncertain.[54] Tertullian, less liberal, accepted Abraham only during the period when he was a monogamist and uncircumcised,[55] and Methodius saw polygyny as part of a sequence of evolution. Man started by marrying his sister, and then with God's grace moved to polygyny, monogamy, continence, and, at last, the pinnacle—virginity.[56]

The New Testament, unlike the Old Testament, slights concubinage. In addressing the Galatians, Paul points out that, of Abraham's two sons, one was born of a free women (Sarah), the other of a bondwoman (Hagar). The one born from "promise" led to Christ, but the one born "after the flesh" led to bondage. That is why, he maintained, the city of Jerusalem had fallen under Roman rule.

THE PROBLEMS OF MARRIAGE

Adultery

Unlike the Romans, the Church officially adopted a single sexual standard, which had once been favored by Aristotle, Plutarch, Seneca, and the Roman Emperor Antonius Pius. This was the first time, however, that an institution as far-reaching as the Church had adopted such a policy. The Church was also influential in getting Emperor Constantine to enact a law that made adultery by the man punishable by death.[57]

In practice, however, as opposed to official policy, both the Church and society tended to support the traditional bias favoring the man. Basil condones the custom of urging the wronged wife to take back her husband, but he expects the husband to expel the sinning wife as "polluted." Similarly, when a separated wife cohabits with another man, she is obliged to do 14 years' penance. Yet the separated husband and his mistress, in a similar situation, need incur only 7 years' repentance. Referring to the double standard, he reluctantly comments: "The requirement is not easy, but custom has so obtained."[58]

Divorce

The Christians, associating the degradation of the Roman nobility with the laxness of divorce, resolved to make divorce difficult to obtain. The ultimate criterion was the New Testament, but unfortunately it proved to be ambiguous and contradictory. Jesus says, according to the report of Mark, "Whosoever shall put away his wife, and marry another, committeth adultery against her. And if a woman shall put away her husband, and be married to another, she committeth adultery."[59] Matthew, however, reports Jesus as saying, " . . . whosoever shall put away his wife, *saving for the cause of fornication,* causeth her to commit adultery: and whosoever shall marry her that is divorced committeth adultery."[60] Whether the Apostles actually disagreed, or whether one of them has been a victim of the numerous translations and editions of the Bible, is a moot point.[61,62] In any event, this ambiguity led to continuing debate among the early Fathers.

Paul adhered to the view that divorce was not possible, as expressed in Mark, except for the earlier-mentioned case of a Christian married to a pagan who deserts the Christian. Hermas, in 140, argued that apostasy, covetousness, adultery, and idolatry constituted valid grounds for divorce. Origen, less than a century later, permitted husbands to divorce wives guilty of adultery. Jerome agreed with Hermas, and Chrysostom with Origen. Augustine at first recognized divorce in case of "unlawful lusts" on the part of either husband or wife, though later he said that marriage was indissoluble because it was somewhat sacramental in nature.

Legislation under the Christian Emperors

The basic principles of the liberal Roman laws on marriage largely survived the ascendency of the Christian Emperors. It was easy for theologians, mostly unmarried, to talk of the indissolubility of marriage. The Emperors, on the other hand, knew that to enact these views into civil law would be largely ineffectual and would anger and agitate a population dominated by men.

The traditional Roman custom had been to accept divorce and subsequent remarriage when the mutual consent of both partners had been obtained. A one-sided divorce was no more difficult except that, if the woman initiated action without cause, a goodly portion of her dowry was withheld from her, whereas a husband desiring divorce without cause had to return the entire dowry.

The first important changes were made by Constantine, who wished to halt the inequities he perceived in one-sided divorces. His law of a.d. 311 was intended to eliminate divorce for any superficial reason. Henceforth a woman could obtain a divorce only if her husband failed to communicate with her for four years while in the military service, or if he was a murderer, a poisoner, or a violator of tombs. If he was an adulterer, as in the past, he was killed. A man had sufficient reasons for obtaining a divorce if his wife was a procuress, a poisoner, or an adulteress. In case of divorce for reasons other than the above, the woman violating the statute lost all claim to her dowry and was transported to an island. The man, if responsible for the divorce, surrendered the dowry and was not allowed to remarry. If he did remarry, his former wife could invade his house and acquire the dowry of her successor.[63]

Although the valid reasons for divorce were modified by succeeding emperors, the Church itself moved toward a confirmation of the strict indissolubility of marriage at the Council of Carthage in 407. A test case presented itself some 45 years later. The campaigns of Attila in Italy in 452 had caused huge casualties in dead, wounded, and captured to the Roman armies. In the years that followed, the wives of many prisoners received no news of their husbands who had been carried away. Assuming that their husbands were dead, they remarried. When conditions gradually improved, many husbands who had been thought dead returned. When Nicetas, Bishop of Aquileia, went to the Church Fathers to seek a judgment, they supported the dictum of St. Basil that "a woman whose husband has gone away and disappeared, and who married another, before she had evidence of his death, commits adultery."[64] Therefore, in agreement with the decision of the Council of Carthage, the verdict of indissolubility of marriage was affirmed.

Ignoring the Church's edict, Theodosius II, in 439, abrogated his predecessor's law and restored the traditional Roman law. The thankful populace responded with such an increment in the divorce rate that an alarmed Theodosius restored Constantine's laws, but with slight modifications. He granted a man two additional reasons for divorce: if his wife spent the night outside of his house, and if she attended a public spectacle without his permission. Divorce without official sanction resulted in the loss of dowry and prewedding gifts. In addition, the woman—not the man—was prohibited from remarrying for five years.

Justinian, 100 years later, added abortion as a valid reason for divorcing a wife. Influenced by his wife Theodora, he passed other amendments that favored women. A woman could now divorce a husband who was impotent, was five years in captivity, tried to induce her to commit adultery, falsely accused her of adultery, took another to live in his house, persisted in frequenting other houses in town with another woman despite warnings, or entered a monastic order. For the woman, divorce on nonapproved grounds resulted in the loss of dowry as well as life-long confinement in a cloister; but for the man it meant only the loss of the nuptial gift and one-third of the dowry.

Reflecting a strong ecclesiastical influence, Justinian denied, for the first time, the right of divorce by mutual consent except for any of three conditions: if the husband was impotent, if either he or his wife wished to enter a monastic order, or if he had been in captivity for five years. A subsequent revision provided that if both parties agreed to a divorce on other than the approved reasons, both would be forced to enter a monastery or convent; also, two-thirds of their property went to their children, and one-third to the monastery to which they were confined. By the time of the reign of his successor and nephew Justin II, however, the number of attempted poisonings of spouses was so alarming that Justin repealed the prohibition of divorce by mutual consent.

In retrospect, the legislation of the Christian emperors reflected the opposing pulls of the populace and the clergy. While by the time of Justin the right of divorce still remained, increasing inroads were being made by the state, largely influenced by the clergy. Although a number of emperors showed considerable vacillation with respect to women's position in divorce, the overall picture shows a strengthening of women's rights vis-a-vis men—to a point somewhat short of equality. But both sexes suffered curtailed freedom in proportion to the growing influence of the Church.

Remarriage

The Christian Fathers differed greatly among themselves regarding the possibility of remarriage after divorce, just as they did about the possibility of divorce. The problem of semantics troubled many. Did "put away" mean that the couple was divorced or only separated? When Augustine talked about marriage as a *sacramentum,* his use of the term was not as strong as its subsequent connotation for theologians who followed him. In addition, attitudes differed toward remarriage after the death of a spouse and after divorce.

Remarriage after the death of a spouse. The Church preferred that neither a widow nor a widower remarry—that they lead a life of continence—but it did not forbid remarriage. Theology was doubtless mixed with expedience here, for widows (and even widowers) were more likely to name the Church as heir to their property than those who remarried. Nevertheless, since formerly married women seemed particularly unable to resist the charms of the marital state, the Fathers reluctantly condoned a second marriage.

Tertullian at first followed the official Church position on remarriage after the death of a spouse. Later, as an adherent of the harsher Montanist sect, he attacked the Church's acquiescence with regard to remarriage after death of the spouse, arguing that nuptial ties, if they existed beyond divorce, also existed beyond the grave. The Church never countenanced this view, and regarded it as heresy. The rigid Jerome, however, could not see why any religious person would want to clap the once-severed chains of matrimony on himself.[65]

To conclude, remarriage was at first regarded as lawful and without sin; but with the increase of Gnosticism and asceticism, attitudes toward remarriage became harsher. A first marriage was justified as necessary to populate the planet; a second marriage was sinful and unfortunate but could be forgiven as due to weakness of the flesh; a third marriage was no better than fornication; a fourth was an unbelievable sin or scandal.

In later years, the Byzantine Church penalized remarriage by imposing a mild penitential discipline; the crowning was omitted for second marriages, and presbyters often signified their disapproval by not attending the wedding festivities. Eventually, however, the view prevailed that the carnal bond uniting man and wife was considered to be severed at death, permitting remarriage without retribution.

Remarriage after divorce. We have seen that, notwithstanding that "the twain (man and wife) are one flesh," if a Christian married a pagan and the pagan departed of his own free will, "the brother or . . . sister is not under bondage in such cases." But did "putting away" someone for reasons of fornication mean that the individual was free to remarry? Did being freed from "bondage" countenance remarriage? There is no doubt that the Ambrosiaster (a commentary of uncertain authorship) favors this view: "The marriage in which God is not honored is not indissoluble; and for that reason he who is dismissed for God's sake does no wrong if he marries another, since contempt for the Creator . . . cancels the obligation of matrimony so far as the deserted partner is concerned, and he is not to be blamed if he forms another union."[66]

Gradually, there was acceptance of Paul's view that if the pagan spouse deserted the Christian of his own will, the bonds of matrimony were dissolved and the Christian was free to remarry (Pauline privilege). Technically, of course, there was no divorce, for the marriage was held to have existed under spurious circumstances.

The question of remarriage after adultery was also not clarified immediately. The Council of Elvira, in 306, ruled that a divorced woman who had put away a guilty husband and had remarried was to be excommunicated. She was not to be admitted to communion again until her first husband died, except in case of her mortal sickness. If, however, she had divorced him without justification and had remarried, she was not readmitted to communion even on her deathbed. The Council of Arles (314), more generous to the husband of an adulterous wife, *advised* against, but did *not prohibit* him from marrying again in her lifetime.

Less than a century later, Jerome conveyed the stiffening position of the Church when he said, "A husband may be an adulterer, or a sodomite, he may be stained with every crime and may have been left by his wife because of his sins; yet he is still her husband and, so long as he lives, she may not marry another."[67] By 407, the Council of Carthage, in reaffirming the doctrine of the indissolubility of marriage, forbade remarriage because of adultery by either mate, and thus committed the Church to the position from which it has not vacillated since.

In time, however, the rich and wealthy found a practical way to "divorce" and remarry. The unfavored marriage could be annulled by the Pope, as reported earlier, for consanguinity, affinity, or spiritual affinity. Strictly speaking, of course, this was not considered a divorce, because the marriage was held never to have truly existed. Such technicalities merely served to enable the Pope to rationalize his action in return for such earthly concessions as he might obtain from the nobleman or king requesting the annulment.

To summarize, the indissolubility of marriage was proclaimed on the basis of the New Testament, but it gathered momentum and universal acceptance within the Church largely from the fourth century on. Henceforth, only the rich and powerful could shed a wearisome spouse with legal and religious impunity; the average person had to make do with what he contracted "for better or for worse." Marriage, after all, was not an unpardonable sin provided it was committed only once.

The Ideal Spouse

The ideal wife, in Clement's view, "loves her husband from the heart, embraces, soothes, and pleases him, acts the slave to him and is obedient to him in all things except when she would be disobedient to God."[68] Though revering him, she submitted to sex only out of marital duty to help fulfill her function as a woman.

The ideal husband, as a superior creation of God, did not take advantage of his wife. He never made her submit to sex except when, in a calm mind, he could focus on the lofty procreative result of his mating, and not on the base means by which it was attained. Consequently, there was no justification for sex with a menopausal woman. The husband who could restrain himself from stealing the pearl of virginity from his wife, however, was much honored.[69]

CONCLUSIONS

There is considerable difference of opinion concerning the effect of early Christian doctrine on marriage and on the sexual-emotional relationship between men and women. It has been claimed that Christianity improved man's barbarous nature, provided new opportunity for women in Church life, and gained them respect as saints and martyrs.[70] To others—e.g., Bertrand Russell[71] and Joseph McCabe[72]—the doctrine has been a thorn in the progress of the relationship of the sexes for almost 2000 years. As is usually the case in polarized issues, there is something to be said for both sides.

To the proponents of the anti-Christian faction, we must inquire: how it came about that a concept of marriage which, in their view, crushed the spontaneity of relationships, forced a negative view toward sex, and in its celibastic and ascetic leanings mangled the marital relationship, could yet have prospered. We must assume that, at least at its onset, Christianity met certain needs that were not satisfied by earlier religions. It cannot have been simply the promise of eternal life, for other religions had promised that. Rather, its unique contribution lay in its code of ethical behavior applied equally to both sexes, and in its assertion that all mankind was conceived in sin.

The last-noted contribution may appear to be of dubious value. However, Langdon-Davies[73] opined that man, as a congenital neurotic, suffers almost universally from guilt and seeks out institutions or creates them in accordance with his capacity to regulate this sense of sin. While this philosophy smacks of teleological magic, it does make sense after some modification. In most societies, man develops the need to go beyond his own immediate needs (unless he is totally immersed in the task of earning his daily bread) and to contribute toward some purpose other than self-interest. Since life is brief and precarious, it is concern for others that saves life from seeming absurd, what with its strains and inevitable progression toward decay and death.

Early Christianity provided such a purpose—else it would not have succeeded, for at first it was a religion of the poor, without friends or allies. Since the Christian revolutionaries, a hunted, weak minority, lacked the power and means of communication to bring about changes in the physical world, their battleground became the self and the control of interpersonal relationships, and their revolution became one of the spirit. Sexual regulation, unlike military insurrection, was within their power and gave them the chance to deprive themselves of sensual enjoyment. Sacrifice thus assuaged the feelings of guilt in the face of sensual decadence (peculiar to their time) and of impending death (peculiar to all times).

In retrospect, this contribution seems of limited value, and it must seem sad that the altruistic motives of mankind should have been harnessed so inefficiently. How many poor were helped? Was it necessary to frustrate natural biological and psychological urges to achieve a state of grace? These questions are legitimate, viewed in today's perspective. They are less damaging to Christianity when examined relative to the period of their origin, when social progress and economic justice were hardly possible.

Another plus for Christianity was the fact that the treatment of women in civil law improved, and for the first time their participation in the Church was welcomed. Although the more established Church later excluded them from any leading role in its affairs, the antifeminism that manifested itself was not indigenous to Christianity, but was transmitted by the pagan philosophy regarding their inferiority. In the after-life, which at that time was more important than the earthly one, woman would be rewarded by being literally no different from man. Even on earth, however, the Church enhanced woman's status by attacking the double standard of sexuality and elevating marriage to the status of a sacrament (in succeeding years it was actually declared a sacrament).

On the debit side, it must be acknowledged that attitudes cherishing virginity, condemning women as strumpets of the devil, and disparaging the physical in man caused severe difficulties that have lessened appreciably only in recent times.

Moreover, it has never been shown that sensual satisfaction is an impediment to man's social productivity, and self-privation is no longer taken as infallible proof of one's holiness and one's love for others. As Fromm says, man, in loving himself, does not love others less.[74]

The Church's strong prohibition against divorce, and its almost unilateral opposition to remarriage after divorce, produced little benefit for women, men, or their offspring. We know today that the children of unhappily married parents, whose marriage is technically intact, are considerably worse off emotionally than the children of divorced parents.[75] In opposing divorce on theological grounds, therefore, the Church contributed to the misery of innumerable millions of the faithful. Moreover, the rich and powerful, then as now, could still obtain divorces through "annulment."

We may conclude that the contribution of Christianity to marriage was mixed. Its egalitarian philosophy was counterbalanced by the restrictive measures denigrating man's mammalian ties. Man, however, did not grow more virtuous in the ensuing millennium. Instead, as belief in the immediate reappearance of Jesus faded, the licentiousness of clergy and laity increased. The Church determined to take a more active role in regulating marriage, which became possible during the Middle Ages, when its temporal and moral influence became even stronger.

REFERENCES

1. H. Jonas, *The Gnostic Religion.*
2. Matthew 19:12. Note: throughout this chapter, all biblical citations refer to the King James translation.
3. John 8:7.
4. John 8:11.
5. Matthew 12:48-50.
6. Luke 9:59-62.
7. I Corinthians 7:7-9.
8. Tertullian, *Treatises on Marriage and Remarriage.*
9. I Corinthians 7:38.
10. P. D. Bardis, "Family forms and variations historically considered."
11. Augustine, *The Confessions, the City of God, and on Christian Doctrine.*
12. Ibid., p. 57.
13. Ibid., p. 42.
14. Ibid., p. 61.
15. Romans 13:13-14.
16. Augustine, op. cit., pp. 394-395.
17. Ibid., p. 396.
18. Matthew 24:19.
19. Tertullian, op. cit., p. 17.
20. Ibid., pp. 56-57.
21. Ibid., p. 58.
22. Chrysostom, *Works,* pp. 103-104.
23. D. S. Bailey, *Sexual Relation in Christian Thought.*
24. Jerome, *The Letters of St. Jerome,* p. 152.
25. Matthew 19:12.
26. Jerome, op. cit.

27. W. E. H. Lecky, *History of European Morals.*
28. Jerome, *Select Letters of St. Jerome*, p. 249.
29. M. M. Hunt, *The Natural History of Love.*
30. Gregorius I, *The Dialogues of St. Gregory.*
31. D. S. Bailey, *op. cit.*
32. I Corinthians 11:9.
33. Ephesians 5:22-23; I Timothy 2:9,11.
34. *Fathers of the Third Century*, p. 16.
35. P. D. Bardis, *op. cit.*
36. Ephesians 5:25.
37. Clement, *Fathers of the Second Century*, p. 211.
38. Ibid., p. 420.
39. W. L. George, *The Story of Woman.*
40. D. S. Bailey, op. cit.
41. Augustine, op. cit., p. 520.
42. Revelation 14:4.
43. I Corinthians 7:34.
44. Jerome, *The Letters of St. Jerome*, p. 158.
45. Ibid., p. 147.
46. Jerome, *Select Letters of St. Jerome.*
47. G. E. Howard, *A History of Matrimonial Institutions.*
48. J. Muirhead, *Historical Introduction to the Private Law of Rome.*
49. M. M. Hunt, op. cit.
50. Jerome, *The Principal Works of St. Jerome.*
51. W. Goodsell, *A History of Marriage and the Family.*
52. I Corinthians 7:15.
53. P. D. Bardis, op. cit.
54. Augustine, op. cit.
55. Tertullian, op. cit.
56. Methodius, *The Symposium and a Treatise on Chastity*, p. 44.
57. G. E. Howard, op. cit.
58. D. S. Bailey, op. cit., p. 70.
59. Mark 10:11-12.
60. Matthew 5:32.
61. G. H. Joyce, *Christian Marriage.*
62. O. Collins, *Divorce in the New Testament.*
63. G. E. Howard, op. cit.
64. Basil, *Works*, p. 239.
65. Jerome, *Select Letters of St. Jerome.*
66. D. S. Bailey, op. cit., pp. 96-97.
67. Jerome, *The Principal Works of St. Jerome.*
68. W. Goodsell, *Problems of the Family*, p. 55.
69. *Fathers of the Third and Fourth Centuries.*
70. E. M. White, *Women in World History: Her Place in the Great Religions.*
71. B. Russell, *Marriage and Morals.*
72. J. McCabe, "How Christianity has treated women."
73. J. Langdon-Davies, *Sex, Sin and Sanctity.*
74. E. Fromm, *The Art of Loving.*
75. F. I. Nye, "Child adjustment in broken and in unhappy homes."

7
The Middle Ages:
The Church and Marriage

The fall of the Roman Empire brought political chaos to Western Europe, and the early Middle Ages witnessed countless roving tribes and bands that pillaged and burned villages when not at war with each other. But the Church managed to flourish in the midst of all this unrest because the semibarbaric chieftains, who had seized huge parcels of empire land, recognized the Church as a politically useful ally in maintaining stability. In turn, the still youthful Church generally adapted itself to the customs of the barbarians, provided that the latter accepted the Church's basic theological principles.

As in earlier times, marriage was considered to be a private and civil affair, although the Church encouraged the presence of the priest as a mark of religiosity. After the marriage ceremony, the couple was encouraged to attend Church services so that the priest could offer a special blessing (the blessing did not itself constitute a marriage ceremony).

Among the Teutonic tribes, the two ceremonies were given specific titles. The *gifta,* the traditional ceremony in which the father gave the bride to the groom, was followed on the day after the wedding night by the *brautmesse,* or bride-mass, at which the couple received the benediction of the priest. While neither ceremony had any legal bearing, their omission could result in reprobation by the Church. By the tenth century, the Church, sensing its ability to control the populace through the regulation of marriage, instituted the custom of holding the *gifta* in front of the Church door, with the priest presiding. After he blessed the newlyweds, the wedding party marched into the Church for the bride-mass and a second benediction. Still, the fact that the wedding ceremony occurred *outside* of the Church signified its continuing temporal character.

With time, however, the father's role became more ceremonial than intrinsic to the wedding, and the *self-gifta*—the gift of the bride by herself—emerged; this was followed by the custom of having *any* third person officiate. When the Church appropriated the regulation of marriage into its domain, the *third* person present became *only* the clergy; thus, in 1076 Archbishop Lanfranc ordered that "no man give his daughter or kinswoman in marriage without the priest's benediction (or) the marriage shall not be deemed legitimate but as fornication."[1] By the fourteenth century, the parties concerned no longer married themselves, but were married *by* the priest, who stated, "*I* join you in the name of the Father, the Son, and the Holy Ghost."[2]

WHAT CONSTITUTES MARRIAGE?

As the Church came to be the sole arbiter in marital problems, certain nagging questions, unanswered for hundreds of years, pressed for solution. Perhaps the most important was what constitutes a marriage. The clergy agreed that consent of the involved parties was necessary, and that certain impediments might forbid marriage. On the question of the necessity of sexual intercourse to validate a marriage, however, there were strong differences. Alluding to the sacramental nature of marriage and the Biblical reference that "the twain shall be one flesh," Paul clearly expected that coitus would be a necessary function of marriage. On the other hand, the ascetic-minded held that continent marriage was on a much higher plane than the carnal kind. They offered three arguments. First, although marriage had existed in Paradise, there had been no carnal interaction between Adam and Eve. Only after the Fall did they indulge in physical intimacies. Therefore, sex could not be intrinsic to marriage.[3] Second, the new interpretation of the Gospel had deprived Jesus of the company of his siblings, for the union of Mary and Joseph was now judged to have been unconsummated. And if the "first family" of the Church never engaged in sexual relations, sex must not be very important to marriage. Last, it was clear that sex was basically an inferior act, if not necessarily disgusting, and so shameful an act could hardly be a prerequisite for a grace such as marriage.

There was heated debate on this issue,[4] culminating, in the twelfth century, in the emergence of two systematists, Gratian and Lombard, who became influential leaders of Christian thought. Gratian, an Italian monk, after reviewing 3,800 texts relating to Church matters, concluded in his *Decretum* that while consent initiated a marriage, only the *copula carnalis* ratified it. The former act, therefore, was equivalent to the Roman betrothal. Under certain conditions it could be dissolved, but once the sexual act had occurred, marriage was indissoluble.

The theologian Peter Lombard wrote a similar compendium, *The Sentences.* Regarding marriage, he made a sharp distinction between *sponsalia per verba de praesenti* and *sponsalia per verba de futuro.* In the former, the couple take each other as husband and wife *from the present moment on.* This consent is sacramental in nature because it signifies the joining of Christ to the Church in charity. The fact of intercourse extends the sacramental nature by representing the Incarnation whereby the members of Christ's body are joined to their Head. *Sponsalia per verba de futuro,* however, was merely a promise to wed, and could be withdrawn unless coitus had taken place after the promise. Lombard's views prevailed. His good friend, Pope Alexander III, ruled that once consent was given, even if the woman later married another in a Church ceremony and entered into sexual relations with him, she was still married to the first husband.[5]

The new philosophy offered two advantages. First, it displaced the idea of the mystical bond, *henosis*, in carnal relations whereby man and wife became one. The Church now had a definition of marriage that permitted full sway to the antisexual leanings of the hierarchy. In addition, the ecclesiastical courts at last had what seemed to be a simple and effective means of ascertaining the validity of a marriage. Whether coitus had taken place at some time in the relationship was impossible to determine, but consent in the presence of witnesses had an indisputable, evidential value.

Going still further, and disregarding civil laws, the Church held that parental consent, witnesses, a religious ceremony, or even a record of the event were not essential to the validity of a marriage. So long as the couple had agreed to be man and wife—publicly, privately, even secretly—the marriage was valid.

It soon became apparent that individuals who were motiviated to marry secretly were not likely to be careful in ascertaining that there were no impediments to the marriage. Subsequent ecclesiastical legislation, therefore, forbade priests to marry a couple privately, under pain of suspension from office for three years; and by the year 1200, Archbishop Walter of England ruled that no marriage could take place unless the banns had been published on three successive Sundays preceding the marriage.[6] The purpose of banns was to permit anyone who knew of any impediment to voice his objections to the match. However, the bishop possessed the power to dispense with the banns, and in return for financial considerations he was often pleased to do so.

THE CURSE OF THE SECRET MARRIAGE

Despite the fact that the Church no longer officiated at "secret" marriage ceremonies, it continued to recognize secret marriages, which burgeoned from the thirteenth to the sixteenth centuries. Individuals who became tired of their spouses would leave them, claiming that they had formerly been secretly married to someone else. Contrariwise, an impetuous youth, eager to seduce a damsel, might secretly marry her by saying "I do," jump into bed with her, and later swear to the Church that he neither had matrimonial thoughts in his mind nor had pledged anything. Since the Church was forced to render purely arbitrary decisions as to whether a couple was married or not, it began to consider the total abolition of secret marriages.

Despite the fact that many secret marriages unwittingly violated the impediments of consanguinity, affinity, and spiritual affinity, the Church found itself overlooking these faults if the case came to its attention after years of marriage. After all, it was not reasonable to stigmatize the children of the marriage as bastards because of the misdeeds of parents. The Church found itself forced to maintain one rigorous standard for those contemplating marriage and a "softer" one for those already "married." To resolve the difficulty, the Council of Trent in 1563 decreed that henceforth all marriages not contracted before a priest and two or three witnesses would be void,[7] thereby ending the era of secret marriages. In England and Scotland, however, the practice persisted, although in waning form, until the eighteenth and nineteenth centuries.

MARRIAGE AS A SACRAMENT

Although Paul had demeaned marriage in comparison to virginity, he did suggest that it had allegorical meaning as a symbol of the unity of Christ (the Bridegroom) and his bride (the Church). Augustine had enhanced the dignity of marriage in claiming that its indissolubility stemmed from this *sacramentum* or symbolism. By 1164 we find, in Peter Lombard's *Sentences,* that marriage was not regarded as one of the seven sacraments. To Lombard it did not, like the Eucharist and Holy Orders, confer grace and virtue—it was purely remedial. But most Church Fathers held it to confer sanctifying grace, and Lombard's view rapidly lost favor.[8]

The recognition of marriage as one of the seven sacraments had a profound significance on the possibility of divorce. Heretofore the Church had proclaimed that marriage *ought* not to be dissolved, but had in practice permitted divorce. Henceforth, marriage *could not* be dissolved, which in practice meant that the Church did not recognize divorce except by papal dispensation.

CHILD MARRIAGES

In declaring that parental consent was not necessary for marriage, the Church not only weakened parental influence over children but also strengthened its own position as the main regulator of marriage. One effect of this policy was an increase in child betrothals and marriages. Parents were anxious to achieve beneficial alliances for themselves and their children, and wished to act while their children were still young enough to be manipulated.

Although canonists defined the age of reason as seven, children of even more tender years were sometimes married. John Ridgmarden, for example, married a girl of five who was carried to the ceremony in the arms of the priests. The young lad, finding the whole thing rather tedious, said he would "learn" no more that day. The priest answered, "You must speak a little more and then go play you."[9]

As long as marriages were carried out under Church auspices, the Church did not strongly oppose child marriage (it did make a rather weak plea that babies in the crib should, as a rule, not be married unless there was some pressing need).

One saving grace was that a marriage between children could be dissolved if it had not been consummated. Since there was always some doubt as to whether this had happened, a rule of thumb was arbitrarily applied. If the boy was more than 14 and the girl more than 12, and they had bedded together, the presumption was that they had had intercourse. If only one was above this arbitrary age of puberty, the marriage could be voided by the younger partner.[10]

IMPEDIMENTS TO MARRIAGE

The adoption of the seventh-degree limitation of consanguinity for prospective marriage proved most difficult to comply with, especially among the nobility. Since hardly a monarch in Europe was unrelated to another ruler, the papacy was under continuous pressure to loosen the consanguinity restrictions. But the restrictions could not be liberalized on grounds of practicality, for this would have implied that marriage was a contract at the disposition of man to alter as he saw fit. Consequently, theologians tried to rationalize the desire for liberalization on a foundation of natural law. Peter Lombard argued for a sixth-degree limitation on the grounds that there were six ages of the world. Finally, the fourth Lateran Council (1215), after due consideration, allowed those related beyond the fourth degree (less related than first cousins) to marry. One argument in support of the decision was that there were four humors (fluids) in the body, as well as four elements in the world.

THE CHURCH'S ATTITUDE TOWARD SEX

Regulating Sex among the Laity

The civil courts, which regarded women as valuable chattels, maintained a list of prescribed compensatory payments for various sexual misdemeanors that injured the "property" of the husband or father. The Church, on the other hand, concerned itself with the sinner's soul, which might be in mortal jeopardy of not attaining salvation. The recently converted English tribes seemed rather unconcerned about sexual sins, and St. Boniface, himself English, regretfully noted: " . . . English people . . . refuse to have legitimate wives, and continue to live in lechery and adultery after the manner of neighing horses and braying asses."[11]

Under the Romans, marriage problems had been handled in the civil courts; but with the ascent of the Christian emperors, the bishop, on invitation, was entitled to hear marriage cases. By the ninth century the bishop's court was issuing its own decrees on marriage, and in the eleventh century Pope Gregory VII was granted formal recognition from William the Conqueror of the ecclesiastical court's right to try all matters pertaining to the "soul." By the twelfth and thirteenth centuries, the "soul" was interpreted to include the deadly sins of fornication, adultery, and the like.

Punishment could involve corporal or pecuniary penance. In rare cases, the threat of excommunication was raised against sinners who failed to heed Church rules. It was a threat few cared to test, for to be excluded from the society of Christians in a God-fearing era was tantamount to being exiled to a living hell.

There were three methods for proceeding against a sexual offender: inquisition, accusation, and denunciation. Inquisition involved the judge acting as the accuser, although he often had help from the apparitor, who ferreted out most of the evidence. In the accusation method, anyone could come forward and say that the accused had sinned. This method was not very popular because if the accusations proved groundless, certain penalties might rebound to the accuser. Denunciation was the most-favored method because the Churchwarden would present the official indictment, using the informer merely as a "friend of the court." Unlike the civil court, the sinner could be made to testify against himself. Evil thoughts as well as acts were punishable.

Refusal to answer a charge might lead to a punishment greater than that meted out for confessing to it. In most cases, denial of a charge meant little to the court unless the accused could produce a large number of compurgators who would vouch for his credibility and uphold his innocence of the charge. Since the trials were held infrequently, often at considerable distance from the home of the accused and with delays in the hearing, the poor were severely handicapped in availing themselves of proper defense. In addition, witnesses were rare, legal counsel almost entirely absent, and injustice quite common.

The rich were usually able to surmount these difficulties with payments of contrition or through bribery. During the later Middle Ages, England was infested with swarms of "quaestors," or papal pardon-mongers. Chancellor Gascoigne complained in the fifteenth century: "Sinners say nowadays, I care not what or how many evils I do before God, for I can get at once, without the least difficulty, plenary remission of any guilt or sin whatever through an Indulgence granted me by the Pope, whose written grant I have bought for fourpence . . . for these grantors of Indulgence run about from place to place and sometimes give a letter for twopence, sometimes for a good drink of wine or beer, sometimes to pay their losses at a game of ball, sometimes for the hire of a prostitute, sometimes for fleshly love."[1][2]

To make it easy to determine what was prohibited and what punishments should follow each type of transgression, penitentials were instituted. The most famous of these is Theodore's Penitential, issued in the seventh century. Some penances were mild—for example, a man who had lain with his wife should not enter Church without a bath. The "sin" of marriage required the couple not to frequent the Church for 30 days, followed by 40 days' penance and the bringing of an offering. Childbirth, an unclean act, also required 40 days' absence from Church.

Peccant parishioners who were too poor to purchase indulgences, or those whose sin was too public or too great to be bought off, became targets for sadistic sport. The erring man could be made to promenade barelegged in a white shirt to the altar; there, holding a heavy two-pound candle, he recited numerous psalms, confessed his sins aloud, led the congregation in prayer for his soul, and asked forgiveness of all. After his absolutions, he placed the candle in front of a suitable ikon and received a certificate denoting that he had satisfactorily completed penance.

The woman sinner was apt to be punished more severely. At York, a woman judged guilty of fornication received 12 floggings before a procession in the cathedral, 12 more in her parish church, and 12 in the marketplace; in addition, she incurred a stiff fine.[13]

Officially, penance was not a punishment, but an expression of contrition on the part of the sinner. The doing of "good works" was an acceptable act of contrition. Payment of money to the Church was a "good work," thereby leading to the enrichment of the Church in proportion to the lightening of the layman's sins.

Abstinence was a favorite topic among theologians, who vied with each other in drawing up schedules of "refraining" days. One gentleman recommended abstinence during the seasons of fasting and on important festivals, on Thursdays to commemorate the arrest of Jesus, on Fridays to honor his death, and on Sundays in remembrance of the Resurrection. Not to slight his mother, Mary was given one of the remaining open days, Saturday, while Monday was reserved to commemorate the deceased. This left available for copulation only a few scattered Tuesdays and Wednesdays that did not fall on fast or feast days. A more generous soul allowed Monday, Tuesday, Thursday, and Saturday for sexual purposes, but cautioned that married persons should abstain for 40 days before Easter, Pentecost, and Christmas, as well as from the manifestation of conception by the wife until after the birth, and for seven, five, or three days before communion.[14]

When these rigorous proscriptions seemed to threaten the viability of marriage, the liberal divine, Robert de Courson, advanced the radical idea that lawful coitus was meritorious.[15] The liberal wing was strongly supported by the Scholastic, St. Thomas Aquinas. Aided by his teacher, Albert the Great, he developed the idea that coitus was not in itself sinful, even if it was an intense experience. God was the apex of reasonableness, and if he created Adam and Eve with a sexual apparatus, it was not intended merely to serve as an ornament. True, the sin of Adam and Eve had tainted the coital act with evil, but not because of the act per se. Rather, after eating of the apple, man had sustained a debilitating weakness of the will. In the heat of passion and in the experience of orgasm, man had lost the faculty of reason, and in the thrashing of limbs and in sensual cries he behaved like a beast of the field. Had man not sinned, he would have experienced keen sensual pleasure in his sexual relations while at the same time maintaining rational control of the will.

There is a similarity to the thinking of Augustine here, but the distinction lies in the fact that Augustine saw the sin of the Fall resulting in a compulsive desire for self-satisfaction that expressed itself most easily in sexual desires. Aquinas saw the sin as producing only a near loss of the powers of concentration. Accordingly, he was far less harsh in his judgment of the sinfulness of coitus. In fact, if an individual cohabited primarily for the purpose of procreation, for payment of the "marital debt," or to recollect the sacramental blessing of marriage, Aquinas believed that he was absolved from sin. If he was not married, he stood convicted of mortal sin.[16]

Lest Aquinas' leniency toward sexuality be overexaggerated, it should be noted that he made it clear that marriage was still inferior to virginity. Defending the proposition that marriage should receive a "goodness" value of 30, widowhood a score of 60, and virginity a score of 100, he explained: " . . . the married man abstains only from one that is not his, the widow from both hers and not hers, so that in the latter case we find the notion of double, just as 60 is the double of 30. Again 100 is 60 + 40, which latter number is the product of 4 X 10, and the number 4 is the first solid and square number. Thus the addition of this number is fitting to virginity, which adds perpetual incorruption to the perfection of widowhood."[17]

The thinking of the late medieval churchmen on sexuality was a considerable advance over the early Fathers. However, even though the violent hatred expressed by Jerome was replaced by the more moderate views of Aquinas, coitus was never quite legitimized as a proper behavioral function. It was a second-class perfection, belonging to the *operation or function* category, whereas primary perfection rested in the *essence or spiritual* quality of marriage. The married Christian, therefore, could never attain the heights of the cleric because the latter, in avoiding lust, retained his marvelous faculty of reason.[18]

The Church and the Sexual Excesses of the Priests

Starting with the pontificate of Gregory I (590-604), for some 400 years the Church sought to stem the sexual excesses and marriages of the clergy—but with a resounding lack of success.

Even the papacy was not free of sexual license. In 904, for example, a high papal official's daughter, Marozia, had her lover crowned Pope (Sergius III); not to be outdone, in 914 her mother had *her* lover installed as John X. The grandson of Marozia, John XII—the first teen-aged pope—was tried by an ecclesiastical council on the charge of incest and adultery with his father's concubine. It was a time, in sum, when a goodly number of Rome's populace could call the Pope "father" in the literal as well as the theological sense.

While willful violations often went unpunished, clerics were humiliated for minor involuntary "sins." A cleric who experienced orgasm while sleeping had to rise immediately, sing seven prescribed penitential psalms, and, in the morning, sing 30 more for good measure. The unfortunate cleric experiencing orgasm while asleep in Church had to sing the whole psalter.[19]

A reaction against the excesses of the clergy soon set in. Spearheaded by Pope Leo IX and Peter Damiani (1007-1072), an Italian hermit-monk, cardinal, and doctor of the Church, clerics were ordered to banish their wives and stay away from women; also, under some monastic codes, speaking to a woman earned the cleric 100 to 200 stripes.[20] At the same time, the children of the monks' concubines were impressed as slaves of the Church.

The successor of Leo IX, Nicholas II, issued a new sanction in 1059; it enjoined Christians to shun any Mass celebrated by a priest known to keep a concubine in his dwelling. The monk Hildebrand, who assumed the papacy as Gregory VII in 1073, enforced these statutes with fanatic zeal.

By the time of the first and second Lateran Councils in 1123 and 1139, further steps were taken. Hitherto, although monks had been forced to separate from their wives, the sanctity of the marital bond itself had never been in question. Now, not only were monks allowed to enter a monastery without the consent of their spouses (reversing the view of the early Fathers that mutual consent was necessary for such a move), but any marriage contracted in defiance of the canons was held to be invalid.[21]

These measures encountered stern resistance. In 1060, Ulrich, a bishop, attacked the concept of a celibatic clergy, citing the Scripture, which urged priests to take only one wife. Some went to the point of arguing that enforced celibacy prevented achieving the grace of virginity, since such grace could be won only by an act of free will.[22]

An anti-pope arose—Honarius II (1061-1072)—who fought to maintain clerical "privileges." The Milanese clergy, long accustomed to marriage, tried to make the issue one of Rome versus Milan, but in vain—with the support of the emperor, Milan was put down. By 1215 the fourth Lateran Council, under the aegis of Innocent III, decreed that incontinence on the part of a priest must not go unpunished and that the sons of canons should no longer inherit their fathers' Church positions.

In England, however, the elimination of married clergy led to a widespread increase in concubinage. Henry I, authorized in 1129 by a Church synod to execute the laws punishing ecclesiastics who abandoned celibacy, found a new source of revenue to appease his avariciousness. The offenders paid Henry a tax for the privilege of keeping a concubine. An examination of the records of the ecclesiastical courts of the time shows that sexual offenses attributable to the clergy were from 5 to 50 times as great as among the laity on a per capita basis.[23] By the time of the Reformation, it is estimated that there were 100,000 prostitutes in England, whose prime customers were the ecclesiastics. The Beggars' Petition asked, "Who is she that will set her hands to work to get three-pence a day, and may have at least twenty-pence a day, to sleep an hour with a friar, a monk, or a priest."[24]

The situation became so bad that traveling clergy had difficulty in getting lodging among the laity for fear that no man would know his own child. A poem of the period warned:

> Were I a man that house helde,
> If any woman with me dwelde,
> Ther is no frer [friar] bot he were gelde,
> Shuld com within my wones [home]
> For may he til a woman wynne,
> In priveyte, he wul not blynne [stop],
> Er he a childe put his withinne,
> And perchaunce two at ones.[25]

Homosexuality also became such a problem that it was stipulated that any offender would be demoted and deprived of future advancement in the order; habitual offenders were struck with anathema. Only the onset of the Reformation, when priests were permitted to marry, cut down the sexual excesses of the clergy in England.

The prurient behavior of the clergy during this period must be understood in context. In the United States today there is only one priest for about a thousand people; in thirteenth-century Europe, one in twelve was a cleric.[26] This high proportion is attributable not only to the religiosity of the times, but to the fact that the monastary offered one of the few opportunities for a lowborn person to advance himself. How else could he free himself from being tied to the land and its feudal obligations? Moreover, most educational facilities and books were lodged in the monasteries, which remained relatively free from the frequent feudal skirmishes that ravaged the countryside. Understandably, many took the cloth for reasons that were far from spiritual, and many were unable or unwilling to curtail their sexual freedom. Even when we note that many monks lived in sin, a goodly number were faithful husbands to their wives and concubines. In any event, the enforcement of celibacy seemed to result in a new clergy, less interested in the flesh and more dedicated to the execution of papal policies.

CHURCH AND STATE STRUGGLE OVER MARRIAGE

The Middle Ages were marked by intense struggles between the papacy and various kings. In theory, the king was the temporal arm of God, and the Pope was his spiritual arm; but in practice both men sought to control events in Europe. The kings envied the growing wealth of the Church in land and benefices; the Pope, thanks to the aid of Pepin the Short in the eighth century, became a temporal ruler as well as the spiritual head of Christendom. It was the Pope, after all, who crowned Pepin's son Charlemagne as "Emperor of the

Romans" on Christmas day, 800, hoping thereby to initiate a subtle superior-inferior relationship in which the Pope would be the feudal overlord of the vassal Christian kings.

The Pope held a mighty trump card in the forthcoming struggles. Powerful though they might be, the kings were Christians, and their personal lives were subject to the same impediments in marriage as the ordinary layman—unless the Pope chose to give them dispensation. This papal power involved two protracted battles in the Middle Ages, and each time the papacy emerged stronger and more politically influential.

Some 300 years before these power struggles, the first recorded instance of papal intervention in a king's marriage had occurred. Theodebert, King of Austrasia, had violated the impediment of affinity by marrying the widow of his brother. Pope Vigilius (537-555) did not dare to break up the marriage, but contented himself with asking the Bishop of Arles to advise the king to expiate his sin "by a no little affliction of the body."[27]

The year 857 witnessed the beginning of the first real battle between Church and state over marriage—that of Lothair II, eponymous ruler of Lotharingia (a strip of land west of the Rhine between the North Sea and the Jura mountains). The marriage, a political one, soon wearied Lothair, who now wished to marry Waldrada, the concubine of his youth. For 12 years he tried every pretense conceivable to shed his wife, Teutberga. First he charged her with having had an incestuous relationship with her brother, and with not being a virgin at marriage. When the acknowledgement of her virginity at marriage was read to him, he declared that this had been achieved through her occult powers. When this ruse failed, he convoked a council of ecclesiastics and submitted forged documents and a forced confession from Teutberga of many heinous crimes. The "kangaroo" court finally annulled the marriage.

The queen's brother then took a bold step: he asked the Pope to review the proceedings. Eventually a synod was convoked to review the case. Lothair did not object, having heavily bribed the papal emissaries. But the Pope denounced the synod and its meretricious bishop. There followed a seesaw battle between Lothair and his royal relatives, and Pope Nicholas II and his successor, Hadrian II. Eventually, Lothair's position was weakened by the avarice of his relatives, who coveted the heirless Lothair's land, thus proving that property was thicker than blood. Lothair was forced to renounce Waldrada and journey to Rome for forgiveness in 869.

The victory over Lothair signaled the onset of the golden age of the papacy. Nicholas' guiding principle that no subject need obey anyone—be he serf or king—who violated the moral precepts of divine law, was largely carried out. In the succeeding four centuries, the papacy ruled on many marriage cases concerning kings and the nobility, usually with success. In fact, the ceremony in which the Pope invested the king with temporal power increasingly reflected the changing status of the two offices. Whereas formerly the Pope had anointed the head of the king with fine oil, he now anointed only his shoulder blade and arm, signifying that he was but a mere technician in the papal scheme of things. It was the Pope who conferred the imperial emblem, crown, sword, scepter, and ring, and the emperor who swore an oath of obedience to the Pope and kissed his feet. The king thus became the "son" of the Roman Church; the Pope essayed the role of "father." By the twelfth century, the Pope was no longer the "vicar of St. Peter," for such a title could not adequately reflect the papal authority. Rather, His Holiness was henceforth known as the "vicar of Christ," an indication of how high the papacy had risen.

The most epic battle between a king and a Pope came about in the match between Philip Augustus, King of France (the most powerful monarch in the West), and Pope Innocent III, one of the most dynamic popes in history. The story starts with the demise of Philip's first wife. Seeking a useful ally through remarriage, Philip chose the allegedly beautiful and youthful Ingeburg, sister of King Canute VI of Denmark.

On August 14, 1193, Philip, consumed by impatience for the marriage, met the wedding party at Amiens and married her. A chronicler reports that on the next day, during her crowning, "marvelous to behold, the king, instigated by the devil and vexed by the sorceries of evil, began to hate the wife so long desired.... By suggestion of the evil one, he began vehemently to be horrified and to tremble and pale at the sight of her so that, very much perturbed, he sustained himself with difficulty until the end of the ceremony."[28]

Subsequently, in trying to rid himself of her, he claimed that he had tried to consummate the marriage but failed. Whence came this repulsion? To one writer, Philip's anger at Canute's failure to support his plans against England was redirected at Ingeburg. Some believe that the young beauty suffered from halitosis, while others assert that the body of the noble queen stank.[29] Be that as it may, Philip tried to get her to go back to Denmark, but she refused. Philip then had 16 renowned ecclesiastics and nobles swear that the impediment of consanguinity existed. The king's council, predictably, acted on cue and declared the marriage dissolved. Poor Ingeburg, who knew no French, could utter only "Mala Francia, Mala Francia, Roma, Roma"—to convey the idea that she would tell the Pope all. She was finally shipped off to a monastery, and Philip—defying the suggestion of Pope Celestine III to take her back—married Agnès of Meran in June 1196.

The charge of consanguinity was clearly refuted by Canute; he sent the Pope a highly accurate picture of his family genealogy. Celestine did not dare to go further than his mild disapproval of Philip's actions. Ingeburg pined away on a rather pitiful dole, shut off from society. Then Celestine died, and was succeeded by Innocent III. In a letter to Philip, the new Pope briefly recalled his happy youth in France, but terminated the social amenities by stating that if Philip did not take back his wife, the Pope would not hesitate "to do what we owe to our duty."[30]

When Philip disregarded the warning, an interdiction was placed on his kingdom. He tried unsuccessfully to bully the clergy into disregarding it, and in the end, with humble tears, he took back his queen and swore to rectify his ways. Another council was to take place soon, and in the meantime Philip kept the queen in semiconfinement. The Pope learned of this but hesitated to act because there was the possibility that some of the clergy would follow Philip. Moreover, he needed the French king's aid against Philip of Swabia and to help him stamp out the rampant heresy in southern France.

The high officials at the council, fearing the king, were ready to annul the marriage, but because of the courage of a lowly parish priest who ably defended the queen, the proceedings dragged on for 15 days. Philip became disgusted with the excessive duration of the council and mercurially declared that he was keeping the queen. Gratified, the Pope recognized Philip's children by Agnès as legitimate, but stated that this in no way impugned the validity of Philip's marriage to Ingeburg.

Philip, delighted that his children were legitimated, incarcerated the queen again. The years ticked by. In 1208, a full 15 years after his marriage, Philip was still trying to dissolve the strongly forged bonds of matrimony. He now maintained that some magic power prevented consummation of his marriage with Ingeburg. In addition, he claimed that she wished to embrace the religious life. It didn't matter which grounds were used—he wanted the Pope to nullify the marriage without convening a council of judgment.

Innocent, for his part, wanted to punish King John of England for his perfidy to the Church in seizing Church funds. He certainly needed Philip's temporal arm to execute this wish. Therefore, he would gladly nullify the marriage if any objective evidence could be brought forth. But he could not bring himself to turn his back completely on Ingeburg and deprive her of her queenship without an objective trial. He wrote the king that the queen denied that sexual intercourse had not taken place or that consanguinity existed. In addition, he believed that her conversion to religious life resulted from Philip's coercion. Should Philip want to convene an unbiased council, the Pope would send his legate to aid in its preparation. Philip argued that since he had not experienced an orgasm in the act of coupling, the marriage was null. The Pope found these fine distinctions embarrassing, and urged his legate to tell Philip to stop voicing "insanities of this kind."[31]

At this point, the aging 48-year-old Philip made no further plans to shed Ingeburg legally. After being harassed for 20 years, she lived in relative peace as the queen during the remaining decade of Philip's life, although it is reported that they never had "full" conjugal relations.

In retrospect, the victory was less than complete for Innocent III, who, for political reasons, never brought the king to complete submission. Even his loyalty to the queen was tempered by his political policy; nevertheless, he never disavowed her cause, even when his perseverance brought him no clear gain. He had checked the attempt of the most powerful ruler in Western Europe to flaunt the decrees of the Church on the indissolubility of marriage, and he had brought the Holy See to its apogee as a political influence in Europe.

The Church and Apostolic Dispensation

On the subject of allowing ostensibly forbidden marriages to occur, the Church proved much more sensitive to the political climate and to material considerations than it had been regarding the dissolution of the marriages of kings. In 1137, Louis VII, surnamed the Pious, married the most famous queen of the Middle Ages, Eleanor of Aquitaine. Some time later, St. Bernard of Clairvaux discovered that the couple were related well within the seventh degree. Louis was but five generations removed from his ancestor Hugh Capet, who had married a sister of Eleanor's great-great-grandfather. But nothing was done to dissolve the politically expedient marriage, which had served to unite France.

Pope Clement III (1187-1191) was confronted by the case of Count William, who had had his first wife put away on the grounds of consanguinity and had subsequently remarried. Now, ill at ease, the Count confessed that he had perjured himself when he had alleged that a blood tie existed between his first wife and himself. The pontiff, reversing the earlier rule that the husband must return to the first wife, ruled that Count William should remain with his second wife. Musing on a suitable punishment, he concluded that, regarding future copulation with his wife, he must approach her "contritely and with condign sadness and reluctance."[32]

The same Innocent III, who had so stoutly opposed Philip, issued a dispensation allowing the son of the Duke of Austria to wed his cousin, related within the fourth degree, because of the Duke's participation in a Holy Crusade and the political advantage of such a marriage to the duchy. Other French nobles received dispensations for vigorous participation in the battles against the heretical Albigensians.

Later, in 1251, another dispensation was granted to a couple contingent upon the husband's release of prisoners and his joining the papal party in the struggle against Frederick the Emperor. Gregory IX granted one marital dispensation if the recipient donated one-third of his total income for three years for the benefit of the Holy Land; another dispensation was granted when the viscount in question agreed to furnish 40 knights for one year to fight the Moors in Spain.

THE CHURCH AND THE INDISSOLUBILITY OF MARRIAGE

While formally opposing remarriage if the first spouse was alive, in practice the early Church maintained a flexible position. Recent converts to Christianity, such as the Franks, Saxons, and Goths, had long-standing customs permitting remarriage after divorce. The Church, occupied with strengthening its new found position as the spiritual caretaker of the populace, wisely refrained from a direct assault on the customs of converts.

Concessions by the Church are also evident in the Council of Agde at

Narbonne in 506, which, while condemning unlawful divorce, implied that those seeking permission from the bishops for divorce might be permitted to remarry. At the Council of Nantes in 658, however, it was decreed that adultery was a legitimate ground for divorce, but not for remarriage.

Gregory II, in a letter to St. Boniface in 726, stated that if a wife was physically unable to perform the conjugal act, the husband was permitted to marry again even though she was still living. It is clear, therefore, that no unilateral policy was yet in force by the eighth century: some councils affirmed the traditional indissolubility of marriage, while others permitted exceptions.

Under the monarchies of Pepin the Short and Charlemagne, however, the view that marriage was indissoluble gained ground, and eventually, in 1142, Gratian's *Decretum* codified the diverse rulings on divorce. According to him, once the *copula* had occurred, the *sacramentum* entered into marriage, and henceforth neither captivity, postmarital physical incapacity, desertion, imprisonment, choice of religious life, slavery, or even apostacy could sever the bond. At the same time there was also acceptance of Lombard's view that marriage is valid if vows in the "present tense" were undertaken. This kind of marriage could, however, be dissolved by papal dispensation or by taking holy orders *provided* that the marriage had remained unconsummated. These views remain in force today.

Dissolution of the "Mixed" Marriage

The "Pauline privilege," as interpreted from Paul's statements in the New Testament, had been interpreted as sanctioning divorce if a pagan spouse voluntarily left his Christian partner. But as the Church gained strength, its attitude toward "mixed marriage" became increasingly severe. In Spain, where Christianity met little opposition among the native folk religions, and where a considerable number of Jews had settled, the "Pauline privilege" was elaborated considerably. In 633, at the Council of Toledo, one of the canons stated that a converted Jewish woman *must* leave her unconverted Jewish husband, an act never suggested by Paul.

The early Christian Fathers, to be sure, had considered the marriages of unbelievers to be just as indissoluble as those of true believers. A rationale for the new outlook was needed, therefore, and Hugo of St. Victor (1096-1141) provided it. He stated that when one of two pagans is converted, the Christian exists in a more sanctified state than the infidel, because the latter alone is now responsible for the *injuria Creatoris.* The "injury to the Creator" represented the fallen state of all mankind, compounded by the fact that the non-Christian, unlike his mate, was not restored by baptism; hence the Christian was free to dissolve the marriage and remarry "in the Lord" even though the nonbeliever wished to abide in matrimony. Shortly thereafter, Gratian took quite another point of view, as did Peter Lombard. They advocated that the believer should be free to remarry only if the nonbeliever leaves.

Pope Innocent III resolved the issue by stating that if a pagan becomes a Christian, he may not leave his spouse except if the other blasphemes the divine name or draws the partner into mortal sin. If the partner was originally a Christian, however, and only later moved to paganism, nothing could sunder the marriage. Marriage between pagans may be "true," but it is not *ratum* (ratified). Among Christians it is always both "true" and *ratum,* for once the sacrament of marriage is received it is never lost. The basic distinction between pagan and Christian marriage thus revolved around the sacramental quality of the latter. In case of a conflict, therefore, the *ratum* always took precedence over the "true," and a "true" marriage could be dissolved, but not a *ratum* one.[33]

At the close of the Middle Ages, the Church was well on its way to solidifying its position on marriage and adopting a homogeneous policy throughout most of Christendom. The *divortium vinculo matrimonii* came to be considered an act that declared a marriage null and void because of such impediments as a previous verbal contract with another person in the *present* tense, consanguinity within the fourth degree, and spiritual affinity. Because the principals were never really considered to have been married, the taking of another spouse was permitted. On the other hand, *divortium a mensa et toro* (separation from bed and board without the privilege of remarriage) was granted for adultery, heresy or apostasy, and cruelty.[34]

CONCLUSIONS

The Church started the sixth century without temporal power regarding marriage for several reasons: legal control of marriage was largely centered in the civil courts, Church policy regarding marriage was inconsistent because of the lack of strong centralization, and the clergy served the world of the flesh as much as that of the spirit. As we have seen, many of these difficulties were resolved, and the Church emerged as a political and spiritual power of no small consequence.

To fully understand the impact of the Church on marriage, we must understand the thinking of medieval man. Whether peasant or prelate, he regarded himself on earth much as a voyager. He might be visiting for a long or a short time; he might be materially successful or impoverished, happy or sad. But always in the back of his mind was the knowledge that what counted was his ultimate destination: heaven or hell.

The Church had taken over marriage, heretofore a quasi-civil affair, and had made it an integral concern, steeped in symbolic significance and ceremony. With this bold stroke, the way was paved for its control of a considerable amount of secular behavior. Kings ruled by force of arms, but in the age of faith the Church ruled by more powerful means: it could deny salvation and it could instill guilt in those who failed to honor its precepts. As we have seen, these powers could effectively force the most powerful monarch into submission by paralyzing his subjects into compliance on pain of excommunication.

By restricting and defining the conditions for sex, war, and work, the Church hoped to build a better Christian society. The populace was ready to follow the proscriptions of the Church as long as they believed that God responded to human plea and that the Church was the primary mediator between man and God. By the close of the Middle Ages most persons still believed in God, but the conduct of the Church caused an increasing number to question the role of the clergy as valid mediators. Impelled by its taste for growing political power and control of the laity, the Church plunged into the affairs of this world with such rapaciousness that the contradiction between its professed concern for the spiritual salvation of man and its greedy use of Church offices for power and wealth was not lost on the laity. It would not be too long before a fiery spokesman such as Martin Luther would give full vent to this smoldering discontent.

REFERENCES

1. G. E. Howard, *A History of Matrimonial Institutions,* Vol. 1, p. 313.
2. Ibid., p. 310.
3. O. D. Watkins, *Holy Matrimony.*
4. Ibid.
5. C. J. Gellinek, "Marriage by consent in literary sources of medieval Germany." Germany."
6. O. D. Watkins, op. cit.
7. G. E. Howard, op. cit.
8. G. H. Joyce, *Christian Marriage: An Historical and Doctrinal Study.*
9. E. S. Turner, *A History of Courting.*
10. F. Pollock and F. W. Maitland, *The History of English Law before the Time of Edward I.*
11. G. May, *Social Control of Sex Expression,* p. 65.
12. Ibid., p. 150.
13. E. S. Turner, op. cit.
14. D. S. Bailey, *Sexual Relation in Christian Thought.*
15. Ibid.
16. T. Aquinas, *Summa Theologica,* Vol. 19.
17. T. Aquinas, *The Summa Theologica,* 2 Vols., p. 1055.
18. D. S. Bailey, op. cit.
19. G. May, op. cit.
20. M. A. Gist, *Love and War in the Middle English Romances.*
21. D. S. Bailey, op. cit.
22. J. Langdon-Davies, *Sex, Sin, and Sanctity.*
23. G. May, op. cit.
24. Ibid., p. 126.
25. T. Wright, *Political Poems and Songs Relating to English History Composed during the Period from the Accession of Edward III to That of Richard III.*
26. D. S. Bailey, op. cit.
27. C. E. Smith, *Papal Enforcement of Some Medieval Marriage Laws,* p. 54.

28. Ibid., p. 106.
29. Ibid.
30. Ibid., p. 113.
31. Ibid., p. 126.
32. Ibid., p. 103.
33. O. D. Watkins, op. cit.
34. W. Goodsell, *A History of Marriage and the Family*.

8

Marriage among the Medieval Laity

The laity, like the Church, did not esteem the marriage *relationship* very highly, although the marriage institution itself became accepted as a sacrament. However, various factors brought about a change in attitude toward the marriage relationship, and by the fourteenth and fifteenth centuries the concept of marriage as being solely a remedy for concupiscence and for the purpose of procreation was considerably broadened.

LEGAL STATUS OF WOMEN

Because of her "frailty," a married woman in Western Europe could not represent herself in court, nor was she entitled to engage in business transactions or make a will. No matter how wealthy she was, she could not participate in a legislative body—for example, in the English Parliament or in the French Estates-General. In line with her inferior status, any legal offense that she committed usually incurred one-half the fine that would be levied against a man for the same offense.

The tortuous logic used to support these legal prejudices is strikingly illustrated in a French lawyer's defense of the Salic laws,[1] which prohibited any woman from succeeding to the throne of France. He quotes the New Testament (Matthew 6:28): "Consider the lilies of the field, how they grow; they toil not, neither do they spin: And yet I say unto you, that even Solomon in all his glory was not arrayed like one of these." What has this to do with the Salic law? The lawyer first points out that France is the kingdom of the lily, as evidenced by the *fleur de lis* on the royal escutcheon; and according to the Bible, lilies, though gloriously arrayed, cannot spin. Men do not spin; women do. Ergo, women should never inherit the throne.

On the other hand, an unmarried woman of age and a widow were fully competent before the law, with the right to sue and the dubious privilege of being sued. They could also make feoffments and bonds without a guardian, hold lands, and make contracts and wills. The difficulty with their position, however, was that in a somewhat unscrupulous era they did not have men to protect their lands. They also lacked the married woman's security of the dowry and, consequently, only the exceptionally strong willed could risk the "advantages" of remaining single.

Inheritance of Property

Legal discrimination against married women extended to their right to inherit land. Among many Germanic tribes, married women were excluded from ownership, but a widow acquired full possession of her morning-gift (a substantial gift by the husband on the morning after the wedding) for life. Anglo-Saxons showed more generosity toward their married women: the wife had full possession of the morning-gift even while her husband lived. If she bore children, she was entitled, by Ethelbert's law (584-616), to one-half of the family estate. According to the law of King Canute of England, however, she was entitled to a third of the couple's land acquired after the marriage, whether or not children had been born.

For a time there seemed to be a growing recognition of the importance of marriage and women's marital rights; but the rise of feudalism in England, after the invasion of the Normans in 1066, led to a rapid deterioration in the economic status of the wife. Feudalism required an ability on the part of the vassal to maintain order within his fief, collect taxes, defend his territory, and provide troops for his lord in time of war. Few women were physically or psychologically capable of executing these requirements. Since it now became crucial to the lord that his fiefs be at all times controlled by men, inheritance laws were altered to ensure this condition.

Henceforth, in England, the wife could not inherit more than one-third of her husband's land, nor was she able to inherit her husband's domicile—it passed into the hands of a male heir. Also, as a widow without children, she could remarry only with the king's permission. Sometimes the king did not even obtain the widow's consent to a marriage that he arranged. John I of England granted Richard de Lee the right to marry the widow of Stephen Falconbridge (who had an inheritance and a dowry) in return for 50 marks. The marriage did not take place because the widow herself paid the king 50 pounds to change his mind.[2]

SOCIAL STATUS OF WOMEN

The philosophers and theologians of the Middle Ages spent considerable time trying to find a rationale for the inferior treatment of women. Thomas Aquinas considered women inferior because of their more emotional nature and lesser capacity to reason. Hence women were incapable of being clerics—in short, unworthy of education. All this seemed logical enough because, as the Bible indicated, woman came out of man and not vice versa. Aquinas also considered the question of whether woman should have been created in the first place:

... [by] nature, woman is defective and misbegotten, for the active force in the male seed tends to the production of a perfect likeness in the masculine sex, while the production of woman comes from defect in the active force or from some external change, such as that of a south wind, which is moist, as the Philosopher observes. On the other hand, in relation to the universal nature, woman is not misbegotten, but is included in nature's intention as ordered to the work of generation. Now the universal intention of nature depends on God, Who is the universal Author of nature. Therefore, in producing nature, God formed not only the male but also the female.[3]

Aquinas points out, however, that once a child is past infancy, the mother's role in educating the child is largely superseded by that of the father. Due to the "laws of nature" (her inferiority), a woman is a dependent and hence a "natural" subject. A male slave, contrariwise, is a subject only because of the conventions of men. It follows, therefore, that a slave, unlike a woman, is competent to receive holy orders, and that men are better friends of other men than are women.[4]

On the question of whether a man loves his father better than his wife, Aquinas noted that there are different kinds of love. Husband and wife are closer than father and son because of the intimate nature of the parents' relationship. On the other hand, from the point of view of loving the "good," the father takes precedence over the wife.[5]

A man who allowed his wife to gain the upper hand was a disgrace, and male society took steps to punish both the aggressive wife and the timid husband. Among the Teutons, a woman who struck her husband was compelled to ride on an ass through the streets, sitting backwards and holding the astonished animal's tail in her hands. A henpecked husband might one day find his neighbors lifting the roof from his house—a man who could not protect himself from his wife should not be sheltered from the elements.

Moderate physical punishment administered to one's woman was not considered amiss. A Welsh law states that the stick used in such chastisement should not be longer than the husband's arm or thicker than his middle finger. If no bones were broken or the physiognomy of one's spouse seriously marred, little complaint would be raised. In fact, a proverb of the period advises:

> A woman, a dog, and a walnut tree
> The more you beat them, the better they'll be.

If the husband was brutal, the wife was reminded of the counsel of the Lady of La Tour: "She who bears with such a husband patiently, and without discrediting herself, so much the more increases the good renown of herself and of her honors."[6]

Women were characterized as having a feeble intellect and being emotionally labile; they laughed and cried at nothing, and could switch from love to hate in a moment. A strong man could handle a woman and possibly control her with beatings; but alas, this could not educate her. Her limited genetic potential doomed her to be captious, obstinate, perverse, and susceptible to the devil's influence.

Occasionally, some women were fortunate enough to gain an education and then go on to make an impact on history. Such a woman was Héloïse.

ABELARD AND HELOISE: MARRIAGE OF THE MILLENNIUM

The most famous love affair of the Middle Ages was that of Abélard and Héloïse, who lived during the eleventh and twelfth centuries. Much of what we know of them is based on an exchange of letters—three by her, four by him, and one by him to an unnamed friend which somehow passed through her hands. There is some question about their authenticity, particularly that of the first letter, the earliest copies having been written in Latin about a century after the lovers had died. Nonetheless, there are many who believe them to be authentic, and they certainly are consistent with the personalities of the couple as described by others.

Abélard was a theologian and philosopher who became a canon (unordained) of the Cathedral of Notre Dame. By the year 1118, he was 38 years old and the most famous theologian in Europe. Handsome, polished, and above all enthusiastic, he attracted students from every corner of Europe, and their contributions kept him from any want—or almost any want. Until then he had been chaste, but now, almost a demigod, he saw no reason to deny himself the earthly solaces. He heard of an 18-year-old girl in Paris, Héloïse, niece of the canon Fulbert. Despite her youth, she was already well versed in Latin, Greek, and Hebrew, and was regarded as not only brilliant but also lovely to look at. Abélard decided to "join her with myself in love, and I believed that I could effect this most easily. For such renown had I then, and so excelled in grace of youth and form, that I feared no refusal from whatever woman I might deem worthy of my love."[7]

He confidently contrived to become a lodger at Fulbert's house, claiming that his own household was too expensive. Fulbert, delighted to have so great a scholar under his roof, welcomed Abélard and played into his hands by telling him that he could instruct Héloïse at any hour of the day or night. Abélard gleefully noted:

What more need I say? First in one house we are united, then in one mind. So, under the pretext of discipline, we abandoned ourselves utterly to love, and those secret retreats which love demands, the study of our texts afforded us. And so, our books lying open before us, more words of love rose to our lips than of literature, kisses were more frequent than speech. Oftener went our hands to each other's bosom than to the pages; love turned our eyes more frequently to itself than it directed them to the study of the texts. That we might be the less suspected, blows were given at times, by love, not by anger, affection, not indignation, which surpassed all ointments in their sweetness.[8]

At first, Fulbert paid no attention to rumors of the affair between the scholar and his niece. Finally, he took them seriously and sent Abélard away. But Héloïse was pregnant. One night, in Fulbert's absence, Abélard and Héloïse eloped and fled to his home in Brittany, where a child, Astrolabe, was born.

Fulbert was overcome with grief, and enraged that he was impotent to punish Abélard. For the moment, he could do little because he could not pursue the culprit in the latter's home territory. Then Abélard, perhaps out of contrition for the girl and her uncle, perhaps thinking that his career was in jeopardy, came to Paris to see Fulbert. He proposed marrying her provided that the marriage would be by secret vow and no one would hear of it. Abélard wanted to resume his position in the Church without fear of discovery, and he hoped that the child would be cared for by his sister. Héloïse bitterly protested against the marriage: it would interfere with his career and with his contribution to the world. Here too, as in everything else in their relationship, Abélard's wishes prevailed.

Despite the secret marriage, the gossips had already put two and two together and surmised that the absence of the couple was due to an affair and/or a pregnancy. Contrary to his promise, Fulbert leaked the news that the couple were not actually living in sin. But Héloïse, to protect Abélard, swore that she was not his wife but only his mistress. Fulbert was not only filled with shame, he was being made to look like a liar as well!

At the urging of Abélard, and to escape her uncle's contumely, Héloïse fled to the Argenteuil nunnery near Paris and donned the nun's habit, but did not take any vows. There she and Abélard were able to have a few trysts. Fulbert and his family thought that Abélard had grown tired of his wife and was preparing to shed her by having her become a nun. He could no longer stand idly by while it seemed to him that Abélard had made a fool of Héloïse, of Fulbert, and of his family. He bribed Abélard's servant, and as Abélard slept, a band of men sprang upon him and castrated him while he struggled in vain. If Héloïse was to be a nun, then Abélard should be only a monk! Two of the scoundrels were caught and deprived of their genitalia and eyes—testimony to the penchant for mutilation during the Middle Ages.

The disconsolate Abélard found the shame even worse than the pain. He ordered Héloïse, who was not yet 20 years of age, to take the nun's veil; he would then become a monk. He asked her to act first because he did not fully trust her.

The rest of his life was a sad anticlimax. One of his books was burned for its unorthodoxy, and he had continuous trouble with the monks under his supervision (some of them tried to poison him). He died a natural death in 1142. Héloïse became a prioress and was much beloved by the Church and her nuns until her death in 1164.

The Letters

The lovers' letters were written between 1129 and 1132, some years after Abélard's castration. The first two of her three letters have made Héloïse one of the most admired women in history. Why? Above all else, she is unusually selfless—she is willing to do anything and everything for her lover. There are no qualifications, no ethical concerns, no guilt feelings—only full compliance with Abélard's wishes.

Héloïse was beautiful and educated. But she was more than that: she was also an alive, sensuous, vibrant woman who enjoyed the pleasures of the flesh. Note how she addressed Abélard: "To her master, nay father, to her husband, nay brother; his handmaid, nay daughter, his spouse, nay sister: to ABELARD, HELOISE."[9] These are the words of a woman seeking the exact word to convey the well of feeling in her who, finding no word equal to the task, chooses the one that signifies everything—ABELARD.

She admits that she has taken the veil—not for love of God, but for love of Abélard—and she refuses to allow herself the comfort of rationalization:

> So sweet to me were those delights of lovers which we enjoyed in common that they cannot either displease me nor hardly pass from my memory. Whithersoever I turn, always they bring themselves before my eyes with the desire for them. Nor even when I am asleep do they spare me their illusions. In the very solemnities of the Mass, when prayer ought to be more pure, the obscure phantoms of those delights so thoroughly captivate my wretched soul to themselves that I pay heed to their vileness rather than to my prayers. And when I ought to lament for what I have done I sigh rather for what I had had to forego. Not only the things that we did, but the places also and the times in which we did them are so fixed with thee in my mind that in the same times and places I re-enact them all with thee, nor even when I am asleep have I any rest from them. At times by the very motions of my body the thoughts of my mind are disclosed, nor can I restrain the utterance of unguarded words.[10]

Only once does she evidence less than perfect admiration of her lord Abélard. Throughout much of the first letter, there is a plaintive note that he does not love her very much because he has never once written her since she took her vows. She asks, perhaps almost demands, that he write. This "human flaw," like the beauty grain on a lovely face, only serves to enhance her stature. She shows us that she is not a goddess, but a human being with the need to hear from her lover. It is easy to identify with her because, like us, she has plebeian needs and can express them very well. However, unlike many of us, she is capable of rejecting almost all these needs when the interests of her lover are at stake, and we therefore admire her all the more. We may consider her actions unwise and unfair to herself; but we esteem her because she has shown us the power of the will and how it can subject even a strong body to its decision.

It is more difficult to identify with Abélard. He is castrated; we are not. As he himself puts it, " . . . for me no crown remains, since there remains no cause for strife . . . in him from whom is plucked out the thorn of concupiscence."[11] And even though he has our sympathy for the cruel treatment he has experienced, we are struck by his egotism. When Héloïse is pregnant, for example, his primary concern is apparently not for her, but for the effect the pregnancy and their subsequent marriage might have on his reputation.

Unlike Héloïse, Abélard has strong feelings of "rationalization"–"sour grapes." Now that sex is beyond his capacity, he can see no good in it. He chides her for complaining about God's insensitivity in allowing him to be emasculated. God should be glorified, praised, and thanked for this gift of "divine mercy."

What does Abélard think of their sexual relationship now? "Need I recall our earlier fornications and most shameful pollutions which preceded our marriage? . . . Thou knowest to what great infamies my immoderate lust had sacrificed our bodies, until no reverence for honour nor for God even, for the days of Our Lord's Passion or of any solemnity soever could recall me from wallowing in that filth."[12]

We understand Abélard, pity him, but do not admire him. He has adjusted to a catastrophic situation by acquiring the ability to distort. He has shown us that the mind can enable us to continue when we are hurt by clouding our senses so that we do not see things as they really are. Abélard, the *adaptive man*, is much less admirable than Héloïse, the *heroic woman*.

Héloïse represents a precursor of Renaissance Woman. Superficially, she appears to be a model churchwoman, true to her vow of chastity and greatly admired by the Church for her exemplary behavior. Yet if such a great woman has sexual desires, can sex really be evil? Are honor and sensuality really incompatible, or cannot they both exist in the "good" person? Héloïse made sexual honesty respectable, and she foreshadowed a new kind of ideal woman. This new model was pious, but did not shun a natural appetite of sensuality within the holy bonds of matrimony. We shall meet this new type shortly in the works of Chaucer.

THE CHANGING SOCIAL STATUS OF WOMEN

As trade with the East and among the European nations increased, towns sprang up and the nascent bourgeois class banded together to form guilds. Their labors required more skill and less physical strength than agricultural tasks, and many tradesmen were eventually assisted in their work by their wives and children. Of 85 English guilds, 72 included woman members (some were paid less than men for equal work).[13] Widows and children could remain guild members after the father died, but women rarely advanced to administrative functions. The improvement in women's occupational opportunities had an effect on their social status. As an active contributor to the family earnings, she gained a greater voice in family decisions. When she shared the same work interests as her husband, she became that much more interesting a companion.

Changes occurred also among the nobility. By the end of the Anglo-Saxon period, the wives of the lords no longer ate in separate apartments—they could join their lords in the great hall. Widows showed an increasing ability to preserve their estates, resisting the efforts of their overlords to marry them off. In this connection they were aided by the decline of feudalism and the support of the kings, who placed limits on the size of the armies of the nobility in their efforts to establish themselves as absolute monarchs.

As Europe prospered, the wealthy exhibited a thirst for luxuries, and women used their newly gained status to discard the austere wardrobes prescribed for them by the clergy. They began to pay more attention to their toilette, and false hair came into vogue. One churchman swore at the Assize of God that women were using so much color on their faces that not enough was in supply to paint the holy images in Church.

By the fourteenth and fifteenth centuries, women's clothing became quite bold: dresses were so low-necked and breasts laced so high that a normally endowed matron could balance a candlestick on them.[14] Shoes were long and narrow. Agnès Sorel, the mistress of Charles VII, wore her head fashionably shaved in the front. Possessed of magnificent breasts, she introduced the original topless gown: it allowed the full charm of her left breast to be displayed while the right one remained modestly tucked away.

Wealth brought not only material comforts, but the luxury of time for leisure. Woman's companionate role was added to that of sex, procreation, and domestic work.[15] This new attitude is evidenced in the *Book of the Ménagier* (householder), written at the close of the fifteenth century. The husband (the ménagier) is close to 60; his new wife is scarcely 15. The book was written for the instruction of the wife, who humbly entreats him not to correct her in front of strangers.

This treatise on domesticity is superficially similar to the one in which the Greek Ischomacus instructs his teen-aged wife (whom we encountered in chapter 4), but there is no suggestion in the earlier dialogue of any close emotional interaction between the couple. However, the ménagier's instructions reveal a warm emotional feeling for his wife:

> Be careful that in winter he [the husband] has good fire without smoke, and let him rest well and be well covered between your breasts and thus bewitch him . . . and serve him and cause him to be well served in your house; and you shall look to him for outside things, for if he be a good man he will take even more care and trouble over them than you wish, and by doing as I have said, you will make him always miss you and have his heart with you and with your loving service, and he will shun all other women, all other services and households; all will be naught to him save you alone. . . . And so on the road, husbands will think of their wives, and no trouble will be a burden to them for the hope and love they will have

of their wives, whom they will long to see, even as poor hermits, penitents and fasting monks long to see the face of Christ Jesus; and husbands served thus will never desire to abide elsewhere or in other company but will withhold, withdraw and abstain themselves therefrom; all the rest will seem to them but a bed of stones compared with their home.[16]

A more powerful vignette of the mature wife in action is given in Chaucer's *Canterbury Tales.* Prior to Chaucer, there had been heated debates as to whether marriage was of value to mankind. Brunetto Latini, in 1230, had defended marriage as worthwhile because God instituted it; it originated in Paradise; Adam and Eve were free of sin at that time; marriage existed in Noah's Ark; the Virgin was married; Jesus attended a wedding; and marriage was a sacrament.[17] In all these points there is no mention of pleasure as a benefit of marriage, because the association of pleasure with marriage would have been, in the eyes of the Church, a deficit rather than an asset. In fact, in France, the religious woman wore a night shirt, a *chemise cagoule,* which extended to her ankles. The gown contained a suitable aperture through which the husband could impregnate his wife without any other direct physical contact, thus heeding Abélard's call to "engender chastely."

Chaucer was strongly pro-marriage.[18] His chief spokesman in this area, the Wife of Bath, is hardly the type to wear a *chemise cagoule.* She is no shy bride of 15 who meekly adores a ménagier. Rather, she is a highly sensual woman—witness the gap between her upper front teeth, commonly interpreted as a sign of sensuality in the Middle Ages. Her attitude toward virginity is accepting but far from enthusiastic or reverent!

> Tell me also, to what purpose or end
> The genitals were made, that I defend,
> And for what benefit was a man first wrought?
> Trust you right well, they were not made for naught. . . .
> I bear no malice to virginity;
> Let such be bread of purest white wheat-seed,
> And let us wives be called but barley bread;
> And yet with barley bread (if Mark you scan)
> Jesus Our Lord refreshed full many a man. . . .
> In wifehood I will use my instrument
> As freely as my Maker has it sent
> If I be niggardly, God give me sorrow!
> My husband he shall have it, even and morrow,
> When he's pleased to come forth and pay his debt.[19]

The Wife of Bath is sensitive to the inferior status of women. When one of her wealthy husbands (she had five in all) refused to let her know the whereabouts of the keys to the household money, she used what she described as a woman's weapons—her tongue and the withholding of sex. She also has a few scathing words for priests who write of women's wickedness:

> A clerk, when he is old and can nought do
> Of Venus's labours worth his worn-out shoe,
> Then sits he down and writes, in his dotage,
> That women cannot keep vow of marriage![20]

In his "Envoy to the Clerk's Tale," Chaucer takes a surprisingly strong profeminist stand:

> Strong-minded women, stand at your defence,
> Since you are strong as camel and don't ail,
> Suffer no man to do to you offence;
> And slender women in a contest frail,
> Be savage as a tiger there in Ind;
> Clatter like mill, say I, to beat the male.[21]

When it became evident that women were asserting themselves, a reaction set in. *The Fifteen Joys of Marriage,* authored by an anonymous cleric in the mid-fifteenth century, is typical. The fifteen "joys" are, in actuality, fifteen ways in which women take advantage of men.[22]

It was generally supposed that the "new" woman made life so unbearable for her husband that a contented husband was impossible to find. Accordingly, a custom arose at Dunmow in England that "he that repenteth not of his marriage in a year and a day, either sleeping or waking, may lawfully go to Dunmow to fetch a gammon of bacon."[23] Addison, describing the same custom in another locale, claimed that during the first 100 years of the custom only two men collected the prize. The first, a sea captain, did not see his wife from the day of his marriage until he claimed the prize. The second was married to a mute![24] In short, power is rarely relinquished voluntarily, and the average man did not take kindly to the new female assertiveness that threatened his exploitation of her.

PEASANT MARRIAGES

The bourgeois marriage, as we have seen, had the potential of developing into a meaningful relationship based on mutual responsibility and communication between husband and wife at work or in managing the home. The nobility, who arranged marriages for political or economic reasons, often found satisfaction in extramarital relationships.

Practically nothing is known with regard to serfs, because no one thought them worthy objects of study—they were considered beasts of burden, incapable of finer emotions. A baron might plead with his lady amour that he would die of love if she did not grant him a kiss. If a serf were "to die of love," it would signify that he had overstrained himself in bed; thus, the cleric Andreas Capellanus, who wrote an extensive manual on courtly love, did not recommend the use of such techniques with serfs. If a nobleman sees a peasant woman whom he desires, he is advised simply to seize her, drag her behind the bushes, and rape her.[25]

Just how lowly a status servitude (serfdom) was may be gleaned from Gratian's *Decretum.* If a freeman or freewoman married, believing his (her) spouse to be free, and if the spouse was later convicted of being a serf, then the freeman or freewoman was permitted to marry someone else if he (she) could not purchase the freedom of his (her) spouse.[26] Since anyone marrying a person who subsequently became a leper could not obtain a divorce, servitude was apparently considered a very bad station in life indeed.

Frequently, the Church and the nobility had different reasons for ignoring the Church laws that prohibited marriage because of affinity or consanguinity among the peasantry. From the Church point of view, the lack of record keeping among the peasantry made it almost impossible to determine which swineherd was related to which shepherdess in any degree. Also, there was not much likelihood of selling dispensations to such poverty-stricken persons.

This lack of Church involvement led, on occasion, to peasants marrying without priestly sanction. A trusted rustic would ask the couple several times whether they took each other for man and wife, and they would reply several times that they did. While such marriages were strictly forbidden, they were often not punished by the Church, and it is estimated that 9 percent of the villeins of one manor in the reign of Edward III were bastards. In certain situations the Church might urge the serfs to marry, as evidenced by a 1394 petition to the House of Commons, which complained that religious orders were putting pressure on their serfs to marry freewomen with an inheritance. Because the freewoman took the status of the serf, such marriages offered an opportunity for the clergy to claim the estates—a serf could not hold property.[27]

The nobles winked at the marriage restrictions for the peasantry—after all, they wanted manpower for their fields and footmen for their armies. Also, inbreeding assured them that all the offspring resulting from the marriage would come under the lord's domain.

If the serf died without heirs, his parcel of land reverted to his seigneur. Only by marrying could he avert this possibility. Even the birth of a child did not secure the serf's land. If the serf died and left an heiress under 14 years of age, the lord profited further. He held the rights to her land and he could arrange a marriage for her, for which he received benefits from the groom. Upon reaching the age of 16, if the girl did not wish to marry the lord's choice, she could purchase her freedom of choice or "sue out her livery" by payment of a half-year's income from her land.[28]

As has been noted, the lord always sought to implement his manpower for exploitation of the land and for future military needs; hence if a serf did not marry within a certain time, or if he chose to marry someone other than the one selected by the lord, he had to pay a fine. In the interests of money and/or sex, a few bold lords instituted the *jus primae noctis*—"right of the first night." Its meaning is apparent in the following statement by a Norman lord at Bourdet in 1419: "I have a right to take from my men and others, when they marry on my lands, 10 sols tournois and a joint of pork of the whole length from the chin to the ear, and the tail frankly comprised in the said joint, with a gallon of whatsoever drink is drunk at the wedding; and I may and ought, if it pleases me, go and lie with the bride, in case her husband or some person on his account fail to pay to me or at my command one of the things above rehearsed."[29] Whether or not the *jus* was ever exercised is a matter of some dispute.[30]

In cases where two serfs of neighboring fiefs wished to marry and sought permission, it was customary for the two lords to split equally the number of children ensuing from the marriage. This did not mean that the children were necessarily separated from the parents, for it might still be possible for the family to live on one fief and have some of its members go to work on a neighboring one. At other times, unfortunately, no ready solution presented itself, and some of the children were sent to new homes.

The sexual offender was in double jeopardy. The ecclesiastical court could fine him and make him do any required penance. After that, he was turned over to the lord. The lord had no "spiritual" jurisdiction, but he was quite concerned about the depreciation of his property. Accordingly, he might levy a fine, the *lecherwite,* for incontinence on the part of a bondswoman. The rationale was that a nonvirgin represented "damaged goods," and the lord could expect to get more for disposing of a virginal bondswoman in marriage. Hence, the lady in question was obligated to compensate the lord for injury to his income.

The decline of feudalism brought some easement to the marital restriction imposed on the peasant. Villein tenants gradually acquired the mobility to leave their manors and to send their children elsewhere if they desired. Their children could also marry without consulting the lord or paying a fine to him. In this climate of relative freedom, the countryside became somewhat depopulated and the towns grew crowded with the former villeins.

MARRIAGE REGULATIONS

Among the Teutonic and Old English in Roman times, marriage had been essentially by bride-purchase. In the first stage, the *bewedding* or betrothal, the business contract between the suitor and the father of the bride was drawn up and the *weotuma* or transfer price was agreed upon. In the second phase, the *gifta,* the bride was turned over to her husband. Sometimes duplicity occurred, and the newly emerging kings enacted laws to deal with such situations. A law of Aethelbert, King of Kent (560-616), has survived:

> If a man buy a maiden with cattle, let the bargain stand, if it be without guile, but if there be guile, let him bring her home again, and let his property be restored to him.
>
> If a man carry off a maiden by force, let him pay L shillings to the owner, and afterwards buy the object of his will of the owner. If she be betrothed to another man in money, let him make *bot* with XX shillings.
>
> If a freeman lie with a freeman's wife, let him pay for it with his *wer-geld,* and provide another wife with his own money, and bring her to the other.[31]

To the modern mind, the equation of interpersonal malice with monetary compensation may seem rather callous. Seen in context, however, these laws represented a step forward in the institution of law and order. Heretofore, rape or seduction had often led to blood feuds in which two families sequentially killed a member of the other family to avenge their honor.[32] The *wer-geld,* however, gave each family a legal excuse for ceasing the endless carnage.

Eventually the bride-price was fixed according to the bride's station, and then it became the *arrha,* "earnest money," signifying that a contract had been undertaken, with full payment to be made on delivery. The *arrha,* which had small significance, was paid to the bride herself, often in the form of a ring, and it is this custom which has survived to this day.

Between the sixth and ninth centuries, the purchase price itself lost its original meaning, and was now seen as an insurance fund to be put aside for the bride against the time she might become a widow. The *bewedding* was soon called the *wed,* and even the *arrha* disappeared, the contract merely stating that a sum of money or property would be turned over to the bride. The *weotuma* itself underwent a metamorphosis—it was reduced to a token—while the *morgengifu,* or morning-gift, became the heart of the financial concern. It now became a mandatory gift, agreed upon in advance upon fulfillment of the conditions (usually that she was a virgin) under which the bride was transferred to the aegis of the husband.

The forerunner of the dowry, the *gerade,* had persisted from antiquity. It consisted, in its most elementary state, of the necessities of life for a young bride: linen, eating implements, furniture, ornaments, money, and occasionally some livestock. As the economic wealth of Europe increased, dowries became increasingly substantial. Many a middle-class father, graced with a bevy of daughters, therefore sought to put at least one, perhaps more, in a convent to avoid the strain of too many dowries.

In the event of a breach of contract on the part of the groom—if he failed to marry within two years of the betrothal—he usually forfeited the *weotuma* and paid an additional fine. Where the breach occurred on the bride's side, the groom sued for return of the *weotuma,* plus an additional compensation of one to three times the original amount.

In time, the shifting of the payment from the father to the bride herself introduced the concept of *self-gifta.* The parties could marry themselves if need be, although it was far more customary for the bride's father to officiate at the ceremony. Originally, too, the father had had the right to give his daughter to anyone he wished. By the close of the seventh century, however, a man could marry his children off without their consent only before they reached the age of 16.

In the eleventh century, King Canute, the Danish King (1017-1035) who had seized England, had a law enacted which stipulated, "And let no one compel either woman or maiden to him who she herself mislikes, nor for money sell her; unless he is willing to give anything voluntarily."[33] Thorpe advances reasons to suggest that the law was intended to prevent the father or guardian from forcing the girl into an unreasonable union rather than to serve as a declaration of the daughter's independence regarding marital choice. The facts seem to bear him out, in that there was no dramatic breakthrough to a free choice of marriage partner. Nevertheless, it was no longer unusual for the feelings of the bride or groom to influence the choice of marital partner.

By the late fifteenth century, we note that one Margery Paston pledged her faith to Richard Calle, who was in a subordinate position working for her brother, Sir John Paston. The family tried to break up the romance, but was prevented by the fact that she had already pledged her troth and the bishop considered her betrothed.[34]

MARRIAGE CUSTOMS

Courtship customs varied not only from country to country, but from class to class. Because the bride had to be assured of a good future, men in Western Europe seldom married before their mid-twenties, with the average age range being between 25 and 35. Women were considered ripe for marriage shortly after the first flow of menses, with the average age being between 14 and 18.[35] The size of the dowry and the financial status of the family were considered carefully, as was the extent of their political power and whether they were of the nobility (if so, were they of the old or the new aristocracy?).

Very detailed protocol defined the progress of a marriage suit. In England, a suitor came to the parents of his hoped-for bride bearing a leathern bottle of wine. If they accepted it and drank from it, he was free to continue his suit. To clarify his situation further, he would get himself invited for supper and watch the dessert carefully. If the daughter served him walnuts, he knew that he was not wanted.

On the wedding day, the friends of the bride would give her a white hen to symbolize her virginity. At the ceremony, the exciting omen to watch was how readily the wedding ring went on: if easily, she would be submissive; but if it had to be forced, the husband had best beware—this despite the fact that women often cut their hair short as a sign of submission.[36]

After the wedding it was considered, then as now, great sport to put obstacles in the path of the departing couple. In medieval times, however, humor went much further: the groom's "friends" sometimes splashed dirty water on the bride or dropped her in a pile of dung, which was sure to enrage him.

When the couple retired, the husband put his wife's shoe near the head of the bed on his side, as a symbol of his power over her. But they usually did not have much privacy. As the revels continued at the groom's house, the guests might applaud when they heard "the straw move" upstairs, or cheer the groom lustily if they heard the bride's "cry of defloration." The more voyeuristically inclined tried to peer into the keyhole or shimmy up the side of the building for a peek through the window.

The post-betrothal behavior of a typical noble couple has been described as follows:

> At meals he and his beloved are allowed to sit together and above all to eat out of the same porringer, when he delicately leaves to his intended all the best morsels. He consults a competent jongleur, and with his aid produces suitable verses praising his fiancee's beauty. He gives her a gold ring with both his own name and hers engraved thereon. In return, besides a sleeve and a stocking to hang on his lances (gifts which she has already sent in mere friendship to other cavaliers), she bestows a lock of her hair set around a gold ring; likewise a larger lock which he may twine around his helmet. The happy pair are permitted to take long walks together, and to promenade up and down the garden, with [the man] holding his lady in the politest manner by one finger—the accepted method of showing intimacy.[37]

The wedding would preferably take place in June, a good-omened month; May was said to be unlucky.[38] The wedding day found the bride with her hair in two great braids intertwined with gold and worn forward over her breasts. After her marriage she would be allowed to bind her hair in folds over her head, in a style called *valute.*

After the ceremony, if a dowry had been given with the bride, she prostrated herself at the feet of the groom to signify his control over her goods during his lifetime.[39] In other variations, she kissed his foot or had him trod on her foot. The nature of the dowries brought by the bride and groom were read aloud so that no misunderstanding might occur. Silver coins were scattered to the numerous mendicants, burghers, and artisans gathered around.

At last, the Church doors opened, and the wedding party and the attending group proceeded inside for the bridal mass. At the conclusion of the *Agnus Dei,* the groom advanced to the altar to receive the "kiss of peace" from the bishop, which he then transmitted to his bride. The ceremony terminated, the groom led his bride out of the Church. She stayed to his left, his right arm remained free

Courtly love.

"for defense" so that he could draw his sword in accordance with ancient custom, although there was little likelihood that he would have occasion to use it.

The feast in the lord's great hall was resplendent—from a whole peacock, cleaned and reassembled in all its feathered glory, to six or seven courses of soup, numerous game, and, if available, whale meat.[40] The meals were gargantuan by modern standards. The stench of last year's rushes, which had been collecting spittle, vomit, old bones, and dog urine, was swept away; fresh roses and lilacs were scattered about to release their fragrance when walked upon. The groom drank his wine from a goblet and passed it on to his wife to finish. Much time was consumed over gifts for every important guest; they were brought out and distributed with diplomatic speeches.

As the dinner progressed, the voices of guests "in their cups" became louder and louder, and the songs and stories of the jongleurs increasingly ribald. Despite the enormous meals, many leaped to their feet and danced, while others snoozed in alcoves or outside under the trees.

At last the hour grew late, and it became time for the couple to retire. The priest led the entourage to the nuptial couch strewn with roses; he blessed it while the couple piously knelt. The women guests went through the ritual of putting the bride to bed. The couple drank heavily spiced wines or ale that was supposed to have aphrodisiac qualities. In the morning they were given a cup of sack posset to revive their supposedly exhausted energies. Aside from attending chapel to make vows about her future behavior, the wife spent her "honeymoon" in bed for three to ten days, after which she emerged to dine in the great hall. Since the guests had often traveled for many miles, it was not unusual for the festivities to last many days. Important guests were housed in the castle; the lesser lights were assigned to tents pitched on the grounds.

MARRIAGE PROBLEMS

Polygyny

Despite Church pronouncements on the necessity of monogamy, the practice of polygyny continued for some time during the Middle Ages among the Frankish and the Irish tribes who had recently converted to Christianity. In *The History of the Franks,* Gregory of Tours describes the marriage of a sixth-century king, Lother, and his queen, Ingund, as one of great felicity. The queen requested that her lord find a good husband for her sister Aregund. She did not stint in her description of the virtues of her sibling, and she so aroused her husband that he went to the sister's residence and married her on the spot. He explained immodestly to his first wife that "I sought a man wealthy and of good wit, whom I might give in marriage to thy sister, but I found none better than myself.

Know, therefore, that I have taken her to wife, which I believe will not displease thee."[41] His wife replied meekly, "Let my lord do that which seemeth good in his sight; only let his handmaid live in the enjoyment of his favor.[42]

Two hundred years later, Charlemagne, in recognition of his services to the Church, was crowned Emperor of the Holy Roman Empire by the Pope. Because of his special status, he was allowed to operate under a special set of marital rules. He had four wives, the first of whom he repudiated after a year. The others he married sequentially as a widower. His numerous concubines[43,44] were euphemistically referred to as "marriages of the second rank." His daughters never married, for he was very much a family man and could not bear to part with them; but he did permit them to lead a "normal" life in every way, and became a grandfather many times over. To all of this the Church made nary a peep during his lifetime. This was scarcely strange, for the Church never had a friend so powerful and at the same time so faithful.

In Ireland, King Diarmaid MacCerbaill, in addition to numerous concubines, had two legitimate spouses. By the second millennium, however, polygyny had been largely eliminated.

Adultery

England's early laws allowed monetary payment for adultery (in King Alfred's reign it was 120 shillings for a noble's indiscretion, 40 shillings for that of a freeman); but with the disappearance of the Anglo-Saxon kings, these laws were replaced by sterner measures. During King Canute's reign in the eleventh century, adultery by men was still punishable by fine, but for an adulteress the king decreed that "her lawful husband have all that she possessed; and let her then forfeit both nose and ears."[45] The reign of William the Conqueror resulted in an even more punitive law, which stipulated that male offenders were to be castrated.

It was understood that if the husband caught his wife and her lover *in flagrante delicto,* he could dispatch them with impunity. By the thirteenth century, however, it became illegal to kill. Although the cuckold was still considered to be within his rights in emasculating his wife's lover, this also came to be regarded as severe and unusual. Only the civil law—not the Church—sanctioned retribution by the husband. The Church condemned violators to eternal punishment in the hereafter; here on earth, it executed the punishments and reprimands decreed by the ecclesiastical court.[46] The laws became more humane, but the double standard of sexual ethics continued to be interpreted to the disadvantage of women.

A few words need to be said regarding bastardry. Prior to the influence of the Church, children were not socially penalized for being born out of wedlock, although since Roman times they had not been permitted to inherit from their fathers. In 786, an Anglo-Saxon synod decreed that "the son of a meretricious union shall be debarred from legally inheriting, for, in accordance with the apostolic authority of holy decrees, we regard adulterine children as spurious."[47] Because they had been conceived in love and not on the basis of duty, it was thought that a degree of boldness had been passed on to the offspring. Some of the noblest heroes of the literature of this period were bastards: King Conchobar of Ireland, King Arthur, Gawain, and Roland, hero of the Carolingian epics. Among the better-known real-life bastards were Clothwig, founder of the Frankish kingdom, Charles Martel, possibly Charlemagne, and William I of Normandy. William, called the Conquerer by modern-day historians, took no umbrage in being referred to as William the Bastard, an appellation he himself often used.

Because of its considerable power, royalty was for a while able to overrule the official theological attitude. Henry I made two of his bastards earls; Geoffrey, Archbishop of York, an illegitimate son of Henry II, proudly proclaimed himself "son of the king" upon his archiepiscopal seal.[48] By 1483, however, when Richard III was campaigning for the throne of England, he is alleged to have spread the false rumor that the sons of Edward IV were bastards, an argument that abetted his successful seizure of the throne. In time, the term came to connote social, moral, and legal inferiority, and the prejudice persists to this day.

There was a loophole regarding the definition of adultery, thanks to a ruling by Pope Clement III that, in the case of consanguinity, all suits involving marriage should be quashed. As a result, if an adulterer could prove at least a sixth-degree relationship to his spouse, he could escape the charge of adultery because no valid marriage existed. Of course, he had to separate from his spouse, a step many adulterers did not find difficult.

The adulterous peasant, as usual, got the worst of it: the lord could take all the tangible goods of both adulterous parties.

Prostitution

With Church power at its apogee in the Middle Ages, it is hardly surprising that the prostitutes of Paris, along with other professions, had their own patron saint. Naturally, they chose Mary Magdalene. They burned candles before a stained glass picture depicting Sainte Marie l'Egyptienne about to hop into a boat, her skirts pulled up to reveal a luscious pair of thighs. The inscription read, "How the saint offered her body to a boatman to pay for her passage."[49]

Prostitutes were very popular with the students who, according to the medieval writer Jacque de Vitri, took courses on the first floor of the college and attended more stimulating extracurricular courses in debauchery on the ground floor. The standard place of work for a prostitute, however, was a little lodge, a *bord*. When the diminutive is added, it becomes *bordel*, a word that survives today. Another popular rendezvous was the steam bath, licensed and taxed by the state and, as a legitimate and God-fearing institution, closed during Holy Week and Easter.

The *filles de joie* were also quite popular with convicts. The law held that if one of them married a doomed convict, his life would be spared. In 1429 a young man about to be hanged in Paris was claimed by a girl from Les Halles. Unlike many of his contemporaries, he did not view marriage as a fate worse that death, and he married his newfound benefactress.

During the reign of Louis XI, steps were taken to reduce the presence of prostitutes in Paris, particularly after the queen had bestowed a kiss on a splendidly dressed lady after the benediction at Church. The queen learned later that the lady was a prostitute who had defied the regulations forbidding a long train, ornate jewelry, furs, or belts to be worn by harlots. In some cities the prescribed costume was the traditional harlot red of hell.

The Church did not object very strongly to the establishment of prostitution. Saint Thomas compared prostitution to sewers in the palace. Take away the sewers and the palace would be polluted. If there were no prostitutes, the world would be filled with sodomy, and feminine virtue would go down the drain. Such an attitude, needless to say, enhanced the idea of a double standard of sexuality, despite the Church's formal doctrine to the contrary. We need not be surprised, therefore, to note that the "stews" near London Bridge were originally licensed by the Bishop of Winchester, with the girls euphemistically referred to as "Winchester geese." These "stews" survived until Henry VIII ordered them closed in 1546.

The Ideal Spouse

"Of the domestic animals," says the ménagier, "you see how a greyhound, or a mastiff, or a little dog, whether on the road, or at a table, or in bed, always keeps near to the person from whom he takes his food, and leaves and is shy and fierce with all others."[50] Similarly, the ideal wife was expected always to submit humbly to her lord, raise his bastards if he desired, never utter a word of disapproval, and by earnest efforts of love try to win him back from distracting influences. On the other hand, prior to marriage she should be a virgin—chaste but congenial. She should be silent in public regarding any of his secret matters, and should run his house like clockwork. In the street, she should walk with head high, eyelids lowered, and looking about 30 feet straight ahead. She should not kiss young men or allow them to fondle her breasts, nor should she speak to strangers.[51]

Guidelines for the ideal husband are not as readily available as for wives. The Wife of Bath, in her usual straightforward manner, required an obedient husband and one who was "fresh in bed," in addition to the usual health, wealth, and wisdom.[52] The emphasis by a woman on power and sensuality is rather ahead of the times, and, in any event, would not likely have been expected before the end of the Middle Ages.

SUMMARY AND CONCLUSIONS

The Middle Ages brought some relief from the virulent asceticism of the early Christian era. It was essentially a period, nevertheless, in which neither women nor marriage relationships were greatly esteemed. Through such spokesmen as Thomas Aquinas, the Church promulgated and developed the thesis that women were intrinsically inferior to men. Aside from being a wife, a woman could be either a nun or a prostitute, both careers being viewed by the Church as contributing to the maintenance of society, albeit in different ways.

Feudalism, with its emphasis on physical strength and military skill, militated against woman's emancipation, as did the overwhelming dependence of Europe on agricultural economy. Recent cross-cultural research has shown that agricultural societies are associated with differences in the socialization of the sexes.[53] Such societies require the handling of large domestic animals, in connection with which the value of men's strength is at a premium. Indeed, the twin stigmata of being both a woman and a serf in the Middle Ages made the lot of the peasant woman very difficult. In this light, it becomes understandable why a royal chaplain such as Andreas Capallanus could casually condone the rape of peasant women as a justifiable *remedium concupisum.*

Considering the low valuation of women, it is not surprising that, throughout the Middle Ages, there is little mention of real happiness or emotional satisfaction in the marriage relationship. Marriage was essentially a business contract to enhance political and military alliances for the rich and to offer economic security, children, and relief from sexual tension to the poor. The last-named satisfaction, which smacked of hedonism, could not be openly avowed, but such satisfaction was in any case reserved for men.

At the close of the Middle Ages, the dramatic acceleration in commerce and the concomitant rise of the middle class brought into play circumstances that were more favorable to women. Agriculture lost its preeminent position, and various town occupations became available to women. A fuller development of these new opportunities, and their effect on the nature of the marital relationship, was to emerge in the succeeding 100-odd years—1500-1615—which we shall loosely refer to as "Renaissance and Reformation."

REFERENCES

1. P. Butler, *Women of Medieval France.*
2. M. Beard, *Woman as Force in History.*
3. T. Aquinas, *The Summa Theologica,* 1952, First Part, Q. 92, Art. 1, p. 489.
4. T. F. Tout, "Woman's place in the later medieval household."
5. T. Aquinas, op. cit.
6. M. A. Gist, *Love and War in the Middle English Romances,* p. 111.
7. *The Letters of Abélard and Héloïse,* p. 11.
8. Ibid., p. 13.

9. Ibid., p. 53

10. Ibid., p. 81.

11. Ibid., p. 104.

12. Ibid., pp. 96-97.

13. B. B. James, *Women of England.*

14. N. Epton, *Love and the French.*

15. D. Herlihy, "Family solidarity in medieval Italian history."

16. E. Power, *Medieval People,* p. 97.

17. N. Epton, op. cit.

18. D. S. Brewer, "Love and marriage in Chaucer's poetry."

19. G. Chaucer, *Troilus and Cressida and the Canterbury Tales,* p. 258.

20. Ibid., p. 267.

21. Ibid., p. 317.

22. *The Fifteen Joys of Marriage,* p. 24.

23. N. Epton, *Love and the English,* p. 22.

24. H. Thurston, "Mediaeval matrimony."

25. A. Capellanus, *The Art of Courtly Love.*

26. G. C. Coulton, *The Medieval Village.*

27. H. S. Bennett, *Life on the English Manor: A Study of Peasant Conditions, 1150-1400.*

28. B. B. James, op. cit.

29. G. C. Coulton, op. cit., pp. 466-467.

30. C. Brinton, *A History of Western Morals.*

31. B. Thorpe (ed.), *Ancient Laws and Institutes of England,* pp. 23, 24, 11.

32. J. T. Rosenthal, "Marriage and the blood feud in 'heroic Europe.' "

33. B. Thorpe, op. cit., p. 17.

34. D. M. Stenton, *The English Woman in History.*

35. L. Martines, *The Social World of the Florentine Humanists 1390-1460.*

36. W. S. Davis, *Life on a Medieval Barony.*

37. Ibid., p. 106.

38. F. L. Critchlow, "On the forms of betrothal and wedding ceremonies in the old French *romans d'aventure.* "

39. G. E. Howard, *A History of Matrimonial Institutions.*

40. C. Guy, *An Illustrated History of French Cuisine.*

41. Gregory of Tours, *The History of the Franks,* p. 118.

42. Ibid., p. 118.

43. Einhard, *The Life of Charlemagne.*

44. H. W. C. Davis, *Charlemagne.*

45. B. Thorpe, op. cit., p. 407.

46. R. Girard, "Marriage in Avignon in the second half of the fifteenth century."

47. R. Briffault, *The Mothers,* Vol. 3, p. 423.

48. D. Stenton, op. cit.

49. N. Epton, *Love and the French,* p. 49.

50. E. Power, op. cit., p. 93.

51. N. Epton, op. cit.

52. G. Chaucer, op. cit., p. 386.

53. H. Barry, III, M. K. Bacon, and I. L. Child, "A cross-cultural survey of some sex differences."

9

Courtly Love and Its Evolvements

The twelfth century saw the flourishing of "courtly love," a phenomenon whose importance is intensely debated by contemporary medievalists.[1] To some it was a prototype, a precursor of the romanticism that permeated the relationship between the sexes in the nineteenth and twentieth centuries. To others it was a minor art form, never predominant even in the twelfth century, but inflated in importance by the nineteenth-century writer, Gaston Paris, who coined the term "courtly love."[2] Before we can fully assess it, we must first understand its origins, who practiced it, how it was expressed, and how it evolved.

Courtly love embodied the relationship between aspiring lovers and their noble ladies. Its principal exponents, lyric poets or poet-musicians—*troubadours*—composed poems and songs expressing a code whose chief tenets were the ennobling power of love; the conception of love as a burning, rarely extinguished passion; the impossibility of love between husband and wife; the elevation of the beloved to a position superior to that of the supplicant, in imitation of the relationship between feudal lord and vassal; and the idea of fidelity between lovers (at least while they were in love).

Other themes dealt with nature, the naturalness of love affairs, the personification of love as a god or monarch with absolute power over his army of lovers, the incomparable beauty of the woman, and the lover's basic anxiety over the haughtiness of his lady. He feared displeasing his lady because of his unworthiness, emphasized the need for secrecy because of the watchful eye of the "jealous one" (her husband), and stressed his humility and courtesy toward noble ladies. The lover accepted adultery as a consequence of the triumph of love, but vacillated between concern over how long it was taking to win his beloved and stubborn belief that patience would be rewarded by gratification.

The "ennobling power of love" refers to the *process of loving* rather than merely focusing on the beloved herself. The famous troubadour Bernard de Ventadour said, "By nothing is man made so worthy as by love and the courting of women, for thence arise delight and song and all that pertains to excellence. No man is of value without love."[3] Men were believed to be crude and insensitive until love, like a thunderbolt, shook the very marrow of their being; and then they acquired courtesy, a thirst for learning, and gentleness of manner.

Two kinds of acceptable love existed for the troubadour: "pure" love and "mixed" love. "Pure" love refers to the union of the hearts and minds of lovers who experience everything together except physical possession. As Daude de Pradas put it, "He knows little or nothing of the service of women who wishes to possess his lady entirely."[4]

"Pure" love is inexhaustible, because it continually increases tension without satisfying it. The lover may kiss his beloved and embrace her, even without her clothes on, but the final "solace" is omitted. Accordingly, any woman, maiden or married, could indulge in it without fear to her reputation. The tension or suffering of love originates in the eyes (the blind were believed to be incapable of loving) through the perception and the recording of her image in the man's heart. Such passion could occur only between members of the opposite sex and only between the young. After a man reached 60 and a woman became 50, natural heat declined, and they had to console themselves with food and drink.[5]

While "pure" love was the ideal, "mixed" love was also acceptable. "Mixed" love is "pure" love with sex added; but as with the "pure" version, it is the source of the desire to please one's beloved. Although there is good in "mixed" love, there is also danger, for it conflicts with another "good." If, for example, the beloved is already married, she becomes an adulteress. Apart from adultery, however, a case could be made for courtly love as complementary rather than antagonistic to marriage. If love were possible between husband and wife, there might be conflict between courtly love and conjugal love.

According to the code, conjugal love is impossible because love thrives on freedom of choice; it is spontaneous, and not the fulfillment of a contract. Marriage, however, is a relationship with a fixed obligation; hence marriage and love are incompatible. Since love is ennobling, it is good; and since this good cannot be obtained within the confines of marriage, it must be sought elsewhere.

"Mixed" love should not be construed as a vehicle for sexual license, for the latter is an example of "false" love, which is evil, impure, and seeks only to gratify the sensual appetite from any source. This behavior is practiced by dishonorable, debauched dilettantes and, far from being ennobling, reduces man to the level of beasts. The true lover, on the other hand, possesses *mezura*– "measure"–in the sense that he is able to govern his sensual appetite through strength of character. The result of inner passion regulated by "measure" is courtesy, a quality that distinguishes gentlemen from ruffians. The test of character and *mezura* was the elaborate ritual of courtship, whose duration would discourage those whose motivation was merely sex.

Each lover traversed four distinct stages. At first he was an aspirant, a *fegnedor,* who worshipped his love from afar. He would wait for hours, hidden in the shrubs, knowing that sooner or later his beloved would walk along the path. The mere sight of his lady was sufficient reward for any hardships endured. When he could summon the courage to communicate to his lady that he was smitten with Cupid's heavy arrow, he moved to the second stage of being a suppliant, a *precador.* The lady might not notice or encourage him, or she might think it over for hours, days, or months. During this wait, the supplicant had somehow to exist despite the anxiety that beset him. If fortune was with him, his damsel might permit him to court her, to compose songs in her honor. In the third stage, as a recognized suitor, or *entendedor,* the lover might spend a seemingly interminable length of time in a kind of purgatory, waiting for the final favor. Many a lady hoped to have her cake and eat it too—enjoying the enviable position of having her beauty celebrated throughout the land by an adoring swain while maintaining a chaste position at her husband's side. Many a troubadour preferred things to remain that way rather than risk the husband's ire. The more adventuresome and fortunate lover hoped to press on to the fourth stage, the accepted lover, or *drut,* which promised the ultimate intimacy.[6]

The analogy to the feudal relationship between vassal and lord is indicated by the fact that the suitor called his lady *midons,* my lord, rather than *ma dompna,* my lady. Just as the lord was promised fealty in return for the services he supplied his vassal, so the woman was held to be the source of the suitor's bliss, and he did homage to her in loyalty, service, courtesy, and secrecy. As with feudal investure, a ceremony was performed whereby the suitor, kneeling, placed his two hands between those of his lady and, in the presence of witnesses, swore to defend her to the death.[7] Last, the lady and her swain were supposed to be faithful to each other because they were in love, a rule which, naturally, they could not follow with regard to their spouses.

ORIGINS OF COURTLY LOVE

Arab Influence

There is considerable evidence that the concept of courtly love, which first appeared in southern France, was influenced by Arab culture during the rule of the latter in neighboring Spain. Arabs were in frequent contact with southern France from 1031 to 1086, prior to the onset of religious fanaticism after Almoravides' arrival from Africa in 1086. Each of the 20 minor kings in the Moorish territory encouraged literature, and their poets often served as ambassadors to the southern principalities of France.

One of the chief Moorish poets was the Andalusian, Ibn Hazm, who wrote the masterpiece, *The Dove's Neck-Ring,* in 1022. In it, the poet discourses on the ennobling aspects of love; exclusive concern with sensuality is sheer vulgarity, and the lover is a slave unto his lady, addressing her as "my lord" (*sayyidi*) or "my master" (*mawlaya*). Other parallels between Arab and troubadour poetry include a sensitivity to the beauties of nature, the borrowing of personages from Arab love stories, such as Aucassin (Al-Kasim), and the use of musical instruments and presumably, therefore, their lyric forms. As in troubadourian verse, the Arab lover graciously tolerates rejection and, in the words of another poet, Ibn Ammar, the essence of joy is the suffering caused by rejection.[8]

The Crusades offered further opportunities for contact, and it is claimed that the pre- and post-Crusade verse of William IX of Aquitaine differs in rhythm and rhyme in accordance with Arab influence.[9] William must surely have become aware of the fact that the Arabs had a higher esteem for women and more refined courtship practices than the Europeans.

Mere communication or geographic proximity, however, would not suffice for the transmission of a poetic form or spirit unless the ground was already predisposed for such change. This appears to have been the case in southern France. Increasing commerce had brought new wealth to the nobility and, with a decline in local wars, more time for leisure. The combination of the readiness of the French nobility and the new Arab contacts may well have resulted in the introduction of the new poetic form. This view, however, is not shared by Dennis de Rougemont, who, in *Love in the Western World,* expresses a far more original theory of the origin of courtly love.[10]

de Rougemont's Theory of the Origin of Courtly Love

The content of poems of courtly love, says de Rougemont, is not to be taken at face value, but should be searched for an esoteric meaning: the poems are disguised propaganda for the heretical Cathar- religion. At first glance this judgment seems astounding, to say the least. The Cathars opposed sexual intercourse and were strongly ascetic in doctrine, whereas the troubadours extolled love and sex, at least until the advent of the Inquisition. De Rougemont's statement is so bold that the reader might well anticipate newly uncovered evidence to support his assertion. That is not the case. De Rougemont states:

> *What is to be looked for in courtly rhetoric is not natural or precise equivalances of the dogma,* but the lyrical and psalmodic development of the fundamental symbolism.[11]
>   I do not believe that "scientific" history so called can be a criterion of the realities which interest me. Let it be affirmed . . . that such and such a connection cannot be established in "the present state of our knowledge". . . . I am in search of a meaning and hence of illustrative and illuminating analogies.[12]

Among the symbolic and analogical "proofs" he uncovered are the following:

1. The troubadours, like the Cathars, extolled the virtues of chastity.

2. When the troubadours refer to their lady, they are really referring to the Cathar Church of Love.

3. The word "true" appearing before the words "God," "Light," "Faith," or "Church" may be a sign of Catharism.

4. The heresy of Catharism was aflame in southern France in the middle of the twelfth century, when troubadourism also burgeoned.

5. The troubadour Marcabru says that the perpetration of "false" love joins hands with the Devil, who, in the view of the Catharist, is also the creator of material creation and procreation.

De Rougemont also has answers to such questions as "Why is there no reference to Catharism in troubadour poetry?" and "How is it that the overtly earthly troubadours, who spoke of the sexual delights that awaited them in their ladies' chambers, could seriously espouse a doctrine that denounced the importance of the flesh?"

To the first question he replies that the Cathars, upon their initiation into the sect, vowed never to betray their faith even if they had to undergo the cruelest of tortures. The poetry of the troubadours often speaks of never betraying the secret of their great passion. When they ostensibly refer to their lady, in de Rougemont's view, they are actually reaffirming their pledge.

Concerning the second question—the sexual proclivities of the troubadours in contradistinction to the ascetic qualities of the Cathars—de Rougemont points out that some Cathars might seek to encourage sexuality in order to be able to transcend it. We have noted earlier, for example, that some Gnostic sects believed that sexual exhaustion freed the soul to return to the "light." It is possible, therefore, to stifle the Devil by continence or by sexual overindulgence.

De Rougemont's argument is unsound for numerous reasons. For one thing, he treats troubadour poetry as a single entity. The early troubadours, who were quite sensually oriented, did not extol the virtues of chastity. The later troubadours, under pressure from the Inquisition, praised spiritual love when they were *forced* to abjure their anti-Church ideas. These ideas, however, were not Catharistic, but pagan, in that they conceived of love as a quasi-deity and espoused a code of ethics which laughed at the matrimonial institution. Moreover, many troubadours retracted their views on courtly love under pressure. Having done so, why should they not also have confessed their Cathar leanings? It is difficult to believe that if the troubadours really had Cathar ties, not one among hundreds of them ever confessed this allegience. Further, if they were pledged to secrecy, why should they risk danger by broadcasting their beliefs, albeit at a symbolic level? If but one de Rougemont-like sleuth had existed within the hierarchy of the Church, all would have been lost by such behavior.

There is no reason to attribute an intrinsic cause-effect relationship between the rise of Catharism in southern France in the second half of the twelfth century and the proliferation of troubadour poetry at that time. Catharism was an offshoot of Manicheism, which originated long before the Middle Ages. Prevalent in Bulgaria before it reached France, it spread not only to France but to Italy and Spain. Yet there is no evidence of any substantial troubadour activity in these areas at this time. Further, de Rougemont offers no support for his assertions that "lady" symbolizes "love," that "true" before various nouns is a Catharistic sign, and that the statement "false love is the work of the Devil" indicates a Manichean repugnance of sensuality.

Catharist heresy had its taproots in the misery of the poor, who found little rapport with the orthodox and often wealthy clergy. Yet de Rougemont claims that many nobles were enlisted under the Cathar banner. Whence came their motivation? A stronger case can be made for the position that several southern nobles supported the heresy because it gave them greater freedom from the influence of Rome in national affairs. This does not mean, however, that they embraced the Cathar religion, and I am not aware of evidence that any substantial number did so.

The Virgin Mary and Oedipus

Another argument advanced[13] is that the troubadourian code of behavior was the result of the worship of Mary, which was quite pronounced during the Middle Ages. This contention fails to consider the fact that Mary's popularity had commenced some 500 years before. The fact that the references to Mary in the works of the troubadours show up only at the decline of their popularity also weakens the argument that she was the inspiration for their poetry.

Some writers maintain that the perception of women as both angels and tigresses in troubadour poetry stems from unresolved Oedipal problems. According to Hunt,[14] sexual love and incest fear account for the ambivalence toward the lady, whereas Valency[15] sees the conflict as revolving around the mother, who gives love but is also the punisher of the male child. Yet the problem with which most troubadours concern themselves in their poetry is not so much the resolution of ambivalent feelings toward the lady as anxiety over the watchful eye of the husband. Their conflicts are interpersonal rather than intrapsychic.

Was Courtly Love a Revolt against the Church?

In its imitation of religion—the construction of a love god who punishes those who do not practice his religion—it might seem that courtly love was intended as a parody of the Church. Lewis[16] and Turner,[17] in any event, thought that courtly love was a reaction against Christianity and its denial of passion within and outside marriage.

This conclusion does not jibe with the fact that the two classics of courtly love, *Lancelot* and *The Art of Courtly Love,* were written, respectively, by a man who was possibly a cleric and one who definitely was one. It is incontrovertible that the code of courtly love was incompatible with Church philosophy, but the aforementioned contention loses sight of the fact that courtly love was an art form, whereas Church theology was intended as a realistic guide to loving. So long as this distinction was kept in mind, there was no need for serious conflict between the two codes—just as vicarious enjoyment of the female form in photographs can hardly be considered incompatible with marital fidelity.

In conclusion, no simple explanation of the origin of courtly love seems to suffice. The idealization of the lady, and the poetic form of expressing it, were probably borrowed in some degree from the Moors. At the same time, the relative freedom from constant raids and wars at the beginning of the second millennium made it possible to turn to an appreciation of culture and poetry, and the increased wealth of the nobility made it possible to entertain in grand style and to support the luxury of maintaining troubadours. Further, the absence of her lord while on Crusades gave the chatelaine a modest degree of freedom. But castle life, secluded as it was from the growing towns, invited ennui and made the nobility receptive to troubadourian visits. All of these factors probably interacted to produce the phenomenon of court love.

THE TROUBADOURS

History

The first troubadour of note was William IX, Duke of Aquitaine (1071-1127). Returning from the Crusades, where he had proved anything but a success, he took up a new craft: composing songs and poems of love and longing. He wrote his poetry in Provençal, a Latin dialect spoken in southern France. His choice of a language for poetry, according to all tradition, should have been Latin; but his knowledge of this classic tongue was probably too meager for creative expression. In any event, Provençal, even though it was a vulgar tongue, became accepted as the language of love poetry.

Unlike most troubadours, who came from the lower ranks of the nobility or the gentry, or even from the ranks of commoners, William was duke of the most powerful French duchy. As such, he took pains that his songs of longing bore little relationship to his own life. When he was attracted to the wife of one of his vassals, he waited for the vassal to leave the castle and then carried her off in his arms. His own wife took up the veil in protest, but William cared little about what others thought. To the bishop who reprimanded him for flaunting his mistress' figure on his shield, he replied that it would be discourteous not to carry her these few times since she had carried him so nobly in her boudoir on other occasions.

The average troubadour, not quite as saucy as William, often started his craft as a lowly jongleur, employed by a troubadour to sing his songs at various locales. Successful jongleurs, in time, became creators of their own songs—troubadours. The fortunes of the troubadour were risky, for he was dependent on the generosity of the lord with whom he lodged. If times were hard and the castle overcrowded, he might find himself sleeping in an outhouse. Troubadours often communicated their needs indirectly by composing songs for the lord about how the sweetness of one's voice was enhanced if the singer's chest was warmed by a new coat.

The golden age of the troubadour occurred during the time of William's son, William X, that of his granddaughter Eleanor of Aquitaine (who was queen of France and later of England), and of her daughter Marie, Countess of Champagne. One of the most famous troubadours was Bernard de Ventadour. His putative father was a woodsman at the Castle of Ventadour, where Count Ebles III was the lord. The Count took an interest in Bernard—some called it a paternal interest—and sent him to school to become skilled at verse making. He soon took up with Ebles' young wife, the Countess Margarida, and eventually became her lover. Discovered by the Count, he was lucky to get off with banishment. He came to Eleanor's court at Poitiers when the 32-year-old Queen was pregnant with her second child by Henry II, who was away in England. Smitten again, Bernard composed lyrics dedicated to the Queen, in which he suggested "success" with her and with the Countess. After the birth of her child, the Queen was recalled to England by Henry, while Bernard, perhaps thinking that discretion was the better part of valor, remained in France. Throughout his life he seems to have fallen in and out of love repeatedly, justifying the conclusion that his true love was the *concept* of love, and that each corporal copy of the phantasma that moved him resulted in but a short pause in his eternal quest.

The concept of *Frauendienst*—the service of women—was cultivated by the minnesinger (singer of love), as the Germanic version of the troubadour was called. The most noteworthy minnesinger—in terms of life style rather than poetry—was Ulrich von Lichtenstein.[18] Born about 1200 to the lower nobility, he steeped himself in the lore of courtly love at an early age. When he was 12, he became a page at the court of a married princess, having elected her as the lady of his life. He turned pale in her presence and was overcome with emotion when she touched the flowers he had secretly placed before her. He went so far as to make off with the basin of water with which she washed, religiously drinking from it in the privacy of his room.

Upon becoming a knight, he arranged for an intermediary to tell the princess of his love. The highborn lady rejected the suit, declaring that Ulrich was not only presumptuous but ugly. After the latter condition was somewhat improved by an operation on his harelip, he sent his lady one of his new songs and was allowed to attend a riding party and, as an *entendedor,* to speak to her for a minute should the occasion arise. The moment came as he helped her from the saddle, but the poor fellow was so overcome that his tongue vainly tried to lash his jaws into action. Somewhat irritated, the lady called him a fraud and ripped out a handful of hair from his head to show her displeasure. This only convinced the masochistic Ulrich that she was indeed a worthy prize, and the next day he pressed for formal acknowledgement of himself as her "man." She granted this request, but promised neither the slightest physical intimacy nor even a ribbon to carry beneath his clothes.

Several years were spent in pressing for her love, which met with cold rejection. At one point she rebuked him for claiming to have lost a finger in her service. Actually, the finger had only been wounded. When told about her reaction, Ulrich took out a knife and asked his companion to hack off the offending digit. He packaged the tidbit in a velvet case and shipped it off to her. Charmed, she wrote him that it pleased her to gaze at this evidence of his affection each day. Ulrich received her comments in his usual genuflecting position, with bowed head and folded hands. With his lady showing signs of a thaw, he felt that a stupendous feat of derring-do would gain the long-cherished goal. He conceived the idea of dressing himself in white and playing the role of Venus. He dispatched messengers to promise prizes for those who would joust with him, and a grand prize of many horses to the man who could unseat him. In this manner he proceeded from Venice to Vienna, and in five weeks by his own count, he broke 307 lances and unhorsed four opponents but was never thrown.

En route, he visited his wife and children for a few days. Then, refreshed, he continued to Vienna, where news of his feat had preceded him. His lady agreed to see him, although he could expect no special favors; she meant that he must dress as a leper and stand in line with the other lepers and beg alms. In addition, he spent the night in a stinking ditch and, when finally allowed to scale the walls of her chamber, found eight maids-in-waiting attending her in bed. She coyly turned a deaf ear to his pleas to dismiss them and gave him another task. Then, as he was lowering himself out of the window, the princess pretended to kiss him but instead let the rope fall out of her hands, dropping Ulrich back into the moat. She then ordered him to go on a crusade and, when he accepted her command, changed her mind and granted him her love—some 15 years after he had first adored her! Whether he received the final reward, or only the right to caress her naked body, or just a kiss, we do not know.

For some unknown reason the two soon parted, and in the songs of his old age Ulrich turned to invectives against women. He never questioned the value of love itself, as distinct from womankind, believing that he had become a better Christian knight because of his love and service to his lady.

Ulrich was not the only bizarre lover. The troubadour Pierre Vidal fell in love with a lady named Loba de Penautier. Since *loba* meant "she-wolf," he dressed himself in wolf skin and prowled around the premises of her house. His disguise apparently fooled some shepherds, for they set their watchdogs on him and he was severely mauled.

The antics of troubadours suggest that they were a bizarre, highly unorthodox lot. Though imaginative, their occasional attempts to carry their fantasies into actual behavior seem to have ended badly more often than not, and their interpersonal skills were often inferior to their artistic talents.

Poetry of the Troubadours

The troubadour typically expressed himself via the *chanson,* a love song with a melody usually created especially for the poem. While initially its form varied, it almost always had a confessional, ritual character. Each verse was regularly structured and was set to the same melody, expressing the singleness of purpose of the troubadour.

The introduction featured the nature-prelude, in which the return of spring and budding nature reminded man that as one of nature's children he should search out his love. Next, it was customary to mention the effect of the sight of his lady. Pierre Vidal noted that cloudy heavens seemed to clear and that the ice of winter was like rosebuds. Sometimes a glance from his lady froze the troubadour in his tracks; at other times he burned with an insufferable heat.

Despite his hope for speedy acceptance so that love's pleasures could be tasted, the troubadour was often disappointed. He complained that "the more I plead with her, the worse is her conduct toward me."[19] Other themes warned milady that time's winged chariot was drawing near, and that she had better act while she still could. Patience he had, but if the lady took too long, the poet warned, he might die of a broken heart or even become a mendicant.

If this were not enough to change her mind, the embittered lover might unleash a *sirventes* (insulting poem) and cry out that her fine form was offset by a venomous and deceptive nature.[20] If the lady acceded, the troubadour proclaimed himself richer than a king. He might go further and ecstatically describe the red of her lips, the color of her cheeks, and the white of her teeth, skin, breasts, and hands. There was little variation, since every lady was considered flawless.

In sum, the poetry of the troubadour reflects a literary revolt against the rigid social structure of medieval society and a thirst for individual achievement in love, based on the rationale that desire by the man and acceptance by the lady are in accord with nature. However, the stylized, formalistic repetitiveness of the poetry quickly wearies the reader, and most troubadourian verse is not counted among France's literary treasures.

ANDREAS CAPELLANUS AND THE ART OF COURTLY LOVE

The task of codifying the principles of courtly love was undertaken by Andreas Capellanus (Andrew the Chaplain), in a book written probably between 1184 and 1186. Andreas was with Eleanor at her court at Poitiers; later, he went with her daughter, Countess Marie, to Troyes, where she ruled as regent after the death of her husband. The book, divided into three parts, is addressed to a friend Walter, who has never been clearly identified. Walter has been pierced by the darts of Venus, and the book is intended as a guide in these affairs.

In Book I Andreas defines love as "a certain inborn suffering derived from the sight of an excessive meditation upon the beauty of the opposite sex, which causes each one to wish above all things the embraces of the other and by common desire to carry out all of love's precepts in the other's embrace."[21] Love may be aroused in three ways: a beautiful figure, an excellent character, and extreme facility of speech. Despite his contention that only character can be worthy of the crown of love, he contradicts himself by listing a series of fictitious dialogues between men and women of various classes in which the man attempts to seduce the woman through skillful play with words and she attempts to repel his advances by counterarguments.

One dialogue deals with a man of the higher nobility who is trying to seduce a woman of the lower nobility. After interminable verbal jousting, the woman tells him that she is in love with her husband and is not seeking diversion. The man protests—she cannot be in love with a husband!—and when they find themselves hopelessly deadlocked, they write to the Countess of Champagne to serve as arbiter. She replies:

> We declare and we hold as firmly established that love cannot exert its powers between two people who are married to each other. For lovers give each other everything freely, under no compulsion of necessity, but married people are in duty bound to give in to each other's desires and deny themselves to each other in nothing. Besides, how does it increase a husband's honor if after the manner of lovers he enjoys the embraces of his wife, since the worth of character of neither can be increased thereby, and they seem to have nothing more than they already had a right to? [Moreover,] no woman, even if she is married, can be crowned with the reward of the King of Love unless she is seen to be enlisted in the service of Love himself outside the bonds of wedlock. But another rule of Love teaches that no one can be in love with two men. Rightly, therefore, Love cannot acknowledge any rights of his between husband and wife. But there is still another argument that seems to stand in the way of this, which is that between them there can be no true jealousy, and without it true love may not exist.[22]

Another dialogue involves a man of the higher nobility (who is also a cleric) and a woman of the higher nobility, whom he wishes to seduce. Behind their talk of "courtesy," some basic antagonisms break through. To his suggestion that she enrich his and her own character by a little "love," she retorts that she would never commit a deed that injured the Heavenly Bridegroom (Christ) and one's neighbor (husband). The man caustically rejoins that if she is going to play the role of a saint, she should join a nunnery; but if she is going to lead an earthly life, it would be better to "enjoy love thoroughly than to lie to God under cloak of some pretense."[23]

The gentleman recites his assets: he is humble, devoted, generous, and a doer of good deeds—all for the love of her. When she observes that his deeds are all verbal, he explains that he is not boasting but is only trying to give her free access to his virtues. Her objections to his beautiful wife are met easily enough by a quotation from the recent decision of Countess Marie. She then argues that she is too young, but he presents physiological arguments that women are ripe at an early age. As for her contention that the loss of maidenhood before marriage would jeopardize her marital chances, he terms it erroneous thinking and reminds her that such delightful ladies as Anfelis, Isealt, and Blanchefleur all gave their "solaces" prior to marriage, with no ill effects on their marital opportunities.

The maiden then questions whether he is qualified to enter the service of love, since as a cleric he should avoid all desires of the flesh. In reply, he notes, happily, that there is a convenient gulf between what one preaches and what one practices. It is really quite a burden to spread the divine word, and God never meant to make him bear a double burden by living it. Actually, she is lucky to have a cleric as a lover: "We find that a cleric is in every respect more cautious and more prudent than a layman, and conducts himself and his affairs with greater restraint, and is accustomed to keep everything within more proper bounds; that is because a cleric, as the Scripture tells us, has an experienced knowledge of all things. Therefore, in love he is to be preferred to a layman, because it has been found that nothing in the world is so necessary as to be experienced in carrying on all things connected with love."[24]

The argument is not going too well for her, so the noble lady asks him, "Which is the better half of a woman, the upper or the lower half?" Speculating that she will appreciate him more if he chooses the upper part, he defends his choice on the grounds that men are not distinguished from beasts insofar as the lower parts are concerned, but the solaces of the upper parts are unique to man. Unfortunately, he guesses wrong, for the lady points out: "If there were a woman whose beauty was famous throughout the world, but who was found to be wholly useless for the work of Venus, no one would want her solaces, and she would be rejected by everyone as unclean. For the delight of the upper part would be absolutely nothing unless it were indulged in with an eye to the lower and were kept alive by contemplation of it. If you want to deny the truth of this, you will be forced to admit that two men can give each other the solaces of love, a thing which would be disgraceful enough to speak of and criminal to practice."[25]

He has another ready rejoinder, but enough of the flavor of the dialogues has been conveyed and we can proceed to other concerns of Andreas.

Andreas by no means believes that *all* people may love. Anyone who loves a nun, for example, commits a deadly sin. As for peasants, love is simply impossible. Most of them rut like cattle; and if a peasant were really stirred to love, that would be worse, for his farm would go to pot.

In Book II, Andreas describes 21 decisions in cases involving love, which were handed down by such noble judges as Queen Eleanor, the Countess of Champagne, and Queen Adele (the third wife of Louis VII). There has been considerable debate about the seriousness of these court proceedings. Most likely they were quasi-legal and were binding only on those who posed the questions. Some "court" sessions may have been precursors of the seventeenth- and eighteenth-century French salons, where philosophical questions, rather than pressing personal issues, were discussed.

The book ends with a listing of 31 rules for lovers which the King of Love, according to legend, had himself stipulated. The most important rules are the following:

When one lover dies, a widowhood of two years is required of the survivor.

No one should be deprived of love without the very best of reasons.

It is not proper to love any woman whom one would be ashamed to seek to marry.

A true lover does not desire to embrace in love anyone except his beloved.

When made public, love rarely endures.

The easy attainment of love makes it of little value; difficulty of attainment makes it prized.

Every lover turns pale in the presence of his beloved.

When a lover suddenly catches sight of his beloved, his heart palpitates.

A new love puts to flight an old one.

Good character alone makes any man worthy of love.

He whom the thought of love vexes, eats and sleeps very little.

A true lover considers nothing good except what he thinks will please his beloved.

Love can deny nothing to love.

A lover can never have enough of the solaces of his beloved.

A man who is vexed by too much passion usually does not love.

A true lover is constantly and without intermission possessed by the thought of his beloved.

Nothing forbids one woman being loved by two men* or one man by two women.[26]

The third and last book catches the reader by surprise. Andreas declares that he never meant a word of what he said in the first two books; he merely wanted to show Walter all the tricks of the trade so that he could gain greater glory in abstaining from the pitfalls of love! God actually detests sex outside wedlock and any sort of passion whatsoever. Love preoccupies you with gaining wealth, it makes you sin against your neighbor, and it makes you grow old before your time. Mutual love is impossible because "Woman [is] by nature a miser . . . envious, a slanderer of other women, greedy, a slave to her belly, inconstant, fickle . . . disobedient and impatient of restraint, spotted with the sin of pride and desirous of vainglory, a liar, a drunkard, a babbler, no keeper of secrets, too much given to wantonness, prone to every evil, and never loving any man in her heart."[27]

*This does not contradict Countess Marie's earlier cited statement that "no one can *be in love* with two men."

What are we to make of this strange ending? Parry,[28] a translator of Capellanus, and Hunt[29] see this closing as an attempt to imitate Ovid's *The Art of Love*.[30] Sex is the goal in both books, which favor the seduction of married women and the pleasure in deceiving the cuckolded husband. Both also deal with love as pseudo-warfare and talk about the need to perform all manner of services for women. Even the retraction in Andreas' last book follows the pattern set by Ovid. Finally, Ovid's work was one of the best-known books during the Middle Ages, and Capellanus would certainly have read it.

Ovid, however, wrote with tongue in cheek, his many humorous asides leaving no doubt that it was written in levity. Is Capellanus writing in jest? Donaldson[31] thinks Andreas meant to be funny, just like Ovid, except that he unleashed a mace-like wit instead of a rapier-like Ovidian one. Another explanation is preferred by Denomy,[32] who sees Capellanus' writing as reflecting the typical dualist medieval philosophy. The first two books, dealing with the rational and natural world, strongly argue that love is the font of goodness; the last book focuses on man's supernatural aspect. In the world of God and faith, adherence to naturalism is blasphemy and, as a cleric, Andreas argues for the superiority of the divine.

In my opinion, Andreas is neither attempting to be a pale carbon of Ovid, nor is he taking a serious dualist position, or even trying to be funny. His closing diatribe is not a retraction of his jesting, but a rather stereotyped explanation of a traditional Church position. Some of his views may seem ludicrous in the twentieth century, but they appeared quite logical to the medieval mind. Consider, for example, his explanation that he wrote the first two sections of his treatise to acquaint Walter with the ways of love so that he could gain greater glory by rejecting a temptation of which he was fully aware. That this belief was quite common in premedieval and medieval times may be demonstrated by the example of the holy men who took virgins to bed with them to prove the strength of their resolve in refraining from sexual intimacy. Abélard himself points out to Héloïse that she attains a greater achievement in living a life of chastity because her sexual powers are intact, whereas he is a eunuch.

The diatribe against women was consistent with the ecclesiastics' general attitude toward nonvirginal women, as set forth in equally strong language by Saint Jerome. It is the normal and expected conclusion to a cleric's treatise on love.

As to Donaldson's view that Andreas is trying, albeit unsuccessfully, to be funny, I can only say that an exhaustive review of the text fails to reveal any rudiments of humor. I suspect that Donaldson's perception of "attempted humor" rests on his evaluation of Andreas' writing by today's standards, and I submit that the "illogical aspects" were "logical" a thousand years ago.

My own explanation of Andreas' motives would be that by the close of the twelfth century the code of courtly love had become known to most persons in the retinue of the nobility and would have had to be mastered by a cleric who was writing a rejection of courtly love. For this reason Andreas' tactic was to demonstrate that, despite his clerical frock, he knew all about love, and his conservative diatribe at the end would be all the more convincing.

This does not mean to imply that Andreas was any more sincere in his closing attack on courtly love than he was in the first two sections where he extols it. Since he was in the employ of the Countess of Champagne at one time and probably wrote his tome under her patronage, it seems strange that he would so viciously attack the sex of his patron. If, however, she understood that his attack was but a required role for an ambitious cleric,* she may have condoned his denunciation of women. It is thus quite conceivable that Andreas was sincere in both praising courtly love and condemning it. He may have been merely playing a series of roles without having any personal involvement in any of them.

If we examine the numerous dialogues between men and women, we find no clear position taken by Andreas to favor any ideology or either sex. The *combatants* (as I must call them), behind their finery and courtly manners, are full of mutual hostility. They see the "game" as an opportunity to exploit the "other," and little else. The philosophy of the men is to use their knowledge of courtly love to get the women to bed. The women want the narcissistic satisfaction of being courted without granting favors. This is precisely the kind of dialogue that a "marketable,"[33] ambitious personality would create, and it also indicates that Andreas is not seriously involved in either a defense or an attack on courtly love. Instead, his dialogues have become a vehicle for demonstrating Andreas' casuistic talents and little more.

DECLINE OF COURTLY LOVE

The heyday of courtly love corresponded roughly with the lifetime of Eleanor of Aquitaine (1122-1204). Several factors contributed to its decline. For one thing, in 1174 Eleanor, its chief patron, was imprisoned by her husband for almost a decade. For another, there was the Albigensian Crusade (1209-1218), authorized by Pope Innocent III to exterminate the growing influence of the heretical Cathar sect in southern France and northern Italy. Northern French nobles and Crusaders, confident that the rich territory offered untold material gains (unlike the less certain rewards offered by strife against the Saracens), hastened to answer the call. They massacred thousands, as did the Inquisition, a newly developed instrument to handle heretics. The soil of the South was scorched, and the friendly castles, where most troubadours had plied their trade, were razed.

---

*Andreas describes himself as a cleric of royalty. Does he mean that since Marie was the daughter of Queen Eleanor, he is a royal chaplain by association, or did he actually later become a member of the royal household under Philip Augustus? Unfortunately, we do not know the answer to this intriguing question.

Another reason for the decline of courtly love was the troubadours' impatience and weariness at the limitations imposed by the *chanson* on artistic expression. As Gui d'Ussel confessed, "I should make songs more frequently, but it bores me to say each day that I sorrow and die for love, for all know how to say as much. That is why I must find new words set to a pleasant melody; but I can find nothing that has not already been said and sung. How then shall I pray to you, my love? I shall say that same thing in another fashion, so that in this way I may make my songs seem new."[34]

The Albigensian Crusade resulted in an inhibition of sensual expression in troubadourian poetry and in a bowdlerizing of the content of the poems. The lady of the troubadour was no longer a woman of the flesh; she became either the Virgin Mary or a heavenly surrogate. The dichotomy between "mixed" love (containing sensual and spiritual elements) and "false" love (pure lust) was replaced in poetry by a division between "pure" and "sensual" love, with the poet demeaning the latter. To love women as sexual objects was wrong; to love the spark of God in them was good.

Further evolvements in courtly love in the Germanies and in Italy will be considered shortly.

SIGNIFICANCE OF COURTLY LOVE

The Relationship of Poetry to Behavior

A question that has concerned medievalists is whether the troubadour's poetry actually reflected the relationship between the poet and his lady. Some view the poetry as a game or as literature,[35,36,37] others see it as an adequate description of the social behavior of the period.[38,39] In attempting an evaluation, it should be emphasized that courtly love was not a standard, undifferentiated code of behavior, but represented different things to different people.

The verse of Duke William, for example, hardly depicts his real behavior. As the most powerful noble in France—not excluding the king—and as a man who defied the laws of marriage and the clergy in his steadfast pursuit of lust, the Duke can hardly have been sincere when in Poem 9 he said, "I dare not send her a message by another, so much do I fear to annoy her, and I myself have not the courage to declare my love to her, so much do I fear failure."[40]

For William, poetry represented a way of adding variety to simple sex and thus increasing the delight to be obtained from it. Moreover, to be accredited as a poet and a man of letters must have brought considerable pride to a man who already had almost everything the world could offer.

In Bernard de Ventadour and Pierre Vidal, however, we see examples of retarded psychosexual development. Both seem to have been in love—not with people but with the concept of "love" itself. Within this constantly infatuated group, some no doubt took their sexual gratification where they could get it. Perhaps a few thrived more on denial than on gratification, for the latter might reveal the clay feet of an idealized lady.

A considerable number looked to the troubadour's profession as a potential source of achievement and recognition. In an age when commerce was only in its infancy, there was little hope of becoming wealthy unless one was in the clergy or had been born into the high nobility. The majority of troubadours were petty nobles, landless and impecunious. Given a flair for poetry and a reasonably good voice, the opportunity to move from castle to castle must have seemed an exciting, albeit uncertain, adventure.

The desire for adulterous affairs existed then, as it does today, but there was less opportunity to fulfill such aspirations. Would the typical lower-status troubadour really have dared to sing of his love for the lord's lady in the great hall in the presence of the populace and the lord himself or his representative? Surely, genuine love would have required a modicum of discretion.

Not only was such expression contrary to Church precepts, it was contrary to feudal custom. Vassals or lowly employees of a great lord who committed adultery with the lord's wife were like vassals who betrayed their feudal obligations, and even threatened to introduce spurious issue into the lord's lineage.[41]

When Bernard de Ventadour wrote a song with the words, *"per vos me sui del rei partitz"* (Because of you I left the king), he must have meant that he left because of her wishes rather than for her sake. Modern romantic thinking, which disregards status in favor of feeling, simply does not do justice to the importance of and respect for status in medieval times.

The troubadour's verses must be seen, therefore, as an art form that was encouraged by high-status women because it gratified their need for attention and recognition. Nowhere is this more apparent than in *Le Chevalier à la Charrette* (Lancelot), written by Chrétien de Troyes shortly after 1160.[42] The book is replete with instances of courtly behavior superimposed on the skeleton of a story based on earlier legends.[43] When Guinevere is captive, Lancelot tries several times to commit suicide. Pressed into giving his word to sleep with another damsel, he refuses to consummate the relationship. When he sees Guinevere's hair in a comb, he temporarily loses color and the power of speech. For her he crosses the sword bridge, lacerating his hands and knees. His wounds are causing him to lose a fight with a knight for her; but when he looks up and sees her, he is infused with new strength. He even endures the shame of jumping into a cart used for criminals. And when she chastises him for hesitating two steps before he jumps, he accepts her rebuke without complaint. When he leaves her chamber, which he secretly entered to make love to her, he bows and acts as if he were before a shrine. Lancelot, in short, is the true courtly lover.

Yet Lancelot is not typical of twelfth-century literature. Not only were there many other poems written which did not deal with courtly love,[44] but in Chrétien's other poems, *bon bourgeois* that he is,[45] he shows himself highly in favor of marriage and fidelity. Why is Lancelot different? Chrétien gives us the indispensable clue when he tells us that he obtained the *matière* and *sens* (subject matter and spirit) of the story from his patron, Countess Marie of Champagne. The incompatibility of being a true knight and cuckolding one's lord and liege (Arthur) is never touched upon because the audience must have understood the bias of the story and its failure to conform to reality.

The literary value of the troubadours' art varied greatly. Some contributed to the foundations of the poetic art in the vernacular of their country. Others may even be compared to our modern popular singers. Many ladies, charmed by the melodies of a troubadour, doubtless went to bed with their husbands with their minds on some noble knight. Some husbands may also have had the dividend of finding their wives more animated in bed as a result of the evening's entertainment. But it seems wisest to conclude that lovers in the flesh, when they engage in adultery, make love and, if not careful, children—but rarely poetry.

The Church and Courtly Love

Courtly love also proved to be an important secular challenge to the authority of the Church in regulating conduct between the sexes. The threat lay not so much in the glorification of sensuality as in the assertion that, apart from any sensual returns, "good" could come from the adulterous relationship. The lover was believed to become a better man—more courteous, humble, and generous than he had been before love touched him. An extramarital personal relationship was on a higher level than the marriage tie.

Another difference from Church philosophy was in the glorification of passion. To the Church, as Thomas Aquinas was shortly to state, the evil in sexuality was not its carnal enjoyment, but the suspension of the use of one's rational faculties. Courtly love, on the other hand, glorified passion as the source of the troubadour's ennoblement.

Third, ties to nature were stressed in opposition to man-made rules. When spring came and the glands become activated, why should man not heed Mother Nature's call? Did the birds and the bees require dispensation from Rome to mate? Then why should man not unite himself with nature's ways instead of obeying the artifices of other men? In the folk poem "Aucassin and Nicolette,"[46] Aucassin disdains to go to a regimented heaven, with its ill-clad priests and the crippled, maimed, naked, and hungry. He announces that he would rather go to hell, where dwell freer gallant knights, lovely and beautifully dressed ladies, lovers, and happy minstrels.

In a way, the Church had long ago sown the ground for heretical philosophies in emphasizing the importance of the next world and devaluing this one. Now, however, an erotic ideology stressed the joys of sensual life in the present. It is not surprising, therefore, that the Church did not look with favor on courtly love.

The Status of Women

Some writers believe that women were emancipated by courtly love[47] ; others see no relationship between this "literary form" and the actual attitude toward women.[48,49] The disagreement can be reduced by specifying those areas in which women made gains and those in which no progress was apparent. The reference to women covers only women of nobility, for the blandishments of the courtiers were never meant to apply to peasants.

Politically, the effect of courtly love on women's rights appears to have been nil. There is no semblance of legal equality for the lady worshipped by the troubadour. In the area of social relationships, however, there is evidence of a new approach to women. The fact that a woman was worthy of being lauded in poetry could not but enhance the lady in the eyes of her husband and, most important, in her own self-image. Women had been idealized in earlier poetry, but they had usually been unmarried women, Catullus notwithstanding. Now the married woman was being worshipped, and the idea began to take hold that a woman did not disappear into her husband's shadow when she married.

EVOLVEMENTS OF COURTLY LOVE

Even before the Albigensian Crusade, troubadours and their songs spread throughout France to the North, from the Germanies to the East, and from Italy to the West. In each locale, modifications in the old themes reflected the needs and perceptions of indigenous poets.

Le Roman de la Rose

About 1237, Guillaume de Lorris' allegorical poem, *Le Roman de la Rose* (Book of the Rose),[50] appeared; it describes the hero's attempts to win the love (rose) of a fair damsel. The lover (*l'amant*) dreams of the garden of Deduit (Pleasure). Outside the wall are Hatred, Treason, Baseness, Old Age, Poverty, and other obstacles. He gains admittance and is enchanted with a most attractive rosebud. At that moment, Love hits him with five arrows: Beauty, Simplicity, Sincerity, Company, and Kindly Appearance. Fair Welcome, a friendly fellow who becomes the lover's accomplice, fears that the lover is going too far in requesting the rose. Their discussion arouses the ruffian crew of Danger, Shame, Fear, and Jealousy, who drive away both the lover and Fair Welcome. Eventually, when the lover returns and kisses the rose, a huge fortress is erected to separate him from the rose, and Fair Welcome is incarcerated in it in the custody of an old hag. At this point the poem concludes with the death of Guillaume de Lorris.

The narrative follows the finest troubadour tradition. The lover is counseled never to be guilty of uncouth ribaldry, always to be humble and affable, and to combine noble deeds with courteous words.

The thread of the story is picked up by Jean de Meun around 1280. The lover is assisted by Love and his lieutenants, Constrained Abstinence and False Manner. Their aid is accepted since a little deception is always necessary in winning over the ladies. Venus (sex) helps her son Love, who vows to leave no chastity among womankind. Nature and her priest Genius (god of reproduction) are happy to hear that Love and Venus will take the castle, and they deplore the instability and indiscretion of women. True nobility, proclaims Nature in one of her lengthy and numerous digressions, is a quality of the mind and not an accident of birth. She disparages the falseness of courtly love and chivalry, their tournaments and affected mannerisms.

The tale concludes when Genius excommunicates those who resist natural love and throws Love's torch into the castle. Its flame quickly softens the defenses. Venus routs Shame and Fear, Fair Welcome is liberated, and the lover plucks the rose—an obviously carnal meaning.

Jean de Meun was a mediocre poet, and the flowery grace of Guillaume is submerged in tedious discourses on society. Yet de Meun is a powerful critic of his time. He dwells on the evils of marriage and sighs for ancient times, when all was communal and marriage had not yet been invented. Although he is strongly misogynistic, he also grants that society is the cause of this false relationship between the sexes. Women are born as free as men, but man's law has corrupted nature's charter. The mind is more important than beauty, and a man who comes upon a virtuous, intelligent, and witty spouse can live in harmony with her all his days.

Despite his exposé of the sterility and puerile aspects of chivalry, he is unable to arrive at an integrated solution to his tangled frustration, scorn, and visions of "true" nature. He rips open the fabric of distorted relationships between men and women, but the cloth he offers in its place is woven of unrealistic fantasy. "Free love" has been tried by many societies and has never worked. Men and women are not good "naturally"; they are only malleable, carrying within them only the *potential* for meaningful relationships. Jean de Meun, a superb critic, is unable to supply a meaningful substitute for what he has destroyed.

Germany

The changes instituted by the minnesingers, the German lyric poets of the twelfth and thirteenth centuries, are typified by Wolfram von Eschenbach's *Parzival,* adapted from the Arthurian romance. For Wolfram, who has little sympathy for adultery, there is only one kind of faithfulness—that between husband and wife.[51]

In German hands, the treatment of love becomes much more complex and psychological. The troubadours did not concern themselves with *why* people loved. Love occurred at sight and derived from beauty, character, and speech. But that tells us precious little. In the best poetry of Walther von der Vogelweide, love is not akin to man's worship of woman, as troubadourian poetry puts it. It is *mutual, natural,* and needs no reference to perfection.[52] Walther says candidly to his beloved, "Perhaps others are better, but you are good."[53] Intrapsychic conflict between the body and the heart is found in Hartmann von Aue's *Büchlein,* and Gottfried von Strassburg concerns himself with love as a phenomenon in relation to the totality of existence.[54]

The equating of nobility of lineage with nobility of heart is denied. Heinrich von Morungen noted that it was nobility of heart that loved a noble lady, and character rather than birth was the proof of nobility.[55] Wolfram von Eschenbach, in describing the lovers Gahmuret and Herzeloide in *Parzival,* shatters courtly tradition. Herzeloide comes to the tent of Gahmuret, who has just won her hand and estate in a tournament, even though he does not know her. As soon as they are seated, Herzeloide, in an *impulsive* expression of feeling, hugs him. She not only announces that she grants him her love, but asks for the boon of dedicating herself to his service—a complete reversal of the roles of courtly love.

Perhaps the greatest rejection of the traditional code of courtly love comes in a song by Neidhart von Reuenthal, in which a peasant girl wooed by a knight scoffs at him and lets him languish. The circle had come full-round from Andreas Capellanus' advice to knights to rape, not woo, peasant women.

Italian Evolvements

Italian poets, influenced more by papal proximity than by the counts of the Medici, evaluated the consequences of the Albigensian Crusade against heretics and turned away from the carnality of the troubadours. They developed an approach known as the *dolce stil novo* (sweet new style), which emphasized that beauty went beyond the sensual. Love was not merely a *response* to the beautiful flesh of the lady. Her body was but a thin veil for the beauty of her soul, and love came from within the poet in response to appreciation of the soul. Love was an intellectual longing. The *stil novisti* (poets of the new style), who thought of themselves as superior in sensitivity and intellect to the common masses, tried to analyze the emotions engendered by the lady in relation to the scientific knowledge of the times. But science was scarcely advanced enough to permit any meaningful inferences, and the poetry is best described as quasi-scientific, metaphysical speculation. As such, it represented a bridge between "troubadour gallantry and Renaissance intellectualism."[56]

At the risk of oversimplification, we shall describe the transition from troubadour poetry to *dolce stil novo* as follows: The troubadour fell in love with his lady because of her beauty and character. The origins of this beauty and character are never really dwelt upon; but in viewing the lady, the poet is smitten by love. In turn, he is filled with love for his lady. In the *dolce stil novo,* the main difference is that the lady seems to be much more than delightful flesh and blood. She is often referred to as a miracle from heaven, a veritable *donna angelicata.* This subtle modification implies a conflict that can be seen in the sketch first proposed by Singleton:[57]

Love originates in God and is represented by his *donna angelicata,* the sight of whom stirs the poet. The poet then responds by loving (worshipping) the donna. The conflict resides in the fact that although love originates in God, it does not return to Him. The poet's response is focused wholly on the woman, not on God. In fact, much of the "new style" poetry, particularly some poems of Cavalcanti, has a tortured, uneasy cant: the poet grapples unsuccessfully with the problem of attempting to reconcile his sensual striving with the spiritual origins of the lady. It remained for Dante to resolve this impasse by carrying the equation one step further and showing that love for the *donna* was but a step toward the love of God.[58]

Dante (1265-1321)

Dante first saw Beatrice when he was nine and she was slightly younger.[59] He was so taken with her that his whole being trembled. They met again nine years later, and a greeting from the young lady pierced the depths of his soul. To hide his passion, he composed trivia honoring other ladies. Beatrice, irked by his negligence, subsequently refused his salutation. Deeply pained, Dante resolved to express his love in disinterested praise. She married soon after, and died in 1290, while still in her early twenties. Although Dante was grief-stricken at his loss, he was fortunate in another sense, for her memory was sketched indelibly in his poetic eye.

Beatrice's death made one thing clear to Dante. To focus unduly on one's beloved's physical existence was to open oneself to grief and powerlessness. The awesome power of the *donna* on a man came not from the ephemeral flesh but from the spirit of God that shone through her fleshy veneer. The cycle was complete: the poet's love for the *donna* was but love of God, for the *donna* was an analogue of Christ who symbolized sanctifying grace.

Dante fused his love of Beatrice with platonic and Christian ethics and created a new alloy that had hitherto not been experienced in troubadourian art. For the fever of the flesh he substituted fever of the mind. The struggle for love in courtly love is interpersonal and hinges on overcoming the lady's defenses through word and deed, and on duping the husband. In Dante, the struggle for love is internal, vacillating between sensual and spiritual strivings. Through love, the lover's sins may be forgiven by God. In the *Divine Comedy*[60] it is Beatrice who, because of her love for Dante, leads him to experience the presence of God. There is never the slightest hint of any mundane communication between them except on one occasion, when Beatrice undivinely chastises Dante for his earthly carnal appetite after he had lost her. Although his eyes are constantly fixed on her, she looks only upward as she leads him toward the heavenly glory. The troubadour who never received his *guerdon* was left empty-handed. Dante, in giving up his earthly reward, was compensated by being led to God.

Devotion to Beatrice did not keep Dante from physical interest in real women. He married, had children, and acquired a mistress, as befitted any distinguished citizen. His wife never appears in any of his poetry, nor did she accompany him during the last 20 years of his life when he was exiled from Florence. She was flesh and blood, capable of aging, and probably too full of imperfection for the man whose fantasy had scaled such heights.

CONCLUSIONS

The notion that troubadours went about seducing noble ladies (and composed songs about it) is more wish than fact. Both the tradition of courtly love and the songs and poems resulting from it were art forms, and art does not necessarily desire or require a mimicking of reality.

Yet the fact that this particular art form emerged when it did has significance beyond the mere expansion of the repertoire of literature. Courtly love served as a projective technique for eliciting the fantasies, wishes, and desires of courtiers and ladies. From the ladies' point of view, it represented a desire for recognition, attention, and power over men. In the case of men, I suspect that it epitomized their desire for a woman capable of stirring them to the depths. And for both sexes it embodied a wish for freedom of action in heterosexual relations—a far cry from the constraints placed on interpersonal relationships by a stratified class system and arranged marriages.

To the nobility of Aquitaine and its strong women goes much of the credit for making possible this new channel for fantasy. Fantasy deals with that which has not occurred, but the most popular fantasies have been based on a kernel of truth, a truth that could be expanded and projected into the future. The model of the powerful Queen Eleanor, who had managed a divorce from the French king to marry the man who became king of England, must have suggested how attractive an independent, competent woman could be (at least in fantasy) compared to a typically subservient one.

It is no accident, then, that courtly love appeared when it did. It also had antecedents in Moorish literature and in the relative cessation of feudal wars and Viking raids. The emerging peace and the leisure to encourage art afforded the opportunity to focus on interpersonal relations. What made a man attractive now went beyond mere physical strength and courage, and those who were skilled in words and song gained increasing recognition.

Courtly love, however, created a literature of interpersonal struggle that was almost devoid of intrapsychic concern. With time, modifications in the literature occurred in France, in the Germanies, and in Italy. A psychological literature arose, in which the struggle often occurred within the lover himself rather than between two persons.

Strong Church influence succeeded in purging much of the sensuality of the earlier songs. Courtly love literature evolved in its content and became more naturalistic and representative of a wide range of human needs and aspirations. Later poets and singers wrote and sang of nobility of the heart rather than of nobility of lineage, foreshadowing an era when accomplishment, not birth, would be the criterion of social status.

After the rigid concerns and format of courtly love came to an end, the position of women in literature underwent some change. In German literature, peasant girls could reject men of the nobility, and Dante's Beatrice was nothing less than an analogue of Christ. True, the poetic elevation of womankind did not find a parallel in their political and legal advancement. In a sense, however, the concept of woman as an angelic creature represented an advance from her denigrated status in early Christian times. During the Renaissance and Reformation she would at least gain a modicum of progress in the physical world.

REFERENCES

1. F. X. Newman (ed.), *The Meaning of Courtly Love.*
2. G. Paris, "Etudes sur les romans de la Table Ronde."
3. A. J. Denomy, *The Heresy of Courtly Love,* p. 59.
4. Ibid., p. 61.
5. A. Capallanus, *The Art of Courtly Love.*
6. M. Rosenberg, *Eleanor of Aquitaine.*
7. T. Wright, *Womankind in Western Europe.*
8. R. Briffault, *The Mothers,* Vol. 3.
9. J. Langdon-Davies, *Sex, Sin, and Sanctity.*
10. D. de Rougemont, *Love in the Western World.*
11. Ibid., p. 92.
12. Ibid., p. 120.
13. M. M. Hunt, *The Natural History of Love.*
14. Ibid.
15. M. Valency, *In Praise of Love.*
16. C. S. Lewis, *The Allegory of Love.*
17. E. S. Turner, *A History of Courting.*
18. M. M. Hunt, op. cit.
19. M. Rosenberg, op. cit., p. 161.
20. M. Valency, op. cit.
21. A. Capellanus, op. cit., p. 28.
22. Ibid., pp. 106-107.
23. Ibid., p. 111.
24. Ibid., p. 125.
25. Ibid., p. 136.

26. Ibid., pp. 184-186.
27. Ibid., p. 201.
28. A. Capellanus, op. cit., p. 201.
29. M. M. Hunt, op. cit.
30. Ovid, *The Art of Love.*
31. E. T. Donaldson, "The myth of courtly love."
32. A. J. Denomy, op. cit.
33. E. Fromm, *Man for Himself.*
34. M. Valency, op. cit.
35. R. Briffault, op. cit.
36. J. Langdon-Davies, op. cit.
37. E. T. Donaldson, op. cit.
38. A. J. Denomy, op. cit.
39. E. S. Turner, op. cit.
40. J. Langdon-Davies, op. cit., p. 211.
41. J. F. Benton, "Clio and Venus: An historical view of medieval love."
42. C. de Troyes, *Arthurian Romances.*
43. R. S. Loomis, *Arthurian Tradition and Chrétien de Troyes.*
44. S. Painter, *French Chivalry.*
45. T. P. Cross and W. A. Nitze, *Lancelot and Guinevere.*
46. A. Lang, *Aucassin and Nicolete.*
47. W. L. George, *The Story of Women.*
48. R. Briffault, op. cit.
49. J. Langdon-Davies, op. cit.
50. G. de Lorris and J. de Meun, *The Romance of the Rose.*
51. H. J. Weigand, *Courtly Love in Arthurian France and Germany.*
52. M. O'C. Walshe, *Medieval German Literature.*
53. W. Scherer, *A History of German Literature,* Vol. 1, p. 197.
54. W. T. H. Jackson, "Faith unfaithful—the German reaction to courtly love."
55. Ibid.
56. M. Valency, op. cit., p. 208.
57. C. S. Singleton, "An essay on the Vita Nuova."
58. C. S. Singleton, "Dante: Within courtly love and beyond."
59. Dante, *The Early Life.*
60. Dante, *The Divine Comedy.*

10

The Renaissance and the Reformation: 1500–1615

As the sixteenth century dawned, the Church still exerted a major influence on the lives of the populace, but dissatisfaction began to surface. Despite the earlier purging of their wives, or perhaps because of it, the sexual looseness of the clergy remained undiminished. In addition, the accumulation of wealth and the sale of dispensations to absolve sins gave the Church a secular interest that contrasted sharply with Christian philosophy.

Concern with these excesses led to questioning and/or revolt on the part of leading humanists (such as Erasmus) and theologians (Calvin and Luther, among others). Slowly the idea developed that the individual should be able to direct himself toward salvation without the guidance of the Roman clergy.

The laity, of course, shared the clergy's interest in materialism and sensuality, but a few critics felt that some customs went to ridiculous lengths. Montaigne, for example, railed against the custom of men wearing codpieces of inordinate size; he longed for "those days when the tailor took measure of it, as the shoemaker does now of a man's foot."[1]

The ribald sensuality of the period was vividly depicted in *Gargantua and Pantagruel*,[2] by the monk François Rabelais. Much of the book deals with Panurge, a companion to Pantagruel, who asks his lord whether or not he should marry, explaining: "I am in a rage after lust, and after a wife, and vehemently hot upon untying the codpiece point. . . . I itch, I tingle, I wriggle and long exceedingly to be married that without danger of cudgel blows, I may labor my female copes-mate with the hard push of a bull-horned devil."[3]

Pantagruel advises Panurge to marry, as does the "saintly" Friar John, who says:

> I do advise thee to nothing, my dear friend Panurge, which I would not do myself, were I in thy place. Only have a special care, and take good heed thou solder well together the joints of the double-backed, and two bellied beast, and fortify thy nerves so strongly, that there be no discontinuance in the knocks of the venerean thwacking, else thou art lost, poor soul. For if there pass long intervals betwixt the priapising feats, and that thou make

an intermission of too large a time, that will befall thee which betides the nurses, if they desist from giving suck to children,—they lose their milk; and if continually thou do not hold thy aspersory tool in exercise, and keep thy mentul going, thy lacticinian nectar will be gone, and it will serve thee only as a pipe to piss out at, and thy cods for a wallet of lesser value than a beggar's scrip.[4]

Panurge assures the good friar that he is apt at practicing his "placket-racket within the Aphrodesian tennis-court."[5] Still, he is terrified at the thought that other husbands might play Aphrodesian tennis with his wife, just as he has done with their wives.

The fear of being cuckolded is a recurrent theme in the literature of the period. Shakespeare refers to it numerous times. In *The Merry Wives of Windsor,* Mr. Ford is warned by Pistol, "Take heed; ere summer comes or cuckoo-birds do sing."[6] The temporary paranoia of King Leontes in *The Winter's Tale* focused on his fear of wearing horns. Edmund Tilney noted that " . . . a man may shewe his wife and his sworde to his friends, but not to farre to trust them."[7] If he became a cuckold, it was his own responsibility. In Catalonia, he observed, such negligence must be paid for by a fine levied against the cuckold; while in Paris, the cuckold is made to ride through the city in disgrace, with the town crier before him proclaiming, "So do, so haue."

ATTITUDES TOWARD WOMEN

The sixteenth and early seventeenth centuries witnessed a continued improvement in the status of women. A number of women visibly won distinction as powers of state—Elizabeth of England, Marguerite of Navarre, Catherine de Medici, Mary of Scotland, and Dianne de Poitiers. In the spirit of the Renaissance, extensive education in languages and in the arts became available to some. Margaret More, daughter of Thomas More, was among the first to receive an education comparable to that of any nobleman's son. Lady Jane Grey was conversant in any number of languages, as were Mary Tudor and her sister Elizabeth. As a result, a young woman pursuing an education need no longer worry if she married at the ripe old age of seventeen[8] instead of fifteen, as had been the custom a century before.

The advocacy of better education for women, however, hardly constituted a cry for equality of the sexes. Even the most liberal men of the period—such as Montaigne and Shakespeare—were not prepared to go that far. In general, "liberals" sought to increase the opportunities for women to realize some of their potential (aside from child-bearing) without infringing on the traditional rights of men. But even such minor efforts at concessions failed to reverse the age-old image of woman as unstable, stupid, and lascivious. In *Pantagruel,* the physician Rondibilis observes, "When I say womankind, I speak of a sex so frail,

so variable, so changeable, so fickle, inconstant and imperfect. . . ."[9]
  King Lear describes a typical lascivious woman:

> Down from the waist they are Centaurs,
> Though women all above;
> But to the girdle do the gods inherit,
> Beneath is all the fiends';
> There's hell, there's darkness, there's the sulphurous pit,
> Burning, scalding, stench, consumption.[10]

John Knox, the Scottish Reformist, was appalled at the fact that three contemporary women—Catherine de Medici of France, Mary of England, and Mary of Scotland—ruled or played prominent roles in the governments of their countries. That these women were all Catholics probably added to his misogynistic ire. In frustration and rage he wrote, in his *First Blast of the Trumpet Against the Monstrous Regiment of Women:*

> To promote a Woman to bear rule, superiority, dominion, or empire above any realm, nation, or city, is repugnant to Nature; contumely to God . . . it repugneth to nature, that the blind shall be appointed to lead and conduct such as do see? That the weak, the sick, and impotent persons shall nourish and keep the whole and strong? And finally, that the foolish, mad, and frenetic shall govern the discreet and give counsel to such as be sober of mine?. . . . And what I pray you is more able to cause Woman to forget her own condition, than if she be lifted up in authority above man?[11]

Other men, less vituperative, emphasized "rationalized projection"[12] to justify their hegemony over women—that is, they failed to acknowledge their own supremacist role, and projected the responsibility onto "Nature." Luther, for example, noted that women had small, narrow breasts and broad hips because they had been created to "remain at home, sit still, keep house, and bear and bring up children."[13] On the subject of childbirth, Luther could wax lyrical: "Work with all your might to bring forth the child. Should it mean your death, then depart happily, for you will die in a noble deed and in subservience to God."[14] Similarly, Friar Luis de León pointed out that "Nature made women . . . slow in movement so that they might be easy on their clothes."[15]
  Guillaume Bouchet sought a physiological explanation for man's superiority. Women are much more "humid" due to the accumulation of menstrual blood in their organs. The male has a warmer and more dilated system, allowing for greater evaporation of the humors. Women, on the other hand, possess tighter joints that prevent rapid evaporation of the trapped humors, and this is more likely to cause madness, obstinancy, and headaches.[16]
  Even the relatively liberal Montaigne could employ "rationalized" projection

to explain man's temporal hegemony over women: "Reason, prudence, and the offices of friendship are better found among men, and therefore it is, that they govern the affairs of the world."[1 7]

Nevertheless, most men acknowledged that women were their spiritual equals and, if physically and mentally infirm, should be all the more carefully cherished and guided—in Luther's words—as befits an "inferior vessel." But no one marveled that these "inferior vessels," in addition to rearing a brood of children, might be called upon to exercise "skill in physics, surgery, extraction of oils, banqueting stuffe, ordering of great feasts, distillations, perfumes, ordering of wool, hemp, flax, making cloth, dyeing, office of malting, oats, brewing, baking, and all other things belonging to a household."[1 8]

ATTITUDES TOWARD MARRIAGE

Sixteenth-century attitudes toward marriage, which were generally ambivalent or positive, were better than in the Middle Ages. Erasmus thought that few men would put their heads in the "collar of a matrimonial noose" if they had a foreknowledge of marriage. As for the ladies, "what woman would open her arms to receive the embraces of a husband if she did but forecast the pangs of childbirth, and the plague of being a nurse?"[1 9] Despite these admonitions, in his colloquy *Courtship,* Erasmus (who never married) implies that marriage is much preferable to virginity.[2 0]

Francis Bacon is no less ambivalent: "He that hath wife and children hath given hostages to fortune; for they are impediments to great enterprises, either of virtue or mischief. Certainly, the best works, and of greatest merit for the public, have proceeded from the unmarried or childless men, which both in affection and means have married and endowed the public."[2 1]

Therefore, when the question was posed as to when a man should marry, his answer is, "A young man not yet, an elder man not at all."[2 2] Nevertheless, wives possessed considerable flexibility: they could be mistresses to young men, companions during middle age, and nurses in one's declining years. In addition, being single could lead to self-centeredness and to blatant disregard of one's responsibilities toward society and the future. Bacon's personal life mirrored his mixed feelings about the blessings of matrimony: he criticized the institution, but he married.

The advocates of marriage became more numerous. Thomas Bacon advanced the heretical view that marriage was superior to virginity. The German occult, soldier, and physician, Heinrich Cornelius Agrippa (1486-1535), argued that the purpose of marriage went beyond procreation and the prevention of fornication: companionship should not only be added to this list but should head it: "Even men who were somewhat aged, yea and to those that be decrepite, and in who there is no power of generation, no hope left of propagacion, it is nevertheless lawful to marry, and (if a man may say it) oftimes necessary, whereby they maie passe for the later daies of their life, in the company of their well-beloved wyfe with more joye, suritie and less care."[23]

LUTHER'S VIEWS ON MARRIAGE

The most influential pro-marriage advocate of the sixteenth century was Martin Luther (1483-1546). His ideas are permeated by the desire to depict the Catholic Church as a usurper attempting to impose its own laws and rules as if they were God's will. But since the basis for determining God's will should be the Scriptures, many long-standing pronouncements by the Church on marriage were invalid.

Two prime evils had to be eradicated. One was the licentiousness of the clergy, the solution for which was to encourage marriage for all and to attack the concept that God had a special love of virgins. Second, the right of the Church to regulate marriage must be denied, and the idea that marriage was sacramental in nature and hence under the jurisdiction of the Church must be refuted. Did the Church say that virginity was superior to marriage? Luther replied: "If you are able to remain chaste and be pure by your own strength, why then do you vow to be chaste? Keep it, if you can; but it is a mere nothing that you should want to boast about your vow and then plead that they have led you astray. Do you want to know to whom you have vowed to keep chastity? I'll tell you: the miserable devil in hell and his mother."[24]

God gave man freedom, and it was a delusion to imagine that self-imposed vows of celibacy could gain divine favor. Faith alone promised salvation, not dubious "good works." The virtue of celibacy is that it theoretically freed man to devote more time to spreading God's word. If, however, a man vowed celibacy but continually experienced lustful thoughts, he could hardly be free to spread the word. He would be better off with a lawful outlet for his sexual needs. Feelings are not acts, and it is foolish to believe that "anyone who is tempted and whose lust and desire for another woman are aroused would be damned for it. I have often said that it is impossible to be alive and to have flesh and blood without sinful and evil inclination. If an evil thought is involuntary, it is not a mortal sin."[25]

Marriage is not a sacrament, because the act of marriage does not include a word of divine promise.[26] Nowhere in the Bible is it written that married persons, by virtue of their union, receive any grace from God. Further, marriage is of ancient origin and is found among nonbelievers as well as believers, which also contradicts the notion that it is a sacrament and the exclusive possession of the Church.[27] Yet marriage is a holy and spiritual institution, a gift to man which, unlike celibacy, is specifically approved in Scripture. But being approved, Luther makes clear, is not the same as being flawless: "With all this extolling of married life, however, I have not meant to ascribe to nature a condition of sinlessness. On the contrary, I say that flesh and blood, corrupted through

Adam, is conceived and born in sin; as Psalm 51 [:5] says. Intercourse is never without sin; but God excuses it by his grace because the estate of marriage is his work, and he preserves in and through the sin all that good which he has implanted and blessed in marriage."[28]

Marriage, in short, "may be likened to a hospital for incurables which prevents inmates from falling into a graver sin."[29] But if the Church has no business meddling in marriage and divorce, who should provide the necessary regulatory function? In Luther's view, "marriage is a rather secular and outward thing, having to do with wife and children, house and home, and with other matters that belong to the realm of the government."[30] The role of the clergy should be to serve as advisers in questions of conscience when officials and jurists become confused about whether violations exist.[31]

JOHN CALVIN

Another great theologian of the sixteenth century was John Calvin (1509-1564), whose thinking on marriage was strongly influenced by Luther. The two men had different physiques and temperament, which may have influenced their approach to marriage, to the relationship between the sexes, and to sex. Luther was intense, sensual, impulsive, and expressive. Although inconsistent in his attitude to his wife, he was a genial, lively person who liked to eat well, drink, and play the lute. Of Calvin it might be said that his spirit bore the "cross" of his body. Thin, dour, and pallid, he suffered throughout much of his life from dyspepsia, headache, ulcers, and kidney stones, to which were added pulmonary hemorrhages and tuberculosis in his old age. To function despite these ailments required a will of iron, and he expected no less of Geneva's citizens in connection with controlling their inclinations toward life's pleasures. As the leading luminary of the Consistory, which ruled Geneva as a theocracy, he was influential in embodying many of his views into law. He strongly opposed the three "d's"—drinking, dancing, dicing—but did not look askance at an occasional glass of wine. One's dress should be painfully simple, card-playing should be highly restricted, and the theater absolutely avoided. Instrumental music was not to be played in church, but songs could be sung if they passed the censor.

Although, like Luther, he ostensibly favored marriage, Calvin did advise that "every one refrain from marriage as long as he shall be capable of supporting a life of celibacy."[32] For those who had to succumb at some point, marriage was the remedy, but he urged such people to be guided by moderation and modesty.

His own nature was far from sensual. When he passed the age of 30, very likely still a virgin, he decided to marry to avoid the monasticism that he had so criticized in Catholic priests. Also, he wanted someone to free him from cares so that he could devote himself completely to God. His ideal was no voluptuous maiden, but one who was "chaste, agreeable, modest, frugal, patient, and affords me some hope that she will be solicitous for my personal health and prosperity."[33] In 1540 he married the widow **Idelette de Bure**. Their only child died at birth, and his wife, now an invalid, lived only seven more years. On her death, he gave her the supreme compliment: she had never interfered with his work.

It is somewhat difficult, from the perspective of today's more permissive culture, to understand why Genevans adhered to his grim dicta to avoid worldly pleasures and the temptations of leisure. Yet his views spread to Scotland, the Netherlands, England, and then, through the Puritans, to the Colonies. What made these repressive measures so attractive?

His "Puritanism" was not asceticism for the sake of mortifying the flesh. His followers believed that they were pilgrims between two worlds. God had predestined some to salvation, and the elect could prove their status by the frugality and industry of their lives. By making each person responsible for demonstrating his own salvation, Calvin had unwittingly enrolled in his camp the most cogent aid of all—the internal censor.

The Calvinists who migrated to England were also reinforced in their ways by their persecution at the hands of the Anglicans. This persecution furthered the polarization between themselves and the "decadence" of the English Cavaliers, and they sought to make their lives the antithesis of the sensuality and bawdiness that they perceived in their oppressors. (We shall return to these successors of Calvin when we study the Puritans in America.)

In sum, attitudes toward marriage showed an acceptance of marriage and an increased devaluation of asexuality by the Reform movement, which, far more than the Catholic Church, was responsive to the feelings of the populace. Also, Luther's willingness to yield the jurisdiction of theology over marriage to the secular government made inroads into the all-encompassing Church influence.

ARRANGED MARRIAGES VERSUS LOVE MATCHES

Arranged Marriages

The traditional view of marriage was that it represented a duty, and that one's choice should be made on rational grounds. Since parents were more experienced in the ways of the world, it followed that it was they who should choose marriage partners for their children. Many great figures of the period, such as Montaigne, Erasmus, Rabelais, Marguerite of Navarre, and Luther, subscribed to the concept that marriage should be primarily determined by other than the self-interest of the participants.

Even though the Church stipulated that the free consent of both parties must be obtained, in practice this meant that the parents had to make sure that their offspring did not publicly object to the choices made for them. If the parents disapproved of a marriage, they could usually block it by withholding consent.[34]

In Luther's opinion, any one who could marry should do so; but he also favored respect for a father's wishes. As to the problem of a father who opposed his son's desire to marry, Luther said:

> To hinder or forbid marriage and to compel or urge marriage are two quite different things. Although parents have the right and power in the first instance—namely, to forbid marriage—it does not follow that they have the power to compel their children to marry. It is more tolerable to obstruct and block the love which two persons have for each other than to force together two persons who have neither liking nor love for each other. In the first case there is pain for a short time, while in the second it is to be. feared that there will be an eternal hell and a lifetime of tragedy.[35]

Luther counseled that even though a child would be technically justified in refusing to marry the person chosen by his father, he should in fact comply. Scripture, noted Luther, enjoins us to "resist not evil." A "weak" Christian, however, might ask his friends to petition the authorities to prevent such a marriage.

Sir Thomas More advocated strict honesty in arranging marriages. In his *Utopia*, prior to a contemplated marriage, "some grave matron presents the bride naked ... to the bridegroom, and after that some grave man presents the bridegroom naked to the bride.[36] According to John Aubrey, More, to some extent at least, practiced what he preached: "When Sir William Roper came a-wooing early in the morning, More took him to his bedroom where his two daughters lay sleeping. . . . Seizing the bedsheet by a corner he whipped it off to reveal the two still sleeping young ladies lying on their backs, their smocks up to their armpits. Awakening, they rolled over on their bellies. Visibly impressed, Sir William noted sagely, 'I have seen both sides.' Patting the older on the rump he said, 'Thou art mine.' "[37]

Shakespeare, on the other hand, satirized the greed of the arranged, loveless marriage. In *The Merry Wives of Windsor,* Slender, who is being pushed toward a hoped-for marriage by his cousin Shallow, answers a question as to whether he can love the girl: "I will marry her, sir, at your request; but if there be no great love in the beginning, yet heaven may decrease it upon better acquaintance, when we are married and have more occasion to know one another. I hope, upon familiarity will grow contempt. But if you say, 'Marry her,' I will marry her; that I am freely dissolved, and dissolutely."[38]

In *The Taming of the Shrew,* Petruchio exclaims that if a woman has money he will marry her:

> But she as foul as was Florintius' love,
> As old as Sibyl, and as curst and shrewd
> As Socrates' Xanthippe, or a worse.[39]

In sum, when persons of wealth sought a spouse for themselves or their offspring, they saw no reason to sacrifice wealth or family gain for such uncertain commodities as passion, beauty, or virtue.

Marriage for Love

Although arranged marriages continued in vogue, a number of writers called for love and freedom of choice as the chief basis of marriage. In *The Courtier,* Castiglione advocated, through his character The Magnifico, that one should love only a person one could marry. There was nothing radical in this statement— Capellanus had said the same thing more than 300 years before. But most people now regarded love in a more honest fashion than did the troubadours with their formalized ritual of "courtly love." Shakespeare pokes fun at the exaggerations of the courtly lover in *As You Like It.* When Orlando pleads with Rosalind that he will die if his love for her is not requited, she tells him that "men have died from time to time and worms have eaten them, but not for love."[40] Nor does love depend on exaggerating the beauty of one's lover, Shakespeare's sonnet advises us:

> My mistress' eyes are nothing like the sun;
> Coral is far more red than her lips' red;
> If snow be white, why then her breasts are dun;
> If hairs be wires, black wires grow on her head.[41]

For Shakespeare, not only is love the true basis of a relationship between the sexes, but a declaration of love is tantamount to a proposal of marriage. Although his lovers typically fall in love at first sight, they never yield to passion until they have pledged their troth. Despite her passion for Romeo, Juliet says:

> If that thy bent of love be honorable,
> Thy purpose marriage, send me word to-morrow,
> By one that I'll procure to come to thee,
> Where and what time thou wilt perform the rite.[42]

The course of true love never runs smoothly in Shakespeare's plays, but suitors who are not really in love and woo someone with riches or parental support always fail. In advocating love as the necessary ingredient for any marriage, Shakespeare even depicts a king (Henry V) who marries for love rather than for purposes of state. Shakespeare's message that the young should marry whom they choose and that they not bow to parental wishes is repeatedly conveyed in *A Midsummer-Night's Dream, The Winter's Tale, The Merry Wives of Windsor, The Taming of the Shrew,* and *Romeo and Juliet.*

The advocacy of love marriages was not restricted to sonnets and plays. Agrippa, in *The Commendation of Matrimony,* pointed out that if greedy parents forced their children to marry those whom they hated, the inevitable result would be anger, fornication, and adultery. He opined that "love be the cause (of marriage), not substance of goodes; choose a wyfe, not a garment, let the wyfe be maryed not (for) her dowrye."[43]

Remarriage offered the closest approximation to love matches. Since about 45 percent of England's aristocratic women died before the age of 50, there was ample opportunity for choosing a second partner.[44] Financial considerations did not count as heavily at this point as the desire for companionship and a male heir. The widower would already have inherited his first wife's dowry and, if he now married a widow, she was also likely to possess some means. Second marriages at an advanced age were more often based on personal decisions rather than on parental coercion or passionate love.

In sum, parental influence in matchmaking remained paramount in the sixteenth century. Yet Lord Burghley, the minister of Queen Elizabeth, saw the handwriting on the wall when he cautioned his son, Robert Cecil, "Marry thy daughters in time lest they marry themselves."[45]

THE RELATIONSHIP BETWEEN HUSBANDS AND WIVES

As in the past, the first axiom of the marital relationship was that the wife was the physical and intellectual inferior of the husband, A then-current joke concluded: "A Good Woman is but like one Ele put in a bag amongst 500 snakes, and if a man should have the luck to grope out that one Ele from all the snakes, yet he hath at best *but a wet Ele by the Taile.*"[46]

Women who tried to seize the domestic reins were attacked, and husbands who allowed them to do so were mocked. Jean Bodin, the great French political philosopher, noted that "those [women] who take such great pleasure in bossing around their effeminate husbands resemble those persons who prefer to lead the blind than to follow the wise and clairvoyant."[47]

Even Shakespeare, who championed love as the only legitimate basis of marriage, adhered to this doctrine. At the close of *The Taming of the Shrew,* the no-longer shrewish Katharina submits: "Thy husband is thy lord, thy life, thy keeper, thy head, thy sovereign."[48]

A scathing denunciation of the failure to exercise masculine leadership appeared in a letter from Luther to the notary Stephen Roth on April 12, 1528. Roth had moved from Wittenberg to Zwickau, but his wife refused to accompany him. The reasons for her reluctance are not clear. Troubled, Roth asked his wife to consult Luther, but she failed to visit him. Luther waited for some time and then wrote the following letter, which is co-signed by John Bugenhagen, his follower and colleague:

Grace and peace in Christ, and authority over your wife!
My dear Stephen:

Your lord and mistress has not yet come to see me, and this her disobedience to you displeases me greatly. Indeed, I am beginning to be somewhat put out with you too, for by your softheartedness you have turned into tyranny that Christian service which you owe her, and you have hitherto so encouraged her that it would seem to be your own fault that she now ventures to defy you in everything. . . . You should have remembered that you ought to obey God rather than your wife, and so you should not have allowed her to despise and trample underfoot that authority of the husband which is the glory of God, as Saint Paul teaches. . . . By your own fault you are now opening a window in this weaker vessel through which Satan can enter at will and laugh at you, irritate you, and vex you in every way.

You are an intelligent man, and the Lord will enable you to understand what I write. At the same time you will recognize how sincerely I wish you two to come to an agreement and Satan to be driven off. Farewell in Christ.[49]

Despite the universal concordance regarding woman's inferiority, a few men were beginning to suspect that they might be as responsible for her condition as Mother Nature. In Erasmus' *The Godly Feast,* Timothy exclaims, "Often it's our own fault that our wives are bad, either because we choose bad ones or *make them such.*"[50] Montaigne, observing that men and women were equally inconstant in their affections, thought that women were more justified. Nature made both sexes that way—but women did not choose men; it was the men who chose women. From childhood on, women are weaned on romance and stories of love. When their imagination reached a boiling point, they married and became more stimulated by sexual experience. Then the husband went out to sow his seed elsewhere, while he worried about the chasteness of his spouse.[51]

In *Othello,* Emilia complains about the one-sidedness of the marital relationship:

> What is it that they do
> When they change us for others? Is it sport?
> I think it is . . . And have not we affections,
> Desires for sport, and frailty, as men have?
> Then let them use us well; else let them know,
> The ills we do, their ills instruct us so.[52]

Despite the many problems in marriage, Shakespeare sees it as a generally blissful state. Some misunderstandings may even lead to tragic consequences—for example, in *Othello* and *The Winter's Tale*—but apart from a few incidents needed to develop the drama, the everyday relationship between husband and wife is usually good. Faithfulness is the rule; and in the rare cases where it is violated, as in *Anthony and Cleopatra* and *All's Well That Ends Well,* Shakespeare is less than sympathetic to his characters.[53]

A number of important public figures viewed the relationship between husband and wife with considerable ambivalence. According to Montaigne, "Whoever supposes to see me look sometimes coldly, sometimes lovingly, on my wife, that either look is feigned, is a fool."[54]

Luther noted, " 'tis a grand thing for a married pair to live in perfect union, but the devil rarely permits this. When they are apart, they cannot endure the separation, and when they are together, they cannot endure the always seeing one another."[55] On one occasion, when he was away from his family and thought that he was dying, he missed them terribly. Upon his recovery he observed, "A great thing is this bond and communion between man and wife."[56] At another time, however, he said that marriage straightened out all fuzzy minds to one basic idea: "Do and think as she wishes."[57] He vowed that his wife was more precious to him than France and the treasures of Venice, but he also reflected, "If I were to marry again I would carve myself an obedient wife out of stone, for to find one of flesh and blood is not conceivable."[58]

In sum, relations between man and wife had greatly improved in comparison with Greek and Roman times. Men exploited women, but attributed it to Nature's will. The more sensitive ascribed women's foibles to their imitating their lords, but even the most sophisticated did not yet perceive all of women's "inferiority" as having societal rather than biological roots.

Sex Relations

Most writers advocated sexual relations as a means of reducing sexual tensions, provided that procreation was not interfered with and that there was only moderate indulgence. Anyone who aroused himself by looking forward to sexual pleasures was considered a wanton. Vives said, "The solaces and pleasures of those which are married must be rare and sober."[59] Montaigne agreed: "Those shameless excesses that our first heat suggests to us in this sport are not only indecently but detrimentally practiced on our wives. Let them at least learn shamelessness from another hand. They are aroused enough for our need."[60]

As a result, many husbands "dishonored" other women with the excesses of their bestial appetites. Fausto da Longiano, perhaps overoptimistically, thought that wives might consider this a mark of the esteem in which they were held.[61] Erasmus' *Colloquies*[62] mentions a kindly (grateful?) wife who sent tidbits up to the room where her husband was frolicking with a younger playmate.

Sometimes the wife rebelled against this "austere" treatment. Bonaventure des Périers recounts the story of a Parisian doctor who justified his lack of sexual appetite on the pretext that the stars had urged him to make love to his wife only on rainy nights. There must have been a lengthy dry spell, for the infuriated wife finally ordered a servant to pour water on the roof with a watering can. When the recalcitrant doctor soon died of exhaustion, his widow was free to marry a nonastrologically oriented man.[63]

Luther advocated sex as a good remedy for marital stress:

> Is it sinful for a man and a woman to desire each other for the purpose of marriage? This is ridiculous, a question that contradicts both Scripture and nature. Why would people get married if they did not have desire and love for each other? Indeed, that is just why God has given this eager desire to bride and bridegroom, for otherwise everybody would flee from marriage and avoid it. In Scripture, therefore, He also commanded man and woman to love each other, and He shows that the sexual union of husband and wife is also most pleasing to Him. Hence this desire and love must not be absent, for it is a good fortune and a great pleasure, if only it continues as long as possible.[64]

Budding "science" also threw a cloak of respectability over the sexually active. Physicians of the time were constantly concerned with eliminating evil vapors and humors. They recommended regular purges and blood-letting, and prescribed a periodic, though not excessive, evacuation of semen.

Thomas Cogan, in *The Haven of Health,* noted the multiple benefits of the sexual act: "it procureth the appetite to meate and helpeth concoction; it maketh the bodie more light and nimble; it openeth the poares and cundittes and purgeth flegme; it quickeneth the minde, stirreth up the witte, reviveth the senses, driveth away sadnesse, madnesse, anger, melancholy, fury."[65]

As to the negative effects of suppressing sex, Luther said, "It necessarily strikes into the flesh and blood and becomes a poison, whence the body becomes unhealthy, enervated, sweaty, and foulsmelling."[66] But he did not condone lustful behavior in marriage. His was a realistic approach; sex was a force too powerful to oppose, but it could be harnessed for useful purposes.

Sex, in sum, became theologically acceptable in the sixteenth century. While its pleasurability was not directly alluded to, the day when sex was considered intrinsically evil had clearly passed.

SEQUENTIAL POLYGYNY—THE SAGA OF HENRY VIII

One man, Henry VIII, is credited with the most interesting sixteenth-century marriages. His first marriage (at the instigation of his father, Henry VII) was to Catherine of Aragon, widow of his elder brother, Arthur. Although Arthur, a boy of 15, had died five months after his marriage, it was assumed to have been consummated, and the Spanish Ambassador even sent "proofs" to her father, King Ferdinand. When Catherine denied the consummation, there was a question as to whether the princess and her dowry of 200,000 ducats should return to Spain. This potential loss, conjoined with the desire to maintain the alliance between Spain and England, impelled Henry VII to marry 12-year-old Henry to Catherine, six years his senior.[67]

The Bible offered contradictory evidence on the validity of the marriage. The Church cited Leviticus 20:21, which held that it was unclean to take a brother's wife. Henry VII, however, leaned toward the levirate (Deuteronomy 25:5): a brother should marry his brother's widow if she was childless. Apparently, the devil was not the only one who could quote Scripture to suit his purpose. The Pope obligingly granted a dispensation, and in 1503 the betrothal was announced, although cohabitation was postponed because of Henry's youth. In 1509, at the age of 18, Henry VIII succeeded to the throne and publicly celebrated his marriage.

After a number of stillbirths, a daughter, Mary, was born in 1516, and Henry thought a son would surely follow. When the next child was stillborn, he began to mutter that his failure to produce a male heir was a punishment from God for violating the Biblical injunction against marrying his brother's wife. Catherine, her health ruined by the succession of pregnancies, was ill and dour of spirit. By 1524, Henry ceased having physical relations with her and sought ways of shedding her.

Until now, Henry's behavior had caused no great scandal, for it was an unwritten law that kings, who married for reasons of state, could indulge themselves with other ladies. In addition, the desire for a male heir met with sympathetic approval from a populace which recalled the bloody Wars of the Roses, fought over questions of succession.

Somewhere in his extramarital forays, Henry is believed to have contracted syphilis, which plagued him for the rest of his life, and he grew increasingly corpulent as a consequence of heavy eating. The portrait by Holbein shows an unpleasant-looking, heavy-set man with beady eyes—a far cry from the handsome youth who had ascended the throne. Some sexual urges remained, nevertheless, and he took up with Anne Boleyn and installed her as maid of honor to his queen. Anne was about 20, short, and not particularly pretty; but she was well educated and vivacious, and had flashing dark eyes. Her energy captivated the King, but for a time she skillfully put off his advances. When at last he resolved to make her his queen, two problems became rather irksome: (1) he had slept with Anne's sister, Mary (Sir George Throckmorton charged that he had slept with her mother as well), and a long-standing papal ruling forbade marriage to Anne under these circumstances; (2) only the Pope could annul Henry's marriage to Catherine—though a papal ruling prohibiting marriage to a brother's wife had been conveniently ignored at the time of his own marriage.

At that moment, the Pope was a virtual prisoner of Charles, Emperor of the Holy Roman Empire, who had captured Rome. Since Charles was also a nephew of Catherine of Aragon, it was most unlikely that he would sanction his aunt's divorce, and so the Pope did not grant Henry an annulment. Although he consented to a trial to test the validity of Henry's marriage, he secretly instructed his legate to stall for time pending clarification of the political situation.

Infuriated, Henry agreed to an attack on the clergy which culminated, in 1531, in the Convocation of Ecclesiastics and designated him the "protector" and head of the English clergy. Having by this time won over Anne, he ignored the Pope's letters that he give up his adulterous ways and take Catherine back until there was a ruling on the validity of his first marriage.

On January 15, 1533, he married Anne, already pregnant with the future Queen Elizabeth. His dutiful Archbishop of Canterbury, Cranmer, soon declared Henry's first marriage void and the new one fully valid. In fact, the Convocation of 1533, ordered by Henry, declared that marriage to a brother's widow (Catherine) was contrary to divine law and did not admit of dispensation.

Soon, however, familiarity had bred both a child and contempt. Anne's vivacity was now expressed in a hot temper and in imperiousness, and Henry thought regretfully of the peaceful but dull Catherine, who died in 1536. On the day of Catherine's funeral, Anne bore him a dead child. Henry, still desirous of a son, now believed that he had been drawn to Anne by witchcraft rather than lust. When he began to pay attention to Jane Seymour, the queen's maid, and the jealous Anne complained, he told her not to interfere with his kingly franchise. Their strained relations led him to refer the rumors of Anne's infidelity to his council for investigation (whether these rumors were well founded or contrived is unknown). The subservient council found her guilty of adultery with five men, including her brother. In view of her hot temper and emotional lability, it is possible, though not likely, that she sought revenge for Henry's unfaithfulness with one man; but to risk her position and life by carrying on an affair with five men strains credulity.

Henry wrote to Anne while she was confined to the Tower, requesting that she confess and thereby live. She admitted having received two proposals but, she stoutly maintained, she had resisted them. Henry either did not believe her or simply wished to be rid of her. His marriage to Anne Boleyn was declared void, and two days later, on May 19, 1536, Anne lost her head.

Eleven days later, Henry jumped into his third matrimonial venture, this time with Jane Seymour. No outstanding beauty, she is reported to have been intelligent, kind, and modest, and to have spurned the King's advances while Anne lived. She died 12 days after the birth of her sickly child, who later became Edward VI. Henry now looked around for a new wife who could produce the elusive healthy male heir.[68]

At this time, the Emperors Charles of Spain and Francis of France were momentarily reconciled, and Henry's ministers feared a coalition against him. Thomas Cromwell convinced Henry that a league of Protestant states would be needed to counter this threat, and proposed to cement the alliance by having Henry marry the Elector of Saxony's sister-in-law, Anne of Cleves. Henry had never seen her and was somewhat reluctant to marry sight unseen, but was persuaded to send Hans Holbein to paint the young lady's portrait. The portrait showed a large, serious, yet not unattractive woman, and Henry agreed to the marriage. But when he came face to face with Anne on January 1, 1540, he was dismayed by her appearance. However, since things had gone too far for him to back down, they were married and Henry hoped for a strong son. Before the first night had passed, the King realized that he couldn't stand her. According to a letter Cromwell claimed to have received from the king: "I liked her but not well, but now I like her much worse for (quoth your Highness) I have felt her Belly, and her Breasts, and thereby, as I can judge, she should be no Maid; which strook me so to the Heart when I felt them, that I had neither will nor courage to proceed any further in other matters; saying, I have left her as good a Maid as I found her."[69]

Within a few months, proceedings were under way to shed what he called his "Flanders mare." Anne, valuing her life, was quite adaptable: she kept her head and entered into Henry's good graces. She swore that she was still a maid, and the marriage was duly annulled. She continued to live in England on a pension until 1557, not having the courage to return home to Saxony.

Henry's aging eyes next turned to a 20-year-old Catholic girl, Catherine Howard. Catherine was a first cousin of Anne Boleyn, and the law of affinity forbade marrying so close a relative of a former spouse. Henry's need inspired the Act of 1540, which allowed cousins and others not prohibited by God's (read: Henry's) law to marry. This accomplished, on July 28, 1540, Henry, now rapidly deteriorating at the age of 49, entered the marital lists for the fifth time. Catherine was the most attractive of his wives, and he was quite fond of her until he learned that she had led an active premarital sex life with several suitors.

Catherine naively hired one of her former lovers, Dereham, as a personal secretary. Despite his grief, Henry was at the point of forgiving her when Cranmer, his faithful lieutenant, presented "evidence" of her postmarital indiscretion with her cousin, Thomas Culpepper. Catherine admitted having seen him in her chamber only in the presence of Lady Rockford, who testified that nothing had occurred—except that she had once fallen asleep. Her testimony became irrelevant when a letter of endearment to Culpepper, signed "yours as long as life endures," sealed Catherine's doom.

Anne Boleyn had been put to death, despite the questionable nature of the evidence against her, because Henry detested her. Now, even though he was unwilling to part with the young, sensual Catherine, her behavior left no alternative. She was convicted of "treason," but her real sin was that she had robbed the megalomaniacal monarch of his illusions of youthfulness. Catherine had made him painfully aware of the fact that at 51, weighing about 250 pounds, with a girth in excess of 50 inches and a mantle of suet closeting his formerly muscular frame, he was an old man. On February 13, 1542, Catherine's head rolled off the block.[70]

A final effort—on July 12, 1543, Henry took a sixth wife, Catherine Parr, herself twice widowed. She served as little more than a nurse to the unwieldly mass of spreading and putrifying flesh. Henry could rise only with considerable effort. A gaping leg ulcer, possibly due to the syphilis, emitted a stench that kept everyone at a considerable distance.

His death, on January 28, 1547, was mourned by few. His marriages and divorces had changed England from a Catholic to a Protestant state and inspired a formidable series of marital laws. Half a continent away, Luther was proving himself no less influential than this absolute English sovereign in changing marriage laws.

MARRIAGE REFORM

For centuries, Church edicts on marriage had been accepted, often passively, sometimes grudgingly, as in the long struggle for celibacy of the priesthood. At the onset of the sixteenth century, the Holy See seemed unchallenged in its right to regulate marriage. To Luther, however, the Pope, Anti-Christ, and the Devil were three appellations to describe the same basic evil, and he made every effort to tear down the long-standing body of canonical law.

He agreed with the Church in opposing secret marriages, but he believed that the punishment suggested by the Church (banishment and disinheritance were favored by the Synod of Leipzig) was too severe.[71] Those wishing to marry clandestinely did not sin in wanting to marry; they had merely chosen the wrong means. His main thesis was that all those who "want to be married and are also fit and competent to do so, even though they enter the marriage state contrary to human law, do what is right, and nobody should be scandalized by what they do."[72] By "human laws" Luther meant the laws on marriage established by the Holy See, which Luther believed were not inspired by God. Anything not prohibited in Scripture was permitted to man. The Bible said nothing about marriage being forbidden to those related in the third and fourth degree. Consequently, one could marry a first cousin or even a niece (though not an aunt, because God specifically forbade that in (Leviticus 18:6-13).

Affinity, or relationship through marriage, also was interpreted too severely by the Church. After a wife's death, her husband was forbidden to marry into her family to the fourth degree (unless he paid the Church for the privilege). Luther said that God did not forbid marrying any of the wife's relatives, except her mother and daughter. Likewise, Luther claimed that spiritual affinity (i.e., a godson or godparent status) should be no impediment to marriage. Moreover, he felt that Christians could marry adopted persons as well as Turks, Jews, or heretics. He treated with scorn the use of marital prohibitions as a punishment for various crimes, and ridiculed the idea that one could not marry the relative of a fiancee if the latter died before marriage. Another impediment which Luther declared invalid was the enforced celibacy of priests and nuns, and of the blind and deaf. He himself married a nun, making his practice consonant with his preaching. In fact, the only real impediment to marriage, in his opinion, was impotence or physical unfitness for the sexual act.

Most of his suggestions were adopted relatively quickly by the Protestant countries except the sanctioning of marriage between a Christian and non-Christian, which many thought went too far.

In England, Henry VIII had maintained a conservative stance on marital legislation that did not concern his own marriages. In 1539, one of his statutes forbade priests from marrying. The Act of 1540 annulled unconsummated secret contracts and declared that marriages solemnized in church invalidated any contract not yet consummated. Moreover, a secret marriage not followed by a church marriage rendered subsequent children bastards in the eyes of the state, even though the Church recognized them.[73] On Henry's death, Edward VI repealed these laws; but he soon died, and his sister Mary, a Catholic, reinstated them. When Elizabeth succeeded her after five years, she reinstituted marriage for priests and a more liberal Protestant practice. Although marriage legislation was subject to the vagaries of Tudor succession, the net effect was to loosen the restrictions prohibiting marriage.

The Tyranny of Wardship

Shortly after gaining the throne, Henry VII, first of the Tudors, revived his own feudal rights while destroying those of his aristocratic tenants. With respect to marriage, the rule was that after the death of a person holding land from the king as knight-service, his heir, if underage (21 for men, 14 for women), as well as one-third of his land, came under the wardship of the king. In that era of short life spans, one-third of the sons succeeding to the peerage were less than 21; hence wardship posed a potent threat to the heirs of landowners.[74]

While under wardship, the land could be used for the profit of the king. Through his chief officer, the Master of the Ward, the king had the right to offer a bride to an unmarried heir, though not one below him in rank. This offer could not be refused except by payment of a heavy fine. If the wardship was up for sale, the mother could reclaim her offspring for a mutually agreeable price, or a stranger could purchase the wardship. The Master of the Ward could grant wardships at his discretion to high bidders, to his cronies, or to friends of the crown.[75] If the ward waited until the age of 21 and did not wish to marry the bride selected for him, he could pay the value of his marriage as assessed by a jury. If he married before, without the express consent of the king, his land could be held until double the value of the marriage had been realized.

Widows often had husbands suggested to them by the crown. If a widow wished to exercise her own prerogative, she paid for the license to do so: one-third of the annual rate of her dower.

In practice, most peers were unofficially exempt from wardship; the lower gentry and merchants bore the brunt. A striking example of the evils of this system is the case of Walter Aston. In 1597, his father having died, he was sold for 300 pounds to Sir Edward Coke. The "true" price was higher: to obtain the wardship, Sir Edward had to part with an additional 1,000-pound bribe (a healthy sum, since the pound was then worth at least thirty times its current value). In 1600, however, Walter secretly married. His enraged "guardian" had the marriage dissolved and the girl thrown into Fleet prison for a year. Walter persisted, and eventually bought his freedom for 4,000 pounds.

A more tragic story is that of Walter Coverly. Forced by his guardian to abandon the woman of his choice and marry another, he took to dice and the bottle. One day, drunk and despairing, he murdered his two children and stabbed his wife.[76]

The gentry fought back and were partially successful in staving off royal encroachment. One way was to marry off one's heir at a young age while the father was alive, thus eliminating the threat of wardship.[77] Another way was to obtain lands from the king as one's *lord* rather than as one's *king*, because there were fewer (or no) feudal rights under the first method.

A significant diminution in the oppressive use of wardship practices did not occur, however, during the sixteenth century. So long as the king remained an absolute monarch, both he and the nobility profited from wardship, and there was little respect for freedom of choice in marriage.

Other Marital Regulations

With royalty replacing the Church as the regulator of marriage, a variety of laws ensued, depending on the orientation of the monarch. In France, under Henry II, a law was passed (1556) which invalidated the marriage of any minor who did not have the consent of his father or guardian.[78] A minor was anyone under the age of 30, but if the minor was over 25 and less than 30, his marriage was valid despite the lack of parental consent; however, they could disinherit him. *Even after the age of 30,* parents had to be formally notified three times before the individual could marry someone of his own choice.

In England under Queen Elizabeth, unmarried, unemployed women experienced considerable hardship. A statute of 1563 stipulated that any such woman between the ages of 12 and 40 could be forced by municipal officials, on pain of imprisonment, to work at any job for any length of time and for any wage determined by these officials.[79] Paradoxically, Elizabeth strongly opposed the marriage of any of her courtiers or maids of honor.[80] She wanted her court to be the prime concern of her courtiers and attendants, and herself to be the hub of the court.

More freedom in marital choice was found in Scotland, where the clasping of hands was all that was needed to institute a trial marriage. According to the rules, the couple remained married for a year and a day, after which they called in the priest to join them for life. If the trial failed, each went his own way. In case of pregnancy, however, there was no escape.[81]

The Council of Trent

The Church had at first been taken aback by the success of the Reformation, but in the second half of the sixteenth century it was ready to face the twin tasks of refuting the Protestant heresies and instituting reforms within Catholicism. The sessions of the Council of Trent, 1536-1563, resulted more in a defense of traditional marriage laws than in progressive legislation to meet the needs of the times. The Council reaffirmed that marriage was a sacrament, that polygamy was prohibited, that the Church had the power to offer dispensation from impediments of consanguinity and affinity, and that it could also establish impediments to dissolving matrimony. Anyone who dissolved a marriage on his own, however, was to be anathema. An unconsummated marriage could be dissolved by taking vows, but adultery was not a sufficient cause for divorce although separation might be advised by the Church. Clerics could not marry, and if anyone advocated marriage as being superior to virginity, that person was anathema. The Church also reserved the right to prohibit the solemnization of marriage during certain seasons, and reserved for itself and its courts the right to hear marriage cases rather than refer them to secular courts.[82]

The Church's paternalistic approach, while it curtailed individual freedom in many respects, did seek to correct a marriage flaw where autonomy had obviously gone too far. While recognizing all previous clandestine marriages as valid, the Church declared that all future marriages would be valid only if there were three witnesses and if the wedding was performed by a priest who would also keep accurate records of the marriage. The consent of the participating parties must be freely given; parental consent was not needed unless the man was under 18 and the woman under 16. In this respect, the Church was more lenient than Luther and Calvin, who required the father's consent.

The Council also recognized mixed marriages between Protestants and Catholics if the Catholic was left free to retain his faith, if the children were raised as Catholics, and if the Protestant did not object to his partner trying to proselytize him[83] (this one-sided outlook was not modified until 1966). The Council's main agreement with Luther and Calvin was that impotence was a bar to marriage.

MARRIAGE CUSTOMS

One of the major factors militating against free choice in selecting a mate, especially among the rich, was the financial dependence of the bride and groom on their parents. The dowry continued, as did the dower of the groom, now called the "jointure" in England. Where once the latter had amounted to one-third of the husband's estate, its value was now dependent on the market.

During the sixteenth century, the size of dowries increased considerably in comparison with jointures because of the scarcity of unmarried heirs relative to the available number of unmarried heiresses. Several factors contributed to this imbalance. First, since the status of the man rather than that of the woman determined the status of the couple, daughters could marry "up" but not "down," whereas sons could marry "down" without fear of losing status. Second, since the oldest son received the estate under the primogeniture laws, his younger brothers were not very desirable—they were unlikely to bring much in the way of financial security to the bride. Finally, the closing of the nunneries in many Protestant countries made marriage one of the few valid "careers" remaining for women. The net effect was to make sons more sought after than daughters, and many an oldest son was expected to recoup the family fortunes through his marriage.

Since the jointure was so much less than the dowry (a 1:10 ratio was not unusual), the father of the groom was expected to compensate by specifying in advance just how much he intended to give all his sons during his lifetime and how much to the oldest son at his death. The scion of a wealthy father could hardly hope to raise any cash by himself, and was quite dependent, free choice or not, on his father's attitude to his marriage. The dowry was often so large that it had to be paid out in several installments over a period of a year or two. The cost of the trousseau, the feast, and the jewels was also met by the bride's father.

Many noble families found themselves short of cash, and in the last part of the sixteenth century the number of marriages between nobility and gentry increased greatly. As the Earl of Huntington remarked to his son, "Without means, honour will look as naked as trees that are cropped."[84]

Age at Marriage

The basic minimum marriageable age was about 14 for boys and 12 for girls. Many child marriages occurred, as has been noted, in order to escape wardship. On the other hand, there was good reason for postponing very early marriages. It was believed (as it had been among the ancient Greeks) that sperm was essential to mental and physical growth, and that immoderate wastage in early youth would impair subsequent mental and physical development. In addition, parturition by a girl below 16 years of age was considered dangerous both for her and the infant. A solution that resolved these opposing trends was to marry the children when they were young, but to postpone cohabitation until a more suitable age and thus avoid the threat of wardship in the event of the father's death. To accomplish this feat, it became customary to send the bridegroom to make the Grand Tour of Europe immediately after the marriage so that he would not engage in sex with his wife. He would return in a year or two, when the couple had matured physically.

Luther was a proponent of youthful marriage, recommending that a man marry by 20 at the latest and a woman at 15 to 18.[85] However, many unconvinced men heeded Plato's advice not to marry before 30—or even 35, as Aristotle had suggested. Toward the close of the century, the age at marriage slowly rose.

The Wedding Day

Weddings were colorful and festive. An English bride wore a variety of gay colors: her bridesmaids wore the colors of the bride, as well as "two-penny" gloves and scarves which she had presented to them.[86]

Without the "penny wedding," the poor would not have been able to afford a wedding. Announcements of a wedding date meant that the guests could contribute toward the expenses. Some brought cash for the collection that was taken by the best man; others brought sheep, hens, or any commodity of value. Incidentally, strangers were welcome provided they made a contribution.[87]

The Wedding Eve

To the couple retiring to their chamber on the wedding night, Vives offered the following advice:

> After yu hast married thy wife, go thy waye into thy chamber, and abstaynyng thre dayes from her, geue thy selfe to prayer with her, and in the fyrst nyght thou shalt burne the liuer of the fyshe, and the deuil shalbe driuen awaye. The seconde nighte thou shalte be admitted vnto the companye of saynetes. The third night shalt yu obtaine the blessyng of God, so that whole children shalbe borne of you. And after the third nighte be past, take thy wyfe vnto thee in ye feare of God, and moore for the desyre of children, then bodelye lust.[88]

For those not so religiously inclined, other barriers to early consummation had to be reckoned with. A great fear of witchcraft still existed, and one of the most potent fears for the bridegroom was that he might fail to demonstrate his manliness due to an evil person's curse. The most common curse was *les nouements d'aiquillettes*— strips of leather, cotton, or silk, which, when tied in knots by evil-wishers and passed through the wedding ring, had the effect of preventing consummation until the knots were untied.

The usual procedure for counteracting all such curses was for the man to urinate through his wedding ring. Sometimes, in the case of especially powerful curses, extra measures might be needed. Montaigne relates how a friend of his, a count, feared the evil powers of a rival who appeared at his wedding. Montaigne prepared a gold amulet and assured his friend that if he found himself impotent he should signal this fact to Montaigne; the latter would then employ powerful white magic and restore the count's sexual powers. Apparently, several people were present in the room when the couple retired behind their curtains. Sometime later, as was customary, the count was given a caudle, or spiced drink, which was alleged to have aphrodisiacal qualities. The count had more faith in Montaigne than in the drink, for he signaled his friend that all was not well. Montaigne then reports:

[I] whispered him in the ear, that he should rise, under pretence of putting us out of the room, and after a jesting manner pull my nightgown from my shoulders . . . throw it over his own, and when we were all gone out of the chamber he should withdraw to make water, should three times repeat such and such words, and as often do such and such actions; that at every of the three times, he should tie the ribbon I put into his hand about his middle, and be sure to place the medal that was fastened to it, the figures in such a posture, exactly upon his reins (kidneys), which being done, and having the last of the three times so well girt and fast tied the ribbon that it would neither untie nor slip from its place, let him confidently return to his business, and withal not forget to spread my gown upon the bed, so that it might be sure to cover them both.[89]

Montaigne, who did not himself believe in such magic, noted that "their very inanity gives them weight and reverence."[90]

A delightful French peasant custom was the *aillade.* When the couple had retired, the guests quickly boiled water, into which they poured handfuls of garlic, pepper, salt, soot, cinders, spider webs, and whatever else struck their imagination (each guest suggested his favorite "spice"). Then the search went on for the couple, who invariably knew what was coming. When they were discovered, the guests all poured in. The couple feigned surprise when offered the *aillade,* and custom compelled them to sip it at least once and comment on how delightful and fragrant it was. The congregation roared and then regretfully retired, singing such vigorous lyrics as *"Ya pas uno pallio al leit . . ."* (There is not a straw in this bed that will not shake . . . all through the night).[91]

In reviewing the broad variety of marriage customs, two factors stand out. One was the impersonal nature of many marriages that were based on business arrangements. Second, there was a continuing lack of confidence in the power of the individual to surmount hostile influences, natural or supernatural.

MARRIAGE PROBLEMS

Adultery and Fornication

In Luther's view, the moral laxity of the times was aggravated by the increasing boldness of girls who "run after the fellows into their rooms and chambers (at the university) and wherever they can and offer them their free love."[92] But Montaigne reported that the favorite after-dinner topic among *men* was boasting about their conquests. One nobleman, after seducing a lady, awoke in a state of great excitement. When the lady inquired whether the lord was not satisfied, he replied that he was *so* satisfied that he could scarcely wait for everyone to get up so that he could run around and tell everybody just how satisfied he was![93]

In this era of arranged marriages it was commonly accepted that noblemen would have mistresses. Anyone who lived without one, according to Francis I of France, was a "nincompoop"—and Francis himself certainly wasn't one. Henry IV of France had such a good time with some delightful young abbesses while besieging Paris that one rogue quipped that Henry has "slept with our Holy Mother and cuckolded the Almighty."[94]

A number of intellectuals and literary figures, such as Erasmus and Shakespeare, began to see the double standard as being distinctly unfair to women. Castiglione hammers this message home in the dialogue between Lord Gaspar, a male supremacist of the first order, and the Magnifico Giuliano (who speaks for Castiglione). Lord Gaspar says that women, unlike men, must be chaste. If not, "their children would be uncertain, and that tie would be dissolved which binds the whole world by blood and by the natural love of each man for what he has produced."[95] The Magnifico cleverly replies: "But tell me why it is not ordained that loose living is as disgraceful a thing in men as in women, seeing that if men are by nature more virtuous and of greater worth, they could all the more easily practise this virtue of continence also; and their children would be neither more nor less certain, for although women were unchaste, they could of themselves merely and without other aid in no wise bear children, provided men were continent and did not take part in women's unchastity."[96]

Luther was typically forceful, radical, and pragmatic in his attitude toward fornication and adultery. He regarded the former primarily as a sin against the parents, who thereby "lost their daughter."[97] Adulterers, in his opinion, should be put to death by the temporal government.[98] If the government allowed the adulterer to flee to another country, it would be better to permit him to remarry than to have him remain incontinent and debauch other women. On the other hand, rather than automatically permitting a divorce on grounds of adultery, every effort should be made to reconcile the pair.

Under certain circumstances, Luther thought that adultery was permissible. Suppose a woman were wed to a man who was impotent at the time of marriage, but she either declined to embarrass him in court or was unable to prove it to the court's satisfaction. In this situation, the man was not really her husband, in Luther's view, and if she desired children or was unable to maintain continence, she might be counseled to give herself to another man. The woman was to keep this marriage (relationship) secret and ascribe the paternity of the children to the legal father. Such a women did not forfeit salvation, because the impotent man should never have married her in the first place.[99]

Punishment for Adultery and Fornication

The punishment of sexual offenses varied. In northern Italy, a man might both lose an eye and pay a fine for his erring ways, but fines were more common. A woman caught in the act of adultery could be killed with impunity (the wives of several Italian dukes died in this manner).[100] In Geneva a fornicator was exiled, and adultery was theoretically punishable by drowning or beheading. Some persons suffered these extreme penalties and died, but most sexual offenders got by with jail terms and steep fines.[101]

Pope Pius V considered making adultery a capital offense, but contented himself with a milder penalty. One Roman woman of noble birth was sentenced to life imprisonment, while a prominent *male* banker was merely whipped in public, but other men were banished.[102]

Under Edward VI, the English Parliament authorized a commission headed by Cranmer to revise its marriage laws. In their report of 1552 regarding sexual offenses, a man seducing a virgin had to marry her if she would have him and if there were no legal impediments. Otherwise, he forfeited one-third of his property or made some arrangement for the support of any ensuing offspring. In a humane gesture, the commission avoided imposing capital punishment despite the zeal of some reformers. Instead, the adulterous husband had to restore all the property the wife had brought to the marriage and give her one-half of all his other property; he was also sent into exile or incarcerated for life. The wife, for a similar charge, faced banishment or imprisonment, and lost her dower and all rights to her husband's property.

Although these recommendations influenced ecclesiastical policy, they did not become law because of the untimely death of Edward in 1553.[103] As might be expected, a double standard existed in actual practice: many nobles had their sexual offenses taken for granted by their spouses, although the reverse was rarely the case.

Prostitution

Prostitution continued to be as popular as ever at the beginning of the sixteenth century. Rome's 90,000 inhabitants included 6,800 registered prostitutes. Venice, which in 1509 had a population of about 300,000, registered only 11,654 prostitutes, but these were listed in a directory according to name, address, and fee.[104] Catherine de Medici, the Italian bride of Henry II of France, went so far as to organize prostitution as an important arm of diplomacy, employing her maids of honor to achieve her ends.[105]

Governmental sanction of prostitution was soon to end throughout much of Europe. A major incentive for eliminating prostitution was the spread of syphilis, which ravaged Europe from the sixteenth century on. The disease struck most forcefully those who enjoyed unlimited opportunities. Both Francis I and Henry VIII, whose character degeneration paralleled that of their bodies, probably died of syphilis.

Reaction against disease and moral turpitude took the form of severe punishment for adulterers and prostitutes. France ended legal prostitution in 1560, and the province of Toulouse introduced a punishment for harlots—the *accabussade*. The prostitute left the Town Hall, hands tied behind her back, a sugar loaf hat on her head, and a derisive sign pinned to her dress. To the hoots of the jeering citizenry, she was taken to a rock in the middle of the Garonne River, where she was completely undressed and forced into an iron cage. By means of a winch, the cage was submerged in the river three times. As if this were not enough, the half-drowned unfortunate was forced to spend the rest of her life in prison.[106]

The Englishman Stubbes advocated the use of a branding iron for the cheeks, forehead, and other visible parts.[107] In 1566, Pope Pius V issued a decree in Rome that banished prostitutes from the Papal States. When the businessmen of Rome complained that Pius was about to depopulate the city, he relented somewhat and permitted a few selected courtesans to ply their trade in a secluded section of the city, but he gave help to those women who sought to change their profession.[108]

Polygyny

Despite the zeal for marital reform, a surprising number of influential persons—Erasmus, Henry VIII, Luther, and Pope Clement VII—condoned polygyny under certain conditions. Calvin, on the other hand, avowed that not only was polygyny wrong in his time, but it had been equally wrong in ancient times when the patriarchs had taken multiple wives.

While Luther did not favor polygyny, he left a loophole, observing that a Christian should not marry several wives "unless God commands him to go beyond the liberty which is conditioned by love."[109] This philosophy soon led to difficulty. Landgrave Philip of Hesse had married for political reasons in 1523, but because of his wife's "form, fragrance, and manner,"[110] remained faithful for exactly three weeks. His aversion did not prevent his siring seven children by her, but he also indulged in "adultery and whoredom." In 1538, having contracted syphilis, he decided to renounce his wayward life and take a concubine. His theologian, Martin Bucer, went to Wittenberg and asked permission for Philip to marry again without a divorce. Luther tried to dissuade Philip, but the latter swore that his wife had a physical impediment that prevented sexual relations. Moreover, he could not restrain himself from consorting with other women unless he could take another wife; and, if necessary, he would appeal to the Pope. To keep him from taking this undesirable last step (Philip was a leading *Protestant* prince), Luther reluctantly gave his permission. He then rationalized his decision with examples of polygyny on the part of Abraham and the Hebrew prophets. In closing the interview, he reminded Bucer and, through him, Philip that their conversation came under the seal of confession and could not be quoted. Luther then expressed the following hope: "because [Philip] was compelled by his weakness to satisfy his passion in customary fashion with sin and shame, he might secretly keep an honest girl in a house, have her on account of his dire need and for the sake of his conscience in a secret marriage (although, of course, the world would have considered it adultery), and visit her from time to time, as great lords have often done. In like fashion I advised several clergymen under Duke George and the bishops secretly to marry their cooks."[111]

Divorce

The Catholic position remained firm, as it has to this day: apart from separation from bed and board, neither divorce nor remarriage was possible while one spouse was living. This position was unanimously rejected by the Protestant Reformists, who regarded it, from the first, as a papist innovation. Most of these influential leaders—Beza, Brenz, Bugenhagen, Calvin, Chemnitz, and Luther— agreed that adultery was *ipso facto* an inevitable cause for divorce, leaning on Scripture for support. In fact, support for divorce was generally based on the Bible, and rarely justified by reference to difficulty in interpersonal relationships.

Impotence already existing at the time of marriage was a cause for divorce, although, technically speaking, according to Luther, a marriage with an impotent man was invalid from the start. More interesting is the decision, among Protestants, that severe marital difficulties should constitute grounds for divorce. The rationale was found in the Bible in I Corinthians 7:15: "But if the unbelieving depart, let him depart. A brother or sister is not under bondage in such cases." What has this to do with divorce where both partners are Christians? On the surface, very little. It was therefore necessary to reinterpret "unbeliever" in a new and wholly different way: a person who deserted his wife was now said to be committing an un-Christian act and could be regarded as an "unbeliever." Other un-Christian acts, such as refusal by a wife to fulfill her conjugal duties in bed despite repeated warnings, hindrance by one party of the other's attempt to live a godly life, and rejection of conciliation after marital discord had separated the parties, were also grounds for divorce.

On the other hand, chronic marital bickering, which is nowhere mentioned in the Bible as a cause for divorce, justified separation from bed and board, but not remarriage. As long as a man can have his spouse in bed, he cannot complain about her incessant nagging, for "he who wants a fire must endure the smoke."[112]

The English commission headed by Cranmer, in its report of 1552, showed itself more liberal than Luther. In addition to divorce for desertion, adultery, and absence for seven years or more on presumption of death, it admitted divorce "in cases of such violent hatred as rendered it in the highest degree improbable that the husband and wife would survive their animosities and again love one another."[113] As with Luther, incessant or even vehement quarrels were not sufficient grounds for divorce. Even more radical was Martin Bucer, who had represented Philip of Hesse in his plea for a second marriage. Bucer considered divorce a divine institution and favored it for any kind of marital difficulty. His views, however, were too progressive for his time and did not affect English legislation.

In sum, there appears to have been greater awareness that the laws dealing with adultery were prejudicial to women, and some attempt to change—but not to enforce—them was made. For the first time, extreme incompatibility was recognized as grounds for divorce. The extent to which Scripture had to be distorted to support such action reflected the growing concern of the people for more control over their lives.

CONCLUSIONS

The period from 1500 to 1615 was marked by significant advances in the freedom of choice of marital partners. In the early Middle Ages, parents arranged marriages for their children without consulting them. In the later Middle Ages, the Church insisted on free consent of the parties involved, which in practice gave the children a veto over parental choice. In the sixteenth century, the children themselves began to take a somewhat more active role in the selection of a spouse, with veto power usually retained by the parents. After the Council of Trent ruling, however, parental consent could be dispensed with after adulthood had been reached, although some countries, such as France and England, did not hesitate to bypass the ruling.

This increased freedom had many roots. The end of feudalism had reduced the need for military alliances among the nobility of various kingdoms. With the development of relatively "high-speed" coaches and improved roads, young people had greater mobility and could more readily meet eligible partners than had been possible in the day of the isolated castle. The "London season" for marriages, masque balls, and a marriage market testifies to this new freedom of movement. In addition, the field of eligibles broadened for both the nobility and the bourgeoisie.

Financial considerations in marital arrangements began to compete with family line in one's estimate of a marriage partner. Among the wealthy, money still served to restrict the freedom of choice. Where money and estates were important, choice was controlled through the jointure and dowry. Children who did not obey their parents' preferences could end up penniless. In a society with little upward mobility, the power of the purse was a potent influence on the "correct" choice. Also, with the threat of wardship hanging over England, many otherwise liberal parents arranged their children's marriages to safeguard the family inheritance.

More subtly, greater freedom of choice developed because of more favorable attitudes toward marriage, sex, and women. Fewer people believed in the imminent physical coming of Christ, and the focus slowly shifted from the rewards of heaven to those possible on earth. Europe could finally turn its attention to the pleasures of everyday living. Virginity, whose primary reward lay in the next world rather than in the present one, did not enjoy popular support as a lifelong goal, and almost no one objected to the taking of moderate pleasure in sex, congenial company, and food.

The new acceptance of sexuality, in turn, created two problems: fear of being cuckolded and that of being impotent. (Concern about women's sexual enjoyment is almost totally absent in writings addressed to men.) In addition, adultery and prostitution, long tolerated as the inevitable consequence of arranged marriages, suffered a real setback. As psychological compatibility slowly became accepted as a prerequisite for marriage, punishment for nonmarital sexual relationships (e.g., prostitution) became more severe.

Women made continued gains in the social area: protection from physical abuse at the hands of their husbands, and more educational opportunities. While still regarded as basically inferior to men, they profited from the general humanistic climate and its stress on the importance of the individual. Even in the writings of advocates of male supremacy, we see inklings of an awareness of the exploitation of women.

In sum, the period was marked by great turmoil and change, not only in politics but in conceptions about marriage. Many people now considered marriage as a contract that should be entered into without coercion, as an interpersonal relationship that could be severed under exceptionally trying conditions. Nevertheless, the old ways were too solidly implanted to permit a rapid changeover to new marital patterns, and the century can be characterized as one of transition between the old concepts of parental arrangements and theological regulations, and the modern concept of marriage as it was to unfold in the succeeding three centuries.

REFERENCES

1. M. E. Montaigne, *The Essays,* p. 415.
2. F. Rabelais, *Gargantua and Pantagruel.*
3. Ibid., p. 180.
4. Ibid.
5. Ibid., p. 185.
6. W. Shakespeare, *The Plays and Sonnets of William Shakespeare,* Vol. 2, p. 80.
7. C. Camden, *The Elizabethan Woman,* p. 118.
8. W. Durant, *The Renaissance.*
9. F. Rabelais, op. cit., p. 192.
10. Shakespeare, op. cit., p. 274.
11. D. Day, *The Evolution of Love,* pp. 233-234.
12. B. I. Murstein and R. S. Pryer, "The concept of projection: a review."
13. M. Luther, *The Table Talk of Martin Luther,* p. 299.
14. M. Luther, *The Christian in Society,* Vol. II, p. 40.
15. L. De Leon, *The Perfect Wife,* p. 20.
16. N. Epton, *Love and the French.*
17. M. E. Montaigne, op. cit., p. 399.
18. N. Epton, *Love and the English,* p. 102.
19. C. C. Zimmerman, *Family and Civilization,* p. 511.

20. D. Erasmus, *The Colloquies of Erasmus.*
21. I. Brown, *A Book of Marriage,* p. 265.
22. Ibid., p. 266.
23. H. C. Agrippa, *The Commendation of Matrimony.*
24. M. Luther, *Sermons,* p. 362.
25. M. Luther, *The Sermon on the Mount,* p. 88.
26. M. Luther, *Church and Ministry.*
27. M. Luther, *Works of Martin Luther,* Vol. 2.
28. M. Luther, *The Christian in Society,* Vol. II, p. 49.
29. Ibid., Vol. I, p. 9.
30. M. Luther, *The Sermon on the Mount,* p. 93.
31. M. Luther, *The Christian in Society,* Vol. III.
32. J. Calvin, *Institutes of the Christian Religion,* Vol. 1, p. 439.
33. G. Harkness, *John Calvin: The Man and His Ethics,* p. 16.
34. R. M. la Clavière, *The Women of the Renaissance,* p. 49.
35. M. Luther, *Letters of Spiritual Counsel,* p. 264.
36. T. More, *Utopia,* p. 203.
37. E. S. Turner, *A History of Courting,* p. 47.
38. W. Shakespeare, op. cit., p. 75.
39. Ibid., Vol. 1, p. 206.
40. Ibid., pp. 617-618.
41. Ibid., Vol. 2, p. 606.
42. Ibid., Vol. 1, p. 295.
43. H. C. Agrippa, op. cit.
44. L. Stone, *The Crisis of the Aristocracy* 1558-1641.
45. N. Epton, op. cit., p. 94.
46. C. L. Powell, *English Domestic Relations 1487-1653,* p. 147.
47. J. Bodin, "La famille et l'état, d'après J. Bodin," p. 175.
48. W. Shakespeare, op. cit., p. 227.
49. M. Luther, op. cit., pp. 277-278.
50. D. Erasmus, op. cit., p. 60.
51. M. E. Montaigne, op. cit.
52. W. Shakespeare, op. cit., Vol. 2, p. 237.
53. W. G. Meader, *Courtship in Shakespeare.*
54. D. M. Frame, *Montaigne,* p. 100.
55. M. Luther, *The Table Talk of Martin Luther,* p. 301.
56. R. H. Bainton, *What Christianity Says about Sex, Love, and Marriage,* p. 83.
57. M. M. Hunt, *The Natural History of Love,* p. 223.
58. Ibid.
59. R. Kelso, *Doctrine for the Lady of the Renaissance,* p. 88.
60. D. M. Frame, op. cit., p. 92.
61. R. Kelso, op. cit.
62. D. Erasmus, op. cit.
63. N. Epton, *Love and the French.*
64. M. Luther, *The Sermon on the Mount,* p. 89.
65. L. Stone, op. cit., p. 620.
66. M. Luther, *The Christian in Society,* Vol. II, p. 45.
67. W. Durant, *The Reformation.*

68. Ibid.
69. H. Savage, *The Love Letters of Henry VIII.*
70. L. B. Smith, *A Tudor Tragedy.*
71. M. Luther, *The Table Talk of Martin Luther.*
72. M. Luther, *Sermons,* p. 359.
73. W. Goodsell, *A History of Marriage and the Family.*
74. L. Stone, op. cit.
75. J. Hurstfield, *The Queen's Wards.*
76. L. Stone, op. cit.
77. F. J. Furnival, *Child Marriages, Divorces, and Ratifications.*
78. E. Westermarck, *The History of Human Marriage.*
79. C. Camden, op. cit.
80. L. Stone, op. cit.
81. E. S. Turner, op. cit.
82. S. P. Breckinridge, *The Family and the State.*
83. C. C. Zimmerman, op. cit.
84. L. Stone, "Marriage among the English nobility," p. 170.
85. M. Luther, *The Christian in Society,* Vol. II.
86. E. S. Turner, op. cit.
87. B. B. James, *Women of England.*
88. C. Camden, op. cit., p. 102.
89. M. E. Montaigne, op. cit., p. 38.
90. Ibid.
91. N. Epton, op. cit., p. 113.
92. W. Durant, op. cit., p. 761.
93. N. Epton, op. cit.
94. Ibid., p. 105.
95. B. Castiglione, *The Book of the Courtier,* pp. 203-204.
96. Ibid., p. 204.
97. M. Luther, *The Table Talk of Martin Luther.*
98. M. Luther, *The Christian in Society,* Vol. II.
99. M. Luther, *Works of Martin Luther,* Vol. 2.
100. W. Goodsell, op. cit.
101. M. H. Hunt, op. cit.
102. W. Durant and A. Durant, *The Age of Reason Begins.*
103. G. E. Howard, *A History of Matrimonial Institutions.*
104. W. Durant, *The Renaissance.*
105. S. Putnam, "The psychopathology of prostitution."
106. N. Epton, op. cit.
107. N. Epton, *Love and the English.*
108. W. Durant and A. Durant, op. cit.
109. M. Luther, *Letters of Spiritual Counsel,* p. 276.
110. Ibid., p. 288.
111. Ibid., pp. 290-291.
112. M. Luther, *The Christian in Society,* Vol. II, p. 35.
113. G. E. Howard, op. cit.

11

The Age of Reason and Licentiousness: 1615–1789

The seventeenth and eighteenth centuries marked an era of rationalism and enlightenment in Europe. Buoyed by the discoveries of Galileo, Newton, and Leibniz, Europeans postulated that the laws of nature governed not only the interrelationships of physical objects but those of individuals as well. God—the Divine Mechanic, as the deists viewed him—had created a harmonious functioning order, and man's task was to discover these "natural" laws and discard man-made ones which did not accord with nature. New scientific discoveries encouraged the belief that even further progress would be possible if a religious outlook gave way to reason. Through reason rather than faith, men could attain objective truth; thus, rationalism advanced as theology ebbed.

It was now considered rational to seek to maximize pleasure and minimize pain. However, hedonism need not be selfish and amoral; the concerned moralist who cast aside theology as the motivating force for good could replace it by group hedonism. "Good"—as Jeremy Bentham later expressed it—was that which gives pleasure to the greatest number.

Some believed that no matter how diverse societal institutions appeared on the surface, reason suggested that nature employed only a few natural units to form society. The family was one such "natural" unit[1]; the king, according to Thomas Hobbes, was the "father" of his country's families.[2]

Primitive man came into his own in the eighteenth century, thanks to European voyages to the South Seas, whose inhabitants were closer to nature than those in the European societies. Since they lacked technology, it was romantically concluded that they must indeed lead a simple, useful, and happy life. If only "civilized" man could shed his greedy ways and allow his natural goodness to emerge, thought Diderot as he reflected on Bougainville's report of his Tahitian journey.[3] In addition, "civilized" marriage in Western Europe was not very highly esteemed by the rationalists.

ATTITUDES TOWARD WOMEN AND MARRIAGE

Attitudes Toward Women

As the king ruled his subjects, so the hegemony of the husband over his family continued to be recognized as nature's decision.[4,5,6,7] According to John Milton:

> Not equal, as their sex not equal seemed;
> For contemplation hee and valour formd;
> For softness shee and sweet attractive Grace,
> Hee for God only, shee for God in him:[8]

Lord Halifax allowed that men might take advantage of women, but thought that "*Injustice* should be *conniv'd* at in a very few instances, than to break into an Establishment upon which the Order of Humane Society doth so much depend."[9]

Johnson put it bluntly: "one or the other must have the superiority."[10] And a physiologically minded writer attributed women's mental shortcomings to her moist brain; man's dry brain accounted for his superior judgment.[11]

Lord Chesterfield, in letters to his son, offered a similar (albeit less physiological) description: "Women . . . are only children of a larger growth; they have an entertaining tattle and sometimes wit, but for solid reasoning good sense, I never knew in my life one that had it."[12]

In a letter to the newly married wife of a friend, Swift told her that although she could never attain the degree of knowledge of a school boy, under a good man's guidance there was no reason why she could not acquire some knowledge.[13]

Against this formidable array of opinion, a man who exaggerated in using the name Uxorious could only say that the chief virtue of women was that they softened the natural roughness of men.[14]

Many men believed that women were simply incapable of absorbing much knowledge. Fenelon[15] noted that women could neither properly pronounce what they read nor spell correctly; and Rousseau observed that "little girls always dislike learning to read and write, but they are always ready to learn to sew."[16] The average man agreed with Charles II, who, when a man boasted that his wife understood Greek and Hebrew, growled, "Can she make a pudding? That is learning enough for your wife."[17]

In sum, men were not overtly hostile toward women—they merely regarded them as limited and childlike.[18]

Petty Bourgeois and Aristocratic Views of Marriage

Because money was never abundant in petty bourgeois families, arranged marriages based exclusively on property were rare, and children could exercise a degree of independence in their choice of marital partner (subject to parental approval). The husband was the key to the family's economic mobility. If he lacked business acumen, he could blight his family's future; consequently, a prospective bride's family would carefully evaluate the intelligence, character, and financial status of a prospective son-in-law.[19]

Both spouses were expected to work hard, the wife either aiding her husband at his trade or working at home. Middle-class mores were stern, and extramarital liaisons were infrequent. In England, the epitome of the hardworking, God-fearing bourgeois was the Puritan, whom we shall discuss later in the chapters on American marriage. Although he had an undeserved reputation for antisexuality, the Puritan, as part of his Calvinist heritage, opposed any overt manifestations of affection or enjoyment. During the reign of Oliver Cromwell, who was a Puritan, ale houses and theaters were closed, people were fined for swearing, dancing was denounced, and sweethearts were convicted for walking together on the Sabbath or even for sitting on a doorstep.[20]

Among the wealthy, marriage was primarily a business arrangement. With little emotional involvement in each other, the partners often enjoyed considerable freedom after marriage. If the husband preoccupied himself with mistresses, the woman could also pursue an independent social life and sometimes take lovers with her husband's tacit approval.

The Puritan hegemony had ruined the English nobility financially, and with the Restoration the rate of intermarriage with the rich merchant class accelerated—titles could be conveniently exchanged for the pound sterling. The son of the Duchesse de Chaulnes objected to marrying a richly dowered but middle-class lady. His mother explained that "to marry advantageously beneath oneself is merely taking dung to manure one's acres."[21] Sir Anthony Absolute, in Sheridan's *The Rivals,* says to his son, who has complained about the ugliness of the woman he is to marry, "Odds life, Sir! If you have the estate you must take it with the livestock on it."[22]

A description of an arranged marriage is found in the memoirs of Madame d'Epinay.[23] Monsieur de Rinville has a young male cousin, d'Houdetot, whom he wishes to see married to Mimi, the daughter of Monsieur de Bellegarde. A dinner is given by Madame de Rinville for both parties and their families. After dessert Monsieur de Rinville has something to say:

"Best begin with the articles, and our young friends in the meanwhile shall converse...." And they return to the drawing room. There Monsieur de Rinville squares himself to say that the Marquis d'Houdetot gives his son an income of 18,000 pounds a year from his estates in Normandy; and the Marquise d'Houdetot ... adds "all her diamonds, and fine ones they are, and she shall have every last one, every sparkler she can lay her hands on." Monsieur de Bellegarde replies with a dower of 300,000 pounds and a share in the inheritance. They rise. "Agreed. We'll sign the contract tonight, publish the banns on Sunday, obtain a dispensation for the others, and hold the wedding on Monday." The notary and family are informed, and that same evening sees them once more at Monsieur de Bellegarde's, where, amid the constraint of both families (as yet totally unacquainted), the articles are signed.[24]

Marriage at a Low Ebb

As marriage among the wealthy became increasingly a business contract, the educated classes became cynical.[25,26] Burton, in *The Anatomy of Melancholy*, noted: " 'Tis an hazard both ways. . . to live single; or to marry."[27] He chose the former alternative.

La Rochefoucauld observed:

> Convenient marriages there may be many
> Delightful marriages more sure not any.[28]

One bachelor, whose uncertainty was somewhat akin to Hamlet's, soliloquized:

> To wed or not to wed, that is the question:
> Whether 'tis better still to rove at large
> From fair to fair, amid the wilds of passion;
> Or plunge at once into a sea of marriage
> And quench our fires?—To marry,—take a wife,
> No more—and by a wife to say we quell
> Those restless ardours, all those natural tumults
> That flesh is heir to;— 'tis a consolation
> Devoutly to be wished.—Marry a wife,
> A wife,—perchance a devil:—ay, there's the rub.[29]

The list of famous literary personages who were confirmed bachelors is imposing; it includes Boileau, Corneille, La Bruyère, Rousseau,* Voltaire, Addison, Burton, Congreve, Pope, Swift,** Isaac Watts, James Thomson, Horace Walpole, Shenstone, Hume, Gray, and Cowper.

---

*In his old age Rousseau had a private quasi-ceremony performed, but he hardly fits the concept of a married man, as a subsequent section will make clear.

**Swift was persuaded to marry his mistress of 16 years' standing during her final year of life. Yet he never permitted her to live in his house, and so the term "wife" seems an exaggeration of her status.

The vogue of bachelorhood led to a fear of depopulation, but such apprehension was largely unjustified because most of the expenditures for the poor were used to support illegitimate children.[30] Both a tax on bachelors and radical variations of marriage were considered. In Richardson's novel *Clarissa,* one of the characters proposes that marriages be contracted only for a year so that polygyny, as well as a large number of old maids, could be avoided. Men, like flowers, might then be classified as *annuals* or *perennials* (the faithful kind). Men had rarely been more reluctant to take the marital plunge since the days of Augustus of Rome.

Many of those who took the marital plunge seemed to rue their decision soon enough. In Vanbrugh's play, *The Provok'd Wife* (1697), Sir John Brute, a Falstaffian character, grumbles:

> What cloying meat is love—when matrimony's the sauce to it! Two years' marriage has debauched my five senses. Everything I see, everything I hear, everything I feel, everything I smell, and everything I taste—methinks has wife in't. No boy was ever so weary of his tutor, no girl of her bib, no nun of doing penance, nor old maid of being chaste, as I am of being married.[31]

An anonymous poem of 1701 echoed the same theme:

> Wedlock, oh! Curs'd uncomfortable State,
> Cause of my Woes, and Object of my hate.
> How blessed was I? Ah, once how happy me!
> When I from my uneasy Bonds was free. . . .[32]

Although much of the resentment was related to the depersonalized character of the "arranged marriage," the antidote was not deemed to be romance.

THE "RATIONAL" BASIS FOR MARRIAGE

The uxorist and the misogynist could agree on one thing: the supremacy of reason as a basis for marriage. If marriage between unequals for the purpose of acquiring wealth was a poor foundation for marital happiness, so were inflamed passions or romantic conceptions of love. Spinoza had argued that marriage must accord with reason[33], and Milton noted, in connection with the creation of Eve for Adam in *Paradise Lost:*

> What higher in her societie thou findst
> Attractive, human, rational, love still;
> In loving thou dost well, in passion not,
> Wherein true Love consists not; love refines
> The thoughts, and heart enlarges, hath his seat
> In Reason. . . .[34]

The supposition that love is at the beck and call of the rational will, and not of the glands, is made in *The Bachelor's Directory,* where the husband is told, "If she [the wife] loves you, you cannot without ingratitude forbear to love her."[35] Even women, frequently thought to be at the mercy of their emotions, sneered at romance. Mary Astell, although she champions the cause of woman's rights, asks, "what does ... Marrying for Love amount to? There's no great odds between ... Marrying for the Love of Money, or for the Love of Beauty; the Man does not act according to Reason in either Case, but is govern'd by irregular appetites."[36]

Swift favored matches of prudence without passion.[37] In *Gulliver's Travels* he extols the Houyhnhms, a race of horses who possess all the virtues for which men strive, and who marry for purely rational reasons.[38]

Johnson expressed himself quite concisely: "It is commonly a weak man who marries for love."[39] Kant stated that once a couple had the will to enter into a reciprocal relationship "in accordance with their sexual nature, they *must* necessarily marry each other ... in accordance with the juridical laws of pure reason."[40]

What was *reason* in marital choice? The *raison d'être* for marriage was procreation. Children could best be reared in a congenial home, and reason dictated that congeniality was most likely to occur when both spouses were of the same socioeconomic rank. Nothing was said about compatibility of personalities, it being assumed that that might be arranged within the possibilities dictated by status. In any event, since emotional satisfaction was not the purpose of marriage, the partners had little to complain about as long as each one carried out his institutionalized role—the husband that of the provider, the wife that of homemaker and bearer of children.

Even such liberals as Voltaire and Diderot did not refer to interpersonal needs or compatibility as components of marriage: "The *voluntary* union between man and woman contracted by *free* individuals, so as to have children."[41] Defoe, who championed women's rights, nevertheless thought that a woman of menopausal age who dared to marry was a lecher, as was her husband.

Rationalism deemed virginity not a sign of virtue, but a means of increased pleasure. Its value to Jeremy Bentham was that, "by restraining enjoyment for a time, it afterwards elevates it to that very pitch which leaves on the whole, the largest addition to the stock of happiness."[42]

Montesquieu saw reason as the basis for the development of marital customs. In England, daughters sometimes married without their fathers' approval; but he found a rationale for this, because marriage was the only vocation open to women. In France, the father's stronger role was rational since, if the daughter did not like the match he offered her, she was free to enter a convent and take up another vocation. What puzzled Montesquieu was the "irrational" behavior of Italian and Spanish daughters: "convents are there established and yet they may marry without the consent of their fathers."[43]

"Reason" took a somewhat more realistic path in the speculations of Locke and Paine. The former reasoned that if the purpose of marriage was *only* for the procreation and care of children, might not the contract of marriage be broken once this purpose had been achieved?[44] Paine had observed that among some American Indian tribes he knew, unlike among Christians, unhappy marriages were dissolved; their philosophy was that "we make it our business to oblige the heart we are afraid to lose."[45]

Not everyone was ready to abide by a "rational" relationship—minus love. The Swedish scientist and mystic, Swedenborg, tried to bring love back into marriage by distinguishing it from passion: "with those who are in love truly conjugial, conjunction of minds, and therewith friendship, increases."[46] Those who enjoy conjugal love experience this friendship in a mental or internal sense. However, those who love each other only physically experience a loss of conjugal love which "withdraws more and more from the interiors of the mind, and successively departs from them at length to the cuticles. And with those who think of separation it goes entirely away; but with those that do not think of separation, the love abides in the externals, but is cold in the internals."[47]

Swedenborg was unwilling to champion the equality of the sexes in the marital relationship. He saw the function of the sexes as complementary: man represented wisdom and understanding, woman personified love, and their relationship developed "to the end that the will of both may become one, and then that the two be made one man."[48]

In sum, the concept of marriage as an emotional bond and a haven from worldly troubles had not yet evolved. "Radicals" concerned themselves with finding a rationale for dissolving marriage when it became oppressive, but they accepted the concept of marriage as essentially a rational, functional means of propagation.

LICENTIOUSNESS

The increasing wealth of the French nobility and the merchant class in the second half of the seventeenth century afforded them considerable leisure time, and *l'amour* became the national sport. Earlier, the volumes of *L'Astrée,* by Honoré D'Urfé, had established the rule that one must love to excess.[49] Pascal also noted that "passion cannot be beautiful without excess. . . . When one does not love too much one does not love enough."[50]

The rich defended their lechery as rational. Was not sex a natural appetite that knew no artificial restrictions? Was not marriage a civil contract and a business arrangement? Thus, it was hardly surprising that the most interesting kind of sex was nonmarital.

In contrast, the "naturalistic" interest in sex was accompanied by a preoccupation with manners. Europe was experiencing class mobility, and the wealthy bourgeois sought to ape the nobility. The *parvenu* was all the more distinguished if he was engrossed in fine manners and genteel breeding. The affair of the young Boswell and the actress Louisa, with whom he was infatuated, is an example of the comic situation that sometimes ensued:

> Boswell:　I hope, Madam, you are at present a single woman.
> Louisa:　Yes, sir.
> Boswell:　And your affections are not engaged?
> Louisa:　They are not, Sir.
> Boswell:　But this is leading me into a strange confession. I assure you, Madam, my affections are engaged.
> Louisa:　Are they, sir?
> Boswell:　Yes, Madam, they are engaged to you.[51]

Two weeks later Boswell feels that the acquaintanceship is sufficiently developed to begin to take some liberties.

> Louisa:　Nay, but you are an encroaching creature! (Upon this I advanced to the greatest freedom by a sweet elevation of the charming petticoat.) Good heaven, Sir!
> Boswell:　Madam, I cannot help it. I adore you. Do you like me? (She answered me with a warm kiss, and pressing me to her bosom sighed, "Oh, Mr. Boswell!")[52]

Unfortunately, the time and place are not propitious even though the lady is willing. Eventually, the two get together at an inn and, in Boswell's words, "Good heavens, what a loose did we give to amorous dalliance."[53] Six days later he reports, "I this day began to feel an unaccountable alarm of unexpected evil: a little heat in the members of my body sacred to Cupid, very like a symptom of that distemper with which Venus, when cross, takes it into her head to plague her votaries."[54] Louisa admits that she had had gonorrhea, but had wrongly supposed herself to have been cured. Despite his annoyance, Boswell promises not to shame her publicly, and the couple politely, but not amicably, terminate their relationship:

> Louisa:　Sir, this is being more generous than I could expect.
> Boswell:　I hope, Madam, you will own that since I have been with you I have always behaved like a man of honour.
> Louisa:　You have indeed, Sir.
> Boswell (rising):　Madam, your most obedient servant.[55]

A French Love Club

On the institutional level, the most notorious French organization devoted to the pursuit of sexual happiness was the Aphrodites, a club whose membership was limited to 200. Each member paid an initiation to the club commensurate with his rank, plus a membership fee (£10,000 for men, £5,000 for women). Money was not the only requirement: the applicant had to undergo a demanding lovemaking bout for several hours, witnessed by incorruptible judges, before being accepted or rejected on the basis of the performance.

Thanks to its well-stocked treasury, the club purchased an elegant country house with special decor and grounds for amorous purposes. One item of furniture, the *avantageuse,* which was designed to supplant the bed as the foundation of love, had some unusual features:

> The lady must let herself fall backwards after having grabbed on both sides two columns representing two Priapes. A thick, firm pillow, covered with satin supports her from the top of her head to the slit of the buttocks. The remaining portion of her body waves in the air down to the feet which fit into a kind of stirrup which is set a short distance away. Those stirrups are not moveable but are softly stuffed. Thus the legs and thighs are forced to bend into the shape of an inverted V. The feet of the gentleman are supported by a kind of saddle. His knees rest on a cross beam. Lying in this position, he is perfectly within reach of the aim of his exercise. His hands find two cylindrical supports on the woodwork on the outside of the piece of furniture.[56]

The diary of one of the female Aphrodites lists 4,959 amorous encounters over a period of 20 years. That sex can sometimes overcome class barriers is testified to by the breakdown by profession: " . . . 272 princes and prelates, 929 officers, 93 rabbis, 342 financiers, 439 monks . . . 420 society men, 288 commoners, 117 valets, 2 uncles, 12 cousins, 119 musicians, 47 negroes, and 1,614 foreigners (during an enforced absence in London—probably during the Revolution)."[57]

The love clubs never became widespread because they required not only an above-average sex drive and pocketbook, but a willingness to undergo notoriety for one's lechery. To have one lover at a time was fashionable; to have them by droves, without regard to station or publicity, was scandalous. For the average well-to-do person who craved a little excitement without sacrificing security, attendance at a masque proved an admirable substitute.

Masques

Masquerading in magnificent costumes and dominoes, the wealthy were borne to the party in sedan chairs on the shoulders of servants or hirelings; the less wealthy came in bouncy carriages. After each person performed his "party piece" and was applauded, the guests turned to more "unstructured" play—behavior quite opposite to that of the conventional social affair. Formal introductions were not only not required but strongly proscribed.

Whispers, suggestive remarks, squeezes, kisses, and petting were the norm. The timid became emboldened; the frigid, fiery. There were rooms where guests could retire and unmask; usually only the man unmasked. It was even possible to go to bed with a masked stranger, as the playwright George Farquhar did, without knowing who she was.[58]

Occasional outcries against such bawdy affairs sometimes resulted in raids, bringing embarrassment to influential members of the nobility who were exposed; but the magistrates, fearful of their positions, usually dropped any charges of immorality.[59]

The philosophy of the day was summed up by a Mr. Temple in a letter to his friend, Boswell:

> A little occasional amorous dalliance, it is to be hoped, all of us may innocently enough allow ourselves; . . . but then such intercourse ought to be but *occasional,* when nature will not be denied; and the desire being satisfied, the object should be thought of no more. Perhaps this reasoning may shock your delicacy (it once would have shocked mine), but unhappily in our present circumstances it is but common sense and common prudence.[60]

What makes the letter noteworthy is that Temple's full title was the Reverend William Johnson Temple.

MARRIAGE IN THE ENGLISH AND FRENCH NOVEL

Two outstanding novels—one English, and the other French—appeared in the eighteenth century: *Pamela,* by Samuel Richardson, was published in 1740; *Les Liaisons dangereuses,* by Choderlos de Laclos, in 1782. Both works depict their respective societies at that time: the mobility and vitality of British society, the stagnation and decadence of the French.

Pamela

Richardson's novel concerns a 15-year-old farmer's daughter, a servant to a noble-woman in the city. After the death of the lady of the house, her son, Mr. B., pursues Pamela across the pages of two books, alternating between kindness and mistreatment. He hides in closets when she undresses and attempts various stratagems to seduce her. He promises to give her money and to send her home, but instead makes her the prisoner of an accomplice while he plans fresh assaults on her chastity.

The modern reader might wonder why Pamela does not leave her job and return home. But the eighteenth-century reader knew that employment for women was almost nonexistent except as servants or, in the case of the more genteel, as governesses. For Pamela to have left without a reference—under the circumstances, she could hardly have expected one—would have ruled out any possibility of being hired by a respectable household. None of Mr. B.'s ruses succeeds, and he finally marries her.

Pamela is a battleground for two contending life styles: the workers and petty bourgeoisie versus the nobility. Pamela is hardworking, virginal, yet preoccupied with marriage. Mr. B. is idly given to romantic foppery and woman chasing, and uninterested in marriage except to someone of the nobility at advantageous financial terms. They epitomize the Puritan emphasis on chastity, work, and godliness, on the one hand, and the Cavalier philosophy of licentiousness, idleness, and semiatheism on the other. Pamela and Puritanism win out not only in a material sense (she remains chaste and also marries into money), but philosophically (he is converted to the Puritan way of life and acknowledges the error of his ways). Such an ending was quite consistent with the fact that Richardson himself was a bourgeois who preferred women to men in his social relationships. Despite his attack on the wastrel nobility, he embodied many of their esteemed qualities in his heroine—Pamela is wondrously formed, highly intelligent, very fluent, and quite sensitive (a fine appearance and good physique were considered the attributes of the nobility). Pamela proves her innate nobility by fainting when confronted with danger. Since the lower classes were supposed to have no more sensitivity than earthworms, Richardson convinces us that she is a lady in spirit who, through some accident in the divine plan, was born to a farmer.

The book delighted readers—they could eat their cake and have it too. It was puritanical and prurient, both a sermon and a striptease. The heroine was virtuous, but at every possible moment she talked of sex.

The duality of prurience and puritanism permeates the famous rape scene. Pamela is a prisoner of Mrs. Jewkes, a hireling of Mr. B. Mrs. Jewkes, another servant, Mrs. Anne, and Pamela all sleep in the same bed. This evening, Mrs. Anne has been filled with alcohol by the nefarious Mrs. Jewkes. Unknown to Pamela, Mr. B. is in the house and has concocted a vile plot, in conjunction with Mrs. Jewkes. As Pamela prepares for bed she notices Mrs. Anne snoring fitfully in her chair—or is it Mrs. Anne? In the book, she later describes to her parents what occurred: "So I looked into the closet, and kneeled down in my own, as I used to do, to say my prayers, and this *with my underclothes in my hand, all undressed;* and passed by the poor sleeping wench, as I thought, in my return. But, oh! little did I think it was my wicked, wicked master, in a gown and petticoat of hers, and her apron over his face and shoulders."[61]

Mrs. Jewkes and Pamela talk a while in bed; then "Mrs. Anne" seems to be stirring so Mrs. Jewkes calls "her" to bed. Once in bed, "Mrs. Anne" (Mr. B.) grabs Pamela, kisses her, and thunders:

> Now, Pamela; . . . is the dreadful time of reckoning come, that I have threatened.—I screamed out in such a manner, as never anybody heard the like! . . . Sure never poor soul was in such agonies as I. Wicked man! said I; wicked abominable woman! O God! my God! this *time!* this *one time!* deliver me from this distress! or strike me dead this moment! And then I screamed again and again.

> Says, he, one word with you, Pamela; one word hear me but; and hitherto you see I offer nothing to you. Is this *nothing,* said I, to be in bed here? to hold my hands between you! . . .
>
> Said she (oh disgrace of womankind!). What you do, sir, do; don't stand dilly-dallying. . . .
>
> Silence! said he to her; I must say one word to you, Pamela! it is this: You see now you are in my power!—You cannot get from me, nor help yourself: yet have I not offered anything amiss to you. But if you resolve not to comply with my proposals, I will not lose this opportunity: if you do, I will yet leave you.
>
> Oh, sir, said I, leave me, leave me but, and I will do anything I ought to do.—Swear then to me, said he, that you will accept my proposals! and then (for this was all detestable grimace) he put his hand in my bosom. With struggling, fright, terror, I fainted away quite, and did not come to myself soon.[62]

It is an opportune swoon, for Mr. B. becomes concerned and does not ravish his unconscious prey. He begins to change and eventually proposes marriage.

The appeal of *Pamela* went beyond the tandem of lust and lecture, for it also had a sociological message. The symbolic triumph of the bourgeoisie over the aristocracy was not a destructive struggle. Mr. B.'s acceptance of Pamela's mores and the new unity of the two were analogous to the English aristocracy yielding power to the bourgeoisie without violent upheaval. The flexibility of the English emerged from beneath the surface of respect for tradition and pomp, and leadership and membership in the ruling bodies slowly passed from the nobility to the bourgeoisie.

Richardson was attacked by Henry Fielding for making chastity a salable commodity and equating it with virtue.[63] The unkindest cut of all was that his readers were moving toward a romantic conception of life, and the passionate foppery that he detested became indelibly linked with his heroine.

Les Liaisons Dangereuses

Les Liaisons dangereuses describes what happens when a French Pamela *loses* her struggle for chastity. The Vicomte de Valmont receives a note from his former mistress, the Marquise de Merteuil. Having been jilted by a lover who intends to marry a young, convent-raised girl, Cecile Volanges, she seeks revenge and requests a favor: Valmont should seduce the girl. But Valmont is involved with Madame de Tourvel, whose husband is temporarily absent. What excites him more than her beauty is her religious morality, which will make the consummation all the more pleasurable. But Madame de Tourvel, although attracted to Valmont, refuses to yield.

Throughout the lengthy "siege," Valmont engages in other affairs. On one occasion he playfully uses a prostitute's buttocks as a table on which to pen his sentiments. In the course of writing the letter, he becomes so sexually excited that he stops to make love. The letter, faithfully reproducing his feelings, conveys quite another picture of what really happened:

> Never did I have so much pleasure in writing to you; never in that occupation did I feel so soft and yet so keen an emotion. Everything seems to increase my raptures; the air I breathe is filled with voluptuousness; the very table upon which I write to you, which for the first time is devoted to that use, becomes for me the sacred alter of love; how much it will be embellished in my eyes! I shall have traced upon it the vow to love you forever! I beg you to pardon the disorder of my senses. Perhaps I ought to abandon myself less to raptures you do not share; I must leave you a moment to dispel an ecstasy which increases every instant, which becomes stronger than I am.[64]

Meanwhile, Madame de Meurteuil pushes the budding romance between the Chevalier Danceny, a Templar, who cannot marry, and Cecile. Valmont returns and seduces Cecile even though she continues to love Danceny. He also succeeds with Madame de Tourvel after a long and arduous campaign, and she is so taken with his charms that she becomes incapable of defending herself from being exploited in the relationship.

In the end, the fickle Valmont is killed in a duel, Madame de Tourvel dies of a broken heart, and the manipulative Marquise comes to a bad end as a result of smallpox.

Les Liaisons dangereuses, heavily influenced by Rousseau, was intended as an indictment of French society for its corruption of man. Marriage, morals, and the education of women are the cause of tragedies. The Marquise de Merteuil had the wrong kind of education; she entered into a *marriage de convenance* and never loved her husband. Valmont never learned to relate to people except as objects who afford him the thrill of winning and are then cast aside. Cecile can be manipulated because, having been in a convent, she never learned how to cope with the world. The Chevalier Danceny has been forced into unwholesome celibacy by an unrealistic social system. Madame de Tourvel, ostensibly a pillar of virtue, is childless, and the social system has forced her husband into being a "businessman" who has to leave his wife behind. The evils of the old order are too strong for her; she is crushed by them. The demise of the villains seems contrived, as if to satisfy a code that the wicked must pay for their sins.

The only cure for a society which had lost touch with the needs of the bourgeoisie and the peasants and, indeed, with itself was the French Revolution (its influence on marriage will be discussed in the next chapter). Let us now discuss Rousseau, whose ideas about mankind helped to bring about this revolution.

Prostitute entering the accabussade. She will be submerged in the river several times and then imprisoned for life. As usual, the male client went unpunished.

ROUSSEAU

Jean Jacques Rousseau was born in 1712 to the family of a Geneva watchmaker. His mother died shortly after his birth, and Jean very early developed a sense of guilt because his father blamed him for the loss of his wife.

While attending boarding school, young Rousseau was spanked by one Mlle. Lambercier. Recalling the incident, he wrote that "the punishment increased my affection for the person who had inflicted it."[65]

Rousseau became a classical Oedipal case. Strongly attracted to the mother figure, he could acknowledge his right to be near her only by paying the penalty for killing his natural mother and for daring to entertain sensual thoughts toward the present mother figure. A spanking provided the proper blend of attention and chastisement.

After a series of jobs and wanderings, he adopted the Catholic faith and was sent to a recently converted Catholic, Madame de Warrens. Rousseau, 15 years old, expected to see a pious matron but found a comely, 28-year-old blonde who had run away from an unhappy marriage. He stayed at her house on and off for several years.

At age 21, like any normal youth seeking to indulge in harmless venery, he had his eye on the mother of one of the students to whom he was giving singing lessons. His shyness prevented him from taking any decisive steps, but Madame de Warrens got wind of his feelings and decided to initiate the virginal youth into the sacred rites of Venus herself—except that she suggested an eight-day wait so that he could thoroughly consider the offer. As the deadline approached, his confusion mounted. He was anxious to have sexual relations with a woman—any woman—but he *loved* Madame de Warrens. "She was more to me than a sister, a mother, a friend, or even than a mistress, and for this very reason she was not a mistress; in a word, I loved her too much to desire her."[66] For Rousseau, there were two kinds of women: those within whom he discharged his genitories, and those he loved. A fusion would never be possible.

He cried throughout the whole performance, feeling as if he were committing incest. Madame de Warrens took it all quite calmly, and for a time served as a combination mistress and saintly Virgin Mary, a role into which he had cast her.

Rousseau also had paranoid tendences. During a rendezvous in Venice with an attractive courtesan, Zulietta, he discovered to his horror that she had a "withered" nipple on one breast. He became convinced that "I had in my arms a species of a monster, the refuse of nature, of man, and of love."[67] When Rousseau mumbled something about the defect, the lady disdainfully retorted, *"Lascia le donne, e studia la matematica"* (Leave women and study mathematics).[68]

In his thirties, he was attracted to an almost illiterate 22-year-old seamstress, Thérèsa. She was modest, lively, and charming. But his paranoia ran away with him, and he was sure that she had syphilis. He was much relieved, therefore, to learn that her only concern was that she was not a virgin: there had been one unhappy experience. Rousseau assured her that he would neither marry nor abandon her, and he was as good as his word—or almost so—for he finally consented to a private ceremony when he was well into his fifties and the value of marriage had greatly lessened for her.

Throughout their relationship, he never behaved like a married man. He was a frequent participant in "assembly-line" intercourse when his coterie of friends found a willing female subject. Patient Thérèsa bore him five children, all of whom he abandoned to the foundling home. (Such behavior was by no means rare: between 30 and 40 percent of all children born in Paris at that time were abandoned.[69]) In his *Confessions*, Rousseau, though remorseful, defended his action on the grounds that it was better for the children to become workmen and peasants, honest members of society, than adventurers and fortune hunters. He considered himself a citizen and a good father in the tradition of Plato's republic, where offspring were raised by the state.

At 45, Rousseau became almost impotent because of a persistent uremic disorder. But the 30-year-old Countess d'Houdetot filled him with the most delicious, masochistic feelings when she described her lover, M. de Saint Lambert: "Contagious force of love! . . . I was seized with a delicious trembling which I had never experienced before when near to any person whatsoever. . . . she inspired me for herself with all she expressed for her lover."[70]

He courted her day and night for three months. One day, when they were alone in a copse, he tearfully poured out his love. While conceding that there never was a lover like him, she felt that she had to be faithful to her lover. And so all Rousseau got was a kiss—but what a kiss! "This single kiss, this pernicious embrace, even before I received it, inflamed my blood to such a degree as to affect my head: my eyes were dazzled, my knees trembled, and [were] unable to support me. . . I was obliged to. . . sit down; my whole frame was in inconceivable disorder, and I was upon the point of fainting."[71] The ability to transform failure into an ecstatic experience was a Rousseauian trademark. The rest of his life was quite unhappy. His writings brought fame, but they irritated the authorities because of his attacks on the social system. His paranoia frequently manifested itself, and he suspected friends of plotting against him. He lived in many different cities and died near Paris in 1778.

Rousseau's Works and His Philosophy of Marriage

Rousseau's basic theme is that man is naturally good, but society has made him unhappy by subordinating nature and reason to an artificially contrived system. Rousseau never espoused revolution, but his thoughts were revolutionary. In his view, the environment, and not birth, exerts the chief influence on man, and, given a supportive environment, man cannot but prosper.

In *La Nouvelle Héloïse,* the hero and heroine, who were predestined to love, are crushed by the machinations of a society that is estranged from nature. In *Emile,* Rousseau shows us what life would be like in the ideal society where nature holds sway. "Nature," as represented by Emile's tutor, enunciates a philosophy that is suspiciously like the traditional eighteenth-century view of marriage:

> The man should be strong and active; the woman . . . weak and passive . . . her strength is in her charms. . . . Nature herself had decreed that woman . . . should be at the mercy of man's judgment. . . . Works of genius are beyond her reach, and she has neither the accuracy nor the attention for success in the exact sciences . . . woman observes, man reasons. . . . The inequality of man-made laws . . . is not of man's making, or at any rate it is not the result of mere prejudice, but of reason.[72]

The ideal wife for Emile is Sophie: she never expresses her desires but, by modest blushes, conceals them even from him who inspires them. She is not bright, only pleasing. She loves needlework and abhors showy clothes. Her husband Emile will rule her person: she will rule his heart. She parcels out her favors, and by making him champ at the bit, rules him more effectively than by simple authority.

One might gather that Rousseau believed that certain basic differences separate men and women. Yet, in another part of *Emile,* he states, "But for her sex, a woman is a man, she has the same organs, the same needs, the same faculties . . . the difference is only in degree."[73]

Rousseau was a maze of contradictions. He claimed to have loved only once, but he named two women whom he loved ecstatically: Madame de Warrens and the Countess Houdetot. He wrote nostalgically of the family and child rearing, but gave away his five children. In *Emile,* contrariwise, he applauded woman's wit, but observed that female wit is a scourge to husbands. He talked about the hegemony of reason in life, and then wrote to his real-life Sophie (Countess d'Houdetot): "I am never more to feel that heavenly shudder, that maddening, devouring fire . . . oh, inexpressible moment!"[74] He extolled chastity, but did not hestitate to participate in "assembly-line" intercourse.

Despite a personal life most charitably characterized as highly neurotic, he was very influential during his lifetime. His credo, that man is molded to society's specifications and is fundamentally good, inspired those who fought governmental injustice long after his culturally inspired biases against women had been forgotten.

HUSBANDS AND WIVES

At the beginning of the seventeenth century, the husband was still fully acknowledged in theory—and often in practice—as the undisputed lord of the home. The wife, no longer considered a lecherous temptress, was a welcome partner so long as she remembered that she was the *junior* partner. Wife beating, although legal, had been frowned upon even in the sixteenth century. In England, by 1674, Lord Chief Justice Hale's ruling on a case of wife beating noted that "moderate castigation was not meant of beating, but only of admonition and confinement to the house."[75]

"Marriage experts" (mostly male) still urged women to accept the errors of their spouses, even to take the blame themselves, and thereby make themselves both loved and indispensable.[76]

The husband is never really responsible for any defects of character, according to a book by Lady Seymour. If he is unfaithful, it is due to his wife or to bad company. And he should not be driven to adultery by nagging. An irritated husband should be forgiven because, doubtless, outside affairs are troubling him. In the case of the wife, of course, this sin is unpardonable. If the reader thinks that Lady Seymour sounds more like a man than a woman, he is right: Juliana-Susannah Seymour was the pseudonym of John Hill.[77]

Wives Gain Greater Freedom

Despite books like Hill's, wives were achieving a considerable degree of social freedom. A woman's rights movement began to emerge and voiced concern at the inequality of the marriage contract. Lady Chudleigh, probably in an autobiographical account, denounced the role of the wife in a typical marriage:

> Wife and Servant are the same,
> But only differ in the Name:[78]

A lack of compatibility, however, did not have to be a cause of strife, since the couple could lead separate lives. Such was the relationship of Squire Western and his wife, as described in Fielding's *Tom Jones:*

> The squire, to whom that poor woman had been a faithful upper-servant all the time of their marriage, had returned that behavior by making what the world calls a good husband. He very seldom swore at her, perhaps not above once a week, and never beat her. She had not the least occasion for jealousy, and was perfect mistress of her time, for she was never interrupted by her husband, who was engaged all the morning in his field exercises, and all the evening with his bottle companions.[79]

Other wives could lead a more zestful life: they went to the theater, to dances, and to the ever-popular masques unaccompanied or with other gallants. Their independence went so far as to be satirized by a "Friend to the Ladies," who lamented that husbands should erect a statue to the memory of anyone who could get the ladies to return to their traditional role.[80]

The lack of communication between the sexes was only thinly veiled by protocol. Boswell, for example, intensely disliked being called "Jamie" by his affectionate wife. He insisted on the more proper "Mr. Boswell." Duc de la Rochefoucauld observed that in England, when ladies left the dinner table, "it is then that real enjoyment begins—there is not an Englishman who is not supremely happy at this particular moment. One proceeds to drink . . . toasts begin . . . conversation is as free as it can be. . . ."[81]

Women writers, aside from their complaints about male boorishness, offered few real solutions to the lack of contact between the sexes. Mrs. Piozzi[82] urged men to pay attention to their wives' minds and to confide in them. Mrs. Chapone[83] attacked the notion that women should never show the extent of their love; she also objected to Swift's idea that they should never have women friends. Like Mary Astell, these women could never bring themselves to champion equality for wives. If their husbands sinned against them, they urged wives to turn to religion and to their children for comfort, and not to complain.

The liberal men who argued for "equality" avoided all mention of putting power in women's hands. The appropriately named Augustus Lovemore, for example, advised husbands not to shave in the presence of their wives, not to appear with dirty attire and a growth of beard after a trip, and to avoid "strong waters" at the dinner table.[84]

The first institutional attempt at some approximation in equality between husband and wife occurred with the appearance of the Society of Friends. Their marriage vows did not include the bride's promise to obey the groom; instead, each promised to love and cherish the other.[85] The movement, however, seems not to have greatly altered the course of non-Quaker marriages during the period.

Sex in Marriage

During the seventeenth and eighteenth centuries the prevailing attitude toward marital sex was expressed in rules set forth by Daniel Defoe:

1. That it be moderate, so as to be consistent with health.
2. That it be so ordered as not to be too extensive of time, that precious opportunity of working out our salvation.
3. That when duty is demanded it be always payed (so far as in our powers and election) according to the foregoing measures.
4. That it be with a temperate affection, without violent transporting desires, or too sensual applications.[86]

As theological influence waned, an interest in sensual dress and sex developed. Upper-class men dressed in lace, buckles, and jeweled clothing. Women wore high-heeled shoes and bodices with laces in the front to make the bosom swell.

Books dealing with sex began to appear. A Frenchman, Dr. Venette, in *Le Tableau de la Vie Conjugale,* published in 1696, recommended spring as the best time to engage in sex. Winter tended to freeze the genitals, and it also cooled the ardor of most women.[87] Summer and fall were acceptable, though not particularly favored. However, according to the English specialist in these matters, Thomas Cogan (author of *The Haven of Health*), summer, with its excessive heat, should be avoided completely—a rule strongly followed by Samuel Pepys.[88]

Sexual desire was believed to be a function of constitution and nourishment. Dr. Venette noted that the liver, which contained fire and sulphur, was the seat of love. Men with high sex drives were said to possess such fiery kidneys that they inflamed the adjoining organs and dried up the cranium, thereby causing premature baldness. A man with a large nose, the good doctor also notes, will have a large genital organ, and a woman with a flabby breast is generally lascivious. For the sagging bosom he prescribed a decoction of red wine and herbs, as well as the wearing of lead molds smeared with henbane oil. Virginity could be determined by having the girl take a hot herbal bath, which was alleged to close the private parts of a virgin. On the other hand, Dr. Venette thought that nonvirginity might be remedied by putting sheep's blood in tiny balls of skin and inserting these into the bride's vagina before her wedding night. This, he opined, would preserve harmony in the family.

For the first time the frigid male became a problem, because so many husbands were a decade or more older than their wives. The complaint of a young wife to her aged spouse is recorded in a poem:

> You wed us with a fancied fire
> To gratify a base desire,
> And take a Virgin to your bed
> With vigour—only in the head.[89]

In France, a wife could divorce her husband if she could prove he was impotent. The accused party could demonstrate the error of these charges by performing before a *congrès* of a judge, surgeons, and matrons. The Marquis de Lagey failed this test, but in a second marriage he produced seven children.

For those who did not want to leave their spouses but wished to perk up their ardor, most authorities recommended a diet of plenty of egg yolks, cock testicles, shrimp, oysters, chocolate, and milk. Dr. Venette preferred powdered Egyptian crocodile kidneys diluted in wine, but regretfully admitted that transportation posed a problem.

The psychology of sex was not ignored either. Mrs. Aphra Behn suggested, with respect to an indifferent husband: "I would many times myself, by dallying with him and some other pretty Wanton postures, try to provoke him to it; whereby he should surely know that it was neither your coolness nor your want of desire that might be blamed in it."[90] Too frequent sexual activity was also a problem since, according to John Evelyne, it "dulls the sight, decays the memory, induces gout, palsies, enervates and renders effeminate the whole body, and shortens life."[9][1]

MARRIAGE REGULATIONS

In France, the power of the state over marriage evolved slowly; in 1659, by royal decree, abductions and secret marriages were abolished. In England, however, there were sweeping changes in marriage legislation. With the ascension of Oliver Cromwell and the Puritans, the Act of 1653 changed marriage from a religious to a civil contract.

At first, religious ceremonies were proscribed, but this decision was soon revised, and the religious ceremony was made optional after the civil one had been performed. The use of a ring at the ceremony, to symbolize the unity of the couple, was replaced by hand-clasping. The government did not deny the importance of religion, but it emphasized that marriage was more properly a function of the state. Parents, as well as the state, were expected to exercise strict supervision. The couple had to publish the banns for three weeks prior to the marriage and could not marry without parental consent unless both had attained the age of 21.

The Act of 1653 also empowered justices of the peace to determine the validity of the marriages of minors who had been forced or abducted into marriage. Prior to this, a man who had contracted spousals with a young woman could carry her away against her consent and, if he had intercourse with her, they were considered to be married. Many a blackguard had abducted a woman and starved and beat her or put a pistol to her heart until she consented to marry him. Once married, the man acquired possession of her monetary assets. Subsequently, the Act of 1653 stipulated that an offender carrying off a person under 21 years of age for the purpose of marriage would suffer life imprisonment and forfeit his entire estate, to be divided equally between the injured party and the state.

The Restoration returned the country to the laws in force before the Cromwell period, but it did not invalidate earlier civil marriages. In 1660 the much-despised system of wardship came to an end, and henceforth the father, and not the crown, was empowered to name any guardian he wished for his son up to the age of 21.

In 1694, under William and Mary, a marriage tax was imposed upon all couples tying the nuptial knot, and new stipulations prohibited couples from marrying without banns. The latter requirement had long been in effect, but now the state put teeth into it by fining any clergyman the sum of £200 for marrying anyone who did not have a license and had not published the banns.

In 1696, bachelors and childless widowers were taxed by Parliament. One result was the formation of bachelors' cooperative clubs, with annual dues of two shillings plus two shillings for each member's marriage. When they entered the bonds of matrimony, they received an annuity of £200.[92] In 1712, a new marriage act provided that the fine for illegal marriages was to be divided between the government and the informer.

"Fleet Marriages" and Other Travesties

The frequency of marriage legislation testifies to the fact that the government was unable to supervise it adequately. The most notorious evidence was the "Fleet Street marriage." Defrocked and disreputable ministers, imprisoned for debt in the Fleet Gaol, performed marriages to earn ready cash. They could not be removed from office, for most had already been expelled from the ministry. Nor could they be fined and locked up, for they were already imprisoned! (In eighteenth-century English prisons, some inmates were detained in cells only during the night.) Since they dispensed with licenses, banns, or parental consent, young heiresses and their lovers could dash to Fleet Street to avoid their pursuing parents. A man of modest means preferred the "Fleet marriage" as a way to avoid wedding expenses, and the father of many a bride hoped for an elopement to spare him the price of a dowry. And some people simply preferred not to publish banns and announce their marital intentions to the world.

Outside the prison, trade was no less brisk. Shop signs advertised speedy, cheap marriages. One tavern kept a parson on the premises to perform the ceremony gratis if two wedding dinners were purchased. A man and a female companion taking a stroll were likely to be accosted by a marriage tout: "Sir, will you pleased to walk in and be married?"[93]

Here, too, women over the age of 12 who wanted to escape from debts or find a father of record for an unplanned baby could hire husbands. Sailors on leave could marry tarts for sport. The record for "Fleet marriages" seems to have been held by John Gainham, who bore the sobriquet "Bishop of Hell," but nevertheless united 36,000 couples while in prison from 1709 to 1740. A Scottish import, the Reverend Alexander Keith, operated in the Mayfair Chapel and advertised in newspapers. In the same one-year period that he performed 6,000 marriages, only fifty regular contracts were solemnized in the neighboring St. Anne's Church.

Since all marriages were "certified" by certificates given by the parson, the government seemed disinclined to take any punitive action. Moreover, the couple that consummated their marriage and lived together were not likely to separate, for they were clearly married from the point of view of common law. By the 1740s, however, the huge number of these marriages—which avoided revenue payment and often led to marital breakup when one spouse drifted off to marry someone else—led to a demand for reform.

The Hardwicke Act

A bill to end clandestine marriages and the Fleet scandals was passed by the House in 1753. With the exception of Quakers, Jews, and members of the royal family, all marriages could be celebrated only after publication of the banns (with parental permission for minors) or the obtaining of a license from the archbishop. Marriages could take place only during the hours of 8 a.m. to noon before an Anglican clergyman in an Anglican church or chapel where banns had been published.[94] Anyone who married persons in violation of these requirements was subject to 14 years banishment and, more important to the couple, such marriages would be null and void. While the law was progressive in most respects, it was intolerant toward Catholics, who could be legally married only by an Anglican.

The law was opposed by such distinguished men as Henry Fox and Horace Walpole. The populace opposed it on the grounds that in order to prevent the children of the aristocracy from rushing into imprudent, unsanctioned marriages, the poor were being denied a cheap, convenient means of marriage.

In general, the arguments covered a narrow range—from the inane to the ridiculous. Madan,[95] in *Thelyphthora; or, a Treatise on Female Ruin,* saw the law as relegating virgins who made mistakes to the position of fornicators, since clandestine marriages were outlawed. Another argument held that many of the poor would never marry rather than indulge in protracted delays (three weeks), with the result that England would be depopulated.

Some critics called the bill undemocratic: a nobleman desiring to marry a commoner might hesitate if his intentions were publicly proclaimed in the banns. The result would be class inbreeding and a consequent weakening of the stock. Mr. Robert Nugent noted that "it shocks the modesty of a young girl to have it proclaimed through the parish that she is going to be married. . . ."[96]

Failing to stop the bill, Henry Fox tried to make it ineffectual by getting it amended so that Scotland was exempt from the act even though the suit leading to the bill had originated there. The result was a minor repetition of "Fleet marriages": a dash across the border to Gretna Green for a hasty marriage. In general, the law was quite successful in that it provided a ready means of registering marriages and ending abductions and forced marriages.

Discriminatory Regulations against Women

Upon marriage, husband and wife became one—and that one was the man. Her land became his, as did her debts. True, he in turn settled a jointure on her (to support her after his death), but the jointures were quite inferior to the dowries.

Through premarital agreements, the wife could keep special lands or monies out of the hands of her husband. This equity arrangement caused one writer to note glumly that under these inequitable conditions ". . . the husband is debarred from enjoying any of the rights of matrimony, except the person of his wife."[97] Equity was, in short, one of the few means women had to maintain themselves on some equal footing with men.

Legal prejudice against women continued throughout the eighteenth century. Here is part of a bizarre law passed by Parliament in 1770:

> All women, of whatever age, rank, profession, or degree, whether virgins, maids, or widows, that shall, from and after such Act, impose upon, seduce, or betray into matrimony, any of his Majesty's male subjects by the scents, paints, cosmetic washes, artificial teeth, false hair, Spanish wool, iron stays, hoops, high-heeled shoes, etc., shall incur the penalty of the law now enforced against witchcraft and like misdemeanours, and that the marriage upon conviction shall stand null and void.[98]

MARRIAGE CUSTOMS

Among the rich, courtships were florid and mechanical. In Molière's *Les Précieuses Ridicules,* one of the young eligible women advises:

> [The man] should behold, either at church or in the park, or at some public ceremony, the person of whom he becomes enamored, or else he should be fatally introduced to her by a relation or friend, and go from her melancholy and pensive. He conceals his passion for some time from the beloved object, but pays her several visits, at which some discourse about gallantry never fails to be brought upon the carpet to exercise the wits of all the company.... The day comes for him to declare himself, which usually should be done in the walk of some garden, while the company is at a distance. This declaration is met by immediate resentment, which appears by our coloring, and which, for a while, banishes the lover from our presence. He finds afterwards the way to pacify us, to accustom us insensibly to hear his passion, and to draw from us that confession which causes so much trouble.[99]

In England, a book by Samuel Johnson (not related to the Johnson of Boswell fame) gave examples of good letter writing in courtship. The would-be suitor addresses the father of the girl:

> Sir, as I scorn to act in a manner that may bring reproach to myself and family, for I hold clandestine proceedings unbecoming of any man of character, with candour and exultation I take the liberty of avowing my love for your daughter and humbly request permission to pay her my addresses.... I have some reason to believe that I am not altogether disagreeable to your daughter....[100]

Even if he won the father's favor, he might be unwelcome to the daughter, and she would then write, "Let me beg that you will endeavour to eradicate a passion which, if nourished longer, may prove fatal to us both."[101]

Newspaper Advertisements

Bluntness of intent was more apt to be found among the less affluent, who placed advertisements in the English newspaper, *The Gazetteer.*

> A Gentleman turned twenty-eight years who has had a plain education and is no way disagreeable in person, bred to business, hath no fortune except health and a decent employ of *Sixty pounds per annum,* would willingly engage with any *staid maid* or *widow* whose circumstances are so easy as that such an alliance would prove agreeable to both parties, as he is far from considering he merits a Beauty, therefore the *plainer the person* the more *agreeable.* Those under twenty-one need not apply, as he thinks they can scarcely judge for themselves with any degree of steadiness or resolution, particularly those under the direction of parents, and under forty years will be considered no disparity, *provided there be a prospect of issue.*[102]

A lady replying to another gentleman's ad confessed:

> I neither speak Dutch, French nor any outlandish tongue, for as my father always says, "*one tongue is enough for any woman".* . . . I am exactly what you term a *Buxom* Girl and I can assure you am not a little admired on a Sunday at Bagnigge Wells by all the spruce linen-drapers, haberdashers, hair-dressers and Common Councillors that . . . exclaim as I pass them, "Faith she is a Bouncer." By this you will find I am none of your *little skinny dabs* but a *hale, stout, fat, good-looking wench.* I hope you are not so unfashionable as to like those women? . . .
>
> My eyes are very good and when I am in a passion (which happens very often) they spark like diamonds. You say you do not expect a shilling with the lady. That suits me quite! for I can tell you I *haven't a shilling in the world.* . . . So now I have told you all, and if you have not a mind to take me, I beg you will keep this letter a secret.[103]

Many marriage ceremonies included the use of omens and superstitions. The Jewish bridegroom blessed his marriage with a glass of wine—a narrow glass for a virgin, a wide one for a widow. Afterward, he threw the glass on the floor in memory of the fall of Jerusalem. During the festivities a raw egg was thrown in someone's face so that the bride might have children as easily as the hen lays eggs.[104]

The wealthy preferred private home weddings, but the less affluent had public ceremonies. It was common to strew the path from the church to the street with emblems of the groom's profession—for example, wood shavings for a carpenter or pieces of old iron for a blacksmith. The custom of crossed swords forming an archway is a relic of the weddings of military men. It was also common belief that if the bride wore a simple smock, her husband would not be responsible for her debts.

During the reign of Charles II, the elaborate sugar-coated wedding cake made its appearance. At first the cake was broken over the head of the bride, as had been the tradition when the cake was little more than a biscuit. Then the fragments were distributed to the guests, and unwed consumers were supposed to dream of a future spouse that night. Finally, someone hit on the idea of cutting up the cake and serving it to the guests.[105]

The feast included special food and drink to aid the groom in his night's work. In addition to the customary spiced wine, there were such allegedly aphrodisiac dishes as a ragout of green truffles, the root of orchis (dog-stones), and the phallic-looking mandrake.

In the evening, everyone entered the wedding chamber, and the young men vied to get the specially loosened garters off the bride's leg. The lucky ones wore them in their hats to celebrate their triumph. The bridegroom's men took off the bride's stockings, and the bridesmaids did the same for the groom. Then they sat at the foot of the bed and threw the stocking over a shoulder. If any hit the owner, it was a sign that the thrower would shortly marry.

The bridesmaids undressed the bride and threw away all her hairpins—it was bad luck to miss any. A wealthy French groom was sometimes shaven all over his body. The English tended to take a more earthy approach. Charles II instructed his new nephew, William of Orange, as he put him and his niece, Mary, to bed: "Now, nephew, to your worke! Hey! St. George for England."[106]

ADULTERY

The Nobility

Fashion, it is said, travels from the top down. In the business of adultery, the era could boast of two of the best leaders: Charles II and Louis XV. Charles II's amorous activities (and the resulting bastards) inspired a parody, by an unknown writer, about why he was always asking Parliament for money:

> I must speak freely to you: I am under circumstances, for besides my harlots in service, my reformed concubines lie heavy on me. I have a passable good estate, I confess but, gad's fish! I have a great charge upon it. Here's my Lord Treasurer can tell that all the money designed for next summer's guards must of necessity be applied to the next year's cradles, and swaddling clothes.[107]

Louis XIV had not been much of a roué. He needed beautiful mistresses mainly for show, for his love of pomp was unexcelled. After his relationship with Madame de Maintenon became established, he became rather dour and a poor model of an adulterous king. Louis XV, on the other hand, maintained liaisons with the opposite sex to the end. Under his reign, the power of the *maitresse-en-titre,* or head mistress, was unrivaled politically and very strong socially. Many families aspired to place their daughters in such an envied position; it meant not only success for their offspring, but a chance for all kinds of new titles and jobs for relatives. Because a large number of the newly created nobility owed their existence to the king's bedtime frolics, they were called *noblesse de lit*—"nobles of the bed."

The chief barrier to becoming a mistress was that generally, only noblewomen came to the king's attention. It is a tribute to the two great mistresses of Louis XV, Mesdames de Pompadour and du Barry, that they made the big jump from the bourgeoisie to the royal bed. Madame de Pompadour, who concerned herself with foreign policy and domestic affairs, became the real ruler of France because the king had no taste for government. She put France on the side of Austria and against Prussia, in part because the Austrian ambassador treated her with the utmost tact and delicacy, whereas Frederick the Great had slighted her.[108]

Madame de Pompadour incurred tuberculosis during her adolescence, and began to fail while in her thirties. Her sexual capacity waned, and the king took to visiting his Park of the Deers with new "does"—in the main, young girls who could quench the fire in the aging monarch and then be pensioned off and married to husbands in the country. The lack of a sexual relationship between Madame de Pompadour and Louis did not, however, cause her downfall; he was fascinated by her brilliant mind and depended on her knowledge of state affairs.

Madame Du Barry, the most beautiful of his mistresses, did not dominate him to the same extent. Her misfortune was that the king died six years after her elevation. Exiled from Versailles by the new king, she was guillotined in 1793 by the revolutionaries.

Most of the European nobility developed the cult of the steady lover. Lady Montagu, visiting the court at Vienna in 1716, noted that most noble ladies had two husbands: one of name and one of duty. There was little that was secretive about these matters—some arrangements lasted 20 years, and it was considered bad form to invite a woman to dinner with only one of her husbands. Lovers became part and parcel of marriage and were not resented by the husbands, who were themselves deputies to husbands-in-name elsewhere.[109]

French lovers often held the stage to themselves and were presented at the Opéra by their paramours.[110] Indeed, an incident related by Madame de Sévigné indicates the acceptance of spouse swapping, particularly among the new class of actors and actresses: A player was considering marriage even though he had a venereal disease. This greatly agitated one of the thespian's companions, who exclaimed, "Zounds, cannot you stay till you are cured? You will be the ruin of us all."[111]

Adultery among royalty was so accepted that in England, when the people booed a carriage containing what they believed was the king's mistress, Louise de Kéroualle, it was not because she was an adulteress but because she was Catholic and a French sympathizer. Actually, inside the carriage at the time was the more popular Nell Gwynn. She stuck her head out of the window and in her own ingenuous style shouted, "Be silent, good people; I am the *Protestant* whore."[112]

The Bourgeoisie

Since the bourgeois or middle-class wife was more apt to have had a hand in selecting her spouse, she had less motivation to stray than a daughter of the aristocracy. Her husband, although allowed greater freedom by society, was often too concerned over his business to wander. In both cases, the liaisons that occurred were much more likely to be tinged with guilt than was the case among the nobility.

Samuel Pepys, a minor functionary in the admiralty at the time he wrote his diary, was a case in point. He loved his beautiful French wife, whom he married for love, but he also loved attractive women. He describes the following church incident:

> ... where I heard an able sermon of the minister of the place; and stood by a pretty, modest maid, whom I did labour to take by the hand; but she would not, but got further and further from me; and, last I could perceive her to take pins out of her pocket to prick me if I should touch her again—which, seeing, I did forbear, and was glad I did spy her design. And then I fell to gaze upon another pretty maid, in a pew close to me, and she on me; and I did go about to take her by the hand, which she suffered a little, and then withdrew. So the sermon ended, and the church broke up, and my amours ended also.[113]

He once picked up a meaty trollop, Doll Lane; after a few drinks, he found that he could tousel her a bit, which led to the observation that she had "a very white thigh and leg, but monstrous fat."[114] But somebody witnessed their "dalliance" and called out from the street, "Sir, do you kiss the gentlewoman so?" and flung a stone at the window.[115] To protect his reputation, Pepys skipped out the back door "without being observed, I think."[116]

He carried on an affair with Deborah Willet, his maid, but his wife caught him in the act of kissing her. After a violent quarrel his wife made him write a letter telling Deborah that he hated her, that he would not see her again (she had been discharged), and that she might become a whore if she carried on with others as she had with him. He also had to promise never to go to bed without getting on his knees and praying to God for strength against temptation; Pepys found this to be "much the best for my soul and body to live pleasing to God and my poor wife, and will ease me of much care as well as much expense."[117] Truly, the words of a bourgeois! He later noted, with contentment, that he was now having intercourse with his wife much more frequently than in the past year and with a great deal of pleasure. Yet he was soon looking up Deborah for more adventure.

Double Standard in Adultery

The man who led an adulterous existence was envied or admired, but a woman whose adultery was identified was "dishonored." A rationale for this double standard was provided by Dr. Johnson:

> Confusion of progeny constitutes the essence of the crime; and therefore a woman who breaks her marriage vows is much more criminal than a man who does it. A man, to be sure, is criminal in the sight of God: but he does not do his wife a very material injury, if he does not insult her; if, for instance, from mere wantonness of appetite, he steals privately to her chambermaid. Sir, a wife ought not greatly to resent this. I would not receive home a daughter who had run away from her husband on that account. A wife should study to reclaim her husband by more attention to please him. Sir, a man will not, once in a hundred instances, leave his wife and go to a harlot, if his wife has not been negligent of pleasing.[118]

Boswell sympathetically cited the case of a woman who had been brutally mistreated by her husband and who had at last obtained a divorce by an act of Parliament and married another. To Johnson, however, there was no temporizing in such matters: "My dear Sir, never accustom your mind to mingle virtue and vice. The woman's a whore, and there's an end on't."[119] Boswell, who, it is clear, generally defers to the master, poses again as the devil's advocate in asking whether a lady whose husband has committed numerous infidelities is not justified in sowing some wild oats of her own. Johnson notes tersely, "This lady of yours, Sir, I think is very fit for a brothel."[120]

On another occasion Johnson explained why he required more perfection from women than men: "Women have not the same temptations that we have: they may always live in virtuous company; men must mix in the world indiscriminately."[121]

Legal Action against Adultery

Under Elizabeth of England, a High Commission had been formed to supervise the ecclesiastical and temporal courts' actions against "incontinent" persons. In practice, the weakening of the clergy's position in England caused illicit sexual behavior to be increasingly viewed as a civil crime.

A law of 1618 empowered a constable "to take company" with suspects and to haul them to prison if they were found to be illegally cohabiting. Tremendous fines were levied, the smallest reported being £28, including court costs.[122] Despite its apparently sweeping powers, the commission was vulnerable on two counts. The defendant, although guilty until proved innocent, had to appear in court to be punished. If he were not personally served with a mandate, he need not suffer any harm. Moreover, in his absence, his property could not be sequestered for any alleged sexual infraction. In addition, the commission proved vulnerable to bribery and was dissolved in 1640.

In 1650 a Puritan parliament took a more serious view of sexual irregularities. Adultery was henceforth punishable by death; fornication, by three months' imprisonment. The legislators' zeal for punishment, nevertheless, was not matched by that of the juries: most adulterers were released as "innocent" rather than put to death.

The return of Charles II formally ended the unobserved law of 1650, and he attempted to restore the Church to a supervisory position over morals, but its declining influence resulted in ineffective regulation. This task now fell into the hands of societies that prosecuted sexual offenders. The scope of illicit sexual activity in London and Westminster alone was so great that one society effected 100,000 prosecutions there between 1696 and 1730. Ecclesiastical jurisdiction was formally abolished in 1788.

In France, unlike England, legal action rested exclusively in the hands of the husband, who for the most part did not avail himself of this right. A husband who enjoyed several mistresses might choose to extend the same privilege to his wife if she was discreet and had a lover of distinction. Yet woe to the wife who chose to act independently! On proof of adultery, the husband could obtain a *lettre de cachet,* send armed men to abduct her forcibly from her lover's residence, and deposit her in a suitable convent to repent. He had the option of taking her back at any time during a two-year period, after which the unreclaimed wife had her head shaven, her stay extended to life confinement, and her fortune presented to her husband with the stipulation that he pay her a maintenance allowance of £1,200 a year.[123] The wife, however, could not incarcerate her husband for a similar offense; after all, he could not bring spurious issue into the family.

PROSTITUTION

As sin became more socially acceptable during the age of reason and enlightenment, prostitution flourished to the point where, aside from theological and civil considerations, it posed a threat. A large standing army had come into vogue with Louis XIV, and prostitutes were not only needless distractions, from the point of view of a commander, but they also spread venereal diseases which decimated the fighting capacity of the men. Louis XIII had been content to whip and shave any prostitute who could not bribe her way to freedom. But the usually mild-mannered Louis XIV, faced with maintaining his much larger military forces, issued an edict in 1674 that any prostitute caught with a soldier within five miles of Versailles would have her ears and nose cut off.[124] The sanctuary for prostitutes was the Opéra or the Comédie Française, since employment in the arts exempted women from paying fines and having their heads shaved.

Responding to the royal outlook, the ecclesiasts' tolerance of prostitution as a necessary evil gave way to condemnation. Davenant attacked the views of Aquinas, holding that houses of prostitution siphoned off lust that might have been directed against modest maidens.[125] Samuel Johnson agreed heartily, maintaining that severe laws against prostitution would promote marriage.[126]

The proliferation of prostitutes in France prompted many schemes for the state regulation of brothels. One of the most involved was the Code of Cythera, a sort of utopia of sensuality proposed by a Monsieur Moët.[127] The plan called for a membership of 1,200 "love favorites." Applicants had to be over 15 years of age and present a certificate signed by two matrons to the effect that they were no longer virgins. In addition, they would pay initiation fees of £500 and present health certificates. Retirement was voluntary after six years of service, but was mandatory at age 40 (a pension was also provided).

The girls would be divided into age categories: "Young Favorites" (under 20), "Joyous Courtesans" (20 to 30), and "Mature Women" (30 to 40). Supervision would be provided by 340 other women (only "ex-workers," who had never appeared in court, were eligible). These ladies would inspect every client and reject the diseased ones, making them pay a fine of £10 to boot, which would go toward house repairs. They would also conduct clinic sessions to instruct the girls in the art of sensuality.

The girls would wear distinctive uniforms with pink taffeta bonnets appropriately embroidered with a bow and arrow. They could not undress completely—nudity, apparently, was considered immoral. They would be cautioned to avoid rigorous activity with old gentlemen lest it cause their demise. Working hours, strictly regulated, would be much less than the typical 10- to 15-hour day of the time. Young Favorites might service up to three men a day, but for no longer than three hours each. Joyous Courtesans could serve a similar number, but for no more than two hours each. Mature Women would probably serve an older clientele, but, while they might serve four men a day, they could spend no more than an hour with each.

The work schedule was to be geared to biological considerations, with time off during menstrual flow. (To keep the work force at full strength, tryouts would be held for applicants during this period.) Despite its carefully worked-out details, the Code was never adopted.

In England, prostitution reached a new high in popularity: one foreign observer estimated that 50,000 prostitutes worked in London alone.[128] This figure could hardly have been accurate even toward the latter part of the eighteenth century, when London's population was about 400,000. The exaggeration, nevertheless, attests to the omnipresence of commercial sex.

A favorite hangout was St. James' Park. Even though the gates were locked at 10 p.m. 6,500 people had authorized keys and many more unauthorized keys were in use.

DIVORCE

In the early part of the seventeenth century, Europe's Protestant countries, with the exception of England, instituted more liberal divorce laws. The Anglican Church, which had permitted divorce for adultery and desertion, now took a firmer line in prohibiting remarriage after divorce. The more liberal Puritans advocated the right of remarriage not only for adultery but for a new, unheard-of reason—*psychological incompatibility*. A major advocate of the new stand was John Milton, and to understand the impetus for his views we should take a cursory look at his personal life.

JOHN MILTON

Born in 1608, Milton became the prototype of a studious, severe scholar. His smooth, fine features earned him the sobriquet of "the Lady." His morals were as fine as his looks, for he shunned the loose talk and promiscuous adventures of his fellow students at Cambridge. He worked hard and wrote poetry, occasionally of a sensuous nature. Despite his extended student years and a tour of the continent, Milton arrived at his thirty-fourth year still virginal.

Milton did not abhor the thought of sex. Rather, his actions suggest an overidealization, reinforced by the absence of actual interaction with women. Unfortunately, his lack of experience marred his judgment as to the kind of woman best suited for him. After a brief visit with the Powell family, who had owed his father a considerable sum of money for many years, he married their 17-year-old daughter, Mary, an incredibly poor choice. He was twice her age, educated, severe, scholarly, republican, and expecting a madonna. She was youthful, high-spirited, unintellectual, with pitifully few political ideas—and these, alas, were royalist in sympathy.

It is possible that she refused him consummation. It is also possible that his regime of rising at 4 a.m. in the summer and at 5 a.m. in the winter, reading from the Bible, studying until dinner and then studying some more, an hour of walking, organ playing, and early to bed, may have been more than she bargained for.[129] In any event, after a month of marriage, she begged leave to visit her parents. He consented, thinking that a short separation might clear the air. But the separation became protracted, despite letters and messengers. A year later, bitter, frustrated, but tied to his wife by the Anglican code which did not permit divorce and remarriage, he wrote *Doctrine and Discipline of Divorce,* perhaps to prepare the way for a future marriage.

Doctrine and Discipline of Divorce

Jesus had said, "Whosoever shall put away his wife, except it be for fornication, and shall marry another, committeth adultery" (Matthew 19:3-9). On the other hand, in the Old Testament, Moses had noted, "When a man hath taken a wife, and married her, and it come to pass that she find no favour in his eyes, because he hath found some uncleanness in her: then let him write her a bill of divorcement, and give it in her hand, and send her out of his house. And when she is departed out of his house, she may go and be another man's wife" (Deuteronomy 24:1-2).

It had been customary in Milton's day to reconcile the differences between the Old and New Testaments by considering the former as a kind of "pilot study"—a preparation for the more perfect Gospel of the New Testament. Milton had originally subscribed to this view, but now, in his hour of need, he proposed to reverse his course and to revise other interpretations besides.

He interpreted the Scriptures to hold that the world today was different from what existed at the time of Adam, when governments and regulations were not needed because everything was in perfect order. Today, man was imperfect, and God commanded him not to be alone. Because of his somewhat debased nature, man might choose an incorrect mate who, far from being a help, might be a virago. To try to fulfill God's law, it might be necessary to divorce the unsuitable spouse and search for another with whom he might live in compliance with God's wish. In fact, "that indisposition, unfitness, or contrariety of mind, arising from a cause in nature unchangeable, hindering and ever likely to hinder the main benefits of conjugall society, which are solace and peace, is a greater reason of divorce than naturall frigidity, especially if there be no children, and that there be mutuall consent."[130]

As for those who believed adultery to be the only reason for divorce, they affirmed that sex was the highest aspect of marriage; but a spouse's ability to help her partner lead a decent Christian life was more important. And if a woman failed to allow a man to reach that state, was she not worse than an adulteress or an idolatress? The big stumbling block, however, was the disparity between the words of Moses and Christ. Milton now took the position that Christ had sworn "not to abrogate from the Law one jot or tittle."[131] Therefore, we must listen to what Christ *means* and not to what he *says:* "Wherein we may plainly discover how Christ meant not to be tak'n word for word, but like a wise Physician, administering one excess against another to reduce us to a perfect mean: Where the Pharises were strict, there Christ seems remisse; where they were too remisse, he saw it needfull to seem most severe."[132]

According to Milton, by naming adultery as a reason for divorce, Christ did not intend to imply that it was the *only* reason for divorce; but he meant it "as one example of other like cases, than as one only exception."[133] Milton cites Grotius as interpreting fornication in Scripture to mean "headstrong behaviour"... as tends to plain contempt of the husband"[134] and not as simple sexual infidelity. Finally, Christ had said that those whom God had joined should not be put asunder. True enough, but how to tell whom *God* had joined? A marriage ceremony was not necessarily valid, for individuals might join themselves under false pretenses. The only way to divine God's presence for certain would be if both individuals in the marriage were content. If they were not, then surely God had not joined them, "and if he joined them not, then there is no power above their own consent to hinder them from unjoyning."[135]

Milton's enthusiastic advocacy of divorce was geared more to freedom for men than for women. At one point in the *Colasterion*, he implied that the right of divorce may be equal for both sexes; yet he never cited a single example of a woman repudiating a man. In sum, Milton's arguments in favor of his position on divorce are illogical and tortured. On topics such as education and freedom of the press, however, he is much more convincing. Apparently, his inconsistency in his writings on divorce can be traced to his bitterness at having been deserted and to his need to lash back at the sex responsible for his humiliation. (Eventually, he was reconciled with his wife.)

His book was popular but not immediately influential. People bought it for the pleasure of attacking his unorthodox views, and Parliament, to whom it was addressed, did not change any marriage laws because of it.

It was difficult to obtain a legal divorce in England until Cromwell opened the doors with a 1653 act in which the question of divorce would be judged by civil magistrates. In 1670, Parliament was officially invested with the right to grant divorces. As government acts, such decisions had to be preceded by the offended party's successful suits for separation from bed and board in the ecclesiastical court and for financial damages in the civil court.[136] Since very few could afford the legal costs, and not many people wanted the publicity entailed in a Parliamentary judgment, only a handful of divorces were granted. Meanwhile, in France, as in other Catholic countries, divorce was forbidden—only separation from bed and board was permitted.

Increasingly, even though the laws did not change, leading thinkers and the populace came around to a faltering acceptance of the notion of psychological incompatibility. Locke accepted it, as has been noted, and Hume, while ambivalent, observed that "liberty of divorce is not only a cure to hatred and domestic quarrels, it is also an admirable preservation against them."[137]

Swedenborg favored divorce, but for reasons other than adultery: the attempt of one spouse to dominate the other, a man's lack of interest in a business, dissimilar dispositions, and a belief that the partner was uninvolved in onself.[138] While Swedenborg's views seem quite modern, they were couched in mystical, theological language which minimized his influence.

In sum, the period was marked by a slow recognition of the psychological meaning of marriage, but the legislation resisted this trend.

THE IDEAL SPOUSE

The Ideal Wife

Among the characteristics highly esteemed in a nubile woman was the ability to blush easily.[139] Rousseau's ideal, Sophie, was able to conceal desire even from her lover, who inspired her to this state. She was most attractive when shame and emotion made words difficult. Her other ideal qualities were a desire to please and console, and her virtuosity with thread and thimble.

The rich could afford to be less industrious and more picayune. Thus, in Congreve's *The Way of the World,* Mirabell requests that his wife-to-be avoid close friendships with other women and not attend a play alone and in a mask. He abhors tight corsets when his wife is pregnant, which would "mould my boy's head like a sugar loaf and . . . make me father to a crooked billet."[140] He requests that "you continue to like your own face, as long as I shall: and while it passes current with me, that you endeavour not to new-coin it."[141]

Frenchmen were more precise in what they wanted in a spouse: *finesse, sveltesse,* and *gracilité.*[142] For the English woman, the new look in the eighteenth century was a pallid, languid pose. Some ladies had themselves bled regularly to achieve it, while others resorted to cosmetics.[143]

Above all else, the ideal wife should be humble—a quality that endears Sophia, Tom Jones' beloved, to his guardian, Mr. Allworthy. The latter notes admiringly, "Whenever I have seen her in the company of men, she hath been all attention, with the modesty of a learner, not the forwardness of a teacher."[144]

The Ideal Husband

For the most part, a man's physical qualities were secondary; good financial status was necessary, but not sufficient. He should also be seven to ten years older than his spouse.[145] All his time should be devoted to business affairs, but he must not become a dandy who spends his leisure hours at the hounds or talks of nothing but dances and duels. He was not expected to inspire passion but, rather, to be kindly and fatherly.

A wealthy woman like Mrs. Millamant, in *The Way of the World,* could demand certain freedoms as a prerequisite to marriage:

> Mrs. Millamant: [I should like] liberty to pay and receive visits to and from whom I please; to write and receive letters, without interrogatories or wry faces on your part; to wear what I please; and choose conversation with regard only to my own taste; to have no obligation upon me to converse with wits that I don't like, because they are your acquaintance:

or to be intimate with fools, because they may be your relations. Come to dinner when I please; dine in my dressingroom when I'm out of humour, without giving a reason. To have my closet inviolate; to be sole empress of my tea-table, which you must never presume to approach without first asking leave. And lastly, wherever I am, you shall always knock at the door before you come in. These articles subscribed, if I continue to endure you a little longer, I may by degrees dwindle into a wife.[146]

CONCLUSIONS

Church influence over marriage declined as governments took over the regulatory functions of marriage and the administration of punishment for such infractions as adultery. This change proved of small benefit to women's political and legal status, although gains were achieved by women in the social area.

The high priority given to money and property in arranging marriages provided a rationale for new sexual freedom for the wealthy. The emancipated married woman became someone's mistress—there was little other opportunity for individual self-expression.

One would have expected that the new emphasis on rationalism would have led to a reassessment of the prevailing perception of women as stupid, frail, and inferior. For the most part, however, philosophers employed rationalization rather than rationalism, justifying women's inferior social position as "nature's way."

The reluctance to sanction divorce on any large scale reflected the fear of governments that familial dissolution would result in anarchy. There was little place for a woman outside of marriage. Gradually, the faint beginnings of a concept of marriage as a psychological as well as a procreational relationship made headway.

When the concern with great estates lessened, and when the full effects of industrialization (and its concomitant mobility) destroyed the ties to the past, rapid progress would be made. But that was not to begin in earnest until the onset of the French Revolution; nor would it accelerate until the twentieth century. For the moment, the patriarchal concept of indissoluble marriage persisted, but creaks in the marital machinery were evident.

REFERENCES

1. P. Petot, *La famille en France sous l'ancien régime.*
2. T. Hobbes, *Leviathan.*
3. D. Diderot, *Oeuvres Philosophiques.*
4. J. Locke, "Concerning civil government."
5. N. Pasquier, "Recommendations paternelles à une jeune mariée."

6. F. de Sales, "Avis pour les gens mariés."

7. W. Whately, *A Bride-Bush.*

8. J. Milton, *Paradise Lost,* p. 159.

9. L. M. Halifax, *The Lady's New-Year's Gift or Advice to a Daughter,* p. 19.

10. J. Boswell, *Life of Samuel Johnson,* p. 391.

11. B. B. James, *Women of England.*

12. Chesterfield, *Letters to His Son,* Vol. 1, p. 107.

13. J. Swift, *Gulliver's Travels,* p. 166.

14. Uxorious, "Hymen."

15. B. B. James, op. cit.

16. J. J. Rousseau, *Emile,* p. 331.

17. D. F. Manuel, *The Government of a Wife,* p. 87.

18. D. Hunt, *Parents and Children in History.*

19. E. de Goncourt and J. de Goncourt, *The Woman of the Eighteenth Century.*

20. N. Epton, *Love and the English.*

21. W. Durant and A. Durant, *The Age of Voltaire,* p. 290.

22. E. S. Turner, *A History of Courting,* p. 90.

23. E. de Goncourt and J. de Goncourt, op. cit.

24. Ibid., pp. 18-19.

25. *The Maids Complaint against the Batchellors.*

26. *The Batchellors Answer to the Maids Complaint,* pp. 6-7.

27. R. Burton, *The Anatomy of Melancholy.*

28. F. La Rochefoucauld, *Maxims and Moral Reflections,* p. 79.

29. *The Bachelor's Soliloquy,* pp. 4-5.

30. I. Watt, "The new woman: Samuel Richardson's Pamela."

31. J. Vanbrugh, *The Provok'd Wife,* Act I, Scene I.

32. *The Pleasures of a Single Life or, the Miseries of Matrimony,* p. 1.

33. B. de Spinoza, *Ethics.*

34. J. Milton, op. cit., p. 245.

35. *The Batchelor's Directory,* p. 237.

36. M. Astell, *Reflections upon Marriage,* pp. 17-18.

37. J. Swift, "Letter to a very young lady on her marriage," p. 451.

38. J. Swift, *Gulliver's Travels,* p. 166.

39. J. Boswell, op. cit., p. 297.

40. I. Kant, *The Science of Right,* p. 419.

41. N. Epton, *Love and the French,* p. 23.

42. D. Day, *The Evolution of Love,* p. 307.

43. C. de Montesquieu, *The Spirit of Laws,* p. 189.

44. J. Locke, op. cit.

45. T. Paine, *The Writings of Tom Paine,* Vol. 1, p. 53.

46. E. Swedenborg, *Conjugial Love,* p. 225.

47. Ibid., p. 226.

48. Ibid., p. 201.

49. N. Epton, op. cit.

50. D. Day, op. cit., p. 261.

51. J. Boswell, *London Journal,* p. 89.

52. Ibid., p. 115.

53. Ibid., p. 139.
54. Ibid., p. 149.
55. Ibid., p. 160.
56. J. Hervez, "Les Sociétés d'amour au 18-ème siècle"; quoted in N. Epton, op. cit., pp. 256-257 (author's translation).
57. Ibid., p. 241.
58. J. T. Merydew, *Love Letters of Famous Men and Women.*
59. C. J. S. Thompson, *Love, Marriage and Romance in Old London.*
60. J. Boswell, *In Search of a Wife,* p. 47.
61. S. Richardson, *Pamela,* Vol. 1, p. 220 (emphases added).
62. Ibid., pp. 221-222.
63. M. B. Williams, "Henry Fielding's Attitudes toward Marriage."
64. C. Laclos, *Dangerous Acquaintances,* p. 152.
65. J. J. Rousseau, *The Confessions,* p. 10.
66. Ibid., p. 160.
67. Ibid., pp. 268-269.
68. Ibid., p. 269.
69. R. Lewinsohn, *A History of Sexual Customs.*
70. Rousseau, op. cit., p. 377.
71. Ibid., p. 382.
72. J. J. Rousseau, *Emile,* pp. 322, 324, 349-350.
73. Ibid., p. 321.
74. C. H. Charles, *Love Letters of Great Men and Women,* p. 95.
75. A. R. Cleveland, *Women under the English Law,* p. 221.
76. *A Series of Letters on Courtship and Marriage.*
77. J. Hill, *The Conduct of Married Life.*
78. D. M. Stenton, *The English Woman in History,* p. 207.
79. B. B. James, op. cit., pp. 315-316.
80. *Friend to the Ladies, a Dialogue Concerning the Subjugation of Women to Their Husbands.*
81. F. A. F. La Rochefoucauld, *A Frenchman in England,* pp. 30-31.
82. H. L. Piozzi, *A Letter to a Young Gentleman on His Marriage.*
83. H. M. Chapone, *Miscellanies in Prose and Verse.*
84. A. Lovemore, *A Letter from a Father to a Son on his Marriage.*
85. G. E. Howard, *A History of Matrimonial Institutions.*
86. D. Defoe, *The Uses and Abuses of the Marriage Bed,* p. 20.
87. N. Epton, op. cit.
88. L. Stone, *The Crisis of the Aristocracy (1558-1641).*
89. E. Ward, *Comforts of Matrimony, or Love's Last Shift,* p. 63.
90. N. Epton, *Love and the English,* p. 181.
91. L. Stone, op. cit., p. 660.
92. C. J. S. Thompson, op. cit.
93. Ibid., p. 85.
94. G. Howard, op. cit., Vol. 2.
95. M. Madan, *Thelyphthora; or, a Treatise on Female Ruin.*
96. E. S. Turner, op. cit., p. 99.
97. W. Alexander, *History of Woman,* Vol. 2, p. 496.
98. B. B. James, op. cit., p. 318.

99. W. Durant and A. Durant, *The Age of Louis XIV*, p. 108.
100. E. S. Turner, op. cit., p. 115.
101. Ibid., p. 116.
102. C. J. S. Thompson, op. cit., p. 55.
103. Ibid., pp. 69-70.
104. Gaya, *Marriage Ceremonies or, the Ceremonies Used in Marriage in All Parts of the World.*
105. J. Braddock, *The Bridal Bed.*
106. M. Ashley, *The Stuarts in Love*, p. 125.
107. N. Epton, op. cit., p. 157.
108. W. Durant and A. Durant, *The Age of Voltaire.*
109. E. Westermarck, *The History of Human Marriage*, Vol. 3.
110. N. Epton, *Love and the French.*
111. M. R. de Sévigné, *Letters of Madame de Sévigné*, Vol. 1., p. 56.
112. W. Durant and A. Durant, *The Age of Louis XIV*, p. 249.
113. S. Pepys, *The Diary of Samuel Pepys*, 2 vols., 1906, p. 318.
114. E. S. Turner, op. cit., p. 86.
115. Ibid., p. 86.
116. Ibid., p. 86.
117. S. Pepys, *The Diary of Samuel Pepys*, vol. 16, 1896, p. 151.
118. J. Boswell, op. cit., p. 160.
119. Ibid., p. 221.
120. Ibid., p. 304.
121. Ibid., p. 391.
122. G. May, *Social Control of Sex Expression.*
123. E. de Goncourt and J. de Goncourt, op. cit.
124. W. Durant and A. Durant, *The Age of Louis XIV.*
125. D. S. Bailey, *Sexual Relation in Christian Thought.*
126. J. Boswell, op. cit.
127. N. Epton, op. cit.
128. W. Durant and A. Durant, *The Age of Voltaire.*
129. E. J. Hardy, *The Love Affairs of Some Famous Men.*
130. J. Milton, *Complete Prose Works of John Milton*, Vol. 2, p. 242.
131. Ibid., p. 283.
132. Ibid., p. 282.
133. Ibid., p. 330.
134. Ibid., p. 335.
135. Ibid., p. 328.
136. G. May, op. cit.
137. D. Hume, *Essays, Moral, Political, and Literary*, Vol. 1, p. 237.
138. E. Swedenborg, op. cit.
139. C. J. S. Thompson, op. cit., p. 56.
140. I. Brown, *A Book of Marriage*, p. 29.
141. Ibid., p. 28.
142. H. P. Thieme, *Women of Modern France.*
143. *The Matrimonial Magazine.*
144. H. Fielding, *Tom Jones*, p. 360.
145. D. Defoe, op. cit.
146. W. Congreve, *The Way of the World*, Act IV, Scene 1.

12
Romantics and
Victorians: 1789–1918

From 1760 to 1840, Western Europe underwent profound economic changes. The agrarian population flocked to factory work in the cities, where machines required speed and dexterity more than raw strength. The labor force, which now included women and children, struggled to eke out a living in 13-hour work shifts.

It was inevitable that family life would react to the urban environment, especially to the crowded tenements in mill towns. The influence of the extended family declined, and the nuclear family lost much of its cohesiveness. Home care deteriorated, meals became irregular, and drinking increased.

The situation aroused much criticism. In England, William Godwin (1759-1839) wrote that man's true goodness was being nullified by foolish, restrictive laws. Marriage laws which assumed that the attitudes of a couple at the time of their marriage would persist over a lifetime were unrealistic: "So long as I seek to engross one woman to myself and to prohibit my neighbor from proving his superior desert and reaping the fruits of it, I am guilty of the most odious of monopolies."[1] Godwin painted a picture of a more enlightened society in which selfish materialism would vanish. Would a child's paternity be in doubt because of sexual liberty? No! The child would be judged by his own character, not by his father's name. Would the woman with numerous children have difficulty maintaining her brood? Those who earned more would happily share with her. Once the artifices of society were removed, a human rationalism would replace the lewd life of which so many moralists complained.

The conservative retort to Godwin came in 1798 from Thomas Robert Malthus, who formulated the principle that unchecked population increases geometrically, whereas food supplies increase only arithmetically. According to his predictions, Europe would have 50 billion inhabitants in the year 2000, but would be able to feed only 2 billion.[2] Godwin's philosophy, which encouraged early marriage because divorces could readily be obtained, would greatly increase the birthrate. Moreover, the idea that society would support the family would also be an inducement for population growth.

Malthus' remedy for poverty was simple: "If we can persuade the hare to go to sleep, the tortoise may have some chance of overtaking him."[3] Late marriages and separate bedrooms—or at least separate beds—were the answer. As a clergyman, Malthus hardly countenanced premarital sexuality; he preached the exercise of willpower to maintain premarital chastity. After that, the choice was restraint or children, since contraception was also on his list of prohibitions.

The rich were quick to endorse Malthus, especially when the poor agitated for factory reforms. Why give them more leisure when they would merely have more time to get drunk, visit prostitutes, or at best go home with sufficient energy to impregnate their wives and aggravate the population problem? Workers who asked for higher wages were offered the counsel of Malthus as a simple means of raising their standard of living: have fewer children!

A more radical solution to the economic problems of the destitute came from Robert Owen, a wealthy manufacturer who believed that only by changing society along socialistic lines could the evils of mankind be remedied. He reorganized his factory in accordance with humanitarian thinking, to the plaudits of social reformers throughout the world. Unfortunately, his views were extremely iconoclastic; he soon antagonized industrial leaders and the clergy, and failed to achieve any political change.

Owen vigorously opposed "marriages of [by] the priesthood." He also maintained that almost every married couple lived in a state of prostitution. He must have meant that marriage without love, as a commercial transaction, was equivalent to prostitution. But his critics interpreted it as a direct attack on the institution of marriage itself. They counterattacked with pamphlets depicting Owen and his cohorts as lecherous immoral men: *Oh Vice where is thy Shame. The Horrible effects of the Social System with an account of the cruel seduction of the Three Unfortunate Sisters, Mary, Elizabeth, and Catherine Johnson and the Death Bed Scenes of their Wretched Father, Allured by teachings of Owen.*[4]

While Owen undoubtedly was ahead of his time, he was hardly immoral. In the brave new world of the future, as he described it in 1833, couples desiring to marry would make a public declaration at an assembly. After three months, if they did not change their minds, they could marry. If the marriage did not work out and both parties desired to separate, they would have to wait until they had been married for a year before announcing their intention. They would then live with each other for six more months, and then, if both still agreed, there would be a divorce. However, if one partner wanted to continue the marriage, the couple would have to spend another six months together before a final separation. Under Owen's system, children would be cared for by the community. It is noteworthy that although nature was to be the guide for mating,[5] Owen advocated an extended interval before the bonds of matrimony could be either joined or sundered.

Owen sponsored several experimental settlements in America and Europe, where people could live in accordance with his ideas. None of them proved successful or lasted more than a few years, probably because the societies adjoining his settlements, despite a lack of sympathy with their principles, were not hostile enough to isolate the members. Consequently, whenever his followers became disenchanted, they could readily return to a traditional and conventional life.

ROMANTICISM

The plight of the poor was not the only factor mediating in favor of a social reorganization. The French Revolution had signaled the end of the concept of absolute monarchy. The Age of Classicism and Reason had also died. No longer could the various strata of society coexist smoothly, guided by reason and convention.

In the wake of this collapse a new movement emerged—romanticism—which the writings of Rousseau, Goethe, and Thomson had been building and which had some implications for love and marriage. It would lead us too far into literary analysis to attempt a complete definition of romanticism, so we shall have to be content with listing some of its outstanding characteristics. One of its chief elements was protest: Wordsworth protested the organization of civilization; Coleridge, the tyranny of reason; Byron, middle-class respectability; and Shelley, the evils of society.[6] The romanticist worshiped that which was natural to man and that which was *idiosyncratic* with respect to each person. He cherished sensation and emotion as essential to life, and was attracted to contrasts, to oppositions and antitheses.[7] It was human to change one's feeling from moment to moment, from situation to situation. Pastoral life and mysterious forests were venerated as part of nature. Love of the past and of exotic distant lands thrived on the inexplicable; above all, the romanticist fueled his protest with youthful energy. Byron, Shelley, Keats, Wordsworth, Coleridge, Chateaubriand, and Lamartine were all in their twenties or thirties when they made their major contributions.

Romanticism was in some ways similar to courtly love. Courtly love could be "mixed" in the sense that it fused the sensual and the pure. In romanticism, too, sexual love was the hieroglyph of divine love.[8] Love was the key to understanding nature, because it touched on the ultimate mysteries of life. But romanticism differed from courtly love in that the romanticist sanctioned open rebellion against the mores of his time; the more openly he defied these mores, the more he was admired. The troubadour, on the contrary, valued discretion almost as much as he adored his lady. Also, unlike courtly love, the romantic lover could express his love immediately rather than artfully traveling a succession of courtship stages. Last, the troubadour generally manifested cheerful optimism regarding the happiness that awaited him when he finally joined his lady. The romanticist, more conscious of his inevitable end, worshipped death because it represented total fusion with the universe.

The focus on bathos and death in one of the early romantic novels, Goethe's *The Sorrows of Young Werther,* caused an international furor. Werther is in love with Lotte, who seems at one with nature. Werther knows that Lotte loves him "from the first soulful glances, the first hand pressure."[9] Even though she is married to Albert, a friend of Werther's, Werther cries out in a letter to her, "And what does that mean that Albert is your husband?"[10] Werther will have his beloved in Paradise. He borrows two pistols from Albert's household and writes, "They have passed through your hands, you have wiped the dust from them, I kiss them a thousand times for you have touched them."[11] And then Werther takes his life.

A considerable number of romantics were so moved by the novel that they committed suicide, and many countries banned its distribution. In fact, a girl was pulled from a pond in Goethe's own garden with a copy of *Werther* tied inside her scarf.

Many romanticists did not always live up to their philosophy. In his major poem *Queen Mab,* young Shelley echoed the Godwinian tenet: "Love is free: to promise forever to love the same woman is not less absurd than to promise to believe the same creed."[12] Nevertheless, Shelley, like his father-in-law Godwin, married, presumably to avoid public censure.

George Sand, despite her many lovers after an unhappy marriage, could occasionally slip out of the romantic mold into traditional, materialist concerns. Having deserted the ailing Alfred de Musset to run off with the physician attending him, she wrote, "I go nearly mad, I soak my pillow with tears, I hear in the silence of the night your voice calling me.... Good-bye my dearest little one.... Good-bye my Alfred, love your George. *Send me, I beg, twelve pairs of glacé gloves, six yellow and six of colour."*[13]

Implications of Romanticism for Marriage

For the radical romanticist, the marriage of the wealthy European—with its priority on economics rather than on the relationship of the participants—was an infamy. Nature and destiny took precedence over bourgeois conventionality, and lovers should feel free to defy unnatural man-made laws and rebel against authority. The scandalous behavior of Byron and George Sand brought strong reactions. For the public, marriage was the kingpin on which the stability of society rested. The publicized pecadilloes of married persons, particularly those of women, threatened the values of the growing bourgeois class in England and France. The stereotype of the romanticist was that of an egotist, unstable and given to every imaginable excess—from opium to promiscuity. The evaluation was patently unfair because it failed to consider several major contributions of romanticism. Although it carried emotionality to excess, romanticism fostered the idea of a natural relationship between the sexes: protocol was abandoned and true feelings surfaced. The veneration of each individual for what he was reflected a more egalitarian spirit than had the rigid class distinctions of past eras. If each man was a beautiful work of nature, why should those born to riches be allowed to exploit those born to rags? Romanticism as a movement, therefore, was compatible with the idea of upward class mobility. The continued decline of Western aristocracy, conjoined with the rising power of the bourgeoisie, helped to foster this dream for the bourgeois, if not for the lower classes.

Further, the idealizing of the love relationship subtly introduced the concept of woman as both a worthy person and an object of desire, for a man could not truly love an inferior person. In addition, skillful women writers such as Germaine de Staël and George Sand[14] served as models of the hitherto unappreciated and latent talent of their sex. The ambivalent populace was *officially* repelled by unconventional behavior, including the extramarital affairs of the romanticists; yet they were attracted by the emotional richness of the romantics' writings and lives. This dilemma gave rise to different responses.

Literary Reactions against Romanticism

Even during the heyday of romanticism, many writers resisted its lure. Must an individual caught in the web of passion renounce his marital ties and give full expression to his desires?

Goethe struggled with this problem in a novel written in 1809, *Die Wahlverwandtschaften* (Elective Affinities). Attempting to integrate the human experience into a unified science, he likened interpersonal attraction to a chemical phenomenon in which four elements, originally joined in two pairs, are brought together. The result is that each of the formerly paired elements seeks new combinations with a member of the other pair.

In the novel, a wealthy man and his wife's niece feel a mutual attraction, as do his wife and his best friend. Goethe changed the laws of genetics to suit his needs: after the husband and his wife made love while both were under the influence of this "affinity" for nonmarital partners, the child she bore had the eyes of the husband's inamorata and the physiognomy of the wife's lover.

Although Goethe's novel superficially resembles the romantic novel of the period—with its emphasis on aristocracy, landscapes, sentimentality, and philosophical conversations—it departs from the romantic code in a significant way. Goethe, perhaps following Rousseau's *La Nouvelle Héloïse,* does not countenance a surrender to passion and the abdication of moral responsibility in the face of natural and supernatural forces. Although "marriage is a burden . . . [it] is the Alpha and Omega of civilization. It makes the savage gentle, and the gentility of the most civilized finds its highest expression in marriage."[15]

While obviously sympathetic to the husband's passion, Goethe, who three years earlier had himself legitimized his liaison of 24 years, could not permit the violators of marriage vows to escape unscathed: the novel closes on an unhappy note for all concerned, but with the marriage intact.

When French writers such as Stendhal,[16] and later Flaubert, began to dissect the romantic objectively, it was a sure sign that the main thrust of romanticism had ebbed. Stendhal noted that passion was a subjective experience that led to distortion. He had once observed that a bare bough of a tree which fell into a salt pit and lay there for some time acquired a covering of brilliant crystals when it was extracted. The shabby branch appeared at first glance to be a priceless *objet d'art*, but in reality it was worthless. He drew an analogy to the experience of love, which he called *crystallization*. Love was a fantasy, a projection of the individual's ego-ideal onto the often undeserving object. When reality intrudes, crystallization ends—and so does love.[17]

Flaubert's Madame Bovary, married to a dull country doctor, has read too much Rousseau and dreams of being a romantic heroine. But her aspirations are jarred by the reality of being seduced by a frayed roué and a simple clerk. Eventually, her love fantasies gone, she poisons herself.

Romanticism may be said to have waned some years after Queen Victoria began to rule. But there was still something greatly appealing and energetic in it. Could it not be revitalized and made to serve some useful purpose? Such an attempt was made, and I call it "Victorian love."

THE VICTORIAN ERA

The invigorating passion of the romantics had caught the fancy of the middle class, but their attack on long-cherished institutions made the romantics unacceptable to the powerful bourgeoisie. The bourgeois code emphasized personal responsibility for one's actions, respect for one's parents, and formal adherence to religion, if not its enthusiastic acceptance. But the code ignored the growing desire of youth to gain a measure of the excitement and freedom of action that the romantics seemed to personify. An increasing number of writers criticized marriages of convenience as morally wrong and doomed its participants to perpetual unhappiness. The reading public identified with Jane Eyre in Charlotte Brontë's novel when she refused the suit of St. John Rivers, whom she liked but did not love: "Can I receive from him the bridal ring, endure all forms of love and know that the spirit was quite absent? . . . No, such a martyrdom would be monstrous."[18]

The answer lay in a new alloy forged of the driving force of the romantics' sensual passion and tempered by the conservative family sentiment of the bourgeoisie. The florid phrases, energetic manner, styled unconventionality, and languid poses of the romanticist were combined in a synthetic manner with bourgeois morality. Man saw his "bestial needs" elevated not solely for the traditional purpose of procreation, but because these needs had as their object the "angel in the house," as his wife was euphemistically called. His passion was purified because it was expressed only within the confines of holy matrimony, and only when and if its delightful deified object shyly nodded assent. Lust was transformed into treacly sentimentality.

Indeed, heaven itself had never before boasted such earthy features. The poetry of Kingsley, Browning, and Rossetti implied that sex continued even in heaven. Kingsley, an energetic minister, maintained that passion would be acceptable if expressed *within marriage.* In his novel *Yeast,* however, the hero, Lancelot Smith—a thinly disguised Kingsley—bemoans the peccadilloes that led him not only to sin against God but to face the prospect of bringing a soiled corpus to the wedding bed!

> The contact of her stainless innocence . . . made him shrink from her whenever he remembered his own guilty career . . . she would cast him from her with abhorrence if she once really [knew] . . . that she would bring to him what he could never, never bring to her! . . . he would have welcomed centuries of a material hell . . . to buy back that pearl of innocence, which he had cast recklessly to be trampled under the feet of his own swinish passions![19]

Similarly, in Tennyson's *Idylls of the King,* King Arthur pays tribute to the inspirational qualities of womankind and to virginal passion, which "keep down the base in man, but teach him . . . amiable words and courtliness."[20]

The apotheosis of womankind received a great boost from one of the most popular books of the 1850s and 1860s, *The Angel in the House,* by Coventry Patmore.[21] Poets had long sung the praises of love, but had dealt with the unattainable or with premarital or adulterous themes. Patmore's work was far more meaningful to the majority of people because its story concerned married love.

Like Patmore, the poem's hero, Felix, woos and wins a minister's daughter. Felix had had 16 important girl friends before, but sought only his "predestined mate," whose name, naturally enough, is Honoria. She sets him afire with a holy passion, but makes no sensual advances that would "cheapen paradise." The model for the heroine, Patmore's wife Emily, died after a five-year illness. While Patmore missed her, he inadvertently admitted that she was more steady than heady.[22]

Felix, the hero of *The Angel in the House,* remained faithful to the memory of his dear wife after her death, but Patmore found celibacy difficult and wooed a fortyish Catholic spinster, Marianne Byles. His poetic tastes changed and, acquiring a distaste for *The Angel in the House,* he bought all the unsold copies in 1873 and burned them. His basic earthiness, which he tried to fuse with religiosity, became increasingly insistent. He began to collect erotica, including a set of the privately printed and forbidden masterpieces of the Eroticon Biblion Society. In his later years his poetry simmered with sensuality, expressing desire but never fulfillment.

John Ruskin, the noted author, critic, and artist, decried the fact that, because of financial considerations, many wise youths had to defer marriage for many years, while the selfish and foolish married early. He therefore proposed:

Permission to marry . . . should be a public testimony to the fact that the
youth or maid to whom it was given had lived, within their proper sphere,
a modest and virtuous life, and had attained such skill in their proper
handicraft, and in arts of household economy, as might give well-founded
expectations of their being able honourably to maintain and teach their
children. . . .

And every bachelor and rosiere [girl] should be entitled to claim if they
needed it, according to their position in life, a fixed income from the
State, for seven years from the day of their marriage, for the setting up of
their homes.[23]

Ruskin's fantasies were never considered seriously by the government. His
impractical emphasis on earning the right to marry and on a long wait is
understandable in the light of his own experience. He had a basic fear or dislike of
female sexuality. He refused to consummate his own marriage and at various
times told his 19-year-old bride, Effie, that he hated children, that his religious
convictions inhibited him, that he wanted to preserve her beauty, and, finally—a
reason closer to the truth—in her own words, "he had imagined women were
quite different to what he saw I was and . . . the reason why he did not make me
his wife was because he was disgusted with my person the first evening."[24] She
endured the situation for six years in a state of increasing nervousness, and then
had the marriage annulled. Shortly thereafter she married the painter John
Millais.[25] Since she bore him eight children, it is probable that the distortion lay
not in her figure but in Ruskin's expectation of what a woman was like. (Most
nude paintings at that time did not show women as possessing pubic hair.)

As for Ruskin, between nervous breakdowns, he fell in love with a ten-year-old
child he was tutoring in art, Rose LaTouche, who also suffered from a mental
disturbance. Their courtship lasted many years despite the 30-year age
difference, parental opposition, and the lovers' misconceptions of each other. As
Rose became a woman and lost her nymphal qualities, her attractiveness to
Ruskin waned, but they maintained some contact until her death in her
twenties.

In retrospect, the Victorian middle-class attempt to fuse romanticism and
conventional marriage failed. One contributing factor was the tremendous
industrial expansion during the latter part of the Victorian era. For many
middle-class men who married late, the experience of passion had ebbed even
though the language of courtship remained florid.

Victorian love also failed because it forced men and women into constant
turmoil and conflict. It was difficult enough to suppress sexual behavior, but to
excite oneself by talking constantly about passion and then forego the sensual
pleasures was doubly frustrating. The *Westminster Review* could extol the virtue
of "repressed . . . hallowed and elevated passion,"[26] but few living examples
could be found. Patmore, for example, married several ordinary women while he
authored sensual poetry. Like most Victorians unable to integrate passion and
middle-class morality, he was constantly restless. Ruskin's madness probably

stemmed, in part, from his guilt over masturbation[27] and his inability to fulfill his interest in sex with adult women. It proved most difficult to be preoccupied with sex, to sublimate, and still remain well adjusted.

The early Victorian period was characterized by a national preoccupation with avoiding the unpleasant, even the ordinary concerns of people. Train stations were made to resemble churches, as if their function thereby became more sanctified. Women, with little else to look forward to except marriage, were advised: "matrimony should be considered as an incident in life which, if it comes at all, must come without any contrivance of yours; and therefore you may safely put aside all thoughts of it until someone forces the subject upon your notice by professions of a particular interest in you."[28]

Despite such counsel, reality asserted itself, and as the evils of the factory system and their effects on the English family became slowly evident, the veil was pulled down even more tightly. An English magazine commented on Ibsen's *A Doll's House:* "Ibsen discusses evils which we know to exist but which it can serve no useful purpose to drag into the light of day."[29] The "light of day" was just as vigorously avoided with respect to the question of sex.

VICTORIAN SEXUALITY

The Victorians perceived man as a rather weak and base physical animal. Nevertheless, through thrift, self-control, and perseverance, he could rise to the pinnacle of success; that is, he might become a successful Christian businessman. Victorian gentlemen without "decent" livings did not marry. What businessman would give his daughter's hand in marriage to a man of appreciably lower economic station? A young man should work hard and acquire his fortune before thinking of marriage. The result was that he sometimes waited so long that he decided not to marry at all. Since the rate of sexual maturity during the Victorian period did not lag appreciably behind the contemporary rate, regulation of the sexual urge proved a problem.

"Muscular" Christianity

Two antithetical schools of thought emerged: "muscular Christianity" and "nature's laws." The former emphasized that true virility was the ability to control one's passions until marriage, and even then not to unleash them to a frightened spouse.

According to one of the key experts on sex, William Acton, the task should not be difficult: "With most healthy and well brought up children, no sensual idea or feeling has ever entered their heads, even in the way of speculation. I believe that such children's curiosity is seldom excited on these subjects except as the result of suggestion by persons older than themselves."[30]

In his book on male sex difficulties (he never conceded that women had such problems), Acton notes that the chief cause of sexual precocity is the tendency to overeducate the young intellectually at the expense of more valuable physical exercises. It is not the athletic boy, fond of exercise, who shows early signs of sexual desires, but the puny exotic whose intellectual education has been fostered at the expense of physical development. He quotes a "healthy" lad:

> During my university career my passions were very strong, sometimes almost uncontrollable, but I have the satisfaction of thinking that I mastered them; it was however, by great effort. I obliged myself to take violent physical exertion; I was the best oar of my year and when I felt particularly strong sexual desire, I sallied out to take more exercise. I was victorious always; and I never committed fornication; you see in what robust health I am; it was exercise that alone saved me.[31]

Other useful deterrents to sexual urges included daily bathing, fasting after 4 p.m., avoiding sexual literature, abstaining from alcoholic beverages, sleeping on a hard bed with a light covering, and religious teaching.

The perfect example of the virile, restrained gentleman was King Arthur in Tennyson's *Idylls of the King*. Though a medieval monarch, he is the prototype of the admired Victorian patriarch: powerful and masculine, combining manly reserve with passionless demeanor. Guinevere finds him cold and unreponsive, yet faultless. When he discovers her affair with Lancelot, he preaches a condescending sermon of forgiveness. Here is the Victorian superman in whom passion, revenge, and every fiery emotion have been throttled by iron resolve.

Victorian writers had many misconceptions about sexuality. For example, here is Acton's description of a youth who practices masturbation:

> The frame is stunted and weak, the muscles undeveloped, the eye is sunken and heavy, the complexion is sallow, pasty, or covered with spots of acne, the hands are damp and cold, and the skin moist. The boy shuns the society of others, creeps about alone, joins with repugnance in the amusements of his schoolfellows. He cannot look any one in the face, and becomes careless in dress and uncleanly in person. His intellect has become sluggish and enfeebled, and if his evil habits are persisted in, he may end in becoming a drivelling idiot or a peevish valetudinarian.[32]

If unchecked, masturbators could look forward to such physical disorders as a large but frequently flaccid penis, a permanently sunken visage, epilepsy, insanity, heart disorders, and tuberculosis. To prevent these dire effects, parents would occasionally enclose their sons' penises in carefully locked cages. Sometimes these contraptions had spikes on the outside to discourage carelessly wandering hands.[33]

Behind these Victorian misconceptions was a philosophy that saw sexuality as a fixed energy system. One had only so many orgasms in reserve, and those who squandered them in youth would be left "dry" as adults. The deficit perception of ejaculation is apparent in Acton's formulation: *"a lavish expenditure of the vital fluid semen* is most detrimental to a young man's constitution. . . ."[34] A Victorian term for orgasm, fittingly enough, was "to spend"—a deficit concept—rather than the modern "to come," with its more neutral connotation.

Acton was not opposed to sexuality itself. A married intellectual should engage in sex once every seven or ten days; to exceed that rate was unhealthy, because intellectual expenditure drained the nervous system as much as orgasm. The combination was deadly, and since intellectual endeavor stood higher in the hierarchy of values, copulation should be engaged in only sparingly. Persons with exceptionally strong constitutions who did not strain themselves mentally—for example, "those of country stock"—could occasionally indulge twice in a single night. To let one's urges run rampant, however, was to invite physical breakdown, as in the following case:

> Some years ago a young man called on me, complaining that he was unequal to sexual congress, and was suffering from spermatorrhoea, the result, he said, of self-abuse. He was cauterized, and I lost sight of him for some time, and when he returned he came complaining that he was scarcely able to move along. His mind had become enfeebled, there was great pain in the back, and he wished me to repeat the operation.[35]

By careful inquiry, Acton discovered that the patient had been indulging in sex three times a week for the past two years. The result of this "expenditure of vital force" was his physical deterioration. Acton favored a treatment of cauterization, which involved inserting an instrument into the urethra of the patient's penis and flushing it with a solution of nitrate of silver (the caustic). On other occasions, he recommended Spanish fly (cantharides), today regarded as a dangerous drug. Other restoratives included phosphorus to build up nervous energy as well as electricity to charge up sluggish constitutions.

There were other pernicious consequences of lubricity. Acton believed that the sins of the father were often visited on the son. In a Lamarckian vein, he warned that the children of salacious appetites themselves experienced a premature sensuality. In addition, the man who weakened the quality of his semen and of his nervous system through sexual prowess and mental overexertion might sire puny physical specimens. Nowhere was there more misconception surrounding sexuality than with respect to women. Acton noted:

> . . . the majority of women (happily for society) are not very much troubled with sexual feeling of any kind. What men are habitually, women are only exceptionally. It is too true, I admit, as the Divorce Court shows, that there are some few women who have sexual desires so strong that they surpass those of men, and shock public feeling by their consequences. I admit, of course, the existence of sexual excitement terminating even in

nymphomania, a form of insanity that those accustomed to visit lunatic asylums must be fully conversant with; but, with these sad exceptions, there can be no doubt that sexual feeling in the female is in the majority of cases in abeyance, and that it requires positive and considerable excitement to be roused at all; and even if roused (which in many instances it never can be) it is very moderate compared with that of the male. . . . Love of home, of children, and of domestic duties are the only passions they [women] feel.

. . . [A woman] submits to her husband's embraces. . . . to gratify him; and, were it not for the desire of maternity, would far rather be relieved from his attentions. No nervous or feeble young man need, therefore, be deterred from marriage by an exaggerated notion of the arduous duties required from him.[36]

Acton's views were far from unique. The Surgeon General of the United States, William Hammand, wrote that it was doubtful that women experienced the slightest degree of pleasure in even one-tenth of the occasions of sexual intercourse. In a rectorial address at the University of Basel, as late as 1891, Hermann Fehling declared that "the appearance of the sexual side in the love of a young girl is pathological."[37] Not to be outdone, the learned physician Michael Ryan, in his treatise *The Philosophy of Marriage,* warned that when desire was strong, female sterility resulted. Dr. F. W. Scanzoni noted that "immoderate coitus and excessive sexual excitation are not without importance in the etiology of cancer."[38]

Their judgments are in sharp contrast to the description by an anonymous gentleman in *My Secret Life.*[39] Its several thousand pages are filled with the orgastic shrieks of hundreds of women who seem more like lust machines than sedate ladies. If the women of *My Secret Life* were somewhat atypical, they at least serve to point out how badly the experts erred in interpreting Victorian woman's sexual behavior as representing her real potential.

The "Sex Is Healthy" School

Between the extremes of sexual fixation and rigid repression lay the "nature's law" or the "sex is healthy" school led by George R. Drysdale, who anonymously published *The Elements of Social Science.*[40] He, too, speaks of the shrunken and flabby penis and of soft, atrophied testicles, involuntary discharges of seminal fluid, hypochondriasis, depression, nervous weakness, and enfeeblement. Unlike Acton, however, *he saw the cause as the lack of regular employment of the sexual apparatus.*

A London physician agreed, offering the disturbing comment that passion existed in both sexes and that in nine out of ten cases of sickness and five out of six cases of consumption "the proximate cause was want of sexual commerce."[41]

Sex experts proved their expertise by their skill in inventing a goodly number of sexual diseases. An American physician, Charles Knowlton, claimed that the postponement of marriage until an advanced age caused sex organs to be "rendered so irritable by unnatural continency and by too much thinking as to induce a disease *Gonorrhea Dormientium,*" characterized by an emission or discharge of semen during sleep. So that women should not feel left out, he also invented a disease of chastity for them—*fluor albus.*[42] To guard against unwanted conception, he advocated a solution of sulphate of zinc, alum, perlash, or any salt that acted chemically on the semen but would not harm the woman. Another connubial guide guaranteed that an alkaline douche after intercourse never failed.[43]

Knowlton's "expert" knowledge of the woman's body left something to be desired, to say the least. According to him, women were most liable to conceive directly after the menstrual flow, and conception did not necessarily occur only if the semen entered the uterus, because the semen could also be absorbed through the vaginal walls. Women could be impregnated while already pregnant, and the resulting child would show the traits of multiple fatherhood. He further stated, unequivocally, that during female orgasm (he called it "exalted excitation") women experienced an emission quite comparable to that of men.

He found sex to be more debilitating to men than to women—the loss of one ounce of semen was equivalent to 40 ounces of blood. For those actively engaged in sex, a good diet of meat, turtles, oysters, eggs, spirits, and wine was recommended. For the unmarried, or for those with literary pursuits, he suggested a calming diet of cool vegetables and milk so that one could be continent for three or four weeks.[44]

The most conservative wing of the "physical health" school was typified by O. S. Fowler. While agreeing with his colleague Wells[45] that celibacy was inconsistent with health, he argued that platonic love was a necessary adjunct. His advice: "*Have* animal love, and exercise it; but *sanctify* it by having still *more* of *mental* cohabitation."[46]

The superiority of the established mores was seconded by the distinguished British physician, Sir James Paget. In a clash between morality and physical health, he advised, the physician should never support immoral behavior even if the patient suffered thereby.[47] Despite the outspoken views of some radicals, the repressive school was not seriously challenged until the last quarter of the nineteenth century.

Prudishness

Man's animal nature, which was considered despicable, had best be disguised. Language underwent a rapid transformation. The word "piss," for example, which appeared in the *London Times* in 1790, was dropped by the Victorian press. Women no longer became pregnant—they were "in an interesting condition." Ladies nibbled on "*bosom* of chicken." The term "miscarriage of justice," if used by a young girl brought instant admonition from her mother.[48]

It was also deemed important to muzzle "dirty" authors and to alter the writings of acknowledged great writers who had sometimes slipped into objectionable prose. Thomas Bowdler had set the style in the 1820s with *The Family Shakespeare,* which omitted "those words and expressions . . . which cannot with propriety be read aloud in a family because of their indecency or impiety."[49] For good measure, he also "bowdlerized" Gibbons and the Bible! His successors had Flaubert censured for writing "dirty" novels such as *Madame Bovary;* Baudelaire was fined for *Fleurs du Mal,* and a bookseller was imprisoned for selling Zola's *La Terre.* Even *Robinson Crusoe* did not escape the expurgator's scissors.

In *The Law and the Lady,* by Wilkie Collins, which the *Graphic* serialized in 1875, the original read: "He caught my hand in his and devoured it with kisses. His lips burnt me like fire. He twisted himself suddenly in the chair and wound his arms around my waist." It reappeared in a more sedate form: "He caught my hand in his and covered it with kisses."[50]

Art and the human body were no more successful in escaping the moralist's eye. Fig leaves, which had long and admirably suited the prudish, were no longer sufficient. Gods and goddesses, who had endured the vicissitudes of European winters with scarcely more than their epidermis to shield them, were belatedly given dresses, togas, and cloaks to hide their nakedness. To avoid the sensuousness of a physical examination by a doctor, the female patient used a doll to point out where she had pain, and the physician was allowed to touch the spot through her clothing if a chaperone was present.

Dancing, which had been almost respectable in the impersonal steps of the gavotte and minuet, again plunged into disfavor, as in Puritan days, with the emergence of a lascivious new dance—the waltz. As the author of the *Ladies Pocket Book* put it, was it possible for a lover to condone his sweetheart's being "embraced and all but reclining in the arms of another? . . . Could he bear to witness her lips . . . (which, if he has approached at all, it has been almost with a sentiment of adoration) . . . approach near enough to those of each man who may be a waltzer, if not to touch, to taint?"[51]

Repressed sexuality was displaced to such innocuous areas as furniture. Chairs were constructed with broad shoulders and wasp waists, and piano legs were so human in appearance that they were covered with skirts by embarrassed ladies, who by this ploy made them still more noticeable. Victorians approached sexuality like a dog a hot piece of meat—too hot to touch, yet too desirable to turn away from.

Woman, the Physical Being

In her dress the Victorian woman personified the conflict of an age which manifested a strong interest in sex but never wanted to admit it. By the 1860s, schizophrenic attitudes toward ladies' dress were very apparent. The skirt went down to within an inch or so of the ground, and British women began to wear drawers. But to make the waist appear small, the skirts blossomed out—held up by a wire superstructure and/or an endless series of petticoats. All this was spread out so much that it was a 50-50 proposition as to whether she could walk through an ordinary wooden gateway. In the 1880s this outlandish costume was replaced by an even more bizarre one. Formerly, a series of padded pillows had filled out the bustle, which conformed to some extent to the natural curve of the buttocks. Now, fashion dictated the use of a monolithic bustle that jutted out almost a yard at a perfect right angle to the trunk and that could carry a tea tray or at least a good-sized prayerbook!

As regards the torso, nature succumbed to fashion's call for a tiny waist and a pouting pigeon chest, an effect that was achieved by a corset with immense iron stays and strong strings. The compression of the waist to wasp-like proportions forced the redundant material and the bosom into greatly augmented hillocks that must have made it difficult for some women to see their shoes except by extending their foot sideways. It was certainly difficult to bend sufficiently to tie one's shoes. Fully enclosed in material but bulging disproportionately in the erogenous zones, the Victorian damsel resembled a pagan fertility idol.

At the opera, strangely enough, the modest Victorian matron wore a gown so décolleté as to give rise to a standard Victorian joke. Two gentlemen at the opera stare at a décolleté gown that seems to exceed all others in daring. "Did you ever in your life see such a sight?" asks one of them. "Not since I was weaned," replies his companion.

At the beach, scarcely an inch of epidermis showed; even worse, the suits were so baggy that a Bedouin could have traveled across the Sahara with an ample water supply in several of these pouches. The Gay Nineties brought such popular innovations as dainty silk undergarments, smaller bustles, and skirts that were raised off the floor a few inches. The big change in dress, however, was not to occur until the end of World War I and the age of the flapper.

Some Notorious Perverts

The period from 1789 to 1918 marked the public appearance of a considerable number of sexual aberrations. Doubtless, such aberrations had existed since the emergence of man as a species, but in the nineteenth century the globe began to shrink rapidly and news traveled faster. As a result, not only did people learn of the eccentricities of their neighbors, but some of them imitated these eccentricities and fads were created.

One of the most famous "innovators" was Donatien Alphonse François Sade, better known as the Marquis de Sade, who was born in 1740. Although once briefly jailed for cruelty to prostitutes, the situation that first brought him notoriety occurred when he picked up a young girl, Rose Keller, who had been begging in the street. On the pretext of giving her housework, he whisked her off to Arcueil, undressed her, tied her hands behind her back, whipped her until she dripped blood, and then applied a salve to her wounds. The next day he approached the terror-stricken girl with a knife in hand and reopened the wounds. She managed to tear herself free, jump out the window, and report the grisly details to the police. The Marquis explained that he had never meant to kill her, only to frighten her. Furthermore, he was interested in testing the healing properties of his new salve. Unimpressed, the officials incarcerated him, but through the efforts of his faithful but masochistic wife, he was released.

The incident which cemented his reputation as a pervert occurred in Marseilles. Accompanied by his valet, he visited a bordello and distributed chocolate sweets to the prostitutes without informing them that he was conducting one of his "scientific experiments": each bonbon contained a powerful dose of cantharides ("Spanish fly"), an alleged aphrodisiac but, more pertinent, a dangerous internal irritant to the mucosa. Within a short time the girls were rolling on the floor and screaming in agony. One girl threw herself out the window and suffered severe injuries; two others succumbed from internal hemorrhaging. Needless to say, the Marquis and his valet had not lingered to witness the results of the "experiment." A jury condemned them to death in absentia. Though eventually imprisoned, he was not executed, and after further episodes he finally ended his days in an insane asylum in 1814.[52]

Sade gave us the word "sadist," and Ritter Leopold von Sacher-Masoch bequeathed the term "masochist." He was born in Austria in 1836 and, like Sade, came from a distinguished family. While still in his twenties, a noted historian and a writer of comedies and novels, he also managed to have affairs with numerous ladies, married and unmarried. In his thirties he began to seek out women much stronger than himself. His pleasure lay in submitting himself completely to them and encouraging them to maltreat him physically. His writings became rather stereotyped, always featuring a woman in furs (he had a fetish for furs) who, with the instrument of lust (the whip), scourges her lover for their mutual orgastic satisfaction.

In "Under the Whip," we read:

> In a holy night of love he lay at her feet and besought her in supreme ecstasy: "Maltreat me, so that I may endure my happiness, be cruel to me, give me kicks and kisses."
>
> The beautiful woman . . . went across the room, stepped slowly into a splendid loose coat of red satin, richly trimmed with princely ermine, and took from her dressing table a whip, a long thong attached to a short handle, with which she was wont to punish her great mastiff.
>
> "You want it," she said, "then I will whip you."
>
> "Whip me," cried her lover, still on his knees, "I implore you!"[53]

Whipping has been a favorite means of discipline over the centuries, but Victorian literature boasts an array of female discipliners, whose names vividly convey their avocation to the reader: Lady Termagent Flaybum ("Bum"—British slang for buttocks), Lady Bumtickler, Duchess Picklerod, Lady Maria Castigate, Madame Birchini, Lady Harriet Tickletail, and the Countess of Greenbirch.[54]

A Freudian rationale for this literary preoccupation with whipping accords well with Victorian morality. The buttocks serve both as a target for aggressive acts and as an erogenous zone. Indeed, Freud names one of his psychosexual stages "anal-sadistic."[55] A young boy's fantasies may involve incestuous longing for his father, a homosexual tendency that was particularly unacceptable to Victorian thinking. By transferring such thoughts to the unconscious, the boy might fantasize being beaten by his father, which in a regressed sense represents love. In addition, by changing the sex of the whipper to that of a woman, the original longing could be further disguised—hence, there would not be the onus of a youth, or even a grown man, having homosexual fantasies.[56]

The whipper or sadist may be said to have fused his erotic and destructive instincts and directed them outward.[57] The Victorian woman is depicted as an individual whose erotic instincts have been dammed up. When this denied eroticism was joined with destructivism, the result was the excessively cruel behavior of some Victorian mothers or mother surrogates (instructoresses). There are other explanations of sadism and masochism, but the psychoanalytic theory does indicate that one consequence of the Victorian ambivalence about sex was the prevalence of fantasies in novels in which sexual pleasure could be experienced only by experiencing pain.

RELATIONSHIPS BETWEEN MEN AND WOMEN

The key to understanding the relationships between men and women lay in the legal and economic inequalities of woman's position and in the acceptance by both sexes of these inequalities. Poor women were treated as beasts of burden; wealthier ones, as pampered household pets.

The Exploited Woman

The beasts of burden worked in laundries, mills, and factories for from 12 to 16 hours a day, often without sufficient rest periods, ventilation, or sunlight. Their work was dull, their wages often half that of men. They lacked adequate safety precautions and were exposed to the risk of tuberculosis.[58]

The wives of wealthy merchants faced quite another problem. With great wealth and much free time, they were not allowed to do anything of consequence, for the bourgeois considered it a sign of prestige if women did little but command servants. In any event, the only jobs available to an unmarried educated woman was that of teacher or governess, both of which paid niggardly wages.

The emerging socialist movement supported the demands of a few vocal women for increased political rights and economic reform. They did not focus on this problem as a central issue because, according to their philosophy, when bourgeois capitalism would be overthrown, the lot of women would automatically improve.

The Church, on the other hand, was the staunch ally of the status quo. This was particularly the case in France, where the Catholic Church fought birth control, women's suffrage, and the right to more than an elementary education. [59]

For a moment, the fight for women's rights appeared to have a champion in the French Revolutionary Government. While certain gains were achieved—for example, easier divorce—the male revolutionaries resembled their nonrevolutionary brothers when it came to the question of women's rights: the attempt by women to get a "Declaration of the Rights of Women to the National Assembly" accepted in 1789 was rejected by the Rousseau-influenced Assembly, which believed that women were meant to serve in the home. [60] Women were neither enfranchised nor could they hold any high political office under the Revolutionary Government.

A more dependable champion appeared shortly thereafter—Mary Wollstonecraft (1759-1797). A vivacious, passionate woman of English birth, she had observed the French Revolution and been profoundly stirred by its reforms. In 1792 she wrote *Vindication of the Rights of Women*, [61] a bold and provocative book. Its main thesis was that passion must be subservient to reason and that, in opposition to the claims of men, the power of reason is not restricted to one sex. She also denied that men were more sexual and less moral and modest than women. Modesty, she pointed out, was a virtue, not a quality. If women were allowed to receive an education and to function in the world, they could make an enormous contribution. On the other hand, so long as they built their lives around bargain hunting, making caps and bonnets, shopping, and trimming, they could hardly expect the world or their husbands to respect them. They would remain little more than sexual objects, and when the passion had burned out, no meaningful relationship would remain.

Stendhal attacked the reasoning that women were more understanding while men had greater powers of concentration. Such reasoning reminded him of a Parisian who strolled occasionally in the gardens of Versailles and, based on his observations, concluded that the trees there came up already clipped. [62] Wollstonecraft and Stendhal were distinctly in the minority. The majority of writers, either from malice or compassion, described women as helpless and/or pitiful.

The Helpless and/or Stupid Woman

Keats exclaimed, "God! she is like a milk-white lamb that bleats for man's protection." [63] Michelet lamented the pain, languor, and weakness endured by this poor creature because of menstruation. This "cicatrization of an interior wound [resulted in the fact that] 15 or 20 days out of 28 (we may say nearly always) woman is not only an invalid, but a wounded one."[64] Comte saw femininity as a kind of prolonged infancy, and Balzac felt that women were incapable of reason or of absorbing useful knowledge from books. Hegel considered women capable of education in the lower arts but certainly not in the advanced sciences, in philosophy, or even some art forms. He explained:

> The difference between men and women is like that between animals and plants. Men correspond to animals, while women correspond to plants because their development is more placid and the principle that underlies it is the rather vague unity of feeling. When women hold the helm of government, the state is at once in jeopardy, because women regulate their actions not by the demands of universality but by arbitrary inclinations and opinions. Women are educated—who knows how?—as it were by breathing in ideas, by living rather than by acquiring knowledge. The status of manhood, on the other hand, is attained only by the stress of thought and much technical exertion.[65]

Another German philosopher, Arthur Schopenhauer, saw woman as more advanced along the phylogenetic scale. She was definitely of the order *Homo sapiens*—somewhere between a child and a full-grown man. Concerning her specific characteristics, he was less kind:

> The only business that really claims their earnest attention is love, making conquests, and everything connected with this—dress, dancing, and so on . . . the fundamental fault of the female character is that it has *no sense of justice* . . . a woman who is perfectly truthful and not given to dissimulation is perhaps an impossibility. . . . It is only the man whose intellect is clouded by his sexual impulses that could give the name of *the fair sex* to that undersized, narrow-shouldered, broad-hipped, and short-legged race. . . . The sympathies that exist between them and men are skin-deep only, and do not touch the mind or the feelings or the character.[66]

Years later, Charles Darwin was to put evolution on the side of male supremacy when he noted that, through sexual selection, "the chief distinction in the intellectual powers of the two sexes is shewn by man's attaining to a higher eminence, in whatever he takes up, than can woman. . . . Thus man has ultimately become superior to woman."[67]

The Good Woman

Another group of men did not so much emphasize woman's inferiority as her natural goodness: she was meek, gentle, soft, and submissive.[68] In *War and Peace* she was Nicholas' wife, and Nicholas could only "wonder at her spirituality and at the lofty moral world, almost beyond his reach."[69] To Ruskin, "she must be enduringly, incorruptibly good; instinctively, infallibly wise—wise, not for self-development, but for self-renunciation."[70]

All these virtues were already embodied in the stereotype of the good German housewife who rarely went out and centered all her attention on the family circle. Her three functions in life have become a stereotype: *Kinder, Küche, Kirche.*

It is noteworthy that Anton Chekhov, the brilliant Russian writer, saw through the caricature of women that men were creating. He wrote in his notebook: "To demand that the woman one loves should be pure is egotistical: to look for that in a woman which I have not got myself is not love, but worship, since one ought to love one's equal."[71]

The Moderates

A more subtle challenge to woman's emancipation came from professed liberals such as Hannah More, Charles Kingsley, Anthony Trollope, and Alfred Tennyson, all of whom advocated the elimination of legal disabilities against women. They favored a broader education for them, though not necessarily a higher one. To enfranchise women and train them for professional careers would be going too far. After all, the sexes *were* different, psychologically and physically, and there should be no talk of superiority and inferiority. Woman's station in life was in the home, and man's was in the competitive world. Let woman expand her horizons so long as it did not make her dissatisfied with her station in life.

In the typical novel by Kingsley or Trollope, this philosophy sinuously threads its way, with the heroine depicted as intelligent and well educated. Argemone, in Kingsley's novel *Yeast,* is so endowed; but in the hero, Lancelot, "she was matched, for the first time, with a man who was her own equal in intellect and knowledge, and she felt how real was that sexual difference which she had been accustomed to consider as an insolent calumny against woman. Proudly and indignantly she struggled against the conviction but in vain. Again and again she argued with him, and was vanquished."[72]

The argument that woman was inferior only because of a discriminatory environment is cleverly destroyed through this "liberal" philosophy. Even an educated woman is no match for a man. Realizing this, Argemone did what Kingsley perhaps expected of his women readers: she retreated to that area in which she was supreme and Lancelot was deficient—moral goodness.

Unquestionably, the compromise position was gratifying to many. It soothed the consciences of men who did not want to deprive women of their rights but who also relished their long-held prerogatives. By 1869, therefore, thanks to the efforts of the moderates, the basic demands of women for justice had been sacrificed on the altar of moderation, and John Stuart Mill had to state woman's case all over again in *The Subjection of Women*—as if Mary Wollstonecraft had never lived or written. His basic thesis was that "the legal subordination of one sex to the other is wrong . . . and . . . one of the chief hindrances to human improvement; and it ought to be replaced by a principle of perfect equality, admitting no power or privilege on the one side, nor disability on the other."[73]

His line of argument was similar to Wollstonecraft's: because men made the laws, they discriminated against women, with the result that the true ability of womankind was buried beneath the surface, and a false, artificial, "good" but vacuous woman had been created in its stead. His viewpoint was not new, but what was different was that it was being advanced by a man, not a woman—in fact by a man of acknowledged intellectual stature, whose ideas were taken seriously by the literate minority of the country. In addition, as a member of Parliament he had tried to push progressive legislation with respect to woman's rights. A series of property acts intended to improve the married woman's legal status were certainly influenced by his writing.

Relations between Husband and Wife

Victorian husband-wife relationships represented a triumph of role stereotype over reality. Women were gaining increasing competence in the social and educational spheres; yet they were asked to play a role which demanded complete subordination of their selves to the ego of their husbands. The roles were so clear that a random sample of European works shows the basic essentials of the stereotype. Tolstoy's *War and Peace* describes Pierre as having the right to regulate the whole family in accordance with his wishes. *A Doll's House*, by Ibsen, deals with the treatment of a woman as a child-wife by her patronizing husband. "How warm and cosy our home is, Nora," he tells her. "Here is shelter for you; here I will protect you like a hunted dove that I have saved from a hawk's claws! I will bring peace to your poor beating heart."[74] Balzac declares that a husband must be imposing and a despot, whereas "a wife is what her husband makes her."[75]

The female retort—for example, in Sara Ellis' *The Wives of England*—was feeble. She noted that husbands are selfish; but instead of blaming them, the ladies should pity them, for the selfish are never happy. In a similar vein, women are superior to men, who—unlike women—lack empathy or the ability to put themselves in other people's shoes.[76] But the fact that women were more sensitive than men was small consolation. The morally superior were trapped in a tightly prescribed code of behavior, and less virtuous men were expected to transgress against the virtuous from time to time—otherwise they would not be morally inferior!

As a sexless creature, a woman might pity her suitor or husband because he suffered from the sting of lust; she might be grateful for his affection, and she would of course love him as a duty—but she would not *respond*. In the words of Dr. Gregory, even if the woman did love her suitor, "never dis-cover to him the full extent of your love, no, not although you marry him. That sufficiently shows your preference, which is all he is entitled to know."[77]

That the ladies allowed themselves to be forced into this narrow concept of femininity is apparent from magazine comments such as those in the *Quarterly Review,* which lamented that "the more admirable the wives [i.e., the more they fitted the ideal stereotype] the more profoundly bored the husbands."[78] For such bored husbands, prostitutes proved eminently more attractive. A commentary on the times appeared in De Maupassant's story "Au bord du lit"; in it, the husband, to gain some measure of sexual happiness, pays his wife a sum of money to ensure a good sexual performance.

One of the first quantitative surveys on marital happiness was conducted by Gross Hoffinger in Germany in 1847. Of the 100 marriages surveyed, he found 48 couples distinctly unhappy, 36 indifferent to each other but managing to live together, 15 happy, and 1 "virtuous." He placed the responsibility for this sad state of affairs at the doorstep of the men, as opposed to the women, by a ratio of 2.5 to 1.[79]

In a few rare cases, drastic measures could be taken to alleviate marital unhappiness. A folkloric notion existed in England that by putting a wife up for auction (with her permission), the marital ties could be legally snapped. Accordingly, in 1832 a farmer, Joseph Thomson, put his 22-year-old wife on the block, with her consent, for the sum of 50 shillings.[80] The price proved unrealistic, so he finally disposed of her for 20 shillings and a Newfoundland dog.

The possibility that the cause of discord might be the social, political, and legal inequality of the sexes did not at first win much support. Instead, male brutality, drunkenness, or insensitivity was generally blamed. *Fraser's Magazine,* calling for kindness toward women, saw a typical marital quarrel in the following vein: "Imagine the offender a well-dressed gentlemen, tall and powerful . . . the victim shrinking from his blows—a gentle high-bred English *lady.* Great God! Does not the picture make every true man set his teeth and clench his hand?"[81]

In sum, we may say that the Victorian period did not offer a particularly distinguished model of connubial felicity despite its posturing of domestic joy. Victorians, however, no longer regarded marriage as simply an economic arrangement or a means of populating the world. In paying more attention to the quality of the relationship, it was natural that treatises on scientific matchmaking should come to be written.

SCIENTIFIC MATCHMAKING IN PRECOMPUTER DAYS

A Basic Theory

O. S. Fowler, in *Matrimony,* declares that the great prerequisite is that like should marry like. He turns to nature for support and asks, "Do lions naturally associate with sheep, or wolves with fowls, or elephants with tigers?"[82] In certain cases, however, nature, when she sees one of her subjects depart drastically from the norm, creates in that person a powerful attraction for an opposite type. Hence, the exceedingly tall man is drawn to the short, plumpish woman. The same is true with regard to temperament and mental ability. A man who has a great memory but fuzzy conceptual powers should marry a woman with great conceptual ability and a poor memory. Their children, Fowler assures us, will have both conceptual strength and a marvelous memory.

(Fowler, like a famous dancer of the succeeding century, seems not to have considered the other possibility. The ballerina, renowned for her beauty and physical grace but not her mental strength, proposed to George Bernard Shaw, famed for his wit but not his physique, that they should have a child. The offspring, she claimed, would inherit *his mind* and *her body.* Shaw thought a moment and then wondered if the child might not have *his body* and *her mind.* The child was never conceived.)

Fowler's basic principle for marital choice was: "Wherein, and as far as you are what you ought to be, marry one *like* yourself; but wherein and as far as you have any marked *excesses* or defects, marry those *unlike* yourself in these objectionable particulars."[83]

Hegel derived an opposites—attract thesis from his dialectics, according to which two opposite forces interact and result in a new, more viable entity. "The force of generation, as of mind, is all the greater, the greater the oppositions out of which it is reproduced. Familiarity, close acquaintance, the habit of common pursuits, should not precede marriage; they should come about for the first time within it."[84]

Allen maintained that "we fall in love with our moral, mental and physical complement,"[85] as did *Chamber's Journal.*[86] He believed that scientific matchmaking was hardly needed, since natural evolution automatically took care of the problem.[87] Coan agreed with the complementary thesis with regard to "natural organization," by which he meant temperament and physique. He added, however, that in terms of all that is induced (environmental influence), there must be similarity in purpose, thought, and how the couple would live. "The secret of fitness of marriage is *opposition of temperament with identity of aim.*"[88]

It was one thing to talk about complementarity and quite another to diagnose its presence. Admittedly this is a difficult problem even today, since "dating behavior" is often a poor predictor of "marital behavior." In the nineteenth century, the difficulty of assessing a potential partner's temperament must have been considerably greater. Chaperones were often present when the couple met, and physical mobility was more limited. Courtship behavior tended to be artificial and a poor index of future behavior.

Happily, a budding science obviated the necessity of interaction—phrenology. Originally formulated by Franz Joseph Gall about 1800, phrenology held that the character and talent of a person are localized in specific portions of the brain. The size and development of the regions are proportionate to the development of the particular faculty and cause corresponding changes in the skull. Based on an examination of the lumps and crevices of the scalp, an experienced phrenologist believed that he could make an accurate assessment of personality.

In the posterior region of the brain lay the areas related to marriage. As listed by Wells in *Wedlock,* they include Amativeness, Conjugality, and Inhabitiveness. The first is responsible for sexual activity, the second for "the mating propensity or instinct of permanent union,"[89] and the last for the love of home. Physiognomy also played a role: for example, a protruding jaw was a sure sign of sexual strength.

A person with a feeble-sized cerebellum (the seat of Amativeness) should never marry, and the phrenologists did not hesitate to advise certain clients to break engagements if this vital element was wanting in their fiancées. A dull and stupid person would be no bargain in marriage either, and could be detected readily enough if one took a close-fitting measure and found the vertical length of the forehead considerably shorter than the nose.

So accepted was this science that Queen Victoria had her children's heads examined by a phrenologist.[90] It was not until the twentieth century that it was conclusively demonstrated that bumps on the head were in no way related to mental or physical characteristics.

THE CLOSE OF THE VICTORIAN ERA

In the final years of the nineteenth century and at the beginning of the twentieth, the myth of impassioned but controlled gentlemen and asexual, pure women disintegrated, for prostitution and venereal disease had become rampant in Europe. Writers showed a new interest in naturalism and turned to the seamier side of life, which earlier Victorians had tried to conceal. The effects of a brutal and indifferent industrial society were vividly depicted in Gorki's *The Lower Depths* and Zola's *Nana.*

Improvements in contraceptives had a profound effect on sexual attitudes and behavior. Women began to feel a sense of freedom in sexual matters (formerly, fear of pregnancy had dampened their sexual responsiveness). It also freed them to take jobs and gradually become a vital factor in the labor force.

Growing urbanization also helped pave the way for the breakdown of the old sexual morality. One could more readily avoid community pressures, and the migration of young people from farm life removed them from the supervising eyes of parents.

The economic well-being of the middle class and the declining religious influence changed the perception of the purpose of marriage from satisfaction of familial and religious obligations to satisfaction of individual needs. It also became apparent that mistakes are made in marital choice, that needs change with time, and that it is rare to feel completely devoted to one's spouse for a lifetime; hence, divorce became more acceptable as the instrument of release from interpersonal difficulty, although it was by no means without some stigma.

These developments were also instrumental in changing male-female relationships. As is customary in such dramatic shifts, some writers at first confused the need for reform with the value of the institution of marriage itself. George Bernard Shaw stated: "I ... object to the family as a legal institution on the ground that the equality of the wife and child is destroyed by making the husband the unit of State, with powers over them which are often grossly abused."[91]

In some novels written at the close of the nineteenth century, the heroines would have nothing to do with marriage: they "married" through the act of loving and needed no artificial priestly incantation. In F. Frankfort Moore's *I Forbid the Banns,* the heroine who refused to marry the hero explains:

> "I do think that you fail to see that for us to go to the church and to ask the priest to join us in what is indeed a holy bond would be equivalent to an acknowledgement that God had not joined us in that holy bond, the moment we loved one another."
>
> "My God! Bertha, do you mean to say that we should live together as man and wife without going through any ceremony?" cried Charlton.
>
> "Ceremony?" said she after a pause during which her face was suffused with a lovely blush. "Ceremony? O Julian, I am ashamed of you!"[92]

No lovely blush appears on the face of Herminia Barton when she responds to a marriage proposal in Grant Allen's novel, *The Woman Who Did:*

> "Never!" she cried firmly, drawing away. "Oh, Alan, what can you mean by it? Don't tell me, after all I've tried to make you feel and understand, you thought I could possibly consent to *marry* you? ... I know what marriage is, from what vile slavery it has sprung; on what unseen horrors for my sister women it is reared and buttressed; by what unholy sacrifices it is sustained, and made possible."[93]

Despite this stance, Allen did not question woman's complete passivity in sexual matters, nor did he advocate that women work. He wanted them to fulfill their natural function and have children while the state supported them. In reality, most women did not oppose marriage, but they battled in the courts to make themselves more equal partners within marriage.

MARRIAGE REGULATIONS

The changes in marriage law during the Victorian era took cognizance of two key factors: the decline in the power of the Church to regulate marriage, and the gradual emancipation of woman's status in marriage. After the French Revolution, civil marriage became compulsory in France in 1792 and remained so despite the adoption of the Napoleonic Code and, later, the restoration of the monarchy. Obligatory civil marriage for all persons was adopted for Belgium in 1804, for Holland in 1811, for Italy in 1866, for Austria (in a somewhat complicated system) in 1868, for Spain in 1870, for Sweden in 1873, and for Scotland in 1878. England alone did not make civil marriage compulsory during this period, but even in England there were dramatic changes in the legal perception of woman in marriage.

The lot of the English wife before 1839 was hardly enviable, and even minor improvements were often bitterly contested. Before 1839 the wife had more economic security than the spinster, who had no place in the business and professional world. But the wife had the legal status of a minor, and everything she owned, even the clothes she wore, belonged to her husband. She could not dispose of property of any kind without his consent, even in connection with making a will. In at least one case, a husband legally willed his wife's property to his illegitimate children.

If a wife worked, she had to turn over every cent to her husband. If she found life unbearable with him and left, he could bring her back by force and lock her up in the house. If they agreed to separate, the children went with the husband if he wished, and he could deny visitation rights. Her advantages were the secondary advantages of the helpless: she was entitled to be supported, and he was liable for debts she contracted before and after their marriage. Finally, as a legal minor, she could not be sued for anything.

The seeds of reform bore their first fruit in an effort to wrest control of marriage from the clergy. In 1835 there was an attempt to toughen an already existing law prohibiting marriage with a deceased wife's sister. The following year, angered by the continued ecclesiastical influence over Parliament, liberals led by Lord John Russell achieved the passage of a law which permitted civil marriage as an alternative to religious nuptials. Initially, few took advantage of the act: in 1844, for example, the ratio of church to civil weddings was about 40 to 1.[94]

The year 1839 witnessed the beginning of a continuous assault on the legal cretinism imposed on married women. They gained the right to visit children in the custody of their estranged husbands and, in some cases, to retain children under the age of seven if the separation had not been caused by the wife's adultery. In 1840 the court was empowered to place the child wherever it believed the child would fare best.

The Property Act of 1857 gave a deserted woman the right to retain any property she gained after she had been deserted. Prior to that, an errant husband could return, claim any property of his wife's, and disappear with impunity. An effort to repeal the sanction against marriage to the sister of a deceased wife was again beaten back in 1859, when Bishop Wordsworth pleaded that such a law would scatter to the winds "all those tender relationships which import an inexpressible charm and delicate sanctity to our English homes."[95] Such laws would not find acceptance in England for another half-century.

By the decree of 1861, a woman assaulted by her husband gained the right to live apart from him and to manage her own property. The Property Act of 1870 gave a woman the right to her savings and real and personal property up to the value of £200, and the law of 1882 removed this last vestigial limitation. The Jackson case of 1891 resulted in the husband's being forbidden to capture and lock up his wife if she wished to leave him.[96] The married woman in England had come of age!

Impulsive would-be spouses received a jolt in 1856. The celebrated "Gretna Green" marriage was abolished, and a new law provided for a 21-day residency in Scotland before marriage could take place.[97] Gone forever were the nostalgic races from England to the Scottish border, with parents in hot pursuit!

In France, the husband retained more power than his English counterpart. Business-like attention was paid to the marriage contract—for example, even the wife's annual clothing allowance was stipulated in advance.[98]

There were basically three kinds of contracts: joint ownership of property, individual ownership, and a dotal arrangement.[99] Even under the individual arrangement, however, the wife could not dispose of property without her husband's consent. The dotal arrangement left the husband as administrator; and in the event that no formal contract was drawn up, the joint system was held to be in effect, with the husband still in control of his funds.

French parents still wielded considerable influence, as indicated by the reform bill of 1896. It allowed male youths of 25 years of age and women of 21 to dispense with parental consent after they had made *one* formal application for consent instead of the previous requirement of *three.* If the parents differed on the question of consent, the father's view prevailed.[100]

Until 1880, French officers could marry only a bride with a dowry, and only with the consent of the commanding officer. The bride was required to have at least two witnesses vouch for her fitness for marriage.[101] In sum, the civil government almost completely supplanted the Church in regulating marriage, and the myth of the married woman's helplessness was finally pierced by legal enactment.

MARRIAGE CUSTOMS

The French and English were supposed to have very different attitudes toward courtship and marriage. The Englishman, a romantic, harbored the traditional belief that only one girl was *the* one to marry. The French, according to a British author, followed the law of expediency: anyone might do.[102] A skeptic suggested that the French were simply more truthful—that the English married for convenience and called it love.[103]

The actual evidence for differences is scanty. The French were alleged to be more sensuous because of the separation of the sexes during childhood and adolescence.[104] But neither the British nor the French swain proposed to the girl; he had to ask the prospective father-in-law for the hand of his daughter. Always under the watchful eye of a chaperone, the couple was never left alone. A nubile British girl of means did not walk outside without a chaperone. In France, restrictions continued even after marriage; the wife could not appear anywhere socially during the first year of marriage unless escorted by her husband or relatives.

Most Englishmen believed that the French had a commercial view of marriage. The low French birthrate was attributed to their aversion to spending money on children, in accordance with the French proverb, *"Il faut faire la soupe avant de faire l 'enfant* (It is necessary to make the soup [to gain one's livelihood] before thinking of having children).[105] But another British author commented that money is *the* important factor in marriage, and no one should marry without at least two years' earnings pocketed away.[106] The British found it thoughtful to send a check as a wedding present; the French considered it bad taste.

The French tended to be more concerned with physical stock. A sure way to break up a French marriage was to spread a rumor that tuberculosis had occurred in the fiancé's or financée's family. A 45-year-old bachelor, returning from Indo-China to seek a wife, passed over his first choice because she was thin and might be susceptible to tuberculosis; he married his more robust second choice.[107]

Once engaged, the French were apt to be more expressive in affairs of love, while the British maintained a proper decorum as long as possible. A reader of a British magazine asked, "If I receive a proposal and the gentleman asks me if I love him would it be improper to answer 'a little'?"[108] Another girl, inquiring whether it was proper for lovers to kiss at parting, learned that "a lover's privileges ought to be able to bear a Mother's eye."[109]

In most of Europe, the interaction of the sexes was rigidly regulated to the exclusion of spontaneity. In the street, a lady never spoke to a man she knew unless she was positive that he had seen her. If his connections were respectable and he was well bred, he might be acknowledged. Acquaintances of less than impeccable status were to be ignored.

A young man desiring to meet a woman whom he had seen and admired might ask about her discreetly through various sources; but since he was a gentleman, he never mentioned her name. If he attended church and was seen by her on several occasions, a timid blush, a dropping of the eyes, or a half-smile might signal him to pursue the matter further by writing to her father.

Assuming that all went smoothly, most advice in books suggested a series of unobtrusive tests to reveal the fitness of the proposed partner for matrimony.

The suitor is advised to observe how the young lady acts with her parents and siblings. He is told to accompany her to a bookstore and ask her to help choose a book for his sister, and then take note of the kind of book she chooses.[110]

Few, if any, intimacies were allowed before marriage, although the first name could be used once the engagement was official. Courtship letters, perhaps because of the lack of sensual outlet, were fiery, in a rather embellished sort of way. An example of a suitable letter by a gentleman proposing marriage to his beloved is offered by the author of *Courtship As It Is and As It Ought to Be:*

> It is only by a reciprocal striving to meet each other's tastes and to cater for each other's pleasures that the rigorousness of worldly cares can be abated and . . . I call God to witness that . . . your life of love with me shall be as near an approach to the utmost height of enjoyment as my pecuniary competence, my untiring zeal and infinite affection can make it. I have seized the opportunity of the moment and have tried to condense in a few words a momentous proposition which involves the temporal well-being of two mortal creatures.[111]

Most wealthy people displayed their candidates for the matrimonial market at court, balls, and the opera. A dancing craze hit England in the Victorian period, mainly because a dance hall provided a place for many to congregate and scout for matrimonial prospects, often under mama's watchful eye.

We have centered our discussion on the courtship practices of the middle and upper classes, for the poor did not experience the time-consuming formality of visits and letter-writing. They had little leisure time, and flowery language was beyond their educational level.

The weddings of the poor were sometimes held *en masse* to save on "preacher expenses." Sometimes, the minister accidentally joined one or more of the group of 10 to 12 couples to the wrong partners, but if they all left the church in the right order, it didn't matter. The Reverend Joseph Brookes was heard to exclaim at one such multiple wedding: "Pair as you go out; you're all married; pair as you go out."[112] Housemaids were often forbidden to marry on pain of discharge, and many servants married secretly and kept on working.

By the end of the nineteenth century, the improved legal and social status of women enabled them to demand more interaction with potential spouses. Modern technology helped in this connection. Chaperones were soon outdistanced by swift ice skaters, cycling parties, and canoe rides down the river. "Spooning"—often no more than secret but sedate necking—became popular, but it was quite tepid compared to the petting orgies of the post-Kinsey period.

The whole system of economic marriage was satirized by playwrights, a sure sign of its imminent disappearance. In Oscar Wilde's *The Importance of Being Ernest,* we encounter the following dialogue:

> *Jack.* Well . . . may I propose to you now?
> *Gwendolen.* I think it would be an admirable opportunity. And to spare

you any possible disappointment, Mr. Worthing, I think it only fair to tell
you quite frankly beforehand that I am fully determined to accept you.
Jack. Gwendolen!
Gwendolen. Yes, Mr. Worthing, what have you got to say to me?
Jack. You know what I have got to say to you.
Gwendolen. Yes, but you don't say it.
Jack. Gwendolen, will you marry me? (Goes on his knees)
Gwendolen. Of course I will, darling. How long you have been about it! I
am afraid you have had very little experience in how to propose.[113]

In sum, early in the nineteenth century the custom of courtship was based
mainly on the physical attraction of the participants and on their socioeconomic
status. Since little interaction was permitted until *after* the engagement,
selection on the basis of psychological compatibility must have been rare among
the upper classes until the improvement in women's status toward the end of the
century.

ADULTERY AND PROSTITUTION

The tremendous upsurge in extramarital sex in the Victorian era stemmed from
the unrealistic roles prescribed for both husband and wife (they have been
described earlier). It is noteworthy that much of the upsurge involved
prostitution rather than adultery. According to one estimate, the equivalent of
the entire active male population of London was visiting a prostitute at least
once every three weeks.[114]

Adultery was not feasible for most men because (a) all wives were to be
treated as purely as one's own, and (b) while all wives were *really* not so pure,
the social behavior of a matron was so circumscribed, not to mention the
presence of servants, that it would have been extremely difficult for a man to be
seen with someone else's wife without incurring scandalous gossip. By the
creation of two dissociated polarized women, the "pure wife" and the "evil but
enjoyable whore," men found life bearable, albeit expensive.

Another factor in the rise in prostitution was the growth of a poorly paid class
of workers. Women earned so little that it was frequently difficult for them to
live without outside support. An attractive woman who acceded to the advances
of a foreman or a mill official could earn many times her weekly wages. Visiting
dignitaries were taken to a mill to choose their ladies for the night.

For governesses, domestics, and seamstresses, the situation was little better:
they were at the mercy of their employers. Many men who were repulsed by the
idea of going to a prostitute had no compunctions about forcing themselves on
their domestic staff. Refusal meant being fired without receiving a letter of
recommendation, which shut out future domestic employment. It is not
surprising, therefore, that an estimated 8 percent of all the women in London
were said to be prostitutes.[115]

The 2,400 pages of *My Secret Life* are replete with examples of the terrible power of money. The hero continually exploits the economic poverty of young girls of 14 or 15 who work as servants.

> I toyed with her, promised a shilling to shew me her garters—She let me and took the shilling—I'd give another shilling to feel her bum. "No, I won't." But my hand was on it almost before she'd refused—and letting it rest there, she grabbed the second shilling. "Another just to feel that little cunt I have licked tonight." "Oh no." The legs close. The bum goes back, but I feel it—"Oh no now, Surr." Her resistance ceases, my hand roves over the smooth belly, scratches in the moss, rubs the top of her split, and a shilling does it—money, omnipotent money![116]

There is often hesitation, resentment, and shame on the part of the women he has approached, but when he offers five shillings for a brief romp, it is difficult to stave him off and walk proudly in rags.

If the poor accepted prostitution to eke out a livelihood, the middle-class man sometimes avoided marriage to conserve his money and to avoid boredom. The kept woman, the *demimondaine,* became acceptable in the shadows of upright society. Mistresses were judged like racehorses or stock investments: too expensive for one owner, but capable of being maintained by a syndicate. In Paris, the early hours of the evening, from five to seven, were reserved for mistresses. Men would visit them immediately after work and then return home for supper.

The importance of an activity in a society may be judged by the number of words devoted to it in the language and by the subtlety of differentiation between these words. That Victorian whoredom was indeed an important industry is apparent from a perusal of the various species of prostitution.

At the bottom of the pack were common streetwalkers, or free-lancers, who were not registered by the police. In France these were called the *insoumises* and were quite numerous. *Grisettes,* or *midinettes,* were the laundresses, seam-stresses, shopgirls, and the like, who often had three lovers. A wealthy old man paid their expenses in return for most of their time. An attractive student might be seen on an occasional Sunday, and a fellow of one's own class was the proper suitor for marriage when finances permitted. *Gigolettes* were notorious for setting up clients for ambush while their "protectors" waited in a deserted park. *Lorettes* inhabited the vicinity of Notre-Dame de Lorette and specialized in drinking and gambling. The women of the *maisons closes* were officially registered prostitutes who enjoyed the quasi-protection of the government.[117]

The *demimonde* was a term coined by Dumas in one of his plays. It originally referred to a class of strongly sexed but honest wives who commit a fatal step because of an act of passion and henceforth live at the edge of society, between two worlds. They are no longer goodstanding members of society, yet not prostitutes. Eventually, the word came to signify a *poule de luxe*, a high class prostitute. The elite of this class were *les lionnes* (the lionesses), *les grandes cocottes,* or *les horizontales*—the upper crust of whoredom. They owned villas, kept carriages, horses, and servants, presided over literary salons, and usually had only one or two very wealthy lovers.[118]

The spread of prostitution was paralleled by a corresponding increase in illegitimate births and venereal disease.[119] By the 1850s, Vienna could list one illegitimate birth for every two legitimate ones.[120] In Berlin, by the close of the century, it was estimated that 30 percent of the men were suffering from venereal disease[121]; 66 percent of the prostitutes in Western Europe had syphilis.[122]

The public was concerned about moral laxity, but little action was taken. Michelet suggested occasional trips as a prophylaxis against adultery,[123] but the more imaginative Balzac[124] approached the domestic situation in the same way that a general surveys the battlefield on the eve of battle: every weak point must be guarded against. Hence he advises a husband not to live on the ground floor because access is too easy. On the other hand, "liberals" such as H. G. Wells, Havelock Ellis, and James Hinton maintained that adultery was not really undesirable so long as the marriage partners could talk about their experiences.

The British government took the attitude that prostitutes were here to stay, and therefore there might as well be "clean" prostitutes. The army and navy were particularly concerned, for their men were suffering the slings and arrows of outrageous spirochetes.

The concern for health thus triumphed over established morality. In 1864 the Contagious Diseases Bill provided for compulsory examination, in several towns, of any woman whom the police suspected of being a harlot. If found to be diseased, she could be detained for up to three months for hospital treatment. An 1866 amendment stipulated that prostitutes must be inspected each fortnight, as was the practice in many countries on the Continent. In 1869 the period of hospitalization was extended to nine months, and the ladies were to be given moral and religious instruction while being treated.

The bill encountered strong opposition from the women's rights movement headed by Josephine Butler. In their view, this legalized the "double standard." No chastisement or physical examination was required of *men.* The bill implied that it was all right for men to sport, but women were unfairly branded as immoral.

The outcry resulted in an investigating commission being formed in 1870. Its report called for better housing, moral training, and education for prostitutes, but the commission also projected its masculine bias in its conclusion: "No comparison is to be made between prostitutes and the men who consort with them. With the one sex, the offence is committed as a matter of gain; with the other, it is the indulgence of a natural impulse."[125] The 1869 bill was eventually repealed in 1886. Legislators no longer viewed prostitutes as a necessary evil, and morally inferior to men. Prostitution was now believed to be environmentally caused by the economic discrimination against the poor and ill-trained, and by the discrimination of men. Consequently, by the turn of the century, labor legislation, particularly for the protection of women, directed its attack toward the sources of immorality rather than on the prostitutes who were its inevitable result.

DIVORCE

The concept of marriage as a civil contract, and of divorce by mutual consent, had been operative in Prussia since the second half of the eighteenth century.

France

The dramatic shift in France from a no-divorce, ecclesiastical type of marriage to a civil marriage, easy-divorce one occurred abruptly in 1792 as a consequence of the French Revolution. Divorce was granted not only on the basis of mutual consent, but also when only one partner desired it because of incompatibility of temperament. It could also be obtained for desertion, criminal conviction, cruelty, dissoluteness, insanity, emigration, and, during the revolutionary period, for aristocracy and incivism.[126] Pessimists foresaw the end of marriage in such legislation, but they were overly pessimistic. In the first 15 months of the new law, some 6,000 divorces were granted. However, since Paris numbered 700,000 inhabitants and well over 100,000 married couples, it is apparent that the huge majority were content to remain fettered.[127]

In 1804 the law was superseded by the Napoleonic Code, which made divorce more difficult but not impossible. Legal separation short of divorce, which had been abolished, was now restored. Incompatibility of temperament no longer constituted valid grounds for divorce. Mutual consent was sufficient only if the wife and husband were more than 21 and 25 years old, respectively, if they had been married between 2 and 20 years, if they had parental approval, if the wife was not older than 45, and if both participants found life intolerable.

The older-established grounds continued to be recognized, as well as the typical one-sided approach to adultery. An adulterous wife could be divorced for one incident. A husband had to cause a scandal by his debauchery or take his mistress into the conjugal home before he could be divorced.

Restoration of the Bourbon monarchy in 1816 resulted in the abolition of divorce, which was only reinstated under the Third Republic in 1884. The Act of 1884 provided that neither mutual consent nor incompatibility was allowable as grounds for divorce. Recognized reasons included adultery, cruelty, slander, and infliction of a punishment involving corporal confinement and moral degradation. The bias favoring adultery on the part of the man was diminished, but the legislators could not bring themselves to dispense completely with masculine privileges: a divorced man could remarry at once, but a divorced woman had to wait ten months. This restriction was finally removed 23 years later. Again, there was no stampede to the divorce court: only 4,123 divorces were recorded in all of France in 1885.[128]

England

The dawn of the nineteenth century saw England still ruled, in effect, by the ecclesiastic courts on the matter of divorce. Divorce could be obtained only by a special act of Parliament after a writ of *mensa et toro* had been obtained from the spiritual court. The spiritual court recognized only adultery of an exceedingly pernicious nature or abject physical cruelty as worthy of such a writ. But the population grew restive. Many ignored the law and simply took another spouse if they were beset by marital complications; they were rarely called to account for such actions.

A case involving a poor man hauled before the court in 1845 offered Judge Maule an opportunity to issue an ironic commentary on the sad state of affairs. The defense argued that the man, accused of bigamy, actually no longer had a first wife because she had robbed and then deserted him and was now living with another man. Judge Maule gave the man the lightest possible sentence and spoke to him as follows:

> But, prisoner, you have committed a grave offense in taking the law into your own hands and marrying again. I will now tell you what you should have done. You should have brought an action into the civil court, and obtained damages, which the other side would probably have been unable to pay, and you would have had to pay your own costs—perhaps £100 or £150. You should then have gone to the ecclesiastical court and obtained a divorce *mensa et toro,* and then to the House of Lords, where having proved that these preliminaries had been complied with, you would have been enabled to marry again. The expenses might amount to £500 or £600 or £1000. You say you are a poor man, and you probably do not possess as many pence. But, prisoner, you must know that in England there is not one law for the rich and another for the poor.[129]

Finally, Parliament established a divorce court by the Act of 1857. All the old biases remained, including the preference for the male in adultery. Additionally, as a sop to the clergy, while the divorced could remarry, no Anglican clergyman could be compelled to solemnize the marriage of a divorced person, and a great number of ministers actually refused to perform such nuptials.

The succeeding decades were marked by numerous debates on whether divorce should be made easier or more difficult. Advocates of freer divorce argued that children brought up in a loveless home were worse off than those living in a divorced home. To the charge that easy divorce would crumble the institution of marriage, they retorted that, from ancient Sparta to present-day Germany, easy divorce had never destroyed marriage.[130] Besides, with increasing free choice based on true affection, and with education and culture advancing everywhere, fewer people would make a poor marriage choice and want to divorce. Thus, liberal divorce laws would hardly occasion a rush to the courts.[131]

The opponents of easy divorce argued that if divorce were easy—say, but mutual consent—one partner (usually the man) would drive the other to yield.[132] Should the husband, who better retained his vigor, be allowed to kick out the now-fading wife of his youth? The man, since he had a stronger sexual appetite, could start an endless quest for variety.[133] And what of the fatherless children and propertyless wives?[134] What is more, Scripture was against divorce.

While liberal elements saw some merit in the conservatives' argument, they maintained successfully that the solution lay not in prohibiting divorce but in changing the discriminatory laws against women. By the beginning of the twentieth century, therefore, husbands were paying alimony and child support, and women were controlling their own property.

The Latin Countries

In Spain, Portugal, and Italy, divorce did not exist. Adultery, cruelty, and desertion might result in decrees of *mensa et toro,* but marriages were only infrequently annulled. The natural consequence was that extramarital affairs served as partial compensation. In some countries such as Portugal, however, there were divorce laws for non-Catholics.

SUMMARY AND CONCLUSIONS

The collapse of the old order brought on by the French Revolution, and the sweeping change in familial life style occasioned by the Industrial Revolution, left a philosophical void that was filled by the Romantic movement. This was a revolt against the suppression of individuality, and carried within it the seeds of change for the elimination of class and sex discrimination. But it was too diffuse and unorganized a movement to contribute much immediate and practical support for democratic aspirations. Moreover, Gothic fantasies, veneration of the past, love of primeval nature, and contempt for man-made laws were not wholly compatible with the bourgeois code of respect for law and order and economic expansion. Women gained little direct benefit from the movement because the laws discriminating against them were not directly attacked by the literary output of the romanticists.

Utopian socialists such as Godwin and Owens were of little more help. Although, unlike the romanticists, they offered detailed programs for marital change, their iconoclasm irritated many. Their visionary outlook was fuzzy on such practical matters as the care of children and the resolution of families following marital breakup. They piously hoped that, under their systems, people would marry only for love and thus rarely separate.

Victorian love attempted to fuse the spirit of romanticism with the traditional conservatism of a guilt-ridden theological concept of marriage. Women were elevated to the position of earthly angels—venerated but powerless. Was such deification a result of the subtle loss of faith in organized religion and the transfer of religious feeling to more suitable objects? The increasing humanism of the period did find women a more exciting object of veneration than the omnipotent but distant patriarchal deity; and the deification of woman helped to solve the problem of what to do with a healthy, somewhat educated middle-class woman who was not allowed to work or spend much time away from her home.

Nevertheless, Victorian love proved a failure, as documented by the rise in prostitution and the resentment of women against this pale substitute for freedom.

The new technology proved to be the catalyst which shattered the subservient status of womankind. Mobility brought freedom from supervision by chaperones; mass education brought a liberalization of attitudes toward women's rights. The first laws extending the married woman's legal rights engendered a hunger for more potent legislation which would later sweep aside almost all laws subjugating women to second-class citizenship. A cry for spontaneity arose, and the old emphasis on artificiality of manners and behavior gave way to naturalism and to rebellion against all restrictions.

By the time of World War I, the old order was smashed, but the possibilities of a new status for women had not commenced in earnest. Ahead lay the roaring twenties, the time of catharsis for the restrictions of yesteryear, to be followed by the slow beginning of that desired-for status and, inevitably, a new concept of marriage.

REFERENCES

1. W. Godwin, *An Enquiry Concerning Political Justice and Its Influence on General Virtue and Happiness*, Vol. 2, p. 272.
2. A. MoraliDaninos, *Histoire des Relations Sexuelles.*
3. T. R. Malthus, *An Essay on the Principle of Population; or a View of Its Past and Present Effects on Human Happiness*, p. 505.
4. R. H. Harvey, *Robert Owen*, p. 210.
5. R. Owen, *The Marriage System of the New Moral World.*
6. B. D. Grebanier, S. Middlebrook, S. Thompson, and W. Watt, *English Literature and Its Backgrounds.*
7. J. Barzun, *Classic, Romantic and Modern.*
8. R. Huch, *Romantic Marriage.*
9. J. W. von Goethe, "The sorrows of young Werther."

10. Ibid., p. 183.
11. Ibid., p. 181.
12. P. B. Shelley, *Complete Poetical Works*, p. 797.
13. G. Sand, "Letters to Alfred de Musset," p. 499. (Emphasis added.)
14. A. Deguise, "Four French women: from emancipation to liberation."
15. J. W. von Goethe, *Elective Affinities*, p. 80.
16. J. Ortega y Gasset, *On Love*, p. 6.
17. M. H. Beyle (Stendahl), *On Love*, p. 6.
18. C. Brontë, *Jane Eyre*, p. 408.
19. C. Kingsley, *Yeast*, pp. 146-147.
20. A. Tennyson, *Idylls of the King*, p. 379.
21. C. Patmore, *Poems*.
22. D. Patmore, *The Life and Times of Coventry Patmore*.
23. J. Ruskin, *Complete Works*, Vol. 17, p. 420.
24. M. Lutyens, *Effie in Venice*, p. 20.
25. J. Evans, *John Ruskin*.
26. W. R. Greg, *Prostitution*, p. 480.
27. R. Pearsall, *The Worm in the Bud*.
28. E. S. Turner, *A History of Courting*, p. 175.
29. C. W. Cunnington, *Feminine Attitudes in the Nineteenth Century*, p. 259.
30. W. Acton, *The Functions and Disorders of the Reproductive Organs*, p. 2.
31. Ibid., p. 27.
32. Ibid., pp. 15–16.
33. A. Moralli-Daninos, op. cit.
34. W. Acton, op. cit., p. 69.
35. Ibid., p. 191.
36. Ibid., p. 69.
37. H. Ellis, "The sexual impulse in women," p. 195.
38. R. Pearsall, op. cit., p. 204.
39. My Secret Life.
40. G. R. Drysdale, *The Elements of Social Science*.
41. *Every Woman's Book; or, What is Love?*, p. 14.
42. C. Knowlton, *Fruits of Philosophy*, p. 10.
43. Intercidona, *The Connubial Guide; or, Married People's Best Friend*.
44. C. Knowlton, op. cit.
45. S. R. Wells, *Wedlock*.
46. O. S. Fowler, *Matrimony*, p. 459.
47. P. T. Cominos, "Late Victorian sexual respectability and the social system."
48. C. W. Cunnington, op. cit., p. 291.
49. *Encyclopedia Britannica*, 1964, Vol. 3, p. 30.
50. N. Epton, *Love and the English*, p. 305.
51. E. S. Turner, op. cit., p. 144.
52. N. Epton, *Love and the French*.
53. R. Lewinsohn, *A History of Sexual Customs*, p. 306.
54. S. Marcus, *The Other Victorians*.
55. P. Mullahy, *Oedipus, Myth and Complex*.
56. S. Freud, "A child is being beaten."
57. S. Freud, "Beyond the pleasure principle."

58. W. F. Neff, "Through the eyes of Victorian reformers," p. 167.
59. A. Michel and C. Texier, *La Condition de la Française d' Aujourd'hui.*
60. B. J. Stern, "The changing status of women."
61. M. Wollstonecraft, *The Rights of Women.*
62. M. Beyle, op. cit.
63. M. M. Hunt, *The Natural History of Love,* p. 313.
64. A. Michelet, *Love,* p. 48.
65. G. W. F. Hegel, *The Philosophy of Right,* p. 134.
66. A. Schopenhauer, "Of women," pp. 225, 227, 229, 230.
67. C. Darwin, *The Descent of Man and Selection in Relation to Sex,* Vol. 2, pp. 352, 354.
68. J. Clowers, *The Golden Wedding Ring.*
69. L. Tolstoy, *War and Peace,* p. 670.
70. J. Ruskin, *Complete Works,* Vol. 18, p. 123.
71. A. Chekhov, *Notebook of Anton Chekhov,* p. 20.
72. C. Kingsley, op. cit., pp. 143–144.
73. J. S. Mill, *The Subjection of Women,* p. 219.
74. H. Ibsen, *Plays of Henrik Ibsen,* p. 159.
75. H. Balzac, *The Physiology of Marriage,* p. 193.
76. S. Ellis, *The Wives of England.*
77. J. Gregory, "Marks of an honorable lover—a father's advice to his daughters," p. 406.
78. M. Caird, *Marriage,* p. 197.
79. R. Lewinsohn, op. cit.
80. J. Braddock, *The Bridal Bed,* p. 156.
81. F. P. C., "Celibacy vs. marriage," p. 234.
82. O. S. Fowler, op. cit., p. 280.
83. Ibid., p. 295.
84. G. W. F. Hegel, op. cit., p. 134.
85. G. Allen, "Falling in love," p. 454.
86. "The choice matrimonial."
87. "Sir George Campbell on scientific marriage-making."
88. T. M. Coan, "To marry or not to marry," p. 500.
89. S. R. Wells, op. cit., p. 11.
90. E. S. Turner, op. cit.
91. G. B. Shaw, *Collected Letters of Bernard Shaw,* 1874–1907, p. 278.
92. F. F. Moore, "I forbid the banns," p. 108.
93. G. Allen, *The Woman Who Did,* pp. 38, 41–42.
94. J. Braddock, op. cit., p. 170.
95. D. Stenton, *The English Woman in History,* p. 337.
96. C. Rover, *Love, Morals and the Feminists.*
97. F. G. Cook, "The marriage celebration in Europe."
98. E. Zola, *Modern Marriage.*
99. T. Bentzon, *Marriage in France.*
100. E. Westermarck, *The History of Human Marriage.*
101. M. Betham-Edwards, "French brides and bridegrooms."
102. "National views on marriage."
103. "French and English theories of marriage."

104. "Courtship and marriage in France."
105. "French marriage."
106. "Marriage versus celibacy."
107. F. M. Thompson, "Spring days in Paris."
108. C. W. Cunnington, op. cit., p. 184.
109. Ibid., p. 185.
110. E. S. Turner, op. cit.
111. Ibid., pp. 158–159.
112. J. Braddock, op. cit., p. 112.
113. O. Wilde, "The importance of being Ernest," p. 40.
114. G. R. Taylor, *The Angel-Makers.*
115. R. Pearsall, op. cit.
116. *My Secret Life,* p. 1615.
117. N. Epton, op. cit.
118. R. Lewinsohn, op. cit.
119. O. R. McGregor, *Divorce in England: A Centenary Study.*
120. R. Lewinsohn, op. cit.
121. F. Müller-Lyer, *The Family.*
122. R. Pearsall, op. cit., p. 229.
123. M. J. Michelet, op. cit.
124. H. Balzac, op. cit.
125. P. Thomson, *The Victorian Heroine,* p. 149.
126. W. D. Camp, *Marriage and the Family in France since the Revolution.*
127. R. Lewinsohn, op. cit.
128. W. D. Camp, op. cit.
129. G. E. Howard, *A History of Matrimonial Institutions,* Vol. 3, pp. 108–109.
130. M. D. Conway, Debate on Mr. Moncure D. Conway's paper "On marriage."
131. E. R. Chapman, "Marriage rejection and marriage reform."
132. C. S. Jones, "The assault on marriage."
133. "Marriage, is it a failure?"
134. E. Johnston, "Marriage or free love."

13

Havelock Ellis and Sigmund Freud: Philosophers of Sex

As the nineteenth century drew to a close, Victorian prudishness declined, and the emerging interest in sexual knowledge generated a new profession—the sexologist. Two sex researchers achieved world fame: Havelock Ellis and Sigmund Freud. Their very different life styles and personalities led them to favor certain views at the expense of other options. I shall attempt to show that their findings stemmed, in part, from unresolved personal conflicts (in the case of Ellis) or the blinders which Viennese culture placed on otherwise acute observational powers (in the case of Freud).

HAVELOCK ELLIS (1859-1939)

Havelock Ellis began writing about sex in the 1890s, and was a prolific writer throughout his life. At first his books were banned, but society eventually caught up with his views, and by the time of his death he was "the Master" to whom disciples flocked from all over the world.

Personal Life

Ellis' father was a sea captain, away much of the time, and his mother had to be both father and mother. A sensitive, shy child with unusual tastes, Havelock developed a fetish for urination which was apparently transmitted by his mother. She would urinate on her hand—"it was good for the skin"—and occasionally she urinated in the park as Havelock stood guard. To him, urination became a beautiful act, and he extended his appreciation to such symbols of urination as fountains.

As an adolescent, when Ellis observed that his ability to project his urine was feeble compared to that of the average man, he became convinced that there was a direct correlation between vesical power and sexual potency. He seems to have avoided masturbation, but experienced nocturnal emissions from time to time.

282

After reading George Drysdale's *Elements of Social Science,* he noted that "its tone ... was thoroughly uncongenial to me,"[1] and probably concluded that he suffered from the dread disease of those who, according to the author, fail to use their genitories in sexual intercourse—*spermatorrea.* The inevitable consequence, according to Drysdale, was weakness, exhaustion of the brain, memory loss, idiocy, insanity, loss of speech, and death by a kind of apoplexy.[2]

These misconceptions had an unsalutary effect on the shy adolescent. Believing that he was undersexed and possibly wasting away, he rejected physical involvements but became preoccupied with the subject of sex. Freud pointed out many years later that such an intense preoccupation could only have come from an abnormal adjustment. When Ellis learned of Freud's view through his friendship with Freud's didactic patient, Joseph Wortis, he vigorously denied the allegation.[3] But we shall shortly see that Freud was quite accurate in his assessment.

Sexual aberrations had a peculiar fascination for young Ellis. He became involved with followers of James Hinton, who had founded a new religion that advocated polygyny and other innovations. Ellis was probably attracted to the philosophy because sexuality remained a perpetually unsolved problem for him and because Hinton also urged that one should try not to be self-righteous but self-less. "Man," according to Hinton, "is condemned to pleasure; but that does not mean selfishness."[4] It should be man's goal to do pleasant things that are also serviceable to others. In fact, Hinton cheerfully serviced as many attractive woman parishioners as he could.

To Ellis, Hinton's philosophy was more than a rationalization for sex. It fused a vision of life and beauty with a belief in scientific, earthy principles. It was the synthesis he had hoped to obtain from orthodox religion, but had not succeeded in doing.

At one of the meetings of the Hinton group, he met a passionate young novelist, Olive Schreiner. She had had a disastrous affair and was trying to find a man who could both satisfy her sexually and offer intellectual dominance or, at least, equality. In Ellis she found only the latter. He was handsome, with a fine beard, but there was something rather effeminate in his thin, squeaky voice. Even more noteworthy was his passivity, his masochism, and his willingness to endure unfulfilled passion. He never attempted to kiss Olive, and she finally took his head in her hands and kissed him. He responded by giving her his diary to read—his most meaningful way of telling her how much she meant to him. Olive and he spent time alone, presumably engaging in mild sexual petting. Ellis noted:

> I was not fitted to play the part in such a relationship which her elementary, primitive nature craved. I on my side recognized that she realized this and knew that the thought of marriage between us, which for one brief instant floated before my eyes, must be put aside. . . . But the relationship of affectionate friendship which was really established meant more for both of us, and was really even more intimate, than is often the relationship between those who technically and ordinarily are lovers.[5]

Later, he met Edith Lees at the Hinton fellowship. At first they were not attracted to each other, but then they found that their outlook on modern relationships between the sexes was highly compatible. They both believed that marriage should be between equal partners. The woman must not be economically dependent on the man—she should have her own income. There should be no male dominance, no jealousy or secrecy, and no emotional demands. This last requirement was mainly advocated by Ellis, a reflection of his detachment from any woman who might make sexual and emotional demands that would interfere with his work.

Ellis was not passionately involved with Lees. His main goal was a spiritual comradeship, and any sexual intimacy would be considered a bonus. On the other hand, she had been terrified by men of action, as represented by her tyrannical father. She found Ellis' passivity refreshing and admired his gentleness. Ellis rationalized his desire not to have children by claiming that a doctor had said that Edith's temperament was unsuited to maternity.

They spent a delightful honeymoon in Paris visiting art galleries, theaters, and especially concerts, which Havelock said gave them their happiest moments. Despite this initial success, the couple failed to have much of a sexual relationship, what with music rather than sex being the sacrament of their union. He proved inadequate as a lover, and "she found the hygiene of birth control messy and inhibiting."[6]

Ellis had proposed that they live apart for six months each year. Edith found the separations painful, but Ellis found her presence too cloying. Emotionally deprived, and perhaps sexually frustrated, she took a lover who would not threaten Ellis' pride—a woman. Ellis countenanced the relationship, forbidding himself any jealousy because such an emotion would have been contrary to his philosophy that every natural act was beautiful. Nevertheless, his wife's move threatened the vestiges of his manhood. His never-failing rationalization took over, therefore, and he diagnosed Edith as a congenital sexual invert. This was nothing to be ashamed of: many of his closest friends were "inverts." Edith might be an anomaly, but she was not abnormal.

The evidence indicates that Edith was a manic-depressive who had had a breakdown before her marriage and desperately needed Havelock to maintain her emotional balance. When he failed her, a new relationship provided some semblance of stability.

Another difficulty developed when Ellis wrote her that he had kissed, rather chastely, a young lady of 24, Amy, the daughter of a friend. He could not understand why Edith blew up over the incident. Having classified her as a *genotypical* homosexual, he failed to understand that she considered herself a *phenotypical* homosexual who had turned to lesbianism only out of concern for her sexually crippled husband. The cripple was now showing signs of moving his limbs in a healthy fashion. In her view, a kiss from Ellis was the equivalent of rape by a red-blooded man!

They tried to justify their positions in their writings. In *Sexual Inversion,*

A painting by Rubens—"Rubens and His First Wife," ca. 1609.

Havelock described Edith (under a pseudonym) in one of the cases. Edith called his scientific writing on sex mere trash; to her, Ellis was only a poet and a philosopher. She proceeded to defend her life in the novel *Kit's Woman,* in which a normal woman with a paralyzed husband is driven into the arms of another man, but eventually returns to the husband because of his deep spirituality. Havelock was undismayed by the book; he believed that passion triumphed over sex, and he acknowledged his sexual inadequacies. But he did find some sort of sexual rapport with Amy and with several others, as well as an emotionally involved, albeit fatiguing, relationship with Edith.

Ellis seems to have experienced some sexual difficulty because of premature ejaculation.[7] Apparently he satisfied his partners by caresses and cunnilingus.[8] His partners were also willing to indulge his enjoyment of watching them urinate while standing (he called it urolagnia, and it was a truly esthetic experience for him).[9]

After Edith's death in 1916, Ellis became involved with Françoise, a French woman who had been translating some work for her. After lying in his arms during her first visit—without sexual involvement—Françoise went to the adjoining room to use the chamber pot and was startled when Havelock accompanied her. Kneeling, he ministered to her as she gently stroked his head.[10] Françoise, who had no sexual gratification from two previous husbands, now experienced orgasm from his hands and kisses. Eventually, they engaged in sexual intercourse, and, though nearing 60, Ellis discovered that he was not impotent after all.

The liaison prospered except for one incident involving an acquaintance of Ellis'—the author Hugh De Selincourt, who boasted that he could withhold ejaculation indefinitely until his partner had achieved orgasm. Interestingly enough, this alleged power had not sufficed to keep his wife from adultery. Determined to prove his virility, De Selincourt pressed Ellis to introduce him to Françoise and then wrote her to request a visit. When she refused and wrote Ellis about it, the latter insisted that his two comrades be good freinds (oblivious to the threat posed by the younger man, Ellis was at his winter retreat on the Cornish coast).

De Selincourt and Françoise met to discuss collaboration on a book she had in mind to honor the Master. But the book did not progress as readily as their relationship. It is unfair to think of De Selincourt as a seducer, for he, Ellis, and Françoise had never espoused the traditional code of ethics. Rather, in uniting their bodies in sensual bliss, he and Françoise were simply carrying out in practice the tenets of the Master, who had preached that sex was a beautiful thing when engaged in by two beautiful beings. It was, in the words of Calder-Marshall, one of Ellis' biographers, "a transcendental affirmation of faith."

Be that as it may, Ellis reacted furiously to the affair, assuming that he had been replaced in Françoise's affections by the younger man. She was hurt by the reaction of the man she worshiped. After all, Ellis had told her that he would have "dear lady friends" despite their attachment. Should she not have a "dear man friend," especially one who tried to make the Master's philosophy his own way of life?

At last they reconciled, each giving up all outside attachments, with Ellis acknowledging that there was some jealousy on his part—a slight contradiction between his practice and his philosophy—and they lived quietly until his death.

Ellis' Views on Sex and Marriage

Ellis, in the words of Freud, was a man of culture rather than a scientist. As to Ellis' book on dreams, Freud noted that although it contained some good ideas, Ellis simply had no talent for psychology. This appraisal, while basically valid, does not negate Ellis' contribution. He was a popularizer of the new freedom in sexual matters and not a theoretician, and despite his timidity in interpersonal affairs, he was courageous in expressing his thoughts on sexual behavior.

He considered homosexuals as genetically different from the average person, but not as perverts. They should be treated with respect and given the opportunity to lead productive lives. It was ridiculous that the divorce laws in England bound two individuals together permanently because at one point in their lives they had wanted to live together. Love cannot last forever, and adultery is not a crime. Rather, marriage should be a private arrangement between two individuals and no one else's business.[11] It is a fact of conduct, not a contract.

In its idealistic sense, marriage is an erotic companionship whose spirituality transcends any simple sexual act. The truly married couple confide in each other when they engage in affairs with others and rejoice and sympathize in the partner's joy if the new relationship brings extra meaning into their lives. Deception and lies are to be avoided at all cost; and naturalness and honesty, even if they break with traditional mores, should be the new high priestesses of marriage. The marriage of the future will recognize all these things. The state will let people alone and intervene only when the couple have children, seeing to it that they have every benefit and protection, and that the parents fulfill all responsibilities toward them.[12]

If society has not adopted these ideas wholeheartedly, it is at least closer to them today than it was when Ellis advocated them. In expressing the belief that marriage is a private affair except when children are involved, he is in tune with today's most advanced views.

In some respects, Ellis was naive and unrealistic. His belief that husband and wife would confide their extramarital affairs to each other and rejoice in each other's new experiences does not seem to enjoy much approval, though currently a small minority of couples have adopted the open marriage he envisioned.

His use of hyperbole regarding the beauty of sex and passion apart from consummation appears to be a projection of his own sexual problems. Courtship and passion can of course be beautiful, but his excessive emphasis on them sounds very much like that of a man who minimizes the actual sex act because that is the part with which he is least comfortable.

SIGMUND FREUD (1856-1939)

The son of a middle-aged wool merchant and his young second wife, Sigmund Freud became a physician as much by elimination as by interest. For a nineteenth-century Viennese Jew, politics and a university career were out of the question, and Freud had no interest in business matters. Essentially, his choice lay between law and medicine, and medicine won out because it dealt more with the human element. Had he lived today, Freud would probably have been a clinical psychologist rather than a psychiatrist, for he believed that the study of medicine interfered with the study of psychoanalysis.

Prior to the publication of Jones' biography, Freud had the reputation of a surly, cigar-smoking cynic with little human emotion. As revealed in Jones' book, however, Freud's courtship of Martha Bernays shows him to have been a rather passionate lover.

In a letter to Martha in 1884, in response to news that she did not look well, he wrote, "Woe to you my Princess, when I come. I will kiss you quite red and feed you till you are plump. And if you are froward, you shall see who is the stronger, a gentle little girl who doesn't eat enough or a big wild man *who has cocaine* in his body.*"[1][3] In all, Freud wrote over 900 letters to her during their more than four-year engagement, which was necessitated by his lack of funds and his extensive schooling.

In addition to romantic passion, Freud exhibited both intense jealousy with regard to Martha and a compulsive need for perfection, which masked his need for dominance in interpersonal relationships. He forced her to give up contact with a young man who loved her although she did not love him. He also demanded that she criticize her mother and brother and withdraw her affection from them because he, somewhat unrealistically, perceived them as his enemies. When she failed to do this, Freud was distressed; he felt, rather immaturely, that she did not truly love him. Apparently, Freud wanted to swallow Martha, to make her an extension of his own ego; but he failed because, despite her strong attachment to Freud, Martha had a mind of her own and would not reject her family.

When Freud's theories first came to public attention, he was labeled a sex fiend. It would have been more accurate to characterize him as traditional, naive with respect to women, and rather prudish.

---

*Freud took cocaine as a stimulant for the brain and body. He was apparently unaware that it readily causes addiction, and that its stimulating action is followed by depressive effects on the central nervous system and may lead to convulsions and/or death.

Freud considered John Stuart Mill's pro-feminist position regarding women naive and ethereal in blurring the classic distinctions between the sexes:

> It is really a stillborn thought to send women into the struggle for existence exactly as men. If, for instance, I imagined my gentle sweet girl as a competitor it would only end in my telling her, as I did seventeen months ago, that I am fond of her and that I implore her to withdraw from the strife into the calm uncompetitive activity of my home. . . . Nature has determined woman's destiny through beauty, charm, and sweetness. Law and custom have much to give women that has been withheld from them, but the position of women will surely be what it is: in youth an adored darling and in mature years a loved wife.[14]

Toward the end of their engagement, Martha announced that she sometimes had "bad thoughts" which she had to suppress. Freud was genuinely astonished. He had naively imagined her to be so pure that she could not possibly have an evil thought. Witness, too, his prudishness as he reminisced, during his engagement, about a walk 18 months earlier when Martha had had to stop repeatedly to pull up her stockings. He confessed to her that "it is bold of me to mention it, but I hope you don't mind."[15] Later, he forbade her to visit a married friend who, as Martha put it, "had married before her wedding." He even forbade his fiancée to skate: it would necessitate her holding another man's hand. Only after he learned that it was possible for a woman to skate unattended did he grant her permission to do so.

As a married man he began, in his usual compulsive manner, to educate Martha according to his standards, but he could not arouse a passion in her for philosophy, science, or learning English. As time went on, his interest in her waned in proportion to his growing investment in his theories and writing. In his letters to his friend, Fliess, he mentions his ideas, hopes, successes, and disappointments, but rarely refers to his wife except for the conventional greetings. His regular schedule and his use of vacation time confirm his lack of involvement in family life.

Freud received patients from eight in the morning until one in the afternoon. Then came a meal with the family. He loved to collect ancient sculpture and often brought his latest piece to the table to keep him company. After lunch, Freud would take his constitutional, and from 3 to 9 or 10 p.m., would occupy himself with consultation and patients. After the evening meal, he walked with one or more members of the family and then returned to work on manuscripts and correspondence. He never went to bed before 1 a.m.

On Sunday, a day of rest, Freud visited his mother, accompanied by those of his family who wished to come. Afternoons, when his wife received at home, he dropped in for a few minutes if it was someone who interested him. In his later years, Sunday afternoons were reserved for his psychoanalytic cronies. Any remaining time was devoted to writing or, on some occasions, to taking his children to the art galleries of Vienna.

Freud obviously had little interaction with his family. He was neither a severe, authoritarian parent and husband, nor was he completely disinterested. He simply put his work first, and so extensive was this commitment that almost no time was left for his family. One might think that with so little family interaction during the work year, they would all spend a vacation together. But this was not the case. In the summer Freud traveled for many weeks. He visited Italy and other parts of Europe accompanied by his psychoanalytic friends and sometimes by his sister-in-law, but very rarely by his wife and family.

There is no dearth of explanations for this behavior. Freud's biographer, Jones, reports that Mrs. Freud was a poor traveler, unable to keep up with her husband's nervous pace. She had her home and six children to care for; and despite their servants, the family was poor. In defense of his master, Jones notes that Freud often sent postcards to his family to say how much he missed them although he was enjoying himself immensely:

> I am desperately sorry I can't manage to let all of you also see the beautiful things here. To be able to enjoy such things in a company of seven or nine, or even of three, I should have been, not a psychiatrist and allegedly the founder of a new direction in psychology, but a manufacturer of something generally useful like toilet paper, matches or boot-buttons. It is too late to learn that now, so I have to go on enjoying myself egoistically, but with a deep sense of regret.[16]

These statements seem to be a rationalization to disguise Freud's relative uninvolvement with his wife. Note how he "compliments" her in a letter to an in-law: "I have really got along very well with my wife. I am thankful to her above all for her many noble qualities, for the children who have turned out so well, and for the fact that she has neither been very abnormal *nor very often ill.*"[17]

It is clear that the world-renowned expert on sex and love may well have drawn upon his own experiences for his theorizing. His objective, cold appraisal of relations between the sexes parallels the affective quality of his own family experience.

According to Jones, Freud's sex drive was considerably below average. Judging from his stamina and energy level, it seems probable that Freud was genetically capable of strong sexual performance but that, for the most part, his interest in his work diverted this energy into other areas. By the age of 41 he had written his friend Fliess: "sexual excitation is of no more use to a person like me."[18] On another occasion, in his forties, he was surprised to find himself physically attracted to a young lady, and at age 56 he remarked wryly, "Today, naturally, the libido of the old man exhausted itself by distributing money."[19]

In his conduct with ladies, even apart from his therapy sessions, he was no less asexual. The Countess Anna de Noailles, a leading poet of France, was quite disappointed with the noted sex expert's behavior. She remarked, "Surely, he never wrote his 'sexy' books. What a terrible man! I am sure *he* has never been unfaithful to his wife. It's quite abnormal and scandalous."[20]

Even if he was not a Lothario or an Adonis, Freud did possess outstanding courage, and he was convinced that he was on the right road in the pursuit of truth. For ten years he labored alone in his quest to make man rational through a proper understanding of the irrational forces that motivated him. Gradually, the impact of his writings and of his personality gained him a band of disciples and some degree of public acceptance, although to the vast majority he remained a sex pervert and a crackpot. He saw himself, as is apparent in his writings, as a Moses who led the fight for clarity but was not destined to see the Promised Land in his lifetime. For the last 16 years of his life he continued to lead his followers and to write, despite the most excruciating pain caused by cancer of the jaw. Sections of bone were removed, scar tissue, more scar tissue, a prosthesis inserted, another one, and on and on every few months during those terrible years. In his eighty-fourth year, on the eve of World War II, he succumbed.

FREUD'S VIEWS ON LOVE, SEX, AND MARRIAGE

Freud was basically a hedonist: the goal of behavior was the pursuit of pleasurable excitement and the avoidance of pain. Human interaction occurs not because there is a love of mankind or even a desire for contact *qua* contact. It occurs only because relations with other humans are usually the only way in which painful tensions can be reduced to manageable levels. Man is a social animal based on biological need rather than on social choice.

Further, man is often at the mercy of instinctual needs that are irrational in nature. These drives are often wholly unconscious or are visible to the conscious mind only in a distorted form. Man imagines that he rules by utilizing his rational faculties; actually, he mainly rationalizes. Still, in a utopian society, reason would prevail and there would exist "a community of men who had subordinated their instinctual life to the dictatorship of reason."[21]

Freud saw his task as uncovering and describing these basic unconscious forces which, when known, could be controlled and harnessed for human betterment. The forces to be uncovered—for example, the notion of infantile sexuality—clashed with Victorian sensibility and contradicted the middle-class value system. Freud did not believe, as Acton did, that the child was naturally free from sexual feeling. Rather, sexual urges, though not necessarily genital ones, were present from birth and passed through various stages prior to the final adult stage of sexuality.

Falling in Love

Freud considered what was generally called "love" to be a behavioral manifestation of a force or energy he termed "the libido." This energy can be diverted into an innumerable number of channels. When the self is taken as the object of love, we have reference to narcissism. In infancy, however, the boundaries between the self and the other are rather fuzzy. The act of a mother feeding the child is apt to be interpreted by the latter as an extension of the self. In any event, a certain amount of energy or libido comes to be fixed on the nurturing loved object. Freud's term for this type of leaning-against or dependent love is "anaclitic," as opposed to "narcissism" in which the self is the object of love.

What happens when we fall in love? It is essentially an attempt at sexual satisfaction and something more. A certain amount of libido is invested in the love object in the hope of achieving sexual aims. Yet, because of conditioning, a part of the libido is deflected from a direct sexual goal and becomes aim-inhibited. The individual is loved apart from the sexual satisfaction he may provide. The love object is in fact often idealized far above the worth of ordinary man. Indeed, the depth of "love" is often measured by the extent of the aim-inhibited expression rather than by simple direct sexual expression.

If a person is essentially fixated on himself as a love object, he will choose a spouse who has one or more of the following qualities: (a) resembles himself psychologically, (b) resembles what he once was, (c) resembles what he would like to be, and (d) resembles someone who was once part of himself. If he is the anaclitic type, the choice will mimic the former relationship with the parent in that a man may seek a woman who tends him, whereas a woman seeks a protective father-figure.

Typically, according to Freud, men manifest anaclitic object-love with marked sexual overestimation, whereas women are narcissistic; but both kinds of choices are open to either sex. In actuality, all love is narcissistic at the core. The individual employing the anaclitic mode invests part of his libido in the love object and thus lowers his own self-regard in overidealizing the beloved. He who loves has forfeited part of his narcissism.[22] This narcissism, however, may be replaced if the beloved loves the lover in return. The return of the libido to the self represents a restoration of love. Genuinely happy love, therefore, represents the happy state of the infant who cannot distinguish between himself and the breast that feeds him, since his ego is not developed. In successful adult love, too, the object-libido and ego-libido have no line of demarcation. Hence, in its essentials, all love is basically self-love. It varies only in whether the love for the self is unabashed (narcissistic) or whether it requires a more circuitous route of having a narcissistically valued object restore the self-love of the individual by granting its own love (anaclitic).

Is Sexual Gratification Necessary?

The question arises, however, as to whether the complete gratification of instinctual desires is in the best interests of the individual and of society. Freud seemed ambivalent on this point. He held that when sexual instincts are inhibited in their aim, that is, diverted from the goal of sexual release, the energy is still available for more fruitful pursuits from the point of view of society, such as painting, music, and building bridges. Moreover, since the aims are inhibited, they are never completely satisfied; hence, there is no reduction in libido and the sublimated efforts continue unabated. Contrariwise, when the aims are uninhibited, the libido supply is depleted by sexual gratification and must await the passage of time before being renewed.[23]

Nevertheless, although the repression and suppression of the sexual instinct may benefit mankind, it is often injurious to the sensitive individual:

> The position, agreeable to all the authorities, that sexual abstinence is not harmful and not difficult to maintain, has also been widely supported by the medical profession. It may be asserted, however, that the task of mastering such a powerful impulse as that of the sexual instinct by any other means than satisfying it is one which can call for the whole of man's forces. Mastering it by sublimation, by deflecting the sexual instinctual forces away from their sexual aim to higher cultural aims, can be achieved by a minority and then only intermittently, and least easily during the period of ardent and vigorous youth. Most of the rest become neurotic or are harmed in one way or another. . . . In general I have not gained the impression that sexual abstinence helps to bring about energetic and self-reliant men of action or original thinkers or bold emancipators and reformers. Far more often it goes to produce well-behaved weaklings who later become lost in the great mass of people that tends to follow, unwillingly, the leads given by strong individuals. . . . For this reason complete abstinence in youth is often not the best preparation for marriage for a young man.[24]

Masturbation is harmful—not because of any physical consequences, but because it vitiates the character through indulgence. It reinforces the tendency in the individual to choose overly simple solutions to the problem of instinctual gratification instead of taking the trouble to establish meaningful relationships with others.

Did marriage, at least, offer at one stroke a means of instinctual satisfaction and compliance with the rules of the "establishment"? Not so! Society countenances sexuality only for purposes of procreation. After perhaps five years of marriage and the birth of several offspring, the partners develop reservations against further sexual contact because of fear of pregnancy or the guilt of confessing that pleasure, rather than procreation, is the goal of the sexual act. In addition, contraceptive devices impair both psychological and physical sensitivity and, as a consequence, physical affection and sexual satisfaction end. The result: "The spiritual disillusionment and bodily deprivation to which most marriages are thus doomed puts both partners back in the state they were in before their marriage, except for being the poorer by the loss of an illusion, and they must once more have recourse to their fortitude in mastering and deflecting their sexual instinct."[25] It is a moot question, therefore, whether the costs of subduing the sexual passions are more than offset by the gains of society.

Freud on Women

Understanding what makes women tick was a problem that puzzled Freud throughout his life, as he modestly admitted in his unanswered question, *Was will das Weib?* (What Does Woman Want?)[26] His closest approximation to an answer was to consider woman an imperfect man, and hence his inferior. During childhood, a woman believes herself to be a castrated male and spends the rest of her life trying to gain a symbolic penis. Her intellectual inferiority is undoubtedly due to the inhibition of thought caused by sexual repression. Her narcissism is, in part, due to late compensation for sexual inferiority. Shame, a typical feminine characteristic, has at its base the concealment of genital deficiency.

Woman, Freud averred, has a much poorer capability for sublimation than man; consequently, frustration of her instinctual drives leaves her an unproductive neurotic. This explains her failure to contribute significantly to the discoveries and inventions that have affected the history of civilization. In only one technique have women made a possible contribution:

> That of plaiting and weaving. If that is so, we should be tempted to guess the unconscious motive for the achievement. Nature herself would seem to have given the model which this achievement imitates by causing the growth at maturity of the pubic hair that conceals the genitals. The step that remained to be taken lay in making the threads adhere to one another, while on the body they stick into the skin and are only matted together. If you reject this idea as fantastic and regard my belief in the influence of lack of a penis on the configuration of feminity as an *idée fixe,* I am of course defenceless.[27]

In conversation, his views were, if anything, more emphatic. In a talk with Joseph Wortis, who had come from the United States to undergo a didactic analysis, he noted that American women led men around by their noses, which resulted in *Frauenherrschaft* (rule of women) in America. In not fulfilling their true supporting role, women were discontented and unhappy, and unsuccessful marriages and divorce ensued. In Europe, things were better because men ruled. "But don't you think it would be best if both partners were equal?" asked Wortis. "That is a practical impossibility," Freud replied. "There must be inequality, and the superiority of the man is the lesser of the two evils."[28]

In sum, Freud possessed a detached, depersonalized view of love and marriage. Self-love was the basis of interaction with other people and love was essentially a distorted idealization of the partner, which preceded getting into bed and did not long survive the wedding. In addition, he had middle-class notions about lauding the value of saving and suppressing one's impulses, although Freud spoke of libido rather than money. Even affection had to be hoarded and doled out carefully because there was only a fixed supply available. Thus, it was foolish to love a stranger: "If I am to love him (with that kind of universal love) simply because he, too, is a denizen of the earth, like an insect or an earthworm or a grass-snake, then I fear that but a small modicum of love will fall to his lot and it would be impossible for me to give him as much as by all the laws of reason I am entitled to retain for myself. What is the point of an injunction promulgated with such solemnity, if reason does not recommend it to us?"[29]

Finally, we may note that Freud's view of women was clearly a product of Victorian culture. He always prided himself on the carefulness of his observations, but he seems to have abandoned all caution in investigating the *causes* of the behavior observed. In his milieu, there were obvious economic, political, educational, and social advantages in being a man; but Freud saw man's favorable position as biologically determined rather than environmentally caused. He ignored the manifold cultural determinants of woman's inferior position in Viennese society. He failed to grasp the possibility that woman wants a symbolic penis, not because she sees herself as castrated, but because it is the *carte blanche* of admission to the privileges enjoyed by men and denied to women. Karen Horney saw through the egocentric bourgeois biases of Freud's thinking when she remarked that had Freud been a woman, we would have had a theory of vagina envy instead of penis envy.[30]

In general, when he theorizes on love, Freud's views reflect the prejudices of his day and his own inability to give of himself intimately and warmly without reservation. He "spent" a little libido on his family, but reserved a much larger measure for his work. The notion that people can gain in loving others (in addition to satisfying specific instinctual needs) was as foreign to him as taking his wife on a vacation.

This conclusion does not denigrate his contributions to psychoanalytic theory. His work on the unconscious and on dreams stamps him as one of the great men of our time. My point is that a "halo" effect which renders every thought and theory of the Master as inviolable is a deterrent to the furtherance of knowledge. Freud projected the limitations of his own marriage onto his views of marriage in general, and it is here that his contribution is least sound.

A COMPARISON OF ELLIS AND FREUD

Although Ellis rejected Freud's contention that repression is an important aspect of the normal personality, he spoke highly of his work and writing skills. But he regarded Freud as an artist, not a scientist, because Freud did not validate his assertions in a scientific manner.[31] Considering Ellis' aesthetic sensitivity, it is doubtful that calling Freud an artist was intended as an insult.

Freud, who thought of himself as a scientist, reacted to this epithet as if it were an insult, terming Ellis' description "a highly sublimated form of resistance."[32] To Freud, Ellis had neither talent for psychoanalysis nor scientific ability. Also, since Ellis confessed that he found difficulty in making judgments and Freud had information that Ellis' wife was a homosexual, Freud concluded that he must be impotent. Freud's characteristic bluntness is expressed in the following passage:

> I feel sure, for example, that Ellis must have some sexual abnormality, else he would never have devoted himself to the field of sex research. You might of course say the same of me, but I would answer that that is first of all nobody's business, and second of all it is not true. I was drawn to study sex by my study of neuroses—it was years before the importance of sex dawned on me. In fact on three separate occasions I had been told of the importance of sex in the neuroses, without ever reacting to the suggestion.[33]

Freud's patent self-confidence stands in sharp contrast to the insecurity of Ellis. Freud's marriage and sexual adjustment seem to have been beneficial for him, and his family adjusted reasonably well to his schedule. Ellis, on the other hand, appears to have had a rather poor marriage. Although he felt a great deal of affection for his wife, she made more emotional demands than Freud's spouse.

Ellis considered marriage a pure function of the relationship and not defined by legal accoutrements. He suspected that a lifetime attachment between a man and a woman was illusory unless they were free to acquire other partners, a view that seems to have been a projection of his fear of binding intimacy. His concept of an ideal marriage, wherein the partners freely discuss their emotional and extramarital sexual liaisons, each rejoicing in the other's enjoyment, was also wishful thinking. It sounds pleasant in the abstract, but few people are secure enough not to interpret such liaisons by their partner as a sign of their own inadequacy. Ellis himself gave the lie to his philosophy when he objected strenuously to his mistress' taking another lover despite the fact that his fear of too close an intimacy had practically pushed her into someone else's arms.

Freud, on the other hand, saw marriage as a palliative that could free man for more creative sublimative efforts. Not remarkably, his own marriage might well be so categorized: it freed him of tensions so that his main energies could go into his work on psychoanalysis.

History has been kinder to Freud than to Ellis. His genius is acknowledged, and his main theory of the importance of the unconscious and repressed sexual urges is generally accepted. Freud is nevertheless increasingly vulnerable to criticism for his sexist bias, a bias that was normal for his time and culture. His theory of "vaginal orgasm" has been disproved, his concept of "penis envy" is fast disappearing, and science is now showing that man rather than woman is the "incomplete sex." These limitations prove his humanness, but do not detract from his major contributions.

Ellis, however, is fading into oblivion. In many ways this is undeserved. His stress on marriage as a relationship rather than a condition is very modern. His tolerance of sexual aberration and of infidelity (in theory at least), and his freedom in writing about sex in relatively straightforward language rather than in psychoanalytic jargon, made him the leading world spokesman of sex in his time. But unlike Freud, he was neither a systematist nor the founder of a school, and he left few followers to perpetuate his name. The kind of writing that was daring enough to get him arrested in 1897 today seems mundane. And again, unlike Freud, his writing contained no such glaring errors that would make him a *bête noire* to the women's liberation movement. Both men, nevertheless, were invaluable in ushering in a new era of sexuality, one that is still evolving.

REFERENCES

1. H. Ellis, *My Life,* p. 115.
2. G. Drysdale, *The Elements of Social Science.*
3. J. Wortis, *Fragments of an Analysis with Freud.*
4. A. Calder-Marshall, *Havelock Ellis,* p. 79.
5. H. Ellis, op. cit., pp. 230–231.
6. A. Calder-Marshall, op. cit., p. 133.
7. E. M. Brecher, *The Sex Researchers.*
8. H. Ellis, *Impressions and Comments (Third Series).*
9. Ibid.
10. F. Delisle, *Friendship's Odyssey.*
11. H. Ellis, "Eonism and other supplementary studies."
12. H. Ellis, "Sex in relation to society."
13. E. Jones, *The Life and Work of Sigmund Freud,* Vol. 1: *The Formative Years and the Great Discoveries,* p. 84.
14. Ibid., pp. 176–177.
15. Ibid., p. 128.
16. E. Jones, *The Life and Work of Sigmund Freud,* Vol. 2: *Years of Maturity,* p. 396.
17. M. Choisy, *Sigmund Freud: A New Appraisal,* p. 49. (Emphasis added.)
18. E. Fromm, *Sigmund Freud's Mission,* p. 29.
19. Ibid., p. 29.

20. M. Choisy, op. cit., p. 47.
21. S. Freud, "Why war?", p. 284.
22. S. Freud, "On narcissism."
23. S. Freud, "Postscript."
24. S. Freud, " 'Civilized' sexual morality and modern nervous illness," pp. 193–197.
25. Ibid., pp. 194–195.
26. E. Jones, op. cit., p. 98.
27. S. Freud, "Femininity," p. 132.
28. J. Wortis, op. cit., p. 98.
29. S. Freud, "Civilization and its discontents," p. 786.
30. K. Horney, *Feminine Psychology.*
31. H. Ellis, "Freud's influence on the changed attitude toward sex."
32. E. Jones, op. cit., Vol. 3, p. 21.
33. J. Wortis, op. cit., p. 154.

14

American Marriage: From the Colonies to the Civil War

Europeans came to the New World to escape religious and political persecution, to seek new economic opportunity, or simply to find adventure. Even though they initially had no intention of altering their traditional marriage customs, many factors conspired to effect changes. Young people could better endure a hazardous and demanding one- to two-month sea voyage which involved poor food, inadequate sanitation, and physical stress. As they put 3,000 miles of ocean between themselves and their parents, kinship ties weakened and the concomitants of extended-family marriages and parent-dominated marriages, such as the dower and dowry, became minimized. Physical endurance and a willingness to face the challenge of the frontier and to work the land became desirable characteristics in a marriage partner. Chaperones and long courtships were unpopular and then gradually became obsolete.

The emphasis on ritual and tradition was further weakened by the absence of a strongly organized clergy in America. In the more tradition-oriented Northeast, the impact of industrialization tended to weaken nuclear family ties. Finally, free land and a perennial labor shortage meant constant migration and the continued diminution of parental authority.

During the early years of the colonies the settlers were greatly outnumbered by the Indians, and the supply of indigenous farm labor was practically nonexistent. However, the situation was rapidly remedied by the increased immigration and a high marriage and birth rate. Men, at first, greatly outnumbered women, and, in accordance with the law of supply and demand, the woman's importance and power in the community was enhanced.

The need for population was so great that anyone who failed to marry at an early age was regarded as a civic slacker and viewed with distrust and suspicion. In 1638, Massachusetts ordered every town to "dispose of all single persons and inmates within their towns to service, or otherwise."[1] In Connecticut, bachelors living by themselves were taxed 20 shillings per week.[2] At other times, they were not allowed to occupy any living quarters without the express permission of the selectmen of their community. Even as late as the end of the eighteenth century, the Reverend John Witherspoon could intone that "a man who continues through life in a single state, ought in justice to endeavor to satisfy the public that his case is singular and that he has some insuperable obstacle to plead in his excuse."[3]

Since women were expected to marry quickly in the Southern colonies, an unmarried woman of 20 might be called an "antique Virgin."[4] At 30, considered beyond reclamation, she was nicknamed "thornback." However, at least in the New England colonies, recently uncovered evidence indicates that the age of marriage was somewhat older than it is today.[5]

Widows were quite popular, even those with children. One reason was their economic status. The European custom of leaving the major portion of an estate to the eldest son did not survive in the colonies. In the typical family, the widow, guaranteed at least one-third of the husband's estate, was the main beneficiary. Her second husband automatically acquired the usufruct of these lands during her lifetime. Further, since children were a definite economic asset in the largely agrarian society, her proven fertility was no detriment to remarriage. Benjamin Franklin aptly noted that "a rich widow is the only kind of second-hand goods that will always sell at prime cost."[6]

The economic advantages of marriage and the virtual absence of housekeepers and hired hands determined that widows and widowers did not long remain single. The first marriage in Plymouth was between a widow of 12 weeks and a widower of 7 weeks. An extreme example was that of Isaac Winslow, who proposed to Ben Davis' daughter on the same day his wife's casket was lowered into the ground.

Practices and attitudes regarding marriage varied considerably from colony to colony, since many nations, classes, and religions were represented. We shall examine the Indians, New Englanders, and the mid-Atlantic and Southern states during the pre-Revolutionary War period.

THE COLONIAL PERIOD

The Indians

Indian marriage was quite diversified. A considerable number of tribes practiced polygyny[7]; others adhered to a monogamous system. Within monogamy, both matriarchal and patriarchal systems were represented.

Generally, there was more permissiveness about sexual license before marriage, but adultery was severely punished. The status of women was, on the whole, inferior to that of men, but was far from that of a slave. Women were indispensable for the day-to-day tasks of subsistence.

The coming of the white man, however, undermined the position of Indian women. In the fight for survival the nonmilitary became expendable, and women degenerated into breeders of warriors who attended to their physical needs. Unfortunately, this stereotype of the "pitiful squaw" is the one that has survived.[8] The Indians were gradually exterminated or reduced to living on reservations, and it is hardly surprising that, as "hostile barbarians," their marriage customs had no impact on whites.

The Puritans

Puritanism stood for a closely regulated life, with the individual keeping careful watch over his own activities to ensure that God came first in his every thought. According to Jonathan Edwards, a mideighteenth-century minister who sought to revive the Puritan spirit, one's practice of religion should involve "not only his business at certain seasons, the business of Sabbath days, or certain extraordinary times . . . but, the *business of his life.* "[9]

Basic to the Puritan philosophy was the tenet that all must undertake to do God's will, and that this could be achieved by leading an industrious, rational life and mastering one's passions. Couples were severely criticized who were forever "colling, kissing and dallying."[10] The easiest way to avoid being overwhelmed by passion was to keep busy every minute of the day. Preacher Cotton Mather even figured out that much time was wasted in bowel movements, time that might be better employed for God's will. He therefore resolved to make the next such occasion "an opportunity for shaping in my mind some holy, noble, divine thought . . . that may leave upon my spirit some further tincture of piety."[11]

The Puritan was more than an overzealous prude, desperately trying to control his own and everyone else's sex life and leisure activities. He countenanced the expression of passion and sexual interest so long as it did not make man forget God. Some Puritans—the minister Edward Taylor, for example—were extremely skillful at combining passion for a young lady with love of God: "My Dove, I send you not my heart, for that I trust is sent to Heaven long since, and unless it hath woefully deceived me, it hath not taken up its lodgings in any one's bosom on this side of the Royal City of the Great King, but yet most of it that is allowed to be layed out upon any creature doth safely and singly fall to your share."[12]

Love could not play an official role in marital choice because, as a passion, it might make man forget God. If a boy liked a girl, he sought to justify his feeling on rational grounds: she was a good Christian; both would help each other to find God; she was thrifty, pious, and industrious. Love was also not a prerequisite to marriage. *"The Great God commands thee to love her,"*[13] said the divine, Wadsworth. "How vile then are those who don't love their wives."[14] Love was a rational, volitional act, and if it did not precede marriage, it was nevertheless the inevitable product of a decent Puritan marriage. Not to love one's spouse, no matter what his or her shortcomings, was to admit one's failure to be a good Christian.

The Puritans were mostly solid, middle-class merchants and tradesmen; and like all good businessmen, they were jealous of reputation and station. It was important not to fall in love with someone outside the Church or with a person with much less financial means. Thus, Fitz-John Winthrop, on the question of choice between a poor and a rich bride for his brother's son, remarked, "I would . . . advise him to leave the maid with a short hempen shirt, and take hold of that made of good bag holland."[1 5]

The Mid-Atlantic Colonies

The middle colonies were heterogeneous in population: Dutch and English in New York, Scotch Presbyterians in New Jersey, Swedes in Delaware, and Quakers, Germans, and Scotch-Irish in Pennsylvania. On the whole, the marital scene was uneventful compared to that of New England. The Dutch, generally tolerant of religious and social variety, sanctioned both religious and civil marriages. The onset of English rule in 1664, under the religiously tolerant Charles II, brought few changes.

Pennsylvania's Quakers represented the left-wing movement of Puritanism and were accused by members of the Anglican Church of not celebrating marriage in an orderly and decent way. This stemmed from the Quaker belief that marriage, as a civil affair, did not require Anglican observances, a ring, and a minister at the ceremony.

Despite such innovations, the Quakers took marriage very seriously. The Friends, as they called themselves, were not allowed to propose marriage without first bringing the matter up at their monthly meeting. Marital choice was restricted to Friends at the risk of expulsion from the religious fellowship. At the monthly meeting, the boy would rise and say, "I, Joseph Jones, intend to take Mary Smith, if the Lord permit." The intended bride would stand up and make a similar statement. A committee then took this information under consideration and checked carefully to determine if either of the couple was involved in any other entanglements, past or present. If a past flirtation was discovered, the transgressor had the privilege of self-condemnation and the opportunity to ask forgiveness of the congregation at its next meeting. If the committee approved the match, the couple was said to have "passed the meeting." So important was "cleanness" of reputation that a young man seeking a wife in a town where he was unknown was expected to present a certificate of good moral conduct from his own community.

The Southern Colonies

The first settlers in the South, more so than in the North and in the mid-Atlantic areas, had been adventurers. Since most of them had sought no reprieve from religious persecution, as had been the case with Puritans, the regulation of marriage continued to be vested in the religious authority rather than in the state. However, where the clergy was in short supply and civil marriage not permitted, common-law marriages began to take place, particularly in the backlands.

Initially there were so few women that Sir Edwin Sandys, treasurer of the Virginia Company in London, providentially provided for the passage of 90 women advertised as "handsome, honestly educated maids of honest life and carriage."[16] The women were given lodging until such time as they would choose a mate. When marital arrangements had been made, the future husbands prepaid the passage with 120 pounds of good Virginia tobacco leaf. The first shipment sold out quickly, as did several subsequent ones.

The southern climate was not as demanding, and the regulation of life was far less severe than in New England; but the early attitudes toward women did not differ as dramatically as they would later, in the years between the Revolutionary and Civil Wars.

Benjamin Franklin and His Times

Eighteenth-century Americans, like Europeans, enjoyed dabbling in the *bon mot* and in tongue-in-cheek advice on any topic under the sun. Not only politics, but marriage problems and the scandalous behavior of the young, served as targets. In a letter to the *American Magazine,* Hymenaeus Phyz claimed to have discovered the physiological and physiognomic signs of compatibility between couples, on the basis of which he prescribed that very tall people should not take very short mates.[17] Another letter writer to the same magazine, A. Project, was shocked by current dress. Girls were cooling their own breasts to inflame those of the men. Indeed, he noted, if a hundred years hence posterity was shown the dresses of 1757, "they would believe their great-grandmothers were all dwarfs."[18]

More reliable advice on matrimony came from John Witherspoon, a minister who served as president of the College of New Jersey (now Princeton University). He decried the emphasis on physical attraction and argued for equality of age and social status as determinants of a good marriage.[19]

One man whose advice on marriage was taken most seriously was Benjamin Franklin, who venerated common sense and eschewed excessive emotionality because it interfered with maximization of rational behavior. As to matrimony, he concluded that it "is the most natural state of man, and therefore the state by which you are most likely to find solid happiness."[20] A bachelor was the odd half of a pair of scissors,[21] and marriage was the obvious solution to the incompleteness of both sexes. But Franklin was no prude; he sired an illegitimate son[22] and could, on rational grounds, advise a young man to take an old mistress rather than a young one—they were so much more grateful.[23] Nor was he a traditionalist, for he encouraged young people to feel free to reject their parents' advice on matrimony.

Unfortunately, marriages often turned sour, said Franklin, because they "are often occasioned by the headstrong motives of ungoverned passions."[24] The wise swain ought to inspire his beloved with sentiments of rational esteem. Sex was also to be treated in a moderate, rational manner. One of the precepts he set for himself was "rarely use Venery but for Health or Offspring; Never to Dulness, Weakness, or the Injury of your own or another's Peace or Reputation."[25] That Franklin admired women is apparent from his numerous writings, but he in no way regarded them as equal to men in intellectual matters, for "Nature, and the circumstances of human life seem indeed to design for man that superiority, and to invest him with a directing power in the more difficult and important affairs of life."[26] Yet he is never boorish about his greater powers: "A man of sense and breeding will be, as it were, superior without seeming to know it; and support his influence with so great a delicacy, that his wife will ever seem to be his equal."[27] In this respect, Franklin's views are in the earlier tradition of the enlightened sixteenth- and seventeeth-century European male who believed that women, while not intellectually equal to men, should be treated kindly and educated to be companions to their husbands rather than mere seamstresses.

Franklin's own life suggested that his personal control of passion had not come easy: "that hard-to-be-govern'd Passion of Youth, had hurried me frequently into Intrigues with low Women that fell in my Way, which were attended with some Expence and great Inconvenience besides a continual Risque to my Health by a Distemper which of all things, I dreaded, tho' by great good Luck I escaped it."[28]

Even as a widower well into his seventies, Franklin continued to express his erotic needs, albeit in a more rational manner than in his youth. When he fell in love with the widow of the philosopher Helvétius and found it difficult to advance beyond kissing and hugging, he penned her a rational proposition:

> If Notre Dame is pleased to spend her days with Franklin, he would be just as pleased to spend his nights with her; and since he has already given her so many of his days, although he has so few left to give, she seems very ungrateful in never giving him one of her nights, which keep passing as a pure loss, without making anyone happy except Poupon [the cat]. Nevertheless, he hugs her very tightly, for he loves her infinitely in spite of her shortcomings.[29]

A charming letter indeed—and then he sent her another equally charming one, purportedly written by the flies in his apartment. The flies "explained" that they had been happily making love until threatened by spiders. During a recent visit, Madame Helvétius had ordered Franklin to have the cobwebs swept away, and the flies were now gratefully petitioning Madame to marry Franklin and thus assure the stability of their good fortune.[30]

Despite his wit and eloquence, Franklin could not persuade Madame Helvétius to become either his mistress or his wife. He was held in great esteem by many other French women, but apparently his only sensual dividends were a few hugs and kisses.

POSTREVOLUTIONARY AMERICA

On September 1, 1785, the New York *Daily Advertiser* carried an unsigned article, "On the State of Marriage in South Britain":

> If you see a man and woman, with little or no occasion, often finding fault, and correcting one another in company, you may be sure they are man and wife. If you see a gentleman and lady in the same coach, in profound silence, the one looking out at one side, never imagine they mean any harm to one another; they are already honestly married. If you see a lady accidentally let fall a glove or handkerchief and a gentleman that is next to her telling her of it, that she might gather it up, man and wife.
>
> If you see a lady presenting a gentleman with something sideways, at arm's length, with her head turned another way, speaking to him with a look and accent different from that she uses to others, it is her husband. If you see a man and woman walking in the fields in a direct line twenty yards distance from one another, the man strides over a stile, and goes on sans ceremonie, you may swear they are man and wife, without fear of perjury.
>
> If you see a lady whose beauty and carriage attract the eyes, and engage the respect of all the company, except a certain gentleman, who speaks to her in a rough accent, not at all affected with her charms, you may be sure it is her husband, who married her for love, and now slights her.
>
> If you see a gentleman that is courteous, obliging, and good-natured to everybody, except a certain female that lives under the same roof with him to whom he is unreasonably cross and ill-natured, it is his wife. If you see a male and female continually jarring, checking, and thwarting each other, yet under the kindest terms and appellations imaginable, as my dear, etc., man and wife.
>
> The present state of matrimony in South Britain:

Wives eloped from husbands	2,361
Husbands run away from their wives	1,362
Married pairs in a state of separation from each other	4,120
Married pairs living in state of open war, under the same roof	191,023
Married pairs living in a state of inward hatred for each other though concealed from the world	162,230
Married pairs living in a state of coldness and indifference for each other	510,123
Married pairs reputedly happy in the esteem of the world	1,102
Married pairs comparatively happy	135
Married pairs absolutely and entirely happy[31]	9

It is noteworthy that this cynical description, aptly subtitled "Only Nine?", was projected onto the traditional parent-dominated marriage then prevalent in Britain. In the postrevolutionary euphoria, Americans were cheerfully optimistic about business, marriage, and the future, an optimism that came to be almost a trademark.[32] Few boosters have been more enthusiastic or more shallow than the Reverend Mason Weems. Obviously proud that the colonies had thrashed Great Britain, the most powerful nation in the world, he warned, in the introduction to his *Hymen's Recruiting Sergeant; or, the Maid's and Bachelor's Friend* that a rematch might be dangerous:

> List then, ye Bach'lors, and ye Maidens fair,
> If truly you do love your country dear;
> O, list with rapture to the great decree
> Which thus in Genesis you all may see;
> Marry, and raise up soldiers, might and main,
> Then laugh, you may, at England, France and Spain.[33]

MARRIAGE IN THE SOUTH

The emergence of large plantations, while relatively few in number compared to the small farms, were a leading factor in the concept of "southern life." Men and women prided themselves on their manners and gracious living, and the role of the plantation mistress was considerably different from that of the wealthy northern wife. The southern mistress had many servants, most of them black. She wielded greater power over her slaves and/or indentured servants than her northern counterpart, who hired only household help. The southern lady's executive role in domestic affairs, according to accounts of the period, was not otherwise matched by a happy existence. The absence of a close feeling for a spouse often selected by her parents, the isolation of plantation life, and the awareness of her husband's possible liaisons with black women could hardly promote emotional well-being.

Husbands, more patriarchal than in the North, freely indulged in sexual encounters with "bad" women (blacks); they compensated for any guilt feelings by venerating the purity and gentility of the "good" white southern woman, carefully shielding her from the callous business and political worlds. She became the living symbol of the loftiest aspirations of southern life, while in the tough life "below" men dirtied their hands in running the plantations and government and in clandestine love affairs.

The Black in the Antebellum Period

The earliest white settlers on the east coast were too concerned with preserving their lives to worry about social distinctions between themselves and those whose skin bore a non-Caucasian tint. In addition, the shortage of women made men relatively insensitive to color differences—John Rolfe was quite happy to marry the Indian princess Pocahontas.

The early black slaves from Africa were considered uncivilized barbarians, and there was no concern about intermarriage with them.[34] But later on, in an effort to maintain a distinction between the rapidly burgeoning native black population and the white population, miscegenation laws were enacted. In 1691, Virginia declared that a white woman marrying a Negro or mulatto, slave or not, would be permanently banished. Other states joined in the prohibition of intermarriage, including Massachusetts in 1705. Not until 1843 did Massachusetts see fit to repeal this law.[35,36]

Both white and black marriages, as well as heterosexual relationships between white men and black women, were profoundly altered by the institution of slavery. Most young southern white men of some circumstance were initiated into the mysteries of sex by a black woman. Many of them found the casual sexual relationships and the variety so pleasing that they hesitated to marry and even avoided marriage with puritanical white women. When they did marry, many did not give up their easy access to the "children of nature."[37]

If the white wives resented this state of affairs, as was likely, there were no organized complaints. Occasionally, however, a diary has been made public which reveals the domestic strain engendered by slavery. Thus, Mary Bodkin Chesnut fulminated in 1861:

> God forgive us, but ours is a monstrous system, a wrong and an iniquity! Like the patriarchs of old, our men live all in one house with their wives and their concubines; and the mulattoes one sees in every family partly resemble the white children. Any lady is ready to tell you who is the father of all the mulatto children in everybody's household but her own. Those, she seems to think, drop from the clouds. My disgust sometimes is boiling over.[38]

For a woman slave, the economic advantages of satisfying the sexual needs of her white master were incalculably greater than working in the fields. The position of concubine was eagerly sought after, but was usually reserved for the light-colored quadroon or octoroon.

Usually, women slaves were exempted from hard work when pregnant. The reasons were not purely humanitarian. The restrictions against importing slaves raised the price of black flesh so much that by the time of the Civil War a ten-year-old black boy brought $1,525 in Georgia.[39] Rather than buy slaves, it was more economical to raise them. Thus, an advertisement in Charleston read: "For sale—a Girl about twenty-nine years of age, raised, in Virginia, and her two female children. . . . She is very prolific in her generating qualities, and affords a magnificent opportunity to any man who wishes to raise a family of healthy niggers for his own use."[40]

Sometimes, in accordance with the belief that white blood strengthened the stock and brought higher prices, white men were paid to serve as stallions. More often, the master himself designated men in their prime to be studs, with the objective of increasing the number of workers on his plantation. Occasionally, this was achieved by legally marrying blacks to each other. A special wedding ceremony had to be concocted, one that recognized the special condition of the slave. The Reverend Samuel Philips of Andover, Massachusetts, devised a ceremony in which he said:

> I then aggreable to your Request, and wth ye Consent of your Masters & Mistresses, do Declare, that you have License given you to be conversant and familiar together, as *Husband* and *Wife,* so long as God shall continue your places of abode as aforesaid; and so long as you shall behave yourselves as it becometh Servants to doe: For you must, both of you, bear in mind, that you Remain Still as really and truly as ever, your Master's Property, and therefore it will be justly expected, both by God and Man, that you behave and conduct your-selves, as Obedient and faithfull Servants towards your respective Masters & Mistresses for the Time being.[41]

Obviously, marriage between slaves had no legal status in the eyes of the law, since a slave was no more a legal entity than a heifer. More often than not, the black man and woman simply cohabited for as long as they wanted to. Either one could switch to another partner—with their master's indulgence—or the master could switch partners for them without their consent.[42]

The black man's position was seriously undermined. The typical masculine role in most cultures calls for the man to protect and control his woman or women. The American slave could do neither. If his master desired his wife or woman, he was powerless to protest. No southern court would entertain a charge of adultery by a black against a white man. On the other hand, any black male attempting to molest a white woman could be castrated.

The white master could split the black family by selling his entire stock at auction. Many white owners considered this behavior cruel, and took pains not to break up a family; others didn't care at all. Even in a benevolent southern family, a sudden reversal of economic fortune might make it impossible to keep the slave's family intact. As a result of the black male's inability to act effectively in a masculine role, his authority over his family was weak. The dominant figures, indeed the only figure to provide some element of stability in a child's life, was his mother. Black families became matriarchies, and 100 years later, on a psychological test involving story-telling, blacks still tended to depict their mothers as being much more emotionally supportive than did the whites; for both blacks and whites, there were no differences found with respect to fathers.[43]

AMERICAN MARRIAGE AS SEEN BY FOREIGNERS

During the eighteenth and nineteenth centuries, a number of European travelers recorded their impressions of family life in the United States. Some of them visited here for weeks, others for years, but most were very much convinced of the truthfulness of their observations. Perhaps the most dogmatic was Stendahl, who never set foot on American shores.

In the main, their assessments were positive, but the majority were struck by the lack of ardor in American marriage. In *On Love,* Stendhal reported that the Americans' emphasis on rationalism, when combined with their orderliness and avoidance of discomfort, made them dull creatures. He scoffed that 25-year-olds were on the downgrade, sensually speaking, and that they lacked the passion that makes life worthwhile. "Lovers" in America could travel, unchaperoned and without fear, for 15 or 20 miles in a sleigh—nothing ever happened. In fact, *crystallization,* the idealization of the beloved as a function of falling in love, was impossible there because the overemphasis on reasoning precluded it. Patronizingly, Stendhal concluded, "I admire this happiness, but I do not envy it; it is like the happiness of creatures of another and lower species."[44]

In a similar vein, the Frenchman Moreau was astounded to find that a young couple could be left alone without fear. In fact, "sometimes on returning, the servants find them fallen asleep and the candle gone out—so cold is love in this country."[45] Even the English, often regarded by continental Europeans as a chill people, reported the Americans as lacking in passion. J. S. Buckingham wrote that "love, among the American people, appears to be required rather as an affair of judgment than of the heart."[46]

De Tocqueville agreed that American wives were cold and virtuous, not affectionate. This frigidity, he believed, was the inevitable consequence of growing up in a democracy. Due to its looseness of structure, as compared to a monarchy, a democracy requires highly educated and independent men and women if it is to remain viable. When European men paid compliments to their women, it was a sign of superficiality and falseness because they never considered the women to be their equals. American men rarely complimented their ladies, "but they daily show how much they esteem them."[47]

De Tocqueville concluded that marriage was superior in the United States. He attributed this to the greater overall equality of status, which in turn was responsible for a democratic life style, unlimited industriousness, and the enhanced status of women. People who were hard-toiling and God-fearing, qualities fostered by the Protestant work ethic, had no time for adultery. Further, a clear-headed approach to marriage of equals, devoid of familial interference or strong economic considerations, left no rationale for illicit affairs. In Europe, however, the prime excuse for adultery was forced marriages between indifferent partners. De Tocqueville concluded that although the women of the United States are confined within the narrow circle of domestic life, and their situation is in some respects one of extreme dependence, I have nowhere seen woman occupying a loftier position; and if I were asked . . . to what the singular prosperity and growing strength of that people ought mainly to be attributed, I should reply: To the superiority of their women.[48]

Other foreign visitors concurred with respect to the influence of democracy on marriage. Parental pressure on marital choice seemed to be minimal,[49,50] dowries were diminishing,[51] and people were even marrying across social lines.[52] Yet all this had a beneficial effect, according to Chastallux, who visited at the close of the Revolution and declared unequivocally that "there is no licentiousness in America."[53]

While European men were visibly impressed by American marriage, European women were far less sanguine. Mrs. Trollope found lower-class American wives overworked, but upper-class women unrefined and dull because they had nothing to do.[54] The Pulszkys, a visiting husband and wife, found that the *ladies' rule* was a myth propagated by men. These worthy folk, totally absorbed in business, wrapped their wives in silks to distract them and keep them from interfering in their affairs.[55]

Harriet Martineau, the English reformer and champion of women's rights, perhaps because she was a woman, clearly saw that the status of women in America was somewhat exaggerated and that they did not enjoy legal equality with men.[56] True, they had more rights than in England, divorce was easier, and morality was somewhat higher. But this might only be a consequence of the youth of the country. On the Eastern seaboard she already saw the British influence in the increasing number of marriages for wealth, and she concluded that human nature was much the same the world over. True progress could come only when women achieved the same opportunities that men already possessed.

In conclusion, the description of American life by foreign visitors indicates that many phenomena—e.g., unsupervised dating, weak parental role in marital choice, and mobility in marriage—are not recent products of twentieth-century industrialization. In fact, the above-mentioned nineteenth-century phenomena may have served to make available a population suitable to the demands of an advanced industrial era.[57]

The alleged coldness of American men and women may in part have been due to the repressive effects of the Puritan and Anglican heritage. It may also have been due to a more relaxed atmosphere between the sexes. (European women, whose upbringing was more secluded, often experienced a sense of release when they married. But it is questionable whether their ardor could long survive the pronounced inequality between the sexes of continental Europe.)

HUSBANDS AND WIVES, BUT MOSTLY WIVES

The position of the woman and wife in America, as in Europe, was one of considerable inferiority. Two distinct approaches served to achieve this state of affairs during the years with which we are concerned, 1607 to 1865. In the early period, from the first settlements until the Revolutionary War, woman's inferior role was taken for granted and attributed to her physical and mental inferiority as well as to Scriptural precepts.

In the nineteenth century, faith in the Bible and in traditional roles had weakened. Rationalizations were found to justify why woman should not mind staying in the house, enjoy no legal existence if married, or not be permitted to vote whether she was married or single. As in Europe, emphasis was placed not on her inferiority, but on her greater *spiritual superiority* and on the need to protect so pure a person from the degrading experiences of everyday life.

This changeover in argumentation is discernible when we compare the Puritans' attitudes toward women with those of the Revolutionary fathers (whose views were those of a transitional period) and with those of the ladies' magazines which, from 1820 on, spoke for the "new woman."

Anne Hutchinson was violently attacked in the Massachusetts Bay Colony not simply for her independent religious beliefs, but because she, a *woman,* had dared to criticize a *male minister.* Governor Winthrop pointed out the sad effects of book-learning on women by citing the case of the wife of Connecticut's Governor Hopkins. The poor woman went mad, in his analysis, by straining her brain with too much reading and writing.[58]

By Revolutionary times, men no longer defended the status quo so much on physical grounds as by vague reference to the traditional roles that were the foundation of society. Thomas Jefferson wrote that in a pure democracy all citizens would meet to transact business, except for slaves, infants, and "women who, to prevent depravity of morals, and ambiguity of issue, could not mix promiscuously in the public meetings of men."[59] Even though women's advocates such as John Witherspoon and Aaron Burr[60] considered women equal to men in rational powers except for their lack of training, *they never argued that their roles could be similar,* for example, in connection with the right to vote.

What should a woman do when her husband took advantage of her? In the June 8, 1785, edition of the *Pennsylvania Evening Herald,* a female adviser to young married ladies wrote, "Let your tears persuade: these speak the most irresistible language with which you can assail the heart of man." [61]

Occasionally a rare woman advocated bolder means to attain equality. Abigail Adams, writing to her husband John about the drawing up of the Declaration of Independence in 1776, said:

Remember the ladies and be more generous and favorable to them than your ancestors. Do not put such unlimited power into the hands of husbands. Remember, all men would be tyrants if they could. If particular care and attention are not paid to the ladies, we are determined to foment a rebellion, and will not hold ourselves bound to obey any laws in which we have no voice nor representation.[62]

John Adams, who doted on his wife, once wrote her that "nothing has contributed so much to support my mind as the choice blessing of a wife, whose capacity enabled her to comprehend, and whose pure virtue obliged her to approve, the views of her husband."[63] Nevertheless, he reminded her, man's power over woman was right, and he would fight for his belief.

Women's magazines of the nineteenth century helped to spread the stereotype of the "correct" lady and to codify their views from New York to California. The first generation of aggressive women's righters—Frances Wright, Harriet Martineau, and Margaret Fuller—were castigated as unfeminine social misfits. The true woman embodied the four virtues of piety, purity, submissiveness, and domesticity.[64]

It followed that a woman, since she was spiritually superior, would have a much stronger religious sense than a man. If her marriage was unsatisfactory, if her husband appropriated all her funds and mistreated her, there was little she could do legally or socially; but she was encouraged to find solace in religion, the great tranquilizer.

Purity was of crucial importance and could not be guarded too carefully. Mrs. Elizabeth Farrar advised women to "sit not with another in a place that is too narrow, read not out of the same book, let not your eagerness to see anything induce you to place your head close to another person."[65] In the magazine romances, loss of sexual purity often led to madness or death. Whether the woman wanted to engage in the sexual act or not seems not to have mattered—what counted was the physical act itself. It was as if the center regulating emotional equilibrium lay in the hymen instead of the hypothalamus (the midbrain).

Another sign of purity was one's use of language. William A. Alcott, in *The Young Wife,* sadly noted that not only men but women used "coarse, vulgar words . . . such as 'My stars!,' 'My soul!,' 'By George!,' 'Good Heavens!.' Such expressions, besides being indelicate, savor not a little of profanity."[66]

Impurity could occur with young ladies of the most virginal temperament— even from the mechanical effect of a tightly laced corset. So thought the noted phrenologist, O. S. Fowler, whose sagacity apparently encompassed considerably more territory than the cranium: "Who does not know that the compression of any part produces *inflammation?* Who does not know that, therefore, tight-lacing around the waist keeps the blood from returning freely to the heart, and *retains* it in the bowels and neighboring organs, and thereby *inflames all the organs of the abdomen,* which thereby EXCITES AMATIVE DESIRES?"[67]

Apparently the ladies did not believe the professor, or perhaps they longed for the alleged aphrodisiacal qualities of corseting, because tight corsets remained in vogue until the end of the nineteenth century.

Submissiveness was emphasized as an absolute necessity for the wife—even when she knew herself to be in the right and her husband to be wrong. "Reverence his *wishes* even when you do not his opinions," said Caroline Gilman in *Recollections of a Housekeeper.*[68] Woman's submissiveness found clinical support from a Dr. Maige: "Woman has a head almost too small for intellect, but just big enough for love."[69] An important corollary of submissiveness was inconspicuousness, as one book advised: "A woman's name should appear in print but twice—when she marries and when she dies."[70]

The virtue of submissiveness is spelled out in George Fitzhugh's *Sociology for the South:*

> So long as she is nervous, fickle, capricious, delicate, diffident and dependent, man will worship and adore her. Her weakness is her strength, and her true art is to cultivate and improve that weakness. . . . In truth, woman, like a child, has but one right, and that is the right to protection. The right to protection involves the obligation to obey. . . . If she is obedient, she is in little danger of mal-treatment; if she stands upon her rights, is coarse and masculine, man loathes and despises her and ends by abusing her.[71]

The merits of domesticity were pointed out by Mrs. Sigourney: "The science of housekeeping affords exercise for the judgment and energy, ready recollection, and patient self-possession, that are the characteristics of a superior mind."[72] Mrs. Farrar found making beds to be good exercise. Even dreary household tasks were not without their virtue, for they fostered patience and perseverance. Housewifery was really a complex art: "There is more to be learned about pouring out tea and coffee than most young ladies are willing to believe."[73]

Women's education in the seminaries could be defended only by pointing out that it not only did not take the woman away from the home (a woman of good family never worked), but it actually increased her domestic skills. *Godey's Lady's Book* pointed out that cooking could be improved through a knowledge of chemistry, geometry was valuable in dividing cloth, and phrenology might be useful in discovering latent talent in children.[74]

That the four virtues of women were sufficient for all occasions is apparent in an essay that won a 50-dollar prize from *The Ladies' Wreath* magazine on the topic, "How May an American Woman Best Show Her Patriotism." The essay offers a story about how, naturally enough, the wife asks the husband how he would answer the question posed by the magazine. He starts off with a few jokes—a suggestion to call her eldest son George Washington and to speak American, not French. Pleasantries and xenophobic statements aside, he then tells her, more seriously, that she would not be patriotic if she voted because it would lead to chaos and confusion. Instead, she could best demonstrate her patriotism by staying home, studying her Bible, and using the quiet life of home and her natural refinement and closeness to God to raise her sons to be good Americans, while her husband, beset by conflict and evil, was out in the rugged world. The judges waxed ecstatic over this essay and happily paid the prize money, remarking that it was "cheap at the price."[75]

In sum, the literature of the day tried fervently to convince every woman that she had the best of both worlds. She really was worshiped by man as his better half. And what if she was legally invisible and politically disfranchised? There was nothing very interesting about politics and business. The outside world was a jungle in which she would be mauled and buffeted. If she submitted to her husband, it was not out of fear, but because she, being closer to the ways of Jesus, could more readily "turn the other cheek." But despite all such brainwashing, some women were not hoodwinked. A small group of them began to unite for action. The battle for legal equality on an organized scale had begun.

Legal Position of the Wife

The wife's legal position in the colonies and in the early years of the United States was quite similar to that in England. The wife had no legal existence apart from her husband. Her real and personal property became his to control—if not to own—at marriage. But, in contrast to England, American laws began to afford a somewhat higher value to women: a wife had the right to bed and board at the expense of her husband and to be supported even if he deserted her; he was also forbidden to do violence to her.

After the Revolution, the first reforms gave a woman the right to control the property she had brought to the marriage and to dispose of it by will. Because each state made its own laws, the rate of progress was varied. It is questionable how much of these early changes were due to pressure by the still poorly organized women's groups and how much reflected the desire of the wealthy to ensure the financial security of their daughters. The latter motive seems to have been the case in New York.[76]

By the 1840s, however, future leaders of the women's rights movements, such as Lucretia Mott and Elizabeth Cady Stanton, began to establish contact, and the first women's rights convention was held at Seneca Falls, New York, in 1848. The ladies issued their "Declaration of Sentiments," patterned closely after the Declaration of Independence: "We hold these truths to be self-evident, that all men *and women* are created equal."[77] It goes on to declare how married women are civilly dead, that they lose all rights to their property at marriage, and that they must surrender their wages to their husband:

> He has made her, morally, an irresponsible being, as she can commit many crimes with impunity, provided they be done in the presence of her

husband. In the covenant of marriage, she is compelled to promise obedience to her husband, he becoming, to all intents and purposes, her master—the law giving him power to deprive her of her liberty, and to administer chastisement. He has so framed the laws of divorce, as to what shall be the proper causes, and in case of separation to who the guardianship of the children shall be given, as to be wholly regardless of the happiness of women—the law in all cases going upon a false supposition of the supremacy of man, and giving all power into his hands.[78]

The list continues with many nonmarital complaints, and closes with an insistence on complete political and legal equality.

That the majority of men opposed the movement as antithetical to the role of woman will startle few. Perhaps more surprising is the fact that a considerable number of women also rejected the women's movement. Many wives felt that such "goings-on" were "unfeminine," the acts of frustrated spinsters who had no husbands to protect them. The fact that an important leader, Mrs. Stanton, was not only married but had borne seven children was played down. Several minor incursions into the discriminatory provisions of property acts occurred in some states in the 1850s, but by 1865 there was still no significant change.

MARRIAGE REGULATIONS

America boasts a remarkable diversity of marriage laws. The fact that no two states have identical marriage laws can be traced to conditions in the original colonies.

New England's colonists, having suffered harassment for their religious convictions in England, were wary of a repetition in the New World, and despite their theological views, they declared marriage to be a civil contract. Priests were not only unnecessary, they were strictly forbidden to officiate at weddings; marriages were performed by a justice of the peace or other civil magistrate. However, with the termination of religious persecution in England under Charles II, the stern Puritanism began to mellow: by 1692, Massachusetts allowed both religious and civil marriages, and other colonies soon followed.

In Virginia the story was exactly the opposite. Until 1794, its upstanding Anglicans insisted that a marriage must be performed *only* according to Church of England rites. The situation in Maryland and New York depended on who was in power during a particular period. Gradually, the concept of the acceptability of both civil and religious marriage spread, and it was established throughout the colonies by the close of the eighteenth century.

Leaning heavily on Scripture as a substitute for church ordinances, the Puritans tried to practice marriage prohibitions in accordance with Biblical teachings. For example, a bill was passed in Massachusetts in 1695 prohibiting marriage with the sister or niece of a former wife. Punishment for such incest infractions in Connecticut consisted of 40 lashes and the wearing of a big "I" (for incest) on the arm or back.[79]

Anyone planning to marry in seventeenth-century Massachusetts had to provide bond against the possibility of violating any of the marriage impediments. Parental permission was also required. This law was tempered somewhat by the fact that the parents had to show cause why the courtship should not be permitted if the swain petitioned for such an explanation.

Laws were sometimes enforced in somewhat informal surroundings. New London, Connecticut, was once scandalized by a man and woman who moved in together and considered themselves married without benefit of law. One day a magistrate met them in the street, and sternly inquired:

> "John Rogers, do you persist in calling this woman, a servant, so much younger than yourself, your wife?" "Yes, I do," retorted John. "And do you, Mary, wish such an old man as this to be your husband?" "Indeed I do," she said. "Then, by the laws of God and this commonwealth," was the disconcerting reply, "I, as a magistrate, pronounce you man and wife."[80]

If New England led in restrictive laws regarding marriage, the other colonies were not totally wanting. Pennsylvania incarcerated bigamists for life in Benjamin Franklin's time, and at one time also enforced the old English law forbidding marriage for one year after the death of a spouse. Virginia strongly forbade any marriage not only between colored and white persons but between freemen and indentured servants or between two servants, unless the consent of the master was obtained. The penalty for violation of some of these codes, which were passed between 1642 and 1662, consisted of several years of extended service for servants and 1,500 pounds of tobacco or a year's extra service to the master by the freeman. By 1748, however, the extra service of servants had been commuted to £5, and extreme punishment for marital infractions gradually disappeared in the colonies.

MARRIAGE CUSTOMS AND COURTSHIP

Courtship was at first strongly regulated; in the South, the chaperone system prevailed. Among the Puritans, a man wooing without the consent of the lady's parents was subject to fine. Arthur Howland, Jr., paid £5 for courting Elizabeth Prence without her father's permission. But most parents did not force their children to wed against their wishes.[81]

As among the well-to-do in Europe, marriage sometimes involved money as well as affection. Judge Samuel Sewall married three times. One of his courtships became strained when Mrs. Winthrop insisted on having a carriage if she married him. He declined, noting that it would cost £100 per annum; but she insisted that it would cost only £40.[82] When the courtship came to naught, the Judge found another widow with whom he began to negotiate terms: he should be held "harmless" in the administration of her property, and should receive £100 if he survived her. If he predeceased her, she would receive £50 per annum for life. After some negotiation, he agreed to take nothing after her death if her sons by a previous marriage posted bond that she was free of all debts. Naturally, for his generosity he insisted that his payment to her after his death should be cut from £50 to £40 per annum. As luck would have it, she survived the Judge by a number of years, thereby putting a drain on his estate.

By the eighteenth century, wooing had become much more stylized than in Puritan days.[83] A woman was supposed to be shocked by—and even "disapprove"—her lover's initial declaration of affection. As the suitor poured forth his heart in succeeding visits, the woman, according to George Washington himself, in his advice to his stepdaughter, must not even indirectly let him know that she cared for him. If he still continued to court her, he proved his honest intentions. *The Spectator* warned, however, that it was hazardous to persist in this game and to exceed proper form.[84] The ardent swain should also commit himself in writing, because breach of promise could be redeemed in pounds sterling by a successful legal suit.

Bundling

The poor were far less formal in their courtship. A popular custom, "bundling," merits some discussion. To engage in bundling, unmarried couples occupied the same bed, without undressing, for the purpose of carrying on a courtship. Its origins are unclear, but it flourished about the middle of the eighteenth century along the Northeastern and Atlantic seaboard. The area's small farms required work during the daylight hours. How, then, could couples get together for courting? The family generally retired shortly after dark. A parlor and sofa were unknown; guest rooms were almost unheard of. Perhaps the young man and woman had seen each other briefly while on errands or at church. In any event, with their parents' permission, the young man could spend the night with the young lady in whom he was interested in order to get to know her better.

Various ways were devised to forestall physical contact: a wooden board might be placed in the middle of the bed; the young girl might be encased in a type of long laundry bag up to her armpits; or her garments might be sewn together at strategic points. It is doubtful that sex was a convenient product of such arrangements. Certainly, the girl was in little danger, for a well-placed scream would have brought instant aid. The idea of the couple in bed, however, brought prurient visions to the minds of many, and Washington Irving could not restrain himself from satirizing the custom: "To this sagacious custom, therefore do I chiefly attribute the unparalleled increase of the Yanokie or Yankee race; for it is a certain fact, well authenticated by court records and parish registers, that, wherever the practice of bundling prevailed, there was an amazing number of sturdy brats annually born unto the State, without the license of the law, or the benefit of clergy."[85]

In time, bundling jokes made the rounds; in one of them, a mother asked her daughter if she had kept her limbs in the bundling bag, and the innocent Miss replied, "Ma, dear, I only took one out."[86] Neither Washington Irving nor jokes could sound the death knell for bundling. But it perished after the Revolutionary War, the victim of settled communities, increased leisure time, and new courting instruments—the parlor and the sofa.

SEX AND MARRIAGE PROBLEMS

Adultery and Fornication

The Bible treated adultery harshly, and the Puritans, who tried to behave in compliance with Scripture, did likewise. They believed that lax sexual behavior tended to threaten the salvation of the sinner's soul. To put a soul in jeopardy, even one's own, was a heinous crime, and should be dealt with accordingly. The penalty for adultery in every New England colony, except Rhode Island and Plymouth, was death. However, few courts enforced this law fully. In the main they resorted to whippings, fines, and branding. By 1673, Connecticut had dropped the death penalty in favor of the gentler punishment of branding the letter "A" on the foreheads of offenders.[87] Massachusetts, in 1694, formally abandoned the death penalty, but the adulterer had to stand on the gallows with a rope around his neck, undergo a severe whipping, and be obliged to wear the scarlet letter "A." If caught at any time without the letter, he faced another whipping.

On one occasion, a woman who had borne an illegitimate child was forced to stand in the Boston market place with the placard, "Thus I stand for my adulterous and whorish carriage."[88] As an additional punishment for adulterers in New England, they were forbidden to remarry. Usually, however, the adulterer moved elsewhere where he could remarry with impunity.

Severe punishment was not the sole province of New Englanders. Although there were no death sentences, pillories, or scarlet letters in the South, the transgressor was whipped, fined, and forced to wear a rope around his neck. The Great Law of Pennsylvania added a year's imprisonment to the whipping. The notorious Colonel Nicholls of New York stipulated that the persons "offending shall bee beared through the tongue with a read hot Iron."[89] This was an unusual punishment for New York and did not survive Nicholls' time.

The weakening of the New England theocracy and the establishment of the Confederation of States witnessed the end of physical punishment for adultery. By 1835 the punishment in most regions was imprisonment or a fine. The eighteenth century also brought more prostitution to the East, which the Puritans had neither explicitly nor implicitly permitted.

Adultery was now viewed much more casually—at least, as far as men were concerned. Benjamin Franklin sired an illegitimate son, Jefferson was rumored to have an offspring by one of his slaves, and Hamilton was involved with a lady, all without much disparagement to their characters. If the men were discreet, it was accepted that they would go elsewhere for their surplus sexual needs rather than unduly disturb their genteel wives.

The *Lady's Magazine* of 1771 portrayed the typical masculine viewpoint in a little morality play. Honoria, the chaste wife, discovers that her husband Moresus is keeping another woman. Intercepting them at their rendezvous, she makes a big row. The husband, angry at being exposed and embarrassed in front of his mistress, tells his wife that her unladylike behavior has made it impossible for him to continue to live with her: "During the whole course of the years we lived together, you never had the least shadow of a cause to complain of my want either of respect or tenderness."[90]

By the nineteenth century, male discretion and female morality were the key to an understanding of moral standards.

Fornication

The attitude toward sexual intercourse between the unmarried was much less severe than that toward adultery. Despite this, any evidence that a couple had fornicated in the past, even though they were currently legally married, made them liable to punishment. Thus, A. F., having a child born six weeks before the "ordinary time," was fined for uncleanness, and his wife was put in the stocks.[91] In Plymouth Colony the punishment for fornication was a £10 fine or a whipping.[92]

Many a couple with a legally conceived fetus must have been apprehensive that their child might arrive a few weeks early. On the other hand, the abundance of reported cases of fornication suggests that quite a number of couples considered their betrothal—which preceded the marriage proper by weeks or months—as license to engage in sexual intercourse.[93]

Another fear was that the child might be born on Sunday. It was commonly believed that a child born on Sunday had been conceived on Sunday, the Lord's day. In some churches children born on this day were refused baptism because of the suspected violation.

A considerable number of couples confessed to premarital fornication. Of 200 persons owning the baptismal covenant in the Groton Church between 1761 and 1775, 66 so confessed. The ready number of public confessions attests to the fact that, in a small community, neighbors were able to keep track of wedding dates, and more embarrassing punishment awaited those who failed to acknowledge their guilt openly. In addition, according to Puritan teachings, confession was good for the soul, and the orthodox habitually attempted to cleanse their sins.

Marriage was a saving grace for fornication. In 1642, Samuel Hoskings and Elizabeth Cleverley of New Haven were soundly whipped after confessing their sin. However, they then went before the court to petition for marriage, and the court rendered the following judgment:

> Samuel Hoskings and Elizabeth Cleverley, being desirous to join together in the state of marriage, and not being able to make proof of their parents' consent, but seeing they both affirm they have the consent of their parents, and with having entered into contract, sinfully and wickedly defiled each other in filthy dalliance and unclean passages, by which they have made themselves unfit for any other, and for which they have both received public correction, upon these considerations granted them liberty to marry.[94]

In 1650, Connecticut made it mandatory for fornicators to marry each other. By the time of the Revolutionary War, fornication was a social misdemeanor rather than a civil one, although technically some states consider it a crime even today.

DIVORCE

Colonial Times

Since marriage was considered to be a civil contract in New England, one would have expected a high divorce rate; but that was not the case. The first New England divorce did not occur until 1661, 40 years after the Plymouth settlement. The recognized grounds of divorce were adultery, bigamy, desertion, impotence, and affinity.[95] There was no recognition of such psychological motivations as incompatibility or cruelty. The only concession in that area was the fact that "malicious desertion" was grounds for divorce. Thus, the Puritans did not lightly regard the breaking of the marriage ties for individual satisfaction.

In Massachusetts, the period from 1639 to 1760 showed an average of less than one divorce or annulment per year. From 1760 to 1786, however, there were 96 petitions for divorce, many of which presumably occurred after the onset of the Revolution and the loss of English regulatory powers.[96]

The usual double standard appears to have obtained with respect to divorce for adultery. Massachusetts men divorced women for adultery throughout the period of record keeping, but it was not until 1776 that the first case of a woman divorcing a man for adultery *only* is known.

In southern colonies such as Virginia, South Carolina, and Georgia, Anglican attitudes toward divorce prevailed: there were no divorce courts and no divorces were granted. Separation from bed and board was permitted only for adultery and extreme cruelty.

The mid-Atlantic colonies hovered in policy between Anglicanism and Puritanism. New York, under the Dutch and early English rule, granted a few divorces. After 1675 the records are obscure, but it appears that New York, with one possible exception, granted no further divorces until the revolutionary period. New Jersey and Pennsylvania showed an inclination to allow a few divorces in the early days. During the first half of the eighteenth century, however, the royal governors took over this prerogative and did not permit divorce. The eve of the Revolution found the colonial legislatures once again granting divorces and the royal governors vetoing these laws in an atmosphere of mounting hostility.

The Revolutionary War placed divorce largely in the hands of the colonies' legislatures. The deficiencies of legislative divorce, however, soon became clear. Faced with perhaps 40 or 50 petitions for divorce each session, they sometimes became so embroiled in a single case that all other business was neglected. At other times, anxious to get on with legislative matters, the cases were disposed of with catechismal chant. Finally the state legislators began one by one to cede their jurisdiction to the courts until, by the Civil War, they no longer handled divorces.

One of the earliest treatises in favor of liberalizing the divorce laws was entitled *An Essay on Marriages; or the Lawfulness of Divorce in Certain Cases Considered.*[97] The author is officially anonymous, although it may have been the printer Zachariah Poulson, Jr. Stirred by the suicide of a woman trapped in an unhappy marriage, the author boldly attacked the basic rationalistic foundation of marriage. Reason, he argued, does not and should not rule the affections. We cannot love at will. Rather, the role of reason is to regulate and govern our actions so as best to satisfy our emotional needs. Moreover, divorces should occur where both parties have basically good dispositions but were not matched correctly. A compassionate, understanding man could tolerate a high-strung, emotional woman; two argumentative, dominating spouses were a mismatch. The author downgraded the notion that easy divorce would result in the breakdown of marriage. In nature, he pointed out, many birds mated monogamously without the need for love. Most couples would stay together not only out of mutual affection, but for the practical reasons of settling estates and caring for children. He shrugged off the argument that marriage was divine; after all, it had existed for millennia before Christ without benefit of divinity. He also noted: "If our creator . . . seeketh or requireth our infelicity, he hath then no longer the attribute of a God, but of a devil."[98] He did acknowledge that, despite all his arguments, some individuals would insist on being tormented in unhappy marriages: "To such we must freely own that all our wits are exhausted, and arguments are at an end; we can only leave them to enjoy what they take to be their greatest good, and assure them, they will not be envied or molested in their so doing, if they do not molest others, in the enjoyment of what they take to be their good."[99]

For every anonymous author who spoke out for freer divorce, there were many distinguished gentlemen who viewed with alarm the growing laxity of the marriage laws. They urged their brethren to hold the line against the sweeping tide of immorality that must follow any weakness in the bulwark of conservatism. Thus, about 1816, Timothy Dwight, President of Yale, declared that Connecticut citizens had become morally corrupt: witness the fact that one couple in a hundred divorced.[100]

The Greeley Debates

From 1840 to 1870, the mantle of conservatism was worn by Horace Greeley, founder and publisher of the *New York Tribune* and later, in 1872, a presidential aspirant. Although, for humanitarian reasons, he championed socialist-utopian communities, his religious background determined his narrow view of divorce.

In 1853 he engaged in a tripartite debate on divorce with Henry James and Stephan Pearl Andrews. Henry James is best remembered as the father of two distinguished sons, Henry James, Jr., and William James. Henry Sr. was independently wealthy and a professional metaphysician[101] who had been influenced by the Swedish mystic Swedenborg and the French prototypal socialist, Charles Fourier. Andrews was a brilliant eccentric whose major obsession was Universology, an attempt to correlate all the sciences of mankind and thus deduce the fundamental principles of the universe. Failure never daunted him, and in 1843 he tried to persuade Great Britain to provide money to free the slaves in exchange for the annexation of Texas. Despite these eccentricities, he proved to be a superb representative of the anarchist position on divorce.

The debate started with James' translation of a Fourierist pamphlet, which had been denounced by *The New York Observer,* a Presbyterian newssheet. Mutual salvos were exchanged between the *Observer* and James. The former claimed that James was attacking the institution of marriage by supporting easy divorce. James maintained that he favored easy divorce, not because he wished to weaken marriage but because he wished to preserve it. Marriage was a spiritual relationship between a man and woman.[102] Its fidelity rested not on artificial restraints but on reciprocal inward sweetness and spiritual appreciation. If true marriage was of the spirit, why force people to stay together who were not really married? Easy divorce would not encourage family breakdown, for the truly married did not need artificial laws to make them toe the mark. Since monogamy was the best way of life, if individuals were left to themselves they would automatically respect the marriage institution.

This view was published in the *Tribune,* Greeley having magnanimously opened its pages to intellectual controversy on the marriage question. Greeley's own position in the debate was that divorce was a sure sign of societal decay, as witnessed, for example, by the Romans. He favored divorce only for adultery, the one circumstance approved by Jesus. The indissolubility of marriage kept out the dissolute, the wicked, and the unscrupulous, who otherwise might prey on the unwary and, after taking advantage of them, skip off to another wife (victim). With divorce a near impossibility, however, they would hesitate to plunge into matrimony.[103]

Greeley conceded the unfortunate fact that there were unhappy marriages. Then let the buyer beware! The fault lay not with the institution, but with the kind of people who married. Probably, if free divorce were permitted, few of those who were *presently* married would want divorces. But future generations would fall victim to the vices enumerated above, and there would be unhappiness and divorce aplenty. Society must be preserved, if need be at the expense of the unhappiness of a given individual.

Andrews' position was that no one should dictate to anyone else what to do in the affairs of the heart or anything else. Who was Greeley to tell him not to cohabit except for progency, or how many lovers to take? As for the fuzzy James, what did he mean by marriage? If he meant the pure state of honest relationship, then let him join Andrews in tearing down the false inhibitions of society. If, however, James meant that marriage was really correct only when it was monogamous and approved by society, then his talk about marital spirituality was nonsense. Which was it?

James' explanations proved more vague than his initial formulations, and Andrews retorted sharply that when Andrews tried to talk sense with him, "he cuttlefishes by a final plunge into metaphysical mysticism."[104] The debate ground to a halt when Greeley refused to print a communication from Andrews which he found too risqué. When Andrews published it himself, the disturbing passage turned out to be a doctor's wife's claim that uterine tumors stemmed from "amative excess."[105]

Despite Greeley's efforts, by 1865 the machinery already existed for relatively easy divorce. True, there was great variety among the states. In contradistinction to the liberal West, South Carolina had not yet granted a single divorce at the time of the Civil War; but the country as a whole was poised to take its place as one of the "divorcingest" in the world.

The Ideal Spouse

We have already indicated that the chief qualities of a good wife, as described in Eastern magazines, were piety, purity, submissiveness, and domesticity. To the farmer, however, industry and vigor were the optimum features. A young farmer, sadly noting the demise of his wife, remarked, "I had rather lost the best *cow I have*, because she [the wife] made so much and such *good butter.*"[106]

The Westerner prized not only industry but physique and a certain uninhibited quality that the "Eastern magazine ladies" lacked. Through the eyes of one of his characters, the hillbilly Stut Lovingood, George Washington Harris, a Tennessee humorist, describes an ideal:

Such a bosom! Just think of two snow balls with a strawberry butt into both of them. She takes exactly fifteen inches of garter, clear of the knot, stands sixteen and a half hands high, and weighs one hundred and twenty-six in her petti-coat tail before breakfast. She couldn't crawl through a whiskey barrel with both heads stove out or sit in a common armchair, while you could lock the *top* hoop of a churn or a *big* dog collar around her waist. Her hair was as black as a crow's wing at midnight, slick as a bottle and long as a hoss's tail. Her skin was as white as the inside of a frog stool and her lips as rosy as a perch's gill in dogwood blossom time. . . .[107]

As usual, there is not much emphasis on desirable male qualities, except that he should be manly, a good provider and, hopefully, a good Christian. As O. S. Fowler described it, "Woman, patronize *muscle,* not dandyism. Smile on strength, not delicacy."[108]

CONCLUSIONS

The two-and-a-half centuries of the development of the United States, from 1607 to 1865, inevitably brought changes from the marriages experienced by immigrants in their native lands. European visitors to America testified to the significant difference between European and American marriages: American women were freer, yet there was less immorality than in Europe. They saw less passion and more friendship between men and women, but only a few deduced the obvious conclusion that European passion might be an artifact of past restrictions in the choice of marital partner. In Europe, after all, passion was rarely directed toward the marriage partner.

Although free choice in marriage was becoming an American standard, it did not carry the same implications that it currently connotes. The choice of partner for purely *individual and idiosyncratic reasons* had not yet become acceptable. Physical passion was still officially taboo as a determinant of marital choice. Instead, normatively acceptable traits were emphasized: kindness, purity, being a good Christian, and being a good provider (in the case of men). However, there were already some advocates of the right to satisfy individual preferences even if they ran counter to the norm. In a brilliant essay at least 100 years ahead of his time, Zachariah Poulson questioned the current mores which denied the validity of feelings as a cause for divorce. Though his treatise had little immediate effect, it did foreshadow the functionalist philosophy of individualism, mobility, and the abandonment of "projects" (marriages) that didn't work in favor of those that did.

The treatment of the black family is one of the saddest examples of human indifference. The disruption of black families as a result of economic factors, the exploitation of black women by their white masters, and the psychological castration of black men all left a residue of antagonism which still exists today within the black community. In fact, the "Negro matriarchy"—a creation of antebellum days, when the black male was robbed of masculinity—has survived to the present era.

Considering that the position of American women compared favorably with that of European women, it may seem paradoxical that such an active women's rights movement emerged in the 1850s and afterward. The paradox is resolved, however, if we hypothesize that reform movements are not based so much on discriminatory practices toward the agitators as upon the discrepancy between what the agitators are seeking and what they perceive they are getting. The level of American women's expectations, in short, rose more rapidly than their perceived gains from 1850 to World War I. Conscious of the growing affluence of their country, women realized that little provision was being made for their development. Slowly, a tide of anger swept over them, and they determined to gain a status independent of that provided by a husband.

The movement could not succeed in the first half of the nineteenth century because there were few economic opportunities for women; moreover, the educational level of women qualified them mainly for unskilled labor. In midcentury, seminaries and full-fledged colleges for girls were established. Shortly thereafter, rapid industrialization greatly increased economic opportunity for women. The invention of the first practical typewriter just after the end of the Civil War also had a significant effect on the employment of women.

Having overcome the initial obstacles to full independence, women pursued their goals with greater determination. The legal nonexistence of women was attacked, and many inroads were made to eliminate discriminatory statutes. The right to divorce was for a time rigorously opposed by many; it would surely not have been achieved in the absence of the possibilities for economic independence. By 1865, women's legal existence was no longer seriously questioned, progressive divorce legislation was making headway, and the full power of the women's rights movement awaited only the cessation of the Civil War. After that, women would additionally profit from the general social movement for greater individual freedom—the totality of which would later shatter many old bans and attitudes regarding marriage and women.

REFERENCES

1. *Records of the Governor and Company of the Massachusetts Bay in New England,* p. 186.
2. J. H. Trumbull (ed.), *Public Records of the Colony of Connecticut.*
3. J. Witherspoon, *Letters on Marriage,* p. 101.
4. J. C. Spruill, *Women's Life and Work in the Southern Colonies,* p. 139.
5. R. Seward, "The Colonial family in America: Toward a socio-historical restoration of its structure."
6. D. Day, *The Evolution of Love,* p. 374.

7. A. Hollander, *Among the Indians.*
8. J. R. Larus, *Women of America.*
9. V. Fern, *Puritan Sage: Collected Writings of Jonathan Edwards,* p. 447.
10. R. M. Frye, *The Teachings of Classical Puritanism on Conjugal Love.*
11. C. Mather, *Diary of Cotton Mather,* p. 69.
12. E. S. Morgan, *The Puritan Family,* p. 16.
13. Ibid., p. 12.
14. Ibid., p. 12.
15. *Winthrop Papers,* p. 396.
16. C. W. Fergusen, *The Male Attitude,* p. 98.
17. H. Phyz, Letter to *American Magazine,* 1757.
18. A. Project, Letter to *American Magazine,* p. 126.
19. J. Witherspoon, "Necessity of equality and rank and age in the matrimonial union."
20. B. Franklin, "The old mistresses' apologue."
21. B. Franklin, "A letter to John Alleyre Esq. on early marriage."
22. C. Van Doren, *Benjamin Franklin.*
23. B. Franklin, "The old mistresses' apologue."
24. B. Franklin, "Reflections on courtship and marriage," p. 24.
25. B. Franklin, *Autobiography,* p. 150.
26. B. Franklin, "Reflections on courtship and marriage," p. 61.
27. Ibid., p. 63.
28. B. Franklin, *Autobiography,* p. 128.
29. C. Lopez, *Mon Cher Papa: Franklin and the Ladies of Paris,* p. 259.
30. Ibid.
31. "Only nine?" p. 113.
32. A. H. Everett, *New Ideas on Population with Remarks on the Theories of Malthus and Godwin.*
33. M. Weems, *Hymen's Recruiting Sergeant,* p. iii.
34. E. F. Frazier, *The Negro Family in the United States.*
35. E. F. Frazier, *The Negro Slave Family.*
36. L. Ruchames, *Race, Marriage and Abolition in Massachusetts.*
37. W. J. Cash, *Mind of the South.*
38. M. B. Chesnut, *A Diary from Dixie,* p. 21.
39. C. W. Ferguson, op. cit.
40. *The Suppressed Book about Slavery,* p. 175.
41. G. E. Howard, *A History of Matrimonial Institutions,* Vol. 2, pp. 225-226.
42. E. F. Frazier, op. cit.
43. H. E. Mitchell, "Social class and race as factors affecting the role of the family in thematic apperception test stories of males."
44. H. Beyle, *On Love,* p. 196.
45. M. L. E. Moreau de Saint-Méry, "The bitter thoughts of President Moreau," p. 99.
46. J. S. Buckingham, *The Eastern and Western States of America,* Vol. 1, p. 479.
47. A. de Tocqueville, *Democracy in America,* Vol. 2, p. 213.
48. Ibid., p. 214.
49. A. Calhoun, *A Social History of the American Family.* Vol. 2; *From Independence through the Civil War.*

50. I. Löwenstern, "A savant from Austria."
51. M. Chevalier, *Society, Manners, and Politics in the United States.*
52. K. T. Griesinger, "A historian's forebodings."
53. A. Calhoun, op. cit., p. 150.
54. F. Trollope, *Domestic Manners of the Americans.*
55. F. A. Pulszky and T. Pulszky, "The Friends of Kossuth."
56. H. Martineau, *Society in America,* Vol. 2.
57. F. F. Furstenberg, "Industrialization and the American family: a look backward."
58. E. S. Morgan, op. cit.
59. D. Day, op. cit., p. 374.
60. A. Burr, "Aaron Burr to his wife."
61. S. L. E., "Hints for young women, particularly those newly married," n.p.
62. D. Day, op. cit., p. 379.
63. Ibid., p. 379.
64. B. Welter, "The cult of true womanhood."
65. Ibid., p. 155.
66. W. A. Alcott, *The Young Wife,* p. 82.
67. D. Day, op. cit., pp. 398-399.
68. B. Welter, op. cit., p. 160.
69. Ibid., pp. 159-160.
70. A. Calhoun, op. cit., Vol. 2, p. 326.
71. G. Fitzhugh, *Sociology for the South,* p. 2.
72. B. Welter, op. cit., pp. 164-165.
73. Ibid., p. 165.
74. Ibid., p. 165.
75. Ibid., p. 172.
76. A. Sinclair, *The Emancipation of the American Woman.*
77. S. Ditzion, *Marriage, Morals, and Sex in America,* p. 257.
78. Ibid., p. 228.
79. A. Calhoun, op. cit., Vol. 1, p. 100.
80. Ibid., p. 63.
81. C. Holliday, *Woman's Life in Colonial Days,* p. 257.
82. S. Sewall, *Sewall's Papers,* Vol. 3.
83. A. H. Wharton, *Colonial Days and Dames.*
84. J. C. Spruill, op. cit., p. 149.
85. W. Irving, *Knickerbocker's History of New York,* p. 189.
86. A. M. Aurand, Jr., *Little Known Facts about Bundling in the New World,* p. 12.
87. G. E. Howard, op. cit.
88. Ibid., p. 174.
89. Ibid., p. 286.
90. J. C. Spruill, op. cit., p. 174.
91. E. S. Turner, *A History of Courting.*
92. J. Demos, *A Little Commonwealth: Family Life in Plymouth Colony.*
93. C. L. Powell, "Marriage in early New England."
94. C. J. Hoadley, *Records for the Colony and Plantation of New Haven,* pp. 77-78.
95. N. M. Blake, *The Road to Reno.*

96. G. E. Howard, op. cit.

97. Z. Poulson, Jr., *An Essay on Marriage.*

98. Ibid., p. 20.

99. Ibid., p. 23.

100. N. M. Blake, op. cit.

101. F. H. Young, *The Philosophy of Henry James, Sr.*

102. J. L. Blau, *Men and Movements in American Philosophy.*

103. S. P. Andrews, *Love, Marriage and Divorce and the Sovereignty of the Individual.*

104. S. Ditzion, op. cit., p. 164.

105. N. M. Blake, op. cit.

106. O. S. Fowler, *Matrimony,* p. 242.

107. D. Day, op. cit., pp. 383-384.

108. O. S. Fowler, op. cit., p. 240.

15

Nineteenth-Century Experiments in Marriage in the United States

By the nineteenth century the Rousseauian message that man's troubles stemmed not from his evil nature, but from malformation by society, had permeated Western thinking. But Europe seemed too moribund to allow much hope for innovation, and the eyes of reformers focused on unsettled America.[1] Where else but in America was land cheap, life full of opportunities, and society sufficiently democratic to allow the formation of a more perfect life? Immigrants flocked to the New World, driven by religious persecution, famine, politics, and the displacements of the Industrial Revolution. New ideas advanced by European socialist-oriented writers, such as Saint-Simon and Charles Fourier, also came to America's shores. Some radical groups—for example, the Mormons and the Oneida Community—were products of the indigenous religious revival that swept the country at the beginning of the nineteenth century.

A small number of Americans elected to live communally—sometimes as a result of economic need, but more often because of a desire to chart a path for their own salvation and for future generations.[2] Fascinating as an evaluation of these experimental societies may be, we must restrict ourselves here only to those which professed to change the relationship between the sexes and/or had implications for the institution of marriage. Even with this restriction, which eliminates the more or less exclusively economic utopias of New Harmony and Brook Farm, we shall describe only a few groups that altered the marriage form.

Our sample may be generally classified as having basically a secularist or a religious orientation.

The secularists did not favor violent overthrow of existing governments, preferring to demonstrate the superiority of their own society by practice; they assumed that the rest of mankind, witnessing their success, would soon emulate their example. Some of them believed that the good life could be achieved by doing away with traditional government in favor of socialism: private property would be abolished and all property held in common or in joint stock. Other secularists were anarchists who perceived all regimentation as odious; if left alone, man would inevitably gravitate toward just and equitable relationships with his fellow men. Their approach to religion ranged from tolerant indifference (Fourier) to implacable hostility (Owen).

The religionists believed that they were the elect of God and were destined to lead to salvation those who would be saved. The Moravians, the Shakers, and the Oneida Community believed that communal life followed the path of Jesus; the Mormons settled for the tithe to the Church rather than communal ownership. The religionists' attitudes toward sex and marriage varied immensely, but all of them believed that their views benefited from divine guidance.

The secular communities of Nashoba, the Fourieristic communes, and the anarchical views of Warren, the Nicholses, and Lazarus will be dealt with first, followed by a discussion of religious groups—Moravians, Shakers, the Oneida Community, and Mormons. An evaluation of the strength, weaknesses, and significance of these communities will also be presented.

THE SECULARISTS

Frances Wright, the Priestess of Beelzebub

Born in 1795, the remarkable and dynamic Frances Wright had managed, by her mid-twenties, to become the protégée of none other than the internationally celebrated hero, the Marquis de Lafayette. She was not only a critic of private property, restrictive religion, and traditional marriage, but a fearless fighter for women's rights and a champion of the cause of blacks.[3] In 1826, with her sister Camilla, she founded a settlement on the Wolf River near Memphis and called it Nashoba (the Chickasaw Indian name for the Wolf River). Nashoba was open to both whites and blacks (the latter were purchased slaves). Although the earnings of Nashoba were to be communal, the blacks' share would at first go to pay off their purchase price. The community began with the encouragement of rather prominent people: Madison, Monroe, Lafayette, and Jefferson, among others.

It soon became apparent that things were not working out very well. The slaves were not idealists and had not been selected for their interest in the project. Nor were they ardent workers. In addition, malaria, floods, constant rain and dampness, and poor soil made Nashoba a wretched place in which to live and work. Frances became so ill that she left for Europe for her health. Meantime, one of the trustees, James Richardson, had sent records from Nashoba's files to an abolitionist publication, which printed a story on the settlement's ideas about the unsoundness of marriage and religion, and the fact that Richardson, a white man, was living openly in sin with the mulatto Josephine. The other newspapers called Nashoba "a great brothel."[4]

When the news reached Frances, she boldly proclaimed that blacks and whites were already living together in southern society, albeit surreptitiously. She envisioned that a happy blending of black and white would yield a new, cream-colored race. Marriage laws outside of Nashoba had no meaning for that community, she declared, and its men and women, unlike the rest of the world, enjoyed equal rights.

But upon her return to Nashoba, she discovered some variations from the true path. One of the slaves, Redrick, had unidealistically tried to force his attentions on another slave, Isabel. Richardson and Josephine had left to try their fortunes in the capitalist world. Only one white woman and one white man were left: Camilla, Frances' sister, and a man named Whiteby. As Camilla explained, to forestall talk they had married. Within a few years Nashoba failed, and Frances and Camilla accompanied the remaining slaves to Haiti and freedom, where the sisters were royally feted for their deed.

After an unhappy marriage, Frances returned to the platform to resume her role as America's foremost woman lecturer. In her talks she explained that it was not marriage per se which she opposed, but its evils. She argued for women's right to education, self-respect, dignity, freedom of divorce, abolition of imprisonment for debt, and just about everything that is taken for granted today. But such a stance 130 years ago was shocking, particularly to men. "A female monster," cried the *New York American.* "A bald blaspheme and a voluptuous preacher of licentiousness," gasped the *New York Commercial Advertiser.*[5]

Some people felt that words were not enough. At one of her lectures the lights were turned off, leaving 2000 souls in darkness. On several occasions small fires were started and an attempt was made to stampede the audience by shouting "Fire!" When all else failed, and it did, vegetables and other projectiles were thrown as she stood on the stage. She survived with the courage of a lioness, but some slippery ice in Cincinnati finally brought her down and she died in 1852. Frances Wright was a remarkable person, but she had preceded the *Zeitgeist* by too great a time span and, as an intense individualist, had failed to develop a coterie of followers. Unfortunately, the women's movement was not directly affected by her efforts.

FOURIER AND THE PHALANX

At the onset of the nineteenth century, a pinched, frigid (possibly impotent) French salesman, François Marie Charles Fourier (1772-1837), was busy constructing a grand scheme for the salvation of the world. We shall touch briefly on his world scheme, concentrating on those aspects that deal with marriage.

Fourier's approach was psychological. Man possessed a vast complex of passions and desires. Good! He must be accepted as he is. The good life comes about by understanding these passions and employing them to benefit both the individual and society. Fourier therefore opposed the idea that a rational life was the means to happiness.

He paid lip service to the existence of God, but observed that God, busy with his multitudinous planets, does not intervene in earthly activities—He is the silent partner of Fourier. Civilization has become a cesspool of corruption, vice, and economic malfunctioning. It must be destroyed, and 16 stages successfully passed through in order to achieve the utopia of harmony. Marriage, in the civilization of his day, is "pure brutality, a casual pairing off provoked by the domestic bond, without any illusion of mind or heart."[6] The idea of monogamy made little sense because it would be difficult to match people perfectly, and few would desire a constant diet of satiety with only one spouse. To compel a Don Juan to obey a law intended for the benefit of the monogamous-minded was a blasphemy against God. Did not God instill passions in man? Would anyone care to question his omniscience? To understand God's ways better, Fourier went to some lengths to describe the passions.

The Passions

In *Le Nouveau Monde Industriel,* Fourier defined passionate attraction as "the drive given us by nature prior to reflection; persistent despite the opposition of reason, duty, prejudice, etc. . . ."[7] The passions were divided into three categories—luxurious, groups, and serial—and many subdivisions. There were, in all, 810 basic combinations of passions, and in the ideal state there should be perhaps two of each combination in a commune, which he called a phalanstery. Each person traveling from one phalanstery to another would be interviewed by an expert in passion matching[8] and have his passional combination recorded. He would then be introduced to his appropriate number of the opposite sex, and quickly initiate an amorous relationship.

Obviously, Fourier was much more of a hedonist than Freud: the latter saw some benefits in repressing and sublimating instinctual drives, but the former could see none. Here is Fourier's definition of happiness:

> What does happiness consist of but to experience and satisfy an immense quantity of passions which are not harmful? That will be the destiny of the human race when they will be delivered from the civilized, barbarous, and savage states. Their passions will be so numerous, so fiery, so varied, that the rich man will pass his life in a sort of permanent frenzy, and the days, which today are twenty-four hours long, will pass as if they were one.[9]

Fourier did not banish the family from his utopia. Those who wished to live in perpetual fidelity could do so, but few would want it. A beautiful woman who, in the space of 30 years could bestow her favors on 30,000 men at the rate of three a day, and leave 30,000 fond memories, would hardly settle for the selfish act of limiting her gifts to only one man.

In the established utopia, vast "harmonious" armies would be forerunners of the modern "Peace Corps," building dams, harnessing rivers, and reforesting mountains. But they would draw undreamed-of benefits: an auxiliary corps of women would cook and dabble in fine arts, and each one would be accessible for sexual favors to three or four men. To Fourier, that ratio was proper for a 25-year-old woman. Mock wars would be an outlet for aggressive passions, but no one would be killed. Prisoners would be at the disposition of the conquerors for up to three days. If the captors were women and the prisoners men, the latter could be "borrowed" by older women. The reverse situation might occur if young ladies were captured.

Infidelity would be a crime only if it were committed secretly. Even then it was not a very serious violation, since it had extended the range of amorous relationship of the parties concerned; and this, after all, was desirable. A court of love might dole out a fit "punishment": a convicted young man might have to perform for a crone, who might otherwise have a difficult time. If he failed to service her properly, he was only undoing himself, since his release from "punishment" depended upon her signature on his "good conduct" certificate.[10]

Even the problem of two men loving the same woman was not insurmountable. In ordinary civilization, the loser might become a misogynist, soured on all womankind. Fourier's treatment for the loser might have inspired an adage such as "It is better to have loved and lost than to have loved and won—much better!" A special corps of trained women acquainted with the "loser's" passional makeup would "work" on him to such an extent that he would soon be diverted from his previous lover.

Many individuals admire systematists, but almost all the world loves sex. To find a systematist who posed love—that is, sexual love—as his keystone was unique. Marx later proposed economics as the key to socialism, but how dull this is compared to the systematist who could say that, in the phalanstery, "Love is no longer, as it is with us, a recreation which detracts from work; on the contrary, it is the soul and the vehicle, the mainspring, of all works and of the whole of industrial attraction."[11]

A pure Fourieristic phalanstery, with the stipulated 1,700 participants and a capital of £500,000, never materialized. Nevertheless, his philosophy had immense appeal as an economic doctrine, and Fourieristic societies sprang up all over the world. The man who edited Fourierism for American consumption was Albert Brisbane.

The Americanization of Fourier

Since his adolescence, Albert Brisbane had longed for a great cause. He found it in Europe, and he paid Fourier five francs a lesson to assimilate all that he could. Upon his return to America at about the age of 30, he joined Horace Greeley in spreading Fourier's associationist gospel: he wrote several books and used Greeley's newspaper, the *Tribune,* as a forum.

Phalansteries sprang up all over the United States. In 1843, when the movement was at its height, some 34 communes were opened.[12] But poor Fourier must have turned over in his grave, for Brisbane[13] and liberals such as Greeley and George Ripley distorted his views to accommodate their conservative stance. In their view, associationism would wipe out "economic" marriage and its concomitant ill effects, as well as emphasize the spiritual harmony between man and wife by increasing the equality between them.[14] As to Fourier's love courts and sensual promises, they would occur in the final stage of harmony, which was nowhere on the horizon. That bridge could be crossed at the proper time, but in the meantime, chasteness was the watchword in the American phalansteries, where single men and women were housed separately. Further, family life in association offered substantial economic advantages, so no one should hesitate to join.

THE ANARCHISTS

"Marital anarchists" who moved to communes were a much more peaceful breed than political anarchists. The fetters which they urged the downtrodden to throw off were not forged by capitalist oppressors but by civil and religious magistrates. To be free, man must break the bonds of matrimony.

Josiah Warren

The father of American anarchism, Josiah Warren, had been present at New Harmony, where Robert Owen's communards had debated endlessly while no one harvested the crops. Sick of meetings, he determined to organize a commune based on the following premise:

> INDIVIDUALITY, definiteness, disconnection, disunion is the great principle of social harmony, order, and progress. . . . It is only when DIFFERENT notes are sounded together that we produce HARMONY. . . . I draw the conclusion, that each individual should be at all times free to differ from every other in thought, feeling, word, and deed; and free to differ from himself, or to change from time to time; in other words . . . the SUPREME "LAW UNTO HIMSELF."[15]

At Brentwood, Long Island, in 1851 he founded a colony called Modern Times. It did not want for individualists. The Reverend S. C. Hewitt found his vision improved when his clothes were off, so he went around unclothed. A lady inhabitant wanted to prove to the world that one could live for a year on a simple diet of water and unsalted beans. Unfortunately, her premature death in the eleventh month was interpreted as detrimental to her position. A man moved into a cozy house with three women, but the quartet made so much noise that everyone was glad when they left. The *laissez-faire* approach appealed so much to several New York criminals that they made Modern Times their home base. The anarchical establishment was sustained because its factory prospered from Civil War orders, but it collapsed during the depression that followed the end of the war.

Apart from his feeling about labor and individuality, Warren was hardly an intense reformer. He lived contentedly enough with his wife and children and was willing to leave the marriage institution as it was except that, so as not to impose upon individuality, he favored a two-year contract, after which the participants had the option to renew.

The Nicholses

One of the most unusual and influential couples of the period were two hydropaths, Mary and Thomas Nichols. Self-styled marriage experts, they also advocated wet packs to cure any ailment.

Mary, born in 1810, had married Hiram Gove, with whom she had five children (only one survived) but little intellectual inspiration. She left him, he divorced her, and at the age of 37 she married the 32-year-old Thomas L. Nichols, an ex-newspaperman and soon-to-be medical doctor. Despairing of curing the world by the judicious use of water, they elected to attack the cause of so much disease and poverty: marriage!

In their epic work *Marriage,* written in 1853, they modestly stated, "The writers of this work . . . have lived for six years in a marriage of ever-increasing love and uninterrupted happiness; as blessed a union, probably, as now exists, or ever existed upon this earth."[16] They went on to attack the present "monogamic system of marriage, with the isolation of families, the shutting up and tabooing of men and women which almost annihilates society."[17] Marriage, alas, is like playing a single tune incessantly on one instrument when a multitude of musicians and instruments are available.

The individual is encouraged to look beyond laws. "What the law calls fornication, when it is the union of mutual love, may be the holiest action two human beings can engage in."[18] On the other hand:

> In the Medical College, at Albany, there is an exposition of indissoluble marriage, which should be studied by all those who begin to see that a legalized union may be a most impure, unholy, and consequently, unhealthy thing. In glass vases, ranged in a large cabinet in this medical museum, are uterine tumors, weighing from half a pound to twenty four pounds. A viscus that in its ordinary state weighs a few ounces, is brought, by the disease caused by amative excess—in other words, licentiousness and impurity—to weigh more than twenty pounds. Be it remembered, these monstrosities were produced in lawful and indissoluble wedlock. The wives and mothers who perished of these evils, and left this terrible lesson

to the world, knew only of legal purity. *They* lived in obedience to the Law of Marriage—pious, virtuous, reputable, ignorant women. God grant that their suffering be not in vain![19]

Contrariwise, women who had children by men they loved escaped not only tumors, but the pains of childbirth as well.

As to the kind of society that would save mankind, the two were in complete agreement: "The society that we want is men and women, living in freedom, sustaining themselves by their own industry, dealing with each other in equity, respecting each other's sovereignty, and governed by their attractions; no one presuming to interfere in the delicate, the private, and personal matters of the affections."[20]

The Nicholses had little patience with complaints that anarchy would result in licentiousness, incest, and assassination. Freed from the distorting restrictions of society, man's inherent good nature would conquer all. What if a women had children by different lovers! The children made lovely gifts. "When a woman loves a man, the most beautiful keepsake he could give her would be a living likeness in a child. It is better than a daguerreotype."[21]

Despite their pleas for money to start their ideal community of Desarrolle, none was forthcoming, and they were forced to settle for a small school in Yellow Springs, Ohio. Having once been residents of Josiah Warren's unsuccessful Modern Times colony, they reluctantly concluded that while their community's ultimate goal would be anarchy, for the present there would have to be a dictatorship under the hegemony of the Nicholses. The group was small, never numbering more than 20 and most were Modern Times refugees. They failed at this community also, and in 1857 many were shocked—not just because the community had closed, but because Dr. and Mrs. Nichols were joining the Catholic Church!

When the Civil War started, they sailed discreetly for England. Dr. Nichols lived on almost to the onset of the twentieth century, but his radical days were behind him. In his old age, he concluded that monogamy was the law of nature.

M. Edgeworth Lazarus

A more extreme radical was Dr. M. Edgeworth Lazarus. The title of his chief work clearly announced his message: *Love Versus Marriage.* The universe was a blooming, buzzing conglomeration of conjugation: the sun and the moon did it, as well as the ocean and the earth, not to mention light and air. Who could doubt that rivers had coitus with islands?

He went much further than the usual diatribes against marriage. Even the Scriptures proved that marriage is vile, but sex is acceptable. For example, Christ "is not recorded to have ever married, nor yet to have avoided women, by whom he was cherished with the most cordial affection. It will be answered that these relations were exclusively spiritual. About this the record is silent. It would detract nothing from His character to consider otherwise."[22]

The Fourierist and anarchist communities were generally short-lived (the reasons for which we shall discuss later). In contrast, the religious communities lasted much longer; it is their story that we shall now chronicle.

RELIGIOUS COMMUNITIES

Religious communities were established in the colonies as early as the seventeenth century,[23] and one of the first European communal groups to entrench themselves firmly were the Moravians, who settled in Bethlehem, Pennsylvania, in 1741. Theirs was a pietistic tradition which emphasized that the Bible was the source of truth, and piety and ethical conduct were more important than specific religious beliefs. The Christian priesthood was considered universal, and the laity would share in the spiritual leadership of the Church. The act of sharing by those filled with brotherly love for one another, and the social emphasis on good behavior rather than dogmatic belief, led easily to an acceptance of a communal form of life as the best approach to these goals.

In the Moravian society, the choir replaced the family as the basic unit of society. Count Zinzendorf, their early leader, had formed choirs to enrich the spiritual life of the community by creating an environment conducive to "prayer, song, study, and testimony."[24] This was achieved by a rigid stratification on the basis of age, sex, and marital status. Everyone ate, slept, worked, and prayed within his own choir. At the age of 12 to 18 months, children were placed under institutional care. At age five or six, the sexes were separated into choirs, with other choirs for ages 6 to 12 and ages 12 to 17. After that, inhabitants moved to Single Choirs; and upon marriage, they moved to the Married People's Choir.

The Moravians recognized that not everyone was suited by temperament for marriage. Count Zinzendorf maintained that sexual desire, even within marriage, was detrimental to the soul. However, "given natural temperaments there are situations where marriage is to be encouraged even under such circumstances."[25] Though married, couples generally did not live together, but were given the opportunity to get together privately once a week.

Marriage was looked upon as a religious goal because it gave individuals a legitimate avenue to minister to the religious needs of the opposite sex. The supervisors of Single Choirs would meet from time to time and recommend certain members for marriage to each other, based on estimates of the individuals' capacities to carry out religious assignments. Compatibility of personality was not taken into consideration.

The decision of the supervisors was not final if not ratified by God. God spoke through the lot: the populace received the names of the two candidates and gave or withheld their approbation. The lot, however, was binding only upon those who specifically requested it. Thus, if a Brother requested a marriage partner, he was bound to comply with the lot's decision. The Sister proposed by him as his bride was not obligated to accept his proposal even if the lot favored the marriage. But the fact that God had expressed his will might make her think twice before rejecting the Brother's suit. It sometimes happened that the lot ratified a man's desire to marry, but not to the woman he had requested. He would then be bound to marry any person ratified for him in a subsequent lot.

Within 20 years, the Choir system and marital choice patterns ran into difficulty. An important factor was the imbalance in the sex ratio. Although the emigrés who streamed from Europe were promised spouses quickly, the immigrants' ratio was such that at one point there were seven single men for every single woman. As a result, marriage was delayed for most, and impossible for many. Despite the fact that congregation members were at first forbidden to marry outsiders, the negative sex ratio required some exceptions. Moreover, complete segregation from the outside world proved impossible. Missionaries sent out to convert others were themselves impressed by the notion of free choices in marriage and economics which they found elsewhere, and these ideas filtered back into the community.

In time, the communality of the Choir system was abandoned even though the Choir system continued. The Single Brothers' Choir died out in 1817, and the Single Sisters' Choir followed suit in 1841. The marriage rate declined, religious enthusiasm waned, and outsiders steadily infiltrated Bethlehem. The Moravians survived as a religious sect by adapting themselves to the "American way" of life, but the "experiment" was over well before the end of the eighteenth century.

Mother Ann and the Shakers

Ann Lee grew up in English slums where, having worked from the age of six, she was not spared the sight of wretched poverty and depravity. She developed such a disgust of marriage and sexual intercourse that she extracted a promise from her mother that she would never have to marry. But her mother died, and her father, a blacksmith, married her off to another smith, Abraham Stanley. She bore four children, all of whom died in infancy.

After assuming the leadership of a radical Quaker sect, and guided by a vision, she set out in 1774 for the United States with her husband and a few followers. Her group of Quakers, who trembled with religious ecstasy during meetings, became known as the Shakers. They held that God was both male and female. Christ, appearing in Jesus, represented the male spirit. Mother Ann represented the female spirit and fulfilled the promise of the Second Coming. (When celibacy became mandatory for all members, husband Abraham buckled under the strain and eventually ran off with another woman.)

Other tenets of Shakerism included the common possession of property, a belief in power over physical disease, separation from the world, and confession.[26] A "family" was composed of "brothers" and "sisters," and could total from 30 to 90 individuals. The sexes were strictly segregated and lived in separate stories of large houses. Life was thoroughly regulated: one rose "at the first trump" at 4:30 a.m. in summer, put the right foot out of bed first, and kneeled in prayer with the right knee placed where the right foot had touched! Everyone dressed with their backs to the center of the room to avoid seeing the nudity of the others. The "second trump" signified that women could open their doors, for the men had removed their chamber pots, which were, after all, suggestive of sex.

Each "brother" had a "sister" who mended his clothes and did his laundry. In a world of celibacy, however, interaction between the sexes had to be carefully regulated: men and women had separate stairs and were not allowed to pass each other unless a third person, aged ten or more, was present.[27] If a person of the opposite sex offered a hand, it could be shaken for the sake of civility, but the incident had to be reported to the elders.

The chief form of social interaction was the "room visit." The women of one room would be assigned to visit a room of men. During the "bacchanal," they sat in rows, facing each other in their drab garments, handkerchiefs on laps to protect their clothing. The men praised the women for their cooking, and the group engaged in riddle-spinning, singing, and the like. The men carefully avoided talking about "men stuff," which would have been too deep for the ladies.

Intellectual activity was frowned upon; even Bible-reading was discouraged. Yet the outside world was not condemned for sexuality and private enterprise. The Shakers had assumed the task of saving man and preparing him for life in heaven, where presumably the Shaker life of celibacy would continue. Shakers welcomed visitors with friendliness, honesty, and cheer. They admitted failure from time to time in separating men and women, and would even send away such "fleshing off" couples with good wishes and some money.

In their heyday in the middle of the nineteenth century, the Shakers had several thousand members and more than 50 communities. They were a tourist "must" for great personages and for other experimenters in marriage. De Tocqueville, De Beaumont, Dickens, Martineau, and Robert Dale Owen were among those who praised the Shakers' piety, honesty, and friendly spirit but criticized their celibacy, rigidity, and intellectual vacuousness.

The Shakers slowly declined in number after midcentury, even though they prospered financially because of their manual skills and superb craftsmanship. They succumbed because the religious revival that had once swept the country went into decline. Women, who had been the core of the sect, now found opportunities to lead an interesting life in the outside world—even those who had no desire to marry. Married women, weary of childbirth, no longer felt impelled to join the movement because contraceptive methods offered a more pleasant solution than a radical flight from the real world. By 1950 less than 100 Shakers remained, and by the time of the writing of this book it is possible that the last Shaker has died.

The religious groups we have so far described were not sympathetic to gratification of the flesh. There were, however, two communities which seemed to combine the best of both worlds, religion and sex—the Oneideans and the Mormons.

THE ONEIDA COMMUNITY

An Antecedent: Spiritual Wives

The great religious revival of the United States was in full swing in the 1830s. A far-flung population, sweating and straining to carve out the West, needed a special kind of emotional contact to overcome the loneliness of the isolated farm. Frontier settlers had no need for the "stuffed-shirt" Episcopalian ritual or the Congregational sermons of the East.

Into this breach stepped a lawyer-turned-preacher, Charles Grandison Finney (1792-1875). His Perfectionism espoused a permanent state of consecration of the soul toward God.[28] He also stressed that man could, by his own choice, remold himself and become a constantly improving person.

Miss Lucina Umphreville, nicknamed "Miss Anti-Marriage," went much further than Finney. She preached celibacy as the only means to salvation. This did not preclude love between men and women: brotherly and sisterly affection could replace carnality. Lucina traveled everywhere with the Reverend Jarvis Rider, her spiritual mate, and they kissed each other on the one theologically approved area—the forehead. But the celibatic siren's song offered little attraction—nineteenth-century America needed and wanted marriage.

But what was marriage? To the religious it was a perfect and eternal union of souls. The marriage of those who wed because of parental pressure, economic reasons, or lust was not a spiritual union. What should be done? The ultraconservative view was that the yoke of matrimony, no matter how onerous, must be borne in this world, even if it meant that only in the next world could one find a true spiritual mate. A more extreme solution was favored by John Humphrey Noyes (1811-1886).

John Humphrey Noyes

Noyes was the son of a Vermont banker and congressman. After attending Yale and becoming a minister, young Noyes started out as a Finney Perfectionist; but instead of striving to be perfect, he developed the philosophy that man was already perfect! Why? Because Jesus had returned to earth for his Second Coming shortly after 70 a.d. Hence, all true Christians were now saved or perfect, and any remaining sinners were of the devil.[29]

In support of his contention, Noyes noted that Christ had said he would soon return, and all signs of the approach of the Second Coming were evident within the age span of the apostles. By an affirmation of simple faith, it must be concluded that he had indeed come. Many people were confused because they expected that his return would be physical, whereas actually it was spiritual.

Such heresy was enough to have his preaching license revoked, but Noyes had much more to say. Even though he is redeemed, man must earn in his earthly life the state of perfection already assured him.[30] People must live like the early Christians: abjure self-seeking and promulgate full spiritual equality. Concerning marriage, Noyes noted that death ends it. When Christ died, he died for all and, in essence, all died. All were resurrected with Christ, and marriage, as it existed earlier, was no longer recognized.[31] What then?

> When the will of God is done on earth, as it is in heaven, *there will be no marriage.* The marriage supper of the Lamb is a feast at which *every dish is free to every guest.* Exclusiveness, jealousy, quarreling, have no place there, for the same reason as that which forbids the guests at a thanksgiving dinner to claim each his separate dish, and quarrel with the rest for his rights. . . . I call a certain woman my wife—she is yours, she is Christ's, and in him she is the bride of all saints.[32]

In less allegorical prose, Noyes spelled out what he perceived to be the truth that all were afraid to enunciate:

> All experience testifies (the theory of the novels to the contrary notwithstanding), that sexual love is not naturally restricted to pairs. . . . Men and women find universally (however the fact may be concealed), that their susceptibility to love is not burnt out by one honey moon, or satisfied by one lover. On the contrary, the secret history of the human heart will bear out the assertion that it is capable of loving any number of times and any number of persons, and that the more it loves, the more it can love. . . .
>
> The law of marriage "worketh wrath." 1. It provokes to secret adultery, actual or of the heart. 2. It ties together unmatched natures. 3. It sunders matched natures. 4. It gives to sexual appetite only a scanty and monotonous allowance, and so produces the natural jealousy. 5. It makes no provision for the sexual appetite at the very time [puberty] when that appetite is the strongest. . . . This law of society bears hardest on females, because they have less opportunity of choosing their time of marriage than men. This discrepancy between the marriage system and nature is one of the principal sources of the peculiar diseases of women, of prostitution, masturbation, and licentiousness in general.[33]

Noyes' marriage proposal to Harriet Holton was consistent with his philosophy: "We can enter into no engagements with each other which shall limit the range of our affections. In fact, the object of my connexion with her shall be, not to monopolize and enslave her heart, or my own, but to enlarge and establish both in the free fellowship of God's universal family."[34] Harriet agreed completely and the nuptial knot was quickly tied.

By the early 1840s, Noyes, Harriet, a few friends, a printing press, and a farm represented a new colony of "Bible communism." In some ways Noyes seemed irrational—for example, his rejection of the idea that illness might have a physical cause. Illness, in his view, was the product of licentiousness, and Noyes claimed the power to heal the sick.

On the other hand, his analysis of the strengths and failures of other communes shows a talented, analytical mind. Religious revivals, he said, bred social revolutions. While theocratic in nature, the energy aroused by religious enthusiasm wishes to go beyond religion unless it is suppressed. Religious love and sexual love are close neighbors.[35] Hence, the religions that tempt men without satisfying them usually culminate in disaster. Actually, revivals, which are divine, require a complete reorganization of society to complement them. Interestingly enough, Noyes pointed out, the direction taken by a particular religious society depends on whether its leader is a man or woman. In the purely feminine case of Mother Ann, the Shakers adopted celibacy because women love courting and love to talk about love. Men want the love itself. In Mormonism, where men held command, a man's form of marriage—polygyny—was instituted.

Noyes proclaimed that his society would embody the principles of association as advocated by the Owenites and Fourier, combined with a religious view of life that did not deny the value of sex. A happy blend of science, spirituality, and sex would soon rule the world.

To trace the development of Noyes' theory into practice, we shall introduce Mary Cragin.

Sexual Communism and the Cragins

Mary Cragin, a schoolteacher, and her husband George, who was an office manager and accountant for the New York Female Moral Reform Society, read some pamphlets by Noyes and became converted. When the Society fired George for his new views, the destitute couple were invited by Abram Smith, a Noyes disciple, to live on his farm near Kingston, New York.

Smith soon began to send his new farmhand George to a more distant farm for overnight stays, and the angry Mrs. Smith left him. Even when George was at the main farm, Smith would summon Mary for "spiritual counseling" in his room. He told her that deception was necessary because Brother Cragin was such a new convert that he was not yet able to accept the Noyes doctrine fully.

Into this *ménage à trois* came Noyes himself. Divining everything, he rebuked Abram and Mary for having deceived George and not obtaining his permission. George, too, was rebuked for his possessive and legalistic spirit toward his wife. Despite the criticism, the adulterous couple found themselves again entwined in the net of Venus, with the result that Noyes read Abram and Mary out of the Church.

Mary wrote such contrite, misery-ridden letters that Noyes softened, envisioning her as another Mary Magdalene—he may also have been experiencing the same attraction that had struck Smith earlier. As for Smith, he continued to be one of the few all-out supporters of Noyes. Noyes forgave them again, and after diagnosing their relationship he had them sign the following proclamation:

> The transaction between Mr. Smith and Mrs. Cragin was characterized by two vices—*licentiousness* and *deception*. . . . Mrs. Cragin took the lead and was the principal agent in the licentiousness, and Mr. Smith took the lead and was the principal agent in the deception. . . . This is exactly in accordance with the respective tendencies of the two sexes. Woman is strong in the department of susceptibility; man, in that of intellect. Do the parties heartily accede to this judgment? J. H. Noyes
>
> I do subscribe most fully to the above decision, and do wish to take on myself the most of the evil. A. C. Smith
>
> I think that Mr. Noyes is correct in his judgment; and that I took the place of Eve in tempting and seducing man, who is made in the image of God. I sincerely ask Mr. Smith's forgiveness for having dragged him down into sensuality. M. E. Cragin.[36]

The Noyes and Cragin couples, joined by several others, moved to Putney, Vermont, and established a colony with money Noyes had inherited from his father and his wife's grandfather. At the beginning, the group lived in economic communism, but under strictly monogamous conditions. Noyes always claimed to have been a virgin at his marriage and, after that, strictly monogamous until the adoption of complex marriage by the group.

The fuse for the transition was lit by a letter written by George to Noyes' wife, Harriet, while George was out of town. George may have found Mary's taste in men too catholic for him (she was already flirting with others). In any event, his letter to Harriet expressed his love for her as a sister in Christ. Harriet told her husband John about the letter and admitted that she reciprocated George's feelings. Commending her for her honesty, he arranged a meeting of the two couples when George returned.

As befitted such an auspicious meeting, Noyes addressed words of caution to the group and the discourse began. Cragin read his letter aloud, and Mrs. Noyes responded that her heart now belonged to him. Then Noyes asked permission of Cragin to express some words of love to Mrs. Cragin, and Mr. Cragin acceded. Mrs. Cragin then confessed that she had loved Noyes so much that she was afraid he would discover it.

The four now considered themselves reciprocally engaged, and Mrs. Cragin noted in her diary that "we have formed a circle which it is not easy for the Devil to break. We find this evidence that our love is of God; it is destitute of exclusiveness, each one rejoicing in the happiness of the others."[37]

Noyes decided that the time was not yet ripe for physical expression, and warned against kissing and other physical signs of affection. For a short time, sexual tensions were sublimated in a rising din of expressions of brotherly and sacred love.

Suppressed sexuality led to hypermobility, and John and Mary found themselves taking increasingly long walks while pondering the theological complexities of the world. One summer day their tension was so great that they walked a considerable distance from their village and had to rest on a flat rock. The last ounce of restraint melted away, and talk gave way to embraces and to inarticulate moans of pleasure. In the midst of the torrent of libido that flowed from both of them, Noyes' conscience, which would have done Thomas More proud, reasserted itself. Was he no better than an Abram Smith? "I will not steal,"[38] he said to himself, and with superhuman effort separated from Mary, and the two started home. They embraced again and in Noyes' words, "Mrs. Cragin distinctly gave me to understand that she was ready for the full consummation."[39] Noyes decided to tell the group what had transpired so that he could "offer the transaction for criticism."[40]

Cragin was a little taken aback, thinking that he was dealing with another Abram Smith in a preacher's habit. Soon, however, respect for Noyes' honesty—or perhaps lust for Noyes' wife—won out, and he gave his approval, as did the joyful Mrs. Noyes. As soon as was decently possible, the quartet repaired to two separate bedrooms and performed the rites of Venus in a manner befitting true Christians.

By 1847, word of the partial establishment of the Kingdom of Heaven on earth (sexual communism) spread to other members. This proved disastrous, because jealousies and intrigues broke out among the newer converts. Lawyers were consulted, and soon a warrant was out for the arrest of John Humphrey Noyes on the charge of adultery. Noyes and his followers fled rather than stand trial. In 1848, they purchased land on the old Oneida Indian Reserve, and the approximately 50 colonists began anew.

Philosophy and Life at Oneida

Unlike most other communes, Oneida was not completely dependent on agriculture, for various light industries (such as the packing and canning of vegetables and fruit) were introduced. The community achieved financial security because of the talent of one of its members, Sewell Newhouse, who perfected a steel trap that was vastly superior to those made by competitors.

Life at Oneida involved a curious blend of practicality and idealism, and sometimes the mixture led to behavior inconsistent with Oneidan precepts. Basically, its philosophy was anarchical. Laws, Noyes said, were necessary only for the lawless. God reigned over man not by threat, but by instilling in his heart grace, truth, and love. The community, therefore, rejected the Constitution of the United States as infringing upon the freedom of man.

The Oneida community, nevertheless, lived in perfect harmony with its neighbors, obeying all the laws of the township. Moreover, the administration of the colony was far from anarchical. Life was strictly regulated, tasks were assigned to each person, leisure taken at fixed hours, and at the head of the organization was the benevolent dictator Noyes.

Sex

Noyes was profoundly disturbed by the fact that in the early years of his marriage his wife had produced four stillborn children in five pregnancies. Had he the right to inflict such torture on her? The solution he hit upon was *male continence.* In explaining the concept, he first repudiated the idea that sexual congress should occur only in the interests of propagation. The amative function was a legitimate goal in its own right. In fact, the *Oneida Circular* boldly proclaimed that "amativeness takes precedence of Philoprogenitiveness, and parental feeling becomes a usurpation when it crowds out a passion which is relatively its superior.[41] He acknowledged, however, that the nonfunctional emission of semen was contrary to nature. The solution: intercourse without male emission.

Many advantages were claimed for this method. The woman was protected from the physical debilitation of childbirth unless she wanted children, yet the physical expression of love could enjoy extensive latitude. The woman could receive full sexual satisfaction without any consequences. Another consideration was the fact that the colony was financially hard pressed in its early days and hoped to restrict the birth rate until the advent of more favorable times. "Male continence" provided a ready answer.

Many outsiders scoffed at this approach, but Noyes and his colleagues stubbornly maintained that a trained man could stop at any stage of sexual intercourse. Indeed, *very few* children were born at Oneida until the group's plan for scientific propagation. If there seemed to be no large-scale sexual frustration there, a deeper probing of Oneida's sex practices may offer some explanation.

To begin with, it should be noted that not everyone obeyed Noyes' injunction to the letter. Men did lose control from time to time, and a few babies were born. In addition, sexual intercourse with male orgasm was permitted under certain circumstances. For the alleged purpose of teaching self-control—and probably for the realistic goal of sexual relief—men, young men in particular, were allowed to "train" with older, menopausal women.

Oneida's sexual philosophy also dictated that the young should mate with the old. The community was opposed to "selfish" love, with two individuals becoming involved in each other to the exclusion of the rest of the group—a practice known as "horizontal fellowship." It was more desirable to seek spiritual uplift in an "ascending fellowship": a young person improved himself by associating with an older, more spiritual individual.

To the criticism of neighbors that "free love" ran riot at Oneida, Noyes calmly replied that at Oneida everyone was married to everyone else and felt a strong responsibility to help everyone else. There were no known cases of infidelity and practically no surreptitious lovemaking.

The actual mechanics of sexual affiliation involved the presentation of a petition to a committee. If it approved the liaison, an older member would then be appointed to serve as an intermediary for the man. Since women were free to choose anyone they desired (even no one), the presence of an intermediary softened the blow if the suit was rejected. In view of the relative lack of sexual discord reported at Oneida, it seems reasonable to assume that few individuals were turned down by the lady of their choice. Living survivors of the colonies recall that the traditional mores of the man pursuing the woman were adhered to in the overwhelming majority of cases, despite the abolition of traditional marriage.[42]

Once the liaison was established, no permission was needed for continued contact unless the committee thought that an exclusively selfish love was occurring, in which case the couple might be asked to separate. This could be accomplished without much publicity, since the couple did not share a common room. Typically, a rendezvous was carried out by the man appearing at the woman's room and departing an hour or so later.

The freedom of women to reject or accept each supplicant prevented the men from regressing to the usual lethargic state of husbands who, after a few years, take their wives for granted. On the contrary, a continuous state of courtship and gallantry prevailed.

Stirpiculture

For 20 years, the colony adhered to its policy of nonpropagation. During that period (1848-1869), Darwin and Galton had published extensively, and a stirring for the betterment of man through selective breeding began to be felt throughout the world. When the colony achieved a sound financial position, in 1869, Father Noyes announced that all was in readiness for the great experiment—*stirpiculture,* from the Latin *stirps:* root, stock, or strain. Fifty-three women and 38 men attested to their willingness to serve the community. The women signed the following document:

1. That we do not belong to *ourselves* in any respect, but that we *do* belong first to *God,* and second to Mr. Noyes as God's true representative.
2. That we have no rights or personal feelings in regard to childbearing which shall in the least degree oppose or embarrass him in his choice of scientific combinations.

3. That we will put aside all envy, childishness and self-seeking, and rejoice with these who are chosen candidates; that we will, if necessary, become martyrs to science, and cheerfully resign all desire to become mothers, if for any reason Mr. Noyes deem us unfit material for propagation. Above all, we offer ourselves "living sacrifices" to God and true Communism.[43]

The men signed a similar statement.

In the decade that followed, 58 live births and 4 stillbirths were recorded, of which 45 were "stirp" children (the remainder were "accidents").[44] Father Noyes, belying his 60 years, reputedly sired ten children. Of the 100 participants in the project, 81 became parents. Their progeny have been and continue to be unusually long-lived. In 1921, 52 of the 58 offspring were still alive (their age range was 41 to 51).[45] This figure represented 13.3 percent of the expected deaths, by actuarial tables, for a United States population. Of the six deaths, one was killed flying a plane during World War I and another was run over by a train. When William M. Kephart, the eminent sociologist, visited the Oneida Community about 1960, some 13 members were still alive, all of whom were in their eighties and nineties.

What factors are responsible for these long-lived Oneidans? Were they a select stock of hardy New England types? The men in the experiment were, on the average, 12½ years older than the women, suggesting some degree of selectivity for longevity. In addition, participation in the colony must have assumed an above-average interest in sex; sexual interest is probably correlated with both overall energy level and longevity.

Were there effects of scientific mating beyond the effects of natural selectivity? It is impossible to say because the two factors cannot be separated. The only *bona fide* test would have been to allow some volunteers to mate without any selection by the control committee and then to compare them with the arranged matings. Since 81 percent of the applications by couples to sire an offspring were approved, the committee's selection would probably not have been markedly different from the natural selection within the community. Thus, it appears likely that the longevity stemmed primarily from genetic factors indigenous to the Oneida population, plus a rigorous, healthy environment, rather than from selective matching.

In general, life at Oneida was, aside from its sexual aspects, far from monastic. The basic sin was the cult of personality. Smoking and coffee drinking were forbidden as "individualistic and appetitive in nature."[46] On the other hand, dancing was warmly encouraged, because it involved the participation of more than one person.

Despite Noyes' perception of women's inferior status (based on Scripture), in practice he accorded them a generally equal share in administrative matters. But the most important posts were held by men.[47] It must be remembered that at that time women received less education than men, and that for women to seek actively to rule over men would have seemed both unfeminine and un-Christian.

The women took to their new freedom with enthusiasm. They abandoned the traditional, impractical floor-sweeping dress and petticoats for the more practical "bloomer" costume of a shorter skirt superimposed over a pair of pantaloons. Warm though this garment may have been, it did permit unrestricted movement. The ladies also cut their hair short, so that the time normally spent on their toilettes could more usefully be used for community matters.

End of the Experiment

For many years various clerics and other sanctimonious persons had been attacking the Oneida Community and its philosophy. Its enemies gained new strength from the efforts of 28-year-old Anthony Comstock, who, in 1872, organized the New York Society for the Suppression of Vice (also endorsed by the Young Men's Christian Association). In 1873 he was influential in getting Congress to pass an anti-obscenity bill that made use of the mails to disseminate information on contraception illegal on the grounds that such information was lewd, lascivious, and obscene.

Noyes and his colleagues reluctantly stopped using their newspaper, the *Oneida Circular,* to discuss sexual problems and techniques. Inspired by Comstock, Professor John W. Mears of Hamilton College wrote newspaper articles and delivered sermons, demanding to know how long the Empire state was willing to tolerate lust and religious fanaticism. He organized conferences of Methodists and Presbyterians to consider legal means of crushing the sinful community.

The clamor of these reformists did not meet with universal sympathy. The non-Noyes Oneida community, including its newspapers, generally thought favorably of the colony: its people worked hard, paid their bills punctually, and hired many local residents. But the colonists became frightened by Mears and his cohorts. The pioneering spirit was rapidly being undermined.

Noyes, the powerful heart of the colony, was becoming increasingly distant and slowly losing his grip over the group. He had not become senile nor did he undergo any profound change of heart over the tenets of Biblical communism. Rather, time was the chief culprit. Now in his late sixties, his throat was so painful that he could scarcely speak above a whisper. His hearing was failing, and he had to be shouted at to gain his attention.

The children, unlike their parents, were not selected for their commitment to group living. They had merely inherited a tradition, and they varied in allegiance. Their elders, at the start of the experiment, had practiced sex with persons of approximately their own age. By the time of the "stirps," when the youngsters reached puberty—in accordance with the principle of "ascending fellowship"— they had to start servicing the much older men and women. While it was possible technically to refuse these propositions, they were usually made by older, powerful members of the central committee. To refuse these aged lovers on esthetic grounds would have been contrary to the religious foundation of the group and might have fostered the suspicion that "exclusive love" with a young age-mate was the reason.

In addition, unlike many other deviant societies, the youth of Oneida were not isolated from contact with the outside world. Many attended Yale and other universities, and acquired romantic notions of exclusive monogamy. Finally, the religious fervor of Noyes, of the elders, and of the youth slowly gave way to the impact of science. Darwin was replacing Christ as the Lord of creation, and the religious intensity of some of the older converts seemed increasingly naive. A factional wing developed within the colony after it accepted 12 members of a Cleveland "free-love" colony under the leadership of James William Towner, an attorney. Towner became the spokesman for many complaining members who could communicate with Noyes only by written messages.

In 1877 Noyes gave up the presidency of the community, moved to the branch at Wallingford, and named his physician-son, Theodore Noyes, as his successor. Theodore unconvincingly attempted to reconcile his scientific training with Oneida's religious views. Alas, he had none of the leadership or charisma that characterized his father. Instead of mingling and trying to stem the tide of disaffection, he lived in monogamic isolation with his "exclusive" wife and asked the members, including the children, to submit reports so that he could keep abreast of the goings-on.

The senior Noyes was called back out of retirement to end the fiasco, and Mears, the reformer, tried in every way to strike at the colony. Finally, on June 23, 1879, Noyes, counseled by two of his old colleagues that he would soon be arrested, secretly fled across the border to Canada.[48] His shocked and disappointed groups received a letter on August 20, 1879, in which he advised that "complex marriage" be given up to avoid persecution by the state and federal authorities, but that economic communism should be retained. The suggestion was adopted, but it seriously impaired the whole superstructure. The spirit of brotherly love expired as each individual began planning and scheming about what portion of the industrial complex would fall his way when the community went under. On September 1, 1880, assets amounting to $600,000 were divided as shares of stock in Oneida Limited, a recently organized spoon-manufacturing business.

In the midst of all this, the old war-horse Noyes and a faithful aide, Theodore Pitt, made a last stab at reviving Perfectionism. Noyes sent out appeals to former subscribers of the *Circular* to meet him in Chicago. When Noyes and Pitts registered at the Palmer House one day in 1879, they found that only one person had answered the call. Noyes retired to the Canadian side of Niagara, where he died in 1886.

In retrospect, the audacity and skill of the man in almost singlehandedly withstanding three decades of hostility from the outside world and dissension within the colony seem amazing. The social scientist hungers to know what success many of his innovations had. It may safely be assumed that most of the men liked the sexual variety. But what about the women? They have been reported as sexually active on the average every two to four days—some as frequently as seven times a week and more.[49] But was this their real desire, or was it conformity to the subtle pressures of the powerful male members? Women have traditionally been more identified with monogamy than men. Is this identification simply due to indoctrination, or is there something in woman's biological makeup that predisposes her toward monogamy even when society does not countenance it? Did the men really attain control and inhibition of their ejaculatory process, or was there a great deal of coitus interruptus and other sexual practices?[50]

Until about the 1950s, a huge collection of diaries, journals, and letters regarding community life were stored in the vaults of Oneida, Ltd. (diary-keeping was much more prevalent in the nineteenth century than it is today). What happened to this stockpile was related by a company officer to Professor Kephart in an interview:

> I went through some of the stuff—old diaries and things—and a lot of it was awfully personal. Names and specific happenings were mentioned— that kind of thing. Anyway, I reported these facts to the company and it was decided that in view of the nature of the material it should all be destroyed. So one morning we got a truck—and believe me, there was so much stuff we needed a truck—loaded all the material on and took it out to the dump and burned it. We felt that divulging the contents wouldn't have done ourselves or anybody else any good.[51]

Thus, incredible as it may seem, a wealth of priceless data on the state of interpersonal relations in Oneida disappeared forever.

THE MORMONS

The Prophet

The Northeast, and particularly western New York, were hotbeds of religious revival in the early nineteenth century. Mother Ann had traveled through the region with the Shakers, John Humphrey Noyes with his Perfectionists, and Charles Finney and Lucina Umphreville with the Revivalists. William Miller and the Millerites spent the 1840s waiting atop the hills for the floods that would annihilate the nonbelievers. Later on, when revivalism waned, the Fox sisters reported mysterious rappings on tables from the other world, and the Age of Spiritualism was ushered in.

In this atmosphere, religious prophets were almost commonplace, and when Joseph Smith, Jr. (1805-1844), began talking about visits from angels he was scoffed at but hardly regarded as crazy. At the age of 21, after several interviews

BEFORE MARRIAGE

Before Marriage. Turn upside-down for post-wedding outlook.

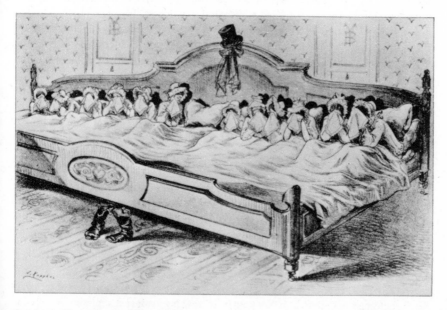

Brigham Young's death in 1877 inspired this artistic comment on the Mormon custom of polygyny.

with angels, he was led to Cumorah Hill, not far from his home in Palmyra, New York. Here he received instructions from an angel as to where the gold plates of the Book of Mormon were buried. This book described the American Indians as the descendants of the ancient Hebrews, who had sailed to America via the Pacific. The book, written in "reformed Egyptian," would have posed a problem for the barely literate Smith except for the fact that he obtained two stones in silver bows fastened to a breastplate, called the Urim and the Thummin. By squinting through these spectacles, the reformed Egyptian was automatically transformed into English.

Most modern scholars regard the book as a hodgepodge of local Indian-origin legends, autobiography, anti-Masonry, and plagiarism from the Bible. Nor does it make for inspired reading. Mark Twain, who described it as "chloroform in print,"[52] also noted the repetitiveness of the language: "Whenever he found his speech growing too modern—which was about every sentence or two—he ladled in a few such Scriptural phrases as 'exceeding sore,' 'and it came to pass,' etc., and made things satisfactory again. 'And it came to pass, was his pet. If he had left that out, his Bible would have been only a pamphlet."[53]

There are also quite a few anachronisms. The use of steel precedes its historical origin by many centuries; the Jaredites sail using a compass centuries before it is first mentioned in other sources; various phrases are the same ones employed by Shakespeare and Pope; and Jesus and Mary are spoken of familiarly by one Nephi, who preceded both by 600 years. Apparently, God has a strong esthetic preference for the kind of English spoken at the end of the sixteenth century. Although the translation was made in the late 1820s, the English used is strangely akin to that of the King James Bible, which is 200 years older.

Moreover, it has become apparent over the years that Urim and Thummin did not provide Smith with 20-20 vision. More than 2,000 changes have been made in the original manuscript, including the deletion of many cases of "and it came to pass."[54]

One passage in the book bearing on marriage (Chapter II, Book of Jacob) states that the Lord found the ancient Hebrew practice of having many wives and concubines abominable; consequently, he ordered that "there shall not any man among you have save it be one wife; and concubines he shall have none."[55] We shall soon see that God would have second thoughts about the incorrectness of many wives.

In addition to his numerous religious duties as a prophet, Joseph Smith drank occasionally and played around with the ladies. He is alleged to have said, "Wherever I see a pretty woman I have to pray for grace."[56] Obviously, his affairs with women preceded his revelation of polygyny by a good number of years. Brigham Young was to say of him years later:

> That the Prophet was of mean birth, that he was wild, intemperate, even dishonest and tricky in his youth, is nothing against his mission. God can, and does, make use of the vilest instruments. If he acts like a devil, Joseph

has brought forth a doctrine that will save us, if we abide by it. He may get drunk every day of his life, sleep with his neighbor's wife every night, run horses and gamble . . . but the doctrine he has produced will save you and me and the whole world.[57]

The prophet was handsome, over six feet in height and more than 200 pounds in weight, all bone and muscle. His most impressive characteristic, however, was his effusiveness. He was a thoroughgoing, friendly extrovert whose commanding presence and magnetic charm, combined with a magnificent physique and a streak of the unconventional, impressed all who came in contact with him.

On July 12, 1843, Smith received the revelation, according to Mormon theology, that God would stand 100 percent behind every act of Joseph Smith. "And again, verily I say, whomsoever you bless I will bless; and whomsoever you curse I will curse, saith the Lord; for I, the Lord, am thy God."[58] After showing that Abraham, Isaac, Jacob, Moses, David, and Solomon had had plural wives and concubines, justifiably,* since the Lord gave them permission, the Lord went on to say, "If any man espouse a virgin, and desire to espouse another, and the first give her consent; and if he espouse the second, and they are virgins, and have vowed to no other man, then is he justified; he cannot commit adultery, for they are given unto him."[59]

The Lord did not forget that Smith's wife Emma had been giving him a hard time about his prerevelation concubines and, in fact, had driven several of them from her house. Therefore, the Lord commanded, "Let my handmaiden Emma Smith receive all those that have been given unto my servant Joseph."[60] The Lord also indicated adherence to a double standard: "And I command mine handmaid, Emma Smith, to abide and cleave unto my servant Joseph, and to none else."[61] When Emma was shown the revelation by a disciple of Joseph, she snatched it and threw it into the fire. As usual, however, Joseph was one step ahead of her: he had taken the precaution of having several copies made.

The revelation, as well as other pronouncements by Smith and his disciples, elaborated the theory of celestial marriage. According to this doctrine, man was at first an ego born into a world of spirits,[62] and his full development ensues from a fusion of spirit and element. Thus, at the appropriate time, a plan in heaven (the spiritual world) called for man to inhabit the earth. Each spirit entered the earth through the process of natural birth. At death, the spirit, if it has lived a good life, passes to the celestial world. The celestial world is variegated and extensive.

Every superior person will be a God and rule as the patriarch of his own kingdom of subjects. However, marital status is decisive. Without marriage one

---

*The Lord was inconsistent in that, in the Bible, He gave Isaac only one wife. In addition, He had apparently changed his mind about the "abominability" of many wives and concubines after what He said in the Mormon Book of Jacob.

could only become a servant angel ministering to those who are far more worthy of glory, the truly married. But even those who have married on earth are not truly married. They are married for *time only,* and in heaven are as if they were single—hence no better than bachelors and spinsters. Those who are married by the prophet in the temple, however, are sealed to each other and married for *time and eternity.* They will remain married in eternity and have separate kingdoms. It was also possible to marry for eternity and not for time; in that case one did not live as man and wife on earth but would do so in heaven.

If a recently converted widower, whose wife had died before his conversion, wanted to reign in heaven with his deceased wife, he could be sealed to her in eternity via a proxy and thereby be reunited with her in heaven. Even a spinster who died without marrying could be saved by a kindly male friend who would marry her for eternity. A spinster who lived alone by preference could be sealed to a man for eternity only, and share his glory in heaven without ever being troubled by his bestial approaches on earth. Naturally, such a man could have other wives to satisfy his sensual needs in that glorious state, for the spiritual world was hardly the antiseptic-asectic place portrayed by most Christian sects. On the contrary, it differed from the ordinary world only in that it was composed of matter so fine that no earthling could see it. In the spiritual world, all the sensations were present—man ate and begat to his heart's content.

God was not viewed as essentially different from man, but as a wiser and older ego who had progressed further than man but could be relied upon for help and advice. A favorite quotation of the Latter Day Saints, as they styled themselves, was, "As man is, God once was; as God is, man may become."[63]

The system was thoroughly masculine in that only men could hold the divine priesthood, and God sent messages to man only through priests. The salvation of each woman was dependent upon her marrying a priest. However, since every male over the age of 12 could become a priest, a woman had only to marry to gain entrance to salvation.

It was also understood that members of the original spirit world were constantly pressing to enter this world via an orderly progression of five stages of development: (1) egos waiting to be born in the spirit world; (2) spirits waiting to be born on earth; (3) humans; (4) disembodied spirits after death; and (5) resurrected beings. The resurrection was taken quite literally to mean that the flesh and spirit would be permanently united. Presumably the already happy disembodied spirits reigning in their kingdoms would enjoy this last state even more.

To return to the earthly sphere, we now see another theologically acceptable reason why the Mormon Church should support polygyny and a patriarchal state and condemn contraception. Countless spirits in Stage 2 were pressing to be born so that they could move on to all the subsequent stages. Each unmarried woman, by not having children, was hindering some spirit from progressing through the cycle. To ensure that spirits were given a fair chance to progress, therefore, every woman should marry and bear children. This was possible only under polygyny and polyandry. For reasons best known to Him, God had forbade polyandry in His revelation to Joseph Smith. Ergo, we are left with polygyny.

The Mormons accepted the Old and New Testaments but interpreted them as strongly supportive of polygyny. God himself quoted Isaiah 4:1 in support of polygyny in order to counteract the effects of war casualties:[64] "And in that day seven women shall take hold of one man, saying, We will eat our own bread, and wear our own apparel: only let us be called by thy name to take away our reproach."

Orson Pratt, an eminent Mormon theologian, reasoned that Jesus himself must have had several wives. True, the Gospels did not say so explicitly, but

> There were several holy women that greatly loved Jesus—such as Mary, and Martha her sister, and Mary Magdalene; and Jesus greatly loved them, and associated with them much; and when he arose from the dead, instead of first showing himself to his chosen witnesses, the Apostles, he appeared first to these women, or at least to one of them, namely Mary Magdalene. Now it would be very natural for a husband in the resurrection to appear first to his own dear wives, and afterwards show himself to his other friends.[65]

Smith's revelation about polygyny was not made public, except for the apostles and a few others. The news was nevertheless electrifying. Many leading Mormons felt it to be a terrible burden that they could comply with only because of their faith in Joseph Smith and the Mormon religion. One may be inclined to say, "He doth protest too much," in examining some typical published reactions, such as this one by Brigham Young: "It was the first time in my life that I had desired the grave, and I could hardly get over it for a long time. And when I saw a funeral, I felt to envy the corpse its situation, and to regret that I was not in the coffin, knowing the toil and labor that my body would have to undergo."[66]

Good Mormon that he was, however, Brigham Young married eight women within one year, and hardly shirked his duty in later years. In the meantime, Joseph Smith and one of his followers, John C. Bennett, had had a falling out, and Bennett published an exposé of the licentiousness of Smith and the Mormons. Smith, who virtually ruled the city of Nauvôo, Illinois, the headquarters of the Mormons at that time, had Bennett's press destroyed. After he fled from state officials who had a warrant for his arrest, Smith was persuaded to return in order to avoid being considered a deserter of his people. He did so with reluctance and was jailed in Carthage, 20 miles from Nauvôo, under the protection of the governor's troops. When a mob of 100 stormed the jail, the troops, who had no liking for Smith, fired a few perfunctory shots over the heads of the attackers and then retired. Smith defended himself with a pistol that had been smuggled in and managed to hit three men, but he was cut down by a fusilade. At the age of 38 the Prophet was called to the next world, leaving 49 wives, 12 of whose former husbands were still living.

Brigham Young

If the enemies of Mormonism thought that Smith's death would finish off the movement, they were mistaken. Brigham Young ascended to the leadership after a brief power struggle. Slightly shorter than Smith and not quite as imposing physically, Young was more stable, a much better administrator, and a great deal more proficient in not antagonizing non-Mormons. The story of his herculean efforts to organize the bitter winter march out of Nauvoô and across the plains to Utah is well known and need not be repeated, and we shall, instead, focus on his attitude toward women and marriage.

In 1852 the practice of polygyny was announced publicly. It had long been an open secret, all too apparent to the increasing number of visitors who stopped at Salt Lake City. In short order it became the chief subject of gossip across the country.

In time, a prosperous trade in exposés of the evil of polygyny developed. A Mormon wife who criticized polygyny was reported as having been kidnapped, carried off into the woods, gagged, "stripped nude, tied to a tree and scourged until the blood ran from her wounds to the ground."[67] She allegedly died a year later. W. Jarman, in his book *U.S.A. (Uncle Sam's Abcess)*, described the murder of a Mrs. Maxfield on the altar for revealing Mormon rite secrets.[68]

The vicious verbal attack of the accusing populace was as extreme as the behavior they attributed to the Mormons in largely falsified tales. The Cincinatti Methodist Conference called Mormonism "a system of masked sensuality subversive of every principle of morality, and abhorrent to every feeling of virtue (which) can only be removed by a resort to arms."[69] The daughter-in-law of Brigham Young told the *New York Times*, "If Salt Lake City were roofed over, it would be the biggest whorehouse in the world."

The violence of these attacks was quite revealing. Some were motivated by genuine religious concern and the supposed bondage of women. Many others, perhaps unconsciously, simply envied and resented men who were enjoying all the sexual privileges that state and church denied to the "moral." Their jealousy is openly mirrored in the humorous commentary of Richard Burton, the noted adventurer, who wanted to become a Mormon and taste the delights of sensuality. Denied the privilege, Burton gazed at the women around him and sighed, "Water, water everywhere, And not a drop to drink!"[71]

Not all the comments were antagonistic or envious. Some pointed to the burdens of husbandhood in a sympathetic vein, as the ficticious experience of the brilliant humorist Artemus Ward illustrates:

> It was leap-year when I was there—and seventeen young widows—the wives of a deceased Mormon—offered me their hearts and hands. I called on them one day—and taking their soft white hands in mine—which made eighteen hands altogether—I found them in tears.

And I said—"Why is this thus? What is the reason of this thusness?"
They hove a sigh—seventeen sighs of different size—They said—"Oh—soon thou will be gonested away!"
I told them that when I got ready to leave a place I wentested.
They said—"Doth not like us?"
I said—"I doth—I doth!"
They then said—"Wilt not marry us?"
I said—"Oh—no—it cannot was."
Again they asked me to marry them—and again I declined. When they cried—
"Oh—cruel man! This is too much—oh! too much!"
I told them that it was on account of the muchness that I declined.[72]

Those who poured into Salt Lake City expecting to see the "new Turkey" were gravely disappointed. The official view of the Mormon Church was that the purpose of sex was procreation. Hence, sexual intercourse was forbidden during pregnancy. Indeed, most of the leaders of the movement were from New York and New England and were quite puritanical. Somehow, thanks to the boldness of Joseph Smith, a rare sexual opportunity had been thrust upon them, but their stern Puritan background forbade them to enjoy their sensual advantages without appropriate rationalization.

Fanny Stenhouse, who married a Mormon official, offered the following example:

I discovered several never-failing signs by which one might know when a man wished to take another wife. He would suddenly awaken to a sense of his duties, and would have great fears that "the Lord" would not pardon him for any neglect. He would become very religious, attend to his "meetings"—testimony meetings—singing meetings, and various *other* meetings! . . .

The young lady was at last selected. She was very pretty, and very *youthful.* The last qualification is very necessary in a Mormon's wife, for then it is expected that she will have more time to bear children to the glory of the kingdom. It must not be supposed that any other consideration influences a Mormon mind. O dear! no. They are such very pure-minded men.[73]

Another means to reduce guilt feelings was to project all lustful sensations onto the rest of the United States. Mormons never tired of harping on the prostitution, fornication, and adultery of the Gentile world.

One of the chief Puritans was the "sultan of the harem," Brigham Young himself. Inevitably dressed in his homespun black suit, President Young loved to attend the frequent dances. He never danced the polka or waltz—they were too lascivious. His preference ran to the more genteel cotillion and quadrille. Moreover, according to John Hyde, Young slept alone in the belief that sexual desires could best be controlled by avoiding the company of a woman when the opportunity was present.

Young had strong feelings about women's fashions:

> The women say let us wear hoops because the whores wear them. I believe if they were to come with a cob stuck in their behind, you would want to do the same! . . . There is not a day I go out but I see the women's legs, and if the wind blows, you see them up to their bodies. . . .
>
> How do you think I feel about it? Who cares about these infernal Gentiles? If they were to wear a s–t pot on their head, must I do so?
>
> I know I ought to be ashamed, but when you show your tother end I have a right to talk about tother end. If you keep them hid, I'll be modest, and not talk about them.
>
> There are these fornication pantaloons, made on purpose for whores to button up in the front. My pantaloons button up here (showing how) where they belong, that my secrets, that God has given me, should not be exposed.[74]

In his attitude toward women, Young was not only puritanical but the stereotype of the patriarch. He advised young men to set up log cabins ten feet square and then "get you a bird to put in your little cage."[75] Wives should obey their husbands and not meddle in their business. As to the wife who thought she knew as much as her mate, Young advised, "Get out of my path, for I am going yonder, and you may whistle at my coat-tail until you are tired of it."[76] A wife should not care too much whether her husband loved her or not. She should "cry out . . . in the joy of (her) heart, 'I have got a man from the Lord! Hallelujah! I am a mother–I have borne an image of God.' "[77]

Young once lost patience with women who constantly whined about their unhappiness with polygyny and their difficulty in accommodating themselves to the presence of other wives. He gave them two weeks to leave, his own wives included, advising them in a sermon that he would supply cash for their needs. The women remained, and their whining continued.

At another time he pointed out that were it not for polygyny he would have had only three sons instead of his ample brood. It must have been hard for him to keep track, for he apparently forgot that his first wife had borne him two daughters, not three sons. According to his last wife, Ann Eliza Webb Young, who later divorced him, Young was surprised one day when a woman greeted him cordially in the street. He stared vacantly at her and at last confessed, "I know I have seen you somewhere; your face is familiar, but I cannot recall you." The lady replied, "You are right; you have most certainly seen me before; I was married to you ten years ago."[78]

Ex-Mormons such as Fanny Stenhouse and Ann Eliza Webb Young considered the status of Mormon women as abject slavery. Strong-willed and able to manipulate men easily, it is hardly surprising that they found it impossible to tolerate polygyny. Their views were reinforced by a number of noted liberals who came to Salt Lake City with built-in prejudices, stayed a few days, and then wrote negatively of the status of women. William Hepworth Dixon, the worldwide traveler and author of *Spiritual Wives* remarked, "I have never seen this sort of shyness among grown women, except in a Syrian tent."[79]

Mark Twain noted sadly:

> With the gushing self-sufficiency of youth I was feverish to plunge in headlong and achieve a great reform here—until I saw the Mormon women. Then I was touched. My heart was wiser than my head. It warmed toward those poor, ungainly, and pathetically "homely" creatures, and as I turned to hide the generous moisture in my eyes, I said, "No—the man that marries one of them has done an act of Christian charity which entitles him to the kindly applause of mankind, not their harsh censure—and the man that marries sixty of them has done a deed of open-handed generosity so sublime that the nations should stand uncovered in his presence and worship in silence.[80]

The evidence indicates, however, that the picture appeared darker than it actually was. Consider the case of the elder in the town of Paragoonah who wanted a second wife, but hesitated to broach the subject with his first wife. It was always necessary to have the first wife's permission as well as that of the President of the Saints and the parents of the prospective bride. The elder eventually summoned up his courage and told his wife that he had had a revelation to marry again. In requesting her compliance, he reminded her that to refrain from carrying out a divine ordinance was a most heinous sin. She postponed her decision for a day, and then told him that she too had had a revelation "to shoot any woman who became his plural wife."[81] They agreed that her revelation took precedence over his, and the matter was dropped.

During the Federal persecution of the Mormons, the women repeatedly petitioned the government to stop "liberating" them. It is hardly conceivable that these petitions would have been so strenuously pushed by "abject slaves." Finally, Brigham Young's own life indicates a considerable gap between his speeches and his behavior. His favorite wife, Amelia Folsom, exercised tremendous power over the patriarch. She agreed to marry him only after he promised her a private carriage and mansion, a box at the theater, a place beside him on special trips, an expensive wardrobe, and a handsome allowance—and she got them all. At the theater she threw apple peels about, and at teatime she threw peanut shells out of the windows. When Young reprimanded her, she told him, "I'll do as I please"—and said to a companion, "Come, let's go upstairs and let him *grunt* it out."[82]

According to his last wife, Ann Eliza Webb Young, Amelia threw a sewing machine at Young when he brought her one of a dubious make instead of a Singer, and threatened to thrash him if he did not comply with her wishes.

But it was Ann Eliza Webb Young who caused him the most grief. He married her in 1869 when he was 68 and she was 24. The prettiest of all his wives, she had been divorced because of the alleged cruelty of her husband. She seems to have become disenchanted with Young almost from the beginning. The aging patriarch did not see her much, and when he took her driving on rare occasions, he avoided streets where he might be seen by Amelia's confidantes. She complained that the house he had built for her was too small, that it was furnished with used carpets from the Lion and Bee Houses where most of his wives dwelt, and that the pine furniture was the cheapest kind obtainable.[83]

Young sent her mother to live elsewhere and gave Ann Eliza very little money. The final straw snapped when he denied her request for a stove. It was a very expensive action: she moved to a hotel on July 15, 1873, and four days later sued for divorce. The story of their legal battles was top news for years. Some newspapers, "influenced" by the Mormons, painted Ann as a strumpet with many Gentile lovers. Others depicted her as a heroine who, through courage and resourcefulness, had escaped the Mormon chamber of horrors.

It took four years to settle their dispute and, in the end, both lost. The court finally agreed with Young that Ann was not legally married to him, thereby saving his estate from settlement and alimony claims. On the other hand, he had to admit in court that he had only one legal wife. The legal position of polygyny, already under heavy attack by the Federal government, was further weakened. The predicted mass breakaway of Young's wives did not occur. Even his discontented wives knew that Brigham, 76 years old, was a very rich man and that they would not have to wait long. Young succumbed suddenly to an attack of *cholera morbus*—acute appendicitis. The Lion of the Lord did not live to see the "principle" crushed.

The Law and the "Principle"

When the "principle" was first officially announced in 1852, it was hoped that the Federal government would agree that polygyny, as part of a religious belief, was permitted under the constitutional guarantee of the inalienable right of religious conscience. However, most non-Mormons did not view the situation in the same light. The platform of the Republican party in 1856 called for the removal of the twin relics of barbarism: slavery and polygyny.

The government differentiated religious belief from practice. Only the former was guaranteed by the Constitution, not the latter. But the country was for a time preoccupied with the slavery issue, and the first antipolygyny legislation was not signed into law by Abraham Lincoln until July 8, 1862. Lincoln would have preferred to let the Mormons alone, but Congress favored action. The bill, which stipulated that a man married to more than one wife at a time was liable to a fine of $500 and four years' imprisonment, also had some loopholes. Enforcement of the law was in the hands of local (i.e., Mormon) courts, not Federal ones. Second, male polygynists claimed, with justification, that according to the laws of the United States they had never been married twice. Finally, Lincoln did not press for enforcement because of the war, his tolerance, or his uncertainty about the constitutionality of the measure. As a result, only two polygynists were ever convicted under this legislation.[84]

Nevertheless, the Mormons could see the handwriting on the wall, and in 1867 they tried unsuccessfully to have the bill repealed. When Ulysses Grant became President and called for the elimination of "licensed immorality," new attacks followed: the Poland bill of 1874 eliminated the jurisdiction of territorial courts over polygyny cases and allowed prospective jurors to be challenged for belief in or practice of polygyny.

Both the Mormons and the Federal government were eager to have the antipolygyny measures tested in the courts, and Brigham Young's secretary, George Reynolds, volunteered to be the guinea pig. Having just married for the second time, he turned himself over to the Federal authorities. He was fined $500 and sentenced to two years' hard labor. The Supreme Court denied the appeal, and poor George had to serve out his time despite 30,000 clemency petitions sent to President Rutherford B. Hayes.

A series of restrictive laws followed, and between 1885 and 1900 more than 1000 Mormons were jailed. The end was near: Church funds were frozen, and the Mormons lost many of their civil rights. The *Salt Lake Tribune* called for a new revelation as a means of saving "face," although the Mormon *Deseret News* denounced the supercilious cynicism behind this plea. In 1890 the new Mormon president, Wilford Woodruff, decided to yield: he issued a manifesto to give up polygyny. Three years later, at the dedication of the Salt Lake Temple, he observed that the manifesto had actually been in response to a revelation. The Lord had sent him a vision of the disasters that would ensue if the Church continued to sanction polygyny. The religious saw the manifesto as a punishment, and the loss of the "principle" as a result of their failure to lead righteous lives.

Persecution of the Mormons ceased, and Utah was admitted to statehood in 1896. Only a small number of Mormons continued to practice polygyny, and a new manifesto was issued in 1904 to provide for their excommunication. Nevertheless, the practice still persists in clandestine form, albeit in very small numbers and in inaccessible areas.

It is noteworthy that some 70 years after the official abolition of polygyny, two small polls taken of Mormons showed considerable sympathy for past polygynous practices. While few favored polygyny for the present era, many were prepared to practice it in heaven in accordance with Mormon theology. The overall conclusion was that polygyny, far from being viewed as sensual opportunism for men, was about equally supported by men and women, which is what would be expected if its roots were religious rather than sensual.[85,86]

Would polygyny have survived internal stresses without the presence of external ones? First, it should be noted that the vast majority of Mormons did not practice polygyny. Estimates vary, but the true percentage probably lay between 3 and 15 percent of the families. Selection seems to have involved such variables as wealth, prestige in the community, leadership qualities, and virility. Polygyny was a prestigious factor in the community; and for some persons, quantity counted as much as quality. Heber Kimball remarked that he thought no more of marrying another wife than of buying a cow. For others, it represented an opportunity to escape the consequences of severe interpersonal difficulties without the need to obtain a divorce. Last, since children were so important for economic and religious reasons, polygyny helped overcome the problem of a sterile wife.

Kimball Young, a social psychologist and sociologist who was the grandson of Brigham Young, attempted to assess the success of polygyny based on his experience in living in polygynous households, on observation of neighbors, on interviews, and on the reading of family records. Using a five-point classification system, he rated 53 percent of the marriages as "moderately successful" and 23 percent as embodying "considerable conflict" or "severe conflict."[87]

These figures cannot be taken very seriously. Young himself states that he did not know how representative his data sample was. In addition, he neither defined his criterion of "success" nor offered any index of the reliability of his measures. About all that can be concluded, conservatively speaking, is that the polygynous household was not necessarily the unhappy cage for women that the Gentile world believed.

In comparing "successful" and "unsuccessful" households, Young does suggest some important factors that influenced success. The successful household was of above-average economic wealth, had partners of similar ages, who were firmly committed to the "principle," and had no wives of grossly disparate ages. An important consideration was the presence of a young, pretty, blushing bride among one or more middle-aged or older wives. This combination made for tremendous jealousy on the part of the older wives and much antagonism toward the new wife and the husband.

In conclusion, it is clear that polygyny was hardly the cesspool painted by the Gentile world, but it did have some advantages and disadvantages. The advantages were mainly on the male side and the disadvantages on the female side, but not exclusively. The asexual spinster, for example, was able to find the comfort and protection of a home, with a minimum need, if any, to engage in sexual intercourse. Such is the variety of human needs and constitutions that no one marriage system could satisfy everyone. Had the external pressures against Mormonism not been present, their religious convictions of the validity of polygyny probably would have ensured its continuation well into the twentieth century.

How the system would have adapted to the emerging insistence of women for greater social, economic, and political equality is a moot question. The theological machinery of Mormonism did not provide the means for women to alter dramatically their position in the Church. Equality would perhaps have manifested itself through a new revelation calling for monogamy.

CONCLUSIONS REGARDING EXPERIMENTS IN MARRIAGE

By the close of the nineteenth century, most marriage experiments had terminated in failure. In attempting an assessment, we must recognize the fact that marital variations were usually accompanied by variations in economic management and life styles. This makes it difficult to ascertain which aspect of the system was primarily responsible for its failure. The societies under consideration, however, may be categorized with respect to their economic, religious, and marital innovations.

The shortest-lived experiments, which rarely survived a decade, were the Owenite and Fourieristic groups. They emphasized economic socialism but, in practice, ignored marital innovation and were either opposed or indifferent to religion. Frances Wright's Nashoba went contrary to the then-current American mores in practically every respect, advocating economic communism, unregulated sexual expression, association of blacks and whites, and an absence of religion. Effectively, it lasted one year; technically, three years. The Owenites and Fourierists had the added misfortune of attracting cranks and misfits who came to talk rather than to work. They also relied too much on agriculture as their main source of income, and were often unable to be self-sustaining.

Fourier and Brisbane, vigorously denying that Fourierism had failed, argued that the genuine conditions for the existence of the phalanstery had never been realized. The truth of this statement, however, merely testifies to how impractical the system was in its very conception.

The Oneida Community advocated economic and sexual communism in conjunction with fervent religious belief and fidelity to the charismatic leadership of Noyes. It was eventually harassed for its sexual practices. In addition, as an open society, its offspring mixed freely with the outside world and did not share the religious enthusiasm of their parents. When Noyes grew old and the Gentiles attacked the community, the younger people lacked the conviction to maintain the society, and it collapsed after about 33 years.

The Mormons were essentially conventional from an economic point of view, and their few small attempts at economic communism were abandoned early. They, too, were characterized by intense religious belief and polygyny, but did not succumb to internal weakness as happened with the Oneida Community. They were, however, forced after sixty years to yield to societal objections to one tenet—polygyny. Since giving up polygyny, they have prospered in terms of wealth and converts.

In a monograph on cooperative group farming, Eaton and Katz[88] have listed the length of life of a number of societies. Calculations from their data yield the following mean years of longevity by category: religious, 35.4; Fourieristic, 3.0; and Owenite, 1.8. Religious groups clearly fared best; the Shakers, who combined economic communism, intense religiosity, and celibacy, lasted the longest—slightly less than 200 years. Their success probably lay in the fact that they did not attack social mores and their religious commitment was strong. The practice of celibacy may be exceptional, statistically speaking, but it does not violate traditional American norms. After some initial difficulty during the Revolutionary War due to their British origin, the Shakers were left in peace because they were industrious, paid their bills, and violated no laws. The keys to longevity for new societies, thus, were *religious involvement* and an *absence of marital innovation.* With these two conditions present, the only danger was from internal collapse.

The survival of the Old Order Amish[89,90,91] testifies to the durability of a society possessing religious fervor and a lack of marital innovation even if its customs seem anachronistic and outmoded today. Dedicated to agrarianism, Biblical literalism, rigid observance of the *Ordnung* (rules for living), and *Meidung* (shunning of the outside world), this group has survived from the eighteenth century to the present day. No member carries insurance or uses electricity in any form, automobiles, tractors with pneumatic tires, central heating, or telephones. Education beyond the eighth grade is discouraged. The men shave their moustaches, but beards are grown after marriage. They dress in old-fashioned and unpressed black suits with suspenders, and wear wide-brimmed hats. The dress of the women is similarly sober.

The group has had difficulties with Federal and state officials over their avoidance of military service, compulsory education, and social security contributions, but it has surmounted these tribulations. It stands in sharp contrast to the Mormons, whose only foible was polygyny and who were hounded ceaselessly for that single expression of deviance.

In sum, the experiments in marriage we have described should not be viewed as total failures. Many of the radical ideas of Robert Owen, Frances Wright, and their colleagues are commonplace today. Most Americans today do not oppose the right of marriage partners to sunder their bonds if they wish to, provided the children are adequately cared for. And this is precisely what Owen advocated in 1825.

A great deal of what women's liberationists have campaigned for in the 1970s was equanimously achieved in the Oneida Community more than a century ago. If these communards were ahead of their time, will the current rash of communes and marital innovations also point the way to the future? There are no easy answers, but we shall deal with that problem in chapters 23 and 24.

REFERENCES

1. J. Bryce, *The American Commonwealth.*
2. A. E. Beston, Jr., *Backwoods Utopias.*
3. R. Riegel, *American Feminists.*
4. H. B. Woodward, *The Bold Women,* p. 40.
5. E. Webber, *Escape to Utopia,* p. 157.

6. F. E. Manuel, *The Prophets of Paris*, p. 219.
7. F. M. C. Fourier, *Le Noveau Monde: Industriel et Sociétaire. Oeuvres Complètes*, Vol. 6, p. 47 (translation by author).
8. N. V. Riasanovsky, *The Teaching of Charles Fourier.*
9. C. Pellarin, *Lettre de Fourier au Grand Juge*, p. 22 (translation by author).
10. F. E. Manuel, op. cit.
11. F. M. C. Fourier, *La Phalange IX*, p. 200.
12. E. Webber, op. cit.
13. A. Brisbane, *Association.*
14. S. Ditzion, *Marriage, Morals, and Sex in America.*
15. H. B. Woodward, op. cit., p. 54.
16. T. L. Nichols, *Marriage*, p. 16.
17. Ibid., p. 109.
18. Ibid., p. 184.
19. Ibid., p. 207.
20. Ibid., p. 300.
21. Ibid., p. 367.
22. M. E. Lazarus, *Love vs. Marriage*, p. 140.
23. M. Holloway, *Heavens on Earth.*
24. G. L. Gollin, "Family surrogates in Colonial America: The Moravian experiment."
25. G. L. Gollin, *Moravians in Two Worlds*, p. 110.
26. W. A. Hinds, *American Communities and Co-operative Colonies.*
27. C. Nordhoff, *The Communistic Societies of the United States.*
28. G. F. Wright, *Charles Grandison Finney.*
29. E. Achorn, "Mary Cragin, perfectionist saint."
30. W. D. Edmonds, *The First Hundred Years.*
31. C. N. Robertson (ed.), *Oneida Community: An Autobiography.*
32. R. A. Parker, *A Yankee Saint*, p. 44.
33. J. H. Noyes, *History of American Socialisms*, pp. 628-629.
34. E. Achorn, op. cit., pp. 498.
35. W. H. Dixon, *Spiritual Wives.*
36. R. A. Parker, op. cit., p. 87.
37. Ibid., p. 121.
38. Ibid., p. 123.
39. Ibid., p. 123.
40. Ibid., p. 122.
41. C. N. Robertson, op. cit., p. 102.
42. W. Kephart, "Experimental family organization: An historico-cultural report on the Oneida community."
43. R. A. Parker, op. cit., p. 257.
44. M. L. Carden, *Oneida: Utopian Community to Modern Corporation.*
45. H. H. Noyes and G. W. Noyes, "The Oneida Community experiment in stirpiculture."
46. W. Kephart, op cit.
47. M. L. Carden, op. cit.
48. P. Noyes, *My Father's House.*
49. M. L. Carden, op. cit.

50. W. Kephart, *The Family, Society, and the Individual.*
51. W. Kephart, "Experimental family organization: An historico-cultural report on the Oneida community."
52. M. Twain, *Roughing It,* p. 110.
53. Ibid., pp. 110-111.
54. M. R. Werner, *Brigham Young.*
55. *Book of Mormon,* p. 111.
56. F. M. Brodie, *No Man Knows My History,* p. 297.
57. I. Wallace, *The Twenty-seventh Wife,* p. 39.
58. F. Stenhouse, *Exposé of Polygamy in Utah: A Lady's Life among the Mormons,* p. 213.
59. Ibid., pp. 214-215.
60. Ibid., p. 213.
61. Ibid., p. 214.
62. J. H. Evans, *Joseph Smith, An American Prophet.*
63. K. Young, *Isn't One Wife Enough?,* p. 30.
64. M. Cable, "She who shall remain nameless."
65. K. Young, op. cit., pp. 39-40.
66. B. Young, "Plurality of wives—the free agency of man," p. 266.
67. K. Young, op. cit., p. 25.
68. W. Jarman, *U.S.A.: Uncle Sam's Abcess.*
69. K. Young, op. cit., p. 4.
70. I. Wallace, op. cit., p. 15.
71. R. F. Burton, *The City of the Saints, and across the Mountains to California,* p. 448.
72. C. F. Browne, *The Complete Works of Artemus Ward,* pp. 379-380.
73. F. Stenhouse, op. cit., pp. 110-111.
74. B. Young, "Extract from a sermon delivered by Brigham Young."
75. B. Young, *Discourses of Brigham Young,* p. 301.
76. B. Young, "Source of true happiness—prayers, etc.," p. 45.
77. B. Young, "The gifts of God—home manufactures—word of wisdom—happiness," p. 37.
78. A. E. W. Young, *Wife No. 19,* p. 155.
79. I. Wallace, op. cit., p. 90.
80. M. Twain, op. cit., p. 101.
81. K. Young, op. cit., p. 123.
82. I. Wallace, op. cit., p. 208.
83. Ibid.
84. Ibid.
85. J. R. Christiansen, " Contemporary Mormons' attitudes toward polygynous practices."
86. V. A. Christopherson, "An investigation of patriarchal authority in the Mormon family."
87. K. Young, op. cit., p. 56.
88. J. W. Eaton and S. M. Katz, *Research Guide on Cooperative Group Farming.*
89. V. R. Tortora, *The Amish Folk of Pennsylvania Dutch Country.*
90. J. A. Hostetler, *Amish Society.*
91. J. A. Hostetler, "Persistence and change patterns in Amish society."

16

The Dawn of Women's Liberation and American Marriage: 1865–1918

With the onset of the Civil War, the nascent women's rights movement temporarily suspended activity and turned its attention to the abolition of slavery. Its advocates also demonstrated considerable competence in replacing—in farms, schools, and shops—the men who went off to war. After the war, liberals hoped for widespread marriage reforms as well as the right to vote in national elections.[1] But the states were slow to amend the property acts discriminating against married women, and for more than 50 years bills granting suffrage to women continued to be defeated.

Despite agitation by the numerically small women's rights groups, a growing number of marriage manuals—written mainly by conservative male clergymen and ministers—took an optimistic view regarding marriage. According to these manuals, an individual contemplating marriage was confronted by religious, physical, and moral criteria.[2] Religious considerations meant that the couple should be not only devout but of the same Christian denomination. Little mention was made of intermarriage, because it was considered altogether out of the question.

Strong emphasis is placed on physique and physical habits in *The Science of a New Life,* published in 1869 by John Cowan, M.D. In his view, men were too physically immature to marry before the age of 30, whereas women, who matured earlier, could consider matrimony after 24. The most revered law in Cowan's book was continence. Sex weakened a person and should be resorted to only sparingly. In addition, a man could not be too careful in choosing a spouse, and the wise man would avoid a woman with a narrow waist as he "would the plagues of Egypt, for they encompass sickness, premature decay and death."[3]

Character deficits, according to L. N. Fowler, included "idleness, intemperate use of intoxicating drinks, smoking, chewing, snuffing tobacco, the taking of opium, licentiousness in every form, gambling, swearing, and keeping late hours at night."[4] Cowan also was annoyed by tobacco and warned his female readers that they should "avoid marrying a man . . . exuding from his breath, his clothes, his body, his very soul, the dirty effluvia of tobacco, the excreted essence of his selfish, unnatural, perverted desires—with the intention of marriage, with a hope of uniting his foul body to your pure existence."[5]

Even if some undesirable prospective partners were to conceal their noxious traits, they could be ferreted out in this scientific era. S. R. Wells, a publisher who doubled as a phrenologist, could not countenance marriage with someone who lacked the Domestic Propensities. The bumps on the brain comprising this cluster of traits were called Amativeness, Friendship, Parental Love, Inhabitiveness, and Union for Life, and could be found in the posterior region of the brain.[6]

The manuals made little mention of problems caused by the considerable difference in status between men and women. But public attention soon focused on the "woman problem," as seen in the behavior of Victoria Woodhull.

THE SAGA OF VICTORIA WOODHULL, ALIAS MRS. SATAN

Victoria Woodhull's father, Ruben Buckman Claflin, was a confirmed psychopath; her mother Roxanna was a superstitious mystic who experienced visions. Not surprisingly, Victoria, born in 1838, became a psychopathic mystic.

At the age of 15, endowed with a beautiful face, magnificent eyes, and a mature physique, she was married to Canning Woodhull, a physician who proved to be an alcoholic lecher. Consequently, Victoria often traveled with her parents, who sold cancer cures when they were not promoting their "clairvoyant" youngest daughter, Tennessee.

In the course of her travels, Vicky met Colonel James Harvey Blood, a disciple of free love, who put his beliefs into practice by abandoning his wife and children. Vicky divorced Woodhull and took out a marriage license to wed the Colonel after his divorce. Whether the marriage was ever performed is not known.

In 1868, she and her sister met the 76-year-old Commodore Vanderbilt, and Tennessee became his bedmate. He helped establish both of them as the first women stockbrokers in New York, and with their newfound affluence they began to publish *Woodhull and Claflin's Weekly*. But Vicky wanted more than money and, having made some influential friends in Washington, fought actively for women's rights. Proudly her paper announced that she would run for president in 1872.

Mrs. Elizabeth Cady Stanton, acknowledged leader of the major women's organization, the National Woman's Suffrage Association, admired Vicky and attracted her to the organization. However, within a short time, when Victoria's emphasis on the marriage problem in the association's platform clashed with Susan B. Anthony's views, she left the organization.

Vicky spoke out on such questions as social freedom, free love, marriage, divorce, and prostitution—topics which titillated the Victorian imagination and attracted large audiences. Most of her speeches, written by the anarchist Stephen Pearl Andrews, were logically and calmly presented and included some historical analysis. On one occasion, in the course of a speech, she was baited with the question, "Are you a free lover?" She departed from her written text to reply: "Yes, I am a free lover! I have an inalienable, constitutional, and natural right to love whom I may, to love as long or as short a period as I can, to change that love every day if I please."[7] In short order, she acquired the reputation of an immoral sex fiend, and the eminent cartoonist Thomas Nast depicted her with horns, hoofs, and bat wings—a Mrs. Satan. Her brokerage business collapsed, her weekly journal circulation withered, and she became fair game for newspaper attacks. Deserted by Commodore Vanderbilt and her old friends, she fought desperately to keep the journal alive.

A newsworthy story about Henry Ward Beecher came to her attention. Beecher, a noted minister, had a weakness for the ladies, one of whom happened to be Libby Tilton, the wife of his protegé, Theodore Tilton. Unfortunately, Libby confessed all to Theodore. Confronted with these facts, Beecher denied all; then he admitted all on another occasion, and later denied everything again! A brooding Tilton leaked the information to some people, and Libby also talked to friends. The story spread, and finally Vicky, who had been sleeping with Tilton for three months, learned the details.

Tired, worried about finances, and irritated by the press attacks on her character—especially by Henry's sisters, Cathy Beecher and Harriet Beecher Stowe—Vicky spoke up in the columns of her weekly. She made it clear that she was not condemning Beecher's act. In fact, since she had slept with Beecher and could attest to his potency, it was not difficult for her to announce in print that "passional starvation, enforced on such a nature, so richly endowed . . . is a horrid cruelty. Every great man of Mr. Beecher's type, has had in the past, and will ever have, the need for and the right to, the loving manifestations of many women."[8]

To counter her boldness, Anthony Comstock, the self-appointed censor and enemy of smut, dashed off to the authorities to have Vicky apprehended for sending obscene literature through the mails. The suit was dismissed on a technicality, but the issue of Beecher's culpability raged on in a suit brought by Tilton against him. The trial was marked by assertions by Beecher's counsel that even to think that his client could have committed adultery was "wicked, wicked as it can be, wicked in heart, wicked in soul, wicked in hate to God, to society, to human nature, wicked in everything."[9]

The backers of Beecher had good cause to wonder how many "wicked" people there were in America. They held stock in one of the most profitable churches in the country, the Plymouth Church in Brooklyn, where Beecher was minister. His publisher had advanced him $25,000, a not inconsiderable sum in those days, to write a life of Jesus. Fortunately, the jury rejected Tilton's suit by a vote of nine to three, and Beecher resumed a profitable lecture tour, none the worse for a few scars.

Vicky also went back to lecturing, fervently espousing the cause of sexual rights for women:

I need not explain to any woman the effects of unconsummated intercourse. . . . But every man needs to have it thundered in his ears . . . that the other party demands a return for all that he receives, demands that he shall not be enriched at her expense, demands that he shall not, either from ignorance or selfish desire, carry her impulse forward only to cast it backward with its mission unfulfilled to prostrate the impelling power and breed nervous debility or irritability and sexual demoralization. . . .[10]

Suddenly, for unexplained reasons, the nature of her talks began to change. Marriage, once a "consummate outrage," now became a "divine provision."[11] At one talk she appeared with a Bible and stood in front of a statue of the Virgin Mary.

The transformation in Vicky's outlook probably stemmed from an almost fatal illness in 1873, which left her with a permanently reduced energy level. Financial losses, the closing of her weekly, and constant attacks by the "respectable" world had at last worn her down. Unable to defeat the powerful forces of conservatism, she was preparing, consciously or unconsciously, to join with them. In 1878 she divorced Blood for "adultery," and blamed him and Andrews for having published their treatises on free love under her name. She asserted that "during no part of my life did I favor free love even tacitly."[12]

The remainder of her life was uneventful and anticlimactic. She married an English banker, John Biddulph Martin, and died in 1927 in obscurity. A brilliant speaker, she lived 75 years ahead of her time, and might have been another Mary Wollstonecraft if she had not used her talents primarily for self-advancement.

FREE LOVE, WOMEN, AND DIVORCE

From 1865 to World War I, the major marital issues were questions of free love as opposed to wedlock, the role of women in society, and the decision as to whether divorce should be made easy or difficult to obtain.

Free Love and Marriage

The free love versus marriage controversy was but the tip of the iceberg of a much deeper fundamental conflict. The strongest adherents of the free-love movement were the anarchists, who believed that each person should be free to live his life in his own way, without governmental regulation. Free love was especially needed, maintained Emma Goldman, a leading anarchist, because marriage was so legally detrimental to the woman's welfare. Indeed, its motto, borrowing from Dante, should be "Ye who enter here leave all hope behind."[13]

On the question of sex for the unmarried, Goldman was unequivocal:

> Can there be anything more outrageous than the idea that a healthy, grown woman, full of life and passion, must deny nature's demand, must subdue her most intense craving, undermine her health and break her spirit, must stunt her vision, abstain from the depth and glory of sex experience until a "good" man comes along to take her unto himself as a wife?[14]

This redoubtable woman was once heckled at a meeting by the question, "Is it true you believe in free love?" Turning a contemptuous gaze at her interrogator, she replied, "Do you mean *you* have to pay?"

Somewhat to the right of the anarchists were the socialists. Their position was typified by the writings of Kate O'Hare, known to the press as "red Kate." In her book, *The Sorrows of Cupid*,[15] she charged that capitalism was the foe of marriage. The poor could not afford to marry, and even those who did marry could not be happy because of the strain of worrying whether they would be working the next week. Marx and Engels had earlier stressed that the wife was exploited by the husband, who pressed her into service as a domestic. When the new era of socialism arrived and the humiliation of women came to an end, there was no guarantee that monogamy would survive, but it would surely be given a fair trial.

The most conservative of the reform movements were the women's rights organizations. Their adherents ranged from the Reverend Antoinette Brown, who favored legal emancipation for women but not easy divorce, to Ernestine Rose and Elizabeth Stanton, who espoused easy divorce. In general, their position can be characterized as trying to enhance the status of women, politically and maritally, within the established legal structure of society.

In a broad sense, the marriage problem could be viewed as that of hedonistic individualism versus duty to society. Whereas a few individuals thought that whether or not they married was nobody's business but their own, the vast majority felt that each person had a duty to marry, to preserve the fabric of society, and to rear sons and daughters for the sustenance of the republic.

The struggle between individualism and duty was a major focus of novels written during or after the period, describing the situation in the last quarter of the nineteenth century. Wharton's *Age of Innocence*,[16] Dreiser's *Jennie Gerhardt*,[17] Howell's *Indian Summer*,[18] and Cather's *My Antonia*[19] describe individuals who cannot follow their heart's dictates because of their need to adhere to the mores of their class or to conform to social dictates.

Many articles expressed concern about a marked disinclination of people to marry.[20-23] Writers attributed this reluctance to selfishness, to the allures of the modern age and its competing temptations for the unmarried, and to the greater independence of women. The question of duty thus became entangled with the question of women's proper societal role, and the arguments focused on both the biological and the social origins of this role.

Role of Women in Society

Biological Origins. Darwin's theory of evolution, a staggering blow at orthodox religion, surprisingly failed to disturb the orthodox perception of woman in society. In fact, the theory was used to defend the status quo, and scientific reasoning was used to justify the biblical description of woman's submissive role. Darwin himself had set the pace by suggesting that the privileged social position of men stemmed from their preoccupation with problems of survival, whereas women had been spared the trials of the hunt and war, and that man had therefore evolved as the superior and craftier sex.

Other writers stated that men were taller, heavier, and endowed with bigger brains than women—proof of evolutionary superiority. In a similar vein, a writer in the 1878 *Quarterly Journal of Science* characterized the women's movement as "an attempt to rear, by a process of 'unnatural selection' a race of monstrosities—hostile alike to men, to normal women, to human society, and to the future development of our race."[24]

A more involved proof of the biological bizarreness of women's rightists came from Otto Weininger in his *Sex and Character*.[25] He argued that since each person was a mixture of male and female cells, he sought to complete what he lacked through his choice of a marital partner. A masculine man would be drawn to a feminine woman; a feminine man would seek a masculine woman. The pure woman, he argued, wants neither independence nor equality with men, for such things are foreign to a woman's sexual nature. It is only women with inherited masculine characteristics who aspire to express themselves in masculine ways by competitiveness and forceful intellectual expression. The women's movement should thus be understood as a product of genetic inferiority.

Some friends of women's rights resorted to defensive genetic explanations. J. H. Browne noted the "general wantonness and ferocity of masculine passion which made him polygynous and polyerotic, whereas the woman was by nature monogamous and monerotic."[26] The editor of *The Nation* expressed a similar sentiment, noting that the purpose of marriage was a civilized attempt to regulate that brutish passion.[27] Henry James, Sr., could do no better than spout the traditional view that women were innately superior spiritually, whereas men were innately more worldly.[28]

More imaginative support came from the early American sociologist, Lester Frank Ward.[29,30] He pointed out that among all the lower phyla, the females were larger and stronger than the males. Hence, he concluded, the same situation obtained for all phyla. Women had had a dominant role as the life-bearing and life-maintaining segment of society when the relationship of sex and birth was unknown. In choosing a man for sexual purposes, a woman was influenced by esthetic factors and by a desire for the most worthy specimen. In the struggle of men for the right to her favors, both cunning and physical strength were involved. Through this sexual selection, man emerged somewhat physically and mentally superior to woman. This did not influence the *gynaecocracy* (rule of women) until, through man's evolving brain, a connection was finally made between sex and birth. At this point, men seized control of decisions regarding their offspring and, by virtue of their now superior physical and mental ability, proceeded to subjugate their wives and establish the rule of men (*androcracy*).

Men now practiced sexual selection, paying little attention to brains in women and more attention to physical beauty. The present sad state of women was due in part to their sexual selection by men, and in part to the cultural deprivation incurred at the hands of their masters. Ward felt that the nadir had been reached and, with a better environment, women would gain greater status and be less subject to sexual selection. In the future, both sexes would rule equally in a *gynandrocratic* society.

The attack on the perception of personality as a resultant of genetic endowment was brilliantly led by Simon N. Patten, who pointed out that social attraction could be better explained by learning and social conditions than by vaguely postulated genetic factors.[31] Increasingly, writers began to deal with the relationship between personality and the cultural milieu. In the past, it may have been necessary for a woman to forego nondomestic pursuits because of an ever-augmenting brood.[32] By the eve of World War I, however, the birthrate had declined, and industry needed women. There could no longer be any excuse for nailing women to the genetic cross of subservience.

Social Origins. Without relying on biological proofs, most persons believed that it was desirable for women to remain in the kitchen. No doubt L. G. Noble was intoxicated by his own florid prose when he warned that, to young girls, "the treacherous breath of these [women's] reforms . . . will be as the last quittance of conscience to launch them on shame's dark whirlpool"[33] However, even a liberal such as Ralph Waldo Emerson, although he would vote for every franchise for women, would not "wish women to wish political functions, nor, if granted, assume them."[34] In a similar refrain, "A Married College Man" noted that the educated American woman was a good comrade but a poor sweetheart.[35]

Liberals such as Lord Bryce[36] and W. I. Thomas[37] applauded the "new woman," but others[38] believed that women would not be happy with work. Finley Peter Dunne gently satirized the "new woman's" desire for work by having one of his characters, Mr. Donahue, the "new man," relax in bed while he urged his wife and mother to work the "pile of slag" at the mill.[39] The end of the story finds the ladies only too glad to return to their traditional roles.

While the typical male writer urged domesticity on women, the unmarried educated woman was finding that the drawbacks of an inferior marital status were an inducement to seek the new professional opportunities awaiting her.[40] A bachelor young female professor noted sarcastically that "certain of the young men whose studies I have shared have with fervor and tenderness held out to me the alluring prospect of broiling their beefsteak while they went on with their studies."[41]

In the New York school system, angry wives were fighting the rule that no married woman could hold a teaching job unless her husband was physically incapacitated.[42] World War I witnessed the collapse of the notion that it was unnatural for women to work. Most women were not thrilled at the idea of working—but it was a way to earn much-needed money. The professional woman, however, met with greater resistance, because the professions were more competitive and the presence of women was more threatening to men's egos. However, by World War I, a woman's right to work at a job of her choosing could scarcely be contested, though many a middle-class man promised himself that he would never undergo the embarrassment of a working wife.

The Battle over Divorce

Divorce in the United States was rare prior to the Civil War. In 1860, only 7,380 divorces and annulments were recorded. The number continued to climb until, by 1920, it reached 167,105, an increase of almost 2,300 percent in 60 years.

Behind this dramatic upsurge were the expanded employment opportunities which allowed women to support themselves, the legislation which improved their legal status, the availability of mass education which gave women valid job credentials, and the changing ideology which slowly became pro-feminist and encouraged the treatment of women as the equals of men.

The battle over the ease of divorce was fierce, especially between 1880 and 1915. On one side were the conservatives, who perceived the issue in moral and societal terms. They saw the rising rate of divorce as threatening the foundation of society—the family, patriarchal style. Divorce was sacrilegious and immoral, and reflected a sensate search for personal satisfaction at the expense of duty to society. Even though unhappy marriages might bring suffering to the participants, this was in considerable measure related to their hedonism and was not an intrinsic part of marriage itself. As George Geglinger explained in the *Catholic World*, "When people understand that they must live together they learn to soften, by mutual accommodation, that yoke which they know they cannot shake off. They become good husbands and good wives, for necessity is a powerful master in teaching the duties it imposes."[43]

The reasons for the increase in divorce, according to the conservatives, included the unholy trinity of "isms"—"individualism," "socialism," and "anarchism." The first "ism" led to pleasure-seeking; the last two "isms" represented an organized plot to destroy the heart of society preparatory to changing the political system. Other alleged culprits were the women's rights movement, the erosion of belief in morality and future punishment, the taste in cheap novels, the sybaritic interest in luxurious living, and increased facilities for travel, as well as the hodgepodge of state laws.

The idea of psychological distress as a cause of divorce was lampooned by the brilliant Finley Peter Dunne's Mr. Dooley: "Ye can always get a divorce f'r what Hogan calls incompatibility iv temper. That's when husband an' wife ar-re both cross at th' same time. Ye'd call it a tiff in ye'er fam'ly, Hinnissy."[44]

Women were singled out for special attack for their extravagance, for their desire to dominate men,[45] and for insensitivity[46] and unreasonable demands.[47] But a few insightful writers saw the increased divorce rate as the inevitable consequence of women's improved legal status, a lower birthrate, and her increasing ability to achieve economic independence.[48]

The liberals tried to accelerate the winds of change by emphasizing the hypocrisy of the laws. The Reverend Westbrook was able to point out, for example, that while South Carolina prided itself that it allowed no divorce, a husband in that state could still leave property to his concubine.[49] Hugo Münsterberg, the transplanted German psychologist, correctly noted that divorce was not associated with immorality: "This is a higher individual morality, which ends marriage when it has lost its inner sanctity."[50] Eugenicists also joined the fray; according to them, divorce would prevent the breeding of a tarnished strain.[51,52]

A more mixed blessing to the liberal movement was the support of such controversial figures as Havelock and Edith Ellis and their friends Edward Carpenter and Olive Schreiner. In their view, divorce—a kind of epiphenomenon—was needed now because the wrong people mated and made the mistake of being offended by adultery. Once the millennium arrived, such "escape clauses" would no longer be needed.

Less individualistic and more respected in the scientific community were the sociologists Lester F. Ward and George E. Howard. They claimed that divorce, the product of an imperfect society, would one day cease. In the meantime, divorce was a necessity.

The struggle came to an end by 1915, as the burgeoning divorce statistics testified. We have discussed the role of ideology, of industrialization, and of women's economic and legal freedom in this victory. There were, in addition, two catalytic factors which hastened the decline of conservatism.[53] The first was the inability of the conservatives to mount a united front. The many diverse religious sects could not agree on a basic platform. Catholics opposed divorce under any circumstances. Some Episcopalians sanctioned divorce for adultery; others did not. Some considered only desertion as justifiable grounds, while others wanted to include extreme physical cruelty. The conservatives attempted to get a Federal bill passed to regulate divorce, but the bill failed to pass Congress because no basic standards could be agreed on. Those who opposed Federal control sought voluntary agreement by the states, but each state was influenced by differing religious and moral viewpoints, and this move also failed.

The second factor that buried the hopes of the conservatives was the change in perception of marriage from that of a theological covenant with God to a legal contract, with psychological and sociological implications. As a result, the right of social scientists to speak out on marriage and divorce was increasingly accepted, whereas the right of the clergy to "pontificate" was increasingly questioned.

Birth of the Reno Divorce

In the absence of a Federal law, divorce procedures varied from state to state. South Carolina granted no divorces until after World War II. The New York law, passed in 1787, stipulated adultery as the only grounds for divorce. With the onset of a divorce boom at the turn of the twentieth century, wealthy New Yorkers who lacked the influence or sufficient grounds for an annulment were forced to look elsewhere. Eager to capitalize on the economic potential of such "guests," various states vied for the privilege of lowering the barriers. The winner was the sunshine state of Nevada, which in 1875 recognized six easy grounds for divorce and required only six months' residence. In the 1890s, North and South Dakota laws provided for a three-month residency, but reformers soon succeeded in raising the requirements to one year.

In 1911, reform began to threaten Nevada. The struggle was not between liberals and conservatives but between merchants and conservatives. The rationale of the merchants is expressed in a poem of the period:

> Have you ever thought about the Reno Colony
> And what we owe this little fad, divorce?
>   Fair plaintiffs oft advising,
>   Forever criticizing,
> Yet their money helps us on a bit, of course.
>
> If you legislate against the Reno Colony,
> To other fields the fair ones you will drive
>   For ill-advised propriety
>   Brings poverty with piety,
> And some of us would much prefer to thrive. . . .
>
> A necessary evil is the Colony.
> It must exist when Love has sullen grown,
>   So quit the foolish knocking,
>   Your own prosperity blocking,
> And learn to let what's well enough alone.[54]

Despite continuous pressure by reformers, the challenges were beaten off.

Love

It may seem somewhat odd that an era in which divorce increased greatly also witnessed the widespread advocacy of love marriages. But the contradiction is more apparent than real, for the newly won status of women enabled them more easily to choose a spouse for love rather than economic security. The romantic ideal dictated that an unloving or unlovable mate should be shed for a better matched one. In the past, when love had been associated with marriage in the United States, it had actually been a label for compatibility of temperament, station in life, or interests. The act of marriage pushed the participants into the role of loving husband or wife, and the importance of love was considered greater *after* marriage than prior to it. Now, however, the importance of attraction and of love *prior* to marriage rose in proportion to the opportunity of the sexes to mingle before marriage and to the lessening of parental influence.

Lester Ward saw romantic love as an evolutionary product confined to the "Aryan race" and having its genesis in courtly love.[55] In the *Ladies' Home Journal* of 1905, Alice Preston remarked that "no high-minded girl and no girl of truly refined feeling ... ever ... admits the advisability of marriage without love."[56] The *Woman's Home Companion* of 1911 advised: "Since we know that Love—that divine presence—may come, it is only rational and wise to be ready for his coming."[57] Romantic love marriage thus followed hard on the breaching of the walls of discrimination against women.

Husbands and Wives

In fighting for her rights, the American housewife had asked for more help from husbands with regard to household tasks and for an end to legal discrimination, but most women did not aspire to leave home and compete in the business world with men. Like the wife in Edith Wharton's novel, *The Custom of the Country*,[58] the educated woman was unhappy with material comfort as a substitute for contact with the interesting outside world of her husband.

On the other hand, an author called "married man" decried the lack of respect and courtesy shown by husbands who read the paper while their wives were at the table; but he confessed that he never could stand the "silly chatter of women."[59]

Traditional stereotypes still persisted, as is apparent in a 1903 survey of the marital preferences of young people. When 100 young women were asked to list the qualities desired in a spouse (they could list more than one), the highest number of votes (42) went for strength of character. Second place (25) went to business ability; respect for women garnered a mere 18 votes; and love (17) came in a weak fourth.[60]

A similar poll among young men[61] found a large majority (74) favoring *domestic tendency* in their spouse, with love coming in second (45 votes). Obviously, equality was more talked about than real. The tipoff is in the relative position of "love." Many people erroneously believe that women are more romantic in their marital choices. The truth, however, is that romantic choice presupposes a secure status and the satisfaction of more basic needs, such as economic security. Since men did not need women to achieve these needs, they could afford to marry for love. Despite all the prattling about love in the women's magazines, many women could not act romantically if they were dependent on a man for economic security. Nevertheless, within a few years after the poll, gains in economic security and self-confidence began to be reflected in the literature. Although in 1908 The *Ladies' Home Journal* still cooed that women should try "to keep the world gentle and kind for men,"[62] a feature article in the *Independent* a year later depicted men as wishy-washy and dull.[63] By 1911, Gertrude Atherton was describing a man as a "big child."[64] The "battle of the sexes" began in earnest in the 1920s, and reached a peak on the eve of World War II.

Sex

The conservatives sought to stem the tide of change by controlling the media and bringing pressure on the Federal and state governments. If organized religion could no longer guard the moral frontiers, self-appointed zealots must rise in defense of the old order. A vigorous censorship movement, led by Anthony Comstock, succeeded not only in quashing obscene literature but in enacting anticontraceptive laws in 24 states. In another 22 states, new legislation defined the dissemination of information about contraceptives as obscene.[65]

At first, this effort by the conservatives hardly seemed necessary, for husband-wife sexual relationships at the end of the Civil War did not seem to have progressed much beyond traditional perceptions. A wife, even though she did not enjoy sex, was supposed to do her duty. A husband, considerate of the discomfort he imposed on his wife, made demands only when nature forced him to act. "Experts" still propounded a quasi-scientific mixture of puritanical ideas and misconceptions. Dr. Cowan, for example, advised his readers to think forcefully of the qualities they wished to pass on to their offspring. When the time came, they should choose a clear, bright day, and make love only when at the height of physical and mental strength—by Cowan's definition, between 11 a.m. and noon.[66] Dr. William A. Alcott assured his readers that the man who made love twice a week was doomed to an early death.[67]

Even by the 1890s, when a new liberalism and the bicycle threw men and women together more frequently, little happened. As H. S. Canby described it, men and women on camping trips slept innocently in the same room; there was an air of general excitement, and the men never thought of approaching their refined female companions. Love and lust had not yet become bedfellows.[68]

Nevertheless, the weakening of religious mores, the growing economic independence of women, improved contraceptive methods, urbanization and its shelter of anonymity, and the automobile and its ability to transport individuals to more permissive environments—all these presaged the freer sexual expression that followed World War I.

The pattern of progress can be traced in the sex manuals. Prior to 1865, the one unequivocal justification of sex was procreation.[69] By World War I, sex as pleasure was clearly acceptable, but women were still regarded as passive creatures who needed awakening. This led to the "sex as work" ethic (mostly for the man). By touching sensitive areas and muttering sweet nothings in the service of technique, he sought to arouse his partner. That his own excitement might abate during protracted foreplay, during which he received little stimulation, was not considered. Men, presumably, were regarded as hypersexed, and women were sexually inferior.

CONCLUSIONS

The period from 1865 to 1914 saw considerable advances in the legal emancipation of wives, the opening up of work opportunities for women, and ideological acceptance of the equality of the sexes. The verbal acceptance, however, far outstripped the actual changes in behavior. Change *was* occurring, but it took many years for progressive attitudes to be reflected on a large scale in everyday life. Most magazine articles advocating the cause of women were written by highly educated men and women for select audiences.

It is incorrect to assume that Americans were by and large unaware of these new ideas, but they probably did not consider them relevant to their immediate lives. Few women (or even men) were attending college, and a great number of both sexes were not even enrolled in the newly emerging high schools. The average woman did not aspire for equal professional rights with men—she mainly wanted greater respect and consideration for her domestic role.

The Declaration of Independence of the women's liberation movement was enunciated in 1848, but the number of activists was quite small until the post-Civil War period, when the seeds of the current movement were planted. The women's movement of the 1960s and 1970s witnessed the carrying out of radical ideas that had been propounded decades earlier, and women could still point, with justification, to the disparity between ideology and fact. But their task now faces less opposition because the ideology, at least, is beyond cavil, thanks to the late nineteenth-century feminists.

After World War I, sex had almost surreptitiously moved into the realm of the acceptable, although it was still bad form to focus attention on it. All this changed soon, with the flapper and the importation of the ideas of Sigmund Freud.

REFERENCES

1. S. Ditzion, *Marriage, Morals, and Sex in America.*
2. M. Gordon and M. C. Bernstein, "Mate choice and domestic life in the 19th century marriage manual."
3. J. Cowan, *The Science of a New Life,* p. 52.
4. L. N. Fowler, *Marriage, Its History and Ceremonies,* p. 131.
5. J. Cowan, op. cit., p. 65.
6. S. R. Wells, *Wedlock.*
7. J. Johnston, *Mrs. Satan,* p. 133.
8. E. Sachs, *The Terrible Siren,* pp. 174-175.
9. J. Johnston, op. cit., p. 233.
10. E. Sachs, op. cit., pp. 223-224.
11. J. Johnston, op. cit., p. 245.
12. Ibid., p. 264.
13. E. Goldman, *Marriage and Love,* p. 234.
14. Ibid., p. 237.
15. K. R. O'Hare, *The Sorrows of Cupid.*
16. E. Wharton, *The Age of Innocence.*
17. T. Dreiser, *Jennie Gerhardt.*
18. W. D. Howells, *Indian Summer.*
19. W. Cather, *My Ántonia.*
20. "Why is single life becoming more general?"
21. K. G. Wells, "Why more girls do not marry."
22. An Unwilling Celibate, "Why do not educated women marry?"
23. C. W. Thwing, "The American family."
24. L. F. Ward, "Our better halves," p. 267.
25. O. Weininger, *Sex and Character.*
26. J. H. Browne, "To marry or not to marry?"
27. "Society and marriage."
28. H. James, Sr., "The woman thou gavest me."
29. L. F. Ward, "Genius and woman's intuition."
30. L. F. Ward, *Pure Sociology.*
31. S. N. Patten, "The laws of social attraction."
32. V. Lee, "The economic dependence of women."
33. L. G. Noble, "Free marriage," p. 664.
34. S. Ditzion, op. cit., p. 272.
35. A Married College Man, "The dislike to be waited on."
36. J. Bryce, *The American Commonwealth,* Vol. 3.
37. W. I. Thomas, "The older and newer ideals of marriage."
38. B. M. Hinkle, "Marriage in the new world."
39. F. P. Dunne, *Mr. Dooley in Peace and War.*
40. "The strike of a sex."
41. A Bachelor Maid, "Why I do not marry," p. 1484.
42. A Married Teacher, "Should the married woman teach?"
43. G. Giglinger, "Divorce and its effects on society," p. 97.

44. F. P. Dunne, *Mr. Dooley Says,* p. 4.
45. H. H. Davis, R. T. Cooke, M. Harland, C. Owen, and A. E. Barr, "Are women to blame?"
46. A. A. Rogers, "Why American marriages fail."
47. R. Pike, "Husbands and wives."
48. I. H. Harper, "Changing conditions of marriage."
49. R. B. Westbrook, *Marriage and Divorce.*
50. H. Münsterberg, *The Americans,* p. 523.
51. R. H. Johnson, "Marriage selection."
52. H. M. Stanley, "Artificial selection and the marriage problem."
53. W. L. O'Neill, *Divorce in the Progressive Era.*
54. L. Curtis, *Reno Reveries: Impressions of Local Life,* p. 60.
55. L. F. Ward, op. cit.
56. A. Preston, "The ideals of the bride-to-be," p. 26.
57. A. B. McCall, "The tower room," p. 24.
58. E. Wharton, *The Custom of the Country.*
59. "The autobiography of a married man."
60. C. Halsted, "The man we want to marry."
61. C. Halsted, "The kind of girl they want to marry."
62. A. Preston, "What a girl should expect of marriage."
63. A. S. Quaesita, "The unattractiveness of American men."
64. G. Atherton, "American husbands."
65. C. F. Brooks, "The early history of the anti-contraceptive laws in Massachusetts and Connecticut."
66. J. Cowan, op. cit.
67. S. Ditzion, op. cit.
68. H. S. Canby, "Sex and marriage in the nineties."
69. M. Gordon, "From procreation to recreation: Changes in sexual ideology, 1830-1940."

17

Marriage and Love in Contemporary America

Sweeping changes in family size and living habits have occurred in recent years. The entrance of women into the work force, the perfecting of contraceptives, and the changing status of children from economic assets to liabilities have drastically affected the birthrate. From 44 births per 1,000 in 1860, the figure dropped sharply to a little more than 17 per 1,000 in 1971[1]; preliminary reports for succeeding years indicate even lower rates.

The effect of mobility on the geographical proximity of parents and married children was dramatic. The proportion of in-laws living with children was traditionally quite high until World War I; by 1947, only 7 percent of U.S. families lived with their in-laws, and by 1967 this figure declined to 1.6 percent.[2] With fewer economic cares, the age at marriage became continually younger, and by 1955 the median male married for the first time at 22.5 years of age and the woman at 20.2. In 1971 there was a slight upward trend: the respective values were 23.2 and 20.8.

Although many of the old reasons for marriage—for example, complementary economic roles; religious and sexual pressures—had eased, the percentage of people marrying increased steadily. In 1890 approximately 60 percent of those 14 and over were married; by 1963 the percentage was approximately 70. It was estimated in 1968 that among the current generation of youth, no more than 3 to 4 percent will never have married by the time they reach the age of 50.[3]

If more Americans were marrying, they were not contemplating the traditional marriage of pre-World War I days. Interest in marriage of a more egalitarian and interactional nature was heightened in the 1920s when a Denver judge, Benjamin B. Lindsey, proposed "companionate marriage."[4] His model would allow divorce by mutual consent provided there were no children, and it would forbid alimony payments to the divorced wife. If there were children, divorce would be granted only when safeguards for their welfare had been assured.

The conservatives deemed Lindsey's proposal an incitement to promiscuity. Joseph Collins,[5] physician and self-appointed marriage expert, considered the Lindsey formula an inducement to lower the birthrate. It was a social duty to bear children, he insisted, and women, who by nature did not like to work, would be forced to do so in lieu of alimony. Fortunately, he warned, nature struck back at contraceptive users by making them permanently sterile.

W. McDougall,[6] the eminent psychologist, foresaw the mass desertion of women, especially of the no-longer-attractive middle-aged, under the Lindsey regime. Without marriage, such women would be lost.

Society did not accept Lindsey's proposal, and his views cost him his job. Time, however, has borne out his conviction that "what may seem radical in this book will be the conservatism of tomorrow."[7]

Though marriage in the past 50 years has become ostensibly quite free in terms of choice, it must be understood that this freedom is exercised within rather narrow limits. Most people still choose someone who is close in age and is of a similar religion, race, education, and socioeconomic status—as well as within a convenient courting distance!

Even within these limits, what is it that determines choice of marital partner? Nine out of ten would reply, without a moment's hesitation, that Americans marry for love. But what is love? In recent years we have begun to study this concept more extensively and to subject it to empirical investigation.[8]

LOVE

Various definitions of love can be roughly classified under three headings: *romantic love,* defined by W. M. Kephart as "a strong emotional attachment to the opposite sex, a tendency toward idealization, and a marked physical attraction."[9] Freud, as noted in Chapter 13, referred to this kind of love simply as aim-inhibited sex. The second type is *conjugal love,*[10] which most writers agree is the sort of affection existing between a man and woman who have been married for a number of years. There is less passion but more spirituality, respect, and contentment in the enjoyment of each other's company. A third kind of love is *agape,* a spontaneous self-giving love which strives to develop the partner to his or her maximum potential, without considering the advantages or costs to oneself.[11,12]

For most Americans, however, "love" is romantic love. A range of corollary notions have developed, many of which have proven to be patently false:

1. *Love occurs at first sight.* Burgess and Wallin, in their monumental study of marriage, found that three-quarters of engaged persons had experienced no strong physical attraction to their partner after they had known each other for a month, and only one-fourth described themselves currently as head over heels in love.[13] It is noteworthy that despite the lack of confirming evidence, the treatment of love in recent fiction perpetuates the myth of love at first sight. A random sample of magazine romance fiction from 1911 to 1915 showed a mere 1.5 percent of occasions when the participants fell in love on the basis of a

one-day acquaintance.[14] An identical survey for 1951 to 1955 showed a figure of 18.4 percent.

2. *Love conquers all.*[15,16] If individuals marry for love and, in a representative sample of married men and women, love led the next highest reason for marriage (to have children) by 76 to 24 percent, then our current extremely high divorce rate suggests that love is not enough. Many other studies have shown that differences in age, religion, and economic status may readily supersede love and bring unhappiness and divorce.

3. *Women are more romantic than men.* If women were truly more romantic than men, one might expect that they would be less likely to contemplate marrying without love. Yet, when Kephart asked a sample of college students, "If a boy (girl) had all the other qualities you desired, would you marry this person if you were not in love with him (her)?" Sixty-five percent of the men said "no," as compared to 24 percent of the women. Most of the women, unlike the men, were "undecided."[17]

4. *For each person there is one predestined true love.*[18] Albert Ellis, in a study of college women, found that 25 percent of his sample reported being in love with two or more men at the same time.[19] Kirkpatrick and Caplow also reported that many men and women had experienced more than one love affair. The chief cause of breakups was a loss of mutual interest, but another important reason was interest in a new person.[20,21]

5. *Romantic love is a sign of immaturity.* In a series of studies, Dean[22,23] was unable to find any relationship between various measures of emotional adjustment and a scale of romanticism. Apparently, romanticism, as measured by his scale, is a function of sociologically determined orientation that is independent of personality adjustment.

Granted that there is much that is inaccurate in the folklore of romantic love, we should ask if it is, by and large, compatible with marriage. Opinions on this question vary considerably. Among those who see it as incompatible are de Rougemont,[24,25] Lerner,[26] van den Haag,[27] and Schlesinger.[28] At the center of their arguments is the perception of love as a drive or a state of tension which, with a minimum of satisfaction, keeps the individual in a hyperactive state. He is not nourished by tangible reward, but by hope and expectations of bliss. Passion, far from being diminished by external barriers, thrives on them. The separation of lovers by geographical distance, the opposition of parents, the necessity of finishing school before marrying—all this permits lovers to fantasize the bliss that will be theirs. Moreover, Lerner sees love as an acquisitive drive. Americans have a great need to achieve per se, as well as the desire to acquire material possessions. The competitive struggle for a mate is in keeping with the belief that competition brings out the best in individuals. Loneliness is considered not so much an unfortunate state due to external events, but the personal stigma of the underachiever in the area of love.

When the lover is finally won, there is great joy for, in America, "love and marriage go together like a horse and carriage." But the joy is short-lived.

Consummation destroys the pleasant anticipatory tension and, in the absence of external barriers, withers away, the victim of intimacy and possession. When there has been no real community of spirit other than passion, marriage now becomes a bond, a yoke that the condemned must wear until death or divorce. Escape lies only in continued fantasies and/or extramarital affairs, where the difficulties of arranging trysts can rekindle the flame of passion and longing.

The only solution, according to de Rougemont, is to *love,* not to *be in love.* Whether marriage is based on rational or irrational reasons is not crucial. What does matter is that the individual makes a decision, commits himself, and then sticks to it. Such a display of volition is, of course, quite incompatible with the concept that love (passion) is irresistible.

Not everyone weighs romantic love so negatively. Kolb[29] and Beigl[30] see it as a necessary positive force. The latter points out that it has evolved from an adolescent stirring outside of marriage, as in courtly love, to a position of integration within marriage. It serves as a homeostatic mechanism, compensating for the vagaries and isolation caused by industrialization and life's frustrations.

To other writers, love is neither a panacea nor a destroyer, but a necessary function of our society. According to Greenfield, every basic need supplied in marriage—food, clothing, sexual gratification—can be purchased in the market. Then why marry? Individuals must marry to form families, for without them "the mechanism for distributing and consuming the valued goods and services, reproducing and socializing the population and maintaining the stratification system . . . would cease to operate."[31]

Greenfield believes that the only way to get people to maintain American culture is to devise a romantic-love complex that would be a reward motive and induce individuals to fulfill the necessary roles of husband-father and wife-mother. Within this framework, for example, while sex could be obtained in the market, it is usually found in the love-complex only after marriage, or at least after a commitment to marriage. Similarly, Parsons[32] sees the function of love as the replacement of kinship ties, which once served to direct the behavior of young adults into proper spheres. To make sure that love occurs only with the "right people," sons and daughters of wealthy parents are sent to the "right" schools, lodged in the "right" sororities and fraternities, and guided to the "right" marital choice under the illusion that their choice is wholly free.[33]

Proof of the effectiveness of love as an inducement to marriage is strikingly apparent in an article by Theodorson.[34] Students of the United States, Burma, India, and Singapore received questionnaires measuring their attitudes toward marriage. By compiling a romanticism index, Theodorson was able to show a perfect relationship between this index and the desire to marry. Among the Americans, by far the most romantic, only 1.6 percent of the men and 1.4 percent of the women did not wish to marry. The comparative figure for India was 30.4 percent and 23.3 percent, respectively. It must be concluded that insofar as the preservation of marriage and the family is a goal of society, love proves to be a strong ally. To understand the development of love, we now turn to a consideration of courtship.

DATING AND COURTSHIP

The twentieth century brought dramatic changes in dating and courtship. Until then, chaperones had sometimes been present, but they had generally been unnecessary because the limited mobility of teen-agers usually kept them pretty much under the surveillance of parents. The advent of the bicycle—and especially of the automobile, now referred to as "a bedroom on wheels"— changed all that. While the traditional mores limiting the interaction of young people remained, the ability to maintain surveillance declined, and a highly independent youth emerged.

Koller's[35] interviews of three generations of women in 1949 found that the youngest generation more frequently saw boys whom their parents did not approve of, less frequently met boys in the immediate neighborhood, and increasingly "played the field" in the sense that more than one boy was likely to be seriously considered for marriage. In addition, age differences between spouses narrowed through the years, and the length of engagements became shorter. This was interpreted as being due to the emergence of the phenomenon of association between young men and women: it preceded serious marriage courtship and was called "dating." Dating involved more or less informal associations without a specific commitment to marry.

Dating has been negatively assessed by many who liken it to a fencing match: the opponents stalk each other, feigning commitment in an attempt to get the other to commit himself irretrievably, and thus be at the mercy of the uncommitted person. To Waller,[36] who made his studies in the 1920s and 1930s, the struggle is aim-inhibited—it does not always lead to sexual consummation because of the youth and inner taboos of the participants. The more common goal is the "thrill" for the man, a physical or sensual experience after contact with the woman's body. For the woman, sex is less likely to be a goal; more important is the self-esteem gained by the boy's attentions, by his willingness to spend time and money on her. The interaction is based on the "line,"[37] a verbal attempt by the man to convince his "date" that he is skillful, interested, and eminently desirable. The girl parries his "line" with her own "line" and maintains her independence.

Theoretically, a successful date should result in both individuals gaining skill in successful role-playing and in retiring from the field of battle unscathed but with enhanced self-esteem. A more likely result, however, is that the boy considered the girl a "dog" or she thinks that he's a "creep." Headaches, fatigue, and/or "school tomorrow" are ill-concealed disguises for the rejection, and many individuals are frightened, depressed, and insecure when dating.[38] Failure brings little sympathy if it appears that it stemmed from ineptness, for dating success is a highly prized status, apart from any intrinsic values in the relationship itself.[39]

If any relationship develops after dating, it is likely to be settled by the "principle of least interest." The individual who cares least about the relationship is often able to dominate the partner who cares most. Another important dating factor is the rating of the partner. On a college campus, according to Waller, class A men generally date class A women. The class A fellow is a member of a high-status fraternity, has plenty of money, and a smooth "line"; he is also a good dancer and has a fine automobile. The girl must be attractive, possess a good "line," dance well and, most important, be popular.[40] To Waller, love was an unanticipated quirk of dating. Sometimes, in the midst of the dating game, the individual found to his surprise that his "line," *mirabile dictu,* actually reflected his true feelings, and the dalliance of dating might unwittingly lead to matrimony.

Waller never subjected his observations at the Pennsylvania State University campus to any empirical test. This void has been filled by others in more recent times, and their findings do not support Waller's conception of dating. Modern college youth view dating as recreational, educational, preparational for marriage, and adjustive.[41-44] The emphasis on competitiveness, looks, manners, neatness, dress, fraternity or sorority membership, and popularity, as spelled out in Waller's theory, is not apparent in the students' evaluations. Further, while many men may be recreationally oriented, women are more often seriously seeking a mate and are much less likely to accept a date with a potentially nonmarriageable man.[44,45] If there is a kernel of truth in Waller's assertion, it resides in the orientation of fraternity and sorority members who, to a slight degree, emphasize the "rating" characteristics described by Waller somewhat more than the non-"Greek," independent students.[46]

An attempt to integrate Waller's views in a historical framework has been made by McCall.[47] He notes that in the nineteenth century premarital sexuality could ruin one's reputation and was sufficient to disqualify an individual for a desirable marriage. Divorce was a rarity, and since one had to marry for life, great care had to be taken to make the right decision.

Waller's observations on dating occurred close to the demise of this phase of the courtship system, which had already begun to wane at the turn of the century. The competitive boy-girl maneuvers occurred in fraternities and sororities—they were more conservative because the wealth of the parents meant that more was at stake. It was natural, therefore, that this group would experience a slight cultural lag in the changing courtship pattern. In addition, since youth enjoyed considerable freedom of choice—but few alternatives after marriage—they understandably developed the complex exploitive bargaining techniques described by Waller.

By the 1930s, the intermediate phase had undergone changes from Waller's perceptions in the previous decade: courtship could now emphasize ongoing satisfactions and avoid the more rigid, uncomfortable competitive struggle it had once been. In this newer context, courtship became a progressive narrowing down of eligible partners until the final and most deeply involved relationship was achieved—marriage.[48]

By the 1960s, a new perception of courtship and marriage was introduced by

Farber—the "permanent available" model.[49] Marriage is not an immutable contract, but a restrictive agreement whereby the participants agree to maintain a certain behavior pattern vis-à-vis the world so long as the benefits from the relationship outweigh the disadvantages. Each partner constantly assesses his social relationships in terms of rewards and costs. If the costs exceed the rewards and the barriers against movement are weak (e.g., our divorce laws), the individual may elect to exchange the unfavorable-ratio relationship for a more favorable one.[50-52] Thus, the individual never disappears from the marriage mart entirely, and the romantic notion of a one and only predestined mate is shelved.

Because marriage does not permanently take an individual out of the market, it behooves him to keep himself available "just in case." Farber suggests that this is the reason for the mania for youth and glamor in the United States. In the search for desirability, "commercials" have replaced kin as teachers of attractiveness; hygiene is far more important to interpersonal success than the quality of the relationship. Perhaps the marriage vows should be changed from "until death do us part" to "until breath do us part."[53]

THEORIES OF MARITAL CHOICE

After World War II, America prospered, belief in the impenetrable mystery of love waned, and research monies flowed. Social scientists for the first time were emboldened to probe, on an empirical basis, the problem of who married whom. Almost all researchers agreed that individuals largely tended to marry homogamously with respect to such variables as age, race, religion, socioeconomic status, and education. But did this mean that personality factors did not strongly influence choice? Yes, according to Reiss[54]; and to the extent that personality played a part, it was because certain personality needs are derivatives of sociological facts. Another sociologist, Robert F. Winch, disagreed, holding that the sociological variables determine and narrow the field of eligibles but do not themselves influence the specific choice, which is determined by psychological factors. Winch formulated a simple theory to describe its operation: (a) we are attracted to those whose needs match our own differing needs (thus dominant and submissive persons are drawn to each other); and (b) when focusing on a single need, those high on the need are drawn to those low on it (a very submissive person seeks out as a partner one whose need to be submissive is low). In a somewhat oversimplified fashion we may speak of this as the "opposites attract" theory.

Winch conducted a study of 25 married undergraduates at Northwestern University and concluded that his thesis was supported.[55] His methodology, however, has been severely criticized, and the overwhelming majority of researchers have obtained results quite contrary to those called for by his theory.[56-58] These later findings are also largely drawn from college populations and range from reporting no correlation between the personalities of the couples to a moderate positive (similars attract) relationship.

Kerckhoff and Davis have attempted to integrate the sociological and psychological viewpoints by utilizing a "filter" theory.[59] Their data suggest that, in the first stage of relationship, a couple choose each other on the basis of similarity of values and those who fail to agree break off. If these short-term relationships are analyzed for psychological compatibility at this early stage by comparing the expectations of one partner with the role which the other desires to play, no degree of compatibility above chance is found. If, however, couples who have been going together for a considerable length of time are studied (longer than eighteen months in the study), the *values* held prove to be no longer selective, but the *psychological compatibility* principle takes over. Presumably, at this point, those with different values have broken off, and the couples have had enough time to test their mutual expectations for a spouse and their partner's ability to fulfill them. The neatness of these findings lasted some eight years, until a replication of the study failed to duplicate the earlier findings.[60] Obviously, the "filter" effects are more complex than originally thought.

None of the theories discussed so far have been able to tell us what common observation dictates: some people are very much like their spouses; others marry individuals who are quite different. To resolve this problem, as well as others, I have proposed the Stimulus-Value-Role (SVR) theory of marital choice.[61] The two principles forming the scaffold of the theory are that (1) marital choice involves a series of sequential stages (at least three) labeled *stimulus, value,* and *role,* and (2) at any given point of the relationship, its viability can be determined as a function of the equality of exchange subjectively experienced by its participants.

Sequential Stages

Stimulus. In an "open field" where interaction is not forced, an individual may be drawn to another, based on his perception of the other's physical, social, mental, or reputational attributes. Because attraction is based largely on noninteractional cues, this stage refers to *stimulus* values. This is crucial in an "open field" situation, for if the other fails to provoke sufficient attraction, further contact is not sought. Although the "prospect" in question might be potentially a highly desirable person, the first person—foregoing opportunities for further contact—never finds this out; consequently, physically unattractive individuals or persons whose stimulus value may be low for the individual (e.g., other races and religions) are unlikely to be seriously considered as marital candidates by a societally determined, high-stimulus value person.

Value stage. If mutual stimulus attraction exists between a man and woman, they initiate or increase their interaction so that they enter the second or "value comparison" stage, so named because the individuals assess their value compatibility through verbal interaction.

The couple may compare their attitudes toward life, politics, religion, sex, and the role of men and women in society and marriage. The fact that the couple is now interacting also permits more continuous and closer scrutiny of physical appearance, as well as other important factors: temperament, "style" of perceiving the world, and ability to relate to others.

It is possible that closer appraisal of physical qualities and temperament will lead to a changed opinion regarding the desirability of the partner, and this may result in an attempt to terminate the contact gracefully but as soon as possible. If contact has been made on the basis of strong stimulus attraction, however, it is more likely that the couple will remain in the second stage, continuing to assess the compatibility of their values.

Should the couple find that they hold similar value orientations in important areas, they are apt to develop much stronger positive feelings for each other than they experienced in the "stimulus" stage. One reason for this is that when an individual encounters another person with similar values, he gains support for the conclusion that his own values are correct; his views are given social validation. Further, many values are intensely personal and are so linked to the self-concept that rejection of these values is experienced as rejection of the self; and acceptance of them implies validation of the self. In sum, the holding of similar values should be a major factor in drawing two individuals together.

Role stage. The couple may decide to marry on the basis of stimulus attraction and verbalized value similarity. However, for most persons, these are necessary but insufficient conditions for marriage; it is also important that the couple be able to *function* in compatible roles. In the premarital phase, the partner's ability to function in the desired role is not as readily observable as his verbalized expression of views on religion, economics, politics, and how men should treat women. Knowing, for example, how much emotional support the partner will give when the individual fails a history examination presupposes an advanced stage of intimacy. It is for this reason that the "role" stage is placed last in the time sequence leading to marital choice.

Exchange Principle

Although romantics may believe that love overrides all material considerations, the second principle of SVR theory holds that love depends on equity of exchange. Each person tries to make social interaction as profitable as possible. *Profit* is defined as the *rewards* gained from the interaction minus the *costs* one must pay. By *rewards* are meant the pleasures, benefits, and gratifications an individual gains from a relationship. *Costs* are unpleasant experiences that inhibit or deter the performance of more preferred behaviors.

A man who is physically unattractive (cost), for example, might desire a woman who has the rewarding asset of beauty. Assuming, however, that his nonphysical qualities are no more rewarding than hers, she gains less profit than he does from the relationship, and his suit is likely to be rejected. Rejection is a cost to him because it may lower his self-esteem and increase his fear of failure in future encounters; hence, he may decide to avoid attempting to court women whom he perceives to be more attractive than he.

Contrariwise, he is likely to feel highly confident of success if he tries to date a woman even less attractive than himself, thereby risking little chance of rejection (low cost). However, the reward value of such a conquest is quite low, so that the profitability of such a move is also low. As a consequence, an experienced individual is likely to express a maximum degree of effort, and also obtain the greatest reward at the least cost, when he directs his efforts at someone of approximately equal physical attractiveness, assuming all other variables are constant.

During the first moments of contact, the individual may attempt to supplement his visual impression of the other with information regarding the other's role in society, professional aspirations, and background. Persons attracted to each other are likely to be balanced for the total weighted amalgam of stimulus characteristics even though, for a given trait, gross disparities may exist. Men, for example, tend to weight physical attractiveness in a partner more than women do, whereas women give greater weight to professional aspiration in the partner; accordingly, although physical attraction may play a leading role, it is hypothesized that the weighted pool of stimulus attractions that each possesses for the other will be approximately equal if individuals are to progress in courtship.

RESEARCH FINDINGS WITH SVR THEORY

One of the most important assertions of SVR theory is that both the theories of need complementarity (opposites attract) and homogamy (similars attract) are inadequate in accounting for marital choice, because the individual seeking a marriage partner is concerned with neither similarity nor complementarity of needs. Rather, he seeks a partner who represents a fusion of his ideal-self and ideal-spouse, although he may be prepared to lower his aspirations somewhat if he perceives himself as not possessing very high marital assets in his own right.

In general, however, when one is about to marry, he does tend to idealize his partner and to see him as close to his ideal-self and ideal-spouse concepts. This being the case, the tendency of an individual to marry someone whom he perceives as similar or different depends largely on how closely his self-concept is to that trinity of desiderata—his ideal-spouse, ideal-self, and perceived partner. This state of affairs may be readily seen in Figure 17.1.

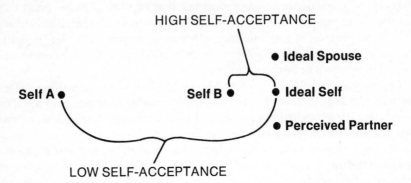

Figure 17.1   *A, whose self and ideal-self concepts are far apart (low self-accept-*
ance), will also see partner as unlike him, whereas B, whose self
and ideal-self are close together (high self-acceptance), will also see
partner as highly similar to the self.

This figure shows that individual B, who is highly self-accepting, is likely to
perceive himself as closely similar to his partner. Individual A, who is not highly
self-accepting (a greater distance between his self and ideal self-concepts), tends
to view himself as relatively dissimilar to his partner. This model has been
strongly validated in my research.[62] The model also tends to explain the
contradictory nature of earlier work which sometimes supported the "opposites
attract" theory and sometimes the homogamy theory. The present model
suggests that dissatisfaction with the self should result in complementary
perceptions by the person in question, whereas a highly self-accepting person
will perceive his partner as similar to himself.

Another tenet of SVR theory is that men occupy a greater status than women
in present-day American society; consequently, the confirmation of their self
and ideal-self concepts by their partners should be more influential than
confirmation of the women's concepts for couples making good courtship
progress. Further, where the man has personality difficulties (say, a neurosis),
the effect should be more inimical to the probability of marriage than neurosis
on the part of the woman. Both of these hypotheses have been confirmed for
my sample of college couples. Concerning neurosis, the man's degree of neurosis
affected the courtship progress of the couple significantly, but the woman's
mental health showed no significant association with courtship progress.

In accordance with the exchange theory aspect of the theory, it has been
shown that a greater than chance similarity of physical attractiveness,[63]
self-acceptance,[64] values,[65] and neurosis[66]—to name just a few variables—exists
among persons in advanced courtship. Moreover, it was predicted and verified
that courting couples would show a greater than chance equality for the
weighted sum of variables judged important for marital choice.[67] In sum,

empirical data have supported the theory, but the research efforts of others will be necessary before its validity can be assessed further.

The theories described are conspicuous by their lack of focus on "love." This probably reflects the fact that "love" has been promiscuously used to describe so many affective states and types of relationship that its connotative utility is quite limited. In any event, "love," insofar as it involves marriage, hardly appears as a spontaneous bolt of lightning. From my own research and that of others, however cynical it may sound, it seems appropriate to conclude that we generally love or at least marry the best bargain we can get.

HUSBANDS AND WIVES

The relationship between American husbands and wives has changed considerably since World War I. The greater freedom of women made them much less sympathetic to the traditional patriarchal role espoused by their husbands, and conflict became inevitable.

In the 1920s, Dr. Schmalhausen could declare that the sexes were at war with each other.[68] According to H. L. Mencken[69] and David Cohn,[70] the war was apparently going badly for the men. Cohn noted that many wives

> regard their husbands not as mates, or men, or even mice, but as mats; not as comrades, but as providers; not as friends, but as a combination redcap, dragoman, butler, escort and animated meal ticket; . . . They demand all that the traffic will bear and give as little as possible in return, except what they whiningly allude to when challenged as "the best years of my life."[71]

Not that husbands were much better, what with their tendency to

> play footie under the table with the nearest woman and thereby spoil both her evening slippers and her evening, tell off-color stories to uninterested females on the theory that this is daring and the stories are fatally aphrodisiacal; and act, in general, the role of the suburban Gay Dog. They care nothing for ideas, humor, conversation, or any wit more subtle than captions to *Esquire* drawings. But at home they want to be mothered by their wives—a process that freezes their already arrested development and makes impossible any relationship on an adult man-woman basis.[72]

To document this sad state further, two surveys by The *Ladies' Home Journal* in 1939[73,74] documented what each sex thought of the other. Some 55 percent of the men thought that women were spoiled, and 59 percent thought that they spent too much time away from the home. Not to be outdone, 54 percent of the women thought that men lose romantic interest in their wives after marriage, and 64 percent saw them as more interested in sports and business than women.

Cuber and Haroff, surveying over 400 middle- and upper-class marriages, likewise concluded that "the evidence forces us to an extremely depressing conclusion: 'there are very few good man-woman relationships. . . .' "[75]

Despite these dismal portraits, a *Saturday Evening Post* national survey in the 1960s revealed that 75 percent of the sample believed that husbands and wives could love each other all their lives.[76] How, then, can problems be avoided? Margaret Mead has suggested that marriage must be worked at every day: a wife must strive to remain desirable and a husband should "not put himself in positions where other women may become desirable to him."[77] On the other hand, Dorothy Dix, the erstwhile syndicated newspaper expert on love, told couples, "Let well enough alone is a fine matrimonial slogan, and as long as husband and wife are good actors it is the part of wisdom for their mates not to pry too deeply into the motives that inspire their conduct. . . ."[78]

If we turn to some recent data (rather than rely on opinions)[79,80] and to earlier data by Terman, Locke, and Burgess and Wallin, we do not find complete support for the gloomy description of marriage cited above. For one thing, the overwhelming majority of subjects are satisfied with their marriages. Even though, in general, only intact marriages are surveyed, this does not severely impair our conclusions about overall satisfaction. Most Americans who have been divorced remarry quickly, and many studies report that second marriages are almost as happy, or only slightly less so, than intact marriages.

Perhaps one reason that married couples are not as unhappy as is imagined is that they are not quite as wrapped up in each other as the romance and women's magazines suggest. In one survey of Chicago suburban housewives, over four times as many women saw the male role in marriage primarily as that of "breadwinner" first and "husband" second. In addition, a little more than half these women saw their own primary roles as that of "mother" rather than "wife."[81]

In the study of Blood and Wolfe, the number one problem in marriage, as described by their women respondents, was not compatibility, but money. Children and personality were less troublesome, with sex a distant fourth in the hierarchy. Contrary to the stereotype of the henpecked husband, most marriages were reported as egalitarian in terms of power structure, and when there was an imbalance the husband was more likely to be the dominant figure. When the woman was dominant, she was not happy; this dominance, in her opinion, was due to a vacuum left by the husband's refusal or inability to assume responsibility.

Further evidence that many homes are still tradition-centered comes from a survey of college students.[82] About 90 percent of the men and 84 percent of the women thought that the husband should be the head of the family; 67 percent of the men and 54 percent of the women said that this was the case in their own families. Hence, if we wish to find unequivocal evidence for the dissidence between the sexes referred to earlier, we shall have to look at specialized segments of society.

The Lower Class

More than 50 years ago a writer who was surveying workers' conditions in the 1880s concluded that mill workingmen did not see fit to aid their wives at home even when they were out of work.[83] Since then, things have not changed much in the lower class, where carefully defined and segregated roles are the rule. Unlike the middle class, interpersonal compatibility is no substitute for the performance of institutional roles. After work, there is little exchange about current happenings; the wife does not have much interest in her husband's job, and he has little inclination to discuss "men's things" with a woman. Both are tired from the full day's chores, and the evening is usually devoted to watching TV, with very little communication.[84] The women perceive their husbands as domineering, controlling, jealous, impulsive, and given to too much drinking with "the boys." The men see their wives as temperamental, emotional, demanding, irritating, and irrational; if they are young, they must be watched or they will "step out on a man."[85]

Occasionally there will be disagreements about money, the children, or the husband's job. A general anxiety pervades the arguments. Security is a very tenuous thing, and the couple do not envision their future as resting in their hands. Life is imposed on them by events external to their own wishes. A sudden layoff at the plant can jeopardize the entire future of the family.

There are no outside activities or organizations to distract them from the ennui of domestic life. Lower-class people are not joiners, except perhaps for a church and/or union. Individuals outside the family are looked upon with suspicion; the small number of friends are often drawn from among parents, brothers and sisters, or other relatives. The few other friends are almost automatically of the same sex. Not only does jealousy prohibit opposite-sex friendships, but the unflattering stereotypes regarding the opposite sex would make communication a near impossibility except for sexual purposes.

Arguments are seldom resolved by intensive verbal communication and expressions of feeling. The wife may yell at the husband, and he is likely to ignore her or escape from the house for some physical activity. If he stays, there may be a flareup, even physical violence. Rather than tackling the problem together, each partner may go off to a same-sex friend and recount his or her grievances.

Black People

Black people, many of whom belong to low-income social strata, experience not only the difficulties endemic to these strata but the problems caused by racial discrimination. As a result, there is considerable evidence of disorganization and instability in the black family. In 1965, the Moynihan report noted that nonwhite illegitimacy rates were eight times that of whites. One-third of nonwhite children lived in broken homes, whereas the figure was 10 percent for whites. Fourteen percent of Negro children received aid under the Aid for Dependent Children program as opposed to 2 percent of white children; and 56 percent of nonwhite children and 8 percent of white children received such aid at some time in their lives.[86]

Other data, both old and new, are hardly encouraging. In 1969, women were the heads of 9 percent of white households as compared to 27 percent of nonwhite households,[87] and there is evidence that children from such black homes are at a disadvantage with regard to scholastic performance[88] and occupational success.[89] Replacing the husband in the lower-class black household may be the "boy friend," whose financial contribution, permanency of living quarters, and relationship to the children vary from noninvolvement to strong "quasi-fatherhood."[90,91]

Research on husband-wife interaction among blacks, as reported by Blood and Wolfe,[92] posed various problems. In their Detroit study they found that the black husband exercised less power and dominance in the home than his white counterpart. The black wife was not only less likely to tell her troubles to her husband than was the case with the white wife, she was also less satisfied with his companionship, understanding, and love. Research on decision making, however, depends somewhat on the types of decisions involved, on how they are measured, and on the kind of subjects used. Middleton and Putney, whose study differed from that of Blood and Wolfe on each of these variables, found no racial differences in decision making.[93]

Aldous, in a more recent study,[94] found that Negro husbands were more likely to abdicate family responsibilities when their wives worked than when they were the sole breadwinners, whereas no such distinctions were found for comparable white families.

Previous investigations of the factors associated with marital adjustment of whites show that the list contains such variables as the happiness of parents' marriages, happiness in childhood, high income, high social status, high education, and the tendency of one member to validate his spouse's self-concept by seeing him in the same way as he sees himself.[95,96] Since fewer blacks have had much success in attaining these desirable conditions, it is not surprising that fewer black marriages are successful. Although approximately one-half of all black marriages end in divorce,[97] it is difficult to establish this figure precisely because a considerable minority of poor blacks cohabit, have children, and part without any legalities.

The world of the lower-class black does not breed positive attitudes to marriage. One writer reports that the relationship between the sexes under such conditions is characterized by mutually polarized and exploitive attitudes.[98] In a survey of those black women whose marriages were intact, 47 percent said they would not marry the same man again. When the entire sample of black women was asked which status they would choose—"wife" or "mother"—given only one choice, 67 percent of the intact group chose "mother" and only 20 percent opted for "wife."[99] It is hardly surprising, therefore, that when a group of 16- and 17-year-old black males were asked whether they would like to get married someday, only 58 percent gave an affirmative reply.[100]

Since the black father tends to be more absent from the family (due to desertion, divorce, or economic reasons) than the white father, the black male child is more often socialized in a fatherless condition. Pettigrew[101] has reported that a distinguishing characteristic of such boys is a marked inability at adult age to maintain a marital relationship. Thus the black seems caught in a vicious cycle.

Moynihan concluded that the Negro family was now caught in a "tangle of pathology [which] is capable of perpetuating itself without assistance from the white world."[102] The nation's efforts, in his opinion, should be to strengthen the Negro family so that it can rear and support its members in a manner comparable to other families.

The Moynihan report and some of its explicit statistical findings and implicit remedies have been savagely attacked by an army of black and white writers.[103-106] There appears to be some basis for the belief that the data of which they complain are not wholly objective.

First, it should be emphasized that in focusing on the matriarchal aspects of the black family and on the various measures of instability, the fact that *the typical black family is a stable one* with both parents present, seems to have been overlooked. Nonwhite families where both husband and wife are present totaled 69 percent in 1969, outnumbering female-headed families by 2.5 to one[107]—a far cry from a matriarchy! Thus, although black families are more unstable than white ones, the typical black family *is* stable.

Second, while the statistical findings are not false, they can lead to false conclusions in the absence of explanations. In 1968, for example, illegitimate births among blacks outnumbered those among whites by 6 to 1 (among blacks—31.2 percent; among whites—5.3 percent.[108] This one-sided ratio makes it sound as if whites were models of propriety. But when we press our investigation, we find that the number of black illegitimate births increased about 29 percent from 1960 to 1968, but the total number of births declined 11 percent. Had the black birthrate continued at its earlier pace, the percent of increment in illegitimate births would have been considerably reduced. In sum, the illegtimacy percentage depends, in part, on the overall birthrate.

Consider, too, that a premaritally pregnant black women is much less likely than a white woman to legitimize her child by marriage. In a world fraught with economic threat, it is of dubious value for some black men to gain "moral respectability" at the expense of the economic responsibilities of marriage and children. Moreover, the knowledge and the ability to bear the cost of effective contraception are more apt to be available in the white community. In addition, if pregnancy occurs, abortion costs are more easily met by whites. Finally, if the pregnancy is carried to full term, adoption agencies can more readily place a white child, and the records of illegitimacy are more likely to be favorably adjusted for whites than for blacks.

Despite all these "cover-ups," the percent of illegitimate births among whites from 1960 to 1968 rose 139 percent (from 2.3 to 5.3 percent)! Hence it is difficult to sustain the myth of black lust and white chastity. The safest conclusion would be that illegitimate births are still increasing somewhat, but their consequences fall more heavily on less affluent blacks. Many of the other statistics also suffer in one way or another from biased reporting that exaggerates racial differences. It should not be concluded, however, that these differences are solely statistical artifacts. Serious scholars do not question the existence of true differences in indices of family breakdown, but they do question the reported magnitude of such differences and their causes.

Perhaps the one study which has proved most irritating to black scholars has been the Moynihan report, which at first glance sounds like an eloquent plea in favor of more concern on the part of white society for the plight of blacks. Blacks are offended by what they perceive as a paternalistic tone in the report and by Moynihan's conclusion that, as a result of generations of discrimination, the condition of the black family is now pathologically self-sustaining apart from the factors of economic discrimination. He calls for an effort to strengthen the structure of the black family, particularly the status of the black man, and for eliminating economic discrimination vis-à-vis blacks.

Black social scientists have focused more on the need to overcome economic and social discrimination against blacks, at which point they believe the "tangle of pathology" will unravel itself and disappear without the patronizing help of whites. The data support this view. Evidence of a separate culture of lower-class blacks, a culture existing independently of economic status, has not been uncovered.[109,110] Rather, lower-class blacks seem to be more asocialized and more resistant to societal mores rather than promulgators of a separate culture. Among middle-class blacks, family concerns are very similar to those of whites. Apparently, the disorganization and the outlook of blacks are a *reaction* to and a *result* of discrimination rather than a *cause* of it. Both black and white writers have observed that lower-class blacks give little emphasis to putting today's pleasures off for tomorrow's greater rewards—in other words, there is no *career strategy*, but a more basic *strategy for survival.*[111] Nevertheless, given the uncertainties of the future for many blacks, who can say that a push for immediate gratification is not the best strategy?[112]

In sum, no one can say for sure that some aspects of lower-class black culture or, for that matter, of lower-class white culture are not harmful to family development. However, when so much of this disorganization seems attributable to discriminatory practices and attitudes, the question of pathological culture seems relatively unimportant. Many present-day familial difficulties among blacks will surely diminish in proportion to their acceptance on a more equal basis by society. Once this has been achieved, the question of independent pathological components would be more readily testable by those interested in pursuing such matters.

The Erosion of Happiness over Time

Most studies of satisfaction in marriage over time dealt with middle-class couples. Because the characteristics of the population, the questionnaires, and the measures of marital adjustment differed, lack of unanimity in the findings is not surprising.[113-118] However, all but one study indicated a progressive dissatisfaction with marriage, which reaches a nadir about the time when there are school-age children in the household. From that point on, while results varied somewhat, there was generally a plateau of satisfaction. When all the children had grown up and left the house, an upswing took place and continued to advanced age. These results, somewhat similar to those found in England[119,120] and Japan,[121] may be typical of marriages other than those in the USA.

The one dissenting study[122] measured the responses of aged couples who, in addition to describing their present satisfactions, recollected their feelings about the past. From their young adulthood to the present day, there was a rising positive feeling. However, the memories of these couples may well have screened out the unhappiness of their middle years—a kind of "whistling in the graveyard" syndrome. All other studies, however, saw the middle marital years as relatively bleak ones.

One possible explanation might be that people become soured on life as they age, and the loss of marital satisfaction is but a part of a general downward trend. Eventually they become reconciled to their lot, and happier as their responsibilities to society and to their children decline. A study by Pineo tested the first part of this thesis for the period from young adulthood to the middle years.[123] Working on a follow-up of the Burgess and Wallin couples who had been married for varying periods up to 20 years, he found a slight but nonsignificant tendency to see oneself and one's spouse in a less favorable light with the passage of time, compared to the time when the couples had been tested during their engagement period. Apparently, it is the satisfaction with marriage itself rather than with the personality of the partner that suffers profoundly with time.

The second most noticeable drop with time was the sharing of interests and activities, but this was not highly related to marital adjustment. To determine the items most related to marital adjustment which were affected by time, subjects with the highest marital adjustment were compared with those who were lowest in marital adjustment. The most differentiating items, not surprisingly, were, "Would you marry the same person again?" and "Do you ever regret your marriage?" Other less obvious items that differentiated the groups related to demonstrations of affection, confiding in one's spouse, kissing one's spouse, and settling arguments by give and take. The unsatisfied individual stops confiding in his spouse, is insufficiently involved in trying to settle differences, stops kissing the spouse, markedly decreases the frequency of sexual relations, and, in short, ceases to react to his or her partner with much positive expression.

The same individual experiences very slight, if any, feelings of unhappiness with himself and only slightly more with his spouse. It is not so much that he dislikes his spouse as the fact that he simply is no longer very involved with her and presumably now finds the bonds of matrimony rather wearisome.

What accounts for this disenchantment? Pineo suggests that it is predicated on a marriage of free choice. Two individuals may date, find that they like each other's company, and have much in common. Let us hypothesize that both are religious, both like music and sports, and both seem well matched in terms of equal sex drive. As their relationship develops and each reveals himself more and more to the other, each perceives the other as being more and more what he desires in a spouse. At the moment in time when the discrepancy between the spouse desired and the perception of the partner is at a minimum, they decide to marry.

Once married, what can the future bring? Closer compatibility? Possibly, but not likely. They were married when differences were at a minimum. At best, they can keep the discrepancy between the expectations of the partner and the perceived fulfillment of these expectations at a minimum. But time changes people's needs, expectations, and philosophies without guaranteeing a parallel change on the part of the partner. Let us look at our hypothetical couple a decade later.

The husband has grown less religious or more involved in other matters, and rarely attends church. His wife still maintains an intense religious feeling and attends regularly. He used to like music, and it is not so much that he dislikes it now as the fact that it has been superseded in the hierarchy of preferences by the monthly meeting of the Rotarians or other organizational interests. His wife, on the other hand, a local symphony booster, must now go to the symphony alone or with friends. The husband still maintains an interest in sports, but more as a spectator than a participant. The wife's time is too taken up with the children to become involved in "games." During the first two years of their married life, they had an equal desire for sex, but now he finds that business worries, golf, and getting ahead make him feel tired. His wife seems more interested than he is, and he feels guilty. It's really no serious problem—just another difference due to the passage of time.

If marriages were made not on the basis of free choice but by parents (without consulting the bride and groom, as in some societies), there would be no reason to expect such a decline in satisfaction with time. Indeed, the couple might more likely feel happier because they expected little and were pleasantly surprised. However, the trend the world over today is in the direction of free choice.

Nothing has been said to suggest that married people are necessarily unhappy. One study indicated that married men were in the happiest of all states[124]; married women and single women were equally happy; and unmarried men were the least happy. Thus, when we say that marital happiness, on the average, declines with time, we mean that the individuals concerned are *less happy* than at the beginning of the marriage, not that they are *unhappy*. Marriages are much more likely to bring more happiness to their participants than does bachelorhood.

DIVORCE

The awesome steady climb in the divorce rate can be fully appreciated by examining Table 17.1. Between 1860 and 1972, the number of divorces and annulments rose about 112 times, whereas the population increased only between 6 and 7 times. In fact, the number of divorces has more than doubled since 1960.

Table 17.1— United States Divorce and Annulment Rate, 1860-1973

Year	Number of Divorces	Rate per 1,000 Population
1860	7,380	0.2
1870	10,962	0.3
1880	19,663	0.4
1890	33,461	0.5
1900	55,751	0.7
1910	83,045	0.9
1920	167,105	1.6
1930	191,591	1.6
1940	256,692	2.0
1950	371,309	2.5
1960	393,000	2.2
1966	499,000	2.5
1967	534,000	2.7
1968	582,000	2.9
1969	660,000	3.3
1970	715,000	3.5
1971	768,000	3.7
1972	840,000	4.0
1973	930,000*	4.3*

Sources: Paul H. Jacobson, *American Marriage and Divorce,* New York: Rinehart, 1959, p. 90: *Vital statistics of the United States,* Washington, D.C.: United States Department of Health, Education and Welfare.

*Estimated by the author.

There are 40 recognized grounds for divorce, but none are exactly the same from state to state.[125] There is also regional diversity: the Northeast has a little more than only one-fourth the divorce rate of the West. The reasons for the higher Western rate are complex: a more liberal tradition; the presence of younger adults, less set in their ways; the effects of migratory life styles; and the fact that religious groups (such as Catholics) which prohibit divorce are more numerous in the East.

The most common ground for divorce is cruelty (60 percent), followed by desertion (30-33 percent) and adultery (2 percent).[126] Some three-fourths of the plaintiffs in divorce actions are women. (These statistics are meaningless because convention dictates that the man usually permits the woman to sue, regardless of who primarily wishes the divorce.)

The divorce capital of the United States is Reno, Nevada, which in 1927 lowered its residence requirements to three months. In 1931, its hegemony was threatened by news that Idaho and Arkansas, thirsting for "tourist gold," were also about to lower residence requirements to three months. Millions of dollars hung in the balance. On March 6, with the speed that only truly dedicated legislators can muster, a bill stipulating a new six-week requirement was passed by the Nevada State Assembly by a vote of 34 to 0. On March 16, the Senate overrode the objection of one unpatriotic soul and approved the bill, 13 to 1. The governor signed it on March 19, along with provisos that divorces could be tried behind closed doors and that wide-open gambling would be sanctioned.[127]

Meanwhile, for varying reasons, some New Yorkers decided to divorce in accordance with New York laws, which accepted only adultery as grounds. The couple might agree on collusive measures to facilitate such action. In the "hotel adultery" ploy, the husband and wife arranged to have the husband meet a woman who served as a professional witness for a fee. The woman would remove a few outer garments and hop into bed with the man, whereupon, by prior arrangement, a private detective, a professional process server, and someone who knew the husband (half the time this person was the wife herself) would burst into the room.

Other more exotic but difficult maneuvers were described by a retired professional witness, Dorothy Jarvis, in the *New York Mirror* Sunday magazine under the title "I Was the 'Unknown Blonde' in 100 New York Divorces." Where the husband was unwilling to cooperate, a technique called "push and raid" was employed. A woman was shoved into the victim's room; she whipped off her coat, revealing scanty clothing, and the detective burst into the room. The "shadow and shanghai" routine consisted in following the victim until he could be seized and brought to a suitable location for a raid. In the "dance and dope" arrangement, the girl doped the victim's drink in her apartment, and when he passed out, she signaled the raiding party.

These charming but expensive collusive episodes are now presumably a part of history's dusty pages since New York's recent widening of the divorce grounds. What persists, however, is the antiquated perception of the divorce seekers: they are not two incompatible individuals—one is the guiltless, pure victim and the other a guilty marriage wrecker. The guiltless one, in this adversary system, brings charges against the guilty one in court. The parties are not always full of mutual hatred, but the law does not recognize divorce by mutual consent. Nor is divorce recognized because the individuals are no longer in love, or have grown to dislike each other, or found someone else more appealing—despite the fact that these reasons account for the majority of divorces.

Laws are extremely difficult to change, even when the conditions which gave rise to them no longer apply. The law, for example, has still not come to grips with the phenomenon of the "working wife." She must live where her husband wants to, even though both work. And the husband may be required to pay alimony even if his wife works. In addition, the Catholic Church has been blamed, with some justification, for halting legislation on more lenient divorce, not to mention birth control. Yet even though today more and more prelates have issued statements that Catholics should not attempt to influence legislation regarding non-Catholics, we do not see any drastic changes. The role of Catholicism in inhibiting divorce has been exaggerated.

The truth of the matter is that if the American public really wished to make divorce much more lenient, it would have exerted irresistible pressure on state legislatures. The absence of such pressure in many states reflects what polls in the United States and in other countries have consistently shown since the 1940s and early 1950s: most people think that divorce laws are too lenient, and women are more inclined to believe this than men.[128] A national Gallup poll conducted in the United States in January 1966 asked, "Generally speaking, would you say divorce laws in this state are too strict or not strict enough?" The answers (in percentages) were: too strict, 13; not strict enough, 34; about right, 18; no opinion, 35.[129]

Nevertheless, as shown in Table 17.2, the *Saturday Evening Post* did a representative nationwide survey of *married persons* and found much change from an earlier 1937 sample.

Table 17.2 – Replies in Percent, to Question "What Are
Reasonable Grounds for Divorce?"

	1937	1966
Adultery	34	52
Physical cruelty	23	47
Desertion	25	46
Nonsupport	22	42
Mental cruelty	12	39
Incompatibility	16	28
Any reason making the marriage unhappy.	29	20

Source: *Saturday Evening Post,* December 31, 1966, and January 7, 1967.

Little difference was found between men and women, but the overall sample showed only 13 percent unequivocally opposed to divorce compared to 17 percent in 1937. Strong differences were found, however, when social class was taken into account. Among men, 45 percent of the college graduates would grant a divorce for incompatibility as compared to 30 percent of the high school graduates and 14 percent of the elementary school graduates. For women, physical cruelty was sufficient grounds for 69 percent of the college graduates, 50 percent of the high school graduates, and 31 percent of the elementary school graduates. Somewhat surprisingly, only 25 percent of the Catholics flatly opposed divorce.[130] These data suggest that a continuous liberalization of views on divorce seems to be taking place, and it will be of interest to see whether these trends will be correlated with subsequent state legislative actions.

Some Socioeconomic, Cultural, and Psychological Correlates of Divorce

Literally hundreds of variables have been shown to be associated with divorce. Rather than provide an interminable list, and since many of these variables are highly correlated with each other, I have elected to separate them into a few key dimensions based on the repetitiveness of their occurrence in numerous studies.[131-136] I shall first discuss variables that can be classified as noninterpersonal, followed by a discussion of interpersonal ones.

One important variable is "poverty" and its associated variables, such as "lack of education" and "occupation." The lower one is on these variables, the more likely he is to be divorced. It is not difficult to see why this should be so, and William J. Goode has developed a useful schema to account for marital strain.[137] For the most part, the United States does not have a large number of poor, in the absolute sense of the word. Those who are relatively poor, especially since the advent of television, may be said to have the same basic need and desire for material comforts as the wealthy: clothing, housing, medical care, automobiles, and furniture. Income, however, is skewed in its distribution, so that the poor cannot fulfill their aspirations as readily as do the rich. It would be inaccurate to say that the poor share identical desires with the rich, but the former have a greater discrepancy between their goals and what they achieve. To the poor, the "establishment" is omnipotent, and they believe that there is little that they can do to alter their plight. Unfortunately, one of the few places they can give vent to their frustrations is at home, and this displaced anger leads to heightened tension for the whole family. Further, the lower-class wife, who is more likely than the wealthy wife to be working, needs more help in the home. She is less likely to get it because masculine and feminine roles are more strongly stratified in the lower class than in the upper classes.

The middle- and upper-class wife, accustomed to comparative luxury, is less likely to allow interpersonal differences to build up to the point of a possible divorce. She has too much to lose; if divorced, she is less likely to earn as much as her husband. Then, too, there are such external influences as friends, colleagues, and community forces, all tending to weigh more heavily on the upper classes. Unlike the worker, the network of social communication is very strong between professional and social life, and divorce news is quickly transmitted to all members of the network and can lead to embarrassing interaction. The lower-class worker has less interaction with his fellow workers or superiors and is less traumatically affected by a change in his marital status.

Another important factor differentiating the divorced and the nondivorced is the greater social conventionality of the latter, as typified by membership in community organizations and by church attendance. Since divorce is still a slightly unconventional act, the association between divorce and unconventionality is not surprising. The nondivorced, as compared to the divorced, seem to have had a much more optimistic outlook on life since childhood. They recall their childhood as happy and remember their parents as happily married. Whether it was the actual environment that was good, or whether their rosy outlook makes everything seem good in retrospect, is a moot point.

In any event, there can be little doubt that temperament is associated with marital stability. A study by Vincent Glaudin and myself[138] suggests strongly that the presence of marked "masculine" righteous attitudes by both men and women is associated with marital breakdown. Also, hysteric-type women and psychopathic character disorder-type men are candidates for marital breakup.

The nondivorced also appear to be more sociable than the divorced, mixing easily with people and having many friends of the opposite sex without arousing jealousy in their spouses. One spouse feels no jealousy, perhaps because the other thinks of him as equal or better than she is (this is another differentiating characteristic). In addition, the length of acquaintanceship and engagement was far longer for the nondivorced. There was less impulsive acting out, which is not to say that these relationships were passionless but only that the passions did not lead to hasty marriage. Next, the sexual adequacy of the nondivorced is high, which is clearly related to the quality of the interpersonal relationship, although biological factors may also contribute. Finally, the presence of strong dominance drives in women has been shown to be associated with divorce in two different studies.[139,140] It appears that the reason for this finding is that dominant women tend to be most dissatisfied with the men they marry. If they are able to marry others of comparable dominance, all goes well; but because of their high drive, the odds are against much success in their choice. In the typical case, dominance or even egalitarian expression by the woman is contrary to the more passive, nurturant stereotype of women held by men, and the average husband is threatened by such behavior.

While all these factors are important, they cannot tell the whole story. To illustrate, let us turn to some available data on remarriage, which indicate that the majority of these marriages, perhaps 70 to 80 percent, turn out to be quite happy.[141-143] Since these newly happy individuals cannot change their background to make their childhood happy, their parents happy in marriage, and so on, there must be other factors to account for this new facility for marital happiness.

One factor may be presumed to be the housekeeping skills and the experience of living with someone else acquired in the first marriage. Another factor may be a change in the motivational structure of personality, leading the second pair of spouses to seek to avoid those behavioral responses which brought on the first marital disaster. There may be more involvement in protecting the marriage after one failure.

A final important factor, not yet discussed, is the relationship between the marital partners in terms of values and drives. Research has shown that the more homogeneous the partners are with respect to age, education, race, occupational and socioeconomic background, religion, basic philosophical values, and sex drive, the more likely they are to avoid the divorce court. It would seem that compatibility with respect to personality is also important, but there has been little study in this area. What work has been done indicates that perceptual confirmation of one's own role in marriage by the spouse, and perception of the spouse as fulfilling one's own expectations regarding a spouse, are associated with avoidance of divorce. This is undoubtedly the area on which much of the marital research will focus in the future.

THE WIFE AND EMPLOYMENT

By the 1940s, the educated but functionless wife had degenerated into the malevolent caricature depicted by Philip Wylie as "Mom":

> She is a middle-aged puffin with an eye like a hawk that has just seen a rabbit twitch far below. She is about twenty-five pounds overweight, with no sprint, but sharp heels and a hard backhand which she does not regard as a foul but a womanly defense. In a thousand of her there is not sex appeal enough to budge a hermit ten paces off a rock ledge. She nonetheless spends several hundred dollars a year on permanents and transformation, pomades, cleansers, rouges, lipsticks, and the like—and fools nobody except herself. . . .
>
> She smokes thirty cigarettes a day, chews gum, and consumes tons of bonbons and petits fours. The shortening in the latter, stripped from pigs, sheep and cattle, shortens mom. She plays bridge with the stupid voracity of a hammerhead shark, which cannot see what it is trying to gobble but never stops snapping its jaws and roiling the waves with its tail. . . . But it is her man who worries about where to acquire the money while she worries only about how to spend it, so he has the ulcers and colitis and she has the guts of a bear. . . .[144]

As Will Durant had foreseen, the end of the purely domestic wife was at hand.[145] Slowly but steadily, the ranks of working wives swelled, augmented in particular by their demonstrated competence during World War II, when Rosie the Riveter was the heroine who compensated for the paucity of men on the industrial front.

Women seemed to be at the crossroads—between traditional domesticity and a working girl's life. In that hour of need, the Freudians stepped forward to defend the traditional woman. In the 1920s, psychoanalysts had been in the avant garde of sexual liberalism; two decades later, they became the apologists of reactionary, patriarchal feminism. America had become child-centered, and psychiatrists and pediatricians warned mothers that the emotional security of their children was in jeopardy if they went to work. Since, according to Freudians, the adult's personality and sexual adjustment were more or less determined by childhood experiences, mothers who "abandoned" their children were dooming them to perpetual maladjustment. Dr. Helen Deutsch further warned that the intellectual activity of women threatened the soft, yielding emotionality that was feminine.[146] Talcott Parsons and Robert Bales added the weight of functional sociology to woman's dilemma, noting that her role in the family was an *expressive* one whereas that of her husband was instrumental.[147] At a slight risk of simplification, we may say that this is equivalent to the statement that *he* works and *she* makes the family feel good by her presence.

The laurel wreath for dissemination of misinformation, however, belongs to a "best seller" of the immediate post-World War II period, *Modern Woman: The Lost Sex,* by Ferdinand Lundberg and Dr. Marynia F. Farnham, a psychiatrist. In a brief promenade through history, the authors attempt to demonstrate how woman got "lost." They resurrect the long-disavowed myth that "before the Industrial Revolution women had a large and satisfying world of free activity available to them."[148] Under the guise of psychiatric expertism they proceed to prick the dummy of women's rights with the voodoo needles of psychiatric curses. "[Historical] feminism . . . was at its core a deep illness."[149] Mary Wollstonecraft "was afflicted with a severe case of 'penis-envy' "[150] and was a "masochist,"[151] while John Stuart Mill was a "passive-feminine character."[152] Such labeling, of course, saved the authors the more tedious job of documenting the validity of their writings for women's position at that time.

Turning to more modern times, the fact that two-thirds of divorces were initiated by women is taken by the authors as conclusive evidence that women are much more unhappy in marriage than men, although more qualified views have stated that this is merely a function of legal nicety. One expert has gone on record as maintaining that men actually manipulate the conditions leading to most divorces.[153]

The sharp decline in birthrate saddens Lundberg and Farnham, and they attribute it to "psychic sterility" and to the use of contraceptives: "Women cannot make [sexual] pleasure an end in itself without inducing a decline in pleasure. In general, oversimplifying in order to make the point pithily, women who don't want children, whether they have them or not, fail to derive maximal satisfaction from the sexual act."[154]

Finding themselves unable to gain the symbolic penis through childbirth, these women are often led to "sexual freelancing," but without success, while their husbands are in the meantime wooed by "single working women." The authors defend not only the double sexual standard, but also the doctrine that men should be paid more for equal work because they are fulfilling the traditional role of supporting a wife. In the chapter "Ways to a Happier End," they suggest that public honors be accorded women who have successfully raised "well-balanced" families, and mothers should be given sizable subsidies so that they need never work. On the other hand, women may be allowed one kind of work: "All public teaching posts now filled by women would be reserved not only for married women but for those with at least one child. . . . What would happen to the spinsters? They would perhaps be encouraged to marry."[155]

Lundberg and Farnham grant women who wish to enter the "masculine" fields of law, mathematics, business, industry, and technology the right to do so. "Government and socially-minded organizations should however, make it clear that such pursuits are not generally desirable for women."[156] As to bachelors, the authors combined a Puritan stricture with a more modern type of torture: bachelors should be subjected to unfavorable tax rates so that in effect they would be supporting children, and bachelors of more than 30 years of age who are, after all, "a dubious social quantity," should be encouraged to submit to psychotherapy.[156]

While the battle of words for the direction of women's energies continued, the female work force rose sharply. In 1900, about 21 percent of women over 14 years of age worked, but only 5.6 percent of married women did so. By 1963, 36 percent of all women over 14 were working, but the proportion of working married women was well over 60 percent.[157]

Despite this increase, attitudes regarding the roles of men and women have remained traditional and rather refractory to the changes in behavioral roles. In a survey published in 1960, 75 percent of male Pennsylvania State University students and 70 percent of the co-eds agreed that women should be able to cook before marriage.[158] They agreed even more strongly that a mother with a young child should not work (89 percent of the men, 83 percent of the women). A difference was seen in replies to questions about what should happen after the children were grown. Only 31 percent of the men, but 50 percent of the women, thought it all right for the woman to go to work. With respect to the woman's duty to her children as opposed to more personal interests, there was also a difference. To the statement, "It is a mother's duty to devote herself completely to her children even if this hampers her own interests," 45 percent of the men but only 23 percent of the women said "yes."

Obviously, there is much uncertainty as to where women are going. They are interested in working, but when they do, they seek the traditional feminine roles of teacher, librarian, and service clerk.[159] Even though housework is boring, they experience a sense of worth when they do housework.[160]

Margaret Mead addressed herself to the question of the future of women in *Male and Female*, but her message was fuzzy. Each sex has its special contribution, she argues; but "it is of very doubtful value to enlist the gifts of women if bringing women into fields that have been defined as male frightens the men, unsexes the women, muffles and distorts the contribution the women could make, either because their presence excludes men from the occupation or because it changes the quality of the men who enter it."[161]

Pearl Buck expressed a much firmer conviction that women must feel free to work and fight tradition,[162] but Betty Friedan is the one who fired at the problem point-blank in *The Feminine Mystique*.[163] The book is overly long, repetitious, and exaggerated. Yet its great virtue is that Friedan seizes the problem in a vise-like grip and does not relinquish her hold until every aspect of "the problem that has no name" has been explored: what does a woman do with her creative ability other than being a housewife?

The waste of womanpower is staggering. According to *Womanpower,* only one of four women *capable* of doing college work goes to college as opposed to one of two men. Regarding PhD's, of 300 women capable of earning the degree, only one does so compared to one of 30 men.[164] Of all doctoral recipients, women represented 15 percent in 1930; by 1960 it declined to 10 percent.[165]

From 1950 to 1960, the number entering the professions increased considerably for both sexes. Despite the fact that the smaller number of women in the professions would have predisposed women to experience a greater percentage gain than men, exactly the opposite occurred. For example, from 1950 to 1960 there was a 3.6 percent decline in women chemists, in contrast to a 13.5 percent increase in men chemists. In the same period, women engineers rose by 11 percent, whereas their male counterparts showed a 64.3 percent increase. While women geologists declined 27 percent, male geologists increased 81 percent. Physics and mathematics burgeoned in the decade, but although women physicists increased 20 percent, male physicists increased 93 percent. Although the number of women in mathematics more than doubled, male mathematicians more than quadrupled.[166]

The reason for this difference is not difficult to discern. Thirty-eight percent of the women in the Pennsylvania State University survey acknowledged that the primary motive for women going to college was to find a mate.[167] Even this high figure is probably an underestimate, for not a few women probably said "no" when in their hearts they meant "yes." In another study, college women were asked the following question: "An American woman can be very successful in a number of ways. Which of the following would you most like to be yourself?" The answers most frequently given were being the mother of several accomplished children and being the wife of a prominent man.[168]

Consequently, it is hardly startling that only two of five women scientists are married as compared to four of five male scientists, and that many married women scientists quit the profession due to marriage and/or a family, never to return. Some "liberals" advocate that women withdraw from a profession with the advent of the first child and return when the last one is in elementary or high school. But this leaves a gap of 15 or 20 years in many cases. Such an interval poses little problem to a department store clerk, but it is hardly so in the case of a nuclear physicist, many of whom find it difficult to keep abreast of current developments without taking time off. Again, if we are dealing with an exceptionally talented woman, there is an even greater tragedy involved. It has been carefully documented in recent years that the most creative years for scientists are the twenties and thirties, which is also the period of childrearing, when the woman is least likely to stay in the profession.

In a study of career development,[169] college women were given a hypothetical story in which a woman, a brilliant biology B.A., helped her husband through law school by working. Both want children and he now has a good job. However, she would also like to get an advanced degree in biology and pursue a career in research. What should the couple do: start the family first and have the wife get her degree later; have her give up the career goal; get the degree now and postpone child bearing; or combine degree-seeking and child bearing simultaneously?

Only one-fourth of the women thought that child bearing should follow immediately, with the career postponed temporarily or permanently abandoned. Yet one-half thought that these last two alternatives would be chosen by most wives, and three-fourths said that these two alternatives would be chosen by most men. When the attitudes of men were sampled, the women's predictions proved to have considerable accuracy. Moreover, it can be surmised from the fact that so many women quit work between the ages of 24 to 44 that they do, in fact, comply with men's wishes rather than with their own.

To conclude, we may note that there are at least four basic reasons why married women have not done more in the professional world. First, there is the myth that extensive maternal care is crucial to the child's personality development; this has never received empirical verification. Indeed, it is becoming apparent that the *way* the time is spent rather than the *number of hours* logged is more important. Certainly, evidence from the Soviet Union and the kibbutzim of Israel shows that rather than suffering ill effects from all-day child care by trained specialists, the children not only are well-adjusted but possess far more ability to function independently in comparison with exclusively mother-reared children. Moreover, not enough attention has been given to the role of the mother as exemplar. An educated woman who is interacting in a professional world is able to contribute much more to the cognitive development of a child than one who stays at home. She is also able to present the child with the example of a mother who is fully as capable in the intellectual sphere as his father. If the child is a girl, this model may serve as a potent stimulus for her self-perception and professional aspirations.

A third factor holding back married women's professional development has been the attitude of married men. Some of them are unalterably opposed to a wife's working because they believe that a woman's place is in the home with the children, or because they feel it reflects on their "breadwinner" status. They are not necessarily opposed to women bettering themselves, and may even encourage their wives to improve their minds by attending the weekly meetings of the "Great Books" club. Others take the stance that their wives can work at anything just as long as they take care of the children, prepare meals, and see that their shirts are pressed. Naturally, such kindness does not extend to a willingness to make any sacrifices to aid the cause. Finally, a distinct minority of men believe that women are as fully entitled to a professional career as themselves, and that they must make sacrifices for a wife's career just as they expect their wife would do for them.

The fourth point is the failure of our otherwise technologically advanced society to make child-care and house-keeping provisions that facilitate the "twin careers" of mother and professional. Almost all other industrialized nations have day-care centers with modest prices and excellently trained personnel. Too often, in the United States, such facilities are meager and run by profit-oriented, often untrained, individuals; in fact, instead of nurseries or playschools, they could more aptly be called "keeperies." Moreover, in this day of specialization and of a paucity of domestic servants, it seems odd that we have not developed networks of specialized teams that go from house to house and clean up in a fraction of the time that it ordinarily takes a single person to do so.

The small proportion of women in professional life may be related to women's perception of the accomplishments of their own sex. On one occasion, Philip A. Goldberg conducted an experiment in which he presented passages on varying topics to undergraduates in a women's college.[170] The author was identified as "John T. McKay" to half of the girls, and as "Joan T. McKay" to the other half. When asked to evaluate the paragraphs, the girls gave higher valuation to the identical works of the fictitious male author than to the fictitious female author. They obviously considered men intellectually more competent than women.

As the nonprofessional woman ages, she is especially prone to what Jules Henry has called the "40-year-old jitters."[171] Basically the reasoning is as follows: A man does, a woman is. A man validates his role image by getting a good job and, to a lesser degree, by marrying and raising a family. A nonprofessional woman validates herself by getting a man. Since she does not have a career, she gains his esteem by keeping a good home, raising the children, and providing emotional, sexual, and esthetic satisfaction. Obviously, physical beauty plays an important role in her stimulus value as a sexual partner and showpiece to his associates.

In the upper classes, a man's assets may rise with age, when promotions and the scarcity of middle-aged men may raise his market value. On the average, the stimulus value of women declines much more rapidly than that of men, and the woman whose chief forte has been beauty is often rightfully anxious at the depreciation of her chief salable product as she approaches 40.

It is interesting to note that despite the failure of women to crack the professional barrier, they are succeeding dramatically in whittling away at sex differences in other social areas where, since World War II, there has been a continuous decline in sexual dimorphism.[172] Children are given less sex-specific names, scotch is "lighter," and vodka, which has little "bite," has zoomed in popularity to conform to feminine tastes. Young male adolescents with long hair are difficult to distinguish from girls, especially since the former now wear bright colors, beads, and earrings. Women have advanced in sports: in 1946 they accounted for 35 percent of the nation's tennis players, but in 1968 the figure rose to 45 percent. The billiard parlor, formerly a smoke-filled denizen of sleazy hustlers, bookies, and other marginal characters, has become a clean and well-lighted family center. Dancing, where once the man "led" and the woman "followed" in the foxtrot, waltz, and tango, has shown a revolutionary change. Most contemporary dance steps require no leading or following; pure equality or, more correctly, anarchy ensues—one need not look at or even touch his dancing partner.

Such changes, however, are essentially peripheral to the need of the bright young college graduate woman to find meaningful expression of her potential, other than becoming a wife and mother. Between 65 and 70 percent of American married women do not work full time. If we contemplate what the addition of these millions—from sales clerks to surgeons—could mean to our society, we must conclude that the loss is not that of the individuals alone; it is also society's loss.

CONCLUSIONS

The predominant feature of twentieth-century American life has been the growth in the cult of the "individual." The rising divorce rate, the falling birthrate, and increasing sexual permissiveness and social interaction between the sexes have been interpreted by conservative sociologists such as Sorokin and Zimmerman as resultants of our sensate culture, flabby morality, and lack of responsibility to society. Neither of these writers has ever been able to show a connection between these variables and dissoluteness—in fact, there are just as many positive interpretations for these phenomena as negative ones. Increased divorce could represent a rising requirement for compatibility in marriage; a lower birthrate reflects greater concern for the welfare of *each* child. Sexual permissiveness (which we shall discuss in the next chapter) signifies a greater acceptance of the fact that man would be biologically ready for sex in his teens were it not for social inhibitory restrictions.

The new individualism has thrust greater responsibility on the individual in his choice of a marriage partner. Formerly, interaction between nubile individuals was sparse and supervised. Other means of evaluating a potential marriage partner had to be found, one in which interaction could take place without commitment—namely, dating. The increasing interest in interpersonal relationships and the family has also led to theories of marital choice. Finally, with woman's new role as a worker, the traditionally segregated husband-wife roles are becoming less differentiated as men and women develop new ways of relating to each other.

These changes do not appear to have endangered the family. The divorce rate, while high, is matched by high marriage and remarriage rates, and we also see a higher percentage of intact marriages today (thanks, in part, to a falling death rate). All this does not obviate the presence of much marital unhappiness. Apart from problems of psychological incompatibility, which defy simple solutions, it is quite apparent that marital maladjustment is strongly overrepresented in the lower class. To cope with the unhappiness of these millions, most communities offer only a scattering of family service agencies, often staffed by semitrained, middle-class-oriented personnel. The need for communication with families in distress is our number one problem. I do not refer merely to marital counseling, although that would be helpful. One cannot avoid economics in dealing with marriage, since poverty is probably the primary correlate of divorce, and economic well-being must be upgraded through education, training, and better jobs.

A second problem deals with American society's concept of women. Much has been said earlier and need not be repeated. But if we really want to create equal opportunity for women in our society, we must take account of her future dual roles of mother and worker. To date, regrettably, society has failed to realize the need for more flexible educational facilities, jobs, improved child-care centers, and the training of more understanding husbands.

REFERENCES

1. "Annual summary for the United States, 1971: Births, deaths, marriages, and divorces."
2. "Few U.S. married couples said to live with relatives," p. 50.
3. *Two Hundred Million Americans.*
4. "Are changing conventions menacing the marriage institution?"
5. J. Collins, "The doctor looks at companionate marriage."
6. W. McDougall, "Marriage and the home."
7. B. B. Lindsey, *The Companionate Marriage*, p. 391.
8. Z. Rubin, "Measurement of romantic love."
9. W. M. Kephart, *The Family, Society, and the Individual.*
10. W. Waller and R. Hill, *The Family: A Dynamic Interpretation.*
11. E. Fromm, *The Art of Loving.*
12. N. Foote and L. Cottrell, *Identity and Interpersonal Competence.*
13. E. W. Burgess and P. Wallin, *Engagement and Marriage.*
14. R. W. England, Jr., "Images of love and courtship in family-magazine fiction."
15. R. T. L., "Ten reasons for marriage."
16. A. Preston, "A girl's preparation for marriage."
17. W. M. Kephart, "Some correlates of romantic love," p. 473.

18. "What is it that men look for?"
19. A. Ellis, "A study of human love relationships."
20. C. Kirkpatrick and T. Caplow, "Courtship in a group of Minnesota students."
21. C. Kirkpatrick and T. Caplow, "Emotional trends in the courtship experience of college students as expressed by graphs with some observations on methodological implications."
22. D. G. Dean, "Romanticism and emotional maturity: A preliminary study."
23. D. G. Dean, "Romanticism and emotional maturity: A further explanation."
24. D. de Rougemont, *Love in the Western World.*
25. D. de Rougemont, "The crisis of the modern couple."
26. M. Lerner, *America as a Civilization.*
27. E. van den Haag, "Love or marriage?"
28. A. Schlesinger, Jr., "An informal history of love, U.S.A."
29. W. L. Kolb, "Family sociology, marriage education, and the romantic complex."
30. H. G. Beigl, "Romantic love."
31. S. M. Greenfield, "Love and marriage in modern America: A functional analysis," p. 374.
32. T. Parsons, "The social structure of the family."
33. J. F. Scott, "Sororities and the husband game."
34. G. Theodorson, "Romanticism and motivation to marry in the United States, Singapore, Burma, and India."
35. M. R. Koller, "Some changes in courtship behaviour in three generations of Ohio women."
36. W. Waller and R. Hill, op. cit.
37. G. Gorer, *The American People.*
38. L. G. Burchinal, "The premarital dyad and love involvement."
39. T. Parsons and R. F. Bales, *Family, Socialization and Interaction Process.*
40. W. Waller, "The rating and dating complex."
41. R. O. Blood, Jr., "Uniformities and diversities in campus dating preferences."
42. S. H. Lowrie, "Dating theories and student responses."
43. W. N. Smith, Jr., "Rating and dating: A restudy."
44. R. Coombs and W. F. Kenkel, "Sex differences in dating aspirations and satisfaction with computer-selected partners."
45. E. M. Rogers and A. E. Havens, "Prestige rating and mate selection on a college campus."
46. R. O. Blood, Jr., "A retest of Waller's rating complex."
47. M. M. McCall, "Courtship as social exchange: Some historical comparisons."
48. E. W. Burgess, H. J. Locke, and M. M. Thomes, *The Family: From Institution to Companionship.*
49. B. Farber, *Family: Organization and Interaction.*
50. P. M. Blau, *Exchange and Power in Social Life.*
51. J. W. Thibaut and H. H. Kelley, *The Social Psychology of Groups.*
52. G. C. Homans, *Social Behavior: Its Elementary Forms.*
53. E. S. Turner, *A History of Courting,* p. 222.
54. I. L. Reiss, "Toward a sociology of the heterosexual love relationship."

55. R. F. Winch, *Mate Selection.*
56. B. I. Murstein, "The complementary need hypothesis in newlyweds and middle-aged married couples."
57. B. I. Murstein, "Empirical tests of role, complementary needs, and homogamy theories of marital choice."
58. R. C. Tharp, "Psychological patterning in marriage."
59. A. C. Kerckhoff and K. E. Davis, "Value consensus and need complementarity in mate selection."
60. G. Levinger, D. J. Senn, and B. W. Jorgensen, "Progress toward permanence in courtship: A test of the Kerckhoff-Davis hypothesis."
61. B. I. Murstein, "Stimulus-value-role: A theory of marital choice."
62. Ibid.
63. B. I. Murstein, "Physical attractiveness and marital choice."
64. B. I. Murstein, "Self ideal—self discrepancy and marital choice."
65. B. I. Murstein, "Interview behavior, projective techniques, and question-naires in the clinical assessment of marital choice."
66. B. I. Murstein, "The relationship of mental health to marital choice and courtship progress."
67. B. I. Murstein and R. D. Roth, "Stimulus-value-role theory, exchange theory, and marital choice."
68. S. D. Schmalhausen. "The war of the sexes."
69. H. L. Mencken, *In Defense of Women.*
70. D. Cohn, *Love in America.*
71. D. Cohn, quoted in O. Jensen, *The Revolt of American Women,* p. 200.
72. Ibid., p. 39.
73. H. F. Pringle, "What the men of America think about women."
74. M. Cookman, "What the women of America think about men."
75. J. F. Cuber and P. B. Harroff, "The more total view: Relationships among men and women of the upper-middle class," p. 102.
76. S. Brown, "May I ask you a few questions about love?"
77. M. Mead, *Male and Female,* p. 357.
78. R. S. Lynd and H. M. Lynd, *Middletown,* p. 120.
79. H. Z. Lopata, "The secondary features of a primary relationship."
80. R. O. Blood, Jr., and D. M. Wolfe, *Husbands and Wives.*
81. H. Z. Lopata, op. cit.
82. G. A. Theodorson, "Change and traditionalism in the American family."
83. A. Calhoun, *A Social History of the American Family.* Vol. 3: *Since the Civil War.*
84. N. Hurvitz, "Marital strain in the blue-collar family."
85. L. Rainwater, R. P. Coleman, and G. Handel, *Workingman's Wife.*
86. D. P. Moynihan, *The Negro Family: The Case for National Action.*
87. R. Farley and A. I. Hermalin, "Family stability: A comparison of trends between blacks and whites."
88. H. L. Wasserman, "The absent father in Negro families: Cause or symptom?"
89. B. Duncan and O. D. Duncan, "Family stability and occupational success."
90. D. A. Schulz, "The role of the boyfriend in lower-class Negro life."
91. L. Rainwater, "Crucible of identity: The Negro lower-class family."

92. R. O. Blood, Jr., and D. M. Wolfe, op. cit.
93. R. Middleton and S. Putney, "Dominance in decisions in the family, race and class differences."
94. J. Aldous, "Wives' employment status and lower-class men as husband-fathers; support for the Moynihan thesis."
95. E. B. Luckey, "Marital satisfaction and its association with congruence of perception."
96. E. B. Luckey, "Marital satisfaction and congruent self-spouse concepts."
97. J. Bernard, Remarriage: *Marriage and Family among Negroes.*
98. L. Rainwater, op. cit.
99. J. Bernard, *Marriage and Family among Negroes.*
100. Ibid.
101. T. F. Pettigrew, *A Profile of the Negro-American.*
102. D. P. Moynihan, op. cit., p. 47.
103. A. Billingsley, "Family functioning in the low-income black community."
104. A. Billingsley, "Black families and white social science."
105. L. Carper, "The Negro family and the Moynihan report."
106. W. Ryan, "Savage discovery—the Moynihan report."
107. R. Farley and A. I. Hermalin, op. cit.
108. Ibid.
109. C. V. Willie and J. Weinandy, "The structure and composition of 'problem' and 'stable' families in a low-income population."
110. J. H. Scanzoni, *The Black Family in Modern Society.*
111. L. Rainwater, op. cit.
112. S. D. Proctor, "Stability of the black family and the black community."
113. B. C. Rollins and H. Feldman, "Marital satisfaction over the family life cycle."
114. W. R. Burr, "Satisfaction with various aspects of marriage over the life cycle: A random middle-class sample."
115. R. O. Blood, Jr., and D. M. Wolfe, op. cit.
116. G. Gurin, J. Veroff, and S. Feld, *Americans View Their Mental Health.*
117. P. Pineo, "Disenchantment in the later years of marriage."
118. E. B. Luckey, "Number of years married as related to personality perception."
119. E. Chesser, *The Sexual, Marital, and Family Relationships of the English Woman.*
120. D. A. Pond, A. Ryle, and M. Hamilton, "Marriage and neurosis in a working-class population."
121. R. O. Blood, Jr., *Love Match and Arranged Marriage.*
122. N. Stinnett, J. Collins, and J. E. Montgomery, "Marital need satisfaction of older husbands and wives."
123. P. Pineo, op. cit.
124. G. Knupfer, W. Clark, and R. Room, "The mental health of the unmarried."
125. W. M. Kephart, "Legal and procedural aspects of marriage and divorce."
126. G. R. Leslie, *The Family in Social Context.*
127. N. M. Blake, *The Road to Reno.*
128. W. M. Kephart, *The Family, Society, and the Individual.*

129. G. Gallup, *The Gallup Poll: Public Opinion 1935-1971.*
130. S. Brown, op. cit.
131. W. J. Goode, *Women in Divorce.*
132. J. T. Landis, "Social correlates of divorce or nondivorce among the unhappy married."
133. J. T. Landis, "Some aspects of family instability in the United States."
134. L. M. Terman, *Psychological Factors in Marital Happiness.*
135. E. W. Burgess and P. Wallin, op. cit.
136. H. J. Locke, *Predicting Adjustment in Marriage.*
137. W. J. Goode, op. cit.
138. B. I. Murstein and V. Glaudin, "The use of the MMPI in the determination of marital adjustment."
139. A. H. Maslow, "Self-esteem (dominance feeling) and sexuality in women."
140. A. H. Jacobson, "Conflict of attitudes towards the roles of husband and wife in marriage."
141. H. J. Locke, op. cit.
142. J. Bernard, *Remarriage, A Study of Marriage.*
143. W. J. Goode, op. cit.
144. P. Wylie, *Generation of Vipers,* p. 189.
145. W. Durant, "Breakdown of marriage."
146. H. Deutsch, *Psychology of Women: A Psychoanalytic Interpretation.*
147. T. Parsons and R. F. Bales, op. cit.
148. F. Lundberg and M. F. Farnham, *Modern Woman: The Lost Sex,* p. 126.
149. Ibid., p. 143.
150. Ibid., p. 149.
151. Ibid., p. 160.
152. Ibid., p. 193.
153. W. J. Goode, op. cit.
154. F. Lundberg and M. F. Farnham, op cit., p. 271.
155. Ibid., p. 365.
156. Ibid., p. 370.
157. M. G. Benz, "United States."
158. G. A. Theodorson, op. cit.
159. F. T. Empey, "Role expectations of young women regarding marriage and a career."
160. R. S. Weiss and N. M. Samuelson, "Social roles of American women: Their contribution to a sense of usefulness and importance."
161. M. Mead, op. cit., p. 379.
162. P. Buck, *Of Men and Women.*
163. B. Friedan, *The Feminine Mystique.*
164. A. Roe, "Women and work."
165. A. S. Rossi, "Women in science: Why so few?"
166. Ibid.
167. G. A. Theodorson, op. cit.
168. A. S. Rossi, op. cit.
169. Ibid.
170. P. Goldberg, "Are women prejudiced against women?"
171. J. Henry, "Forty-year-old jitters in married urban women."
172. C. Winick, "The beige epoc: Depolarization of sex roles in America."

18

The Sex Explosion in America

From a zoological point of view, the sexuality of humans exceeds that of their fellow apes. Whereas the female baboon is sexually available for only one week of the monthly cycle, woman is always accessible, even when pregnant or nursing. She is also the only female of the mammal phyla that incontrovertibly experiences orgasm.

The human mammal's precopulatory pattern is much more erotically developed than that of most mammals, lasting between several minutes to several hours. The male *Homo sapiens* has not only the longest erect penis of the 192 species of apes, but also the thickest[1] ; consequently, its pressure on the female's clitoral region aids her in achieving orgasm. Her breasts, lobes, nose, and lips, all richly endowed with nerve endings, undergo transformation during the sexual act. These organs seem to have been designed so as to heighten the sensual effect of the sexual encounter, although there is no unanimous agreement on this point.[2]

Perhaps the most important contribution to human sexuality is the brain. Man alone is not dependent on sensory stimulation or glandular secretions to experience arousal; he alone is capable of internal stimulation. By erotic fantasizing, he can *induce* hormonal secretion and self-arousal. Indeed, some people are capable of achieving orgasm solely by fantasy. And since the brain, as a two-edged sword, is equally capable of suppressing or repressing sexuality, man can deny his mammalian heritage, though perhaps not without cost.[3]

By the dawn of the twentieth century, even though sex was no longer regarded as evil or wicked in America, it was still not a topic fit for everyday conversation. World War I brought in its wake a new receptivity to sex, and with amazing speed the Victorian era breathed its last. What killed it?

CAUSES OF THE SEXUAL REVOLUTION

War. Wars are noted for a slackening of sexual morality. The uncertainty of survival engenders a psychology of "live tonight, for tomorrow we may die." Exposed to the excitement of World War I and to the smell of death in Europe all about them, 2 million male Americans shrugged off the puritan code of their forefathers. The conformity-inducing pressures of stable homes and communities were replaced by liquor, women, and the urge to live each moment to the hilt. When the war ended, the thirst for stimulation lingered on, and the soldiers brought it back with them. Perhaps, if the goals of the war had been accomplished and if living conditions at home had not changed so dramatically, these veterans might have been reabsorbed into the old culture: But the United States did not join the League of Nations, and disillusionment with the failure to achieve worldwide democracy confirmed the need to reject the old morality.

Rise in the status of women. The nineteenth amendment, giving women the right to vote, was ratified in 1920. It symbolized the giant strides they had been making in getting an education and becoming a greater part of the work force (understandably made easier during wartime conditions). The "new" woman was equally responsive to the need for excitement engendered by World War I. She became more aggressive, demanding the role of a sex partner, not of a concubine.

In her drive for sexuality, the length of her skirts rose during the 1920s from a few inches off the ground to knee height. Corsets, petticoats, and cotton garments were cast aside and replaced by flesh-colored rayon and silk stockings; she also took to an array of cosmetics to make herself more alluring: lipstick, rouge, creams, perfumes—all became vital. Incredible as it may sound, only two persons in the beauty culture business paid an income tax in 1917; but by 1927 over 18,000 firms and individuals were listed on the tax rolls![4]

The "new" woman wanted freedom too, and she emulated the paragon of freedom—man. Adopting a flat-chested "look," she bobbed her hair short and appeared in long-waisted flimsy dresses to proclaim both "freedom" and sexiness. She took to smoking, a necessary prop for a new image: the youthful, dynamic, casual, sexy playmate who was so blasé! Moreover, there was something sexy about moist lips holding a dangling cigarette (Freud would call it a phallic symbol). And since alcohol eased her residual childhood inhibitions, she also accompanied her boyfriend to the "speakeasy."

Sigmund Freud comes to America. Freud visited America only once, in 1909, to participate in a symposium at Clark University. His trip did not cause much of a furor at the time. By the end of the war, however, his writings had become increasingly known. Science was the new god of the United States, and for growing numbers of Americans, Freud's therapeutic observations and theories seemed to bear the mantle of science. His theories were denounced by psychologists as unscientific, and his view on infantile sexuality appalled the older generation, as did his emphasis on the pervasiveness of sex in all behavior. Largely overlooked was the fact that Freud acknowledged that some of the greatest contributions to the cultural heritage of mankind had resulted from sublimating libidinal drives to other creative channels. No matter! That part of Freud's teachings which fit America's need for expression was adopted. He gave respectability to sexual feeling and behavior simply because, as an established physician-psychologist, he developed theories about these questions. Suddenly, instead of being a lecher if he experienced persistent sexual urges, an individual saw himself in danger of becoming a "neurotic" if he did not express his basic libidinal drives. Youth may not have understood everything Freud was saying, but they interpreted him as a destroyer of inhibitions; as America's number one guilt-killer, he was deified by a generation of flappers.

The metamorphosis of communication and transportation. In times past, a sexual revolution involving a change in mores and behavior would have been more aptly named a sexual *evolution,* because it would have taken years, perhaps decades, for new ways to filter down on a large scale. Thanks to the industrial era, not only were the new ways transmitted rapidly, but new means for promoting premarital sex came into being.

The telephone became a potent stimulus to interpersonal relationships. Even though physical distance might make it difficult for a man and woman to see each other for long periods, they could keep in touch via the telephone. "Blind dates" could also be arranged. Magazines and films spread the word, teaching millions how to flirt, how to kiss, how to caress. The sales of "true confession" magazines, offering clarity on the right and wrong men to love, skyrocketed overnight.

Dancing, which had slowly evolved from a rigid set of movements to the somewhat more flexible waltz and polka, now moved boldly forward. It was a superb way for couples who had not yet reached the stage of talking freely to communicate their feelings. A squeeze on the hand, the woman's head leaning on the man's shoulder, the more intimate "button shining" and syncopated embraces—all marked the progress of courtship and the ripening of feeling.

Not to be overlooked was the car. Not only was it a "bedroom on wheels" if the need arose, but it could transport the couple to another locale where privacy was assured. In one study of a Dallas motel clientele, only about 6 percent of the registering couples gave their real names.[5] There were no Kinseys to record the sex explosion at the time, but years later his data, based on the recollections of older subjects, confirmed what most flappers in the twenties knew: sex had come to stay.

Not that the old order gave way without struggle. There were the usual warnings about the grave consequences of a sensate culture. In Philadelphia, a Dress Reform Committee of leading citizens polled more than a thousand clergymen regarding a "moral gown" for ladies. Despite some divergent opinions, a dress was endorsed if it was loose fitting, if the sleeves reached just below the elbows, and if the hem plunged to within 7½ inches of the floor.

In 1930, the zoologist Harmon De Graff and a psychologist, Max F. Meyer, were dismissed and suspended, respectively, from the University of Missouri for circulating a questionnaire on sex. The president of the school described their work as "sewer sociology."[6]

Marie C. Stopes' *Married Love,* imported from England in 1918, ran into trouble at the customs office for being obscene. Presumably, her charts of women's periodicity of sexual desire were obscene—it surely could not have been her flowing, metaphorical description of the orgasm: "The half-swooning sense of flux which overtakes the spirit in their eternal moment at the apex of rapture sweeps into its flaming tides the whole essence of the man and woman, and as it were, the heat of the contact vaporizes their consciousness so that it fills the whole of cosmic space. For the moment they are identified with the divine thoughts, the waves of eternal force, which to the Mystic often appear in terms of golden light."[7]

The 1930s marked a turning point in the freedom of the press to discuss sex. In 1931, Judge Woolsey ruled that Mrs. Stopes' book was not obscene. In *Ideal Marriage,* a sex manual published in 1937, the Dutch physician Van de Velde broke away from discussion of the standard sexual man-over-woman, ventral-ventral position. He described ten sexual positions and dared to advocate the "genital kiss" as an acceptable part of foreplay.

The "sex as work" ethic, which focused on the man working diligently to arouse his sexually dormant wife, was modified somewhat to become the cult of "mutual orgasm," according to which the idea of one partner preceding the other to climax was looked upon as an artistic failure.

In 1948, a book appeared whose impact was sufficiently strong to classify all data before it as "pre-Kinseyan." Authored by Alfred C. Kinsey, an Indiana zoologist, and his associates Wardell B. Pomeroy and Clyde E. Martin, the book was entitled *Sexual Behavior in the Human Male.* It was followed five years later by a companion volume, *Sexual Behavior in the Human Female.* The titles are indicative of the authors' approach. Why did they use the terms "human male" and "human female" instead of simply "men" and "women"? Apparently because they wished to give a detached, factual account of a species rather than a moralistic value-biased interpretation of human sexual behavior.

Among the findings reported[8,9] was the fact that, contrary to the impression given by Hollywood, sexual behavior persisted into advanced age. Also, aberrant sexual behavior was much more common than the social mores suggested. Homosexuality, for example, was indulged in by a considerable proportion of the population at one time or another. The stricture that intercourse was to be avoided until marriage was more honored in the breach. Some 90 percent of the men and about 50 percent of women engaged in intercourse without benefit of matrimony. Through intercourse, masturbation, or petting, some 64 percent of the women achieved orgasm before marriage. Little guilt was reported with regard to these experiences by the majority of respondents.

In general, men and women were depicted as having considerably different sexual behavior patterns. Both sexes were capable of orgastic behavior as children, and the onset of puberty did not mark as dramatic a change in erotic sensitivity as had been traditionally depicted. Men, however, showed a much higher orgastic rate than women as teen-agers, and then manifested a slow, linear decline with age. Women, on the other hand, showed a slight rise in their twenties and maintained this level without change until their late fifties. The two curves of orgastic behavior never crossed, on the average, but were far apart in early adulthood and relatively narrowly apart in late middle age and early old age.

Kinsey and his associates have been criticized strongly on several counts.[10] It has been claimed that their sample of volunteers is not typical of the American population. This is undoubtedly true, particularly in the case of their women subjects. Nevertheless, Kinsey was aware of this fact and acknowledged that the nature of the questions asked and the financial limitations led him to eschew a probability sampling. Few researchers would fault him on these grounds. He was, after all, the *first* to present a thorough coverage of sexuality even with a biased sample. While some of his findings may be slightly different from what would have been obtained by a probability sampling, the data are of immense interest even if based on a volunteer population.

He has also been criticized for a mechanical approach to the study of sex. There is little emphasis in his work on the quality of the interpersonal relationship between men and women, and on their perception of sex in the context of this relationship. The primary focus appears to be on outlet and on the number of orgasms achieved through various sources. Yet it is difficult to fault him for this, for Kinsey was essentially a taxonomist of sexual behavior who presented valuable, hitherto unknown data. It is presumptuous of others to insist that a man and his staff who spent 15 years in gathering data are guilty of serious transgressions because they did not *also* collect data on interpersonal relationships.

The Kinseyites have been attacked also for the use of self-reports, which some writers claim has little relevance to actual behavior. Kinsey has shown, however, that the individuals are remarkably consistent within their own reports and also tend to agree highly with their spouses, whose reports were collected separately.

There *is*, nevertheless, a serious flaw in the work, one that has drawn scant attention from the experts, with the exception of Shuttleworth[11] and Kirkpatrick[12]; despite the fact that Kinsey has engaged in an essentially actuarial study, he has ranged far beyond his data in his conclusions, and his assiduity in collecting data is in extreme contrast to his cavalier manner of drawing interpretations from his data. One such example is his interpretation of the fact that coitus occurs with regularity as suggesting that it is the male partner who is primarily responsible for this state of affairs, since this regularity is often found in male behavior but not in the female. He ignores the findings of Terman[13] and of Burgess and Wallin,[14] which indicated that, on the average, the man was not getting as much intercourse as he desired and the woman was getting more than she desired. These findings clearly suggest that the frequency of intercourse in most cases is a compromise between the greater desire of the man and the lesser desire of the woman.*

---

*An article by Bell in *Family Life Coordinator* appears to contradict this finding.[15] He reported that among the college-educated women whom he studied, 65 percent stated that

Another problem is his vacillation in attributing differences in the sexual behavior of men and women to psychological and biological factors. He does claim, however, that most differences are due to learning, conditioning via previous experiences, and social pressures. Kinsey arrives at this conclusion in the following manner: First he notes that he is unable to find any anatomical, physiological, or neurological differences and only very slight hormonal differences that might account for differences in sexual behavior. The average woman, for example, achieves orgasm by masturbation in just under four minutes, whereas it takes the average male between two and four minutes by this method.

In addition, interviews yielded the information that men were more aroused than women by viewing members of the opposite sex, nude figures, genitalia of the opposite sex, their own genitalia; by observing portrayals of sexual action; and by making love in the light rather than the dark. Moreover, males were more likely to experience sexual fantasies concerning the opposite sex while daydreaming or masturbating; they were more likely to be erotically aroused by reading sex-oriented books; and they were less likely to be diverted by external stimuli during coitus. All this, according to Kinsey, is due to the greater susceptibility of men to psychological conditioning. So far it sounds as if male-female differences are learned; however, Kinsey also states that the sexes may well differ in their capacity for psychosexual stimulation, hinting that these capacities may depend on neurochemical properties of the cortex.

Another possible explanation that I should like to suggest is that the greater reported sexuality of men is a function of the interactive effect of a more easily activated (though not necessarily stronger) drive, the physical nature and location of the genitalia, and the socialization effects of the masuline and feminine roles. We proceed now to a consideration of the evidence for this conclusion.

One fair test of drive is the length of time to achieve orgasm. It is reported that, in intercourse, most males are much quicker in this regard than women. This

---

the frequency of intercourse was "about right," 6 percent said it was too frequent, and 25 percent said it was too infrequent. He also cited Burgess and Wallin as supporting this finding, since 16 percent of their women were oversatiated with sex as opposed to 19.6 percent who showed some degree of sexual hunger. This led Bell to conclude that the sexually ravenous woman of the future may be too much for the average man. It also indirectly appears to confirm Kinsey's contention that it is the man who determines frequency of sexual intercourse. However, Bell's data are quite misleading. Terman, for example, illustrates clearly, in *Psychological Factors in Marital Happiness* (pp. 272-273) that the average man is not having intercourse with the frequency desired, whereas the average woman is having it just about as desired. Also, if we look further into the data of Burgess and Wallin, we discover that the number of satiated husbands was 2.5 percent and the number of "hungry" husbands was 42.2 percent. The safest overall conclusion, therefore, is that there are many more people not making love as often as they would like (for whatever reason) than there are people making love more often than they would like. Men, however, are more likely to be in this deprived group than women. The error in Bell's conclusion would have been immediately apparent had he sampled men in his own study or reported the reactions of men in the Burgess and Wallin study.

fact, however, is not necessarily due to inhibitions on the part of women, as Kinsey implies, but stems from the fact that the location of the clitoris and its surrounding hood makes physical contact with this organ not nearly as direct or intense for women as is the sensory contact achieved by the penis, the homologous male organ. A better test, therefore, is the speed of achieving orgasm through masturbation. The average speed for men reported by Kinsey is faster than that reported for women. In addition, most men, when deprived of sexual outlet, tend to become morose and irritable. Many women, on the other hand, rarely suffer such distress from abstinence, and many are capable of indulging in sexual activity freely and then abstaining for weeks or even months without acute physical discomfort.

Men who do not ejaculate do not leave descendants. For women, the orgasm is not necessary for procreation. It is possible, therefore, that, through evolution, men have become "sexier" without a corresponding evolution on the part of women. There are almost no young men incapable of orgasm, whereas somewhere between 5 and 10 percent of women have never experienced orgasm.

There are considerable physical differences between men and women which have received scant attention from Kinsey. Men's sexual organs are external, and are susceptible to ready stimulation by any kind of physical contact, including such unintentional sources of arousal as binding underwear and tight pants. Women's genitalia are not nearly so available to accidental external stimulation.

The sheer variety of measures attesting to men's greater sex drive makes it unlikely that all of these are resultants of "cerebral conditioning," as Kinsey claims. The majority of husbands state that they never refuse their wives intercourse, while the vast majority of wives say that they have refused intercourse at one time or another. Some three-quarters of married men admit to a desire for extramarital intercourse, whereas only a quarter of the married women state that they have ever desired an extramarital partner. More husbands than wives describe themselves as experiencing sex daydreams and eager longing for sex before marriage. Many men enjoy sex with just about *any* woman. Most women enjoy sex only with their lover. More women than men feel they are having too much sexual intercourse; more men than women feel they are not getting enough. Religious belief serves to lower sexual interest in women, but not in men.[16]

Can conditioning in the man really account for all these differences? If men were truly more influenced by psychological factors than women, as Kinsey states, we should expect greater variability across different measures of sexual outlet for men than for women, because our constantly changing environment offers an infinite variety of learned sexual behaviors. Contrariwise, evolution has assured a certain regularity in the expression of biological need for sexual outlet. Actually, women show much greater variability; thus, marriage increases the orgasm rate of men by 63 percent, and that of women by 560 percent.[17] Widowers do not suffer a marked decrease in the number of orgasms; widows do.

Our conclusion (opposite to that of Kinsey) is that because the need of men

The belated return of a husband of the Victorian period.

for sex and their orgastic rate are so much more constant than that of women, it is the *woman's rate* that is more influenced by learning. While the increased sexual interest shown by women in the past decade can scarcely reflect changes in biological capacity, they are readily accounted for by the decreased inhibition in expressing sexuality.

Even the differences in response to erotic stimuli found earlier by Kinsey have largely failed to stand the test of time. Research sponsored by the Presidential Commission on Obscenity and Pornography[18] resulted in data varying from no male-female differences in sex arousal and in orgasmic reaction in the hours following the presentation of stimuli, to slight statistical differences showing greater male reaction. The type of population used and the means of recruitment appear to make a difference in the findings.[19] The younger the subjects, the less their sexual experience, the lower the social class, and the less selective the recruiting procedure, the greater was the male reactivity compared to the female one.

The differences in responsivity by the sexes to the various stimuli are noteworthy. The work of Schmidt and Sigusch and colleagues,[20,21] in particular, indicates that women, more than men, respond much more strongly to moderately erotic stimuli which focus on love or suggest some kind of interpersonal relationship between the sexes, as compared to more overtly sexual material which either gives no clues as to the relationship of the partner or shows only the opposite sex. Although men also respond strongly to sexual interaction between the sexes, they respond less strongly than women to heterosexual scenes in which the sexual organs are not displayed. They do, however, respond more strongly to pictures of women in varying degrees of dress than do women in response to comparable male pictures. These data suggest that interpersonal relationships are more important in triggering erotic arousal for women than for men.

It thus appears that much of the data favoring male reactivity in Kinsey's study were due to cultural inhibitions of women, lack of familiarity with erotic materials, and the male bias in selecting stimuli for comparison which favored men rather than women.

SEXUAL ADJUSTMENT AND MARITAL HAPPINESS

Judson T. Landis, investigating the length of time required to achieve marital adjustment in a broad spectrum of areas, concluded that it took more time for the area of sex than for any other.[22] It might be expected, therefore, that there is a high relationship between sex adjustment and marital adjustment, but that depends on what is meant by sexual adjustment. Terman[23,24] found a very, very slight relationship between frequency of intercourse and a questionnaire score of marital adjustment. The wife's orgasm adequacy showed a somewhat higher relationship to marital adjustment, and the relationship of sexual "satisfaction" to marital adjustment was still higher. The reason for this finding is apparent in a study by Wallin,[25] who found that sexual satisfaction in women was to some degree independent of orgasm adequacy. It would seem that some women do not need to achieve orgasm in every act of intercourse to attain sexual satisfaction. Psychological and physical contact may be quite enjoyable even when sexual release does not result. Even when orgasm is achieved, apparently the sensation may be less valued than those experienced in building up to a climax.

This position contrasts greatly with the image perpetuated by D. H. Lawrence in *Lady Chatterly's Lover,* namely, that a woman's orgasm was experienced as "deepening whirlpools of sensation, swirling deeper and deeper through all her tissues and consciousness till she was one perfect concentric fluid of feeling, and she lay there crying in unconscious inarticulate cries."[26]

Many women who experience much more prosaic orgasms, or even no orgasm at all, may feel that they are being robbed of their natural right. That such frustration may be the result of expectation is evident in Wallin's[27] finding that educated women were more frustrated by the lack of orgasm than less educated women.

Further light on the question is cast by Thomason[28] and Gebhard;[29] they found that as the percentage of orgasms for the wife increases, the marriage adjustment score also increases. Gebhard, however, has also shown that if he categorized women's marital contentment as "Happy to Moderately Happy," "Moderately Happy," "Average," "Moderately Unhappy," or "Very Unhappy," the number of women in each category experiencing orgasm 90 to 100 percent of the time did not vary greatly. Each category contained between 35 to 40 percent of women who achieved orgasm always or almost always. Only another category, "Very Happy," showed a greater frequency (about 60 percent) of high-orgasm rate women. These data suggest that the extra 20 percent of the women with high orgasm rate in the "Very Happy" category probably resulted from their happy relationships.

Another noteworthy research finding is the deleterious effect of high sex drive on marital adjustment for men[30,31] and the positive effect of a high sex drive for women.[32] Given the greater cultural acceptance of sex interest by men, the greater imperiousness of the male drive, as well as women's greater tolerance of sexual abstinence, I posit the following explanation. The male ego interprets a high sex drive in a woman as evidence that she really likes him, since he has probably noticed that few other women in his earlier experience expressed such an interest in sex. She is agreeable almost any time he wants sexual relations; but when he does not want intercourse, provided he meets a certain minimum of his partner's needs, he does not frustrate her. Both are happy with their sexual life, all other things being equal. On the other hand, the high-sex-drive husband is apt to find rejection by a low- or average-sex-drive wife very frustrating. If, however, he insists on having sexual relations, his wife is apt to perceive him as insensitive and "just using her."

In my own studies on marital choice,[33] I have found evidence consistent with the findings reported above. Men with above-average sex drives were less likely to be seen as approaching the woman's ideal-spouse concept than were men with below-average sex drives. On the other hand, women with high sex drives were apt to be much more pleasing to their fiancés than women with below-average drives.

Kinsey sees one of the major causes of unhappiness as lying in the difference in strength of sex drive between men and women. In the early years of marriage, the man may constantly pressure the woman for sexual relations and experience frustration in her lesser interest. In later years his descending sex drive may cross with her more or less constant sex drive, and eventually she may be more desirous of intercourse than he is.

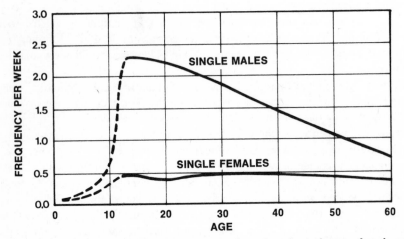

Figure 18.1   Comparison of aging patterns of total outlet in human female and male, showing active median frequency of orgasm in total sexual outlet. Data estimated for preadolescence are shown by broken lines. Based on A. Kinsey et al., Sexual Behavior in the Human Female, *p. 714.*

In my opinion, this perception of sexual crisis arises from Kinsey's failure to recognize the flexible nature of woman's sexual responsiveness. Using Kinsey's curves derived from data on single men and women, we may note that, in the average case, the curves do not cross despite the descending male drive with the passage of time; consequently, there is little to worry about. Even in the exceptional individual case, where the curves might intersect with the passage of time, we must take cognizance of the flexibility in sexual behavior that the woman possesses and assume that she could adjust to her spouse's lowered drive level without much difficulty. In this respect, I would ask, as did Kirkpatrick earlier, whether the woman, like the man, really does not suffer a diminishing biological sex drive as a function of time.[34] Since her sexual behavior is often considerably conditioned by experience, particularly that of a positive nature, it might be expected that when her experience with sex is of short duration, she would not show as much interest as after some years of coital experience. In the latter case, "love" for her spouse and the concomitant meaningful sex experience might keep her sexual interest at a plateau for many years, despite a declining biological drive. For the more biologically oriented male, such plateau-maintenance behavior is not to be expected.

A study by Clark and Wallin bears on this question.[35] The authors reported that women whose marriages were happy were increasingly likely to be sexually responsive with the passage of time. Women who were sexually responsive initially, but whose psychological relationship with their husbands changed from positive to negative, were less likely to maintain this sexual responsiveness through time.

PREMARITAL SEX

Until quite recently, many textbooks on marriage, cautioned against the evils of premarital sex: unwanted pregnancy, loss of respect, and the disappearance of the "aura of holiness." But young people have apparently not been impressed by these edicts. A generation ago, Rockwood and Ford found that only about half of their male college sample wanted to marry a virgin[36]; the figure was the same during the 1960s, when Reiss conducted his survey.[37] However, in the 1970s, in response to a slightly modified question—"I wouldn't want to marry a girl who isn't a virgin at marriage"—a national probability sample of 13- to 19-year-olds showed only 30 percent "yes" answers.[38]

The incidence of premarital sexual intercourse has also climbed relentlessly. Davis,[39] working with women college graduates in the 1920s, found only 7 percent stating that they had indulged in premarital intercourse. Hamilton, a short time later, found that 35 percent of his female volunteer population and 54 percent of the men were nonvirgins at the time of marriage. In the 1930s, Terman found 37 and 64 percent of the men and women, respectively, in this category. More startling was his finding that the incidence of virgins was plummeting downward. Of the women born before 1890, 86.5 percent were virgins; but of those born in 1910 or later, a scant 31.7 percent reached the nuptial bed without being deflowered. At any rate, in Terman's estimation, virginity would be close to the vanishing point for men born after 1930 and women born after 1940.

The rise in nonvirgins continued, but not quite at Terman's projected rate. Burgess and Wallin published their book in 1953, but much of their research was done in the late 1930s. They show rates of 47 percent for women and 68 percent for men with respect to nonvirginity. Kinsey's data show percentages of 50 and 90 percent, respectively.

Kinsey had reported that about half of his female subjects had intercourse before marriage, and about 20 percent while they were college students. More recently, two research teams[40,41] have reported that the incidence of female coitus for college women still in school ranged between 40 and 50 percent, about double that found by Kinsey for comparable ages. The rate for college men was 58 and 60 percent, respectively, slightly higher than the incidence of between 44 and 49 percent for men reported by Kinsey for the comparable age range of 20 to 21.

An admittedly atypical sample of *Psychology Today* readers indicated that only 9 percent of the male respondents and 12 percent of the female ones arrived at the nuptial bed *virgo intacta.*[42] These figures correspond to Kinsey's findings for premarital men, but exceed his reported premarital female rate of about 50 percent.

Very recent surveys suggest that Terman's prophecy of the vanishing American virgin may not have been very much in error after all—only a bit late in arriving. In 1971, a normal probability sample of teen-aged women aged 15 to 19 showed 28 percent to have had coital experience.[43] By age 19, however, 46 percent were no longer virgins. In 1972, another normal probability sample of boys and girls aged 13 to 19 found 59 percent of the former and 45 percent of the latter no longer virgins.[44] Focusing on the "elder statesmen" of the group aged 16 to 19, 72 percent of the boys and 57 percent of the girls had had coital experience. Since very few marry at such young ages, it seems inescapable to conclude that, barring a revival of child marriages, the vast majority of Americans in the immediate future will have had coital experience prior to marriage.

It is not difficult to pinpoint some contributing factors to the accelerated rate. One is the birth control pill, which completely eliminates fear of pregnancy. Until fairly recently, the pill was not as important as one might imagine. It was dispensed by physicians, a notoriously conservative lot as a profession, who usually granted it only to married women. Within the last few years, however, the tide of sexual freedom has changed medical practice: not only do many private physicians readily dispense the pill, but college medical personnel are increasingly making it available to co-eds. Their reasoning—most co-eds requesting the pills will engage in intercourse anyhow, and the pill will avoid the greater inconvenience of abortion—seems logical, but it pushes the acceptability of premarital sex to still greater heights.

Another factor is simply the breakdown of theological influence and the cult of honesty and sexual candor that separates modern youth from many in the older generations. Indirect confirmation of this point is found in the work of Robert Bell and Jay Chaskes, who studied Temple University co-eds: the number experiencing guilt (they felt they "went too far") was cut in half from 1958 to 1968.[45]

A primary question arising from these findings is: what are the effects of premarital sex on subsequent sexual adjustment and marital satisfaction? At first glance the data appear paradoxical. Kinsey, as well as Kanin and Howard,[46] found that premarital sexual experience is clearly associated with postmarital sexual adjustment for women. Other researchers have found slight *negative* associations between premarital sex and engagement success, stability of marriage, and marital adjustment. Kinsey also reported that premarital sexuality was more likely to lead to extramarital sexuality than was virginity.

The issue is confusing because various controls are lacking.[47] Even though many more lower-class men than higher-class men engaged in premarital sex, the opposite was true of women. Yet class was not considered in the above findings. Further, it seems reasonable to conclude that individuals engaging in premarital sex have greater sex drives than those who refrain; hence it is hardly surprising that they achieve a better orgasic rate after marriage than do virgins. However, it was reported earlier that high sexuality in women was associated with good marital adjustment. True, but this figure was quoted for *all* women sampled after marriage. The women engaging in premarital sex represented a more select group of women who not only had high sex drives but were willing to express their drive in behavior even though social mores condemned it. These women would also be more likely later to express their sexuality outside marriage. In sum, in view of the failure to control these crucial variables, it would be hazardous to conclude that premarital sex per se may be causally related to anything.

Sex Differences in Premarital Attitudes and Behavior

There have been striking differences reported between men and women in their attitudes and behavior regarding premarital sex. Ehrmann,[48] in a survey done in the late 1940s and early 1950s, noted that 29 percent of his college women were either indifferent to or disgusted by sex, but only 8 percent of the men were so affected. Men were also more likely to show a higher relationship between attitudes and behavior than women. Apparently, a considerable number of his women were more involved in sexual activities than they ostensibly wished to be.

The importance of the identity of the partner in determining sexual satisfaction was quite different: of those who had had intercourse, 56 percent of the men and only 2 percent of the women had done so with mere acquaintances. The exclusivity of the sexual expression of women was further emphasized by the finding that the more persons they dated, the less *likely* they were to engage in sexual intercourse, whereas the opposite was true of men. The men apparently dated a large number of persons in the quest for sexual release; the women dated many men because they were not involved and were out to have a good time without granting "favors." The lack of importance as to who the sexual partner was for men was emphasized in their rating of pleasure experienced in intercourse. Using a rating scale—"1" signified no or very little pleasure, "2" was below average, "3" was average, "4" was above average, and "5" was very much pleasure—men gave acquaintances an average rating of 4.2; it increased slightly for friends—4.4, and a bit more for lovers—4.9. Women who had experienced intercourse rated their pleasure with acquaintances as 1.0, with friends as 4.0, and with lovers as 4.4.

In a similar 1970 study with Connecticut and Virginia students, Lawrence Sutton and Ariel Leshem found a notable shift:[49] 10 percent of Connecticut College women had intercourse with acquaintances, as opposed to Ehrmann's 2 percent. More surprising was the fact that 51 percent of the Connecticut women with lovers had intercourse with them, whereas the comparable figure of Ehrmann's sample was 17 percent.

The figures for men also showed some reversal. Although 56 percent of Ehrmann's men had had intercourse in the "acquaintance" stage, only 21 percent of the Connecticut sample had done so. Yet slightly more Connecticut men in the "lover" stage had had intercourse (32 percent) than the 29 percent reported by Ehrmann. Since the Connecticut men were on the average two years younger than Ehrmann's male sample, it is highly probable that the Connecticut figure would have doubled if comparable ages had been utilized. Rates in the Virginia sample generally ranged between the Ehrmann and Connecticut samples.

The comparisons suggest that the increasing willingness of college women to engage in sex with those with whom they become emotionally involved has resulted in a sharp decrease in men's relations with superficial contacts. By way of support of this position, Kinsey had found that 22 percent of his college men had frequented prostitutes, but Packard's sample of college men drawn from 26 colleges showed a mere 4 percent who frequented prostitutes.[50] As to the degree of enjoyment, there seemed little change except that both the Connecticut and Virginia women had a neutral or slightly negative reaction to sex with acquaintances, whereas Ehrmann's women had evidenced nothing short of utter disgust in such relations.

Views of Society

Some writers, whom we might characterize as "doom prophets," perceive a high correlation between the vitality of a culture and the limitations placed on amorphous sexual freedom. They see the current sexual permissiveness as a harbinger of the decay of our civilization.[51-53] Whatever opinion one may hold, the adult population has made no serious attempt to curtail this behavior. Granted that it is quite difficult, if not impossible, to keep constant watch over today's teen-ager, this does not suffice to explain the increase in premarital sexual activity. Not only are the peer mores of teen-agers supportive of premarital sex, but adults themselves have been affected by the liberal climate and do not see premarital sexuality as conflicting with their outlook. Contrary to the notion that people usually grow more conservative with age, a recent study demonstrated that the today's adults were more conservative in their youth.[54]

Mothers and daughters do differ with respect to outlook on premarital sex,[55] but this difference has been shown to be a function of specific role relationship between parents and teen-agers. In a study by Reiss,[56] 44 percent of single adults were highly permissive regarding premarital sex. Among married persons whose children were all preteen, 22 percent were permissive, as compared to 13 percent for those with all teen-age or older children. This trend held even where age differences between the groups were controlled.

Both the Protestant and Catholic churches have taken a tactically different approach to their traditionally negative orientation toward sex. They now stress that it is "the personal responsibility of the Christian to find God's will for himself."[57] The Church may inform, but it does not judge. As to premarital sex, liberal theologians and educators no longer automatically condemn it, but ask, "Is it meaningful? Does it work toward the creation of trust, confidence, and integrity in relationships?"[58] Does it, as the Presbyterian pastor of the University of Colorado asked, establish a "covenant of intimacy"?[59] If so, it can be condoned.

Unfortunately, these views, while indicating a more liberal position, seem to lack practical utility. They pose questions to which few can give answers. Suppose a young man is alone with a girl he has begun to know. They are friends, but are not engaged to be married. As they experience a growing mutual attraction and the desire for physical intimacy, will they stop to ask themselves whether the sex act will eventually work in the direction of trust, confidence, and integrity, and whether it will establish a covenant of intimacy? Can they really foretell what only time can determine?

In some cases, where a couple has been extremely close, sexuality enhances and enriches the relationship. Some couples find that sex is a catalyst and turns a moderate friendship into love. Some react negatively to sexuality when they learn that their partner was interested *only* in sexual gratification. And a goodly number of such experiences lead neither to a profound deepening nor a severing of the relationship. Some couples grow closer when they realize that they can cooperate in a pleasureful venture: they are interested in each other's company, in the joy of sexual release, but never really believe they will marry and/or become wholly enamored of each other. Was the momentary pleasure bad because it did not lead to a deepening relationship?

In practice, according to Reiss,[60] contemporary young unmarried adults have adopted a standard midway between the traditional double standard and the conservative single one: this is the *transitional* double standard, according to which it is acceptable for a man to sleep with anyone, but a woman should be in love or at least emotionally involved. Hence, while engaged men have quite often had intercourse with other women, Kinsey reported that 46 percent of the women had had intercourse only with their fiancés.

ADULTERY

In varying societies, past and present, adultery has been condemned and prohibited far more than premarital sexuality. So strong were the prohibitions against it among the Jews that the Talmud could excuse it only if a man looking over a parapet accidentally fell off, and accidentally landed on a woman, and accidentally had intercourse with her! Any other extramarital coitus was strictly prohibited.

In view of the emphasis on sexuality in America in recent decades, it is interesting to examine how ancient taboos have changed. Current novels suggest that half the housewives in suburbia are promiscuous and aggressive—no milkman or stray male is safe.[61] Some reports[62,63] on spouse-swapping parties (where housekeys are put in a bowl and randomly drawn for a one-night sleeping partner) and newspaper ads for "switchers" are enough to make the nonadulterous couple wonder if they are out of step with the times.

Apparently, according to Terman, and to Burgess and Wallin, more husbands than wives have at one time desired extramarital coitus. But what about their actual behavior? For his various age ranges, Kinsey found that 27 to 37 percent of the married men had engaged in extramarital relations on at least one occasion. Having only active-incidence data, he could surmise only that the cumulative incidence data would have been somewhat higher. Believing that many men were covering up, he concluded, somewhat arbitrarily, that about half of the married men had engaged in extramarital relations at least once. For women, Kinsey found a cumulative incidence of 26 percent by age 40; the incidence rose consistently for those born more recently. If this incidence is less than the novels would have us believe, it is still hardly a puny figure.

A recent questionnaire of the rather sexually liberal *Psychology Today* sample indicated that 40 percent of the men and 36 percent of the women had engaged in extramarital relations. Even allowing for the possibility that this married sample is below the ages for which Kinsey compiled his figures (*Psychology Today* did not give a breakdown of age), the incidence was not as high as one might expect from a sexually permissive sample more than 20 years after the Kinsey studies.

In fact, when the Kinsey data are examined closely, it appears that the United States is far from being a Zion of adultery. The number of women actively involved in extramarital coitus varied between 6 and 17 percent of the population of women ever involved. On the average, these women engaged in extramarital sex about once in ten weeks during their peak years. Among these adulteresses, almost half were engaged in such activity only a year or less of their lives, and about the same proportion were unfaithful with only one man.

The truth of the matter is that adultery in America is a very chancy affair. A convention, a vacation, or an ocean voyage may provide an escape from the numbing influence of one's immediate environment and its risk of detection. In addition, the American woman, with her high expectations with respect to men, cuts a poor figure as an adulteress. Sex, for her, is fused with a meaningful relationship; if she likes a man, she soon wants to be his wife, not a furtive bed companion. With more liberal divorce laws, many people think it foolish to resort to adultery as the only alternative to an unhappy marriage.

It seems likely, therefore, that most long-term adulterous relationships serve to maintain marriages more than to sunder them. About half the women Kinsey interviewed stated that their husbands knew or suspected their infidelity, and, of these women, 42 percent stated that no difficulty ensued. Apparently, a considerable number of individuals have weighed all the alternatives and have found that the security and comfort of marriage outweigh the importance of their partner's fidelity. Indeed, an attitude survey of youth suggests that many of them are tolerant of adultery so long as it does not jeopardize the viability of the marriage.[64]

For a behavior so intrinsically a part of marriage, it is remarkable how little research has been undertaken on the topic. One obvious reason is that religious officials have almost universally condemned extramaritality. Another is that until recently, many marriage counselors interpreted extramaritality as a sure sign of neurosis or immaturity.[65] Rather than risk bearing the stigmata assigned by theology and the psyche, few individuals volunteered to acknowledge their extra-marital liaisons, and few researchers had the courage to risk the epithet of "research voyeurist" and undertake the difficult tasks of collecting such data. As a result, we know little of the causes of adultery. However, Ralph E. Johnson, in checking 60 case histories from the Family Service Agency, came up with the following reasons: "(1) the spouse was unable to have sex because of a physical handicap; (2) the spouse was having an affair with someone else; (3) the spouse was unaffectionate or sexually frigid; (4) the spouse was extremely obese or "too fat"; (5) the spouse did not keep herself (himself) physically clean; (6) there was a separation because of the armed services, extended business trips, or imprisonment; (7) the spouse was incapable of satisfying the other one sexually; (8) the spouse was convinced that the only time to have sexual intercourse was to have children; (9) the spouse looked at sex with contempt."[66]

I might add these factors: (10) prescribed norm behavior—for example, when an advertising man for an erotic magazine attending an office party might feel it incumbent to live up to the company image; (11) curiosity about how others make love; (12) a need for novelty and variety; (13) uncertainty about one's masculinity or feminity, and the need to test oneself; (14) a need for excitement and adventure; (15) an unusual opportunity—one's spouse is away or one is traveling; (16) a high sex drive that is considerably stronger than that of the spouse; (17) a feeling of alienation from the world and a need for escape; (18) fear of aging; (19) lack of total commitment to one's spouse; (20) lack of theologically inspired inhibition; (21) a tendency to act unconventionally without unbearable guilt feelings.

Albert Ellis[67] has suggested standards for differentiating the healthy adulterer from his nonhealthy counterpart. He depicts the healthy adulterer as (1) undemanding and noncompulsive; although he likes extramarital affairs, he does not need them; (2) not unduly disturbing his family, marriage, or his general existence; (3) accepting his affairs and not suffering from guilt; (4) sexually adequate with his spouse. Ellis, however, presents no data to justify his standards. In fact, one finds very little data at all on the reasons for adultery.

In one of the few empirical studies, Gerhard Neubeck and Vera Schletzer[68] investigated 40 couples, one of whose members had been at the University of Minnesota about ten years earlier. Using a scale from a personality inventory which measured the tendency to disregard social mores (unconventionality), the authors discovered an association between a high score on this scale and adultery. No association, however, existed between a high score on unconventionality and marital satisfaction.

In the study by Professor Johnson, of the 100 middle-class, middle-aged couples who were interviewed, 20 husbands and 10 wives reported having been involved in extramarital relations. When opportunities for extramaritality were questioned, however, it developed that 72 percent of the husbands acknowledged having such an opportunity, whereas only 29 percent of the women reported in the affirmative. The ratio of women engaged in adultery compared to perceived opportunity was thus actually *slightly greater for women than for men.*

Husbands engaging in adultery showed significantly less sexual satisfaction in marriage than those who did not; no such association was found for women. This finding leads to the speculation that one important reason for extramarital relations by men is low sexual satisfaction; women, however, may be more drawn to extramaritality for interpersonal reasons. Finally, categorizing his subjects by interest or noninterest in extramaritality, Johnson found no relationship between desire for extramaritality and dissatisfaction in marriage.

In sum, despite Dorothy Parker's verse,

> Hoggamous, higgamous, men are polygamous
> Higgamous, hoggamous, women monogamous

it is conceivable that the difference in interest in fidelity might narrow or disappear if women were not brought up to be monogamists and had as many amorous opportunities as men. Also, the belief that adultery is *prima facie* evidence of an inadequate marriage does not jibe with the few facts we now possess. Further research on this topic is past overdue.

SEX, SOCIOECONOMIC CLASS, AND BLACKS

Differences in the sexual behavior of the lower and middle classes have been the subject of many studies. According to Kinsey, lower-class men and women are much more likely to have premarital sexual experience than those in the middle class, and are also more prone to engage in extramarital activity during the early years of marriage. However, middle-class people in their thirties and forties surpass the lower-class group in this respect. The latter, particularly the men, sow their wild oats in their youth. Later, job and family responsibilities, or the lack of time or money, prevent any "extracurricular" activity. For the middle-class, extramarital liaisons probably depend on the breaking down of conditioned inhibitions.

Dramatic differences are found in love-making styles. In general, the lower class is much more conservative and indulges in a smaller variety of practices. Broken down by educational class,* Kinsey found that 82 percent of men with more than 13 years of education kissed the female breast frequently, but only 33 percent of those with elementary schooling or less had done so with any degree of frequency. About 45 percent of the highly educated men had made oral contact with their wives' genitalia, whereas only 4 percent of the lowest educated class had done so. "Deep kissing" in marriage was practiced frequently by 77 percent of the highly educated men, but by only 40 percent of the lowest educated group. It is evident that these groups have differing views about sex: To learn more about these differences, we shall discuss some studies of attitudes toward sex as a function of social class.

First, it should be noted that the lower class does not enjoy sex as much as the middle class. Rainwater,[69] surveying couples in several U.S. locales, found that 78 percent of the middle-class men stated that sex was a source of great interest and enjoyment. Members of the upper-lower class did not differ appreciably, but only 44 percent of the men in the lower-lower class found sex very enjoyable. For women, the comparable figures were 50 and 20 percent, respectively. Indeed, whereas 3 percent of the middle-class women rejected sexual relations altogether, some 20 percent of the lower-lower class did so. There is no evidence of any physical or physiological reason for this difference in attitudes and behavior. Possibly, the greater physical strain experienced by the lower class in attempting to cope with everyday living may have some bearing on this lack of enthusiasm. Another reason, for which there is some clear-cut evidence, is the lack of interaction and communication between husband and wife, as was noted in chapter 17. Where lower-class couples may be categorized as either "jointly organized" or "immediately segregated," there is a considerable amount of sexual enjoyment for both partners. Where there is great segregation of role function, with little joint functioning as a couple, there is considerably less sexual satisfaction. Moreover, when the reactions to intercourse are dichotomized into the categories "socio-emotional closeness and exchange" or "psycho-

---

*Much of the above findings are drawn from Kinsey's work. In some cases he gives breakdowns by educational level rather than by socioeconomic class. There is, however, a fairly high relationship between class and educational level, and the findings of educational-level differences undoubtedly would also hold for analysis of socioeconomic class.

physiological pleasure and relief only," 16 percent of the "highly segregated" husbands fell into the former category and 84 percent into the latter, whereas for the middle class the respective percentages were 75 and 25. Similar figures were found for women.

Not only is the emphasis on sex physical in the lower class, it is also depersonalized.[70] This accounts for the fact that Mirra Komarovsky, in her book *Blue-Collar Marriage,*[71] was able to show that a considerable minority of uneducated "blue-collar" women stated that their sexual satisfaction exceeded their satisfaction in marriage, while only a very few educated "blue-collar" women said that.

The lower-class man also makes little attempt to satisfy his partner sexually, which probably accounts for the Kinsey finding that orgastic ability in women is correlated with amount of education. It is not that the lower-class man opposes his wife's right to orgasm; it is just that he does not see it as his responsibility to make sure that she attains it. Thus, Masters and Johnson, in their *Human Sexual Response,*[72] state that whereas 214 of 216 college-matriculated men in their study were concerned about coital-partner satisfaction, only 7 of 51 noncollege men expressed concern. These data serve to support the contention of many marriage counselors that it is very rare for sexual maladjustment to exist independently of the quality of the interpersonal relationship of the couple.

One final point regarding socioeconomic class and permissiveness toward premarital intercourse. It is commonly assumed, based on Kinsey's data, that permissiveness and socioeconomic class are inversely related: the higher the class, the less likely that premarital sexuality will be sanctioned. However, Kinsey's middle- and upper-class subjects were largely volunteers and members of clubs. Such individuals are quite apt to be conservative in their outlook and to adhere strongly to traditional mores. Reiss' representative national sample[73] corroborated Kinsey's findings only for individuals whom Reiss classified as "conservative." For conservatives, the higher the class, the less permissive the individual. For individuals classified as liberals, however, the higher the class, the more liberal the outlook on sex. The two gradients did not intersect, but were closest for the lower class and diverged most sharply for the upper class. The relationship was more clearly marked for the student sample than for the adult sample, offering support for predictions of increased permissiveness as more individuals move from the lower to the middle class and as a liberal atmosphere pervades the United States.

Alas, this finding was not replicated in two studies, American and Dutch.[74,75] Both pointed out that whereas they measured liberalism and conservatism by attitude scales directly, Reiss' measures of liberalism and conservatism were indirect in that he used subjects from what he called "liberal" and "conservative" settings. A liberal setting, for example, included being divorced, being Jewish, living in New England, living in a town of 100,000 or more, and so on. A host of variables, such as urbanization, religion, and region may have been confounded with liberalism in Reiss' findings. For the present, therefore, no conclusions can be drawn regarding the interrelationships of liberalism-conservatism, economic class, and sexual permissiveness.

Black People and Sex

In *Notes on Virginia,* Thomas Jefferson stated, "Negroes are more ardent [than whites] after their female, but love seems with them to be more an eager desire, than a delicate mixture of sentiment and sensation."[76] Current folklore has extended the stereotype. Among many whites, the belief persists that the black male possesses a giant phallus and great potency. Further, according to the stereotype, he is lazy and happy-go-lucky; but when he becomes sexually aroused, he is apt to give full rein to a vigorous appetite, undeterred by social restraints.

If premarital sexuality, illegitimacy, and rape qualify as indices of vigorous sexuality, this stereotype might have some validity. By age 15, 60 percent of black girls had had premarital intercourse, and by age 20 some 80 percent of unmarried black women are no longer virgins, compared to 20 percent of white women.[77] About one-fourth of all black births are illegitimate, compared to one-fifteenth of all white births. Blacks are also overrepresented in the rape statistics.

The stereotype does not hold up, however, when we discover that the "sensual" black man turns out to be more romantic than the white man on the scales of romanticism. Moreover, although he is more religious than his white brother, unlike the latter, religious conviction does not impede premarital sexuality.

It has become fashionable to claim that black-white differences with regard to sex are primarily a function of socioeconomic differences because so many blacks are in the lower class. However, it has been observed that blacks are more permissive in sexual matters even when class differences are controlled.[78] This finding is marred by the fact that class differences are often measured by family income. Blacks, however, have a higher birthrate than whites, and it is therefore likely that the standard of living may be lower for a typical black family than for a white family with the same income.

In sum, there is no research evidence to support the belief that blacks are more sexual than whites. Indeed, insofar as other data suggest that low economic status is correlated with sexual maladjustment, and in the light of the relatively weak position of the black man in the black family, there is reason to surmise that blacks should be less adequate sexually than whites. However, since no evidence has come to light on this question, too, one should presently conclude that higher premarital and illegitimacy rates among blacks do not necessarily reflect their sexuality so much as their disaffection with respect to the institution of marriage.

THE TREATMENT OF SEXUAL PROBLEMS

The sex explosion, which began in the 1920s and continued steadily into the 1950s, liberated many, but for some people it became threatening. Nineteenth century women may have experienced little sexual satisfaction, but they expected little and managed to live with this lacuna. With the advent of the sex explosion, and with the media conveying the impression that the sophisticated were living a life of sexual ecstasy, people became increasingly conscious of their sexual shortcomings. At first it was too embarrassing to talk about, but bit by bit the popular magazines began to discuss such problems. Unfortunately, they were so discreet that they never got down to brass tacks. Men were encouraged to prepare their wives for the hour of embrace with gestures, flowers, praise, and considerate actions. Wives were advised to take a more active sexual role, to let their husbands know how much they enjoyed them—in sum, to be responsive.

It is questionable whether anyone was helped by such advice, although the mention of sex problems on the covers of magazines undoubtedly sold millions of copies. Sensitive persons did not learn much by reading, and those who were insensitive to their partners probably avoided such articles. Most people with problems such as unresponsiveness, premature ejaculation, and vaginismus could find little practical help—either in magazines or in the more specialized marriage manuals—because very little factual knowledge existed.

Into the breach stepped the gynecologist William Masters, who was soon joined by a psychologist colleague, Virginia Johnson. In the 1950s they embarked on a twofold plan: to provide an adequate description of the physical aspects of an orgasm, and to develop a means of treatment of individuals with sexual problems.

In their study of the orgasm, the authors utilized such helpful aids as an artificial plastic penis which permitted a simulated study of the interaction of genitalia during intercourse. Among their most important findings was the confirmation of the view of recent sexologists that Freud's theory of two kinds of orgasm in women was false.[79,80] Freud had postulated a mature (vaginal) orgasm and an infantile (clitoral) orgasm, but Masters and Johnson showed that vaginal contractions were merely accompaniments of an intense clitoral orgasm. They also determined—by actual films of women using the artificial translucent phallus—that the common belief that direct contact between the penis and the clitoris caused the woman to experience orgasm was in error. The penis was not found to touch the clitoris, which retracted during intercourse. Instead, the thrusting action pulled the hood of the clitoris against the clitoris, which in turn eventually led to orgasm.

Masters and Johnson also established a clinic which utilized their findings and those of others to treat such sexual problems as frigidity, impotence, vaginismus, and premature ejaculation. The treatment is short-term, intensive, and expensive (typically $1,000 to $2,000). The standard treatment consists of daily meetings for two weeks, where instruction on sexual techniques is combined with educative psychotherapy dealing with attitudes toward sexuality. In the treatment of premature ejaculation, for example, the woman learns to stimulate the male partner extravaginally until the warning sensation of impending ejaculation. After a rest, stimulation is repeated until better control is eventually achieved. The couple "graduate" to intercourse, again with practice in inhibiting ejaculation. One effective technique is for the woman to pinch the erect penis between her thumb and index and middle fingers at a point just below the glans. For an erect penis, this is not painful and serves as a kind of erotic inhibitor to reduce the feeling of imminent orgasm.

This particular problem has been successfully treated in more than nine out of ten cases. Overall, Masters and Johnson achieve substantial improvement in four out of five cases. Considering the large number of sexual difficulties experienced by many couples, it is not surprising that sex clinics are opening throughout the country, promising some measure of hope for a problem once considered too delicate to talk about.

CONCLUSIONS

The sex revolution has entailed a series of explosions within a continuing evolution. America's sexual mores changed greatly after World War I, and a period of consolidation and slow evolvement followed for three decades. Sex thrives on leisure and prosperity, and the depression required more attention to bread-and-butter issues. The renewed sexual emphasis in the 1960s, which continues today, cannot wholly be attributed to "the pill," although it owes much impetus to it.

A primary agent in both periods of sexual emphasis has been the change in women's attitudes. The flapper strove for social equality in connection with smoking, drinking, and dress, as well as in employment. But she could never achieve full sexual equality because even though she and her partner might have "fun," only *she* had the baby. For this reason, couples who indulged freely in premarital sex tended to be those who intended to marry. Other encounters were generally commercial or exploitive.

In the 1960s and 1970s, sex has become the private concern of two people. Although promiscuous sex has increased slightly, the overall increase in sexuality has come mainly from lovers and good friends who are not necessarily engaged to be married. The myth that sex can be enjoyable only within marriage has all but disappeared, as is evidenced by the plethora of premarital and extramarital couples.

While many people are quite concerned about being adequate sexually, orgasmic ability has shown but a modest relationship to marital adjustment. It seems likely that sexual adequacy in a woman is very much related to the quality of her interpersonal relationships. At least, most studies of the relationship of sexual techniques and habits—including length of foreplay, ability to withhold ejaculation, and capacity for multiple orgasm—have shown little relationship to marital adjustment.

In sum, in an affluent society in which men and women are becoming more equal, it is not surprising that sex is commanding greater interest than ever before. Yet sex is not reducible to physique, to the size of glands or organs, or to skill. Sex is mainly psychological, and good sex is rare in the absence of a genuine interpersonal relationship. Even in those rare cases where a technically perfect sexual relationship exists, it is still rarer to find that it holds a marital or nonmarital relationship together when everything else is lacking.

REFERENCES

1. D. Morris, *The Naked Ape.*
2. B. I. Murstein, "The sexual image in marriage throughout history."
3. E. Morgan, *The Descent of Woman.*
4. F. L. Allen, *Only Yesterday.*
5. E. S. Turner, *A History of Courting.*
6. S. Ditzion, *Marriage, Morals, and Sex in America,* p. 396.
7. M. C. Stopes, *Married Love,* p. 96.
8. A. C. Kinsey et. al., *Sexual Behavior in the Human Male.*
9. A. C. Kinsey et. al., *Sexual Behavior in the Human Female.*
10. D. P. Geddes, *An Analysis of the Kinsey Reports on Sexual Behavior in the Human Male and Female.*
11. F. K. Shuttleworth, "A biosocial and developmental theory of male and female sexuality."
12. C. Kirkpatrick, "The sociological significance of this research."
13. L. M. Terman, *Psychological Factors in Marital Happiness.*
14. E. W. Burgess and P. Wallin, *Engagement and Marriage.*
15. R. R. Bell, "Some factors related to the sexual satisfaction of the college educated wife."
16. P. Wallin and A. L. Clark, "Religiosity, sexual gratification, and marital satisfaction in the middle years of marriage."
17. F. K. Shuttleworth, op. cit.
18. *Technical Report of the Commission on Obscenity and Pornography.* Vol. 8: *Erotica and Social Behavior.*
19. G. Kaats and K. Davis, "Effect of volunteer biases on sexual behavior and and attitudes."
20. G. Schmidt and V. Sigusch, "Sex differences in reactions to pictorial and narrative stimuli of sexual content."
21. V. Sigusch et al., "Psychosexual stimulation: Sex differences."
22. J. T. Landis, "Length of time required to achieve adjustment in marriage."
23. L. M. Terman, op. cit.

24. L. M. Terman, "Correlates of orgasm adequacy in a group of 556 wives."
25. P. Wallin, "A study of orgasm as a condition of women's enjoyment of intercourse."
26. D. H. Lawrence, *Lady Chatterly's Lover*, p. 125.
27. P. Wallin, op. cit.
28. B. Thomason, "Marital sexual behaviour and total marital adjustment: A research report."
29. P. H. Gebhard, "Factors in marital orgasm."
30. H. J. Locke, *Predicting Adjustment in Marriage.*
31. G. V. Hamilton, *A Research in Marriage.*
32. L. M. Terman, *Psychological Factors in Marital Happiness.*
33. B. I. Murstein, "Sex drive, person perception, and marital choice."
34. C. Kirkpatrick, op. cit.
35. A. L. Clark and P. Wallin, "Women's sexual responsiveness and the duration and quality of their marriage."
36. L. D. Rockwood and M. E. N. Ford, *Youth, Marriage, and Parenthood.*
37. I. L. Reiss, *The Social Context of Premarital Sexual Permissiveness.*
38. R. Sorensen, *Adolescent Sexuality in Contemporary America.*
39. K. B. Davis, *Factors in the Sex Life of Twenty-Two Hundred Women.*
40. E. B. Luckey and G. D. Nass, "A comparison of sexual attitudes and behavior in an international sample."
41. G. Kaats and K. Davis, "The dynamics of sexual behavior of college students."
42. R. Athanasiou, P. Shaver, and C. Tavris,"Sex."
43. J. F. Kantner and M. Zelnik, "Sexual experience of young unmarried women in the United States."
44. R. H. Sorensen, op. cit.
45. R. R. Bell and J. B. Chaskes, "Premarital sexual experience among coeds."
46. E. J. Kanin and D. H. Howard, "Postmarital consequences of premarital sex adjustments."
47. R. L. Hamblin and R. O. Blood, Jr., "Premarital experience and the wife's sexual adjustment."
48. W. Ehrmann, *Premarital Dating Behavior.*
49. L. Sutton and A. Leshen, "A comparative study of premarital dating behavior."
50. V. Packard, *The Sexual Wilderness.*
51. J. D. Unwin, *Sex and Culture.*
52. P. Sorokin, "The depth of the crisis: American sex morality today."
53. D. Mace, "Does sex morality matter?"
54. S. Rettig and B. Pasamanick, "Changes in moral values as a function of adult socialization."
55. R. R. Bell, "Parent-child conflict in sexual values."
56. I. L. Reiss, op. cit.
57. A. Whitman, "Is marriage still sacred?"
58. L. A. Kirkendall, *Premarital Intercourse and Interpersonal Relationships*, p. 6.
59. H. A. Grunwald, "The second sexual revolution: A survey."
60. I. L. Reiss, *Premarital Sexual Standards in America.*

61. M. M. Hunt, *Her Infinite Variety.*

62. P. Avery and E. Avery, "Some notes on 'wife-swapping.'"

63. W. Breedlove and J. Breedlove, *Swap Clubs.*

64. H. Christensen, "A cross-cultural comparison of attitudes toward marital infidelity."

65. O. S. English, "Values in psychotherapy: The affair."

66. R. E. Johnson, "Some correlates of extramarital coitus," p. 450.

67. A. Ellis, "Healthy and disturbed reasons for having extramarital relations".

68. G. Neubeck and V. Schletzer, "A study of extramarital relationships."

69. L. Rainwater, "Some aspects of lower class sexual behavior."

70. L. Rainwater, *And the Poor Get Children.*

71. M. Komarovsky, *Blue-Collar Marriage.*

72. W. H. Masters and V. E. Johnson, *Human Sexual Response.*

73. I. L. Reiss, *The Social Context of Premarital Sexual Permissiveness.*

74. G. M. Maranell, R. A. Dodder, and D. F. Mitchell, "Social class and premarital sexual permissiveness: A subsequent test."

75. C. P. Middendorp, W. Brinkman, and W. Koomen, "Determinants of premarital sexual permissiveness: A secondary analysis."

76. J. Bernard, *Marriage and Family among Negroes,* p. 99.

77. R. R. Bell, *Premarital Sex in a Changing Society.*

78. I. L. Reiss, op. cit.

79. W. H. Masters and V. E. Johnson, op. cit.

80. W. H. Masters and V. E. Johnson, *Human Sexual Inadequacy.*

19
Marriage in the Soviet Union

There are other contemporary societies apart from the United States which are currently experiencing rapid industrialization and governmental involvement in family affairs. The character of marriage and the relationships between the sexes in these societies are also changing. We shall consider three such examples: the Soviet Union (in this chapter) and then China, Japan, and the Black African polygynous marriage (in subsequent chapters).

PREREVOLUTIONARY PATTERNS IN RUSSIA

The key to understanding prerevolutionary Russian marriage is the fact that the conversion of Russia to Greek Orthodox Christianity in about a.d. 1000 also involved the absorption of the Oriental, Byzantine perception of woman. An impure, sinful, inferior person, she was relegated to a special place on the *left* in church. A girl received little education; her father arranged her marriage and handed the groom the *durak,* a whip of male authority, which sometimes hung over the bridal bed.[1] She wore an iron wedding ring, but her husband's ring was golden, and until her death she wore a headdress to cover her hair.

The husband was the father-protector of his wife, much as the Czar was of the Russian people. According to the *Domostroi,* a sixteenth-century collection of rules of family conduct, the father was responsible for the spiritual and worldly salvation of the entire family and enjoyed considerable leeway in attaining these ends.[2] Among the serfs in the village of Viriatino, the patriarch might hold the switch in one hand during meals and swat anyone who laughed too loudly or talked too much.[3] If a wife opposed her husband, Pope Sylvester, who lived during the time of Ivan the Terrible, counseled him to:

> beat her with a whip, according to the measure of her guilt, but not in the presence of others, rather alone. Do not strike her straight in the face or on the ear, be careful how you strike her with your fist in the region of the heart, and do not use a rod of wood or iron. . . . Keep to a whip, and choose carefully where to strike: a whip is painful and effective, deterrent and salutary.[4]

Progress came very slowly in Russia. It was only in 1704 that Peter the Great decreed that parents could not force their daughters to marry. A wife still remained under the "tutelage" of her husband, and she could not obtain a passport under her own name. She was not allowed to work without his permission and was enjoined to follow him wherever he went.

The Code of the Russian Empire noted tersely that the husband was obliged to "love his wife," but the wife was commanded to "obey her husband as the head of the family, to be loving and respectful, to be submissive in every respect and show him compliance and affection, he being the master of the house."[5]

Prerevolutionary attitudes toward women may be summarized by the following representative Russian proverbs[6]:

> A woman's hair may grow long but her common sense stays short.
> A dog is wiser than a woman: he won't bark at his master.
> Marry a wife who can read, and she'll find all the holidays on the calendar.
> A good husband is father to his wife.
> A wife isn't a jug—she won't crack if you hit her a few.

Changes toward a more progressive view did not wait for the Revolution. By the middle of the nineteenth century, the intelligentsia began increasingly to reject the authoritarian and property basis of husband-wife relationships and to stress the emotional quality of marriage, freedom of choice, and the ethical necessity for equality of the sexes.[7] By the second half of the nineteenth century, much inspiration came from the socialist writers of Western Europe.

THE SOCIALIST VIEW OF
PREREVOLUTIONARY MARRIAGE

The socialist view of marriage, as described by Engels, was that it derived from the economic system within which it existed. In ancient times, in primitive communistic societies where work in the house was a public necessity, the societies evolved into matriarchies. When property became important, men wanted to pass their possessions on to their children, and they therefore initiated a patriarchal society. In Engels' view, "the overthrow of mother-right was the *world historical defeat of the female sex.* The man took command in the home also; the woman was degraded and reduced to servitude; she became the slave of his lust and a mere instrument for the production of children."[8] In the *Communist Manifesto* Marx and Engels state that the bourgeois husband sees her as a mere instrument of production to be gainfully exploited.[9]

The solution, according to Engels, is clear. The female sex must be brought back into industry, and the monogamous family must no longer function as the economic unit of society. Then each working person will have a newfound dignity, and there will be no squabbling over the bequeathing and inheriting of property because the state will own the property. Prostitution will disappear as women are restored to the status of respected citizens.

Monogamy, in the millennium, will not necessarily be weakened. On the contrary, individuals will freely choose each other, and sex will become an enriching experience when people love without fear of pregnancy and economic responsibility because the state will care for all children, legitimate or not. The important fact will not be whether sex takes place in wedlock or not, but whether reciprocal love exists.

In Engels' day, socialists perceived the indissolubility of marriage to be a consequence of economic and theological influences. In their opinion, theological views were absurd because of the prevalence of adultery and prostitution. But the coming of the socialist Utopia, as described by Jaurès in 1908, "will unquestionably eliminate from the relations between man and woman all legal restraints; but at the same time it will fortify the moral obligations of fidelity, which is the ideal of sincere and true monogamy."[10]

If Utopia failed, the consequences would not be tragic because marriage would be viewed not as a millstone but as a state of understanding. When understanding no longer existed, voluntary separation would be in the interests of both parties and unattended by the reciprocal recriminations of bourgeois divorce.

In sum, the three steps to the communist marriage of the future were as follows:

1. The unit of production must become society rather than the family. In denying the family the right to accumulate wealth, selfishness will give way to a concern for society.

2. The end of the economic function of the family will also free woman from economic bondage. Kitchen work and the rearing of children will become functions of the state, freeing women for productive labor.

3. When woman becomes the economic equal of man, the relationships between the sexes will greatly improve and a new and more ethical monogamous relationship will ensue.

REVOLUTIONARY AND POSTREVOLUTIONARY
FAMILY LEGISLATION, 1917-1926

The first laws guaranteeing equal legal status to women were passed by the Kerensky government, but it was so short-lived that effective legislation was enacted only with the advent to power of Lenin and the Soviets. The laws of 1917 and 1918 stressed the fact that marriage is a private affair in which the state plays the role of a bystander and intervenes only to ensure that the welfare of the weaker members of the family (usually the wife and children) is not endangered. Children, for example, received full legal rights whether born in or out of wedlock, and fathers had joint responsibility with their wives for children under both conditions.[11]

There was one exception. Whereas religious marriage had been the only form recognized by the Russian Empire, the new regime recognized only civil marriage. Religious marriage was acceptable as a vestigial custom for those so interested, and marriages entered into before the new laws went into effect, even if religious, were recognized.

Men and women were declared equal before the law. If the husband decided to change his domicile, his wife was not obliged to follow him. After marriage, she did not have to take his name unless she so wished. There was no community property, and in case either spouse was unemployed, the one who was working had to support the other.[12]

Equality was also apparent in divorce. According to the decree of 1917,[13] a marriage could be annulled when both members or at least one member appealed to the court, provided the marriage was childless. If the whereabouts of one of the parties was unknown, the machinery of divorce was in no way impeded: a divorce notice was mailed to the last known address of the missing party. If children were involved, or if one party opposed the divorce, the court decided the case according to its concept of justice and assigned custody and child-support payments as the situation warranted.

In 1918 a law was passed forbidding the adoption of children.[14] It was feared that some individuals might use adoption as a cheap source of labor because the hiring of others was prohibited. Another reason was that the state had promised to rear children according to the scientific principles of Marxism, and millions of war and famine orphans would not have parents to interfere with their training.

In the three years following the Revolution there were a large number of abortions—a result of economic deprivation, civil war, lack of knowledge about contraceptives, and "wartime" morality. To reduce the alleged 50 percent infection rate and the 4 percent death rate because abortions were often performed by unskilled, nonmedical personnel, the state, although it disapproved of abortion, legally recognized it on November 18, 1920.[15]

THE BATTLE OF CONTRASTING THEORIES OF THE FAMILY

The philosophy of Marx and Engels had been enacted into law, and all Soviet theorists could agree with Lenin that "none of the most advanced bourgeois republics . . . could . . . achieve in the course of decades what we did during the first year after coming to power."[16] Marriage and divorce were recognized as private affairs, independent of politics. Houses were built without kitchens, for it was believed that everyone would soon eat in state-owned restaurants and that the community would provide all sorts of social services for the family.

Marx and Engels, however, had never spelled out whether the family was really necessary. Theirs had been a philosophy of eliminating evils, but they were distressingly vague on what to do about regulating the relationship between men and women once this had been achieved. They assumed, rather simplistically, that interpersonal problems between men and women would vanish with the coming of communism. According to Engels, the new race of people would determine their own behavior, but he ventured no prediction about the nature of this behavior.[17]

Some individuals took the view that monogamy was the epiphenomenon of the private enterprise system. By analogy, if collective ownership replaced private enterprise, should not women be publicly owned as well? Thus, we note the "nationalization of women" act passed by the City Soviet of Vladimir in 1918:

> Any girl 18 or older and not married must . . . register at the Free Love Office of the Commissariat of Welfare. Those registered will have a choice of males between 19 and 50. The men in turn are granted the right to choose among the girls. The selection of husbands and wives will take place over a month. . . . Males between 19 and 50 will, in the government interest, be allowed to choose their partners regardless of the latter's consent. Any children born of such unions will become the property of the Republic.[18]

Although this act represented an extremely atypical action, Alexandra M. Kollontai, in her writings and novels, popularized a slightly less radical view and found support among a larger minority. Marriage was outdated because lovers "cannot provide material security for each other. . . ." The family in the bourgeois sense "deprives the worker of revolutionary consciousness"[19] and will die out. A new family of the collective of workers will take its place in which people will be bound together not by blood relationships but by common work.[20] In addition, "as marriage ceases to be of material advantage to the married, it loses its stability."[21] Marriage will, however, exist as "a sublime union of two souls in love with each other."[22]

Kollontai fiercely defended the woman's right to do everything the man did. In her fictional work, *The Love of Three Generations,* the heroine Zhenia, pregnant by one of her lovers and soon to have an abortion, is discovered by her mother in the act of making love to the mother's husband Andrei (Zhenia's stepfather). Her mother begins to lecture her about ideals and proprietary attitudes, and then a nonplussed Zhenia asks, "But what has the Party, or revolution, war with the White Guards or the depression . . . to do with my kissing Andrei or someone else?"[23]

Kollontai's philosophy became a rationalization for escaping interpersonal commitment under the guise of involvement in the revolution. Lunacharsky describes the plight of the virginal but politically active girl who is propositioned by a male colleague. "Well," she says, "what if I do, and you leave me, and I get a baby? What do I do then?" He answers, ". . . what philistine thoughts! What philistine prudence! How deeply you are mixed in bourgeois prejudices! One can't consider you a comrade."[24]

Lenin was able to see through the theory that "sex is no more than a glass of water":

> Many of them call their attitude "revolutionary" and "communistic." That does not impress us old people. Although I am nothing but a gloomy ascetic, the so-called new sexual life of the youth—and sometimes of the old—often seems to me purely bourgeois, an extension of bourgeois brothels. . . . This glass of water theory has made our young people mad, quite mad, . . . this . . . theory is completely un-Marxist. The relations of the sexes to each other are not simply an expression of the play of forces between the economics of society and a physical need, isolated in thought by study from the physiological aspect. . . . Will the normal man . . . lie down in the gutter and drink . . . out of a glass with a rim greasy from many lips?[25]

To Lenin, sex was a necessity, but one which must be controlled and regulated by the individual. Lenin was no puritan; he simply did not think that dedicated workers should divert their badly needed energies from revolutionary pursuits. Moreover, realizing the inability of the impoverished state to care adequately for the children of such affairs, he was scarcely anxious to encourage their production.

Perhaps most typical of the views of the Party leaders was the idea that although the family would probably disappear with the advent of a classless society, an attempt to dissolve it summarily at this stage of the revolution was premature. In the thinking of A. Slepkov, presocialist relationships still existed, and the state, weakened by civil war, had not been able to create the communal resources (public restaurants; the rearing of children by the state) that would do away with the need for the family. Hence the immediate goal was to coordinate the family with the activities of the state in preparation for the eventual transfer of the functions of the former to the latter.[26]

Lenin died in 1924 and was succeeded by Stalin. Preoccupied at first with consolidating his power, there was little governmental interference in the individualistic orientation that marriage was taking. The law of 1926 allowed a small measure of joint community property and also recognized de facto marriage. The struggle to legalize de facto marriage was not won lightly. Comrade Solz, during the deliberations of the Party in 1926, voiced the fears of many that recognition of de facto marriage would lead to promiscuity and a cavalier attitude toward marriage.[27] On the other hand, it was argued that Engels' gospel that men and women would live together harmoniously and/or freely should be legally recognized now that the millennium had arrived. Further, a very small number of comrades had already presented the Party with a *fait accompli* and were living together as man and wife without recourse to the ZAGS (marriage registry office).

Divorce was simplified even further by being channeled to the ZAGS instead of to courts.[28] A divorce cost three rubles and could be obtained by one person without discussing it with the other. Within three days the ZAGS would send out the following form:

ZAGS of the _____District Soviet _____(Date)
To Citizen_____(Name)
You are informed that your marriage, contracted_____ _____(Date)
with the citizeness_____(Name) has ended____(Date);
and that your last name previous to your marriage has been assigned
to you_____(Name).

    According to Paragraph 24 of the Code of Law Regarding Marriage, Family and Guardianship, you can apply to the Tribunal of the People, according to your dwelling place, for the decision of questions regarding children and the amount of support money in case of need and of your incapacity to work.

               _____(Name), MANAGER[29]

To the Western world, the U.S.S.R. had become a twentieth-century Sodom and Gomorrah, where men and women bathed together in the nude[30] and lived in a continuing sexual orgy, and where women were constantly running to the abortionist so that their bodies could be renewed for tomorrow's lover or husband. But Soviet citizens looked at the situation quite differently. Nude bathing, while not widespread, was a custom that had to do with sun, not sex. Subsequent to the Revolution, men and women experienced much longer courtship periods than in Czarist times, when arranged marriages were the vogue.[31] As for abortions, it was claimed that these were primarily for married women with several offspring who, because of the difficult times, could not support more children.[32] The Soviets, in short, considered themselves sufficiently superior in "intrinsic morality" to bourgeois states and, unlike them, had no need for external constraints.

Two examples of selflessness are cited by Anna Louise Strong, who married a Russian and lived in the U.S.S.R. for some time. She relates an encounter with a champion female tractor driver whose husband had a similar position with another brigade. Once a week during their honeymoon, the husband walked 12 miles to his bride, spent some time with her, and walked back to get to his job in the morning! Why didn't she meet him halfway? She did not want to fatigue herself unduly and jeopardize the work record of her championship brigade. Why not join the same brigade? Both exclaimed, "Desert my brigade at sowing time!"[33]

In the love poem *Tanya,* a young collective farmer visits a knowledgeable woman farmer for technical advice. As he is leaving after a pleasant scientific discussion, he blurts out, embarrassed, that he loves her. She shouts to the departing suitor:

Listen lad! / as farewell / I want to tell you something.
If you win in competition, / Send your go-between, /
But if not, / If you lag behind, /
Don't come near me![34]

In the late 1920s it was still possible for Soviet writers to lampoon the attempt to regiment spontaneous emotional expression. The playwright Katayev, in *Squaring the Circle,* describes a situation in which two men, Abram and Vasya, sharing a dingy room, decide to marry without informing each other. They bring their brides home to share the one room, since other housing is unavailable. Soon enough, Abram discovers that he really loves Vasya's bride, Ludmilla, and Vasya falls in love with Tonya, the bride of Abram. In a reflective mood, Abram ponders:

> What is needed for a durable marriage? (Counts on his fingers.) Class consciousness, a common political platform, labor solidarity. . . . Is there character similarity? There is. Is there mutual understanding? There is. Is there membership in the same class? There certainly is. Is there a common political platform? How could it be otherwise? Is there labor solidarity? And how! Then what is lacking? Love, perhaps? Why that's a social prejudice! A lot of banana oil, rotten idealism—and by the way. . . . (Sniffing hungrily.) Ugh! The room reeks of sausage which belongs to Vasya. Should I? Or is it unethical?[35]

Throughout the play, the characters frequently correct each other for the slightest expression of spontaneity that might smack of capitalist decadence. Once, on the question of responsibility of action, Tonya says to Abram, "You're the husband, aren't you?" And he snaps back, "Kuznetzova, no bourgeois tricks!"[36] Later, Ludmilla spontaneously exclaims that Abram fell off his bicycle because "God punished you," and Abram retorts, "God is a medieval concept."[37]

The clash between individualism and institutional loyalty is strikingly presented in the scene in which Tonya and Abram confess their love for each other.

> Tonya (securely): Wait a minute, Vasya. Wait! Sit down! Let us discuss the new situation objectively and calmly. Very well, let us suppose that you should leave Comrade Ludmilla and I should leave Comrade Abram and that you and I should come together, on the basis of . . . eh . . . (Indecisively). Will it be the right thing to do from the point of view of Communist family morality?
>
> Vasya: Absolutely right.
>
> Tonya: Absolutely wrong. Today I register with one man. Tomorrow I divorce him. The next day I register with another man! What kind of an example are we setting to our Party comrades, and to the most active

elements amongst the nonpartisan youth and the poorer peasantry?

Vasya (embraces her violently): And perhaps the poor peasantry will not even notice it!

Tonya (recovering for a moment): This is pure and simple opportunism.

Vasya: What's the difference?[38]

The play ends on a happy note as the Party theoretician of the local cell, Comrade Favius, assures the participants that they can rush off to the registry and exchange their spouses, because it "won't harm the Revolution."

By the mid-1930s, however, the fight for individualism at the cost of commitment to the state was officially frowned upon. The wars, economic difficulties, suppression of the kulaks, and high abortion rate demanded that every possible effort be made to strengthen the state. In the prescribed code of interpersonal behavior, love was deeroticized. Kollontai fell into disfavor, as did Freud, and the ideal of sublimating sex so that one's energy could be more productively employed for the benefit of the state, triumphed. Individualism, if it ever proved to be acceptable, would prevail only in a distant utopian and classless society.

Signs of the abandonment of utopian goals were already evident. In 1927 the state permitted parents to adopt children, a tacit admission, for the moment, of its inability to raise children adequately. Millions of homeless children were wandering through the countryside in bands, and state orphanages could handle only a fraction.[39] Indeed, even those raised by the state did not seem to function as well as those reared by parents.

The long-awaited communal kitchens and restaurants did not materialize and, as late as 1925, crèches were caring for only 3 percent of the nation's children.[40] Last, the divorce and abortion rates were increasing steadily, while the birthrate dropped; this was particularly the case in such large urban centers as Moscow and Leningrad. In 1934 the Medical Institute of Moscow delivered 54,000 children and performed 154,000 abortions. The divorce rate in Moscow in the first half of 1935 was 38.3 per hundred.[41] Since the country was rapidly becoming urbanized, the threat of family breakdown and population growth stagnation appeared quite real.

THE SOVIET UNION AS "FRIEND" OF THE FAMILY

In 1936 a series of laws was enacted to discourage liaisons and cavalier marital ventures. A financial penalty was imposed on divorce seekers: 50 rubles for the first divorce, 150 for the second, and 300 rubles for the third. Since the average monthly wage was 238 rubles,[42] it was hoped that divorce would not be entered into lightly. Henceforth, both parties had to appear at the ZAGS office to obtain a divorce, thus avoiding the shock of a postcard divorce. For the first time, an official stigma was attached to divorce: it was noted on one's passport. Child support for the man was to be one-fourth to one-half of his income, depending on the number of children, and failure to pay resulted in two year's imprisonment.[43]

Legal abortion was ended except for medical reasons. Public discussion revealed a great deal of opposition to the termination of legal abortion,[44] but the Stalinist regime rationalized that the bases for tolerating it, such as "moral heritage of the past," economic hardship, and the inadequacy of contraceptive methods, was no longer valid.[45] The effect of these laws on the divorce rate was swift. When the divorce law was passed on June 27, 1936, the number of divorces granted in Moscow that month was 2,214! In July, it was 215; from January 1 to June 30, 1936, it was 10,313. The total for the same period the following year was 3,860.[46]

Changes in the behavior of government officials and of marital experts were as noteworthy as the legal changes. Amidst publicity and fanfare, Stalin went to the Georgian mountains in 1934 to visit his mother—until then, hardly anyone had known that she was alive. Wedding rings, once regarded as the symbol of the yoke of womanhood under capitalism, quietly reappeared in shops.

A leading Soviet expert on marriage, Wolffson, wrote an article in 1936 to admit his grievous error of 1929, when he had written that socialism entailed the extinction of the family.[47] Svetlov, also a sinner in this respect, now wished to make it clear that socialism does not absolve parents of the responsibility of bringing up their children.[48]

Another writer stated:

> The State cannot exist without the family. Marriage is a positive value for the Socialist State only if the partners see it as a lifelong union. So-called free love is a bourgeois invention and has nothing in common with the principles of conduct of a Soviet citizen. Moreover, marriage receives its full value for the State only if there is progeny, and the consorts experience the highest happiness of parenthood.[49]

There was probably no single explanation for the change. The regime was quite sensitive to the falling birthrate and saw it as an impediment to the realization of its economic goals. In addition, many parents did not wish to have their children raised by the state. It was probably concluded that this new generation of parents, already inculcated with communism, would be an adequate and inexpensive means for transmitting the communist ideal.[50] Above all, the government was too involved with the accelerated industrialization to be able to deal with such time-consuming and expensive ideals as the raising of children.

Legislation during World War II

In 1944 the Soviet army was tearing the Nazi forces to shreds, but the U.S.S.R. wartime losses included 20 million men. Convinced that the birthrate could be most effectively increased by making divorce more difficult, the regime pressed its social engineering of the family still further. On July 8, 1944, the government quietly abolished every liberal law. Divorce became not only difficult to obtain, but costly. It was not so much that the grounds for divorce were different or difficult (they were, in fact, unspecified), but that the procedure was both laborious and humiliating. First, notice had to be given to the People's Court of intention to divorce and a fee of 100 rubles paid. Next, there was an interview with the judge to ascertain motives and to establish witnesses. If the judge thought reconciliation was possible, he might attempt to dissuade the parties from divorce. If nothing could be done, the active party had to publish in the local newspaper, at a cost of 400 rubles, a notice about his divorce action. This notice was sure to be seen by friends and relatives, who might try to reconcile the couple. In due time, the People's Court heard the case and, where feasible, tried to reconcile the couple. If not, the case was passed to the Regional or City Court. If the divorce was granted after a hearing, the couple proceeded to the ZAGS, where their divorce was entered into their passports and a fee of 500 to 2,000 rubles was paid.

Another important act of 1944 was the prohibition of de facto marriages. Unmarried mothers could no longer bring paternity suits against putative fathers. Presumably, the idea was to spare the man and his legal family the financial and emotional distress of paternity suits that might undermine its stability. On the child's birth certificate a bar was placed where the father's name was supposed to be entered. On the other hand, financial aid to all mothers, wed or unwed, was increased—after all, the needs of children were primary. As an incentive to have children, greater taxes were levied on single and childless people, and taxes diminished progressively with the birth of each child. In addition, honorary designations were instituted. A mother of five received the Medal of Motherhood, Second Class, which became "First Class" with the birth of her sixth child. A woman who bore seven, eight, or nine children was entitled to the Order of the Glory of Motherhood, third, second, and first degrees, respectively. For ten children, nothing less than the designation of Mother-Heroine would suffice.

With this legislation, the regime turned its back on the tenets of Marx and Engels in three vital respects. The separation of private and public life was no longer held justifiable. In fact, a sure way to hinder one's advancement within the Party ranks was to get a divorce. The concept of morality as an epiphenomenon of the economic order was likewise rejected, as was Lenin's favorite point that social equality for women could be achieved only by getting them out of the kitchen. It is difficult to imagine many a Mother-Heroine straying far from the domestic hearth. Indeed, "housework," once an epithet of derogation, was now redefined as "socially useful labor."[51]

No one dared say that the "holy trinity" of Marx, Engels, and Lenin was wrong. Rather, their writings on the subject were ignored, or emphasis was placed on the fact that the current era of "socialism" was not to be confused with the as yet unattained millennium of "communism." Finally, the rejected policies of the 1920s were often attributed to fallen idols, and frequent references in this regard were made to Trotsky and other "fascist hirelings."[52]

AMELIORATION IN POLICIES TOWARD THE FAMILY

With the death of Stalin, family legislation was again liberalized. Permission to marry foreigners, revoked in 1947, was reinstated in 1953. Abortions for nonmedical reasons were legalized in 1955, and the law taxing the childless and those with small families was annulled as of January 1, 1958.

Because of difficulties in getting a divorce, many estranged couples simply went their separate ways and eventually established new families. Rather belatedly, in response to this de facto rejection of the divorce laws, a new law was promulgated in 1965: the obligation and cost of announcing one's divorce in the newspaper were abrogated, and the divorce procedure was simplified by having it handled in one court rather than in two. If the couple had no minor children, divorce by mutual consent would be granted three months after application.

In 1968 a major overhauling of marriage laws was achieved. The 1944 law, preventing the name of the father of an illegitimate child from appearing on the child's certificate and not allowing the mother to sue for child support, was revoked. Henceforth a 30-day premarital "reflection period" was required, and a pregnant woman could not be divorced until a year after the birth of her child.[53] In addition, the obligation to support minor children could be imposed on relatives if the child had no parents. On the other hand, adult children were required to support their parents or those who had raised them if they were needy or disabled.[54]

Another noteworthy change has been the locale in which marriages are performed. During the 1920s, when formalized unions were considered unimportant, ceremonies took place in the ZAGS office—in the same dirty and poorly lit rooms where the couple waited in line with others who came, for example, to report deaths. The populace complained about the drabness of ZAGS weddings and often turned to supplementary church weddings to mark this important event in their lives.[55] In the late 1950s and in the 1960s, marriage palaces were opened, equipped with lavish carpeting and decorous surroundings.

The significance of these changes is severalfold. On the one hand, they represent a continuous evolution toward greater protection for women in marriage and a more positive evaluation of the institution of marriage itself. On the other hand, the regime realized that the growing tide of illegitimacy and divorce represented a thirst for individual freedom of action which repressive legislation had forced underground but failed to quench. The legislation simply recognized an existing condition. Last, by making relatives responsible for each other's care, the state acknowledged that it was cheaper and easier to make family members responsible for each other than to have the state do it. The family was no longer viewed as being in the process of withering away.

THE RUSSIANS AND SEX

In the first days of the Revolution, despite publicity in the West, there were few proponents of "free love," and their influence largely disappeared by 1930. In their place came a new amalgam of traditional Russian romanticism and "Party ethics." The romanticism was reminiscent of nineteenth-century Victorianism: the thrill of a touch, the searing look, the excitement of a pounding heart, the shy downward gaze of a modest maiden.[56] The emotion of love was emphasized rather than physical contact. In the Soviet film *Ballad of a Soldier,* Shura and the hero of the battlefield, Alyosha, fall in love. After a series of adventures, however, the two finally part because neither has been bold enough to express his or her feelings for the other.

Russians are dismayed at exposing the body, as in burlesque houses, or at making love in public.[57,58] Khrushchev was shocked, during his Hollywood visit, to see women on a movie set doing the "can-can." When the editor of the magazine *Soviet Women* was asked whether articles on dating or sexual problems were treated in her magazine, she replied, "We Russians do not write about such intimate things."[59]

Even a leading Soviet marriage sociologist, Kharchev, seemed to rationalize the Russian awkwardness in dealing with personal matters when he explained that Russian researchers do not ask questions about sexual life because of "the moral trauma which we could inflict upon people by such questions."[60]

For knowledge, the Russians have substituted polemic. In 1939 the editor of a symposium on Soviet youth asked, "Is it not clear that the smashing of former sexual relationships by the proletariat is leading towards a new, healthy, socialistic sexual relationship, which will wholly abolish confusion in sexual matters, sexual looseness and sexual perversion?"[61] If the confusion was lifted in subsequent years, it was not through enlightened sex-education courses or manuals. Sex education in the Soviet Union made a hesitant start only in the 1960s.[62]

The "new, healthy" approach to sex was not really new at all; it was merely a stronger emphasis on Lenin's dictum that sex should come second to the Revolution. Sex in itself was not evil, but it could so preoccupy an individual that he would be distracted from his commitment to the socialist goals of the country. A student's goal was to attain the highest grades of which he was capable. If romance and sexual escapades hindered him, they must go. In addition, no decent, sound man would engage in sexuality for its own sake, for that would mean exploiting women, which was also a cardinal sin. However, if a man was about to graduate from the university, and if he intended to marry a girl, some people would not object to their living together for a few weeks or months *if* they were fortunate enough to get a room.[63]

This is the official image. How much it is adhered to in actual behavior is not known. There is reason to believe that discreet premarital sexuality was and is prevalent in college dormitories.[64] A study in Leningrad revealed that 65 percent of the men and 28 percent of the women applying for divorce admitted having had intercourse with someone other than their marital partner before marriage.[65] Although divorcees are not a representative sample of even the Leningrad population, they are a substantial minority. The divorce rate in Moscow is currently almost two times the United States national rate. Moreover, the number of illegitimate children was estimated at from 6 to 11 million in 1961.[66,67] In 1945 the number of unwed mothers receiving grants for children was 281,700; but in 1957 the figure climbed to 3,312,000 and then dropped to 2,445,000 in 1961. These figures underestimate the actual number of out-of-wedlock children because state aid was paid only until the child reached the age of 12. This sharp increase is most likely the result of an imbalance in the male/female ratio due to the severe war losses. It is certainly clear, nevertheless, that there is a considerable divergence between reality and the official portrait of sexual behavior painted by various writers.

Even a "Party" writer such as Kharchev, after making the rather rash statement that "in Soviet society there are no objective social causes giving rise to sexual license,"[68] goes on to say, "But the conduct of young people is by no means always directly dependent upon the economic, social, and ideological relationships existing in society."[69] Kharchev correctly attributes sexual problems to the formerly sexually segregated school system and to the total lack of sex education. He also blames the nefarious influence of the capitalist press, radio, and art. What he fails to grasp is that the Russian increase in premarital sexuality is part of a worldwide movement of growing individual freedom.

The effects of this movement are so strong that Soviet social scientists have recently begun to bend theory again so that it can fit current trends. Recent research on the premarital sex lives of 620 young people in Leningrad indicated that only a minority of the respondents were opposed to premarital sex.[70,71] Over 85 percent of the men and 47 percent of the women had already experienced sexual intercourse—figures strikingly similar to those recently found in the United States.[72,73] Also similar is the plaint that "men are more liberal toward their own sexual behavior than toward that of women, and women are more liberal toward male sexual behavior than toward their own."[74]

In view of these data, the Leningrad researchers Kharchev and Golod argue for a single moral code that will permit premarital sexual freedom to both sexes. They do not propose libertinism but, rather, the freedom of mature individuals to harmonize "individual freedom in behavior (including that of sexual love) and moral responsibility to society."[75] This is referred to as no more than what Engels predicted when he said that future generations would determine their own mores. A safe prediction!

In keeping with the new sensitivity to sexuality, the first Sexology and Sexopathology Laboratory recently opened its doors. The writer reporting the event noted that the U.S.S.R. had no books on sex for the general public and that there were a total of ten doctors trained to treat the sexual problems of a population of 240 million.[76] Clearly the Soviet Union seems about to enter the Age of Kinsey, if not that of Masters and Johnson.

HUSBANDS AND WIVES

Although the Soviet Constitution in 1918 guaranteed equality for all women, it has not been possible to achieve this goal. One reason that the promised emancipation from the kitchen has not materialized is that the regime has been unable to supply all the crèches, restaurants, and home services needed. Also, the Russian husband has not pitched in to share the domestic chores on a 50-50 basis when both mates are working. David Mace, who studied the time records of household work in 1931, found that employed women spent four times as much time on domestic work as men. When only the heads of households were studied, the ratio was about 8 to 1.[77] Mace's more recent observations in the 1960s, as well as those of others, have confirmed the inequality of time devoted to housework.[78,79]

Another reason for the disparity is that attitudes toward equality have lagged behind the laws. Only about 20 percent of the total membership of the Communist Party are women,[80] and women on the average do not earn as much as men.[81] An editorial in 1965 complained that although 56 percent of the collective farmers are women, less than 2 percent serve as collective farm chairmen and state farm directors.[82] Moreover, a tendency still persists among the rural peasant population to retain some aspects of the patriarchal family: minimal emotional involvement, a double sexual standard, and physical threat to the woman.[83] The rural woman's response is to picture her husband as hot-tempered and childish, but to insist that he really needs her. In the 1950s, in the country as a whole, a considerable number of marriages resembled mother-son relationships, but this is scarcely surprising if we recall that after World War II millions of Soviet boys were raised by their mothers alone.

Despite the tendency for men to try to hold on to their age-old privileges, the regime has continually applied pressure to implement nondiscriminatory laws in work and marriage. A 1961 survey by Kharchev[84] revealed that, according to his observations (no quantitative data are presented), 60 percent of 300 Leningrad families could be classified as practicing equal responsibility for husband and wife, with only 36 percent classified as husband-dominant. However, a recent poll in Kostroma showed that only 28 percent of the men approve of production jobs for women and 61 percent find it an *acceptable necessity*. For women, the percentages were essentially reversed.[85] In sum, it may be concluded that most women would like to work, but they find it extremely exhausting to have a full-time job plus being a housewife. Their solution is not to stop working, but to demand better child care from the government and more help at home from their husbands. Husbands, who seem willing to accept the income brought in by their wives, are much more reluctant to share household tasks on a 50-50 basis. Not surprisingly, recent Soviet articles have a women's liberation flavor.

Concerning the sexual relationships between husband and wife, next to nothing is known because a veil of modesty is drawn over this topic by most Russians. There are no marriage counselors to describe their clients' behavior. However, talks with Russian refugees suggest that there appears to be little difficulty and, in the words of the British marital expert H. V. Dicks, "genital failure is not one of the anxieties that overtly beset the Russian male."[86] It is noteworthy that Russian women have in the past been described as charmless and thick-waisted Amazons, dressed in shapeless, dowdy garments faintly reminiscent of the 1930s. René MacColl, a journalist who spent 77 days in Russia, remarked, "Even were I twenty years younger and a bachelor, I would as soon think of trying to kiss a Soviet woman as a thistle."[87] Other writers[88] report that Russian girls are quite sexy, but in a modest, feminine, unpretentious way. In recent years, miniskirts and pants suits have been making an appearance, and women are exhibiting a strong penchant for cosmetics. One can only speculate as to whether dieting and the emaciated fashion-model look will ever come into vogue.

DIVORCE

Komsomolskaya Pravda declared in 1919, "The Soviet family lives amicably and knows no strife."[89] Be that as it may, it cannot be denied that the Soviet divorce rate has risen steadily despite a "strifeless society" and, until recently, very formidable divorce laws. The divorce rate was 0.4 per 1,000 in 1950,[90] 0.6 in 1955, 1.3 in 1960, 1.5 in 1964,[91] with a sharp rise to 2.7 in 1967, which equaled the capitalist United States figure of that year.[92] In 1969 it decreased slightly to 2.6. Yet the reported rate is acknowledged by even the Soviet expert, Perevedent, as an underestimation of the actual rate and the rate to be expected in the near future. One reason for judging the figures to be conservative is that the urban centers show a considerably higher rate than the national average (Moscow's is 6.0). Since the U.S.S.R. is rapidly becoming urbanized, it is more than likely, for this reason alone, that the divorce rate will increase in the future. Second, a considerable number of marriages formerly broke up without the participants notifying the authorities.[93] Despite recent reforms, a divorce still entails some difficulty, cost, and red tape, and Communist Party members are still stigmatized by it. If the present trend toward liberalism continues, therefore, the rate may keep climbing. In any event, the data hardly warrant the proud Soviet boast of a strifeless marital environment.

On the positive side, it should be stressed that some current features in Soviet life that are conducive to divorce will be alleviated in the near future. The importance of sex education is just being realized. The lack of adequate housing after World War II placed a heavy strain on marriage. Some years ago a survey reported that only 5 percent of newlyweds could hope to have their own house or apartment in the near future.[94] The typical new family lived in one room in the 1960s (housing space in 1960 was still equal to that of 1926).[95] Sometimes five or six families have had to share a kitchen, and an even larger number have had to share one toilet. The lack of privacy and the overcrowding could easily have augmented tensions to the breaking point. However, a massive housing construction program is making headway and, with more space, interpersonal tensions should decrease.

Another major cause of dissension is excessive drinking by men, which figured in 29.2 percent of the total number of divorce suits initiated in the city of Leningrad[96]; next in line was coarseness and cruelty on the part of the husband (26.6 percent). While the government has emphasized its disapproval of drunkenness, the efficacy of its efforts along these lines has not been measured. In view of these "imperfections" in Soviet society, it may be interesting to see how their social scientists have tackled the problem of reconciling their sweeping generalizations about the inevitability of marital happiness under socialism with the discordant evidence.

THE RUSSIAN MARRIAGE EXPERT: NAIVETE AND PROJECTION

The paramount feature in the writings of Russian marriage specialists is that Marx, Engels, and Lenin have already shown, beyond argument, the dialectical inevitability of the strengthening of the family under socialism.[97] In an earlier study on the defensive uses of perception, Dr. Pryer and I have indicated that there are several mechanisms available for defending the commitment of the "self" once a firm position is taken.[98] One possibility is to interpret more or less ambiguous data in accordance with one's needs (need-misperception). That is the only justification I can find for the statement by the dean of Russia's marriage lawyers, the late G. M. Sverdlov, that "procreation ... may be most freely manifested, unaltered by economic considerations [i.e., in the Soviet Union]. The above is vividly manifested by a steady growth of the population in the U.S.S.R. and by a permanent increase in the number of families with many children."[99] The truth of the matter, however, is that most countries have shown a steady increase in population without the benefit of a socialist government, and that the birthrate has been dropping steadily in the Soviet Union since the 1950s.

When the "offending" data are too far out of line with the prescribed position, it is too unrealistic to deny their existence. In this eventuality, it is possible to use *complementary rationalized-projection,* in which the *responsibility* for the sad state of affairs is projected onto others; accordingly, premarital sexual looseness may be ascribed to neofascist, imperialist, capitalist influences.

Western scientist-colleagues who are not adherents of socialist philosophy have been dismissed with contempt as "bourgeois scholars—vulgar materialists, Freudians and outright idealists of the religious stripe."[100] A. G. Kharchev explains that the difference between Soviet and Western scholars lies in the fact that Soviet theoreticians believe that theoretical generalizations are more important than supporting data.[101]

Kharchev unwillingly offers some insight into how these theoretical generalizations are derived. He acknowledges that certain tendencies, such as the decrease in family size and the eradication of the patriarchal structure, are common to both the U.S.S.R. and the West. He then states categorically, without any substantiating evidence, that these findings are conditioned by similar economic conditions in both countries. Then he uses this opinion as if it were an established fact and concludes, "Thus the existence of these aspects merely confirms the dependence of marriage and family relations on the economy of society."[102]

An important corollary of the fact that marriage in the Soviet Union *must* always be good is that marriage in the capitalist countries must always be based on private property and, therefore, must invariably be bad. In enumerating the "proofs" of how good marriage is under socialism, Kharchev exhibits a rather astounding ignorance of the fact that the same "proofs" also exist in capitalist marriages. In a study of 500 couples marrying in Leningrad, for example, Kharchev found that 76 percent of the individuals regarded love as the major condition for a happy marriage.[103] In his opinion, "love" is chosen because, in the Soviet Union, there is no economic reason for marriage. He seems to be totally unaware that most women in the United States do not marry solely for economic support, and that when a national survey on the reasons for marriage was carried out (see the chapter on modern American marriage), about the same percentage of Americans said that love was the major reason for marriage.

In like manner, Kharchev[104] cites the fact that the age difference between spouses in Russian marriages has dropped between 1920 and 1960, and that the number of mixed marriages (European and non-European) has increased, as proof of the superiority of the socialist system. He also states that over 90 percent of Russian marriages involve couples in which the members have an "approximately equal educational level."[105] Missing in these boasts about the splenders of socialism is an awareness that the same conditions exist in what he derisively calls "the show window of the capitalist world, the United States."[106] The newer breed of Soviet social scientists, however, seem more data-oriented and less polemical. Hopefully, more empirically based and useful findings will be forthcoming in Soviet writings on marriage.

CONCLUSIONS

With respect to the treatment of women, it cannot be denied that the Revolution accomplished a great deal. If the Russian woman has not yet been fully emancipated from the kitchen, she has in fact been granted full legal equality with men. In addition, the government has granted her special protection, (maternity leaves and benefits) taking cognizance of her special situation to assure and encourage her professional aspirations. As a result, women have achieved an eminence in professional life and in the government which, while certainly not equal to that of men, is nevertheless matched by few other nations in the world.

Legislation specific to marriage has not fared nearly as well. Although there were voices bent on eliminating the family as an institution as rapidly as possible, the basic attitude of the Soviet government in the early years can best be characterized as *laissez-faire*. The attempt at "self-regulation" brought a host of family problems, including illegitimate children and a falling birthrate.

Subsequent legislation aimed at strengthening the family and preventing marital breakup by a range of penalties and restrictions. The most recent legislation continues the protection of the family, but abandons the unpopular and humiliating restrictions that attempted to dissuade any but the most determined from seeking divorce. Soviet marriage today, from a legal point of view, strongly resembles the situation in many liberal industrialized Western nations.

Western writers, as noted by Bronfenbrenner,[107] have tended to exaggerate the Russian shifts in the philosophy of marriage. Too much weight has been accorded to the "free love" theorists of the period immediately following the Revolution. In truth, the breakdown in traditional family values and morality during those days was much more the result of war, famine, financial crises, collectivization, forced industrialization, and urbanization than of the government's strong antimarriage policy.

Writers such as Inkeles have exaggerated the corrective legislation of 1936 and 1944 as evidence of a return to a position on marriage that is "very close to that held in many of the states which form Western society."[108] These laws were instituted, despite their unpopularity (particularly the antiabortion laws), by a Stalinist regime more concerned with raising the number of properly inculcated citizens than with family interaction. Indeed, even today there is not much concern on the part of the government with advancing individual happiness where it is not beneficial to the state. Very recent writings denounce bachelorhood, small families,[109,110] the increasing divorce rate, marriage bureaus, and computer matching.[111] There is little to suggest that the government now regards love, marriage, and the family as apolitical. Citizens are still officially exhorted to marry good communists and to raise their children in accordance with the true communist ideal.

The so-called progressive legislation has come about because the population, acting in its own interests, has taken matters into its own hands, with the government's tardy legislation reluctantly limping after public demand. There are signs, however, that authorities are finally becoming more sensitive about consulting the people prior to the introduction of new legislation. The 1968 legislation, in contrast to that of 1936 and 1944, followed large-scale meetings and discussion throughout the country.

In conclusion, it is evident that the abolition of private property has not *ipso facto* improved family relations.[112] The high divorce rate in the Soviet Union today, which merely makes official the more surreptitious breakups of yesterday, cannot be attributed to capitalism because that has been abolished. It stems, rather, from the stresses of industrialization and urbanization, and from the wish for individual freedom and happiness, which seems highly correlated with the rate of industrialization.

There have been gains in family life, probably reflecting in part the low level from which it started in Czarist times. Similar gains have been achieved in the United States, in Scandinavia, and in many other countries. It is questionable, therefore, how much of these gains in the U.S.S.R. can be attributed to socialism and how much to the benefits of industrialization.[113] Perhaps the safest conclusion is that the people of any country, capitalist or socialist, when freed from poverty and back-breaking labor, will crave individual freedom and push their government until it gradually complies with their wishes.

REFERENCES

1. F. W. Halle, *Woman in Soviet Russia.*
2. H. K. Geiger, *The Family in Soviet Russia,* p. 244.
3. V. U. Krupianskaia, "Family structure and family life."
4. E. W. Burgess and H. J. Locke, *The Family,* p. 156.
5. S. Wolffson, "Explanation of the new family policy by Soviet theorists," p. 281.
6. *Russian Proverbs.*
7. P. E. Mosely, "The Russian family: Old style and new."
8. F. Engels, *The Origin of the Family, Private Property and the State,* p. 50.
9. K. Marx and F. Engels, *Manifesto of the Communist Party,* p. 427.
10. J. Jaurès, "Marriage in socialistic society," p. 407.
11. K. Hulicka, "Marriage and family law in the U.S.S.R."
12. "The original family law of the Russian Soviet Republic."
13. "Decree on the introduction of divorce of December 19, 1917."
14. A. V. Makletsov, "Marriage and the family in Soviet Russia."
15. "The original family law of the Russian Soviet Republic."
16. N. B. Krilenko, "The family in Soviet Russia," p. 209.
17. F. Engels, op. cit., p. 100.
18. E. Pawel, "Sex under socialism," p. 92.
19. H. K. Geiger, op. cit., p. 51.
20. A. M. Kollontai, "Excerpts from the works of A. M. Kollontai," pp. 56-57.
21. Ibid., p. 58.
22. Ibid., p. 68.
23. Ibid., p. 74.
24. A. Lunarcharski, quoted in H. K. Geiger, op. cit., p. 70.
25. K. Zetkin, "Excerpts from *Reminiscences of Lenin,*" pp. 76-77.

26. A. Slepkov, quoted in H. K. Geiger, op. cit., p. 45.
27. A. V. Makletsov, op. cit.
28. Y. Mironenko, "The evolution of Soviet family law."
29. D. Mace and V. Mace, *The Soviet Family*, p. 214.
30. W. C. White, "Moscow morals."
31. S. Kopelianskaia, "Marriage in the U.S.S.R."
32. R. M. Frumkin and M. Z. Frumkin, "Sex, marriage and the family in the U.S.S.R."
33. A. L. Strong, "We Soviet wives," p. 419.
34. V. Sandomirsky, "Sex in the Soviet Union," p. 202.
35. V. Katayev, *Squaring the Circle*, p. 135.
36. Ibid., p. 137.
37. Ibid., p. 166.
38. Ibid., p. 176.
39. H. Selehen, "Soviet family life."
40. H. K. Geiger, op. cit., p. 58.
41. N. S. Timasheff, "The attempt to abolish the family."
42. H. K. Geiger, op. cit., p. 255.
43. R. Maurer, "Recent trends in the Soviet family."
44. P. Juviler, "Family reforms on the road to communism."
45. M. Fairchild, "The status of the family in the Soviet Union today."
46. H. K. Geiger, op. cit.
47. R. S. Lynd, "Ideology and the Soviet family."
48. V. Svetlov, "Explanations of the new family policy by Soviet theorists."
49. N. S. Timasheff, op. cit., p. 59.
50. L. A. Coser, "Some aspects of Soviet family policy."
51. H. K. Geiger, op. cit.
52. H. K. Geiger, op. cit., p. 104.
53. J. P. Waehler, "Neues sowjetisches Familienrecht."
54. "Revised principles of marriage and family legislation."
55. E. Stevens, "Love and marriage—Soviet style."
56. J. Novak, "Sex, marriage, and divorce in Russia."
57. N. Kolbanovski, "The sex upbringing of the rising generation."
58. J. Gunther, *Inside Russia.*
59. A. W. Langman, "Love and marriage Soviet style," p. 107.
60. A. G. Kharchev, "Problems of the family and their study in the U.S.S.R.," p. 544.
61. A. V. Makletsov, op. cit., p. 97.
62. P. Stafford, *Sexual Behavior in the Communist World.*
63. A. G. Kharchev, *Marriage and Family Relations in the U.S.S.R.*
64. P. Juviler, Personal communication.
65. P. Frank, "Soviet divorce."
66. P. Juviler, "Marriage and divorce."
67. P. Juviler, "Family reforms on the road to communism."
68. A. G. Kharchev, "The nature of the Soviet family," p. 17.
69. Ibid., p. 17.
70. S. I. Golod, "Sociological problems of sexual morality."
71. "Russia."

72. E. B. Luckey and G. D. Nass, "A comparison of sexual attitudes and behavior in an international sample."
73. G. R. Kaats and K. E. Davis, "The dynamics of sexual behavior of college students."
74. S. I. Golod, op. cit., p. 13.
75. Ibid., p. 20.
76. A. Baskina, "Neither beast nor angel."
77. D. Mace, "The employed mother in the U.S.S.R."
78. D. Mace and V. Mace, op. cit.
79. M. G. Field and K. I. Flynn, "Worker, mother, housewife: Soviet women today."
80. Ibid.
81. J. Cuisenier and C. Raguin, "De quelques transformations dans le système familial russe."
82. K. Hulicka, "Women and the family in the U.S.S.R."
83. H. K. Geiger, op. cit.
84. A. Kharchev, *Marriage and Family Relations in the U.S.S.R.*
85. M. Pavlova, "Woman's lot, man's responsibility."
86. H. V. Dicks, "Observations on contemporary Russian behavior," p. 142.
87. R. MacColl (quoted in D. Mace and V. Mace, op. cit., p. 112).
88. G. Frost, "What Russian girls are like."
89. D. Mace and V. Mace, op. cit., p. 210.
90. "Marry early, down with bachelors."
91. P. Juviler, "Soviet families."
92. "Soviet population expert deplores the rising divorce rate."
93. H. K. Geiger, op. cit.
94. Ibid., p. 260.
95. Ibid.
96. P. Frank, op. cit.
97. A. V. Makletsov, op. cit., p. 97.
98. B. I. Murstein and R. S. Pryer, "The concept of projection: A review."
99. G. M. Sverdlov, "Changes in family relations in the U.S.S.R.," p. 55.
100. E. G. Balagushkin, "The building of communism and the evolution of family and marital relations," p. 46.
101. A. G. Kharchev, "Problems of the family and their study in the U.S.S.R."
102. Ibid., p. 548.
103. A. G. Kharchev, "On some results of a study of the motives for marriage."
104. Ibid.
105. A. G. Kharchev, "Marriage in the U.S.S.R.," p. 15.
106. Ibid., p. 22.
107. U. Bronfenbrenner, "The changing Soviet family."
108. A. Inkeles, "Family and church in the postwar U.S.S.R.," p. 36.
109. "A plan to encourage large families."
110. "Newlyweds, young couples."
111. "*Pravda* says no to marriage bureaus."
112. H. K. Geiger, "The Soviet family."
113. R. A. H. Schlesinger, *Changing Attitudes in Soviet Russia. The Family in the U.S.S.R. Documents and Readings.*

20

Marriage in China: Past and Present

In ancient China, before the advent of the imperial period, women are said to have enjoyed a rather high status in society.[1-3] Indeed, the character for a man's family name is still formed from the radical for "woman,"[4] and the word for wife meant "equal." The wife kept her own name after marriage and gave it to the children. Women occasionally held high administrative posts in the government and, among the upper classes, received considerable education.

CONFUCIAN MODEL OF THE FAMILY

By the time of Confucius (551-479 b.c.), the advent of property consciousness and the feudal system had done much to weaken the position of women. The influence of his writings accelerated this process; they stressed patriarchal family ancestor worship and filial piety. A woman was considered inferior to a man, and the key word describing her function was *obey:* in childhood she obeyed her father; in adulthood, her husband; when widowed, her son. Buddhism, which became a prominent religious influence in China after the first century a.d., also taught that women, basically inferior to men, were the personification of all evil.[5]

Chinese cosmology reinforced these views by attributing the creation of the world to the interaction of two fundamental elements—*yang,* the male principle, and *yin,* the female. The positive male elements—heaven, sun, height, light, strength, and activity—were superior to the negative counterparts of the female: earth, moon, depth, darkness, weakness, and passivity.[6]

Confucianism was slow in spreading, and in the years following Confucius' death the typical Chinese family was not characterized by filial devotion.[7] Foreseeing a correlation between weak family ties and social instability, the early and later Han dynasties (202 b.c.-220 a.d.) gave official sanction to the ethic of filial piety. Despite the subsequent decline of imperial authority, the powerful nobles used "filial piety" to rationalize the accumulation of vast landholdings that were alleged to provide in perpetuity against want by family members.

The Clan

By the middle of the eleventh century, with the waning of the hereditary aristocracy, state officials were recruited by competitive examinations and the economy became more diversified.

The power of the clan (a group of families whose heads claim common descent) rose rapidly; they accumulated funds and maintained ancestral halls, clan schools, and properties. Their poor were cared for, and penniless but talented clan members were provided with advanced education at clan expense. But there were limitations to the clan's effectiveness. It sometimes comprised thousands of members, and its great size precluded detailed attention to the individual. Also, it depended on voluntary contributions from its more successful members. Because financial success varied from generation to generation, the clan was not always able to maintain its services.

The clan never replaced the stem family as the basic economic unit.[8] The typical household included the husband, wife, children, and occasionally one or both of his aging parents. Although the average household consisted of only about five persons throughout much of China's history, the wealthy were able to accommodate many nuclear families within the same extended family compound; unlike the peasants, they could practice the Confucian model of the large family living together and linked by mutual obligations.

The model consisted of a patriarch (grandfather or father) as the ruling head who presided over his family: a wife, concubine(s), sons, grandsons, their wives and children, unmarried daughters, relatives, slaves, and servants. In his role as family priest, he exercised both economic and spiritual control.

Individual interests were subordinated to those of the extended family and, to a lesser degree, to those of the clan. As a result, the tendency among the wealthy was to avoid chopping up the estate into smaller parcels when the patriarch died. If no agreement could be reached, the estate was divided equally among the sons (daughters were ineligible to inherit because they did not carry on the family name).

Parent-Child Relationships

The most important relationship in the household—between the patriarch and his eldest son—rested on a foundation of respect more than affection. The model son obeyed his father without question; most important, he owed him every possible material comfort until the day his father died. The intensity of filial piety may be garnered from the "Twenty-Four High Examples of Filial Piety."[9] One example tells of a son who, bare-bodied, lay down on the ice to melt it so that his ailing father could taste some fish. Another son, lacking enough food to support both an aged father and a young son, elected to bury his son in a pit; fortunately for the youngster, however, the pit yielded a hidden treasure. These tales may not all have been true, but they reflect the status of the father in traditional Chinese society.

The patriarch himself was not without obligation toward his son. As an expression of filial duty to his own parents and ancestors, he was expected to train his son as his successor. He also had to provide him with a wife and with an inheritance so that he could marry and have sons to perpetuate the line.

The mother-son relationship was somewhat less intense and less formal than that between father and son. The mother was responsible for caring for her son during his early years, eventually relinquishing him to his father when the time came for schooling and training. Since the father-son relationship was formal, with little spontaneous emotional interaction, the early years with his mother, when no restrictions were placed on him, were warmly regarded; while the mother-son relationship was officially supposed to be formal, in actuality it often served as an emotional safety valve for the son to convey feelings that could not be expressed elsewhere.

The daughter's relationship in the family was much less significant than that of the son. Women were regarded as inferiors—a daughter was unable to carry on the family name. She would eventually marry, join another household, and rarely return to visit. She could be regarded with affection by other family members, but she played no special role in the family, and her main asset lay in her potential marriage. To this end her chastity, essential to a gentry marriage, was guarded by segregating her from males during her formative years. Her parents and other family elders made the marriage arrangement for her that would best further the family interests.

The Husband-Wife Relationship

Unlike the modern Western marriage, the traditional Chinese gentry's husband-wife relationship was neither the strongest nor the most emotionally meaningful in the family. Since neither spouse had chosen each other, it mattered little whether or not they were sexually attracted to each other. Their primary duty was to procreate.

The husband was assumed to be biologically destined to seek satisfaction with a variety of women; among the wealthy, concubinage was a necessary accompaniment of marriage. The woman was not biologically so destined; her chief function was to produce children, and she was expected to remain faithful to her husband.[10]

The wife raised her husband's children under her mother-in-law's supervision, endured her husband's concubines in silence, and gave her husband complete obedience; but his parents' commands might take priority over his wishes. Considering the unequal status of husband and wife, it should come as no surprise that their relationship could be described as "correct" rather than cordial. Each knew the order of things and tried to follow his or her prescribed role. Beyond that, the development of mutual affection was uncertain. The wife usually felt a stronger attachment to her father or brothers than to her husband, just as the husband remained more deeply committed to his mother.

The extent of this commitment is illustrated by comparing the reaction to the mother's intervention in a son's marriage in the United States and in prerevolutionary China. In the United States, the mother who rules her married son's life is described as an emasculating "busybody," and her passive son is contemptuously viewed as lacking any backbone. But in the precommunist family system in China, a mother who disliked her son's wife could demand that the son divorce her; despite his unhappiness, her wishes were executed.

Even in the unlikely event that the partners were highly attracted to each other, it was contrary to custom to express the slightest degree of public affection. An old Chinese saying states, "When you ascend the bed, act like husband and wife; when you descend to the ground comport yourself like a Chün tzu" (the Confucian ideal of persons of reserved, dignified, superior conduct).[11]

There is a case recorded of a violation of this code. A man who had been away from the mainland for some time was so happy to see his wife again that he had the affrontery to hold her hand, whereupon one disgusted member of the populace crowned this obscene gesture by pouring a bucket of human excrement on the unfortunate Don Juan.[12]

The upper-class father generally took his meals apart from his wife and family except on rare occasions. He was the absolute master of his household; during the imperial period, he had the right—if not social sanction—to put his children to death. He could also sell his wife and children into servitude.

The wife, on the other hand, had little real power. She was the administrator of the household, but only on the sufferance of her spouse, and was dependent upon him for approval and financial support. She seldom ventured from the family compound, leaving the shopping and other errands to servants.

For the mother, the acquisition of a daughter-in-law meant that, after all the years of frustration as an underling, she could now let out her pent-up aggression on a passive subject who was obliged to wait hand-and-foot on her. The need to compensate usually took precedence over empathy for a predicament that she herself had experienced as a bride. The mother-in-law accepted her new, more powerful status, rationalizing that her daughter-in-law was merely being trained in the philosophy of respect for ancestors, which also included filial piety for living ancestors. The daughter-in-law's turn to receive the benefits of such a situation would come if she could produce a son and, in time, become a mother-in-law herself. The difference in the relative status of groom and bride is expressed in the proverb, "A son-in-law must do one-half the duty of a son, but a daughter-in-law must do twice as much as a daughter."[13]

Against the weight of these difficulties, the wife could count on no one in the household, including her husband, to check her being abused. Her family might intervene in the case of severe abuse, but the physical distance, in addition to the reluctance to disrupt alliance patterns, made this unlikely. As a last resort, however, the wife might attempt suicide.

The most reliable Chinese statistics on suicide are for Peking in 1917. The data show that men, more than women, committed *successful* suicide.[14] If, however, we examine the 21 to 30 age range, in which the stresses of child care and household tensions for women must have been paramount, the women lead men in suicide per 100,000 people—53 to 16. Consider also that a transition to a more industrialized society was under way in 1917, and many abuses were being corrected. Also, women attempt suicide more often than men, although they usually do not succeed as often. The statistics, therefore, lead us to conclude that traces of women's unhappy condition remained even at this late date.

The suicide attempt of the wife was a powerful protest against mistreatment in a culture where loss of "face" was a devastating moral blow. The investigation by the magistrate was taken as firm proof that the *li* (the system of reciprocal family responsibilities in accordance with the Confucian ideal) had broken down. By subjecting the family to an unwelcome spotlight, it usually had the effect of improving the wife's situation and diminishing her exploitation.

Despite the strain on the husband-wife relationship, certain factors served to make life bearable. For one thing, the expectations in terms of anticipated rewards from interaction were so low that disappointment in the event of coldness or even hostility on the part of the partner was relatively slight. Moreover, the absence of intense affection between the couple might be beneficial in a culture that frowned on individualism. If a couple's love motivated them to support each other against their parents in a situation where neither had the means to maintain their opposition, the result would be tension in the household and a crushing defeat for the couple in any event. In addition, divorce was complicated and rare, and the unhappy spouse simply tried to adjust as best he could.

The passage of time usually brought the couple closer together. As the older generation began to die off, their mutual allegiance rose in importance. The couple, now assuming the position of the older generation, generally supported each other vis-à-vis the younger generation in a dispute.

Marriage among the Peasants

Only the barest shadow of the Confucian model trickled down to influence the peasant class, the vast majority of the population. Without the economic and political strength of the gentry patriarch, the peasant patriarch could exert little leverage over his family. The husband-son relationship was much more equal and informal, and sons felt freer to leave their fathers if economic prospects were more promising elsewhere. Unlike the gentry wife, the peasant wife had to work very hard to sustain the family, and she exercised correspondingly greater power in family decisions.

PURPOSE OF MARRIAGE

From our preceding discussion, it may be concluded that the purpose of marriage was to assure the continuity of the family line under as favorable circumstances as possible—for example, the accumulation of property and the founding of politically and economically useful family alliances. This is corroborated by a survey of clan views on marriage in the twentieth century, in which the most desirable quality in marriage is a "spotless family background."[15] Interestingly, the most inappropriate reason for marriage was "marriage motivated by craving for the wealth and influence of the other family."[16] Considering the economic concern of most families, this Confucian ideal seems to have been honored more in the breach than in the observance.

Among peasants, the purposes of marriage were much more personal and less lineage-oriented. The need for an additional field hand at harvest time took precedence over the quality of the family tree.

One aspect of marriage that lacked crucial importance was love. To the Chinese, love between a man and a woman signified a state of sexual excitation. Even though the elders did not object to sex per se, they recognized it as a powerful impetus to action. The young and the inexperienced could hardly be expected to handle passion and at the same time bear the family's welfare in mind; thus the choice of partner was a matter for parents to decide. Such a decision was more than a prerogative; it was their responsibility to see to it that a suitable mate was provided. Indeed, under Chinese empire law during the early eighteenth century, a family elder who did not provide a spouse for any girl in his household—a daughter or a slave—was keeping the joy of a fulfilled life from her, and could risk receiving 80 bamboo blows.[17]

MARRIAGE CUSTOMS

The marriage contract, a document that involved two families rather than two individuals, did not require the signatures of the couple. In fact, the bride and groom usually did not see each other before the ceremony, and their parents did not negotiate directly, for there was a possibility that one of the suggested marriage partners might be rejected. Outright rejection was regarded as so insulting that it was avoided at all costs, or a vendetta against the insulting family might be necessary. As a consequence, professional matchmakers were called in; they could be rejected while representing a client without the client losing "face."

The matchmaker on the groom's side, after memorizing his client's and family's good qualities and preparing elaborate rationales for any familial weak spots, would bring gifts to the girl's family. If they were amenable, they retained the gifts and furnished the matchmaker with vital information about the girl: the names of her father, grandfather, and great-grandfather, and the eight characters denoting the year, month, day, and hour of her birth.[18] After the girl's family was given similar data about the prospective groom, both matchmakers checked everything for conformity to standard exogamous and endogamous rules. Generally, persons with the same surname could not marry unless they were at least five generations removed. On the other hand, a cross-cousin marriage between a girl and her paternal aunt's son was permissible and often encouraged. Marriage between a boy and his paternal aunt's daughter was not allowed because of the belief that a girl carried only her mother's blood and that such a marriage could be incestuous. Parallel cousins (offspring of two sisters or two brothers) with the same surname also could not marry.

> Another hurdle to be overcome was the comparison of horoscopes. The eight characters standing for [the girl's] name, hour, day, month, and year of birth were compared by a specialist with the corresponding data of the boy. The particulars about birth included the so-called horary and cyclical characters symbolizing animals like the rat, ox, tiger, and hare. If the girl's birth, for instance, took place on the day and hour ruled by the serpent or tiger, and the boy's by the sheep or dog, the match would be considered inauspicious: a tiger is likely to devour a sheep or a dog. The written name may contain symbols of wood, earth, water, fire, etc. A fire symbol in the girl's name would burn the wood symbol in the boy's name, but earth or water would be favorable to wood.[19]

Happily, horoscope matching is not an exact science; and, if the families wanted the match very badly and the initial horoscope did not look promising, a horoscope consultant was called in. After considerable discussion, it was possible to find a new meaning in the horoscope matching. And, *mirabile dictu,* these new interpretations, much more promising than the original readings, permitted the marriage to take place. Of course, if the marriage turned out to be unsuccessful, the parents could always revert to the original horoscope interpretation as a rationalization for their error.

Once the horoscope problem was solved, betrothal gifts (a wild goose, a roll of silk), sometimes accompanied by cash, were sent to the bride's family, and a legally binding betrothal contract was signed. The fortune teller announced the most propitious day for the wedding, and a red chair was sent to the bride to convey her to her future home. She was carried to the sedan (or sometimes walked to it) on covered ground—symbolically she was in a state of limbo until safely deposited in her new home. She now became an outsider to her natal home, and ritual acts were performed to prevent her taking its prosperity with her. Before she entered the sedan, it was inspected to assure its freedom from evil; once ensconced in it, she used various instruments to ward off evil influences. Upon entering her new house, her father-in-law performed a ritual to cleanse her of adhering evils (e.g., mirrors were flashed).[20] Her absent family signified that they had not gained a son but lost a daughter.

It was not unusual for the groom's parents to incur a large debt in connection with the wedding feast and ceremony. A poor peasant sometimes spent as much as a year's income[21] for the festivities and bride-price. The bride-price, often a very handsome sum, served several purposes: it saved "face" and emphasized to the newlyweds the extent of their indebtedness to the groom's family.

If both families were rich, "face-saving counter-gifts (dowry) were made by the bride's family, sometimes equivalent in value to the groom's gifts. The girl's family often used the entire bride-price to outfit her.

Poor families had to patch the bride together in as skimpy a manner as possible and pocket the remainder of the sum for more pressing needs. Sometimes, a poor family would sell a young girl to a couple who had no son but had high hopes of producing one in the future. The girl became a "daughter-in-law-in-anticipation."

Almost everyone married—bachelors and spinsters had little prestige in the community. The few bachelors extant were usually those who were too poor to pay the bride-price. A widower, for example, might think twice about remarriage, and a family with a large number of sons might also have difficulty in scraping together the means to launch their youngest ones into matrimony. Prior to the 1949 revolution, the average age at marriage in the twentieth century was approximately 19 to 20 for men and 17 to 18 for women.[22]

MARRIAGE EXPECTATIONS

The Husband

A man expected his wife to be fertile; but this criterion could not have been empirically demonstrated, for another prerequisite was virginity. Nevertheless, even if a woman had some character deficiencies, if she could produce male heirs her position in the household would be solidified. Other desirable qualities included submissiveness, industriousness, and filial devotion to his ancestors and parents.

In terms of interests, there was little communality. The husband did not expect an educated companion or someone with whom to exchange views on government and politics. In fact, a wife rarely met her husband's friends or business associates. If he traveled on a business trip lasting months or years, it was customary for the wife to remain behind.

The Wife

Based on her inferior position, the wife could expect little from a husband other than security and sustenance. If he did not beat her and was polite and considerate, she counted herself lucky. The Chinese wife would doubtless have been pleasantly surprised to find a mate who was romantically attentive and affectionate (such husbands did exist). However, the combination of an arranged marriage, in which the participants did not previously know each other, together with the ritualized nature of the interaction, made a romantic union quite improbable.

MARRIAGE PROBLEMS

Divorce

Three kinds of divorce existed in old China: a divorce initiated by one party, divorce by mutual agreement, and divorce by compulsion of the authorities. In practice, divorces initiated by the husband were the overwhelming majority. The basic philosophy behind divorce was that it was deemed to be in the best interests of the family. Divorce due to personal feelings or incompatibility on the part of either partner was rather unlikely.

The legal code of divorce under the Manchu dynasty (1644-1912) was based on the writings of Confucius and stipulated the following seven grounds for divorcing a woman: improper respect toward his parents, failure to bear children, adultery, jealousy with regard to the husband's other women, a repulsive disease, garrulousness, and thievery. On the other hand, there were three conditions under which a wife could not be divorced: if she had mourned the husband's parents for three years; if the husband's family, initially poor, had now become rich; and if she had no family to which to return.

In feudal and early imperial times, a husband could be divorced by his wife; later, she could do this only if she and her husband came to a mutual arrangement. In practice, innumerable restraints made divorce a rare phenomenon. To send a wife back to her parents without good reason, for example, might cause both her family and her to lose "face." In addition, if he remarried, his family would have to incur a second round of wedding expenses.

Lacking legal recourse to divorce, most wives found it difficult to cope with a mother-in-law's authority and with having to work from dusk to dawn without appreciation. A wife could do little about it except consider suicide. She could not leave and take the children with her, because they were considered part of her husband's family. Finally, a divorcée depreciated a great deal on the marital market, and her chances of remarrying someone in her social status were practically nil.

Concubines

Since the Chinese considered sex to be not only a natural body function but a very powerful one, if the husband felt the need for an especially stimulating sexual partner or if he had no male heirs, it was acceptable for him to take a concubine. The concubine represented the husband's free choice, and even if a strong emotional attachment sprang up between them, it could not be officially acknowledged. Needless to say, the possibility of a lover for the wife was never entertained except, perhaps, in her fantasies.

The status of the concubine varied considerably. In its lowest form, the concubine was little more than a servant who did the most menial work, incurred the enmity of the wife, and was the object of the husband's sexual needs. On the other hand, she might enjoy a high status if there was a strong emotional and sexual interaction with him. In addition, if she bore a male heir and his wife had not, she could be treated like a second wife, although legally she was always subservient to the first wife.

The existence of concubinage over several thousand years in China is best understood in the light of the services it performed for both parties. For the man it provided sexual variety, a chance for emotional involvement, and the possibility of additional sons. The advantage to the concubine and her family lay in the fact that most concubines were purchased by rich men at a handsome price. She usually came from an impoverished household, and her new status meant a step upward in social mobility. Although abuses of concubines were not unknown, among the wealthy she was not required to work too hard because it would obviously impair her sexual attractiveness and vitality. Further, although she could not worship at the shrine of ancestors, her children enjoyed quasi-legal status and could inherit from the father. If the legal wife died, the husband sometimes married her.

THE SEEDS OF CHANGE

For centuries the pyramid of the nuclear family, the extended family, and the clan rested on an uneasy balance with the state. It was advantageous for the state to communicate its wishes to the citizenry via the clans, who could then relay advice to the patriarchs. The fly in the ointment, however, was the fact that the clans themselves could snowball into powerful political entities, control large territories, and tolerate little governmental interference. Over the course of centuries, many clans, spread out through entire villages, found it expedient to oppose the creation of a strong centralized government. The stumbling block for the government was the simple fact that family ties were much more important than ties to the government.

Industrialization and nationalism in the nineteenth century brought the government and the family into mortal battle. By 1898 K'ang Yu-wei pointed out that the traditional family hindered the proper execution of public duties. Although his reform efforts did not succeed, the nascent nationalist movement continued.

The process of industrialization slowly undermined the foundation of the old family system. By leaving his father's household to take a factory job, the son weakened the clan ties. New cultural contacts with Westerners and the perception of the tangible rewards of a materialist philosophy led some to question the validity of traditional familial forms. The dramatic impact of industrialization on the status of women impressed one Western observer as early as 1910:

> The most striking instances I have ever met of the reaction of industrial opportunity upon the position of women is found in three districts in central Kwantung, where women can easily support themselves by silk winding. In these districts, thousands of girls have for a long time maintained antimatrimonial associations in which each member binds herself to leave her husband after the three days required by custom and return to her parents' home. There she supports herself by her labor and does not return permanently to her husband at all unless a child is born. In vain have parents and magistrates sought to compel the girls to return to their wifely duty. The girls threaten to take opium or drown themselves and, if too hard pressed, they carry out their threat. This extraordinary revolt of young women against the hard lot of the Chinese wife seems to be spontaneous and unprompted by foreign influences.[23]

During that period, college students and intellectuals traveled and preached individual liberty, sexual equality, and national solidarity, bringing new ideas to the hinterlands.

Early Family Legislation

The need for family legislation was reflected even in prerevolutionary times by the formation of an Imperial Commission on the Family in 1907. The commission called for separating the *li* from the law and for a legal definition of kinship that would be independent of traditional mourning charts and ancestor worship.

Sun Yat-sen, the first president of the Chinese Republic, saw the traditional family as a hindrance to nationalism; however, due to the political chaos, no sweeping changes occurred immediately. Nevertheless, the May 4th Movement of 1919 included a call for "family revolution." While the movement had no organized platform, its objectives regarding the family were sexual equality in the home as well as in industry, and marriage on the basis of free choice and love rather than by parental arrangement. Confucian orthodoxy was perceived as the backbone of the opposition to progress, and his teachings were increasingly eliminated from the school curriculum.

The period between 1911 and 1931, marked by continuing battles with warlords and the Communists, saw no important legislation. The courts generally took a conservative line, supporting the traditional notion that persons belonging to the same family must live together (a son must live with his parents)[24] and ruling that "the purchase of a woman for the explicit purpose of begetting children is justified and not invalid."[25]

By 1931, the Kuomintang, under Chiang Kai-shek, governed most of China except the areas held by the Chinese Communists. The Code of the Family, which realized many of the objectives of the May 4th Movement, for the first time allowed women to inherit property; it also averred that marriage could take place only with the free will of both participants, forbade marriage as a commercial transaction (including the payment of matchmaker fees), set minimum betrothal ages at 15 for girls and 17 for boys, and granted the right of divorce to both wife and husband.

Although the wife could still be divorced for ill treatment of the husband's lineal ascendants, *she,* in turn, could now sue for divorce if *they* mistreated her. The relationship between husband and wife was at least on the road to becoming central to marriage, with a reduction in the importance of relations with parents. The government even tried to bypass the enormous expense of traditional weddings by providing inexpensive "collective weddings" so that couples could be married *en masse* by city authorities. Most people, however, were reluctant to accept this departure from tradition and ceremony.[26]

Certain vestiges of the "old way" remained: orphans were assigned to wards on the father's side of the family, and when a wife sued for divorce, her children, as in the past, remained with the father. The signatures of the groom and bride were still not necessary to make the contract legally binding. Concubinage did not legally disappear until 1936; in 1931 a wife could divorce her husband for adultery, but she could not do so simply because he had a concubine. Despite the sweeping "paper" reforms, the Family Code had its main effect among the relatively few well-educated intelligentsia. The inferior position of women persisted, not only in rural areas but also in the cities. Olga Lang cites some personal experiences.[27] While living in Peiping (Peking), she told her cook that her husband liked boiled potatoes, but that she preferred them fried. So fried potatoes appeared on the menu—*once,* on her birthday! On one occasion, the chief of police in a Shantung town, whose duties included enforcement of the provision of monogamy in the Family Code, introduced both of his wives to Mrs. Lang in 1936, five years *after* the passage of the code!

There are numerous explanations for the failure to implement the code: (1) the vast majority of the people were illiterate, and communication between government and populace was exceedingly poor; (2) the government, engaged in a struggle for supremacy with the Communists, had neither the energy nor the manpower to enforce the laws; (3) since many reforms had been vigorously supported by the Communists, "their" causes suffered by association; and (4) some areas remained under the control of warlords, who did not especially encourage change because they profited handsomely from the old ways. Finally, legislation itself, in the absence of an appropriate social milieu conducive to free choice in marriage, could have little impact.

Dating, parties, and informal social gatherings, common in the Western world, were all but unknown in China. The opportunities for casual meeting that did exist were found mainly in the cities. The agrarian population, the overwhelming majority of the population, continued to arrange marriages in the traditional manner.

In sum, the method of marital choice, as well as marriage customs, changed little throughout most of China. The less vigorous clans, however, declined in the face of industrialization and the attacks of the intelligentsia and the central government.

Some marriages were made in the modern way, and a study by Lang[28] offers some comparison between the old and the new. After interviewing 203 married college and high school students (194 men, 9 women), she categorized them into those whose marriages were arranged by their parents and who met their spouse for the first time only after the ceremony (87), those who saw their spouses prior to marriage and presumably exercised some choice although the parents officially chose the partners (53), and those who chose their own mates (48, although six of them had to obtain their parents' consent). Of the fully arranged marriages, only 31 percent of the respondents could be classified as satisfied with their marriages. In the middle group, 53 percent were satisfied, whereas in the free-choice group 80 percent were satisfied.

Regrettably, the methodology of this research is quite vague. How were the students selected? What precise meaning shall we attribute to "satisfaction"? How reliable were the measures? Yet, despite the absence of precision, the findings at least suggest that educated men largely supported the new marriage laws. Considering the lot of women, one may safely presume that their support was at least equally vigorous.

A 1925 Shanghai newspaper poll on attitudes toward polygyny while also lacking in scientific sophistication, revealed positive support for the new laws. Of 317 readers who replied, 84 percent of the women and 79 percent of the men were opposed to polygny.[29]

THE COMMUNIST LAWS

The coming to power of the Communists resulted in the Marriage Law of 1950, which added new provisions to the earlier Family Code. The more important changes included the raising of the minimum age for marriage to 20 years for men and 18 years for women, the necessity for both parties to register in person in the subdistrict or village in which they resided, and the awarding of the child (in the event of divorce) to either parent, based on the child's best interests.

The 1950 code, in short, underscored the concept that men and women have equal status, whereas the 1930 code had suggested that each family should have a head, implying that men usually occupy that position.[30] The 1950 code goes to great lengths to spell out every right of women, in contrast to the earlier one which gave only lukewarm support to these rights by not explicitly prohibiting them—for example, widows were not prohibited from marrying in the 1930 code, but custom would have strongly inhibited the likelihood. The 1950 code specifically states that widows are free to marry. The 1930 code required a woman to prefix her name with her husband's unless otherwise agreed upon, and it obligated the couple to live together except under unusual circumstances. The Communist code gives each party the right of name and makes no mention of habitation.

The Communist government, in sum, has added little to the 1930 code, but it has emphasized and enforced the laws much more strongly than the Nationalists did. At first there was widespread opposition to its implementation; officials were killed, and there was resistance in the villages.[31] Since 1953, however, efforts have been concentrated on education and persuasion rather than on strong-arm methods. Apparently this approach, conjoined with the fantastic rise in literacy (in 1958 alone, 100 million persons learned to read),[32] has resulted in substantial acceptance of the new law.

ATTITUDES TOWARD MARRIAGE UNDER THE COMMUNIST REGIME

It is difficult to gain a clear picture of marriage under the new regime because the Chinese have limited the amount and kind of interaction between themselves and the West. What is most readily available are analyses of Chinese films and magazines that amount to little more than propaganda, plus the occasional observations of Western newsmen who are restricted from full access in their search of a story.

All sources agree that the status of women has improved immeasurably. The law now guarantees equal economic opportunity, political rights, and freedom of divorce. Prostitutes have largely vanished from the coastal ports, to the discomfort of foreign sailors.[33] The modern Chinese woman, like the man, works full time, and the image of the woman as belonging exclusively in the household has been eradicated.

The power of parents to regulate their children's marriages has been greatly diminished; in the films, plays, and literature of the 1950s, parents were depicted as holding on to stubborn, feudal ideas to arrange marriages, while their progressive offspring fought for the new communist freedom of choice.[34] In the play *Chao Hsio-Lan,* by Chin Chien, the audience is treated to dialogue that would have been unthinkable a generation earlier.

The following excerpt concerns a village farmer, Chao, who refuses to accept the boy friend of his daughter Lan as a prospective son-in-law.

Chao (shouting after her): I'm telling you plainly, I wouldn't take Yung-kang for a son-in-law if he were a hundred times better than he is!

Your engagement has been arranged, it's all settled.

Lan (lifting the curtain over the door): Who settled it?

Chao: I did. Your father!

Lan: I didn't, and I don't care. (Disappearing into the inner room)

Chao (threatening): You just keep talking like that—

Mrs. Chao: Can't I even speak?

Chao (to the next room): Now get this straight. The engagement will take place today. They're sending some presents. The boy is the third son of Old Wei in the next village. He's a primary-school teacher. (In a softer tone) Of course no parents would let their child come to any harm. Just think of all the care we've given you, ever since you were a helpless baby. For years we've been looking forward to the day when you'd be grown up and married into a good family and we could feel easy about your future. But look how you've turned out—bold and willful. Come now, change your clothes. There are people coming from the boy's family in a moment. (Lan enters from the inner room)

Lan: I also want to make things clear. I don't agree. I'm against the whole thing one hundred percent. Let them send their presents. We'll see who goes as the bride.

Chao: You will—whether you want to or not.

Lan: The government will back me up.

Chao: If you let the village chairman hear about this I'll wring your neck.

Lan: You can beat me to death, but I'm not going to be the bride. (Goes into inner room)

Later on, Mei, the sister of Lan, returns to the brouhaha involving the disobedient Lan, who is now backed up by the chairman of the local village. Why is Mei so happy?

Mei (in high spirits): Ma, I've come back.

Mrs. Chao: Mei-lan, what makes you so happy today?

Chao (confidently): Mei-lan's marriage was also arranged by me. And see how happy she is!

Mei: Pa, I've got a divorce, why shouldn't I feel happy?

Chao: What? (Trembling with rage) So you're all rebelling? You . . . you . . . get out of my house! You're all rebelling!

Chairman (to Chao): Yes, they're all rebelling. It's feudal marriages they are rebelling against. Why shouldn't they? Marriage is something that affects their whole life. They're doing the right thing, making a clean break. Mei-lan, tell us in front of your Pa why you wanted the divorce.[35]

Despite the rather forceful attack on parental power, the government has more recently renewed the stress on filial piety.[36] One might argue that there is nothing strange about this fact. Filial piety is the traditional Chinese approach and, once the power of the parents to determine the marriage partner of their offspring had been broken, the policy of piety could be revived. But such an interpretation ignores the fact that a more Machiavellian motivation may account for the change in attitudes toward parents from the early to the late 1950s. Although the economic status of the average peasant has improved under communism, it can hardly be termed adequate by Western standards. Faced with continuing overpopulation, the government is hard pressed to feed and house its approximate 800 million people adequately. A return to Confucian piety would prove extremely helpful in shifting the burden of economic support of the old onto their children rather than onto the state. The sudden turn from negativism to a more positive attitude toward parents, therefore, might reflect the realization by the government that current economic resources do not permit a complete attack on the family as an enemy of the state. It has been possible, nevertheless, to attack "family individualism" in other ways.

"Free Choice" In Marriage, or the Renunciation of "Selfish Individualism"

The ending of "bourgeois" marriage in China did not lead to lascivious escapades, such as marked its official death in the Soviet Union in 1917. The Chinese have very carefully distinguished between free choice and free love. There does not appear to be much sexual license, and even casual flirtation is considered gauche.

In choosing a spouse, physical attractiveness is immaterial, and love is described in an official booklet as "a psychosomatic activity that consumes energy and wastes time."[37] Simone de Beauvoir further points out:

> Love does not appear to play a major role in the life of the young Chinese. For the Chinese woman the bed for so long signified a slavery so odious that her foremost preoccupation is to have no more of that constraint; it is not socialist enthusiasm that prevents her from dreaming of men, but she enthusiastically welcomes a socialism which frees her from men's clutches.
>
> For every Chinese woman, from the top to the bottom of the social scale, physical love has a negative coefficient. She must be entirely delivered from the weight of the past before she will be able to adopt a positive attitude when, instead of feeling pleased with herself for having escaped love, she will be free to love as she pleases.[38]

This does not mean that happiness is impossible in China. It is simply that "true" happiness "is based on spiritual rather than material enjoyment . . . on public rather than private interest . . . on collective welfare rather than on individual happiness . . . [and on] service for the people and the revolution over the cause of self-actualization and the welfare of one's own family."[39]

The literature amply documents this conclusion. In *The Wedding*, by Chao Li-po, the bride-to-be challenges the groom to a socialist work contest, and he skips the wedding ceremony because of more urgent work at the factory.[40] Another story deals with a marriage deeply in trouble despite the fact that the wife devotes herself completely to her husband and children and also works eight hours daily. When she plunges into committee work with new zeal and helps to turn out 10,000 transmitters in seven days, her husband begins to show revived interest in her.[41]

Even divorce is not a tragedy. Divorcees are told that "some people have the wrong idea thinking that because of divorce they are being deserted. This is wrong. . . . You must remember the great Organization; the big family of revolution will never forsake you, unless you forsake revolution. . . ."[42]

The subordination of family and individual interests to the needs of the collective is illustrated in other ways. Although the legal marriage age is 20 for men and 18 for women, increasing efforts have been made to limit birth by encouraging late marriages, including statements by gynecological experts that the best marriage age is 25 for a woman and about 27 for a man.[43] Production needs play a dominant role in the couple's life after marriage. It is not unknown for couples receiving job assignments in different cities to be separated for weeks, even months. Because of their involvement in the revolution, however, the Chinese seem to acquiesce to diminished family interaction.

The Ideal Spouse

One young commune woman listed her ideal husband as one who met the following criteria: he has correct thoughts, he labors actively; he loves the collective body.[44] A progressive bride is described as a girl who asks for three things for her dowry: "a rifle, a nightsoil pail ("nightsoil" is a Chinese euphemism for human excrement), and a copy of *Chairman Mao's Quotations.*"[45]

Shyness and modesty are valued in both boys and girls in interpersonal and family relations. To fulfill the model of the new woman, girls must now also possess the seemingly contradictory virtue of being *ta-fang,* socially expressive and competent.[46] Homogamy with respect to physical attractiveness, education, and socioeconomic class, all of which have been shown to be associated with material adjustment in the West, are officially disclaimed.[47] The *only* factor that counts is political compatibility, "a shared political consciousness that can lead to greater joint efforts in building socialism and increasing production."[48]

CONCLUSIONS

The Communist revolution has witnessed the final disintegration of the patriarchal-clan system. The ritual bond has been severed, and the head of the clan has recourse to few sanctions to support his exercise of authority. His wife can readily divorce him; his children can leave home with impunity. The wife has gained freedom, not only with respect to divorce but also in the area of equal education and economic opportunity.

The functions of the family have shrunk as the work group, the communal dining room, and the nursery have replaced individual economic effort, the single kitchen, and the parental rearing of children. Although the transformation is astounding in that the customs of many centuries have been reversed in the course of two decades, it is instructive to note that traditional habits are not fully discarded. The respect for authority has been retained, but the object of respect has shifted from one's parents to the government and to Mao Tse-tung. This transition was facilitated by the fact that, even in traditional society, the emperor was regarded as a father-figure. His officials were known as "parent officials" *(fee mee kuan)* and the populace was called "children people" *(tzu min).*[49]

The traditional Chinese focus on family welfare rather than on individual interests has been retained, with the necessary change from the narrow family to the collective family, that is, China. Although "free choice" in marriage might appear to be contrary to a conformist regime, it must be stressed that "free choice" refers to the *object* of the individual's marital intentions, not to the *style of his married life.* Extramarital adventures and preoccupation with nuclear family interests are frowned upon, and concern with family matters is deemphasized in comparison with the focus on concern for the state.

Even that vestige of feudalism, the matchmaker, has not disappeared. The populace is urged to consult Party officials about marital choice to ensure that the partner has "correct" thinking. The Party cadre has become the communist version of the one-time matchmaker.

In assessing the effect of communism on the Chinese family, it must be concluded that the radical reforms have met with considerable acceptance. For the moment, the emphasis on the equality of women and the correction of the exploitation of the peasantry have made available a vast body of labor to raise productivity. The absence of personal freedom is no great loss when the starvation and disease of earlier regimes, "the bitter past," are recalled. The real challenge to the government will come when sufficient economic comfort has been achieved and the luxury of freedom of individual behavior may be contemplated. Whether the frowned-upon individualistic, bourgeois "couple love" secretly exists, and whether it will return with the onset of the economic millennium, are moot points, and may be clarified in the near future, as communication broadens.

REFERENCES

1. M. Granet, *Chinese Civilization.*
2. W. Durant, *The Story of Civilization.*
3. D. Mace and V. Mace, *Marriage East and West.*
4. R. Wilhelm, "The Chinese conception of marriage."
5. O. Lang, *Chinese Family and Society.*
6. D. Mace and V. Mace, op cit.
7. P. Ho, "An historian's view of the Chinese family system."

8. H. Fei, "The case of the Chinese gentry."
9. F. L. K. Hsu, "The family in China: The classical form."
10. D. Blitsen, *The World of the Family.*
11. M. J. Levy, *The Family Revolution in Modern China,* p. 113.
12. F. L. K. Hsu, op. cit.
13. K. Kiang, "The Chinese family system," p. 41.
14. W. J. Goode, *World Revolution and Family Patterns.*
15. H. W. Liu, *The Traditional Chinese Clan Rules,* p. 79.
16. Ibid., p. 80.
17. N. Waln, *The House of Exile.*
18. Y. Lin, *The Golden Wing.*
19. O. Lang, op. cit., p. 38.
20. M. Freedman, "Ritual aspects of Chinese kinship and marriage."
21. C. K. Yang, *The Chinese Family in the Communist Revolution.*
22. O. Lang, op. cit.
23. E. A. Ross, "Sociological observations in inner China," p. 729.
24. W. J. Goode, op. cit.
25. M. Freedman, "The family in China, past and present," p. 330.
26. S. L. M. Fong, "Sex roles in the modern fabric of China."
27. O. Lang, op. cit.
28. Ibid.
29. Ibid.
30. M. H. Fried, "The family in China: The people's republic."
31. D. Mace and V. Mace. op. cit.
32. *Encyclopedia Britannica,* 1964.
33. P. Stafford, *Sexual Behavior in the Communist World.*
34. J. H. Weakland, "Conflicts between love and family relationships in Chinese films."
35. C. Chien, "Chao Hsio-Lan," pp. 21-22, 39.
36. P. Chao, "The Marxist doctrine and the recent development of the Chinese family in Communist China."
37. J. Marcuse, "The love affair of Comrade Wang," p. 46.
38. S. de Beauvoir, *The Long March,* pp. 153-154.
39. L. J. Huang, "Mate selection and marital happiness in the communist Chinese family," p. 5.
40. K. Mehnert, *Peking and Moscow.*
41. L. J. Huang, op. cit.
42. L. J. Huang, "Some changing patterns in the communist Chinese family," p. 143.
43. L. J. Huang, "Mate selection and marital happiness in the communist Chinese family."
44. Ibid., p. 8.
45. Ibid., p. 16.
46. A. S. Chin, "Family relations in modern Chinese fiction."
47. L. J. Huang, "Attitudes of the communist Chinese toward inter-class marriage."
48. J. Marcuse, op. cit., p. 45.
49. C. K. Yang, op. cit.

21
Japan: Confucius and Computers

Japan is of particular interest to students of the family because it is a unique example of a lineal family culture that developed under feudalism and was suddenly subjected to the strains of adjusting to a capitalist-industrial society. Certainly the Tokugawa period (1603-1867) represented a splendid example of a tightly controlled feudal system. The population was inculcated with the official ideology that loyalty to the overlord was no different than loyalty to the family. Japan has traditionally been a country where individualism was frowned upon as being detrimental to the interests of the *ie*, the family structure. Indeed, in a society where the family's importance was attested to, in the language, by the distinction between *Goko* (a regular household) and *Boko* (a dependent household subordinate to *Goko*,)* there was no word to describe the nuclear family.[1]

The patriarch possessed great power over the members of the *ie*, as well as responsibilities toward them. Nevertheless, his absolute power was tempered by custom and tradition, and by the fact that it was used only for the collective well-being rather than for personal reasons.[2] It is noteworthy that respect for authority was so deeply ingrained in most Japanese that when the exploited peasantry of the Tokugawa period finally revolted against the feudal hierarchy, their leaders would occasionally surrender to the authorities despite strong military positions. Apparently, the guilt engendered by revolt against the parent surrogate necessitated a personal sacrifice as payment for the disturbance of the "normal" state of affairs.[3]

The Meiji government's ascent to power in 1868 did not alter the identification of the family with the government. Within a short time an elaborate myth was promulgated: the emperor, claiming divine ancestry, was the head of the main family and the Japanese people were branch families, also deriving their ancestry from the Sun Goddess. Loyalty to the chief of state thus went beyond mere political allegiance, for he was also the mythical father of the nation.[4]

In other respects, however, the government, which had been opened to

*These terms are now obsolete.

486

Western influence and trade in the middle of the nineteenth century, showed a mixed reaction to proposed changes in family legislation. That Westerners had considerable technological superiority was hardly debatable, but the Western *style of life* provoked a rallying to the traditional family standards; hence the Civil Code of 1898 sought to strengthen the family by curtailing nonmonogamous practices while at the same time setting up the samurai pattern of marriage as the ideal for *all* Japanese people. This pattern extolled premarital chastity for women, formalism in family relations, subordination of individual desires to the family welfare, sex segregation in childhood, and strict role segregation for the sexes in adulthood.

Overt concubinage was the first casualty of the reform movement. Next, the wife's permission henceforth had to be secured before the husband's bastard could be legally adopted into the family. The progressive movement even suggested that adultery by the husband qualify as grounds for divorce along with the traditionally accepted grounds of adultery by the wife, but this proposal failed because the prevailing, masculine-dominated climate simply would not tolerate it. It was conceded, however, that the eldest daughter had the right to succeed to the position of family head if no living legitimate or illegitimate male offspring was available.

At the same time, the traditional allegiance to the *ie,* adopted from the feudal warrior class, was now legalized and strengthened. Under this system the eldest son, even after marriage, remained with his parents to inherit the estate and headship of the *ie* when his father died.[5] All other offspring also remained in the original household or received permission to marry and leave the household to form branch families. Although the branch families were relatively independent, close emotional ties with the main family continued, and various services were obligatory for both families.

The head of the *ie* not only led in the rites of ancestor worship but took the responsibility of providing for the continuation of the *ie,* whose extinction would affect the welfare of his own family and of the branch families. Continuation was assured by the birth of at least one male child—preferably several, for the death rate was high. In the event of there being no legitimate offspring, a male not related by blood—for example, a son-in-law or a nonfamily person—or even one of the patriarch's illegitimate sons, might be adopted. To assure continuation of the estate intact, male primogeniture was practiced; upon the death of the patriarch, the widow did not inherit and, together with the inheritance, passed to the care of the eldest son.[6] In the event of marital breakup, continuation of the *ie* necessitated that the children stay with the father.

The primary intent of the Civil Code was to entrench Confucian ideology more strongly in the family,[7] but the doctrine of reciprocal obligations placed its harshest demands on children and women. Children owed their parents complete obedience, as did younger siblings to older ones. The woman was taught to obey her father in childhood, to be a loyal and submissive wife to her husband, and, when he died, to revere her eldest son. Women were generally regarded as being intellectually inferior to men and as being prone to such unattractive behavior as jealousy and slander. Men, on the other hand, were perceived as noble, courageous, intelligent, and dignified. Such disparate sexes were, in the best samurai tradition, carefully segregated and educated apart from each other.

HUSBAND AND WIFE

The marital relationship was marked by social and emotional distance. Sex was not sinful, but the passive-masochistic role of women was not conducive to sexual enjoyment for either partner; however, men, as the superior sex, were permitted to indulge themselves in brothels in order to maintain the purity of the home. Love was regarded as the puerile emotion of an inferior being toward a superior one, and no self-respecting man would allow his dignity and standing to be impaired by emotional demonstrations toward his wife. In fact, even if he did feel positively toward her, it would be expressed only in the privacy of the home. It was considered good form for a man to berate his wife in front of guests, so as to demonstrate that he was truly the master.[8]

The social lives of husband and wife in the idealized samurai tradition were completely independent; a man seen on the street accompanied by his wife would be considered a sorry figure.

The Civil Code of 1898 underscored the low status of the wife by asserting that her right to maintenance was only third in priority after the man's parents and children. The code also prevented any presumptive heir from leaving the family to enter another via marriage or adoption. In effect, therefore, two only children could not marry.

In a seemingly progressive stance, the code permitted men of 30 and women of 25 to marry without the permission of the head of the family. This freedom was more theoretical than actual, however, for by controlling all family property as well as the allegiance of all its members, a patriarch could easily make a rebellious members's position untenable.

The effect of the code was to identify samurai customs, as well as selected Western ones, as national laws and to spread their influence among the lower classes, which had hitherto hardly aspired to such customs. The rural classes, however, did not emphasize chastity for women or the segregation of the sexes to the extent that their urban brethren did, for the poverty and working conditions of the farmers did not make these customs very practical. Nevertheless, samurai customs became the national ideology, if not the national practice.

The Japanese family, in the years before and after the enactment of the Civil Code, reflected the firm position of the patriarch. He was served first at dinner, and he ate better food than the rest of the family. Family members or servants handed him whatever he needed rather than oblige him to get something for himself. The family assembled in the front hall to greet him on his return from work, and he bathed in the evening before the rest of the family could do so.

Most servile of all was his wife. Starting with a deferential bow, which was several notches lower than his own, she always referred to him in the third person as *shujin* (master)[9]; he called her *kanai* (wife). When the couple went to town, she always walked discreetly several paces behind him. In the morning she was the first to get up so that he might not see her in a disheveled condition; and so that she could prepare the family meal. At night she dared not retire before him, lest she be called an idle wife.

It would be an exaggeration, however, to conclude that the wife's lot was no better than that of a menial. Once she had produced a male heir her status improved, and when her mother-in-law died she became the lady of the house. The strict demarcation of masculine and feminine roles meant in effect that she could manage her household affairs with little interference. And since she usually handled the financial matters of the house, her role was more active than the official Confucian ideology suggested.[10]

We have already alluded to the lack of social interaction between husband and wife. In addition, she had little social contact with nonfamily members and was effectively tied to the home for a multitude of reasons. For example, Japanese men love pickles, and to make them at home was the special prerogative of the wife. The job was not easy, requiring that the solution in which the cucumbers were kept be stirred twice a day, thus preventing a wife from straying too far from the house.[11] After the children came, she was more firmly tied down than before. Parent-child relationships were recognized as more important than husband-wife relationships; as the ancient Japanese proverb said, "the womb is only borrowed" but "nothing can break the bond between parent and child."[12] In fact, a man mourned 13 months for his parents but only 3 for his wife.

At night the baby slept snugly between the couple. The Japanese have never regarded this as an intrusion, for the philosophy of family collectivism is much stronger than that of parental privacy, and most Japanese parents find it incredible that Americans can leave their children with a baby-sitter who is scarcely more than a stranger.[13] Such action is viewed as a travesty of Confucian ethics, which demands the subordination of personal pleasures to the raising of children.

There were even more powerful and subtle reasons for a close mother-child relationship. When the bride came to her new household, she came as a stranger and had to adapt to the habits of older people who were very set in their ways. Married to a man who was probably not in love with her and, in any event, more devoted to his parents, the new wife could not expect much support from anyone in the family. The birth of a child, however, especially a male, constituted a step toward acceptance in the family, making it unlikely that she would be returned for displeasing one of her in-laws. Moreover, her own child would be the first person over whom she could exercise any power.

It should also be noted that the absence of social interaction or expression of affection between husband and wife could not but influence relations in the marital bed. With one or two children in their bed, and in a room that had paper-thin walls, complete privacy during the sex act was often not achieved. Pressed by the need for speed and little concerned about the sexual satisfaction of a wife who was culturally defined as self-abnegating, the husband waited his chance until the lights were turned out. Then, lying on his side and grasping his wife in sexual embrace (often from the rear in order to minimize noise), he obtained orgasm as speedily as possible and settled back under his quilts.[14,15] The pent-up sexual tension of wives, deflected as libido to the normal emotional bond of mother and child, led to an extremely powerful feeling of love toward the one object for which society sanctioned open emotional expression. The wife stayed at home, the children at her side, and rarely ventured further than the marketplace. The husband, on the other hand, was free to dine out with friends; even on ordinary workdays it often took him two to three hours to wend his way home.[16]

THE JAPANESE MARRIAGE PROCEDURE

Growing up completely segregated from each other in school and at play, Japanese young people enjoyed few opportunities for premarital contact. Since marriage was of immense importance to the family, the choice of partner could never be left to immature youth, but had to be primarily the responsibility of parents. Families avoided direct dealings with each other, lest one family risk the grave insult of rejection. To avoid such embarrassment, a go-between, the *nakodo,* conducted the arrangements. Although the origin of this role probably goes back to antiquity, the presence of the *nakodo* seems to have strongly manifested itself only since industrialization.

The role of matchmaker is highly regarded, and a Japanese proverb says that every man or woman should serve in this role at least three times in his life. Many *nakodo* are friends or relatives of the family and act in that capacity only when requested to do so. Others are semiprofessionals: they have arranged hundreds of marriages and receive a proportion of the marriage expenses as a "present" or fee.[17]

The three basic functions of the *nakodo* are to introduce the participants, to negotiate the conditions, and to perform a ceremonial function at the wedding. The process usually began with a "social" visit to the *nakodo* by the girl's mother. If the *nakodo* impressed her, the mother casually mentioned that she had a daughter of marriageable age and the *nakodo* decided whether or not to commit himself to the case. If he did, he might resort to his stock of photos of eligible men. Since the woman's physical appearance was important, he might arrange to have the mother go for a walk with the daughter at a prearranged time, so that the prospective groom could unobtrusively view the candidate.

If physical appearance was no problem, the preferred next step was to call in another *nakodo* to represent the man's family, and for each *nakodo* to investigate the qualifications of both sides in more detail. The objective criteria to consider were the family's socioeconomic position as well as its status and lineage. Also important was the health of the potential spouse and the possibility of genetic taint. Was there a history of fertility and especially of healthy sons? Were any ancestors "outcasts"? Were there indices of intelligence and domestic ability for the woman? Did she have a diploma for the tea ceremony and flower arrangement? Was she suitably docile? For the man, a primary consideration was his ability to provide financially for the family, his integrity, his willingness to work hard, and his reliability.

If all the qualities were acceptable, a formal introduction, *miai,* was held, with the potential couple, their parents, the *nakodo(s),* and, sometimes, representatives of the family in attendance. Although efforts were made to keep the conversation light and social, too much was at stake to permit really spontaneous chit-chat. The main participants, who were on trial, were often extremely stiff and forced in their interaction. Despite the light-hearted atmosphere, the *miai* was public recognition that a marriage *could* be in the offing. Nevertheless, the official social character of the *miai* permitted either party to break off negotiations. A socially acceptable reason, such as incompatible horoscopes, might be offered without loss of face. However, anyone who became a "veteran" of several *miai* would find it difficult to find other families willing to risk the embarrassment of potential rejection.

Assuming that the *nakodo's* interrogations of the neighbors and the employer of the young man revealed no hidden defects, that the *miai* was successful, and that the monetary negotiations between the parents were concluded satisfactorily, the wedding could proceed.

The main participants at the ceremony were a female pourer of *sake,* the go-between or the priest, and the bride and groom. The pourer went through the motions of pouring the *sake* into the cups of the bride, groom, and *nakodo.* Each made motions of drinking from the cup three times. After nine sips, a tray of food was placed before the couple. Although etiquette forbade their actually eating the food, the ritual of eating and drinking in public was in essence the marriage ceremony.[18]

Sometimes, despite the earnest attempts of parents to arrange the marriage, a boy and a girl might meet and fall in love without benefit of a *miai.* The behavior of the parents, if the relationship could not be broken off, was exactly the opposite of that in the United States. Love is the primary acceptable criterion for marriage in the United States, and if an American marries without being in love (a marriage of "convenience"), he finds it necessary to avoid embarrassment by feigning love. In Japan, however, in order to avoid embarrassment the couple were often forced to contact the *nakodo* and subject themselves to the *miai* in order to go through the semblance of an arranged marriage. To appreciate the force of social pressure, it is only necessary to consider the case of a university professor who decided to marry during World War II. Applying to the municipality for his wedding rice-wine ration, it was noted that in the space reserved for the name of the *nakodo* he had written "none." The official, apparently holding the view that a wedding without a *nakodo* was no wedding at all, refused to approve the professor's ration until he put down some name in the space.[19]

STABILITY OF MARRIAGE

The divorce rate prior to the Civil Code was as high as 340 per 1,000 marriages in 1897, and declined steadily until 1940, when it hit a low of 76 per 1,000 marriages.[20] The initially high divorce rate had to do with the nonsacramental nature of marriage, the lack of governmental concern with it, and the low status of women. Divorce occurred most frequently by mutual consent; in effect, this meant that the husband's family, if displeased with the wife, would send her back. There were two major requirements of a bride[21]: that she be an efficient homemaker and that she please her mother-in-law. Failure at either might be grounds for divorce.

Technically, the wife could sue for divorce because of unusually bad treatment by the husband, but in practice her economic defenselessness, plus the social stigma attached to a divorcee, made divorce a male prerogative. Divorce was not viewed as negatively as it was in the West, for it did not signify the breakup of the family—only the dismissal of an unwanted wife. She was not difficult to replace and, in the meantime, the *ie,* including the husband, continued to live as usual.

The decline of the divorce rate after the onset of the Civil Code was probably due to the adoption of the samurai code, which emphasized family stability, a later age for marriage, and the unwillingness of families in a commercial economy to have a daughter resettle with them.[22] The low divorce rate during the first six decades of the twentieth century, however, has probably been underestimated because, in the rural areas, couples often did not register marriages until a child was born and therefore could send a childless wife back to her people without having to register a divorce.[23]

THE NEW ERA IN MARRIAGE AFTER WORLD WAR II

The Japanese government had sought to tie filial fidelity to allegiance to the emperor and thus to the government. Japan's defeat by the Allies now rebounded to discredit the ancient *ie* tradition, and there was surprisingly little opposition to the radical innovations introduced by Douglas MacArthur as commander of the occupying force. In fact, the new code imposed little on the

Japanese, for it was in complete harmony with the progressive forces in family legislation which had been suppressed by the military caste when it came to power in the 1930s. Article 24 of the new Code clearly stipulated:

> Marriage shall be based only on the mutual consent of both sexes and it shall be maintained through mutual cooperation with the equal rights of husband and wife as a basis. Laws shall be enacted considering choice of spouse, property rights, inheritance, choice of domicile, divorce and other matters pertaining to marriage and the family from the standpoint of individual dignity and the essential equality of the sexes.[24]

Moreover, the "essential equality" of the sexes was enforced by canceling the husband's right to restrict his wife's property rights, by making adultery a cause of divorce for both sexes, and by putting an end to the wife's legal obligation to accept her husband's bastard into the family. Parental consent for marriage was not needed after the age of 20; below that age, the consent of one parent sufficed.[25] In addition, the eldest son no longer inherited all of the land, since inheritance was on an equal basis. The power of the *ie* and of the patriarch had seemingly received a crushing blow.

To assess the impact of the new legislation, of industrialization, and of ideological changes on marriage and the traditional organization of the family, we shall focus primarily on attitude surveys and other research findings.

Primogeniture. Despite legislation ending primogeniture, a considerable number of Japanese families have continued the practice, not only out of respect for the old ways, but because small landholdings cannot be farmed profitably by subdividing them among several children. The legal ploy used is to have each heir renounce his inheritance in favor of the eldest son.[26] The efficiency of this system depends on the cooperation of the younger members of the household, and a considerable number have refused to do so. It is reasonably safe to conclude that eventually the practice of primogeniture will disappear.

Equality between the sexes. Observation of the family in postwar Japan shows that parents still indulge boys much more than girls.[27] In an investigation of the perception of the concepts of "man" and "woman" across the American, Dutch, Flemish, French, Finnish, Japanese, and Kannada Indian cultures, one study found that only in the Japanese culture did the concept of "man" rate higher than that of "woman."[28] Other surveys reported that Japanese women students had quite egalitarian attitudes, while Japanese men did not.[29,30] Finally, in a survey of the attitudes of 5,000 Japanese high school and college students, the late R. E. Baber asked them whether they would rather be a girl or a boy. Approximately 95 percent of the boys preferred to be boys, and about 70 percent of the girls would also have preferred to be boys.[31] It would seem, therefore, that functional equality of the sexes is far from achieved.

Parent-child relationships. In Baber's survey, about 75 percent of the boys and girls said that in three-quarters of the families they knew, the parent-child relationship was stronger than the husband-wife one. However, four out of five thought that parental influence had decreased since the War, and only slightly less than half thought that married children should live with parents. In case of a quarrel between a spouse and a parent, more than four-fifths thought that the man should support his spouse.

The parents themselves seem to be decreasingly enthusiastic about the prospect of living with children in their old age. A survey found 55 percent willing to do so in 1950, but only 39 percent in 1959.[32]

"Love" marriage versus "arranged" marriage. Before the War, "love" marriages were a rarity. During the 1920s a man's body was discovered, and it was not immediately apparent whether it was murder, suicide, or accidental. Examination of the body revealed a photo of the man's wife, whereby the diagnosis of suicide was made. Apparently, no one in his right mind would carry a picture of his wife![33]

The Japanese tend to think that Americans expect too much from marriage.[34] In the above-mentioned cross-cultural survey, the Japanese evaluated "marriage" less highly than any of the six other countries sampled, with the exception of the Kannada Indians. When it came to an evaluation of "love," however, their evaluation was *lowest of all.*[35]

Despite this low evaluation, several surveys have shown that the vast majority of youth want to marry for love.[36] Part of the apparent contradiction lies in one's definition of love. Consider the reaction of a Japanese professor who learned to his dismay that his nephew had fallen in "love." After agreeing to the role of *nakodo,* his investigation turned out as follows: "I was pleasantly surprised to find that this was a pure love, based only on occasional glances at each other on the streetcar which both rode every day. There were no conversations, no dates, no intimacy. I felt that such a couple should marry because this was not a sordid love affair involving pleasure and self-indulgence in which people have already reaped rewards. Rather, this was a restrained, self-disciplined, spiritual love."[37]

Ambivalence toward love marriages sometimes reflects the strength of emotional dependence on parents. One research team decided to investigate attitudes toward love matches by means of both direct and disguised tests, using rural inhabitants as subjects. Although the majority favored "love" marriages on the direct questionnaire-type test, in the most disguised test, in which the subjects made up stories about pictures of people, strong internalized sanctions against "love" marriages were revealed.[38] Such contradictory expressions help to explain Baber's finding that over 80 percent of the girls in his survey were torn between self-reliance and dependence on their parents in choosing a spouse. The majority of his student subjects felt that in a conflict between parents and children over marital choice, the children's choice should prevail. However, for both sexes, the majority wished to make the choice conjointly with their parents rather than separately. More recent research has compared the courtship practices of husbands born between 1921 and 1935 with those of their fathers.

The chief decision maker in recent marriages has been the son himself, although the father often has the final say.[39]

Attitudes toward the nakodo *and* miai. In a truly "free-choice" society, there should be little need for a *nakodo;* thus, attitudes toward the *nakodo* should reveal the depth of the "marriage-for-love" movement. While only about 3 percent of Baber's students found the *nakodo* essential for marriage, about 80 percent found him either "convenient" or "a nice formality," and only about 15 percent thought that the role should be abolished. Estimates of the number of marriages in which the *nakodo* plays a role vary,[40-42] but he would now appear to participate in less than half of them.

As urbanization and industrialization accelerate, the role of the *nakodo* is increasingly being played by a man's business supervisor.[43] The transition is made easier by the fact that Japanese industrial concerns are among the most paternalistic in the world, with each employee enjoying life "tenure."[44]

The function of the *miai* has changed much in recent years. At one time a positive arrangement at or prior to the *miai* meant that the marriage would take place in a short time, but today the *miai* is not quite as binding. A considerable number of persons participate in more than one *miai,*[45] and it is now perceived as the beginning of a new phase in the relationship—dating. Indeed, marriage bureaus, private and public, now interview prospective marriage applicants, recording their income, health, likes and dislikes, and the kind of partner desired, and then arrange a *miai.*[46] The *miai's* present-day function is to pair off marriageable persons while permitting them to date each other sufficiently so that they can determine if they are really compatible. For many Japanese, dating is much too intimate to be separated from marriage, and even as late as 1959 most Japanese students had never had a single premarital date.[47] In a study published in 1957, it was reported that by age 18 the proportion of Japanese boys and girls who had ever been kissed was only 10 percent, as compared to 90 percent in the United States.[48] The situation has changed considerably since then, and boys and girls now are not only more likely to have kissed, but many may sometimes be seen walking hand in hand, which was unheard of a short time ago.[49]

It may be concluded, therefore, that the *nakodo* has weathered the changes in marriage ideology by modifying his role to permit freer interaction between a couple. While a good many couples date without benefit of a *miai,* the continued existence of this institution probably signifies that the present industrial age has failed to provide the opportunity for young people to meet potential marriage partners in a socially approved manner. A professor Hidaka and his wife, and a wealthy architect, Takeda, offer "Hidaka" and "Takeda" parties to provide young people with a chance to meet. The publicity given these "dating" parties accents the absence of social organizations and youth clubs that have served this purpose in the United States. Greater dating contacts are rapidly being achieved by coeducation in the public schools, and future contact between the sexes will be more spontaneous.

Although marital choice is increasingly determined by the participants, the desire by many youths to make the selection of a partner a cooperative effort between parent and child may seem strange to the Western reader. The explanation probably lies in the fact that Japan's culture does not encourage self-reliance in childhood. In Western cultures a child often believes that he must achieve his identity (selfhood) by successfully resisting the efforts of his parents to regulate his life. In Japanese culture, selfhood is achieved by fulfilling the demands of one's role.[50] Those of a child are to be dutiful and respectful toward one's parents; hence it would be incorrect and anxiety-provoking for the child to ignore his parents totally when choosing a marital partner.

Further, the effects of Japanese child-rearing help to promulgate a kind of emotional dependency (particularly on the part of sons toward mothers[51] — *amaeru,* which is defined by Dei as "to depend and presume on another's benevolence."[52] This emotional need has permeated most adults in Japan today and serves to lessen the impact of the striving for independence seen in adolescents in the United States.

The popularity of the new Seichō-no-Ie religious organizations is in part due to their sensitivity to the disparate pulls of adherence to the traditional ie role and the new opportunities for independence for youth.[53] The religion tries to point out the identity of goals of self and those of the family, and thus stimulates self-reevaluation and a mitigation of guilt on the part of those who have strayed from the traditional path.

The relationship between husband and wife. In some ways there has been a great shift away from the traditional patriarchal conception of husband-wife relations. The Japanese say that "since World War II, women and stockings have become strong."[54] Thirty-one percent of the husbands in one study approved husbands aiding their wives in the kitchen, whereas only 42 percent disapproved.[55] Many husbands accept the idea that their wives work, and the number of such wives has been increasing each year. The sight of husband and wife together in town is no longer noteworthy, and some wives even precede their husbands into taxis. The rural areas are much more conservative. Sixty percent of rural wives, in a Ministry of Labor poll, said that they absolutely never went to the cinema or to any place of amusement with their spouses, whereas only 21 percent of Tokyo residents replied in the same vein.[56] A considerable drop in the percentage of wives who serve their husbands first at mealtime has also been noted.

The democratization of role-functioning has not led to much fraternization between husband and wife. Even in enlightened college circles, few wives know each other because Japanese women seldom attend social functions. Men usually go to parties and to the theater by themselves or with friends, while women stay at home with the children. A survey showed that only 6 percent of married couples had mutual friends come to dinner.[57]

Another survey of well-to-do professionals showed little difference in openness between talking with one's wife and with "others." In both cases, feelings and

鈴木春信画

Japanese courting couple in traditional costumes. (Colored print by Harunobu)

personal problems were rarely discussed. A similar group of American men showed little more openness than their Japanese counterparts in talking to "others," but significantly more willingness to discuss feelings and problems with their wives.[58] It is small wonder, then, that when one woman in a Japanese survey heard that a husband and wife were going on a trip together for a few days, she remarked, "How nice!" Later, she asked, "But what would they talk about for so long?"[59] Apparently, the gains in greater role flexibility and role status by Japanese women have not yet led to greater emotional closeness between husband and wife, as in the United States.

The study by Blood, in which he compared "love-match" couples with "arranged marriage" mates, enables us to determine whether the presumably greater interaction of the former resulted in more marital satisfaction. The result, in the case of couples married nine years or more, showed that *miai* husbands were the happiest of the lot, followed by the "love-match" wives and "love-match" husbands, respectively, while the *miai* wives were least satisfied. Apparently, therefore, for men the emotional interaction at the cost of giving up the traditional privileges associated with "arranged marriage" is not as satisfactory as the retention of the traditional masculine role. For women, for whom emotional closeness is often more meaningful than for men, the love match offers many more rewards than the more stultifying traditional match.

Position of wife versus that of mother-in-law. It would be expected that the improved economic and political status of the wife would alter the age-old position of inferiority in the household, particularly with respect to the mother-in-law. In support of this belief, one Japanese observer concludes that there is no longer any question but that "the wife is much stronger than the mother of her husband."[60]

Divorce. It might have been expected that the divorce rate in Japan would rise significantly with the achievement of greater socioeconomic and political equality for women, but this has not occurred. The Japanese rate has remained at about 0.8 per 1,000 population for the last two decades, and for 1971 showed a modest rise to about 0.96[61] —between a third and a fourth of the U.S. figure.

The continued low divorce rate may be attributed in part to the fact that not every wife works, and the economic status of the population until recently has been too low to support separated households. Further, over 90 percent of divorces are still by mutual consent and without court action,[62] attesting to the lack of financial support that can be gained by going to court. Those women who do go to court may receive a lump sum of money. Since alimony as such is not recognized, the impetus toward divorce is lessened.

The lack of orientation toward individual needs is seen in the divorce court's appointment of a conciliation committee to handle all divorce actions coming to its attention. The conciliators are distinguished members of the community, without necessarily any particular training in family matters.[63] The decisions reached often emphasize the traditional Japanese call for compromise and conciliation on the part of both parties, with little consideration for individual problems. There is, however, a growing awareness of the need for professional skill in this area, and such an orientation may be expected in the future.

Last, the old *ie* tradition of a dutiful wife offers some support to unhappy women; they can achieve a measure of satisfaction in fulfilling the wifely role even if they are unhappy about the quality of their relationship with their spouse. However, it is doubtful that tradition will hold the divorce rate down much longer, for Japanese women are making gains in economic power and can observe on their television sets and in their reading material the gains made by women elsewhere.

CONCLUSIONS

Several Japanese authors have explicitly[64] or implicitly[65] stated that current Japanese family behavior is the result of industrialization and urbanization rather than Westernization. This conclusion may be somewhat extreme. There is evidence of extensive Western and, in particular, American influence in a wide variety of data—from the Civil Code of 1947 to operations that "Westernize" the breasts and eyes of Japanese women, and to the Japanese rock-and-roll bands chanting English words they do not understand.

It would not be unfair, however, to suggest that Western standards have influenced the *instrumental* role of Japanese women more than their *expressive* role. It has become possible for women to vote, to work, and to gain full legal status, changes which have undermined the age-old *ie* tradition that placed them at the bottom of the family power hierarchy. The *expressive* or interpersonal functions of women and men, however, are more dependent on cultural learning and traditions, and yield more slowly than do the instrumental roles—hence the relative lack of social and emotional interaction between husband and wife, though anachronistic, is understandable. In the years ahead, it is to be expected that the quality of the interaction will reflect a more equal status of the husband and wife, and that as the *ie* tradition subsides and urbanization and geographic mobility increase, the husband-wife bond will absorb the emotional commitment that once resided mainly in parental and peer relationships.

REFERENCES

1. M. Kurokawa, "Lineal orientation in child rearing among Japanese."
2. E. C. Masuoka, I. Masuoka, and N. Kawamura, "Role conflicts in the modern Japanese family."
3. M. J. Levy, "Contrasting factors in the modernization of China and Japan."
4. F. Isono, "The family and women in Japan."
5. K. Ariga, "The family in Japan."
6. E. F. Vogel, "The Japanese family."

7. A. M. Bacon, *Japanese Girls and Women.*
8. R. O. Blood, Jr., *Love Match and Arranged Marriage.*
9. T. Koyama, "The changing social position of women in Japan."
10. E. F. Vogel, op. cit.
11. E. H. Cressy, *Daughters of Changing Japan.*
12. R. P. Dore, *City Life in Japan,* p. 98.
13. R. O. Blood, Jr., op. cit.
14. R. K. Beardsley, J. W. Hall, and R. E. Ward, *Village Japan.*
15. G. De Vos and H. Wagatsuma, "Status and role behavior in changing Japan."
16. E. F. Vogel, *Japan's New Middle Class: The Salary Man and His Family in a Tokyo Suburb.*
17. E. F. Vogel, "The go-between in a developing society: The case of the Japanese marriage arranger."
18. R. K. Beardsley et al., op. cit.
19. R. P. Dore, op. cit.
20. E. C. Masuoka et al., op. cit.
21. W. J. Goode, *World Revolution and Family Patterns,* p. 359.
22. I. Taeuber, *The Population of Japan.*
23. W. J. Goode, op. cit.
24. K. Steiner, "The revision of the civil code of Japan: Provisions regarding the family."
25. R. P. Dore, op. cit.
26. S. Koyano, "Changing family behavior in four Japanese communities."
27. B. T. Chandler, *Japanese Family LIfe.*
28. C. E. Osgood, "Cross-cultural comparability in attitude measurement via multilingual semantic differentials."
29. A. Arkoff, G. Meredith, and S. Iwahara, "Male-dominant and equalitarian attitudes in Japanese, Japanese-American, and Caucasian-American students."
30. S. Iwahara, "Marriage attitudes in Japanese college students."
31. R. E. Baber, *Youth Looks at Marriage and the Family.*
32. S. Koyano, op. cit.
33. R. P. Dore, op. cit.
34. M. Evans, "Marriage, Japanese style."
35. C. E. Osgood, op. cit.
36. H. Wagatsuma and G. De Vos, "Attitudes towards arranged marriage in rural Japan."
37. R. O. Blood, Jr., op cit., p. 95.
38. H. Wagatsuma and G. De Vos, op. cit.
39. K. Morioka, "Changing patterns of mate selection."
40. E. F. Vogel, "The go between in a developing society."
41. E. Chapin, "Japanese prince meets girl (by go-between)."
42. "Japanese still follow Shinto wedding customs."
43. E. C. Masuoka et al., op. cit.
44. T. O. Wilkinson, "Family structure and industrialization in Japan."
45. R. O. Blood, Jr., op. cit.
46. "Marriage in Japan takes a new tack."
47. R. O. Blood, Jr., op. cit.

48. S. Asayama, "Comparison of sexual development of American and Japanese adolescents."
49. G. De Vos and H. Wagatsuma, op. cit.
50. J. Pelzel, "Japanese kinship: A comparison."
51. T. Sofue, "Some questions about Hsu's hypotheses: Seen through Japanese data."
52. L. T. Doi, " 'Amae': A key concept for understanding Japanese personality structure," p. 132.
53. H. Wimberly, "Self-realization and the ancestors: An analysis of two Japanese ritual procedures for achieving domestic harmony."
54. "Mrs. Sato holds mirror to Japan."
55. T. Koyama, op. cit.
56. Ibid.
57. R. P. Dore, op. cit.
58. F. Massarik, " 'Saying what you feel': Reflections on personal openness in Japan."
59. R. O. Blood, Jr., op. cit.
60. K. Tanaka and S. Sugiyama, "Power structure of family members in urban areas of Japan," p. 25.
61. "Japanese still follow Shinto wedding customs."
62. D. Mace and V. Mace, *Marriage: East and West.*
63. L. Olson, *Dimensions of Japan.*
64. F. Isono, op. cit.
65. T. Yamane and H. Nonoyama, "Isolation of the nuclear family and kinship organization in Japan."

22
Marriage in Black Africa

Africa has undergone profound political changes since World War II, with concomitant changes in family concepts and relations. In this chapter we shall consider both the traditional black African village marriage and the innovations stemming from industrialization, urbanization and, to a lesser degree, Christianity.

Because of the innumerable tribal societies in Africa and the fact that no two marriage patterns are identical, we shall focus on the more important and more prevalent customs rather than on any one given society. Nevertheless, it should be borne in mind that there are exceptions in our generalizations with respect to a number of societies.

POLYGYNY

A key distinction between Western and African marriage is the monogamy in the former and the polygyny in the latter. The fact that most Africans have only one wife reflects an economic limitation rather than a desired state. In a survey by Murdock,[1] polygyny proved to be the ideal in 88 percent of 154 societies studied. About a third of male Africans are polygynous, and the mean number of wives per married man is 1.5.[2] Where do these "extra" women come from? The typical woman marries between the ages of 15 and 20, whereas the typical groom is well over 25. This age disparity is a function of the bride-price, which we shall discuss shortly. In any event, fewer men than women are available for marriage between the ages of 15 and 25.[3]

The advocates of polygyny maintain that it satisfies a man's vanity and sexual appetite, provides every woman with a husband, and cuts down on illegitimacy. In addition, mothers often nurse their children until the age of two or three; many tribes forbid intercourse during this time, for it is feared that the semen will enter the body fluids and poison the milk.[4] The availability of other wives, it is argued, serves to diminish the probability that the husband will seek extramarital contacts. Another claimed salutary effect of polygyny is that widows are often absorbed into the family of the son or brother of the deceased, especially if they have not reached the menopause.[5] Also, by creating bonds between families, polygyny reduces family feuds[6] and greatly increases the prospects of adding children to the family, a very important factor for Africans.[7] Last, the existence of polygyny in no way prevents the choice of a monogamous life for those who are so inclined.

Polygyny has been strongly opposed by Christians on religious grounds, as well as by advocates of women's rights, who consider it a mark of subjugation. Under polygyny, it is not uncommon for women to take lovers if a spouse fails to satisfy their sexual needs. There is often intense competition and strife among the co-wives—not so much because of sexual jealousy but rather because of concern about the position of their children in the polygynous hierarchy of inheritance.

Although the number of polygynous marriages may be slightly on the wane,[8] the ideology is far from dead. The deleterious effect of expensive city living and Western Christian influence on polygyny have been counteracted by the emerging chauvinistic adoration of everything indigenous to Africa—thus the 1969 Pan-African Cultural Congress strongly affirmed its support of polygyny.[9]

Love has never been a focal point of traditional African marriage. Every woman expected to marry; the *sine qua non* of her existence was to bear children and to function as a wife in a household. The bride and groom might have been betrothed to each other as children,[10,11] or they might have met at religious festivals, in social contacts between age-group clubs, in the marketplace, or at neighbors' homes.[12] In some societies, particularly matrilineal ones, cross-cousin marriages of a man to his maternal uncle's daughter were highly esteemed.[13] Since the groom would inherit from this uncle, it was thought fitting to cement the alliance with a marriage. While the participants were generally not forced to marry someone they disliked, they often welcomed the assistance of parents and relatives in making a match. Although the young man and woman themselves might initiate the interaction that could lead to marriage, their parents invariably played a major role because of the phenomenon of the bride-price.

BRIDE-PRICE

The bride-price is the giving of compensation—in the form of livestock, implements, or cash—to the father of the bride as part of the marriage procedure. In some African societies the practice of payments or "gifts" continues for years and years, an indication that black African marriage is often a process rather than an event. The process involves prescribed behavior by the two families involved, as a result of which the relationship between the bride and groom and between their respective families is intricately woven together ever more firmly.

The bride-price in no way means that the woman has been purchased as chattel. Its significance is quite complex: it may be considered as indemnity to the parents for the loss of their daughter—both in the economic sense and, in a patrilineal society, in the lineal sense as well. In some tribes a counterpayment is expected, which, while usually lower in value than the bride-price, may be of sufficient size to negate the economic consideration in the marriage. Further, the cost of the feast, which often lasts for days, serves to diminish the economic focus of the marriage.

The bride-price also represents the parents' consent to the marriage and is tangible proof that the two families are bound together. It establishes the worth of the bride in the eyes of the groom's family, and is a guarantee against maltreatment by him or his family. If the marriage breaks up through no fault of the bride, the bride-price, often a considerable sum, may not be refunded.

The father of the bride distributes the cattle or other livestock among various relatives according to prescribed rules. The livestock may come from the groom's relatives as well as from his father, thus ensuring the interest of the relatives in maintaining the marriage, for if the bride-price is refunded, an accounting could be quite complicated after several years have elapsed.

The bride-price payment grants the husband both exclusive sexual rights and the usual domestic attention. In the lineal and emotional sense, however, the wife often maintains strong ties with her family of origin; thus, if she dies in childbirth, the husband must pay a fine to them for homicide.[14] Should the wife die of natural causes, the bride-price is not refunded.[15-17] Nor is it refunded after a prescribed number of children are born (usually two). In the event of the death of the husband, a surviving brother sometimes inherits the wife if the children are quite young.[18] If they are grown up, other arrangements are made.

Age at marriage is very much influenced by the bride-price. Women are eligible for marriage immediately after puberty, but men must wait years until they can accumulate the bride-price.[19] Another contributing factor to late marriages for men is the tradition that a father first marries off his daughter and thus obtains the bride-price for his son's marriage. Although wealthy men can afford the highest bride-prices, they frequently use their wealth as an inducement to obtain wives for less than the average bride-price.[20]

TYPES OF MARRIAGE

The typical marriage begins with the betrothal; the groom or his representative gives a gift to the girl or to a member of her family. Then the elders discuss the bride-price, and the amount is fixed. Once the initial payment is made, the marriage is formalized, and the couple can live together.

In another variation, the union of the couple occurs first, and is followed by formalization of the marriage. Sometimes a girl can force a marriage by sleeping with a boy and having her parents pursue him for the bride-price. In the most prevalent marriage of this kind, a previously married woman moves into the man's hut on a trial basis. If the liaison lasts, the marriage is formally acknowledged and a bride-price, less than that for a virgin, is paid.

Among the Bangwa, impecunious individuals may be spared payment of the bride-price. The father of the bride, in this *ngkap* marriage, retains the right to the offspring of the marriage, with the husband granted only uxorial rights. Lineage heads and chiefs often succeed in building up a network of profitable wardships, for they can obtain the bride-price of the offspring of their wards.[21]

A belief in reincarnation leads to reciprocity among the Nyende. A man's marriage to his sister would lead to mutual death since, being of the same clan, both possess a mutual "soul"; hence an exchange of sisters or kinswomen outside the clan is prescribed.[22]

Another marriage form involves abduction, especially when the man does not have the girl's parents' approval or when he cannot meet the bride-payment. The abduction must be understood, however, as an attempt to bargain rather than to avoid the payment altogether: the abductor leaves a token (usually an arrow) to indicate that this is not an aggressive act and returns to his parents' house. Confronted with a fait accompli, both families take up negotiations in earnest.[23]

The levirate, "ghost" marriage, and "female" husband marriage are forms that are adapted to particular circumstances. The levirate—where the widow marries a brother of the deceased husband—has been discussed earlier in the chapter on Hebrew marriage. In a "ghost" marriage[24] the woman is married to the name of a deceased bachelor so that his line will not perish; but a kinsman actually marries the woman, and their children are considered as belonging to the lineage of the deceased and can inherit from him.

Among the Nuer,[25] a barren woman may marry another woman. After paying the bride-price for a wife, she assigns to a relative or friend the sexual rights to her wife as well as the duty of assisting the wife in other matters. But she remains the legal husband, and if daughters are born she is entitled to the bride-price when they marry.

Polyandry, or "village wifehood," is practiced among the Lele, Dinga, Pende, and Mbunda. A woman can have five or six husbands; they, too, can take other wives.[26]

While Christian marriage customs have made some inroads, they have been checked because Christianity is strongly associated with colonialism in the minds of many Africans. Early missionaries conveyed the idea that monogamy connoted spiritual superiority and, not surprisingly, incurred the hostility of polygynists.[27] Moreover, with its emphasis on individual choice, the Church failed to recognize the intricate African kinship ties that afford considerable emotional security.[28] In forbidding polygyny, premarital sexual activity, and sexuality for widows or unmarried divorcees, Christian marriage policy has met with much resistance.[29] Western customs and the greater emphasis on pageantry in Church weddings are generally considered too expensive[30]; in fact, most Africans who decide on a Christian marriage service also have a traditional one.[31] The ability to blend custom and Christianity without a feeling of conflict is described by one writer. He tells of a Nigerian teacher from a Catholic family who returned from abroad to discover that his father had taken a second wife. The son was shocked, but the father explained, "I am not an Irish Catholic; I'm a Nigerian Catholic."[32]

IN-LAW RESTRICTIONS AND TABOOS

Two basic principles guide a young couple in their relations with in-laws. Toward those of the same sex, the key motif is exaggerated respect and the extension of many services. Among the Nyoro[33] and Ambo,[34] however, in-laws are treated with avoidance. A man who suddenly encounters his mother-in-law on a path will dive into the bushes to avoid gazing at her. Among the Bagenda, the husband and his mother-in-law may not take one another by the hand, pass each other in a doorway, or look at each other's faces.[35] After the birth of the first child, the restrictions and taboos are gradually lessened; after the second or third child, the relationship may reach a relaxed, informal stage.

Prospective suitors among the Nuer must carry their own spoons and not use those of the villages in which they are courting.[36] Food is a potential source of conflict in some underdeveloped countries. It is also associated with sexuality: a man ingesting his food is symbolically related to the penis, which is said to "eat of the milkpail" that is the vagina.[37]

Apparently, by the avoidance of intimacy and the substitution of exaggerated respect, contact that might lead to quarrels and disruption of the marital alliance is avoided. Once the marriage is on a relatively secure footing (i.e., several children have been born), the threat is weakened and more normal relationships can develop.

THE IDEAL SPOUSE

In some societies the ideal wife should be a virgin,[38] but others are not concerned with this. In fact, some boys want to impregnate their girl friends to be sure of fertility before marriage. On the other hand, a boy who is not seriously involved with a woman might be very reluctant to deflorate her. Not only could he be liable for a virgin penalty fee, but, in the absence of payment of bride-wealth, if a child should result, it would belong to the woman's lineage.[39] In the West it is usually considered undesirable to be "stuck" with an illegitimate child; but in Africa the economic and lineal value of a child, particularly a male, means that little, if any, stigma will be attached to illegitimacy.

Tribal life, with its paucity of mechanical aids, depends largely on physical strength. Hence it is not strange that, compared to Western societies, there is less emphasis on beauty in choosing a spouse. The ideal wife is, above all, fertile, strong, and eager to work for the economic prosperity of the household. She has a stocky frame and good, "workable" legs, and is hardly frowned upon for being plump, big-hipped, and buxom. Most important, she is respectful and submissive to her husband. The Ibo of Nigeria say, "Good manners constitute beauty."[40] Good manners often mean that the wife does not eat with the husband or join him when he is entertaining friends. She always provides him with a sitting stool, but does not sit in his presence; nor does she burden him with idle chatter—she speaks only when spoken to.[41]

It goes without saying that the ideal wife must be a good cook. In patrilineal societies, a betrothed girl often lives with her future husband's family for a few months, even a year, to learn how to prepare food in the family style. Some women have been rejected by their potential fathers-in-law because they could not cook well enough.[42]

The emphasis on utility rather than appearance or personality was demonstrated experimentally by Jahoda. When boys were shown pictures of African women and asked to select those preferred as marriage partners, and girls were shown the same pictures and asked which they would want to be like, both sexes preferred pictures of women carrying pans on their heads to those without pans.[43]

As regards the ideal husband, little data are available, perhaps because most women have been less concerned about physical qualities than men; more important, they are in less of a position to exercise any preference. However, potency is a key requirement. An impotent or infertile man is looked upon with derision, for he contributes nothing to perpetuate his lineage.

RELATIONS BETWEEN MEN AND WOMEN

Male and female roles are quite rigidly institutionalized; each partner knows what duties are expected of him or her. Since marriage is more concerned with kinship than with the interaction of spouses, affection is not necessarily present. The ties to the family of origin often remain stronger than those to the spouse—witness the saying, "Your sister is always your sister; tomorrow your wife may be another man's wife."[44]

Although the woman is often a legal minor and submissive behavior toward her husband is expected, the relationship is more egalitarian than the rules of behavior might suggest.[45] The difficulties of earning a livelihood require that the woman expend a great deal of energy in farming or trading in addition to her cooking and housekeeping chores. Given the relative ease of divorce in most societies, overly suppressive behavior on the part of the man might result in his wife leaving him.

Another stabilizing factor in the wife's status is the bride-price, which the husband risks losing if he drives her away by abuse. Contrariwise, wives would have great difficulty in dominating their husbands. Women who seem to have the upper hand in marriage are considered to be expressing a masculine role, which leads to the suspicion that such cross-sex identity could be achieved only through witchcraft.[46] Practicing witchcraft against a spouse is grounds for divorce in most tribes.

Because of the emphasis on institutionalized roles rather than on the quality of interpersonal relations, a wife who has borne no children stands in low favor, and a fertile wife can be forgiven some indiscretions. Africans, by and large, attribute more power to outside forces than to individual efforts. Hence, in the recent past, if an individual failed to have his love for someone else reciprocated, he never questioned his own shortcomings—he was more apt to consult a witch or wizard to cast a spell or give him a magic potion that would control the feelings of the one he longed for.

Among the Kgatla,[47] a method guaranteed to attract a boy was for a girl to mix dirt and the moisture from between her thighs and genitals, and discreetly slip this potion into his porridge or beer when she invited him to her home. Those desiring more professional service consulted the "doctor" (professional magician), who prepared a lotion made from the heart of a hummingbird (it never deceives the hunter and guarantees that the boy's suit will be honest) and the fat of a hedgehog (this animal is rather sluggish, so the boy will keep hanging around the girl's house). One part of the medicine can be burned in a potsherd, with the girl inundating her face in the smoke. Another part can be smeared on her face while she calls his name. And to leave no stone unturned, still another part may be put into his food.

SEX

Sex is considered natural, but very powerful and potentially dangerous if not treated with ritual respect. Prudishness and phobias about touching the genitalia of children are largely nonexistent. Adults comment favorably on a child's finely shaped genitalia; in the very young, these parts are often kissed as a sign of affection. Prepubertal children often play at coitus, to the amusement of their elders.

Attitudes toward premarital sexual intercourse vary greatly. Few societies openly condone it, but it appears to be more prevalent than the mores officially allow. Virginity, however, is sufficiently prized so that, in many societies, a bull is paid as a fine by any male found responsible for deflowering a virgin.[48] On the other hand, a bonus may be added to the bride-payment to reward parents for having safeguarded their daughter. Sex play, even leading to orgasm, is much more accepted so long as the vagina is not penetrated. Many tribes permit the man to ejaculate on the girl's thighs but not to penetrate the vagina.[49,50]

Circumcision is generally performed on men either at puberty or before marriage. Some tribes also have girls clitoridectomized in preparation for marriage.[51] Removal of the woman's "little penis" may perhaps further the differentiation of sex roles.

Puberty, menstruation, and intercourse involve a great deal of ritual to ward off the potential evil influence of discontented shades (the spirits of ancestors). The Nyakyusa, for example, prescribe that after her initial sexual intercourse with her husband, the bride wipes his genitals with her hands and then wipes her hands on a fowl and some millet. The next morning, without washing, she goes off with the fowl and millet to her parents' house. The fowl is killed and eaten by the parents and daughter; then the parents, who have refrained from sexual intercourse since the girl's first menstruation, may resume sexual relations. If the girl comes without the fowl and drinks from the same calabash of water as her mother, she could give her mother diarrhea because the girl is "heavy" (filled with semen). Hence, unless the proper ritual is adhered to, contact with a "heavy" person is always fraught with danger for someone who is not.[52]

Adultery was countenanced by the Ruanda when a spouse was away for a considerable period of time, even for legitimate reasons.[53] However, most tribes do not permit it, and a number of them consider it dangerous to touch an adulteress who has recently lain with her lover. Among the Lele, a girl fresh from a rendezvous in the bush would never touch her child before her mother performed a magical rite, lest the touch of the child's mother kill it.[54] A difficult childbirth is universally thought to be a sure sign of previous adultery, and women usually confess during labor to ward off the evil spirits.[55]

In sum, we may conclude that the physical act of sex itself arouses little guilt in most Africans, but the symbolic significance and magical consequences are often sufficiently anxiety-provoking to demand a complicated set of rituals.

DIVORCE

The African family varies greatly in its stability. The Zulu permit no divorce on any grounds, whereas other societies allow divorce simply by mutual consent[56] or even if the husband alone requests it.[57] Divorce among many tribes has traditionally been indistinguishable from absence of co-residence. If one of the spouses leaves home for a considerable length of time, in particular because of a bad relationship, either spouse is free to start new relationships that may result in a new marriage.

The frequency of divorce varies with the kind of tribal society. As a general rule, where jural rights over a woman are not transferred by marriage to her spouse and his descent group, her tie to her family remains stronger than the affinal tie. In case of stress, the affinal tie is more likely to break.[58]

There are, however, powerful factors that inhibit divorce in traditional society. In the first place, marriage involves not only two people but two families.

Marriage is best conceived of as a process rather than an event. And the passage of time further cements the alliance in a complex network of gifts and obligations. To undo the marriage necessitates determining the culpability and deciding what portion of the payment, if any, should be returned and how the gifts should be redistributed to the donors. It is most unlikely that the parents of the married couple will agree on the responsibility for marital breakup, nor is it likely that the bride's father would have an easy time getting the bride-price cattle back from his kin. Accordingly, all the families concerned usually strive to preserve the marriage. This may account for the reluctance to consider simple adultery as legitimate grounds for divorce. Even repeated adultery by the man is not considered sufficient grounds, and only rarely so when the woman is the offender.

Another deterrent to divorce is the fact that in most patrilineal societies (and the majority of African tribes are patrilineal) the children remain with the father after divorce. Even in cases where the wife has run away and borne one or more children by another man, the children belong to the husband as *pater* rather than to the *genitor*. In such a case, the husband is also entitled to collect a fine from the lover for damages.

Barrenness is rarely direct grounds for divorce. Although children are highly valued, a pleasant, hardworking but infertile wife is usually kept and another wife added. Among the Swazi,[59] a relative (preferably a younger sister) is provided in order to avoid returning the bride-price. If the husband prefers to get rid of the wife because of barrenness, he might offer other grounds—e.g., he accuses her of witchcraft in preventing conception.[60]

Technically, a wife in a polygynous household can sue for divorce if her husband skips her marital turn among his wives or if he curtails it for any reason. In practice, however, this never happens because it would be viewed by the village as a sad commentary on the inability of the wife to keep her husband; thus the aggrieved wife is more likely to demand some favor or a gift as compensation from the man.[61]

The legally recognized grounds for divorcing a woman among the Iteso, typical of those found in many tribes, include (a) refusal to perform such wifely duties as cooking, housekeeping, and cultivating; (b) refusal to cohabit; (c) continued adultery despite admonitions; (d) desertion; (e) witchcraft; (f) repeated arson; (g) syphilis; (h) epilepsy; and (i) assault upon the husband's elderly relatives. A woman and her guardians can bring suit against the man for (a) excessive cruelty; (b) refusal to cohabit; (c) desertion; (d) failure to provide her with the necessities of life; (e) assault upon her elderly relatives, and (f) witchcraft.[62]

It should be noted that adultery on the part of the woman need not be sexual. Among the Yao, the fact that a woman cooked in her home for a man other than her husband, without the husband's permission, would be considered an adulteration of his uxorial rights.[63]

An example of witchcraft among the Tiv involved a case where a woman claimed that while she was sleeping, her husband had cut off bits of her hair and fingernails (evidently she was a heavy sleeper) and buried them in front of her hut. The intent was either to prevent her from running away or, failing that, to bring her back against her will. She was granted a divorce.[64]

The problem of desertion in old age is common among the Gonja. As the wife ages, the probability of her leaving her husband to return to her kin increases. If she becomes ill, it is her husband's duty to provide medicine for her care. Should these prove ineffective, the witch doctor may prescribe long journeys in search of other herbs and medicines. If the journeys become more protracted, she is more likely to remain with her kin; they are obligated to provide her with food, shelter, and medicine, but *only* if she is not living under her husband's roof. If her husband becomes too old or ill to care for her, she is also likely to seek the support of relatives.[65]

CHANGES SINCE WORLD WAR II

In the post-World War II decades, almost all the former European colonies in Africa gained their independence and moved toward industrialization and urbanization. The thirst for freedom has also spilled over into the area of women's rights, an emphasis on education, and a drive to "get ahead." These factors have profoundly affected the concept of the traditional family, and we shall consider a number of these changes.

Polygyny

There is little question that polygyny is on the wane empirically, if not ideologically. There has been a mass migration, especially of men, to the cities; but the high cost of living makes the expense of multiple wives prohibitive,[66] and small urban flats are hardly geared to accommodate multiple-wife families.

Along with the physical and financial difficulties, the status of the polygynist has waned. At one time, a man's prestige was based on the number of his wives. Today, Christian influence has downgraded polygyny somewhat; but Western concepts of love and of equality of the sexes have had a greater impact. Two student surveys in Ghana, and one in Sierra Leone,[67-69] reported that between 73 and 93 percent of the respondents favored monogamy. As might be expected, the percentage of women favoring monogamy was close to 100 percent. The result is that, among the Yoruba, after the first wife, succeeding ones are increasingly drawn from the ranks of divorcees.[70] Their main attraction is the relatively smaller bride-price required—no small matter in an era of rising costs.

In addition, the migration of men to the city (leaving multiple wives behind) tends to strengthen matrilateral ties even in patriarchal societies.[71] When problems arise during the absence of her husband, the rural wife is more likely to rely on her own kin rather than on her affines. Since the wife's social absorption in her husband's kin is a paramount feature of polygyny, the effect is an impairment to the polygynous foundation.

On the other hand, it is possible to exaggerate the influence of ideology and urbanization on polygyny. For one thing, most surveys have focused on high school and college students, who constitute only a small percentage of the total population. A vast majority of Africans have remained relatively refractory to the monogamic ideal. Recent studies indicate that even in the cities, polygyny does not necessarily disappear.[72,73] Young migrants, it is true, do not possess the wealth to assure themselves wives, and highly educated civil servants may have departed from polygynous ideals in favor of monogamy; however, some men with moderate education and adequate wealth have managed to maintain polygynous households in the city. This has occurred particularly where the wife is also able to work, for one factor that made polygyny feasible was the ability to extract economic return from the wife's labor.

Urbanization has had varying effects on different tribes, depending on whether they were matrilineal, and on the role that polygyny played in their cultures. These effects are quite complex, but it is safe to say that there is no simple cause-effect relationship between urbanization and the decline of polygyny.[74]

Family Influence on Marriage

The ability of families to choose their children's marital partner and to control the marital relationship has weakened considerably. Western norms of individualism and achievement-orientation in love and work are beginning to supplant village mores, with their traditional loyalties based on lineage and obligations toward all kin. In a relatively stable society with little economic mobility, a system of responsibility and obligations worked fairly well. Indeed, in the absence of any social welfare system, kin-responsibility was an absolute necessity for the indigent or disabled.

In Africa today, this system is slowly breaking down with the migration from the village. Education is the key to success, and a wide range of occupational levels has replaced the narrow and fixed occupational range of the village. The possibility of reciprocity has broken down as those who are more secure economically do not find any important services supplied by village kin.[75] Some kinship obligations still persist in the city.[76] The African city dweller is often caught between the competing philosophies of individualism and collectivism: he feels guilty if he rejects his relatives, but frustrated if he allows them literally to eat him out of house and home. Over half of the sample interviewed in Lagos, for example, reported that at least 10 percent of their income went to assist their kin[77]; this included food and housing for visiting relatives, many of whom expect this, as well as a job, from their city kin.

A despairing man from Salisbury, where overcrowding in homes is a legal infraction, periodically makes anonymous phone calls to the police and acts as surprised and shocked as anyone when his premises are cleared.[78] A Freetown

study showed that in one year about 25 percent of the households had received
visits of from one week to a month, and about 8 percent had had visits of more
than a month.[79]

Bride-Price

The bride-price, the key determinant of family alliance in marriage, still exists,
but its role has changed drastically. Cattle are hardly practical in a city, so the
payment is now made in currency. But the bride-price has risen so steeply that
almost no one can pay the full sum (sometimes as much as a year's salary) at
once, and installment payments are now customary.[80] Indeed, among the
Okrika, the question of whether the children belong to the husband's or wife's
family depends on how much has been paid.[81] In short, the bride-price has
become highly commercialized.

The groom's father no longer pays the bride-price. Since the son himself must
labor to raise the amount and even delay his marriage for several years,[82] he
now feels that he can choose anyone he wishes. The mass media now reach into
every corner of the once "dark" continent, spreading the message of liberality
and free choice. For example, in a situation in which a son and his parents had
selected different brides, the influential Northern Rhodesian (now Zambia)
newspaper columnist Josephine advised:

> Since you are paying the *lobola* [bride-price] I think you have the right to
> choose the wife. It is one matter to follow tribal custom if you live in the
> villages and your parents help with *lobola*. But these ways do not always
> suit people who live in town. Stand firm—marry the girl of your choice.
> Why let old customs spoil your life? Apologize to your parents and send
> them gifts.[83]

The role of the parents is becoming much like that in Western society:
approval of choices already made.[84] Urban and student samples indicate an
overwhelming belief that *love* is the key reason for marriage, and that the main
role of parents should be to "give presents."[85] Asked what they would do if
parents opposed their marriage, however, only 24 percent of a Ghanian student
sample stated that they would disobey their parents, while 31 percent were
uncertain.[86] In an educated Sierra Leone sample, when the group was asked
about their attitude in the event of a quarrel between their relatives and spouse,
only 7 percent of the men and 4.5 percent of the women would commit
themselves to the spouse's side, whereas 25 percent of the men and 15 percent
of the women would be "impartial."[87] In sum, parents cannot dictate whom
their children go out with,[88] but they still retain considerable influence and veto
power over whom their children marry.

Relations between Men and Women

The destruction of tribal authority in the cities and the growing emphasis on individualism and equality have tended to decrease the status of men and to increase that of women. Advanced education, formerly a male prerogative, is now increasingly available to women. Nevertheless, stereotypes of the dominant husband and the submissive wife persist not only in rural areas but in educated circles as well. Asked who the chief marital authority should be, 73 percent of married Ghanian respondents thought it should be the man, 2 percent named the woman, and 22 percent called for a 50-50 relationship.[89] Yet male Ghanian students seemingly desired the best of both worlds in choosing "educated and intelligent" as the characteristics most desired in a wife. The traditional stereotype of "obedient, patient, and humble" was third, and the desire for a "beautiful, good-looking" spouse scored no better than fourth.[90]

The shortage of educated women precludes the satisfaction of this primary wish for most educated men. In fact, newspaper marital-problem columns are replete with tragic arranged marriages between educated government functionaries and illiterate wives.[91] The problem is that for most of the country, except in the case of college students, education in a wife is not as popular as sturdiness and obedience. Further, if a girl pursues a career, she will be in college while most of her friends are marrying. After she completes her schooling in her twenties, she is viewed with suspicion as being beyond the prime marrying age.[92] Moreover, because monogamy is becoming increasingly prevalent in the city, men are reluctant to marry a woman whose fertility is untested. Many men, therefore, wait until a woman conceives before undertaking marriage. Obviously, a woman who wishes to have a career or continue her education will find pregnancy and/or the possibility of ending up unmarried a very threatening situation.

In addition, educated wives tend to be much less submissive than uneducated ones, which leads to conflict with a traditional, patriarchically minded husband. As a result, educated women are not always regarded as very desirable spouses. In fact, at the University of Nigeria, in 1967, a debate was held on the proposition that marriage to an educated woman was inimical to a man's happiness.[93]

The actual experience of city life, away from the eyes of others, has tended to weaken institutionalized sex roles. The wife no longer observes the ritual of placing the stool for her husband when he enters a room, and the relationship has become more informal and spontaneous. In the absence of formal age-groups and kin, the couple are of necessity forced to talk to each other and to engage in joint social functions. However, the extent of their interaction is much less than in Western societies. The Bantu husband and wife, for example, do not generally eat together and still spend most of their free time in monosexual gatherings. All in all, the transitional status of the masculine and feminine roles has made the achievement of marital harmony between the couple a most difficult task. In this transitory period, the attainment of somewhat greater equality by women has not resulted in more felicitous unions, but it has brought greater leverage for the woman in her attempt to overcome the traditional limitations of her status.[94]

STRENGTH OF THE INSTITUTION OF MARRIAGE

Decline of the Sexual Code

The presence of many more men than women in the city has enhanced the value of women's sexual services. Women, nevertheless, lag in education, and African society is slow in providing jobs for them. If one adds the fact that tribal mores have greatly weakened in the city, it is hardly surprising that prostitution and promiscuity have flourished. Recalling the high valuation of children in Africa and the tendency on the part of men first to impregnate a girl friend and then decide whether to marry, it is not unusual, among the Bantu in Johannesburg, that between 20 and 50 percent of the couples cohabiting are not married.[95]

Married men, influenced by a polygynist ideology but restricted to monogamy by economic conditions, are tempted to compromise by acquiring mistresses or pickups (the "Jaguars" of Accra, Lagos, and Ibadan). Men separated from wives left in the village are apt to establish semipermanent relationships with what the Africans call, with trenchant honesty, "half-wives" or "outside wives." Finally, the once powerful respect for the supernatural forces that would punish the sexual transgressor has eroded somewhat in the realism of the city.

Divorce

The societal forces and economic factors that once counteracted a liberal philosophy toward divorce have greatly diminished. Since the bride-price is now often paid in cash, it is held exclusively by the father or the oldest male relative rather than divided among various relatives. This new pattern reflects the fact that some relatives no longer live nearby and that the cohesive force of the extended family is not as strong as it once was. Quite often, the entire bride-price is spent at once and can no longer exert a restraining force on the couple's separation. Further, the husband's relatives, having contributed little or nothing to the bride-price, and having had little to say about the choice of bride, are not strongly involved in maintaining the marriage. They are more apt to see the bride as an interloper who has stolen their kin's affections; thus, both the bride's and the groom's families now have less vested interest in supporting the marriage.

There is little question that the philosophy of polygyny is incompatible with the full exercise of women's rights. With greater educational and economic opportunity, she is less likely to adhere to the passive-submissive sex role of the village.[96] In the freer city environment, she is less likely to fear being held at home by physical force, with no place to go except to relatives who would probably send her back because of the bride-price.

The importance of physical violence in precipitating divorce is emphasized by the fact that a Ghanian college sample cited physical cruelty as the most valid reason for divorce: adultery garnered only between 20 to 25 percent as many votes.[97] It would appear reasonable, therefore, to expect that the divorce rate in black Africa will increase significantly in the next decade or two, as women gain sufficient economic independence to terminate marriages in which they suffer physical abuse.

CONCLUSIONS

Black Africa comprises a group of societies in transition. Because the values in the old tribal societies do not jibe well with Western values and urban conditions, cultural conflict is inevitable. In addition, since Western values are questioned because of their association with "colonialism," the situation is highly complex.

Polygyny is incompatible with equality and companionship between the sexes, nor is it wholly compatible with urbanization; and because these last two variables are in the ascendancy throughout Africa, polygyny will gradually disappear. The rate at which this will occur is difficult to predict, for it depends not only on ideological climate or urbanization, but also on interacting variables: thus, patrilineal societies have resisted monogamy in towns more than matrilineal societies.[98]

Until an adaptive fusion of African and Western concepts of the family emerges, we are likely to see considerable turmoil and social disorganization, the inevitable price for an underdeveloped continent seeking to adapt itself to an industrial era.

REFERENCES

1. W. Goode, *World Revolution and Family Patterns.*
2. V. R. Dorjahn, "The factor of polygyny in African demography."
3. K. Hughes, "The Church and marriage in Africa."
4. J. Gunther, *Inside Africa.*
5. H. Ashton, *The Basuto.*
6. T. Price, "African marriage."
7. P. Bohannan, *African Outline.*
8. M. Hunter, *Reaction to Conquest.*
9. "Polygamy backed at Africa parley."
10. A. B. Ellis, "West-African marriage customs."
11. E. E. Evans-Pritchard, "Zande bridewealth."

12. *Social Implications of Industrialization and Urbanization in Africa South of the Sahara.*
13. R. A. Lystad, *The Ashanti: A Proud People.*
14. E. E. Evans-Pritchard, *Kinship and Marriage among the Nuer.*
15. R. F. Gray, *The Sonjo of Tanganyika.*
16. R. F. Gray, "Sonjo bride-price and the question of African wife purchase."
17. J. C. D. Lawrance, *The Iteso.*
18. O. Otite, "Processes of family formation among the Urhobo of midwestern Nigeria."
19. P. Bohannan and L. Bohannan, "The family in Negro Africa."
20. J. Goody, " 'Normative,' 'recollected,' and 'actual' marriage payments among the Lowili of Northern Ghana, 1951-1966."
21. R. Brain, "Bangwa (Western Bamileke) marriage wards."
22. H. Huber, "Le principe de la réciprocité dans le mariage Nyende."
23. *Social Implications of Industrialization and Urbanization in Africa South of the Sahara.*
24. E. E. Evans-Pritchard, *Kinship and Marriage among the Nuer.*
25. Ibid.
26. M. Douglas, "The Lele of the Kasai."
27. J. B. Webster, "Attitudes and policies of the Yoruba African churches toward polygamy."
28. I. O. Delano, *An African Looks at Marriage.*
29. M. Hunter, op. cit.
30. D. H. Reader, *Zulu Tribe in Transition.*
31. H. Feldman, *The Ghanian Family in Transition.*
32. E. E. Lord, "Emergent Africa," p. 59.
33. J. Beattie, *Bunyoro: An African Kingdom.*
34. B. Stefaniszyn, *Social and Ritual Life of the Ambo of Northern Rhodesia.*
35. L. P. Mair, *An African People in the Twentieth Century.*
36. V. Fergusson, cited in T. Beidelman, "Some Nuer notions of nakedness, nudity, and sexuality."
37. E. J. Krige, "Girls' puberty songs and their relation to fertility, health, morality, and religion among the Zulu."
38. E. E. Lord, *Queen of Sheba's Heirs.*
39. W. Trobisch, "Attitudes of some African youth toward sex and marriage."
40. V. Uchendu, *The Igbo of Southeast Nigeria,* p. 52.
41. M. Fortes, *The Web of Kinship among the Tallensi.*
42. G. F. Pfister, "Marriage among the central Basukuma."
43. G. Jahoda, "Boys' images of marriage partners and girls' self-images in Ghana."
44. M. Gluckman, "Estrangement in the African family," p. 466.
45. I. Schapera, "Bushmen hunters in the Kalahari Desert of Africa."
46. R. A. Lystad, op. cit.
47. I. Schapera, *Married Life in an African Tribe.*
48. J. Middleton, *The Lugbara of Uganda.*
49. E. J. Krige, op. cit.
50. M. Wilson, *Rituals of Kinship among the Nyakyusa.*
51. P. Rigby, *Cattle and Kinship among the Gogo.*

52. J. Kenyatta, *Facing Mount Kenya.*
53. J. J. Maquet, *The Premise of Inequality in Ruanda.*
54. M. Douglas, op. cit.
55. A. Philips, *Survey of African Marriage and Family Life.*
56. P. Bohannan and L. Bohannan, op. cit.
57. H. Miner, *The Primitive City of Timbuctoo.*
58. E. R. Leach, "Aspects of bridewealth and marriage stability among the Kachin and Lakher."
59. H. Kuper, *The Swazi.*
60. P. Bohannan, *Justice and Judgement among the Tiv.*
61. R. Linton, "The family among cultivators in the hills of Madagascar."
62. J. C. D. Lawrance, op. cit.
63. J. C. Mitchell, "Marriage, matriliny, and social structure among the Yao."
64. P. Bohannan, op. cit.
65. E. N. Goody, "Conjugal separation and divorce among the Gonja of Northern Rhodesia."
66. W. C. Hallenbeck, *The Baumannville Community.*
67. T. P. Omari, "Changing attitudes of students in West African society towards marriage and family relationships."
68. H. Feldman, op. cit.
69. K. Little, "Attitudes towards marriage and the family among educated Sierra Leoneans."
70. P. O. Olusanya, "A note on some factors affecting the stability of marriage among the Yoruba of Western Nigeria."
71. E. Colson, "Family change in contemporary Africa."
72. R. Clignet and J. Sween, "Traditional and modern life styles in Africa."
73. R. Clignet, *Many Wives, Many Powers.*
74. R. Clignet, op. cit.
75. P. Marris, "Individual achievement and family ties."
76. R. A. Le Vine, "Intergenerational tensions and extended family structures in Africa."
77. J. Aldous, "Urbanization, the extended family and kinship ties in West Africa."
78. L. Fellows, "Kenya report: Market in brides."
79. M. Banton, *West African City: A Study of Tribal Life in Freetown.*
80. "High bride prices annoy Africans."
81. K. Williamson, "Changes in the marriage system of the Okrika Ijo."
82. K. Little, "Some urban patterns of marriage and domesticity in West Africa."
83. B. Hall (Ed.), *Tell Me Josephine,* p. 66.
84. K. Little and A. Price, "Some trends in modern marriage among Western Africans."
85. H. Feldman, op. cit.
86. T. P. Omari, "Role expectation in the courtship situation in Ghana."
87. K. Little, "Attitudes toward marriage and the family among educated young Sierra Leoneans."
88. J. J. Schmidt, "Marriage customs among the Bantu in the housing project in the municipality of Klerksdorp."

89. H. Feldman, op. cit.
90. T. P. Omari, *Marriage Guidance for Young Ghanians.*
91. G. Jahoda, "Love, marriage, and social change: Letters to the advice column of a West African newspaper."
92. A. Southhall, *Social Change in Modern Africa.*
93. E. E. Lord, "Emergent Africa."
94. R. Clignet, *Many Wives, Many Powers.*
95. A. F. Steyn and C. M. Rip, "The changing urban Bantu family."
96. P. C. Lloyd, "Divorce among the Yoruba."
97. H. Feldman, op. cit.
98. R. Clignet and J. Sween, "Social change and type of marriage."

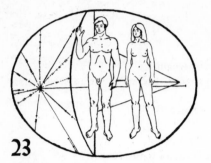

23

The Future of Marriage: Some Literary and Theoretical Approaches

We have considered marriage from the dawn of time to the present day. But what of tomorrow? We shall approach this question from three points of view. To begin with, we shall consider the concept of marriage in the literary utopias of the past 100 years—books which not only depict the concerns and unmet needs of the times in which they were written but also show how, when viewed in perspective, marriage values have changed. After that, we shall discuss several leading theorists and their views on the family of tomorrow. In the final two chapters, we shall examine some present-day variations in marriage, review major historical trends, and then attempt to integrate these findings into a prediction on the nature of marriage in the future.

MARRIAGE IN UTOPIA AND ANTI-UTOPIA

In 1889 Charles Bellamy wrote *Experiment in Marriage,* a novel about a hidden Western Shangri-La—Grape Valley—where a new kind of socialistic society has evolved.[1] Unlike Plato's republic, marriage in Grape Valley is based on personal wishes rather than on the needs of the state, and divorce is much freer. But as in Plato's utopia, women work equally with men, and state nurseries raise children.

Strongly influenced by Darwin's theory of evolution, Bellamy argued for a survival of the fittest in love as in life. Residents of Grape Valley are constantly divorcing and remarrying, and each remarriage seems to be on a more compatible plane than the previous one, with partners moving toward a more perfect union. Today, Bellamy's utopia does not seem far-fetched. Two of his three utopian tenets—free divorce and equal working rights for women—are in the process of being achieved in the United States. The third, the communal raising of children, may be partly realized in a future network of all-day nurseries.

In the post-World War I period, the cheerful optimism of the late nineteenth- and early twentieth-century socialist thought, with its confidence in the progress of mankind, lay buried in the horrors of World War I. Material progress was achieved, but closer regulation of people's lives—the inevitable concomitant of industrialization and modern government—seemed to be a terrible and unanticipated price for economic well-being.

In the 1920s, the Soviet Union was the foremost exponent of governmental regulation, but for a few brief years it was too weak internally to supervise the works of its writers effectively. It was then that a brilliant Soviet writer, Eugene Zamiatin, wrote his utopian novel *We*. But by the time it was ready for publication, he was being harried by the forces of orthodoxy; the novel was never printed in the Soviet Union, although it appeared in an English translation in the United States in 1924.[2]

The main theme of Zamiatin's novel is that the principles of freedom and happiness are incompatible. Freedom leads to irrational behavior and irrational concepts—for example, the square root of minus one, as the hero D-503 points out in his diary. Unfortunately, D-503 meets the atavistic I-330, and she elicits certain irrational hungers in him. In the end, however, along with those remaining persons afflicted with the sickness of freedom, he undergoes an operation for his soul and emerges cleansed, happy, vegetable-like, and in the good graces of the great leader, the Well-Doer.

This theme is repeated in the more popular *Brave New World*,[3] written by Aldous Huxley in 1932. The story takes place around the year 2500, in the year of "Our Ford" 600. It is a world without individuality or political and economic freedom. Marriage and uterine birth are relics of the past. Babies are reared in test tubes, and shallow erotic adventures have replaced the need for a spouse.

The setting of *Walden Two*,[4] by B. F. Skinner, is a contemporary rural environment in the United States just after World War II. Among its features are a *kibbutz*-like arrangement for children and equal opportunities for women. Although the family has lost most of its functions, it is permitted to continue as an emotional bond. The personalities of the inhabitants are somewhat puritanical by current standards, and sexual play among adolescents and the unmarried is frowned upon as a sign of immaturity. Instead, marriage at a young age is encouraged. A couple contemplating marriage visits the Manager of Marriages, who checks to see that they are homogamously paired in terms of interests, school records, and health. If their abilities and temperaments are compatible, they marry. If not, they are advised against marrying, and this usually terminates the relationship. Divorce, while not encouraged, is permitted if genuine extramarital relationships develop.

Walden Two differs from earlier utopias in its use of experiments to improve the quality of life. The superiority of separate or common bedrooms for husband and wife is tested: volunteer couples are randomly assigned to joint or individual bedrooms, and the reactions are checked over a period of years. The results show unequivocally that separate rooms mean greater contentment for both spouses.

In keeping with the experimental terminology, "love" is described as the use of "positive reinforcement." Such definitions appalled several reviewers, who foresaw a sinister depersonalization at work and the mystique of love trampled underfoot. However, Skinner's equating love with "positive reinforcement" served to emphasize his belief that it was a *volitional* response and could be a most efficient way of motivating its recipient in every aspect of life.

In *1984*,[5] also written after World War II, George Orwell depicts a bleak anti-utopia, Oceanis, where the behavior and thinking of the populace are rigorously "shaped up" with less happy consequences for the individual than in *Walden Two*.

> the only recognized purpose of marriage was to beget children for the service of the Party. Sexual intercourse was to be looked on as a slightly disgusting minor operation, like having an enema. . . . There were even organizations such as the Junior Anti-Sex League which advocated complete celibacy for both sexes. All children were to be begotten by artificial insemination . . . and brought up in public institutions.[6]

Orwell repeats the theme of technocracy overpowering man. He becomes the servant of an elite dedicated to the eradication of individuality and the transformation of the population into humanoid robots.

By 1960 a successful revolt of the human spirit against the stifling bureaucracy had begun in the utopian literature. The main thrust was not against governments as villains that oppress man, but against insincerity, materialism, and such artificial institutions as exclusive monogamy.

In *Stranger in a Strange Land* (1961), Robert Heinlein depicts a group where bacchanalia, mate-swapping, and communal living are wholly moral. In the words of Jubal Harshaw, the wise patriarch in the story, "This 'growing-closer' by sexual union, this plurality-into-unity, logically has no place for monogamy."[7]

Another variation of group marriage, which takes place on the moon in the year 2075, is described in Heinlein's science-fiction work, *The Moon Is a Harsh Mistress.*[8] A "line" marriage is one that endures beyond the life span of any one of the participants. New members of either sex may be adopted from time to time by a unanimous vote of the members. The average age of husbands is 40, that of wives 35; the estimated range, from about the age of 15 to senility. Each member is free to sleep with anyone else, except that after a wedding the oldest man usually spends the night with the bride. Children are cared for by all members of the family, and when they grow up they leave and marry elsewhere. Occasionally a grandchild might marry within the family. Divorce is rare because it requires the unanimous consent of all members of the opposite sex.

The reported advantages of a "line" marriage include financial security and emotional stability for children, who rarely face the threat of a broken home. The availability of many members gives the child companionship with persons of all ages and a variety of adult models. Last, death is never the overwhelming tragedy it is in a temporary (nuclear) family.

In the 1960s, too, the novels of Robert H. Rimmer, which focused on interpersonal relationships and marriage, achieved much popularity. His widely read novel, *The Harrad Experiment,*[9] traces the growing friendship of six students (three men and three women). They contract monogamous marriages, but actually establish a group marriage; they share a house and the men rotate to the bedroom of a different woman each week.

The members of the new group, Insix, write a paper for their final year at Harrad to set forth their philosophy (also described in a sequel, *Proposition 31*)[10] of what marriage will be like in a new society. Children will be raised in the Harrad manner, with heterosexual rooming in college, freedom from false modesty about nudity, and emphasis on humanistic values in education. Marriage, always optional, would be mandatory at the birth of a child. Divorce is simple for the childless, or if the children are over 18; but if the children are under 20,* the parents must renounce all rights and the children are adopted into "happier environments."

An important innovation is the possibility of group marriage, limited to six couples. The arrangement can be dissolved if the remaining couples are willing to care for all the children. Bigamous marriage—two men and a woman, or vice versa—is to be permitted, but in case of divorce all children under 18 come under the custody of the state.

In the utopias and anti-utopias we have briefly described, one is struck by the preoccupation with the dilemma of individual freedom versus obligations to society. In Plato's time, when Athens, a moribund state, was torn by internal dissension, his ideal—renunciation of individual wishes for the good of the state—is not surprising. By the time of Bellamy's *Experiment in Marriage,* however, it became acceptable to pursue individual goals, especially for women, who in real life had endured the most restrictions. Utopian though it may have been, Grape Valley's only form of marriage was monogamy because, at the close of a century strongly influenced by Darwin, monogamy was considered to be *the* evolutionary marriage form of mankind.

We and *Brave New World* depict societies in which science has run amok; conditioning techniques, pills, and hypnosis make people into dull robots, except in their choice of bed partners—but here, too, there is pressure not to become involved with any one person. The books convey the fear that, in the industrial bureaucracy of tomorrow, the individual will be unable to preserve his privacy when the ruling powers become increasingly remote.

In *1984,* the individual has all but disappeared. Not only is his thinking controlled, but that last vestige of individuality, his sex life, is taken from him.

Walden Two shows the other side of the coin. Individualism is not encouraged unless it can be supported through the use of the experimental method. New ideas are permitted, but must be verified by an objective assessment of the costs and gains for society. Skinner, however, is rather conservative: he tests the

---

*The discrepancy in ages is found in Rimmer.

incidentals of marriage—such as separate or common bedrooms—rather than the idea of monogamy itself. As to the latter, in a most unexperimental manner, he accepts it explicitly, albeit grudgingly.

The relentless pressure for greater personal control over one's life abated momentarily during the post-World War II boom and the security-minded 1950s. By the 1960s, individualism made a strong return: men wore long hair, earrings, necklaces, and women dressed like men. It was inevitable that the quest for individual development would at last lead to questioning the heretofore solid pillar of society—monogamy. In *The Harrad Experiment, Proposition 31,* and *The Moon Is a Harsh Mistress,* individualism is expressed in the need for variety and in the realization that, for some, one person cannot satisfy every emotional need. Hence, a group marriage is the logical successor to monogamy. The *leitmotif* of the new marriage utopias is that complete self-actualization can be achieved only through multiple emotional attachments.

MARRIAGE THEORISTS

Changes in individual and family behavior in the post-World War I period led to serious treatises on the future of the family. I shall now discuss the approaches taken by several writers.

"Doomsday" Prophets

In *Lysistrata, or Woman's Future and Future Woman,*[11] written in 1925, Anthony M. Ludovici predicts the dire consequences of the emancipation of woman. Sex will be abolished as too degrading, and children will be reared in the wombs of cows and donkeys, which will lead to mankind's "intensified bovinity or assininity."[12] To avoid this nightmare, Ludovici advocates eugenic breeding, infanticide for inferior stock, and legal concubinage to satisfy man's greater sexual appetite. Women will withdraw from industrial and public life and be happily mated to diligent breadwinners. If the woman feels the need for extra activity, she will revive the ancient industries of the home: "bread, cheese, butter, jam, and confectionary making."[13] Children will be raised mostly by their parents and taught the old-fashioned virtues. This better-selected race will attain a new and higher intellectual and cultural level.

Surprisingly, the views of both H. L. Mencken,[14] an eminent observer of the human condition, and the distinguished sociologists Sorokin and Zimmerman have not varied much from this theme. The latter maintain that the family is influenced by society but also has a vital impact on the destiny of a culture. Regrettably, they say, the family gives every indication of breaking down in the second half of the twentieth century. Man has abandoned moral virtues in favor of unbridled hedonism and the pursuit of sensate and material goals. Few children are being born to the most educated classes, whereas the uneducated reproduce prolifically. To ensure continuity of a social class, according to Zimmerman, each mother should bear three to four children.[15] He advocates that a responsible society must be led by men with children, because childless persons are not as immersed in fundamental humanism. Sorokin pessimistically concludes, nonetheless, that catastrophe is inevitable:

> The family as a sacred union of husband and wife, of parents and children will continue to disintegrate. Divorces and separation will increase until any profound difference between socially sanctioned marriages and illicit sex-relationships disappears. Children will be separated earlier and earlier from parents. The main sociocultural functions of the family will further decrease until the family becomes a mere incidental cohabitation of male and female, while the home will become a mere overnight parking place mainly for sex-relationship.[16]

All is not lost, according to Zimmerman, because this inevitable catastrophe will be succeeded by a rebirth. The family undergoes three cyclical variations: the trustee family, the domestic family, and, finally, atomism—the disintegration of family obligation into narcissistic self-concern. Sometime in the next century or two, he believes, the primitive trustee family will be resurrected and the cycle will resume. Surely, says Zimmerman, man can avoid the huge losses in human efficiency in allowing families to disintegrate and then start rebuilding. The masses should be educated to understand that the domestic family, as a sort of happy compromise, blends individual autonomy with strong familial responsibility.[17] Nevertheless, he is not optimistic.

The Functionalists

The functionalists believe that the needs of society, particularly of the economy, dictate the form and mode of family interaction.[18,19] An early functionalist, William F. Ogburn, took the American colonial family as his starting point. Most of the services it had provided in the past—economic, religious, recreational, educational, and status-conferring—had been weakened or removed.[20] Despite these losses, the modern family exercises a greater role in the molding of personality than did the colonial family; the latter, because of material difficulties, the division of labor by sex, and the long hours of work, could not concern itself too much with the emotional quality of the relationships of family members. Simpler considerations, such as instilling an appreciation of religion, work, clean living habits, and sobriety, took precedence.

The emotional importance of the family was also spelled out by Burgess,[21] who designated the emerging new type of family as the "companionship" family because intimate interpersonal association appeared to be its primary function.

He saw this as a process stemming from the decline of the small patriarchal family in pioneer times, when the emphasis was on individual initiative. Other contributing factors were the growth of political independence, industrialization, and economic independence for women. Two indisputable functions of the family still remain: reproduction and the early socialization of children.[22] In addition, the family is still the most preferred means of providing child care, affectional-companionate relations, sexual release, initial status ascription, and the transfer of property.[23]

The fact that the family still performs many functions leads Talcott Parsons to conclude that the family has not persevered simply by giving up most of its functions and trying to make the remaining functions more meaningful for family members. Rather, the family structure tends to reflect the demands of a particular economy.[24] In the present American economy, a high premium is placed on occupational mobility, and status is determined chiefly by the job of the husband. As a consequence, the nuclear family has become relatively isolated and highly differentiated (not disorganized, as some critics claim), and basic patterns within the family reflect the emphasis on "instrumental activism." To follow the "job" involves freeing oneself of family ties and restrictions. A man's primary loyalties are to his wife and children (who follow him on his peregrinations) rather than to his parents and relatives (who do not). Further, his independence of his family of origin is demonstrated in his free choice of spouse.

Proof that the family is not disorganized lies in the fact that a larger percentage of people are marrying and that divorced people usually remarry quickly. Marriage roles are differentiated, with the woman usually not involved in a career although she may work for a time for financial reasons. Her role in the family, according to Parsons, is an expressive one in that she specializes in satisfying the affective needs of the family. The husband specializes in the instrumental function of getting things done: achieving a secure status for the family and earning enough to buy the family home and a car. The importance of upward mobility on the occupational ladder is the result of our focus on "instrumental activism," which encourages members of society to master their environment and develop its resources instead of resigning themselves to the way things are.[25]

The functionalists do not feel that the family is in serious danger of disappearing soon, but their position, particularly that of Parsons, appears vulnerable on several counts. Research on the theory that the masculine role is instrumental and the feminine one is expressive has not strongly supported his theory.[26,27] Instead, the number of married women in careers suggests that dual-career families are characterized by the ability of both husband and wife to adopt both expressive and instrumental roles. Moreover, children have no functional place in Parsons' scheme: they are referred to as the result of "childish elements" in the parents' personalities. Yet children continue to be born, albeit at a slower rate than heretofore.

The functionalists also seem to depict the family as a dependent variable that is influenced by economic changes. This position seems strongly supported by the modification in African family structure with its transition from an agricultural to a more urban society. On the other hand, the functionalists do not adequately consider the contingency whereby the family orientation may influence the nature of society. Thus, the demands of Soviet families for better housing, easier divorce, and greater personal freedom have somewhat modified the overall society rather than vice versa. Another criticism that can be leveled against functionalists is their emphasis on "postdictions" rather than on predictions. It is, after all, easier to find explanations for the status quo than to predict when and why changes in the status quo will occur.

INDIVIDUALISM AND COMMITMENT

A considerable number of writers have concluded that the future of marriage will depend less on the functions served by it than on the commitments of its members. Charles W. Hobart sees the family as weakened by its loss of functions, by increased social mobility, by the decline of status ascription in favor of relationships that are achieved, and by the increased importance of materialist values.[28] Hope for the future, as he sees it, lies in an assertion of human values over production ones—what we *are* becoming is more important than what we *achieve* and what we *own*.

Hobart's position does not bear up under close examination. Some societies with high status ascription, such as the African cultures, also have high rates of marital breakup. Further, material wealth in the United States is *inversely* correlated with rate of divorce.[29] The wealthy apparently reason that what is *achieved,* monetarily speaking, overrides any considerations of what a person *is.*

John N. Edwards concludes, "If, indeed, contemporary marriages are based more on what the marital partners *are* rather than what they *do,* as Hobart suggests, the major disjunctive feature of current family life is that what individuals *are* is primarily reward-seeking organisms."[30] Economic abundance and the full economic emancipation of women are thus perceived as having a suppressive effect on the marriage rate in general because they offer attractive alternatives to matrimony.[31]

In a movingly pessimistic treatise, Barrington Moore, Jr., portrays the heavy burdens of ascribed relationships in a more functional world in which the individual builds his relationships where they benefit him the most. In such a society, obligations to give affection to family members as a function of accident of birth is a barbaric residual. In Moore's opinion, our future may possibly be "a world of reduced family burdens ... of shallow and fleeting erotic intrigues, based really on commercial interests."[32]

Another vision of the present and future is Farber's "permanently available" model, according to which the marital partner, and not marriage, is a transient phenomenon. When the gains yielded by a relationship are exceeded by the costs, the individual then transfers, via divorce and remarriage, into a marriage that is subjectively more rewarding.[33]

Christopher Alexander has argued that "intimate human contacts are essential for human survival, and... each person requires not one, but several given intimate contacts at any one time. [Therefore] it is essential that we invest new social mechanisms consistent with the direction that society is taking, and yet be able to sustain the intimate contacts which we need."[34] But will this not disrupt the family? Ralph Borsodi provides one answer by denying that the family is the be-all and end-all of life: "The family—like any other institution—is a means. *Not the family but living is the end.* Individual life should not be organized primarily for the benefit of the family; *family life should be organized so that the individual may live as nearly like a normal human being as possible.*"[35]

Combine the need for plural intimacy with the plea for forming the family to suit the individual better, and the result is either group marriage, serial marriage, or sanctioned extramarital involvement. Robert Rimmer, as we noted earlier, advocates group marriage. In *Future Shock*,[36] Alvin Toffler predicts that serial marriage will be the mode of the future. Love, he reasons, involves shared growth across a lifetime; but with the accelerated rate of change in so many areas, it will become increasingly unlikely that two individuals will be able to maintain an equal level of growth throughout ever-lengthening lifetimes. Consequently, he predicts, three marriages will be typical for tomorrow's needs: a trial marriage of youth, which may be short, passionate, and unstable, followed in many cases by a more enduring marriage during one's twenties. There will be fewer children, and they will leave home earlier than today. By their late thirties many individuals will have matured in their tastes and will enter into a third and final marriage. Permanence in marriage, in sum, will be rare and encountered only in those exceptional cases where high expectations for emotional, physical, and intellectual needs are mutually met.[37]

A slightly different stance is taken by those who envision the marriage bond as remaining more stable, but see increased freedom as being mutually available to the couple. There will be no single sex ethic, according to Morton Hunt,[38] but the total diversity—including secret affairs, polygyny, polyandry, swapping, communal experience, and "open" marriages—will be greater than today.

All these marriage structures contain one of two seemingly opposite principles. On the one hand, we see the criterion of commitment, implying an agreement to reside with the spouse and any resulting offspring and to commit oneself to their welfare permanently, barring unusual strains in the marriage. On the other hand, there is a concept of an unstable contractual agreement, one that exists only as long as perceived satisfaction remains greater within the marriage than outside it.

Several writers have tried to combine the two principles into a marriage of two stages. Margaret Mead[39] calls the first stage *individual marriage,* in which the participants are committed to each other for only so long as they wish, but they do not have the right to have children. In order to be able to enter the second stage, *parental marriage,* sanctified by its own license and ceremony, the couple have to demonstrate their economic ability to support a child. *Parental marriage* would presumably involve a life-long commitment and, unlike *individual marriage,* would be difficult to dissolve.

Essentially the same idea has been proposed by Bertrand Russell[40] and James Hemming,[41] except that the trial stage is not called "marriage," which connotes some sort of commitment. Virginia Satir[42] advocates avoiding life-long commitments altogether by having a renewable marriage contract, with an option to extend or cancel every five years.

Russell and Havelock Ellis[43] have gone even further in suggesting that even commitment should not be viewed as necessarily giving the legal right of exclusivity. Subject to the private accord of the participants, extramarital adventures or liaisons would be compatible with life-long marriage.

The Evolutionists

A popular argument of the late nineteenth and early twentieth century was that monogamy was destined to be the most accepted form of marriage in the present and foreseeable future because it had superior advantages to any other form. It was one of the rare occasions when religion and evolution united their forces. Westermarck[44] pointed out, in support of the principle of evolution, that man's closest neighbors on the evolutionary scale, the primates, had also evolved into monogamous unions. This assertion was quite discredited by more careful observations of primates, and for awhile the concept of monogamy as a product of evolution lay in limbo.

However, Desmond Morris, in *The Naked Ape,*[45] has again revived the view that "the forces which compel a man to live within the family are completely intrinsic and fully ingrained in the socio-biological content of the human organism."[46] He theorizes that the key to man's accomplishment has been his ability to work in teams. From the earliest days, when man first hunted, the ability to work as a team made him able to conquer prey that was much more physically formidable than himself. An important motivational factor in the team cooperation was that each man had his own woman; thus the relatively weaker members of the tribe, whose help was needed, could give their attention to the hunt in the confidence that, unlike the situation in the animal kingdom, might did not make right in connection with access to the female population.

For the care of children, "pair-bonding" has obvious advantages, and to ensure that the man would always be around to help the woman, she evolved into a permanently sexually receptive partner. This is in contradistinction to her simian sister, who is interested in sex only when in heat—but the monkey mother is more capable of attending to her young without outside help. There is nothing in Morris' speculation to deny that man might not evolve in a more promiscuous manner if survival conditions change; but since evolution is generally a slow process, his theory would suggest the survival of the monogamous "pair-bond" relationship, at least in the immediate future. His theory is no more than speculation, however, and it remains to be seen whether any empirical data will support it.

CONCLUSIONS

By definition, utopian works indicate a dissatisfaction by the writer with the times in which he finds himself. A common feature of some recent novels has been a lack of confidence in the ability of conventional marriage to provide for human satisfaction and growth. A recurring panacea—group marriage—will be discussed in detail in the next chapter.

Twentieth-century marriage theorists fall into three categories. Advocates of the traditional marriage of the *past,* such as Sorokin and Zimmerman, denounce current behavioral patterns as harbingers of the decay of family and society. Functionalists such as Ogburn and Parsons focus on the *present;* they find support for the present family roles in a symbiotic interaction with our industrial society. The "individualists" differ not only from the others but among themselves, as might be expected from those who focus on the *future.* Their chief point of difference among themselves is the extent to which they emphasize commitment in a relationship as opposed to self-satisfaction. There is, in short, little consensus among theorists as to the direction in which marriage and the family are heading.

REFERENCES

1. C. Bellamy, *An Experiment in Marriage.*
2. E. Zamiatin, *We.*
3. A. Huxley, *Brave New World.*
4. B. F. Skinner, *Walden Two.*
5. G. Orwell, *1984.*
6. Ibid., p. 66.
7. R. A. Heinlein, *Stranger in a Strange Land,* p. 350.
8. R. A. Heinlein, *The Moon Is a Harsh Mistress.*
9. R. H. Rimmer, *The Harrad Experiment.*
10. R. H. Rimmer, *Proposition 31.*
11. A. M. Ludovici, *Lysistrata.*
12. Ibid., p. 84.
13. Ibid., p. 109.
14. H. L. Mencken, *In Defense of Women.*
15. C. C. Zimmerman, *The Family of Tomorrow.*
16. P. A. Sorokin, *Social and Cultural Dynamics,* Vol. 4, p. 776.
17. C. C. Zimmerman, op. cit.
18. R. Hill, "The future of the family."

19. R. Hill, "The American family of the future."
20. W. F. Ogburn, "The changing functions of the family."
21. E. W. Burgess, H. J. Locke, and M. M. Thomes, *The Family: from Institution to Companionship.*
22. M. F. Nimkoff, "The future of the family."
23. L. G. Burchinal, "The rural family of the future."
24. T. Parsons and R. F. Bales, *Family, Socialization, and Interaction Process.*
25. H. Rodman, "Talcott Parson's view of the changing American family."
26. S. Kotlar, "Instrumental and expressive marital roles."
27. M. A. Strauss, "The influence of sex of child and social class on instrumental and expressive family roles in a laboratory setting."
28. C. W. Hobart, "Commitment, value conflict and the future of the American family."
29. W. M. Kephart, "Discussion of 'Commitment, value conflict and the future of the American family.' "
30. J. N. Edwards, "The future of the family revisited," p. 510.
31. E. H. Brill, "Is marriage dying too?"
32. B. Moore, Jr., "Thoughts on the future of the family," p. 401.
33. B. Farber, *Family: Organization and Interaction.*
34. C. Alexander, "The city as a mechanism for sustaining human contact," p. 67.
35. R. Borsodi, *Education and Living* (quoted in R. Rimmer, *Proposition 31*, p. 198).
36. A. Toffler, *Future Shock.*
37. C. Rogers, "Interpersonal relationships: U.S.A. 2000."
38. M. Hunt, *The Affair: A Portrait of Extra-Marital Love in Contemporary America.*
39. M. Mead, "Marriage in two steps."
40. B. Russell, *Marriage and Morals.*
41. "Briton offers guide for happy marriage."
42. "I, John take thee Mary—for the next five years."
43. H. Ellis, "The future of marriage."
44. E. Westermarck, *The Future of Marriage in Western Civilization.*
45. D. Morris, *The Naked Ape.*
46. G. C. Hallen and G. A. Theodorson, "The future of the family," p. 90.

24

Current Marital Innovations

There is growing dissatisfaction with the traditional husband-centered marriage in the United States, but which form(s), if any, will replace it? To ensure a reasonable prediction, it would be wise to examine first some current practices and their relationship to the theoretical alternatives already described. In this chapter we shall consider four major alternatives: unmarried cohabitors,* group marriage, communal life, and homosexual marriage. We shall compare these with the traditional marriage forms, polygyny and monogamy, and assess their strengths and weaknesses.

UNMARRIED COHABITORS

Since the founding of the Republic, a considerable number of men and women have eschewed the bonds of holy matrimony in favor of stable, common-law marriage. Drawn mainly from the ranks of the poor, they were not troubled by middle-class values concerning propriety, and the cost and legal involvements of legitimate marriage and divorce seemed more trouble than they were worth.

Today, however, a new type of unmarried cohabitor has appeared; their ranks, as yet small, are growing, especially among college student couples, and they have varied motivations.[1] A few detest all institutions, including matrimony. Some consider the arrangement a temporary convenience for the sake of companionship and sex until new plans take them elsewhere or until they tire of each other. The majority accept the institution of marriage, but live together to test the strength of the relationship or to prepare for marriage. A few regard themselves as committed, but for a variety of reasons find it expedient to postpone the wedding.[2] Regardless of motivations, the majority of cohabiting couples find living together a natural progression in their relationship; they begin by spending a night at a partner's place and it eventually becomes more convenient to move in.

*Cohabitor here signifies one who lives together with another person without being married.

These couples seem not to have taken Margaret Mead's two-step marriage proposal very seriously.[3] Nor have they been much impressed by her warning that, to the extent that their behavior goes contrary to the laws, they will inevitably suffer and may even be responsible for bringing the "whole social order down."[4]

Although some couples state that their relationships are not restrictive and include the freedom to interact intimately with others, one reporter found that their actual living patterns were quite at odds with their libertine philosophy. He noted that the participants, often from middle-class backgrounds, generally did not dress bizarrely, they remained "faithful" to each other, and they lived a rather bourgeois life in cozy apartments—in fact, they appeared "sensitive, edgy, unhappy and prematurely middle-aged."[5]

A number of the couples are precipitated into marriage by the woman's pregnancy. The fact that middle-class, college-educated couples allow pregnancy to occur doubtless suggests an unconscious wish to change the nature of the relationship. The life style of the unmarried married suggests an attempt to work through a basic conflict. Their living habits convey a sense of family, but their hesitation about marriage bespeaks a lack of basic trust in families.[6] They appear to have an unacknowledged obligation or commitment to their partners, and endure the limitations of marriage without fully savoring the benefits of a societally approved relationship.

Not surprisingly, many couples eventually drift into marriage.[7] Many of the women believe that such an action, when initiated by the man, symbolizes that they are really very much loved. Others, perhaps less in need of assurance, find it annoying to cope with the quasi-status of out-of-wedlock liaisons. They resent the cover-up lies they sometimes have to tell parents, neighbors, or friends. Legalizing the relationship guarantees the status of children and obviates inheritance problems. For many, marriage reduces the all-consuming involvement they have given to the relationship. Once married, they can—with a sigh of relief—get on to other interests.

Empirical Studies

Thus far we have reported the judgments of observers—astute observers, to be sure, but perhaps subject to the biases inherent in impressions. However, some recent empirical studies offer a means of verifying those observations. In the first of these quantitative studies,[8] 18 cohabiting couples were compared with 31 couples who were going together. The answers to background and personality inventories revealed that the going-together couples were more committed to marriage than the cohabiting couples. The women in the latter group, however, were only slightly less committed than the going-together couples, whereas the men in the cohabiting couples were clearly less committed. Only 3 of the 18 males in this group reported any public or private decision to marry eventually. Unlike the going-together men, they exhibited little feeling of respect and need for their partners, although they expressed ample trust and experienced sexual enjoyment.

Compared to the going-together group, the cohabiting couples showed far less reciprocity of feelings, need, respect, happiness, involvement, or commitment to marriage. They also indicated that they had had less happy adolescences, but both groups enjoyed similar degrees of happiness and involvement in the current relationship.

These results suggest that the cohabiting couples did not seem particularly oriented toward marriage even though most of the women had such hopes. While a sample of 18 couples is insufficient for a definitive generalization, the data do suggest caution about accepting earlier views on the sedateness and potential marriageability of the "unmarried married."

This caution is reinforced by Eleanor Macklin's study at Cornell.[9] She defines cohabitation as sharing a bedroom for at least four nights a week for at least three consecutive months. Macklin administered a questionnaire to 104 junior and senior women in a course on adolescent development. There were 86 responses; 29 (34 percent) had cohabited with a member of the opposite sex at least once. Of the remaining 66 percent, over two-thirds had stayed with a member of the opposite sex, but not long enough to qualify as cohabitors. Only one person thought it wrong to live with someone outside of marriage. The vast majority stated that they simply had not yet found the right person to live with. To the extent that these students were representative of Cornell undergraduates, and based on my own observations in New England colleges and universities, it must be concluded that living together has become a serious alternative to dormitory life.

Colleges have abandoned the *loco parentis* role. Sexual interaction is no longer punished, college chaperones are nonexistent, and many college health centers dispense contraceptives freely. Students express little guilt about living together, though half of them hide it from their parents. Since peer approval counts a great deal with young adults, it is noteworthy that most of them say that their friends approve and admire their arrangements.

Very few of the Cornell students who responded were engaged or contemplating marriage at the time of the initial cohabitation. About half were "going steady," and about a third had a strong relationship but were also open to other dating relationships. At the time the questionnaire was administered, a third of the relationships had terminated, a third were married or near marriage, and a third were still in the process of defining the relationship. Over 80 percent considered their relationship "maturing and pleasant," more than 50 percent termed it "very successful," and over 60 percent said that they would do it again with the same person, even where the relationship had broken up.

The data suggest that living together is the wave of the future. It is hard to fault it as a practicum for eventual marriage, for it gives a clearer portrait of one's potential spouse than the stereotyped dating behavior of the preceding generation. It is far from certain, however, that living together will substitute for marriage. Relatively few couples live together for an extended period; they break up or move toward marriage. The one-third who were still defining their relationship at Cornell consisted, in part, of those who no longer lived together but continued to see each other. Also, the college situation tends to favor decision avoidance with respect to marriage, since most individuals are committed to completing their education before marriage. Since only a third of the cohabitors were still living together at the time of the questionnaire, it does not appear that this alternative poses a serious threat to marriage. Rather, for most young people it is a developmental stage on the way to matrimony, a time to love and be loved, to find out more about themselves and their partners before the more serious step of marriage.

GROUP MARRIAGE

Group marriage may be defined as the relationship of three or more persons, each of whom is regarded as married or strongly committed to at least two other members of the group and with whom he or she cohabits. There is no reliable estimate of the number of group marriages in the United States because they are illegal in most states. The most extensive research in the area has been done by the Constantines, a computer scientist and his wife. They spent several years in intensive investigation, uncovered 31 such arrangements, and report the existence of about 50 others (based on a variety of unverified sources).[10-12]

The model participant in such marriages is already married to one spouse and is in his early thirties. The model size is four adults, and the largest reported group consisted of only six adults. Education was somewhat above average; religious interest and conventionality were below average. About half of the participants have tried "swinging" (an exchange of spouses for sexual purposes only) at one time or another, but have rejected it as too impersonal. Unlike swinging, in which the man is usually the instigator, both members of the couple seem to be equally motivated to enter a group marriage.

The Constantines were the first to obtain empirical data regarding the personalities of group-marriage participants. Administering the Edwards Personal Preference Schedule, a psychological test, they found that the average participant manifested greater heterosexual needs, a greater need for change, and less need for deference than the average person in the normative U.S. sample. Contrary to the utopian novels of Rimmer, where participants in group marriages are sexually faithful to other members, in real life this ethic was rarely practiced.

All this suggests that one of the primary motivations for group marriage is an interest in sexual variety. It is not surprising, therefore, that the Constantines found that preference for one's legal spouse as a sexual partner was more typical of dissolved groups than of extant ones. After all, if an individual found no one in the group more enticing than his spouse, he had little motivation to remain if sex was his primary motivation for joining it. On the other hand, if sexual motivation was the *only* factor, it did not seem sufficient to keep the group together for any length of time. Indeed, the overwhelming majority of group marriages do not survive more than a few weeks or months. The major problems appear to be "choice of sexual partner" and sexual jealousy. The Constantines suggest that sexual jealousy is a function of age (all 15 respondents under age 31, but only 9 of 15 over age 31, were jealous) and tends to disappear as a group continues (more enduring groups had fewer problems with sexual jealousy).

The first conclusion is probably true in that, with age, there is less concern over exclusivity about many things, including sexual fidelity. One reason may be the fact that older individuals are less physically desirable than younger ones; consequently, the opportunity to participate sexually with younger partners may be regarded as suitable compensation for allowing someone else to have access to one's relatively older spouse.

The second conclusion—that sexual jealousy is reduced dramatically with group experience (measured in terms of a few months)—is not, as the Constantines seem to think, supported by their data. It may well be that where sexual jealousy is disruptive, most groups soon break up, and that those few groups where sexual jealousy is not rampant are more likely to survive. But the Constantines fail to demonstrate that jealousy was *initially present* in the enduring groups and then disappeared.

In theory, at least, there would seem to be a number of benefits in group living, including the possibility of satisfying the wide variety of human needs. One member may be an especially good listener, a second may be a perfect lover, while a third may be a perfect foil for the "blues." Moreover, intensity of feeling in a group is diffused among many people rather than focused on a single individual; hence, individuals who are incapable or unwilling to enter intense emotional relationships find it easier to select their own pace in a group than in a one-to-one relationship.

The group also offers greater economic and emotional security. It is cheaper to live as a group than as a couple; a lost job is not as devastating and a quarrel with a partner does not leave one emotionally isolated. The potentialities for emotional growth and for getting feedback on how one appears to others are much greater in a group of six than in a couple. An overbearing individual, one who might otherwise dominate or bully a spouse, is more likely to be challenged in a group situation.

In the case of differences of opinion, the disputants can benefit from a more objective evaluation by the group. The Constantines found that children in group marriages thrived on the extra attention and affection of other adults, and the parents themselves were more relaxed and less harried due to fewer responsibilities.

The Constantines found a great deal of instability (in addition to jealousy) in connection with the sharing of spouses. A free choice of partners, for example, albeit democratic, presents certain problems. After all, three men and three women can form heterosexual couples in nine ways, and there are six ways of ordering choice patterns for the opposite sex for each person. The very process of selecting partners for the night could consume half the night! Consequently, some groups report that a fixed rotation of partners, even though it limits freedom and spontaneity, is preferred.

Another problem is that it is very rare for two persons to be matched in intellectual compatibility, sex interests, values, and psychological and social status. I have suggested earlier that couples function best when they have equal ability to reward each other even though they may not be equally matched in any given quality. Since our mounting divorce rate demonstrates how rare it is for a couple to maintain this balance over any period of time, is it reasonable to expect to find four or six individuals who are well matched with each other? Furthermore, granted that such an unusual quartet or sextet could be found, would they remain compatible for very long when needs are satisfied to different degrees and group members "grow" at different rates?

Another difficulty is the possible rejection, harassment, and ostracism by peers, neighbors, and society. Faced with a precarious legal status in most states, participants in a group marriage would encounter child-custody and/or property complications in the event of dissolution. Also, the emotional demands of living with other people can be very trying; a six-adult group has to contend with a total of 57 different relationships among two to six people! Many individuals, report the Constantines, simply cannot handle such a "sensory overload."

In a physically and socially mobile society, employment status has become the chief motivating force in life for many. "Getting ahead" often involves frequent job changes—for example, one-third of the membership of the American Psychological Association changes jobs, on the average, every two years! Occupational mobility often causes problems when husbands and wives have independent careers. Consider the complexities and the effects when six people live together, particularly in an era when our society is becoming ever more mobile.

Because group marriage appeals to the need for novelty, intimacy, and security, it will become somewhat more prevalent, especially if legalized. However, there are too many drawbacks ever to make it a mass form of marriage.

THE UTOPIAN COMMUNE: BIRTH AND DECAY OF THE COUNTERCULTURE

To understand the role of marriage in the utopian commune, we must first understand the significance of the modern utopian commune. Dissatisfied with the "establishment" and with the present structure of society, and lacking the power to change it, a small number of these heirs of the historical drive toward greater individuality have decided that they have two alternatives: to go underground or to "drop out" and build a counterculture.[13] Most dissidents have opted for the latter type of revolt.

Throughout the United States, communes with a great diversity in membership and in codes of behavior have sprung up. There are, for example, evolutionary communes and religious communes which work within the framework of society, or withdraw from it but do not actively attack it.[14] Not so with the utopian commune: despite their variability in life style, its members espouse a common philosophy, deriving from the hippie influence:

1. *Universal love.* Love, a most precious commodity, is to be shared with all rather than restricted to the family. Children are loved regardless of their biological parents, and the communal raising of children is encouraged.

2. *Unique value of the individual.* Leaders, or those who establish dominant-submissive relationships, are avoided.[15] Group decisions are not made by the majority but by consensus, since each individual's opinion is highly treasured.

3. *Natural is good.* Man is good if he lives by his instinctive nature rather than by artificial social pressures. Anything that smacks of adherence to the "games" of the system—e.g., the need to achieve or to "beat the other fellow"—is bad. Naturalism means working with simple hand tools rather than using products manufactured by the industrial complex. "Nature's children," i.e., the Negro and the Indian, are highly valued because of their naturalness (they, too, have been victimized by the industrial complex).

4. *Freedom of expression.* Each person should be sincere, "do his own thing," and avoid establishment prudishness, which puts useless clothing on people and even segregates them in unisex toilets. Sexual freedom is fully acceptable.

5. *Keep cool.* By disengaging yourself from an overconcern with material things, it is easy to keep your "cool": to be surprised at nothing, to accept life's vicissitudes with stoical fortitude.

6. *Sexual equality.* All vestiges of sexual exploitation are abjured. Women have sexual equality in the commune.

7. *Drugs.* This is the secret weed around which rituals of solidarity and mutual love are organized, for hippies believe that taking drugs together can lead to mystical experiences which may link them forever, even if they never see each other again. Drugs prove that the inner state (pleasure, revelation) is the important goal, not trying to change the outside world. Drug takers are privy to a wisdom that is beyond the grasp of any "square."[16]

8. *Nonrational, nonempirical emphasis.* Hippies tend to look askance at logicians, empiricists, and the like. Intuition, on the other hand, is highly respected, as is a fatalistic approach to life. No one questions if a project is rejected at the last moment because a member has bad "vibes" (vibrations) about it, and many hippies are enthusiasts of astrology and numerology.

Conflict and Contradiction

The late 1960s and early 1970s witnessed the growth, changing patterns, and dissolution of many communes. In some, structure and bureaucracy, including work schedules and officers, have replaced group consensus, work arrangements dependent on inspiration, and leaderless groups.

These changes stem from basic contradictions and naiveté in hippie philosophy, including a strong emphasis on the cult of collectivism while at the same time advocating independence of action. Spontaneity is a byword, but so is "keeping cool." It is hardly surprising, therefore, that in actual practice there have been many departures from communal philosophy. Mothers often do not wish to share their children with the group. The notion of self-sufficiency through loving care of the land and the use of simple "natural" tools has been replaced by frequent resort to government-issued food stamps and by attempts to purchase such sophisticated farm machinery as limited funds allow. Independence may be beautiful, but too many "free-loaders" sponged off the few who had the inspiration to work. Some people were never inspired enough to take out the garbage! Finally, when authority and schedules were installed, there was less distinction between the new existence and the establishment life which the communards so strenuously sought to escape. Communal sharing and cooperation often gave way to hoarding and indifference.

Group marriage and orgies never got much of a toehold in any communes. The formation of couples was the typical pattern, with perhaps a 10 percent adultery rate (known as "experiences" and "switching").[17] There are usually many more men than women in a commune, but the sexual conflict that would ordinarily ensue is often lessened by the presence of one or two young women on promiscuous "kicks." Originally, some hippies naively hoped that sex, which is natural and good, could be shared with all. But promiscuous women are usually regarded with amusement rather than veneration. Sex can be natural—in the sense that hippies think of naturalness—only for animals. Human sexuality is hardly a simple biological act; it is profoundly affected by the relationship between two people, by their fantasies, hopes, and grievances. Desmond Morris, in *The Human Zoo*,[18] discusses ten different concepts of sex, and his list is far from complete.

The fact that men and women tend to pair in communes suggests that most persons find it difficult to separate sex and emotions. Moreover, as Erazim Kohàk points out, "Not all sexual expression is necessarily the outcome of the impulse to freedom and joy. Masochism and sadism are the obvious counter-instance. In the terminology of the pop revolution, sex can be 'fascist.' "[19] While equality of the sexes in work is considered a key commune principle, the emphasis on agrarianism has assigned the men to the heavy equipment and to caring for large farm animals, with the women unavoidably thrust back into the kitchen and child-rearing.

Primitivism is objectively less feasible today than in Rousseau's time—and it was naive then. As Kohàk observes, "Primitivism . . . is an admission of inability to cope with the complexity of both society and costuming."[20] While society is assuredly more complex today than it was a century ago, it does not follow that complexity is synonymous with evil. Our society has the tools to build a paradise undreamed of in the past, or it can destroy itself. We are faced with the complexities of choice. A return to primitivism is akin to the ostrich hiding his head in the sand and declaring, "All's well if you don't look."

Perhaps the saddest commentary on the failure of the counterculture is the tale of two communes, as described by an itinerant writer:

> When Reality kept a steady population, Morningstar's had climbed to around eighty. No boundary separated them; legally, all the land was Michael Duncan's. The original understanding was that Reality and Morningstar would cooperatively farm the land. Last summer, when Morningstar didn't get around to planting its side, Reality appropriated it. Later in the season, Morningstar people began to rip off Reality's corn, and Reality reacted by driving off poachers with rifle fire aimed a few inches above the corn silk. Reality accused Morningstar of wasting water from the common irrigation ditch and of needlessly cutting down the mesa's few pinion trees for firewood.[21]

In sum, despite its lofty ideals and its rejection of the old, the counterculture appears to have "carried over from the straight world psychological transience, the fragmentation of lives, immersion in abstractions, self-indulgence, and an atomistic version of individual growth."[22] Its future seems largely limited to serving as a developmental stage on the road from adolescence to adulthood.

HOMOSEXUAL MARRIAGE

In our consideration of marriage we have heretofore restricted ourselves to heterosexual contracts. In other eras, marriage between homosexuals would have led to burning at the stake or to mutilation, but a more humanitarian attitude has been developing. Increasing numbers of homosexuals are emerging from "the closet." "Gay" organizations are fighting discrimination on the part of "straights," "gay" dances are held on many university campuses, and "gay" marriages are "performed" in churches, though they are not legal. Assuming a continuing liberalization of attitudes, it is predictable that homosexual marriage will eventually be legalized.

How many such marriages will take place? To answer this question we need first to know how many homosexuals there are. The best available source on the incidence of homosexuality, pending a forthcoming publication by the Institute for Sex Research, is the somewhat dated Kinsey report. According to Kinsey's findings, 37 percent of his male sample had had at least some homosexual experience to orgasm by old age. To be sure, many were adolescents who may have indulged in mutual masturbation; however, 18 percent of Kinsey's males were involved in homosexual relations in 50 percent or more of their sexual contacts; 10 percent of his males were predominantly or exclusively homosexual; and 4 percent were exclusively so.

For women, the percentages were considerably less for the 20-to-35 age range. Twenty-eight percent experienced homosexual arousal, 13 percent to orgasm. Between 4 and 11 percent of unmarried women and between 1 and 2 percent of married women were engaging in homosexual acts in at least 50 percent of their sexual contacts. Only between 1 and 3 percent of unmarried women and less than 3 in 1,000 married women were exclusively homosexual.

It is clear that a visible minority of the population has participated in homosexual experiences of more than a brief and temporary character. In the expected permissive climate of the future, it would not be very daring to predict an increment in these figures. Will many of these individuals with predominantly homosexual experience participate in homosexual marriages once these are legalized? I think not.

Kinsey's data, at first glance, do not appear to support my position. They show that only 30 percent of his masculine sample and only 10 percent of his feminine sample had had more than five homosexual partners, suggesting that the majority of homosexuals are not promiscuous and that they would be suitable candidates for matrimony. It should be kept in mind, nevertheless, that many of those in the homosexual partner group were not established homosexuals, but persons who may have tried a homosexual experience once (or a few times) as an adolescent and have since established a strong heterosexual orientation. Thus, there are fewer established homosexuals than the "raw" statistics might indicate, and the number of "established" homosexuals with high promiscuity rates is, therefore, higher than the all-inclusive rates indicate.

In support of this conclusion, clinical reports show the typical male homosexual to be rather promiscuous.[23-25] He may have enduring relationships, but these are rarely with the man with whom he engages in sex.

One deterrent to permanent sexual relationships is the fact that, at present, society does not sanction homosexuality. Some homosexuals are hounded by police or preyed upon by blackmailers and "hustlers" who threaten to reveal their status. Moreover, if single men live together past a certain age, they become suspect as to their sexual orientation. A male homosexual could hardly take his male sweetheart to the college prom. Pressures may also be exerted by employers and by the family against an enduring relationship.

Although an increasing number of people may favor the legalization of consentual homosexuality, which a few states have already enacted, legal tolerance hardly affects interpersonal and professional prejudice. How many people would feel comfortable if their department or company was headed by a homosexual? How many would vote for a homosexual president? It should be recalled that only a few years ago Walter Jenkins, an aide of President Lyndon Johnson, was hounded out of his job when his homosexuality was revealed.

Feminine homosexual relationships enjoy relatively more stability because of greater societal tolerance. Although men who live together may be considered less than masculine, women who do so are rarely considered to have lost their femininity. Similarly, the sight of women walking arm in arm, dancing with each other, or heartily embracing in the street raises far fewer eyebrows in the U.S.A. than two men engaged in the same behavior. Perhaps the chief reason for this disparity in attitudes is the subservient status women occupy in our society. A departure from femininity, in the direction of masculinity, is no great loss in status. As Professor Higgins says in *My Fair Lady,* "Why can't a woman be like a man?" But if the higher-status male behaves like a woman, he is ridiculed. The wearing of pants by women is accepted, but men who wear skirts are "queer".

Homosexuality predisposes against stable relationships for both men and women in yet another important way. Why does a person become a homosexual? There is suggestive evidence that hormonal factors may be involved in the etiology of homosexuality,[26,27] but the majority of researchers concur that the psychosexual role is largely a learned phenomenon. When an individual elects a nonsocietally approved choice, it often implies some unusual childhood difficulties or developments. Some people opt for homosexuality because of inadequacy in achieving satisfactory interpersonal relationships with either sex. A relationship with the opposite sex might develop into one with marital expectations. Many homosexual men, fearing or unable to handle intimacy, escape into promiscuous homosexuality. Impersonal sex in the "tea-room" (men's room) with a stranger provides sexual gratification without the need for involvement. One writer reports cases of random encounters between two men: one inserts his penis in the mouth of the other, and after ejaculation they take their leave, without any verbal exchange.[28]

Promiscuous homosexuality is less prevalent among women. Many female homosexual relationships do not entail direct sexual stimulation to orgasm. The relationships are apt to develop on the basis of culturally homogamous education, economic status, and age. Often, it is only after a solid friendship that the couple slowly evolves toward a sexual relationship. Since it is only after it reaches a sexual level that the friendship is classified, either by the participants or by society, as homosexual, it follows that women often engage in relatively long-term liaisons or "marriages" with other women. In fact, one woman writer argues that because of the imbalance of power between the sexes—to the advantage of men—the conditions for women "learning to love fully and without fear are at present met only in a homosexual setting."[29] Although her conclusion is debatable, the observation that women have more enduring homosexual relationships than men is scarcely questionable.

In sum, interpersonally inadequate males may have sufficient sexual drive to seek sexual release, but the excessive guilt, inadequacy, and societal antagonism they confront prevent them from developing enduring quasi-marital relationships. Women, enjoying more societal leeway and being better able to delay sexual gratification until a close interpersonal relationship has been established, are better equipped to maintain quasi-marriages. Although it is conceivable that homosexual marriage will be legalized, subtle and not so subtle pressures will limit the number of declared homosexual marriages to a very small proportion of the population.

CAN PRESENT MARRIAGE FORMS SURVIVE?

In our attempt to predict the future, we have not yet considered the possibility that marriage as it exists today, with its strengths and weaknesses, will continue. Therefore, we shall briefly examine two contemporary basic marriage forms: polygyny and monogamy.

Polygyny

Although polygynous marriages are still quite numerous, their prospects are not very bright. In the past, polygyny was associated with the strengthening of kinship ties, but in an industrial age one's kin no longer bring economic rewards, their influence is waning, and the cost of supporting multiple families is onerous. With urbanization, industrialization, and mobility, the housing and transporting of multiple families become more complicated. Most important, women are increasingly resisting sharing their husbands with other women. The ideology of egalitarian marriages and the stronger economic position of women portend a bleak future for polygyny.

Among the aged, where widows far outnumber widowers, there may be an exception to this predicted decline. Why should the deprivation of family life, companionship, and sex be the price of longevity? Given an era of enlightened legislation, polygyny may be instituted in previously monogamic countries, and such marriages may be permitted among the elderly.[30] Except for this group, it would seem merely a question of time until polygyny becomes a custom of historical interest.

Monogamy (Heterosexual)

In terms of future criteria, it may surprise few to learn that monogamy compares favorably with the various marriage forms already described. After all, monogamy has weathered many millennia; unlike polygamy, it fits the general marriageable population ratio of one man for one woman, and it provides a potential for a wide range of emotional intimacy. Another virtue is its flexibility: many tasks formerly regulated by the monogamous family have been readily given up without undue strain. As to its three chief contemporary functions—procreation, socialization of children, and emotional interaction—only the last seems to be at the heart of the institution. In the future, procreation may take place outside the human body, and children may be raised in communal nurseries. Even with only one function, emotional interaction, monogamy can fulfill this need as well, or better than, any other marriage form. Last but not least, monogamy is also the simplest way to transmit property from one generation to another.

But if monogamy is so roseate, why is the divorce rate so high and still climbing? We have pointed out that multiple intimacy is necessary for the satisfaction of a variety of human needs. Intimacy, however, feeds on continued exposure to another person, and the opportunities for intimacy have decreased. The transitory nature of employment patterns and of interpersonal relations has weakened the supportive role once given by peers, parents, and community. Monogamy is now asked to bear alone a rather overwhelming burden. In addition, all the educational media stress the search for self-actualization, the need to be erotic, and to enjoy every possible experience—as the beer ad puts it, "You only go round once in this world." Some individuals maintain that it is difficult to remain erotically stimulated by one partner, no matter how profound his or her talents. Many marriages become tedious, some are "comfortable," and only a few of long standing are exciting.

Not everyone craves excitement. The individual confronted with tension-packed job problems may desire quiet relaxation at home. But if his wife has been home all day, she may demand that he supply some excitement! Hopefully, with a future increase in dual-career families, this gap in desire for stimulation will decrease.

Even in dual-career families, a certain erosion in the marital relationship can set in with the passage of time. Expectations regarding one's spouse remain high, but the perceived fulfillment of these expectations—or at least their satisfaction—decreases. Adaptation has set in. The spouse is taken for granted. The thrill of fulfillment is replaced by the expectation that certain needs will be fulfilled. Unusual performance or temporary deprivation is required to regain the thrill, but the partner's behavior "repertoire" becomes predictable, unexciting. One knows by heart the little ploys that he or she uses in company; the new jokes for guests are "ancient history" to the spouse.

As boredom sets in, a craving for extramarital experience develops. The fact that these cravings are suppressed because of lack of opportunity, because it would hurt the spouse, or because of fear of inadequacy does not mean they are mere fantasies. If the individual is stimulated by an eroticized culture, if he is taught to express himself more fully, and if opportunities increase in a mobile society, he may attempt to act out his fantasies.

Coming generations, with fewer inhibitions, may find the guilt feelings experienced in the twentieth century quite amusing. In fact, in a *Psychology Today* sample (1969), only 18 percent of the men and 27 percent of the women considered extramarital sex to be unequivocally wrong. The majority of men, and at least a sizable minority of women, have committed or will commit adultery at least once in their lives. Their motivations and their moral acceptance of their actions will vary, for adultery no longer conjures up the unitary connotation of theological or psychological sin that it once did. Adultery, like love, can signify an assortment of relationships among spouses—from unselfish tolerance to deceitful exploitation, as a classification of adultery recently proposed by Gordon Clanton clearly shows:

I. *Clandestine adultery.* Old-style adultery. The spouse is unaware of the extramarital relationship, and it is assumed he would disapprove if he knew.

II. *Ambiguous adultery.* The spouse knows about the extramarital relationship but does not fully approve. The spouse has been informed by the adulterer and tolerates it, or the spouse has discovered the adultery but "officially" does not know it and chooses not to confront the spouse.

III. *Consentual adultery.* The spouse knows and approves of the extramarital relationship. There are three types:

1. *Group marriage.* An agreement which links three or more persons in a common projection of a future together, a future marked by spatial propinquity, emotional interdependence, economic sharing, and sexual access to persons in addition to one's spouse or prime lover.

2. *Open-ended marriage.* A relationship between spouses in which each grants the other the freedom to involve himself or herself in important emotional relationships with others [even relationships marked by sexual sharing].

3. *Recreational adultery.* Extramarital sexual experiences marked by a relatively low level of commitment and by the expectation of relative impermanence.[31]

Included within recreational adultery are swinging (to be discussed shortly) and intercourse with a pick-up or prostitute.

Until recently, clandestine and ambiguous adulteries have been the usual forms. Consentual adultery represents a possible future innovation. Within this categorization, we have already discussed the advantages and liabilities of group marriage.

Another type of consentual adultery, *open-ended marriage,*[32] has been advocated by a number of writers, the most notable of whom was Havelock Ellis; but we have already seen how his personal life was quite at odds with his philosophy. The reasons for the failure of open marriage to become widespread are not difficult to detect. Divorce was once inhibited by concern over the effect on children, and the threat of economic insecurity and social stigma. The importance of these factors is constantly lessening, and the quality of the emotional relationship between the couple is increasingly regarded as the primary bond of marriage. This being the case, the freedom to engage in total relationships with others proves quite threatening to the more insecure spouse. What if the spouse falls in love with someone else? What will happen to the marital emotional bond? If both partners engage in extramarital relationships, they may fall in love with someone else. While such a situation would indeed be egalitarian, it would also suggest that the forces pulling the couple away from their present status might lead them to question the advisability of remaining married.

Some couples practice total open-ended marriage, but no data are available with respect to their marriage stability or their satisfaction with the new arrangement. The paucity of evidence, and the negative reaction of many persons to such an agreement, suggest that only a select few will be able to practice open-ended marriage successfully.

The promiscuity arrangement within recreational adultery would seem slightly less threatening to a marriage, since it assumes that the extramarital contact will be on a purely sexual level without any commitment. Yet there is always the danger that such experiences could develop into affairs of the heart, particularly when an absent spouse cannot exercise a counterbalancing influence. A variation of recreational adultery, "swinging," offers many of the advantages of simple promiscuity and, by virtue of its structure, alleviates worry about the development of a full-blown affair. We shall now review some research findings on "swinging," which has received a great deal of attention in the press and in many recent books as a serious variant of monogamy.

Swinging

Swinging, in the context of our examination, refers to a couple's having sexual relations with at least one other individual.[33] The number of couples who have swung at least once has been estimated at between 500,000 and 8 million.[34] The only relatively "hard" data available came from a random sample of 579 persons in a Midwest community of 40,000. Ten persons—1.7 percent of the sample—had engaged in swinging at least once.[35] Assuming, on the basis of a considerable number of surveys, that the Midwest is relatively conservative, it could reasonably be estimated that between 1 and 2 million persons have swung at least once.

The swingers studied so far tend to resemble other upper-middle-class couples in many respects, such as income and education.[36] They do, however, differ from traditional couples in their preoccupation with sex. In a Chicago sample, 99 percent of the men read *Playboy,* and 10 percent were confirmed nudists.[37] In another sample, 90 percent acknowledged being nude in the presence of other swingers, with 57 percent having engaged in intercourse in the presence of others.[38]

To some extent, the description of swingers has been highly contradictory. The survey of a Chicago sample found that 40 percent admired George Wallace of Alabama, and that the majority strongly opposed drugs. On the other hand, another study in California, which compared 100 swinging couples with 100 control persons on a lengthy questionnaire, showed swingers to be quite liberal[39] in political outlook and in tolerance of drugs, drinking, civil rights protesters, long hair, and abortion.

The California sample was quite deviant in areas other than sex; for example, they opposed religious orthodoxy and Sunday school. Compared to the controls, they were more likely to have engaged in premarital sex, to have conceived their first child before marriage, to have been divorced, and to have had divorced parents (only the men). They favored more freedom for women and thought it proper to take a person of the opposite sex to lunch and to practice nudity around the house. They were not as close to their relatives or to their family of origin as to friends. Also, they were more likely to believe that rights were more important than duties.

Their interest in sex, not unexpectedly, differed dramatically from that of the control group. Many swingers recalled a preoccupation with romance while still in kindergarten or in the early primary grades. They dated earlier and had many more premarital sexual partners. Despite extramarital outlets, they also engaged in sex with their spouse quite frequently: 55 percent experienced four or more copulations per week with their spouse compared to 16 percent of the controls. In addition, they enjoyed sex more.

Both general contentment and relationships with spouses seemed slightly better than the controls, and they suffered less from anomie or time on their hands. They describe themselves as warmer and more affectionate than the controls do. Their marital happiness was slightly higher, but not significantly so; however, the swinging men (not the women) were more satisfied with the affection given by their spouse, and both were more likely to spend time talking to each other and to use such expressions as "I love you." On the other hand, swingers were less happy as adolescents, they struggled more with their parents, and they communicated less with them. Also, swinging women were currently less close to their mothers, as compared to control women.

In conclusion, the only crystal-clear finding is that swingers possess high sex drives. Whether, as a class, they are deviant in areas other than sex and are somewhat detached from their family of origin awaits further studies. Different findings with different samples may mean only that sex makes strange bedfellows as well as bedfellows of strangers!

The Swinger Philosophy

There has been a great deal of fanfare about the philosophy of swingers, namely, that sex and love can be separated and that sex without emotional involvement is enjoyable as recreation. (Sex in marriage is accompanied by emotional involvement.) To assure a minimum of involvement, repeated choice of the same partner is frowned upon, as is "romantic" conversation without sexual activity.

On the basis of published reports and interviews, I am inclined to conclude that such a generalization is patently unwarranted. There are, true enough, an unknown number of swingers who are focused exclusively on sex. Others appear to be searching for an intimacy with others besides their spouses. It is not difficult to understand why, for we have already considered the relative isolation in a mobile and urban environment. Where people are conditioned to respond in highly stylized ways to others, with little involvement and emotional contact, sex may be regarded as the key to surmounting the barriers to a hoped-for emotional contact. For most people, sex is not an impersonal act. Although many individuals will pretend emotional interest in someone else in order to spirit a partner into bed, others may use sex to gain friends and intimacy. Extramarital sexual intimacy—the breaking of a taboo—may be used as a device for entering into friendship, particularly in the absence of kin-neighbor-friendship relational systems that reduce some of the demands on the marital bond.[40]

Many swingers may conclude that a person who can overcome the deep-seated inhibition against sex activity with a stranger will also be the kind of person who can rapidly cut through inhibitions to emotional interaction. There is no evidence of the validity of this assumption, but the literature does indicate that some swingers prefer swinging because it avoids problems of intimacy and involvement with others,[41] whereas other swingers hope to enrich their coterie of friends as well as their sex partners.[42,43] The presence of a dichotomy is suggested by the responses to the above-cited questionnaire.[44] In response to the statement, "expressing feelings of 'love' for a swinging partner is generally considered undesirable or unacceptable in the swinging world," 68 percent of the swinging men and 49 percent of the swinging women disagreed or were uncertain. Some 32 percent of the swinging men and 51 percent of the swinging women agreed with the statement.

Where swingers do develop friendships, their sexual interaction often decreases or is terminated.[45] Why this should be has not been investigated. It may be that when a friendship develops, the vagaries attached to the sex act threaten the new relationship. For example, if one member of a foursome loses sexual interest in his extramarital partner, the friendship of all four might be threatened. Since, to a swinger, sex may be available almost anywhere—whereas friendship is not—he may decide to safeguard the new relationship by avoiding sex.

There is no question, however, that a swinger is very different from the run-of-the-mill adulterer. Most adulterers (who are usually men) do not wish their spouses to mimic their adulterous behavior. Swingers, on the other hand, espouse a single standard, and the swinging wife is accorded equal privileges. If the wife cannot participate in a "social"—for example, if she is menstruating—the husband usually is not allowed to participate. Because of this egalitarian philosophy and the limitations on nonsexual interaction, jealousy is generally not a major problem among swingers.[46]

How Swingers Meet

Getting to meet a fellow swinger is a problem for the novitiate couple: they fear disclosure and, in addition, there is a paucity of couples who actually swing. One way is to insert or answer an ad. One magazine ad read as follows:

> S-225
> Married couple, middle thirties. Wife 37-25-36, husband muscular, Los Angeles area. Willing to try anything. Interested in French, Greek, and Arab culture. No single men.[47]

Much of the ad is self-explanatory. The references to culture hardly indicate a hunger for international esthetics. They represent a code: French culture signifies that the couple likes oral sex, the Greek allusion means that they are amenable to anal intercourse, and the Arab feature points to an appreciation of sado-masochistic practices. Ads, however, are risky. Photos may result in blackmail, or people may send doctored or old photos and misrepresent their age or "vital" statistics. And since there is also no control over the kind of mentality one may encounter on a blind date, many swingers prefer that initial contacts be made at "socials" sponsored by swinger magazines, at swinger bars, or through friends.[48] Once established, future arrangements are simple. There are extensive swinger networks, and a couple moving to a different locale can usually be put in touch with others in the new area.

Most swingers range from 25 to 41 years in age[49]; the average number at a get-together is five to eight couples,[50] with an average frequency of twice a month. Although initially it is the man who persuades his spouse to participate, a good number of women, after a period of time, seem to enjoy swinging more than the men do. The women often become bisexual, which is rather rare among men. In one sample, 65 percent of the women *admitted* having sexual relations with other female swingers. In the swinging sessions which he personally observed, the anthropologist Gilbert Bartell recorded 92 percent of the women becoming sexually involved with one another.

Several factors account for female homosexual relationships among swingers:

Most men are hardly matches for sexually aroused multiorgasmic women. While the men rest, they often experience sexual restimulation if they watch women make love to each other. Presumably the sight of another man making love to their spouse (while they are not similarly occupied) would be too ego-threatening to some men, but practically no men are threatened by the sight of two women making love.

Many women are esthetically disturbed by the concomitants of heterosexual love-making. They find semen messy, and the thought of fellating a stranger or even their own spouse is somewhat repulsive. With other women they can at least avoid semen.

The effect of novelty can be highly motivating. Many women have wondered what it would be like to make love to a woman, but have never had a socially sanctioned opportunity. Homosexuality is often interpreted as an inferior activity in our need-achievement-oriented society, because it assumes that the individual cannot successfully "score" with the opposite sex. Because men occupy a higher status in society, they stand to lose more by such activity than women. As a result, there is rarely any male homosexual interaction at swinger parties, although younger swingers show more "flexibility" in this regard than older ones.

At first glance, swinging seems like the answer to the needs of modern marriage. Its advantages are many[51,52]:

It is less time-consuming and emotionally demanding than an affair.

It is less expensive than an affair.

It offers sexual variety for couples bored with each other.

There is less danger of losing one's spouse as compared to discovered infidelity.

It often rejuvenates sexual interest in the spouse.

It is educative sexually.

It offers a chance for a couple to share the thrill of the risqué as they plan for and attend swinger affairs. It affords a camaraderie that others cannot share.

It is democratic and honest.

It is ideal for those who fear intimacy with their own spouse.[53]

In sum, it is in the best American tradition: "to be popular, to have friends, to be busy."[54]

On the other hand, swinging is not without drawbacks:

There is often a lack of emotional closeness between sexual partners, which robs some individuals of sexual enjoyment and/or the ability to perform adequately.

There is little ego satisfaction when the "other" can be won, not by dint of one's charm and attractiveness but merely by being available.

Fantasy often gives way to disappointed reality as one becomes aware that the "other" is rarely a Venus de Milo incarnate, but is flabbier than he (she) appeared with clothes on, or has bad breath or is addicted to unacceptable sexual techniques.

There is a competitive air which inhibits performance. From the woman's point of view, there is always a woman who is sexier, bigger-bosomed, more curvaceous, and more attractive. From the man's point of view, there is always a handsomer fellow, "better hung," and more potent. Not surprisingly, therefore, Bartell reported that 12 percent of the women never experienced orgasm except with their husbands, while less than 25 percent of the men were fully adequate at all swinger sessions.[55]

There is a cult of youth, and everyone becomes less desirable with age.

Many individuals find that they cannot overcome their jealousy and fear that someone else will appeal more to their spouse.

Some individuals cannot shed their feeling of guilt and lowered self-esteem after engaging in what they believe is basically immoral.

For those who adhere to the dictum of swinging only once with another person, or for those who collect new sexual experiences like trophies, there is a never-ending search for new, beautiful partners. Many fatiguing hours are spent on the phone, in writing letters and driving hundreds of miles for interviews, and then perhaps feeling embarrassed at vetoing unattractive prospects or, even worse, experiencing the ignomy of being rejected.

There is a subliminal fear that swingers may introduce venereal disease.

In sum, swinging is neither a sexual paradise nor the road to perdition. It is, in fact, not even a unitary phenomenon. There are male swingers who become impotent with a woman unless they can talk for hours before attempting intercourse (they are known as "head" men). There are swingers who probably "can't make it" with people after they become too intimate with them. The swingers who have been studied appear more content than the controls or the average man on the street. Moreover, their marriages seem no worse than others, perhaps even slightly better. The difficulty is that no one yet knows much about the attitudes and experiences of those people who try swinging and drop out. How large a number do they constitute, and what is the effect of swinging on their personality and marital adjustment? Rectification of this omission through research will be a major contribution to our ability to predict the viability of swinging marriages.

In my opinion, swinging is a major improvement over clandestine adultery. Its focus on honesty, communication, and shared interests between the marital couple expresses the desire for increased communication between men and women. It does not represent the ultimate in interspousal harmony, for it does contain rigid rules of exchange. Each spouse gets no more and no less than the other. If, for example, the woman dislikes a prospective partner, the couple may not swing even though the man might like his partner.

Ideally, in the perfect open marriage, each partner would feel so secure and committed to his spouse that the other might "freelance" without any concern about his partner's jealousy; thus the tit-for-tat exchange theory is an intermediate step in the potential for a higher relationship between husband and wife. It may well be a transitory practice for couples who were raised with a double sex standard but are trying to be fair to each other. Such couples might be too insecure, or too concerned, about free sexual expression on the part of their spouse to be able to tolerate a more spontaneous, flexible arrangement—hence the need for rules. Yet, practically speaking, the millennium of complete acceptance of each other's emotional and sexual expressions vis-à-vis others, while maintaining permanent and mutual commitment, does not appear to be around the corner. Thus, swinging serves as a transition, and it may well prosper for some time to come.

CONCLUSIONS

Although the variations in male-female relationships reviewed in this chapter differ considerably from traditional monogamy, closer inspection indicates that only one variation—group marriage—is in direct conflict with it. Cohabitors and commune adherents are mainly transients: in moving from a single status to marriage, they have stopped off at way-stations. Cohabitation and, to a lesser extent, communal living involve many patterns of intimacy found in marriage: division of chores, sex, the daily routines of living together and being treated as a couple. As a means of assessing the feasibility of marriage with a prospective spouse, such living arrangements are infinitely superior to the traditional stereotyped dating patterns, which bore little relationship to subsequent marital behavior. Further, since commune members and cohabitors are mainly young adults who rarely continue in such arrangements for more than a year or two, they hardly pose serious threats to eventual marriage.

At their best, recreational adulteries, on the other hand, embody an expansion of traditional monogamy rather than a threatening alternative. The strong taboos against emotional interaction in swinging are indirect tributes to the value placed by the participants on their marriages. The evidence also suggests that although a considerable number of swinging couples drop out, they rarely do so because the spouse has become involved with another swinger; hence, swinging per se is apparently no threat to marriage.

Open marriage does appear to be a possible threat, but it is more apparent than real. There is no research on the number of totally open marriages; based on observation, however, they are much rarer than swinging, and swinging is presently engaged in by only a tiny fraction of the population. In addition, there are probably two kinds of people who engage in open marriage. One kind may be those individuals with extremely limited mutual involvement who, for various reasons, prefer to remain married and also operate freely. Such persons can hardly be said to threaten traditional monogamy, for without an open-marriage arrangement they would probably resort to clandestine adultery or divorce. On the other hand, individuals may engage in open marriage who are not only independent but also secure in their affection for each other. It hardly seems bold to suggest that the number of such individuals in our society is miniscule. This highly self-selecting sample is probably immune to the traditional jealousies and insecurities that known extramarital relationships inflict on the vast majority of married couples, and they are, therefore, unlikely to divorce on the basis of such relationships.

Group marriage, then, is the only form that is incompatible with monogamy; but because of the rarity of achieving compatibility with two or more other persons, it is impossible to consider group marriage seriously as a viable alternative to monogamy. If none of these variations can be expected to supplant monogamy, what will future marriage be like? Before we attempt an answer, we shall review the main themes regarding love, sex, and marriage that have emerged in our historical survey.

REFERENCES

1. D. Block, "Unwed couples: Do they live happily ever after?"
2. A. Karlen, "The unmarried marrieds on campus."
3. M. Mead, "Marriage in two steps."
4. M. Mead, "A continuing dialogue on marriage: Why just living together won't work," p. 52.
5. A. Karlen, op. cit., p. 78.
6. Ibid.
7. D. Block, op. cit.
8. J. L. Lyness, K. E. Davis, and M. E. Lipetz, "Living together: An alternative to marriage."

9. E. D. Macklin, "Heterosexual cohabitation among unmarried college students."
10. L. L. Constantine and J. M. Constantine, "Multilateral marriage: A position paper."
11. L. L. Constantine and J. M. Constantine, "Group and multilateral marriage: Definitional notes, glossary, and annotated bibliography."
12. L. L. Constantine and J. M. Constantine, "Sexual aspects of multilateral relations."
13. W. Hedgepath and D. Stock, *The Alternative: Communal Life in North America.*
14. J. W. Ramey, "Emerging patterns of innovative behavior in marriage."
15. G. Dworkin, "The hippies: Permanent revolution?"
16. J. Pitts, "The hippies as contrameritocracy."
17. J. Pitts, "The counter culture: Tranquilizer or revolutionary ideology?"
18. D. Morris, *The Human Zoo.*
19. E. V. Kohàk, "Turning on for freedom," p. 440.
20. Ibid., p. 439.
21. R. Houriet, *Getting Back Together,* p. 184.
22. D. French, "After the fall," p. 35.
23. A. Karlen, *Sexuality and Homosexuality: A New View.*
24. D. Sonnenschein, "The ethnography of male homosexual relations."
25. M. Hoffman, *The Gay World.*
26. B. Rensberger, "Homosexuality linked to hormone level."
27. R. B. Evans, "Physical and biochemical characteristics of homosexual men."
28. L. Humphreys, *Tearoom Trade.*
29. J. Kelly, "Sister love: An exploration of the need for homosexual experience," p. 475.
30. V. Kassel, "Polygyny after sixty."
31. G. Clanton, "The contemporary experience of adultery," pp. 8, 9, 10.
32. N. O'Neill and G. O'Neill, *Open Marriage.*
33. G. D. Bartell, "Group sex among the mid-Americans."
34. W. Breedlove and J. Breedlove, *Swap Clubs.*
35. G. B. Spanier and C. L. Cole, "Mate swapping: Participation, knowledge, and values in a midwestern community."
36. C. E. Schupp, "An analysis of some social-psychological factors which operate in the functioning relationship of married couples who exchange mates for the purpose of sexual experience."
37. G. D. Bartell, *Group Sex: A Scientist's Eyewitness Report on the American Way of Swinging.*
38. J. R. Smith and L. G. Smith, "Co-marital sex and the sexual freedom movement."
39. B. G. Gilmartin, unpublished tables on a sample of swingers and controls.
40. J. W. Ramey, "Emerging patterns of behavior in marriage: Deviations or innovations?"
41. G. D. Bartell, *Group Sex: A Scientist's Eyewitness Report on the American Way of Swinging.*
42. G. Palson and R. Palson, "Swinging in wedlock."
43. H. F. Margolis and P. M. Rubenstein, *The Groupsex Tapes.*

44. B. G. Gilmartin, op. cit.
45. H. F. Margolis and P. M. Rubenstein, op. cit.
46. G. Palson, "Swingers and non-swingers: Conceptions of sex."
47. R. R. Bell, "Swinging—the sexual exhange of marriage partners."
48. D. Denfield, "How swingers make contact."
49. C. Symonds, "A pilot study of the peripheral behavior of sexual mate swappers."
50. G. C. O'Neill and N. O'Neill, "Patterns in group sexual activity."
51. D. Denfield, "Towards a typology of swinging."
52. D. Denfield and M. Gordon, "The sociology of mate swapping: Or the family that swings together clings together."
53. E. Nemy, "Group sex: Is it 'life art' or a sign that something is wrong?"
54. G. D. Bartell, *Group Sex: A Scientist's Eyewitness Report on the American Way of Swinging*, p. 282.
55. G. D. Bartell, ibid.

25
Love, Sex, and Marriage:
An Overview and Some Predictions

In our review of the history of marriage, we have noted four major factors that contributed to its development: the change from institution-centered to individual-centered marriage; the relationship of women's status to marriage stability; changes in expectations regarding marriage; and the changing perception of sex. We shall consider each of these historical factors as well as some current trends, and will conclude by presenting some ideas on what marriage may be like in the near future.

HISTORICAL TRENDS

From Institution-Centered to Individual-Centered Marriage

Marriage among the ancient Chinese, Japanese, Greeks, and Romans served to further the interests of the extended family rather than of the participants. In time, however, the extended family was undercut by industrialization and urbanization. Geographic mobility separated the nuclear family from the kin network. Services formerly provided by the extended family—for example, education, protection, and employment—were gradually taken over by other institutions and societies which increasingly valued achievement more than fortuitous birth.

It would be a mistake, nevertheless, to assume that changes in family orientation are inevitably a simple function of the industrial structure. Ideology changes over time, not only as a result of industrialization but also because of interpersonal communication and altered values. Individuals are not mere modules in the industrial complex, but are themselves capable of changing society and industry to fit their needs. Recent Soviet divorce law reforms did not benefit the industrial complex, nor did the innovative four-day work week of several American companies. Rather, these changes reflect a desire for freedom of human interaction in the one case, and of greater leisure time in the second. They also reflect a growing awareness of the need to accommodate

555

society and industry to the individual rather than vice versa.

In the future it seems likely that the focus on the fulfillment of individual needs will erode many traditional family patterns. Children will rely more on peer mores than on those of their parents, fewer parents will believe in sacrificing their pleasures for their children, and husband and wife will more readily enter into outside relationships as individuals rather than depending almost exclusively on "couple" relationships.

The Relationship between Women's Status and Marriage Stability

If we trace the rise in women's status through history and compare it with the divorce rate, we discover an interesting relationship. The higher her status, the higher the woman-initiated divorce rate. In the United States and in most Western countries, where divorce is most frequently initiated by women, the correlation extends to all divorces regardless of the sex of the initiator. Nineteenth- and twentieth-century critics who complained that women's rights would lead to a breakdown in family stability were absolutely correct! Where they may have erred was in assuming that family stability, as it existed at that time, was a desirable state of affairs.

As I see it, in the past, family stability generally was more conducive to the happiness of the husband than of the wife, and so long as men enjoyed a vastly superior status, they perpetuated "family stability." Their status rested on three factors: (1) greater physical strength, (2) women's continuing fertility in the absence of knowledge about contraception, and (3) the ideology, perpetuated by men, that the disparity in masculine and feminine roles was God-given rather than power-motivated.

In hunting or agrarian societies, the greater physical strength of the male was used to trap animals or handle large farm livestock, to defend themselves against predators or plunderers, and to intimidate women. We can surely assume that this greater strength was a means to achieve special privileges in marriage. In addition, women spent most of their adult lives in being pregnant and in nursing and caring for children. Life expectancy was short, and many women succumbed in childbirth; hence, little energy or time remained to attempt to alter their inferior status.

Third, ideology served to retard equality in a number of ways. Theology taught that woman (the temptress Eve) was inferior to man—a bias that was hardly surprising because almost all theologians were men. Moreover, since masculine and feminine roles were God-given, attempts to change them were un-Christian. As a result, when European universities began to open their doors in the thirteenth century, only men were admitted; after all, it was argued, education can serve no useful purpose for women, who are destined for the hearth.

Although men generally favored family stability, there were specific instances where divorce was necessary for reasons of incompatibility or family alliance.

Depending on the culture, divorce might be realistically available for the man but not for the woman, or, as in the Catholic Church, it was altogether forbidden. In the latter case, however, annulments could be purchased with money or favors. While not all societies expressly forbade divorce initiated by women, women's lower status and their inability to support themselves made divorce largely a male prerogative. Most societies, nevertheless, could not tolerate large-scale divorce because of women's economic helplessness and the realization that population growth, until recently a prime goal of almost every nation, would be jeopardized by family instability.

Throughout the early Christian era and much of the medieval period, there was little serious questioning of the supremacy of the male in marriage and in relationships between the sexes. In the twelfth century, however, the French chatelaine was elevated in status (mainly in the literary sense) through the phenomenon of courtly love. However, these women were few in number and enjoyed an atypically high station in life. They had serfs to tend their crops, nurses to handle their offspring, and they themselves received a relatively good education at the hands of private tutors. Their gains from courtly love, limited to enhancing their creature comforts, had no profound effect on the status of women in general.

By the end of the Middle Ages and the onset of the Renaissance and the Reformation, women's status improved slightly. Europe was not quite as dependent on agriculture for subsistence. Commerce had developed, and some women worked side by side with their husbands, with the permission of the guilds. Although still regarded as inferior, a woman was no longer stigmatized as the "temptress Eve." A few wealthy women of the bourgeoisie received an education, and a few divorces were granted to women for extreme incompatibility.

From the seventeenth to the middle of the nineteenth century, women's legal and social status slowly rose in the West. The divorce rate increased concomitantly; however, as late as 1860 the number of divorces in the United States numbered only 7,380 out of a population of over 31 million. During the nineteenth century, women made considerable ideological gains. They were celestialized as "angels in the house," and their social status rose accordingly. Moreover, the vociferous women's rights leaders brought an awareness of the discrimination against them to an increasingly sympathetic populace. Still, rhetoric did not profoundly affect the power structure.

Power was eventually achieved through several channels. After the Civil War, college education became increasingly available to women, and industrial expansion made room for them in the labor market. Relatively effective contraceptive methods became more widespread, permitting women to escape from permanent entrapment in the nursery and kitchen. Legal discrimination regarding property, civil rights, and the vote began to yield to the persistent efforts of women's rights groups.

As of the second half of the twentieth century, the foundations for women's inferior status were shattered, but some vestiges still remained. Physical strength counted for very little as far as job advancement was concerned. Contraception had been so perfected that the most industrialized nations were approaching zero population growth. This meant that marriage would no longer mean the abandonment of professional aspirations for women; their children would be few in number and increasingly cared for in child-care centers.

With the basis for discrimination rapidly vanishing, women's rights groups focused on the ideology which assigned them inferior employment and marital roles. A vociferous minority of women would no longer accept inferior pay for the same work done by men, nor would many women consent to do all the housework in addition to holding a job. Women insisted on—and succeeded in getting—more help from men in the home.

The divorce rate has paralleled the growth in women's status because unhappily married women need not fear economic insecurity. Men, too, can consider a divorce without the complicating fear that their wives and children have no other means of support. Last, many governments have become increasingly permissive with respect to divorce, both in response to the wishes of the populace and because population growth has ceased to be an attractive national goal.

Divorce will reach an apogee when the full equality of men and women is achieved—not only legal parity, but the provision by the state of more adequate child-care facilities. Nevertheless, in the absence of full equality, it is highly probable that the divorce rate will continue to climb. Eventually, when fewer people decide to marry and those who do marry (particularly women) do so after careful evaluation rather than out of fear of being unmarried, the rate may again decline.

Greater Expectations Regarding Marriage

When marriage was largely an extended-family function or was contracted because of societal pressures, it did not play much of a role in the emotional life of the couple. Its chief purpose was procreation and the cementing of kinship and political alliances. The accomplishment of these goals left wealthy individuals free to find personal gratification elsewhere if they were so inclined.

As Western civilization progressed, however, the Church, the state, and the community assumed many functions of the extended family and of parents. The family no longer granted benefits to the individual or controlled his behavior; the parents' role in selecting marital partners for their children changed from de facto choice to one of veto. And at the present time, that power is waning still further, and parental influence is becoming more subtle and indirect.

Some of the Church's power rested in the belief that it was the mediator between man and God. The weakening of this belief in the last 500 years has adversely affected its power, with the state increasingly supplanting the regulatory role of the Church in connection with marriage. Society, or at least the powerful bourgeoisie and nobility, clamored for individual freedom, and governmental influence on marriage became slowly but increasingly more liberal.

"Love" matches. The growing power of the individual to choose a spouse did not inevitably result in love matches. At first, the potentialities of a partner were evaluated in traditional terms—economic assets, health, character, and social background—with relatively limited attention to the quality of the personal interaction. Few nubile individuals had enough experience to make meaningful character assessments because, in an era when marriage had often been arranged, opportunities for interaction had been largely irrelevant. Hence freedom of marital choice at first meant that young people merely superseded their parents in weighing the above-mentioned criteria for marriage. As late as the middle of the nineteenth century, in the United States and Western Europe, love was not considered a prerequisite for marriage. If the bride and groom were of good character, love would follow *after marriage.* The concept of good and poor matching of marital partners, judged apart from their positive or negative qualities, is actually little more than 100 years old.

Another factor impeding the emergence of "love" as a criterion for marriage was society's unequal evaluation of the sexes. A rough measure of the relative value of the sexes may be gleaned by comparing the size of the dower accompanying the groom with that of the dowry of the bride. In seventeenth-century England, for example, rich eligible women were a glut on the market, and the size of the average dowry exceeded the dower by more than ten to one. Later, the dower vanished in many countries, but the dowry remained. This signified that divorce was not likely, and no dower or guarantee for the bride was necessary for her support. It also meant that the woman had little economic value—hence the necessity of a dowry as an inducement for the man to take her off her parents' hands.

The dowry was a fast-disappearing phenomenon in the United States by the second half of the nineteenth century; with the sharp rise in women's status, it became socially unacceptable to acknowledge a marriage without love.

Although the twentieth century has become the century of the love marriage, the term "love" is confusing—it has many different meanings. "Love" for the purposes of marital selection, as I have treated it in this book, can generally occur only between those with equal marital assets (a weighted amalgam of physical appearance, intelligence, social status, and personality compatibility). Based on these criteria, love between man and wife must have been quite rare in ancient Athens. Could an Athenian male have loved an uneducated woman who spent most of the day confined to her apartments? When educated Athenians fell in love with their educational equals, they fell in love with other men, not with women. In the past, love between a Japanese or Chinese man and woman was also equally unlikely as a determinant of marital choice. It was only the rise in women's status at the end of the nineteenth century that made the love match feasible on a broad scale.

But love matches do not always mean wedded bliss. An individual experiences marital satisfaction when he perceives that his expectations regarding his marriage are met or exceeded in reality. But since one's expectations regarding a love partner are so much higher than for an assigned partner, it is often difficult to satisfy them in reality. The frustration of these greater expectations leads to even more disappointment. Not surprisingly, therefore, countries that are highly industrialized and grant women almost equal status with men (the United States, the U.S.S.R.) are most capable of nurturing love matches, but they also have the highest divorce rates.

Divorce, nevertheless, is hardly an omen of the dissolution of the family, since in the United States four-fifths of the divorced remarry. It is, rather, an inevitable correlate of love matches: when love vanishes, the partner must be replaced by a new lover (spouse); and as love matches increase in the future, they will also augment the divorce rate.

Sex

The ancient Chinese, Greeks, and Romans were highly erotic and sensual, but rarely so viv-à-vis their assigned wives. The Hebrews treated their wives somewhat more equally and showed more sexual interest in them.

The advent of Christianity sharply deemphasized sex, both as a reaction to the licentious practices of Rome and because of the necessary preparation for the coming end of the world. The devaluation of the body by the Christian Fathers led to a perception of sex as filthy bestiality and to the denigration of women as successors to the temptress Eve. Sexuality was slow in regaining popularity. By the time of Thomas Aquinas it had recovered only sufficiently to be classified as a *second-class* function, and that only when performed for the purpose of propagation.

The phenomenon of "courtly love" was another step forward in that sex was glorified as an adjunct of passion. By definition, however, such love could exist only by free choice. Since marriage, as a contract, could not so qualify, passion could exist only outside marriage.

Luther restored the respectability of sex within marriage by declaring it to be necessary for the preservation of health. Matrimony, in his words, was "a hospital for incurables," and sex was doubtless a potent drug taken by the inmates to ease the burden of their terminal illness. As for those who argued against the use of such a "drug," Luther pointed out that the suppression of sex turned a poison loose in the body, which then became unhealthy and stinking.

The "necessary evil" approach to marital sex continued even into the Victorian period. Women were perceived as pure, pious, submissive, and domestic; in the opinion of learned doctors, "angels of the house" experienced no sex urge. Accordingly, when men wanted passion, they paid for it by keeping a mistress or visiting a prostitute.

The twentieth century brought a resurgence of sexual feeling into marriage.

One contributing factor was the perfecting of contraceptives: the condom was relatively safe but unesthetic; the diaphragm and vaginal jelly were safer and more esthetic; and the intrauterine device and "the pill" have proved even more effective and esthetic. Freed from the risk of unwanted pregnancy, women have manifested a high degree of sensuality scarcely thought possible a half-century ago.

A second disinhibiting factor has been the permissive ideological climate that developed in the World War I period. Freud was the product of a more naturalistic view of sex; and though his theories have increasingly come under attack, he was a catalyst who advanced the acceptability of sexual feeling. In the 1970s, the acceptance of sex has blossomed into an erotization of culture. Sex no longer needs to win grudging acceptance as a natural function—it is now "unnatural" not to feel sexy most of the time. Erotic books and films are not only omnipresent; they are best sellers that apparently satisfy the needs of more than the pathologically prurient. Women are assured that perfumes will turn men into delightful sex beasts, and men learn that hair preparations and even shaving cream can make them sexually irresistible.

All the erotic stimuli in the world would be meaningless unless man felt free to indulge in erotic activities. The key to understanding the appearance of eroticism throughout Western culture has been the growing acceptability of hedonism as a philosophy of life. The rise in women's status is also responsible for the new sensuality. Lust may arise from an appealing physique or from the novelty of the situation. Enduring sexual attraction, in my opinion, however, depends a great deal on the perceived status of the object. The rise in the status of women, therefore, has made them more and more sexually desirable.

Still another factor that has increased sexual gratification in marriage is the improvement in sexual technique. Much has been written to the effect that experts in technique do not necessarily make good lovers, and that technique is no substitute for involvement. But this is a "straw man" type of argument, for few would question the point. It can scarcely be disputed that an involved person, skilled in the art of love, is preferable to an involved but unskilled lover. While, ultimately, success in sex depends on honest communication with one's partner, a certain basic knowledge, not available to the past generation, is currently accessible in many manuals.[1]

It is impossible to close this list without noting an obvious factor in marital sensuality: economic prosperity. People can better express their sexuality when they have the leisure time to pursue eroticism. The eighteenth-century French peasant had an enormous work load, and only the aristocracy could devote their lives to leisure. Today's average working person has more free time than ever before, and it is no accident that the preoccupation with eroticism we are witnessing has paralleled this increased leisure.

Yet one of the deterrents to sexuality, today as always, is physical fatigue. The barber on his feet for eight hours, or the housewife whose day is filled with shopping, laundering, house-cleaning, and tending to small children, is often too

Poet's vision of his beloved: hemispherical breasts, pearly teeth, rosy cheeks.

tired to think of sex. And when they do, their limited energy is very *goal-centered* on the orgasm, without much energy for the byplay that is characteristic of the "erotic." In the future, however, with less physically demanding labor and shorter workdays, more leisure time will be available, and some of it will be devoted to sex activities.

OTHER FACTORS IN CURRENT MARRIAGES

In addition to the historical trends we have traced, there are several contemporary factors that seem likely to affect the course of future marriage. One complex of factors consists of the need for variety, stimulation, and novelty. This complex has doubtless always been present in man, but until the advent of the affluent society, the leisure necessary to indulge these needs was largely absent. The need for variety is extended by the myriad forms of music, language, dress, and friendship. Everything is changing more rapidly than ever before, and it will not be surprising to see more husbands and wives satisfy these needs in the interpersonal sphere by developing an increasing number and variety of extramarital relationships.

Another factor to be reckoned with will be the abandonment of many of the unequal and dreary household tasks of women. True egalitarianism will probably come about not only by men sharing the "dirty" work, but by improved technology. The "pill" and the fear of overpopulation will do much to end the mystique of motherhood.[2] Day-care centers, probably sponsored by the Federal or state governments, will enable women to pursue full-time careers.

Another crucial dimension of future marriage will be the satisfaction of the need for intimacy. We are just becoming aware of how vital this is for normal functioning. Prison practices have amply demonstrated that those deprived of contact with other humans become depressed, apathetic, and sometimes psychotic. People who are reared with a minimum of human contact fail to develop normally. In fact, the Harlows' studies[3,4] have shown that monkeys deprived of contact with maternal figures—and, even more important, with peers—do not develop normally either.

In the preindustrial, preurban era, an individual had several sources of intimate contact: his spouse, the extended family, his peers, and the neighborhood.[5] In the present era of depersonalization, the opportunity for continuous contact and emotional closeness is certain only with one's spouse. Any marriage, therefore, which fails to provide a source of intimacy dooms the individual who does not find it elsewhere to frustration and to feelings of inadequacy.

This review leads me to conclude that marriage in the future will be an individual-centered love match between equal-status individuals. The participants will have great expectations, especially with regard to sex. Cut off from familial ties and long-standing relationships with kin and friends, they will depend heavily on their spouses for emotional satisfaction. But they will need more relationships than just those with a spouse, and they will be living in a culture that fosters change and a thirst for variety. Most important, their lives will provide sufficient leisure to pursue these interests. What form of marriage is most consistent with these factors?

WHAT KIND OF FUTURE MARRIAGE?

In our earlier discussion of theories of marital choice, I have suggested that a social-exchange model was most consistent with premarital data. But does this model continue to operate during marriage? Our divorce rate testifies that many individuals remain in marriage only so long as they perceive that their gains exceed their costs. Many others who remain in marriage, despite unhappiness, are still adhering to an exchange law: they perceive even greater costs in being unmarried than in enduring an unhappy marriage.

Many social-exchange marriages are successful in that the partners find the bargain a good and enduring one, particularly when each partner plays a highly complementary role in the marriage and is considerate and relatively uninvolved emotionally with the other. The wife might run an efficient home, entertain her husband's business associates skillfully, and have a high public stimulus-value. Her private life with the "girls" might be more or less her own affair provided that no scandal besmirches the family name. The husband might be hardworking and highly motivated; he provides ample material means and a good education for the children, and is never home long enough to get under his wife's feet. In the absence of interpersonal tension, such marriages may be long-enduring and viable arrangements.

Of course, satisfaction in a social-exchange marriage depends on the equality of status. Since status may change—for example, due to circumstances outside the marriage—a good bargain may become a bad one. The young minor executive with an unsophisticated but pretty wife may have had no problems; but when at the age of 40 he is promoted to a key executive job, an aging and unsophisticated wife may become a social handicap. The difference in their status now increases the chance of a divorce, provided that his job situation and religion permit this.

Commitment is not necessarily a developmental process. It may commence with the onset of the marriage. The Catholic marriage is the purest example of a committed marriage: neither partner can opt out. Most people who marry believe that they will have a committed marriage; they are marrying for life. The high rate of divorce, however, attests to the fact that they are functioning within a social-exchange model. A certain number do remain married even when they perceive an inequitable exchange ratio, when there are no religious proscriptions, and when it is apparent that they could do better elsewhere. Why? In my view, the exchange principle is overridden by another extremely important factor—the self-concept. The individual seeks to play a role as a loving spouse, and the gratification he achieves from this role may more than offset the negative feedback from interaction with a spouse.[6] The stereotype of this behavior is the wife of an alcoholic; she often endures unusual strains that have no rationale for the unknowing observer. The reward is self-engendered: she gratifies her super-ego by heroically "carrying on."

From the point of view of society, and often from the viewpoint of the married partners as well, a "committed" marriage is much more desirable than an "exchange" one. When there is no divorce, there is no emotional turmoil, no legal complication; it is cheaper to continue the same pattern; and the trauma of divorce for the children is avoided.

What, then, could be done to reverse the present trend? Let us recall that there is no reason why marital choice should not be on an "exchange" basis. It is much easier to build a marriage of commitment when both partners have equal exchange value for the other. The traditional dating relationship, however, provided little information with which to form realistic judgments of each other. As a result, the nubile pair fed on fantasy, imagining all kinds of sexual thrills awaiting them. Not for them the cynic's refrain that *"Le soir tous les chats sont gris"* (At night all cats are gray). The disappointments after marriage, and the realization that fantasied and actual sex are not necessarily equivalent, become a painful learning experience.

In this perspective, the steady increment in premarital sexual experience does not signify dissoluteness in our times; rather, it is an intelligent manifestation. Premarital sexuality within an ongoing relationship involves a learning experience of much more than sex. Indeed, an individual's approach to sex probably is a microcosm of his general approach to interpersonal relationships. A person who engages in more than one such relationship will gain a standard of comparision with regard to the degree to which his needs for giving and receiving are satisfied. Some individuals may find themselves quite satisfied with one premarital partner, whereas others may require more experiences before they find out what they need in a partner.

Unfortunately, at the present time a further increase in premarital sexuality would surely augment the rate of venereal disease, already at epidemic proportions. This problem could be alleviated, however, by universal periodic testing.

The reader with a long memory will recall Kinsey's finding that premarital sex was associated with extramarital involvement. How, then, can I advocate premarital sex as possibly inducing less extramarital involvement in the future? The answer lies in the fact that the same behavior in a different context may have a new significance. In 1940, for example, a young man wearing long hair, beads, and an earring, and carrying a flower would have been considered psychotic, a homosexual, or both; today the reaction would be far less extreme because norms have changed. In the Middle Ages, an individual who ate sparsely once or twice a day would have been regarded as a pious monk; today such behavior suggests a diet.

In the 1930s and 1940s, when Kinsey collected his data, premarital sex was relatively unconventional. It was not surprising that individuals engaging in unconventional behavior should manifest a tendency to extramarital sex activity. In the future, when premarital sex is the norm, there may not necessarily be a high correlation between premarital and extramarital sex. As a student remarked, "I don't mind the fact that any number of people have tried on a pair of shoes before I buy them so long as when I buy them, they are mine." It is likely, therefore, that many persons will experiment widely before marriage, but not necessarily afterward.

We have so far discussed an increase in committed marriages by greater and more profound premarital contact. But I do not wish to imply that committed marriage eliminates all the problems confronting marriage today. Rather, its chief strength lies in that its participants are more highly motivated (than those in exchange marriages) in their attempts to surmount any inevitable problems. We still need to address ourselves to these thorny questions: Even in a "committed" marriage, to what degree will this commitment exclude intimate contact with other members of the opposite sex and even older "committed" relationships? To what degree should interpersonal and sexual experiences outside marriage be curtailed because it is painful to the marriage partner? Let us be realistic and acknowledge that although careful, pretested relationships prior to marriage may decrease the number of marital misfits, even in relatively compatible marriages there is often a desire—indeed, a craving—for variety in all kinds of interaction. Moreover, all needs cannot possibly be satisfied by a single partner.

This, then, is the dilemma of future marriage: the individual must not find marriage a straitjacket that stifles his development and his enjoyment of other relationships. At the same time, if an outside relationship supplies the same gratifications to an equal degree as those in marriage, it may become a threat to the marital bond. The solution seems clear. Whatever the needs gratified outside of marriage, they must not duplicate or compete with what is regarded as the *essence* of the marriage. As for the essence, it will vary from marriage to marriage: for some, sexual fidelity is the core of marriage; for others, it is emotional closeness, intellectual sharing, or value similarity; and for a few others it may be a range of household services.

Group marriage, as we noted earlier, is so unlikely to achieve compatibility among three or more persons that it could not possibly be practiced by more than a few people. From our preceding discussion, we can see that it would not appeal to many already monogamously married couples, since it would involve loss of individual commitment to the original spouse in connection with sexual and emotional exclusiveness. "Swinging," however, limits the extramarital liaison to sex while retaining emotional sharing in the marriage. Sexual infidelity is, in fact, losing its importance as a cause for divorce. It is likely, as theological influence wanes, that sexuality will lose still more of its symbolic significance; it may come to be regarded as an enjoyable recreational pastime which, like tennis or golf, does not have to be restricted to one's marriage partner.

The problem with "swinging" will not be the fact that it involves extramarital sex, but its "democratic" principle, which frowns on selectiveness in extramarital choice. Yet many people are selective about whom they choose for sexual relations. Moreover, the forced, ritualistic nature of swinging "turns off" some people who would rather have their sex activity develop more spontaneously. Swinging, nevertheless, does expand the range of interpersonal satisfactions available to a couple, and may appeal to an increasing number because of its shared egalitarian philosophy as well as its sexual stimulation.

Most individuals will either not wish to go as far as swingers do or to operate within the lesser degree of freedom inherent in a swinging situation. They will stick to monogamy, but a monogamy that will be much more egalitarian than its present-day form. A number of couples will remain—by choice or lack of attractiveness to others—a closed duo. They will engage in sex only with each other and maintain emotional intimacy mainly with each other.

A small number of couples will experience completely open marriages: with mutual blessing, each will be free to engage in any kind of extramarital relationship—emotional, sexual, or both. Since many persons perceive the latter type of relationship as threatening to their security and to the marriage, there are only three types of partners who would countenance such a relationship: one who is so low in status that he must submit or be divorced, one who is completely indifferent to his spouse's relationships, or one who is so secure in himself and his spouse that he is not threatened by such an affair. I believe that since all three types are rare, a completely open marriage will be rare.

The vast majority of monogamists will experience marriages more open than those of today, but less than maximally open. Women, for example, will increasingly enter the professions and find much in common with male colleagues that they cannot share with their husbands. In an era of individualism, such relationships will be far more tolerated than now, where opposite-sex contacts are limited to narrowly prescribed circumstances.

In some cases it will be acceptable for spouses to indulge in occasional sexual experiences—an out-of-town trip, for example. Acceptance is more likely to occur when the emotional involvement is minimized by the short-term nature of the experience. Spouses will more readily accept such behavior when its possibility is acknowledged and discussed, and guilt feelings will be much less prevalent than today.

By and large, therefore, the combination of intimacy and sex will be reserved for marriage. Extramarital intimacy without sex will be more generally accepted, as will extramarital sex without intimacy. Outside relationships that imitate marriage in terms of both intimacy and sex will pose too great a threat for most couples to accept.

In conclusion, it seems likely that a somewhat more open kind of monogamous marriage than exists at present will predominate, but a great variety of types and styles of marriage will exist concomitantly, though their experimental and innovative nature will probably restrict their appeal to a relatively bold minority. The God of Marriage, emulating the early post-revolutionary Mao Tse-tung, will smile and proclaim, "Let a hundred flowers bloom."

REFERENCES

1. B. I. Murstein, "What makes a person sexually appealing?"
2. P. M. Hauser, "Social science predicts and projects."
3. H. F. Harlow and M. K. Harlow, "The effect of rearing conditions on behavior."
4. H. F. Harlow and M. K. Harlow, "Social deprivation in monkeys."
5. C. Alexander, "The city as a mechanism for sustaining human contact."
6. R. Weiss, "Forms of sexual relationships: Going together, living together, and marriage."

Bibliography

A. F. *The ladies' pocket book of etiquette (1838)*. London: The Golden Cockerel Press, 1928.

Abélard, P., & Abélard, H. *The letters of Abélard and Héloïse*. (Trans. C. K. S. Moncrief.) New York: Alfred A. Knopf, 1942.

Aberle, D., Bronfenbrenner, U., Hess, E., Miller, D., Schneider, D., & Spuher, J. The incest taboo and the mating pattern of animals. *American Anthropologist*, 1963, *65*, 253-265.

Achorn, E. Mary Cragin, perfectionist saint. *The New England Quarterly*, 1955, *28*, 490-598.

Acton, W. *Functions and disorders of the reproductive organs* (6th ed.). London: J. & A. Churchill, 1875.

Adams, M. S., & Neel, J. V. Children of incest. *Pediatrics*, 1967, *40*, 55-62.

Aeschines. *The speeches of Aeschines*. London: William Heinemann, 1919.

Agrippa, von Netteshein, H. C. *The commendation of matrimony*. Film, New York Public Library, 1945.

Alcott, W. A. *The young wife*. Boston: Charles D. Strong, 1851.

Aldous, J. Urbanization, the extended family and kinship ties in West Africa. In P. L. Van Den Berghe (ed.), *Africa: social problems of change and conflict*. San Francisco: Chandler, 1965. Pp. 107-116.

Aldous, J. Wives' employment status and lower-class men as husband-fathers; support for the Moynihan thesis. *Journal of Marriage and the Family*, 1969, *31*, 469-477.

Alexander, C. The city as a mechanism for sustaining human contact. In W. R. Ewald, Jr. (ed.), *Environment for man: the next fifty years*. Bloomington, Ind.: Indiana University Press, 1967. Pp. 60-102.

Alexander, W. *History of woman*. 2 vols. Philadelphia: J. H. Dobelbower, 1796.

Allen, F. L. *Only yesterday: An informal history of the nineteen-twenties*. New York: Harper, 1931.

Allen, G. Falling in love. *Fortnightly Review*, 1886, *46*, 432-462.

Allen, G. *The woman who did*. Boston: Roberts Bros., 1895.

American way of swinging, The. *Time*, February 8, 1971, 51.

Andrews, S. P. (ed.), *Love, marriage, and divorce, and the sovereignty of the individual*. New York: Stronger & Townsend, 1853.

Annual summary for the United States, 1971: Births, deaths, marriages, and divorces. *Monthly Vital Statistical Report*, August 30, 1972, *20* (13).

Aquinas, T. *Summa theologica*. London: Burns, Oates & Washbourne, Ltd., 1928. Vol. 19.

Aquinas, T. *The summa theologica*. 2 vols. (Trans. Fathers of the English Dominican province.) Chicago: Encyclopedia Britannica, 1952. Occasional quotes by permission of Benziger, Inc. (New York, 1948).

Are changing conventions menacing the marriage institution? *Current Opinion*, 1923, *74*, 338-340.

Ariga, K. The family in Japan. *Marriage and Family Living*, 1954, *16*, 362-368.

Aristophanes. The plays of Aristophanes. In *Aeschylus, Sophocles, Euripides, Aristophanes*. Chicago: Encyclopedia Britannica, 1952. Pp. 455-642.

Aristotle. *The works of Aristotle*. 2 vols. Chicago: Encyclopedia Britannica, 1952.

Arkoff, A., Meredith, G., & Iwahara, S. Male-dominant and equalitarian attitudes in Japanese, Japanese-American, and Caucasian-American students. *The Journal of Social Psychology*, 1964, *64*, 225-229.

Asayama, S. Comparison of sexual development of American and Japanese adolescents. *Psychologica*, 1957, *1*, 129-131.

Ashley, M. *The Stuarts in love*. New York: Macmillan, 1967.

Ashton, H. *The Basuto*. London: Oxford University Press, 1952.

Astell, M. *Reflections upon marriage*. London: R. Wilkin, 1706.

Athanasiou, R., Shaver, P., & Tavris, C. Sex. *Psychology Today*, July 1970, 39-52.

Atherton, G. American husbands. *The Delineator*, 1911, *78*, 7, 49.

Augustine. *The confessions, the city of God, and on Christian doctrine.* (Trans. E. B. Pusey, M. Dods, and J. F. Shaw, resp.) Chicago: Encyclopedia Britannica, 1952. Occasional quotes by permission of T. & T. Clark, Edinburgh.

autobiography of a married man, The. *Everybody's Magazine*, 1905, *12*, 265-271.

Aurand, A. M., Jr. *Little known facts about bundling in the new world*. Lancaster, Pa.: The Aurand Press, 1938.

Avery, P., & Avery, E. Some notes on "wife swapping." In H. A. Greenwald (ed.), *Sex in America*. New York: Bantam, 1964. Pp. 248-254.

Baber, R. E. *Youth looks at marriage and the family*. Tokyo: International Christian University, 1958.

Bachelor Maid, A. Why I do not marry. *The Independent*, 1904, *56*, 1482-1486.

bachelor's soliloquy, The. *Glasgow:* Brash and Reid, 1796.

Bachofen, J. J. *Das mutterrecht: Eine untersuchung über die gynaikikritie der alten welt nach ihrer religiosen und rechtlichen natur*. Stuttgart: Krais & Hoffman, 1861.

Bacon, A. M. *Japanese girls and women*. Boston: Houghton Mifflin, 1894.

Bagley, C. Incest behavior and incest taboo. *Social Problems*, 1964, *16*, 505-519.

Bailey, D. S. *Sexual relation in Christian thought*. New York: Harper, 1959.

Bainton, R. H. *What Christianity says about sex, love and marriage*. New York: Association Press, 1957.

Balagushkin, E. G. The building of communism and the evolution of family and marital relations. *Soviet Society*, 1962-1963, *1*, 42-48.

Balsdon, J. P. V. D. *Roman women*. London: The Bodley Head, 1962.

Balzac, H. de. *The physiology of marriage*. New York: Grove Press, n.d.

Banton, M. *West African city: A study of tribal life in Freetown*. London: Oxford University Press, 1957.

Bardis, P. D. Family forms and variations historically considered. In H. T. Christensen (ed.), *Handbook of marriage and the family*. Chicago: Rand McNally, 1964. Pp. 403-461.

Barry, H., III, Bacon, M. K., & Child, I. L. A cross-cultural survey of some sex differences. *Journal of Abnormal and Social Psychology*, 1957, *55*, 327-332.

Bartell, G. D. Group sex among the mid-Americans. *Journal of Sex Research*, 1970, *6*, 113-130.

Bartell, G. D. *Group sex: A scientists's eyewitness report on the American way of swinging*. New York: Peter H. Wyden, 1971.

Bartlett, J. *Familiar quotations* (13th ed.). Boston: Little, Brown, 1955.

Barton, G.A. *A sketch of semitic origins*. New York: Macmillan, 1902.

Barzun, J. *Classic, romantic, and modern*. Boston: Little, Brown, 1961.

Basil. *Works* (Nicene and post-Nicene fathers). New York: Christian Literature Co., 1895. Vol. 8, second series.

Baskina, A. Neither beast nor angel. *Current Abstracts of the Soviet Press*, 1969, *1*(8), 12.

batchellors answer to the maids complaint; or the young men's vindication, The. London: J. Coniers, 1675.

batchelor's directory, The. London: Richard Cumberland, 1696.

Beard, M. *Woman as force in history*. New York: Macmillan, 1946.

Beardsley, R. K., Hall, J. W., & Ward, R. E. *Village Japan*. Chicago: University of Chicago Press, 1959.

Beattie, J. *Bunyoro: an African kingdom*. New York: Holt, Rinehart & Winston, 1960.

de Beauvoir, S. *The long march*. New York: World, 1958.

de Beauvoir, S. *The second sex*. New York: Bantam Books, 1964.

Beidelman, T. O. Some Nuer notions of nakedness, nudity, and sexuality. *Africa*, 1968, *38*, 113-132.

Beigl, H. G. Romantic love. *American Sociological Review*, 1951, *16*, 326-334.

Bell, R.R. Some factors related to the sexual satisfaction of the college educated wife. *Family Life Coordinator*, 1964, *13*, 43-47.

Bell, R. R. Parent-child conflict in sexual values. *The Journal of Social Issues*, 1966, *22*, 34-44.

Bell, R. R. *Premarital sex in a changing society*. Englewood Cliffs, N.J.: Prentice-Hall, 1966.

Bell, R. R. "Swinging"–the sexual exchange of marriage partners. Paper presented to the Society for the Study of Social Problems, Washington, D.C., 1970.

Bell, R. R., & Chaskes, J. B. Premarital sexual experience among coeds, 1958 and 1968. *Journal of Marriage and the Family*, 1970, *32*, 81-84.

Bellamy, C. J. *An experiment in marriage*. Albany, N.Y.: Albany Book Co., 1889.

Bennett, H. S. *Life on the English manor: A study of peasant conditions 1150-1400*. New York: Macmillan, 1937.

Bennis, W. G., & Slater, P. E. *The temporary society*. New York: Harper & Row, 1968.

Benton, J. F. Clio and Venus: An historical view of medieval love. In F. X.

Newman (ed.), *The meaning of courtly love.* Albany, N.Y.: State University of New York Press, 1968. Pp. 19-42.

Bentzon, T. Marriage in France. *The International Quarterly,* 1903, *8,* 31-43.

Benz, M. G. United States. In R. Patai (ed.), *Women in the modern world.* New York: The Free Press, 1967. Pp. 489-509.

Bernard, J. *Remarriage: A study of marriage.* New York: Dryden, 1958.

Bernard, J. *Marriage and family among Negroes.* Englewood Cliffs, N.J.: Prentice-Hall, 1966.

Bestor, A. E., Jr. *Backwoods utopias: The sectarian and Owenite phases of communitarian socialism in America: 1663-1829.* Philadelphia: University of Pennsylvania Press, 1950.

Betham-Edwards, M. French brides and bridegrooms. *Living Age,* 1904, *241,* 566-571.

Beyle, M. H. (Stendhal). *On love.* New York: Liveright, 1947.

Bianquis, G. *Love in Germany.* London: Frederick Muller, 1964.

Billingsley, A. Family functioning in the low-income black community. *Social Casework,* 1969, *50,* 563-572.

Billingsley, A. Black families and white social science. *Journal of Social Issues,* 1970, *26,* 127-142.

Blake, N. M. *The road to Reno: A history of divorce in the United States.* New York: Macmillan, 1962.

Blau, J. L. *Men and movements in American philosophy.* New York: Prentice-Hall, 1952.

Blau, P. M. *Exchange and power in social life.* New York: John Wiley, 1964.

Blitsen, D. R. *The world of the family.* New York: Random House, 1963.

Block, D. Unwed couples: Do they live happily ever after? *Redbook,* April 1969, 90 ff.

Blood, R. O., Jr. A retest of Waller's rating complex. *Marriage and Family Living,* 1955, *17,* 41-47.

Blood, R. O., Jr. Uniformities and diversities in campus dating preferences. *Marriage and Family Living,* 1956, *18,* 37-45.

Blood, R. O., Jr. *Love match and arranged marriage.* New York: The Free Press, 1967.

Blood, R. O., Jr., & Wolfe, D. M. *Husbands and wives.* New York: The Free Press, 1965.

Blum, S. The perfect husband. *McCall's,* August 1967, 60 ff.

Bodin, J. La famille et l'état, d'après J. Bodin. In A. Cherel (ed.), *La famille française.* Paris: Edition Spes, 1924. Vol. 1, pp. 173-177.

Bohannan, P. *Justice and judgement among the Tiv.* London: Oxford University Press, 1957.

Bohannan, P. *African outline.* Middlesex, England: Penguin, 1966.

Bohannan, P., & Bohannan, L. The family in Negro Africa. In R. N. Anshen (ed.), *The family: Its function and destiny.* New York: Harper, 1959. Pp. 188-200.

Book of Mormon, The. Salt Lake City, Utah: The Deseret Book Co., 1962.

Boswell, J. *London journal.* (Ed. F. A. Pottle.) New York: McGraw-Hill, 1950.

Boswell, J. *Life of Samuel Johnson.* Chicago: Encyclopedia Britannica, 1952.

Boswell, J. *In search of a wife.* New York: McGraw-Hill, 1956.

Braddock, J. *The bridal bed.* London: Robert Hale, 1960.

Brain, R. Bangwa (Western Bamileke) marriage wards. *Africa,* 1969, *39,* 11-23.

Brandt, P. (pseud. Licht. H.) *Sexual life in ancient Greece.* New York: Barnes & Noble, 1969.

Brecher, E. M. *The sex researchers.* Boston: Little, Brown, 1969.

Breckinridge, S. P. *The family and the state.* Chicago: University of Chicago Press, 1934.

Breedlove, W., & Breedlove, J. *Swap clubs.* Los Angeles: Sherbourne Press, 1964.

Brewer, D. S. Love and marriage in Chaucer's poetry. *Modern Language Review,* 1954, *49,* 461-464.

Briffault, R. *The mothers.* 3 vols. New York: Macmillan, 1927.

Brill, E. H. Is marriage dying too? *Christian Century,* 1967, *84,* 268-270.

Brinton, C. *A history of Western morals.* New York: Harcourt, Brace, 1959.

Brisbane, A. *Association; or a concise exposition of the practical part of Fourier's social science.* New York: Greeley & McElrath, 1843.

Briton offers guide for happy marriage. *New York Times,* October 15, 1967, 3.

Brodie, F. M. *No man knows my history: The life of Joseph Smith the Mormon prophet.* New York: Alfred A. Knopf, 1946.

Bronfenbrenner, U. The changing Soviet family. In D. R. Brown (ed.), *Women in the Soviet Union.* New York: Teachers College Press, 1968. Pp. 98-124.

Brontë, C. *Jane Eyre.* New York: Bigelow, Brown, n.d.

Brooks, C., & Brooks, F. The early history of the anti-contraceptive laws in Massachusetts and Connecticut. *American Quarterly,* 1966, *18,* 3-23.

Brown, I. (ed.). *A book of marriage.* London: Hamish Hamilton, 1963.

Brown, S. May I ask you a few questions about love? *Saturday Evening Post,* December 31, 1966–January 7, 1967, 24-27.

Browne, C. F. *The complete works of Artemus Ward.* London: Chatts & Windus, 1922.

Browne, J. H. To marry or not to marry? *The Forum,* 1888, *6,* 432-442.

Brownmiller, S. Sisterhood is powerful. *New York Times Magazine,* March 15, 1970, 26 ff.

Bryce J. *The American commonwealth.* Vol. 3: *Public opinion–illustrations and reflections–social institutions.* London: Macmillan, 1888.

Buck, P. *Of men and women.* New York: John Day, 1941.

Buckingham, J. S. *The eastern and western states of America.* 2 vols. London: Fisher, Son & Co., 1867.

Burchinal, L. G. The premarital dyad and love involvement. In H. T. Christensen (ed.), *Handbook of marriage and the family.* Chicago: Rand McNally, 1964. Pp. 623-674.

Burchinal, L. G. The rural family of the future. In J. N. Edwards (ed.), *The family and change.* New York: Alfred A. Knopf, 1969. Pp. 409-445.

Burgess, E. W., & Locke, H. J. *The family* (2nd ed.). New York: American Book Co., 1960.

Burgess, E. W., Locke, H. J., & Thomes, M. M. *The family: From institution to companionship.* New York: American Book Co., 1963.

Burgess, E. W., & Wallin, P. *Engagement and marriage.* Philadelphia: Lippincott, 1953.

Burr, A. Aaron Burr to his wife. In A. S. Richardson (ed.), *Old love-letters.* Boston: James R. Osgood, 1883. Pp. 314-315.

Burr, W. R. Satisfaction with various aspects of marriage over the life cycle: A random middle class sample. *Journal of Marriage and the Family,* 1970, *32,* 29-37.

Burton, R. *The anatomy of melancholy.* New York: Tudor, 1938.

Burton, R. F. *The city of the saints, and across the mountains to California.* New York: Harper, 1862.

Butler, P. *Women of medieval France.* Philadelphia: Rittenhouse Press, 1908.

C., F. P. Celibacy vs. marriage. *Fraser's Magazine,* 1862, *65,* 228-235.

Cable, M. She who shall be nameless. *American Heritage,* 1965, *16*(2), 50-55.

Caird, M. Marriage. *The Westminster Review,* 1888, *130,* 167-201.

Calder-Marshall, A. *Havelock Ellis.* London: Rupert Hart-Davis, 1959.

Calhoun, A. *A social history of the American family.* Vol. 1: *Colonial period.* Cleveland: Arthur H. Clark Co., 1917.

Calhoun, A. *A social history of the American family.* Vol. 2: *From independence through the Civil War.* Cleveland: Arthur H. Clark Co., 1918.

Calhoun, A. *A social history of the American family.* Vol. 3: *Since the Civil War.* Cleveland: Arthur H. Clark Co., 1919.

Calvin, J. *Institutes of the Christian religion.* Philadelphia: Presbyterian Board of Christian Education, 1936. Vol. 1.

Camden, C. *The Elizabethan woman.* Houston: Elsevier Press, 1952.

Camp. W. D. *Marriage and the family in France since the Revolution.* New York: Bookman Associates, 1961.

Canby, H. S. Sex and marriage in the nineties. *Harper's Monthly Magazine,* 1934, *169,* 427 ff.

Capellanus, A. *The art of courtly love.* (Trans. and ed. J. J. Parry.) New York: Columbia University Press, 1941.

Carcopino, J. *Daily life in ancient Rome.* New Haven, Conn.: Yale University Press, 1964.

Carden, M. L. *Oneida: Utopian community to modern corporation.* Baltimore: The Johns Hopkins Press, 1969.

Carper, L. The Negro family and the Moynihan report. In R. Staples (ed.), *The Black family.* Belmont, Calif: Wadsworth. Pp. 65-71.

Cash, W. J. *The mind of the South.* New York: Alfred A. Knopf, 1957.

Castiglione, B. *The book of the courtier.* (Trans. L. E. Opdycke.) New York: Immortal Classics, 1929.

Cather, W. *My Ántonia.* Boston: Houghton Mifflin, 1954.

Chandler, B. T. *Japanese family life.* Rutland, Vt.: Charles E. Tuttle, 1963.

Chao, P. The Marxist doctrine and the recent development of the Chinese family in communist China. *Journal of Asian and African Studies,* 1967, *2,* 161-173.

Chapin, E. Japanese prince meets girl (by go-between). *New York Times Sunday Magazine,* March 22, 1964, 42 ff.

Chapman, E. R. Marriage rejection and marriage reform. *The Westminster Review,* 1888, *130,* 358-377.

Chapone, H. M. *Miscellanies in prose and verse.* London: Printed for C. Dilly and J. Walter, 1783.

Charles, C. H. *Love letters of great men and women.* London: Stanley Paul, 1924.

Chaucer, G. *Troilus and Cressida and the Canterbury Tales.* (Trans. J. V. Nicholson.) Chicago: Encyclopedia Britannica, 1964.

Chekhov, A. *Notebook of Anton Chekhov.* New York: B. W. Huebach, 1922.

Chesnut, M. B. *A diary from Dixie.* Boston: Houghton Mifflin, 1949.

Chesser, E. *The sexual, marital, and family relationships of the English woman.* London: Hutchinson's, 1956.

Chesterfield, Earl of. *Letters to his son.* 2 vols. New York: Tudor, n.d.

Chevalier, M. *Society, manners, and politics in the United States.* New York: Doubleday, 1961.

Chien, C. Chao Hsio-Lan. In *The women's representative.* Peking: Foreign Language Press, 1956. Pp. 5-43.

Chin, A. S. Family relations in modern Chinese fiction. In M. Freedman (ed.), *Family and kinship in Chinese society.* Stanford, Calif.: Stanford University Press, 1970. Pp. 87-120.

choice matrimonial, The. *Chamber's Journal,* 1898, *1,* 498-499.

Choisy, M. *Sigmund Freud: A new appraisal.* New York: Citadel Press, 1963.

Christensen, H. T. A cross-cultural comparison of attitudes toward marital infidelity. In J. Mogey (ed.), *Family and marriage.* Leiden: E. J. Bill, 1963. Pp. 124-137.

Christiansen, J. R. Contemporary Mormon attitudes toward polygynous practices. *Marriage and Family Living,* 1963, *20,* 167-170.

Christopherson, V. A. An investigation of patriarchal authority in the Mormon family. *Marriage and Family Living,* 1956, *18,* 328-333.

Chrysostom. *Works* (Nicene and post-Nicene Fathers). New York: The Christian Literature Co., 1894. Vol. 9, first series.

Clanton G. The contemporary experience of adultery. Unpublished manuscript, Rutgers University, 1972.

Clark, A. L., & Wallin, P. Women's sexual responsiveness and the duration and quality of their marriage. *American Journal of Sociology,* 1965, *71,* 187-196.

la Clavière, R. M. *The women of the Renaissance.* New York: G. P. Putnam's Sons, 1900.

Clement. *Fathers of the second century* (ante-Nicene Fathers). New York: Charles Scribner's Sons, 1899. Vol. 2.

Cleveland, A. R. *Women under the English law.* London: Hurst & Blackett, 1896.

Clignet, R. *Many wives, many powers.* Evanston, Ill.: Northwestern University Press, 1970.

Clignet, R., & Sween, J. Social change and type of marriage. *American Journal of Sociology,* 1969, *75,* 123-145.

Clignet, R., & Sween, J. Traditional and modern life styles in Africa. *Journal of Comparative Family Studies,* 1971, *2,* 188-214.

Clowes, J. *The golden wedding ring; or thoughts on marriage in a conversation between a father and his two children.* Manchester: Society of Gentlemen, 1813.

Coan, T. M. To marry or not to marry. *The Galaxy,* 1869, *7,* 493-500.

Cobbett, W. *Advice to young men and (incidentally) to young women.* London: Alfred A. Knopf, 1930.

Cohn, D. L. *Love in America.* New York: Simon & Schuster, 1943.

Cole, W. G. *Sex and love in the Bible.* New York: Association Press, 1959.

Collins, J. The doctor looks at companionate marriage. In C. A. Spaulding (ed.), *Twenty-four views of marriage.* New York: Macmillan, 1930. Pp. 205-217.

Collins, O. Divorce in the New Testament. *The Gordon Review,* 1964, *7,* 158-169.

Colson, E. Family change in contemporary Africa. *Annals of the New York Academy of Sciences,* 1962, *96,* 641-647.

Cominos, P. T. Late Victorian sexual respectability and the social system. *International Review of Social History,* 1963, *8,* 18-48, 216-250.

Congreve, W. The way of the world. In R.M. Smith (ed.), *Types of Social Comedy.* New York: Prentice-Hall, 1931. Pp. 169-266.

Constantine, L. L., & Constantine, J. M. Multilateral marriage: A position paper. Unpublished manuscript, 1969; obtainable through authors, 26 Casey Ave., Watertown. Mass.

Constantine, L. L., & Constantine, J. M. Group and multilateral marriage: Definitional notes, glossary, and annotated bibliography. *Family Process,* 1971, *10,* 157-176.

Constantine, L. L., & Constantine, J. M. Sexual aspects of multilateral relations. *The Journal of Sex Research,* 1971, *7,* 204-225.

Conway, M. D. Debate on Mr. Moncure D. Conway's paper "On Marriage." London: Dialectical Society, 1871.

Cook, F. G. The marriage celebration in Europe. *Atlantic Monthly,* 1888, *61,* 245-250.

Cookman, M. What the women of America think about men. *Ladies' Home Journal,* January 1939, 19 ff.

Coombs, R. H., & Kenkel, W. F. Sex differences in dating aspirations and satisfaction with computer-selected partners. *Journal of Marriage and the Family,* 1966, *28,* 62-66.

Cooper, D. *The death of the family.* New York: Pantheon, 1970.

Cornish, F. W. The wife in ancient Greece. In B. J. Stern (ed.), *The family, past and present.* New York: Appleton-Century, 1938. Pp. 75-81.

Coser, L. A. Some aspects of Soviet family policy. *American Journal of Sociology,* 1951, *56,* 424-437.

Couch, H. N. Woman in early Roman law. *Harvard Law Review,* 1894, *8,* 39-50.

Coulton, G. C. *The medieval village.* Cambridge: Cambridge University Press, 1931.

Courtship and marriage in France. *Westminster Review,* 1877, *107,* 164-185.

Cowan, J. *The science of a new life.* New York: Cowan & Co., 1874.

Cressy, E. H. *Daughters of changing Japan.* New York: Farrar, Straus & Cudahy, 1955.

Critchlow, F. L. On the forms of betrothal and wedding ceremonies in the old French *romans d'aventure. Modern Philosophy,* 1904-1905, *2,* 41.

Cross, E. B. *The Hebrew family.* Chicago: University of Chicago Press, 1927.

Cross, T. P., & Nitze, W. A. *Lancelot and Guinevere.* Chicago: University of Chicago Press, 1930.

Cuber, J. F., & Harroff, P. B. The more total view: Relationships among men and women of the upper-middle class. In H. Rodman (ed.), *Marriage, family and society*. New York: Random House, 1965. Pp. 92-102.

Cuisenier, J., & Raguin, C. De quelques transformations dans le système familial russe. *Revue Française de Sociologie*, 1967, *8*, 521-557.

Cunnington, C.W. *Feminine attitudes in the nineteenth century*. New York: Macmillan, 1936.

Curtis, L. *Reno reveries*. Reno, Nev.: Chas. E. Weck, 1912.

Dante, *The early life*. Florence: Felix le Monnier, 1846.

Dante, *The divine comedy*. Chicago: Encyclopedia Britannica, 1952.

Darwin, C. *The descent of man and selection in relation to sex*. London: John Murray, 1888. Vol. 2.

Davis, H. W. C. *Charlemagne*. New York: Putnam's, 1899.

Davis, K. B. *Factors in the sex life of twenty-two hundred women*. New York: Harper, 1929.

Davis, R. H., Cooke, R. T., Harland, M., Owen, C., & Barr, A. E. Are women to blame? *North American Review*, 1889, *148*, 622-642.

Davis, W. S. *The influence of wealth in imperial Rome*. New York: Macmillan, 1910.

Davis, W. S. *Life on a medieval barony*. New York: Harper, 1923.

Day, D. *The evolution of love*. New York: Dial Press, 1954.

Dean, D. G. Romanticism and emotional maturity: A preliminary study. *Marriage and Family Living*, 1961, *23*, 44-45.

Dean, D. G. Romanticism and emotional maturity: A further explanation. *Social Forces*, 1964, *42*, 298-303.

Decree on the introduction of divorce of December 19, 1917. In R. Schlesinger (ed.), *Changing attitudes in Soviet Russia. The family in the U.S.S.R. Documents and readings*. London: Routledge & Kegan Paul, 1949. Pp. 30-32.

Defoe, D. *The use and abuse of the marriage bed*. London: T. Warner, 1727.

Deguise, A. Four French women: From emancipation to liberation. *Connecticut College Alumni Magazine*, 1972, *49* (2), 6-9, 38-39.

Delano, I. O. *An African looks at marriage*. London: United Society for Christian Literature, 1944.

De Leon, Luis. *The Perfect Wife*. Denton, Tex.: The College Press, Texas State College for Women, 1943.

Delisle, F. *Friendship's odyssey*. London: Delisle, 1964.

Demos, J. *A little commonwealth: Family life in Plymouth Colony*. New York: Oxford Press, 1970.

Denfield, D. Towards a typology of swinging. Paper presented at Groves Conference on Marriage and the Family, San Juan, Puerto Rico, May 8, 1971.

Denfield, D. How swingers make contact. *Sexual Behavior*, April 1972, 60-63.

Denfield, D., & Gordon, M. The sociology of mate swapping: Or the family that swings together clings together. *Journal of Sex Research*, 1970, *6*, 85-100.

Denomy, A. J. *The heresy of courtly love*. New York: D. X. McMullen, 1947.

Deutsch, H. *Psychology of women: A psychoanalytic interpretation*. New York: Grune & Stratton, 1944.

De Vos, G., & Wagatsuma, H. Status and role behavior in changing Japan. In G. H. Seward and R. C. Williamson (eds.), *Sex roles in changing society.* New York: Random House, 1970. Pp. 334-370.

Dicks, H. V. Observations on contemporary Russian behavior. *Human Relations,* 1952, *5,* 111-175.

Diderot, D. *Oeuvres philosophiques.* Paris: Garnier Frères, 1956.

Ditzion, S. *Marriage, morals, and sex in America.* New York: Bookman Associates, 1954.

Dixon, W. H. *Spiritual wives.* 2 vols. London: Hurst & Blackett, 1868.

Doi, L. T. "Amae": A key concept for understanding Japanese personality structure. In R. J. Smith and R. K. Beardsley (eds.), *Japanese culture: Its development and characteristics.* Chicago: Aldine, 1962. Pp. 132-139.

Donaldson, E. T. The myth of courtly love. *Ventures,* 1965, *5,* 16-23.

Dore, R. P. *City life in Japan.* Berkeley Calif.: University of California Press, 1958.

Dorjahn, V. R. The factor of polygyny in African demography. In W. R. Bacon and M. J. Herskovitz (eds.), *Continuity and change in African cultures.* Chicago: University of Chicago Press, 1959. Pp. 87-112.

Douglas, M. *The Lele of the Kasai.* London: Oxford University Press, 1963.

Dreiser, T. *Jennie Gerhardt.* Garden City, N.Y.: Garden City Publishing Co., 1926.

Drysdale, G. *The elements of social science.* London: E. Truelove, 1898.

Duncan, B., & Duncan, O. D. Family stability and occupational success. *Social Problems,* 1969, *16,* 273-285.

Dunne, F. P. *Mr. Dooley in peace and war.* Boston: Small, Maynard & Co., 1898.

Dunne, F. P. *Mr. Dooley says.* New York: Charles Scribner's Sons, 1910.

Durant, W. Breakdown of marriage. *Pictorial Review,* November 1927, *29,* 4.

Durant, W. *The story of civilization.* New York: Simon & Schuster, 1935.

Durant, W. *The life of Greece.* New York: Simon & Schuster, 1939.

Durant, W. *Caesar and Christ.* New York: Simon & Schuster, 1944.

Durant, W. *The Renaissance.* New York: Simon & Schuster, 1953.

Durant, W. *The Reformation.* New York: Simon & Schuster, 1957.

Durant, W., & Durant, A. *The age of reason begins.* New York: Simon & Schuster, 1961.

Durant, W., & Durant, A. *The age of Louis XIV.* New York: Simon & Schuster, 1963.

Durant, W., & Durant, A. *The age of Voltaire.* New York: Simon & Schuster, 1965.

Durkheim, E. La prohibition de l'inceste et ses origines. *L'Année Sociologique,* 1896, *1,* 1-70.

Dworkin, G. The hippies: Permanent revolution? *Dissent,* 1969, *16,* 180-183.

Eaton, J. W., & Katz, S. M. *Research guide on cooperative group farming.* New York: The H. W. Wilson Co., 1942.

Edmonds, W. D. *The first hundred years.* Oneida, N.Y.: Oneida Ltd., 1948.

Edwards, J. N. The future of the family revisited. *Journal of Marriage and the Family.* 1967, *29,* 505-512.

Ehrmann, W. *Premarital dating behavior.* New York: Bantam, 1960.

Einhard. *The life of Charlemagne.* Ann Arbor, Mich.: University of Michigan Press, 1960.

Ellis, A. A study of human love relationships. *Journal of Genetic Psychology,* 1949, *75,* 61-67.

Ellis, A. Healthy and disturbed reasons for having extramarital relations. *Journal of Human Relations,* 1968, *16,* 490-501.

Ellis, A. B. West-African marriage customs. In B. J. Stern (ed.), *Marriage, past and present.* New York: Appleton-Century, 1938. Pp. 44-46.

Ellis, H. *Impressions and comments. Third (and final) series. 1920-1923.* Boston: Houghton Mifflin, 1924.

Ellis, H. The future of marriage. *The Saturday Review of Politics, Literature, Science and Art,* 1927, *143,* 623-624.

Ellis, H. Freud's influence on the changed attitude toward sex. *The American Journal of Sociology,* 1939, *65,* 309-317.

Ellis, H. *My life.* Boston, Mass.: Houghton Mifflin, 1939.

Ellis, H. Eonism and other supplementary studies. In his *Studies in the psychology of sex.* New York: Random House, 1942.

Ellis, H. Sex in relation to society. In his *Studies in the psychology of sex.* New York: Random House, 1942.

Ellis, H. The sexual impulse in women. In his *Studies in the psychology of sex.* New York: Random House, 1942.

Ellis, S. *The wives of England.* New York: D. Appleton & Co., 1843.

Empey, L. T. Role expectations of young women regarding marriage and a career. *Marriage and Family Living,* 1958, *20,* 152-155.

Encyclopedia Britannica. Chicago: Encyclopedia Britannica, 1964.

Engels, F. *The origin of the family, private property and the state.* Chicago: Charles H. Kerr, 1910.

England, R. W., Jr. Images of love and courtship in family-magazine fiction. *Marriage and Family Living,* 1960, *22,* 162-165.

English, O. S. Values in psychotherapy: The affair. *Voices: The Art & Science of Psychotherapy,* 1967, *3,* 9-14.

Epstein, L. M. *Marriage laws in the Bible and the Talmud.* Cambridge, Mass.: Harvard University Press, 1942.

Epstein, L. M. *Sex laws and customs in Judaism.* New York: Bloch Publishing, 1948.

Epton, N. *Love and the French.* Cleveland: World, 1959.

Epton, N. *Love and the English.* Cleveland: World, 1960.

Erasmus, D. Erasmus on Christian marriage. In B. J. Stern (ed.), *The family, past and present.* New York: Appleton-Century, 1938. Pp. 129-130.

Erasmus, D. *The colloquies of Erasmus.* Chicago: University of Chicago Press, 1965.

Euripides. A Greek woman's protest. (Trans. A. W. Way.) In B. J. Stern (ed.), *The family, past and present.* New York: Appleton-Century, 1938. P. 87. (Originally published by Loeb Classical Library and Harvard University Press.)

Evans, J. *John Ruskin.* New York: Oxford University Press, 1954.

Evans, J. H. *Joseph Smith, an American prophet.* New York: Macmillan, 1946.

Evans, M. Marriage, Japanese style. *McCall's,* 1966, *94*(2), 84, 176.

Evans, R. B. Physical and biochemical characteristics of homosexual men. *Journal of Consulting and Clinical Psychology,* 1972, *39,* 140-147.

Evans-Pritchard, E. E. *Kinship and marriage among the Nuer.* London: Oxford University Press, 1951.

Evans-Pritchard, E. E. Zande bridewealth. *Africa,* 1970, *40,* 115-124.

Everett, A. H. *New ideas on population: With remarks on the theories of Malthus and Godwin.* Boston: Oliver Everett, 1823.

Every woman's book; or, what is love? London: R. Carlisle, 1834.

Fairchild, M. The status of the family in the Soviet Union today. *American Sociological Review,* 1937, *2,* 619-629.

Farber, B. *Family: Organization and interaction.* San Francisco: Chandler Publishing Co., 1964.

Farley, R., & Hermalin, A. I. Family stability: A comparison of trends between blacks and whites. *American Journal of Sociology,* 1971, *36,* 1-17.

Farquhar, G. *The beaux' stratagem.* In C. A. Moore (ed.), *Twelve famous plays of the Restoration and eighteenth century.* New York: Modern Library, 1933. Act V, scene 4, pp. 499-511.

Fathers of the third century (ante-Nicene Fathers). New York: Christian Literature, 1890. Vol. 4.

Fathers of the third and fourth centuries (ante-Nicene Fathers). New York: Scribner's Sons, 1899. Vol. 7.

Fei, Hsiao-tung. The case of the Chinese gentry. In R. L. Coser (ed.), *The family: Its structure and functions.* New York: St. Martin's Press, 1964. Pp. 550-569.

Feldman, H. *The Ghanian family in transition.* Unpublished paper, Cornell University, 1969.

Fellows, L. Kenya report: Market in brides. *New York Times Magazine,* February 19, 1967, 12, ff.

Ferguson, C. W. *The male attitude.* Boston: Little, Brown, 1966.

Fern, V. (ed.). *Puritan sage: Collected writings of Jonathan Edwards.* New York: Library Publishers, 1953.

Few U.S. married couples said to live with relatives. *New York Times,* March 24, 1968, 50.

Field, M. G., & Flynn, K. I. Worker, mother, housewife: Soviet women today. In G. H. Seward and R. C. Williamson (eds.), *Sex roles in changing society.* New York: Random House, 1970. Pp. 257-284.

Fielding, H. *Tom Jones.* Chicago: Encyclopedia Britannica, 1952.

fifteen joys of marriage, The. London: Orion Press, 1959.

Fitzhugh, G. *Sociology for the South.* New York: Burt Franklin, n.d.

Flacelière, R. *Love in ancient Greece.* New York: Crown, 1962.

Flugel, J. C. *The psychoanalytic study of the family.* London: Hogarth Press, 1939.

Fong, S. L. M. Sex roles in the modern fabric of China. In G. H. Seward and R. C. Williamson (eds.), *Sex roles in changing society.* New York: Random House, 1970. Pp. 371-400.

Foote, N., & Cottrell, L. *Identity and interpersonal competence.* Chicago: University of Chicago Press, 1955.

Ford, C. S., & Beach, F. A. *Patterns of sexual behavior.* New York: Harper, 1951.

Fortes, M. *The web of kinship among the Tallensi.* London: Oxford University Press, 1949.

Fortune, R. F. Incest. In R. L. Coser (ed.), *The family: Its structure and functions.* New York: St. Martin's Press, 1964. Pp. 70-74.

Fourier, F. M. C. *Le nouveau monde: Industriel et sociétaire. Oeuvres complètes.* Paris: A la Librairie Sociétaire, 1848. Vol. VI.

Fourier, F. M. C. *La phalange. IX Revue de la science sociale.* Paris: Aux Bureaux de la Phalange, 1849.

Fowler, L. N. *Marriage, its history and ceremonies.* New York: S. R. Wells, 1855.

Fowler, O. S. *Matrimony.* Boston: O. S. Fowler, 1859.

Fox, J. R. Sibling incest. *British Journal of Sociology,* 1962, *13,* 128-150.

Frame, D. M. *Montaigne.* New York: Harcourt, Brace & World, 1965.

Frank, P. Soviet divorce. *New Society,* 1966, *8* (215), 718-719.

Franklin, B. A letter to John Alleyne Esq. on early marriage. In B. Franklin (ed.), *Letters on courtship and marriage.* Trenton, N.J.: Daniel Fenton & James J. Wilson, 1813. Pp. 219-223.

Franklin, B. Reflections on courtship and marriage. In B. Franklin (ed.), *Letters on courtship and marriage.* Trenton, N.J.: Daniel Fenton & James J. Wilson, 1813. Pp. 5-80.

Franklin, B. *The old mistresses' apologue.* Philadelphia: The Philip H. & A. S. W. Rosenbach Foundation, 1956.

Franklin, B. *The autobiography.* New Haven, Conn.: Yale University Press, 1964.

Frazier, E. F. The Negro slave family. *The Journal of Negro History,* 1930, *15,* 198-259.

Frazier, E. F. *The Negro family in the United States.* New York: Macmillan, 1957.

Freedman, M. The family in China, past and present. *Pacific Affairs,* 1961, *34,* 323-336.

Freedman, M. Ritual aspects of Chinese kinship and marriage. In M. Freedman (ed.), *Family and kinship in Chinese society.* Stanford, Calif.: Stanford University Press, 1970. Pp. 163-187.

French, D. After the fall. *New York Times Magazine,* October 3, 1971, 20 ff.

French and English theories of marriage. *Living Age,* 1865, *86,* 606-609.

French marriage. *Living Age,* 1873, *118,* 259-265.

Freud, S. Totem and Taboo. In A. A. Brill (ed.), *The basic writings of Sigmund Freud.* New York: Random House, 1938. Pp. 807-930.

Freud, S. "A child is being beaten": A contribution to the study of the origin of sexual perversions. In his *Collected papers.* London: Hogarth Press, 1949. Vol. 2, pp. 172-201.

Freud, S. On narcissism: An introduction. In his *Collected papers.* London: Hogarth Press, 1949. Vol. 4, pp. 30-59.

Freud, S. Why war? In his *Collected papers.* London: Hogarth Press, 1950. Vol. 5, pp. 273-287.

Freud, S. Civilization and its discontents. In *The major works of Sigmund Freud*. Chicago: Encyclopedia Britannica, 1952. Pp. 767-802.

Freud, S. Beyond the pleasure principle. In *The complete psychological works of Sigmund Freud*. London: Hogarth Press, 1955. Vol. 18, pp. 7-64.

Freud, S. Postscript. In *The complete psychological works of Sigmund Freud*. London: Hogarth Press, 1955. Vol. 18, pp. 134-143.

Freud, S. *Moses and monotheism*. New York: Vintage Books, 1955.

Freud, S. "Civilized" sexual morality and modern nervous illness. In *The complete psychological works of Sigmund Freud*. London: Hogarth Press, 1959. Vol. 9, pp. 181-204.

Freud, S. Femininity. In *The complete psychological works of Sigmund Freud*. London: Hogarth Press, 1964. Vol. 22, pp. 112-135.

Fried, M. H. The family in China: The people's republic. In R. N. Anshen (ed.), *The family: Its function and destiny*. New York: Harper, 1959. Pp. 146-166.

Friedan, B. *The feminine mystique*. New York: Dell, 1964.

Friedländer, L. *Roman life and manners under the early empire*. New York: E.P. Dutton, 1908. Vol. 1.

Friedländer, L. Marriage custom in ancient Rome. In B.J. Stern (ed.), *The family, past and present*. New York: Appleton-Century, 1938. Pp. 98-101.

Friend to the ladies, a dialogue concerning the subjugation of women to their husbands. London: J. Wilkie, 1765.

Fromm, E. *Man for himself*. Rinehart, 1947.

Fromm, E. *Sigmund Freud's mission*. New York: Harper, 1959.

Fromm, E. *The art of loving*. New York: Bantam Books, 1963.

Frost, G. What Russian girls are like. *New York Times Magazine*, January 24, 1965, 16 ff.

Frumkin, R. M., & Frumkin, M. Z. Sex, marriage, and the family in the U.S.S.R. *Journal of Human Relations*, 1961, *9*, 254-264.

Frye, R. M. The teachings of classical puritanism on conjugal love. *Studies in the Renaissance*, 1955, *2*, 148-159.

Furnivall, F. J. *Child-marriages, divorces, and ratifications*. London: Kegan Paul, Trench, Trübner & Co., 1897.

Furstenberg, F. F. Industrialization and the American family: A look backward. *American Sociological Review*, 1966, *31*, 326-337.

Gallup, G. *The Gallup poll: Public Opinion 1935-1971*. 3 vols. New York: Random House, 1972.

Gaya. *Marriage ceremonies or the ceremonies used in marriage in all parts of the world*. London: Abel Roper, 1697.

Gebhard, P. H. Factors in marital orgasm. *The Journal of Social Issues*, 1966, *22*, 88-95.

Geddes, D. P. (ed.). *An analysis of the Kinsey reports on sexual behavior in the human male and female*. New York: Dutton, 1954.

Geiger, H. K. *The family in Soviet Russia*. Cambridge, Mass.: Harvard University Press, 1968.

Geiger, H. K. The Soviet family. In M. F. Nimkoff (ed.), *Comparative family systems*. Boston: Houghton Mifflin, 1965. Pp. 301-328.

Gellinek, C. J. Marriage by consent in literary sources of medieval Germany. In *Studia Gratiana*, 1967, *12*, 555-580.

George, W. L. *The story of woman.* New York: Harper, 1925.

Gerson, M. Women in the kibbutz. *American Journal of Orthopsychiatry,* 1971, *41,* 566-573.

Gibbon, E. *The decline and fall of the Roman Empire.* 2 vols. Chicago: Encyclopedia Britannica, 1952.

Giglinger, G. Divorce and its effects on society. *Catholic World,* 1903, *78,* 92-98.

Gilmartin, B. G. Unpublished tables on a sample of swingers and controls.

Girard, R. Marriage in Avignon in the second half of the fifteenth century. *Speculum,* 1953, *28,* 485-498.

Gist, M. A. *Love and war in the middle English romances.* Philadelphia: University of Pennsylvania Press, 1947.

Gluckman, M. Estrangement in the African family. In N. W. Bell & E. F. Vogel (eds.), *A modern introduction to the family.* New York: The Free Press, 1968. Pp. 464-468.

Godwin, W. *An enquiry concerning political justice and its influence on general virtue and happiness.* New York: Alfred A. Knopf, 1926. Vol. 2.

Goethe, J. W. von. *Elective affinities.* Chicago: Henry Regnery, 1963.

Goethe, J. W. von. The sorrows of young Werther. Excerpted in I. Schneider (ed.), *The world of love.* New York: George Braziller, 1964. Pp. 181-188.

Goldberg, P. A. Are women prejudiced against women? *Trans-action,* 1968, *5,* 28-30.

Goldman, E. Marriage and love. In E. Goldman (ed.), *Anarchism and other essays.* New York: Mother Earth Publishing Association, 1914. Pp. 233-245.

Gollin, G. L. *Moravians in two worlds: A study of changing communities.* New York: Columbia University Press, 1967.

Gollin, G. L. Family surrogates in colonial America: The Moravian experiment. *Journal of Marriage and the Family,* 1969, *31,* 650-658.

Golod, S. I. Sociological problems of sexual morality. *Soviet Sociology,* 1969, *8,* 3-23.

de Goncourt, E., & de Goncourt, J. *The woman of the eighteenth century.* New York: Minton, Balch & Co., 1927.

Goode, W. J. The theoretical importance of love. *American Sociological Review,* 1959, *24,* 38-47.

Goode, W. J. *World revolution and family patterns.* Glencoe, Ill.: Free Press, 1963.

Goode, W. J. *Women in divorce.* New York: The Free Press, 1965.

Goodsell, W. *Problems of the family.* New York: Century, 1928.

Goodsell, W. *A history of marriage and the family.* New York: Macmillan, 1934.

Goody, E. N. Conjugal separation and divorce among the Gonja of Northern Ghana. In M. Fortes (ed.), *Marriage in tribal societies.* Cambridge: Cambridge University Press, 1962. Pp. 14-54.

Goody, J. A comparative approach to incest and adultery. In B. Farber (ed.), *Kinship and family organization.* New York: Wiley, 1966. Pp. 54-68.

Goody, J. "Normative," "recollected," and "actual" marriage payments among the Lowili of northern Ghana, 1951-1966. *Africa,* 1969, *39,* 54-61.

Gordon, M. The ideal husband as depicted in the nineteenth century marriage manual. *The Family Life Coordinator,* 1969, *18,* 226-231.

Gordon, M. From procreation to recreation: Changes in sexual ideology, 1830-1940. Unpublished manuscript, University of Connecticut, 1970.

Gordon, M., & Bernstein, M. C. Mate choice and domestic life in the 19th century marriage manual. Unpublished manuscript, University of Connecticut, 1969.

Gorer, G. Love and friendship. In G. Gorer, *The American people: A study in national character.* New York: Norton, 1948.

Gottesman, I. I. Personality and natural selection. In S. A. Vandenberg (ed.), *Methods and goals in human behavior genetics.* New York: Academic Press, 1965. Pp. 63-74.

Granet, M. *Chinese civilization.* New York: Knopf, 1930.

Gray, R. F. Sonjo bride-price and the question of African "wife purchase." *American Anthropology,* 1960, *62,* 34-57.

Gray, R. F. *The Sonjo of Tanganyika.* London: Oxford University Press, 1963.

Grebanier, B. D., Middlebrook, S., Thompson, S., & Watt, W. *English literature and its backgrounds.* New York: The Dryden Press, 1955.

Greenfield, S. M. Love and marriage in modern America: A functional analysis. *Sociological Quarterly,* 1965, *6,* 361-377.

Greg, W. R. (attrib.). Prostitution. *Westminster Review,* 1850, *53,* 448-506.

Gregorius, I. *The dialogues of St. Gregory.* London: Philip Lee Warner, 1911.

Gregory, J. Marks of an honorable lover—a father's advice to his daughters. In *Domestic happiness portrayed: Or a repository for those who are and those who are not married.* New York: Charles Hubbell, 1835. Pp. 404-407.

Gregory of Tours. *The history of the Franks.* 2 vols. London: Oxford University Press, 1927.

Griesinger, K. T. A historian's forebodings. In O. Handlin (ed.), *This was America.* Cambridge, Mass.: Harvard University Press, 1949. Pp. 252-269.

Grunwald, H. A. The second sexual revolution: A survey. In H. A. Grunwald (ed.), *Sex in America.* New York: Bantam, 1964. Pp. 1-15.

Guéhenno, J. *Jean-Jacques Rousseau.* New York: Columbia University Press, 1966. Vol. 1.

Gunther, J. *Inside Africa.* New York: Harper, 1955.

Gunther, J. *Inside Russia.* New York: Harper, 1957.

Gurin, G., Veroff, J., & Feld, S. *Americans view their mental health.* New York: Basic Books, 1960.

Guy, C. *An illustrated history of French cuisine.* New York: Bramhall House, 1962.

Halifax, Lord Marquis of. *The lady's New Year's gift or advice to a daughter.* Kensington: Philip Sainsbury, 1927.

Hall, B. (ed.). *Tell me Josephine.* New York: Simon & Schuster, 1964.

Halle, F. W. *Woman in Soviet Russia.* New York: Viking Press, 1935.

Hallen, G. C., & Theodorson, G. A. The future of the family. *Indian Journal of Social Research,* 1966, *7,* 89-93.

Hallenbeck, W. C. (ed.). *The Baumannville Community.* Durban, Union of South Africa: Institute for Social Research, University of Natal, 1955.

Halsted, C. The man we want to marry. *Ladies' Home Journal,* June 1903, 8.

Halsted, C. The kind of girl they want to marry. *Ladies' Home Journal,* February 1904. 4.

Hamblin, R. L. & Blood, R. O., Jr. Premarital experience and the wife's sexual adjustment. *Social Problems,* 1957, *4,* 122-130.

Hamilton, G. V. *A Research in Marriage.* New York: Albert & Charles Boni, 1929.

Hardy, E. J. *The love affairs of some famous men.* New York: Frederick A. Stokes, 1897.

Harkness, G. *John Calvin: The man and his ethics.* New York: Holt, 1931.

Harlow, H. F., & Harlow, M. K. The effect of rearing conditions on behavior. *Bulletin of the Menninger Clinic,* 1962, *26,* 213-224.

Harlow, H. F., & Harlow. M. K. Social deprivation in monkeys. *Scientific American,* 1962, *207,* 136-146.

Harper, I. H. Changing conditions of marriage. *The Independent,* 1906, *61,* 1329-1332.

Harvey, R. H. *Robert Owen.* Berkeley, Calif.: University of California Press, 1949.

Hauser, P. M. Social science predicts and projects. In P. M. Hauser (ed.), *The future of the family.* New York: Family Service Association of America, 1969. Pp. 21-38.

Hedgepath, W., & Stock, D. *The alternative: Communal life in North America.* New York: Macmillan, 1970.

Hays, H. R. *From ape to angel. An informal history of social anthropology.* New York: Alfred A. Knopf, 1960.

Hegel, G. W. F. *The philosophy of right.* (Trans. T. M. Knox.) Chicago: Encyclopedia Britannica, 1952.

Heinlein, R. A. *The moon is a harsh mistress.* New York: Putnam's, 1966.

Heinlein, R. A. *Stranger in a strange land.* New York: Berkley Publishing, 1971.

Henry, J. Forty-year-old jitters in married urban women. In S. M. Farber & R. H. L. Wilson (eds.), *The challenge to women.* New York: Basic Books, 1966. Pp. 146-163.

Herlihy, D. Family solidarity in medieval Italian history. *Explorations in economic history,* 1969, *7,* 173-184.

Herodotus. *The history of Herodotus.* Chicago: William Benton, 1952.

Herzog, E. Is there a "breakdown" of the Negro family? In L. Saxton (ed.), *The individual, marriage, and the family: Current perspectives.* Belmont, Calif.: Wadsworth, 1970. Pp. 383-392.

Hesiod. *Hesiod.* Ann Arbor, Mich.: University of Michigan Press, 1959.

High bride prices annoy Africans. *New York Times,* December 19, 1965, 7.

Hill, J. (pseud. Juliana-Susannah Seymour). *The conduct of married life.* London: R. Baldwin, 1754.

Hill, R. The future of the family. In H. Becker & R. Hill (eds.), *Marriage and the family.* Boston: Heath, 1942. Pp. 621-650.

Hill, R. The American family of the future. *Journal of Marriage and the Family,* 1964, *26,* 20-28.

Hinds, W. A. *American communities and cooperative colonies* (2nd ed.). Chicago: Charles H. Kerr, 1908.

Hinkle, B. M. Marriage in the new world. In H. Keyserling (ed.), *The book of marriage.* New York: Harcourt, Brace & Co., 1926. Pp. 216-243.

Ho, P. An historian's view of the Chinese family system. In S. M. Farber, P. Mustacchi, & R. H. L. Wilson (eds.), *The family's search for survival.* New York: McGraw-Hill, 1965. Pp. 15-30.

Hoadly, C. J. Records of the colony and plantation of New Haven. Hartford, Conn.: Case, Tiffany & Co., 1857.

Hobart, C. Commitment, value conflict and the future of the American family. *Marriage and Family Living,* 1963, *25,* 405-412.

Hobbes, T. *Leviathan.* Chicago: Encyclopedia Britannica, 1952.

Hobhouse, L. T., Wheeler, G. C., & Ginsberg, M. *The material culture and social institutions of the simpler peoples.* London: Chapman Hall, Ltd., 1917.

Hoffman, M. *The gay world.* New York: Basic Books, 1968.

Hollander, A. Among the Indians. In O. Handlin (ed.), *This was America.* Cambridge, Mass.: Harvard University Press, 1949. Pp. 9-14.

Holliday, C. *Woman's life in colonial days.* Boston: Cornhill Publishing Co., 1922.

Holloway, M. *Heavens on earth.* New York: Dover, 1966.

Homans, G. C. *Social behavior: Its elementary forms.* New York: Harcourt, Brace & World, 1961.

Homer. *The iliad.* (Trans. R. Lattimore.) London: Routledge & Kegan Paul, 1951.

Homer. *The odyssey of Homer.* (Trans. T. E. Shaw.) New York: Oxford University Press, 1956.

Horace. *Satires, epistles, and ars poetica.* (Trans. H. R. Fairclough.) London: Wm. Heinemann, 1929.

Horney, K. (ed.). *Feminine psychology.* New York: Norton, 1967.

Hostetler, J. A. *Amish society.* Baltimore: The Johns Hopkins Press, 1963.

Hostetler, J. A. Persistence and change patterns in Amish society. *Ethnology,* 1964, *3,* 185-198.

Houriet, R. *Getting back together.* New York: Coward, McCann & Geoghegan, 1971.

Howard, G. E. *A history of matrimonial institutions.* 3 vols. Chicago: University of Chicago Press, 1904.

Howells, W. D. *Indian summer.* New York: Dutton, 1951.

Hsu, F. L. K. The family in China: The classical form. In R. N. Anshen (ed.), *The family: Its function and destiny.* New York: Harper, 1959. Pp. 123-145.

Huang, L. J. Some changing patterns in the communist Chinese family. *Marriage and Family Living,* 1961, *23,* 137-146.

Huang, L. J. Attitude of the communist Chinese toward inter-class marriage. *Marriage and Family Living,* 1962, *24,* 389-392.

Huang, L. J. Mate selection and marital happiness in the communist Chinese family. Paper given at the National Council on Family Relations Convention, Washington, D.C., October 1969.

Huber, H. Le principe de la réciprocité dans le mariage Nyende. *Africa,* 1969, *39,* 260-274.

Huch, R. Romantic marriage. In H. Keyserling (ed.), *The book of marriage.* New York: Harcourt, Brace & Co., 1926. Pp. 168-196.

Hughes, K. The Church and marriage in Africa. *Christian Century,* 1965, *82,* 204-208.

Hulicka, K. Marriage and family law in the U.S.S.R. *International Journal of Legal Research,* 1968, *3,* 77-90.

Hulicka, K. Women and the family in the U.S.S.R. *Midwest Quarterly,* 1969, *10,* 133-154.

Hume, D. *Essays, moral, political and literary.* 2 vols. London: Longmans, Green, 1907.

Humphreys, L. *Tearoom trade: Impersonal sex in public places.* Chicago: Aldine, 1970.

Hunt, D. *Parents and children in history: The psychology of family life in early modern France.* New York: Basic Books, 1970.

Hunt, M. M. *The natural history of love.* New York: Grove Press, 1959.

Hunt, M. M. *Her infinite variety.* New York: Harper & Row, 1962.

Hunt, M. M. *The affair: A portrait of extra-marital love in contemporary America.* New York: World, 1969.

Hunter, M. *Reaction to conquest.* London: Oxford University Press, 1961.

Hurstfield, J. *The queen's wards.* Cambridge, Mass.: Harvard University Press, 1958.

Hurvitz, N. Marital strain in the blue-collar family. In A. B. Shostak & W. Gomberg (eds.), *Blue-collar world: Studies of the American worker.* Englewood Cliffs. N.J.: Prentice-Hall, 1964. Pp. 92-109.

Huxley, A. *Brave new world.* New York: Harper, 1946.

I, John, take thee Mary—for the next five years. *Christian Century,* 1967, *84,* 1182.

Ibsen, H. *Plays of Henrik Ibsen.* New York: Books, Inc., n.d.

Inkeles, A. Family and church in the postwar U.S.S.R. *Annals of the American Academy of Political and Social Sciences,* May 1949, *263,* 33-44.

Intercidona. *The connubial guide; or, married people's best friend.* London: John Wilson, n.d.

Irving, W. *Diedrich Knickerbocker's a history of New York.* Philadelphia: J. B. Lippincott & Co., 1871.

Isono, F. The family and women in Japan. *Sociological Review,* 1964, *12,* 39-54.

Iwahara, S. Marriage attitudes in Japanese college students. *International Understanding,* 1964-1965, *2,* 18-22.

Jackson, W. T. H. Faith unfaithful—the German reaction to courtly love. In F. X. Newman (ed.), *The meaning of courtly love.* Albany, N.Y.: State University of New York Press, 1968. Pp. 55-76.

Jacobson, A. H. Conflict of attitudes toward the roles of the husband and wife in marriage. *American Sociological Review,* 1952, *17,* 146-150.

Jacobson, P. H. *American marriage and divorce.* New York: Rinehart, 1959.

Jahoda, G. Boys' images of marriage partners and girls' self-images in Ghana. *Sociologues,* 1958, *8,* 155-169.

Jahoda, G. Love, marriage, and social change: Letters to the advice column of a West African newspaper. In P. L. van den Berghe (ed.), *Africa: Social problems of change and conflict.* San Francisco: Chandler, 1965. Pp. 143-162.

James, B. B. *Women of England.* Philadelphia: Rittenhouse Press, 1908.

James, H. The woman thou gavest me. *The Atlantic Monthly,* 1870, *25,* 66-72.

Japanese still follow Shinto wedding customs. *New York Times,* 1973.

Jarman, W. *U.S.A.: Uncle Sam's abcess.* Exeter, England. W. Jarman, 1884.

Jaurès, J. Marriage in socialistic society. *The Independent,* 1908, *68,* 404-406.

Jefferis, B. G., & Nichols, J. L. *Safe counsel: A complete sexual science and a guide to purity and physical manhood. Advice to maiden, wife, and mother on love, courtship, and marriage.* Atlanta: Guide Publishing Co., 1895.

Jensen, O. *The revolt of American women.* New York: Harcourt, Brace & Co., 1952.

Jerome. *The principal works of St. Jerome* (Nicene and post-Nicene Fathers). New York: Christian Literature, 1893. Vol. 6, second series.

Jerome. *Select letters of St. Jerome.* (Trans. F. A. Wright.) London: William Heinemann Ltd., 1933.

Jerome. *The letters of St. Jerome.* (Trans. C. C. Mierow.) Westminster, Md.: Newman Press, 1963.

Johnson, R. E. Some correlates of extramarital coitus. *Journal of Marriage and the Family,* 1970, *32,* 449-456.

Johnson, R. H. Marriage selection. In *Proceedings of the First National Conference on Race Betterment.* Battle Creek, Mich.: Race Betterment Foundation, 1914.

Johnston, E. Marriage or free love. *The Westminster Review,* 1899, *152,* 91-98.

Johnston, J. *Mrs. Satan.* New York: G. P. Putnam's Sons, 1967.

Jonas, H. *The gnostic religion.* Boston: Beacon Press, 1958.

Jones, C. S. The assault on marriage. *The Living Age,* 1914, *281,* 248-251.

Jones, E. *The life and work of Sigmund Freud.* Vol. 1: *The formative years and the great discoveries 1856-1900.* New York: Basic Books, 1953.

Jones, E. *The life and work of Sigmund Freud.* Vol. 2: *The years of maturity.* New York: Basic Books, 1955.

Jones, E. *The life and work of Sigmund Freud.* Vol. 3: *The last phase: 1919-1939.* New York: Basic Books, 1957.

Joyce, G. H. *Christian marriage: An historical and doctrinal study.* London: Sheed & Ward, 1933.

Juviler, P. Marriage and divorce. *Survey: A journal of Soviet and East European studies,* 1963, *48,* 104-117.

Juviler, P. Soviet families. *Survey,* 1966, *60,* 51-61.

Juviler, P. H. Family reforms on the road to communism. In P. H. Juviler & H. W. Morton (eds.), *Soviet policy-making: Studies of communism in transition.* New York: Frederick A. Praeger, 1967. Pp. 29-60.

Kaats, G. R., & Davis, K. E. Effect of volunteer biases on sexual behavior and attitudes. *Journal of Sex Research,* 1971, *7,* 26-34.

Kaats, G. R., & Davis, K. E. The dynamics of sexual behavior of college students. *Journal of Marriage and the Family,* 1970, *32,* 390-399.

Kagan, J., & Beach, F. Effect of early experience on mating behavior in male rats. *Journal of Comparative Physiology and Psychology,* 1953, *46,* 204-208.

Kanin, E. J., & Howard, D. H. Postmarital consequences of premarital sex adjustment. *American Sociological Review,* 1958, *23,* 556-561.

Kant, I. *The science of right.* Chicago: Encyclopedia Britannica, 1952.

Kantner, J. F., & Zelnik, M. Sexual experience of young unmarried women in the United States. *Family Planning Perspectives,* 1972, *4*(4), 9-18.

Karlen, A. The unmarried marrieds on campus. *New York Times Magazine,* January 26, 1969, 28-29, 77-80.

Karlen, A. *Sexuality and homosexuality: A new view.* New York: Norton, 1971.

Kassel, V. Polygyny after sixty. In H. A. Otto (ed.), *The family in search of a future.* New York: Appleton-Century-Crofts, 1970. Pp. 137-143.

Katayev, V. Squaring the circle. In E. Lyons (ed.), *Six Soviet plays.* London: Victor Gollancz, 1935. Pp. 123-210. Occasional quotes by permission of Houghton Mifflin Company.

Kelen, B. *The mistresses.* New York: Random House, 1966.

Keller, A. G. *Homeric society.* New York: Longmans, Green, 1911.

Keller, S. Does the family have a future? *Journal of Comparative Family Studies,* 1971, *2,* 1-14.

Kelly, J. Sister love: An exploration of the need for homosexual experience. *The Family Coordinator,* 1972, *21,* 473-475.

Kelso, R. *Doctrine for the lady of the Renaissance.* Urbana, Ill.: University of Illinois Press, 1956.

Kenkel, W. F. *The family in perspective* (2nd ed.). New York: Appleton-Century-Crofts, 1966.

Kennett, R. H. *Ancient Hebrew social life and custom.* London: Oxford University Press, 1931.

Kenyatta, J. *Facing Mount Kenya.* London: Secker & Warburg, 1956.

Kephart, W. M. Discussion of "Commitment, value conflict and the future of the American family." *Marriage and Family Living,* 1963, *25,* 412-413.

Kephart, W. M. Experimental family organization: an historico-cultural report on the Oneida community. *Marriage and Family Living,* 1963, *25,* 261-271.

Kephart, W. M. Legal and procedural aspects of marriage and divorce. In H. Christensen (ed.), *Handbook of marriage and the family.* Chicago: Rand McNally, 1964. Pp. 944-968.

Kephart, W. M. *The family, society, and the individual.* Boston: Houghton Mifflin, 1966.

Kephart, W. M. Some correlates of romantic love. *Journal of Marriage and the Family,* 1967, 29, 470-474.

Kerckhoff, A. C., & Davis, K. E. Value consensus and need complementarity in mate selection. *American Sociological Review,* 1962, *27,* 295-303.

Kharchev, A. G. The nature of the Soviet family. *Soviet Review,* May 1961, *2,* 3-19.

Kharchev, A. G. Problems of the family and their study in the U.S.S.R. *International Social Science Journal,* 1962, *14,* 539-549.

Kharchev, A. G. On some results of a study of the motives for marriage. *Soviet Sociology,* 1964, *4* (No. 4), 41-51.

Kharchev, A. G. Marriage in the U.S.S.R. *Soviet Sociology,* 1965, *5,* (No. 4), 3-24.

Kharchev, A. G. *Marriage and family relations in the U.S.S.R.* Moscow: Novosti Press Agency Publishing House, n.d.

Kiang, K. The Chinese family system. *Annals of the American Academy of Political and Social Science,* 1930, *152,* 39-46.

Kiefer, O. *Sexual life in ancient Rome.* New York: Barnes & Noble, 1952.

Kingsley, C. *Yeast.* London: Macmillan, 1881.

Kinsey, A. C., Pomeroy, W. B., & Martin, C. E. *Sexual behavior in the human male.* Philadelphia: W. B. Saunders, 1948.

Kinsey, A. C., Pomeroy, W. B., Martin, C. E., & Gebhard, P. H. *Sexual behavior in the human female.* Philadelphia: W. B. Saunders, 1953.

Kirkendall, L. A. *Premarital intercourse and interpersonal relationships.* New York: The Julian Press, 1961.

Kirkpatrick, C. F. The sociological significance of this research. In W. Ehrmann, *Premarital dating behavior.* New York: Bantam, 1960. Pp. 363-371.

Kirkpatrick, C., & Caplow, T. Courtship in a group of Minnesota students. *American Journal of Sociology*, 1945, *51*, 114-125.

Kirkpatrick, C., & Caplow, T. Emotional trends in the courtship experience of college students as expressed by graphs, with some observations on methodological implications. *American Sociological Review*, 1945, *10*, 619-626.

Knowlton, C. *Fruits of philosophy* (2nd ed.). London: J. Watson, n.d.

Knupfer, G., Clark, W., & Room, R. The mental health of the unmarried. *The American Journal of Psychiatry*, 1966, *122*, 841-851.

Kohák, E. V. Turning on for freedom. *Dissent*, 1969, *16*, 437-443.

Köhler, J. Indisches Ehe- und Familienrecht. *Zeitschrift für vergleichende Rechtswissenschaft*, 1882, *3*, 342-442.

Kolb, W. L. Family sociology, marriage education, and the romantic complex. *Social Forces*, 1950, *29*, 65-72.

Kolbanovski, V. N. The sex unbringing of the rising generation. *Soviet Sociology*, Fall 1964, *5*(3), 51-62.

Koller, M. R. Some changes in courtship behaviour in three generations of Ohio women. *American Sociological Review*, 1951, *16*, 366-370.

Kollontai, A. M. Excerpts from the works of. In R. Schlesinger (ed.), *The family in the U.S.S.R.* London: Routledge & Kegan Paul, 1949. Pp. 45-74.

Komarovsky, M. *Blue-collar marriage*. New York: Random House, 1964.

Kopelianskaia, S. Marriage in the U.S.S.R. *Living Age*, 1935, *349*, 160-164.

Kotlar, S. L. Instrumental and expressive marital roles. *Sociology and Social Research*, 1962, *46*, 186-194.

Koyama, T. The changing social position of women in Japan. In W. Goode (ed.), *Readings in family and society*. Englewood Cliffs, N.J.: Prentice-Hall, 1964. Pp. 237-242.

Koyano, S. Changing family behavior in four Japanese communities. *Journal of Marriage and the Family*, 1964, *26*, 149-159.

Krige, E. J. Girls' puberty songs and their relation to fertility, health, morality and religion among the Zulu. *Africa*, 1968, *38*, 173-198.

Krilenko, N. V. The family in Soviet Russia. *Political Quarterly*, 1937, *8*, 204-226.

Krupianskaia, V. U. Family structure and family life. In S. Benet (trans. & ed.), *The village of Viriatino*. New York: Doubleday, 1970. Pp. 91-126.

Kuper, H. *The Swazi*. New York: Holt, Rinehart & Winston, 1964.

Kurokawa, M. Lineal orientation in child rearing among Japanese. *Journal of Marriage and the Family*, 1968, *30*, 129-131.

L., R. T. Ten reasons for marriage. *Ladies' Home Journal*, 1935, *52*, 58.

Lacy, W. K. *The family in classical Greece*. Ithaca, N.Y.: Cornell University Press, 1968.

de Laclos, C. *Dangerous acquaintances*. London: George Routledge, n.d. (Now Routledge & Kegan Paul Ltd.)

Landis, J. T. Length of time required to achieve adjustment in marriage. *American Sociological Review*, 1946, *11*, 666-677.

Landis, J. T. Some aspects of family instability in the United States. *Transactions of the Third World Congress of Sociology*, 1956, *4*, 174-179.

Landis, J. T. Social correlates of divorce or nondivorce among the unhappy married. *Marriage and Family Living*, 1963. *25*, 178-180.

Lang, A. *Social origins*. London: Longmans, Green & Co., 1903.

Lang, A. *Aucassin and Nicolete*. New York: Holiday House, 1936.

Lang, O. *Chinese family and society*. New Haven, Conn.: Yale University Press, 1946.

Langdon-Davies, J. *Sex, sin, and sanctity*. London: Victor Gollancz, 1954.

Langman, A. W. Love and marriage Soviet style. *McCall's,* September 1960, *87,* 106-107, 192.

La Rochefoucauld, F. A. F. *A Frenchman in England*. Cambridge: The University Press, 1933.

La Rochefoucauld, F. *Maxims and moral reflections*. London: J. Bell, 1799.

Larus, J. R. *Women of America*. Philadelphia: Rittenhouse Press, 1908.

Lawrence, D. H. Benjamin Franklin. In C. L. Sanford (ed.), *Benjamin Franklin and the American character*. Boston: D. C. Heath, 1955. Pp. 57-64.

Lawrence, D. H. *Lady Chatterley's lover*. New York: Signet, 1959.

Lawrance, J. C. D. *The Iteso*. London: Oxford University Press, 1959.

Lazarus, M. E. *Love vs. marriage: Part 1*. New York: Fowlers & Wells, 1852.

Leach, E. R. Aspects of bridewealth and marriage stability among the Kachin and Lakher. *Man*, 1957, *57*, 50-55.

Lecky, W. E. H. *History of European morals*. 2 vols. New York: Appleton, 1905.

Lee, V. The economic dependence of women. *The North American Review,* 1902, *175,* 71-90.

Lerner, I. M. *Genetic homeostasis*. London: Oliver & Boyd, 1954.

Lerner, M. *America as a civilization*. New York: Simon & Schuster, 1957.

Leslie, G. R. *The family in social context*. New York: Oxford University Press, 1967.

Le Vine, R. A. Intergenerational tensions and extended family structures in Africa. In E. Shanas and G. F. Streib (eds.), *Social structure and the family: Generational relations*. Englewood Cliffs, N.J.: Prentice-Hall, 1965. Pp. 188-204.

Levinger, G., Senn, D. J., & Jorgensen, B. W. Progress toward permanence in courtship: A test of the Kerckhoff-Davis hypothesis. *Sociometry*, 1970, *33*, 427-443.

Lévi-Strauss, C. Reciprocity, the essence of social life. In R. L. Coser (ed.), *The family: its structure and functions*. New York: St. Martin's Press, 1964. Pp. 36-48.

Levy, M. J. Contrasting factors in the modernization of China and Japan. In W. J. Goode (ed.), *Readings on the family and society*. Englewood Cliffs, N.J.: Prentice-Hall, 1964. Pp. 225-230.

Levy, M. J. *The family revolution in modern China*. New York: Atheneum, 1968.

Lewis, C. S. *The allegory of love*. New York: Oxford University Press, 1958.

Lewinsohn, R. *A history of sexual customs*. (Trans. A. Mayer.) New York: Harper & Row, 1958.

Licht, H. *Sexual life in ancient Greece*. New York: Barnes & Noble, 1969.

Lilar, S. *Aspects of love in western society*. London: Thames & Hudson, 1965.

Lin, H. W. *The traditional Chinese clan rules*. Locust Valley, N.Y.: J. J. Augustin, 1959.

Lin, Y. The golden wing: A sociological study of Chinese familism. New York: Oxford University Press, 1947.

Lindsey, B. B. The companionate marriage. New York: Boni & Liverwright, 1927.

Lindzey, G. Some remarks concerning incest, the incest taboo, and psychoanalytic theory. American Psychologist, 1967, 22, 1051-1059.

Linton, R. The family among cultivators in the hills of Madagascar. In B. J. Stern (ed.), The family, past and present. New York: Appleton-Century, 1938. Pp. 42-43.

Linton, R. The natural history of the family. In R. N. Anshen (ed.), The family: Its function and destiny. New York: Harper, 1959. Pp. 30-52.

Little, K. Some urban patterns of marriage and domesticity in West Africa. Sociological Review, 1959, 7, 65-97.

Little, K. Attitudes towards marriage and the family among educated young Sierra Leoneans. In P. C. Lloyd (ed.), The new elites of tropical Africa. London: Oxford University Press, 1966. Pp. 139-162.

Little, K., & Price, A. Some trends in modern marriage among West Africans. Africa, 1967, 37, 407-425.

Lloyd, P. C. Divorce among the Yoruba. American Anthropologist, 1968, 70, 67-81.

Locke, H. J. Predicting adjustment in marriage: A comparison of a divorced and a happily married group. New York: Holt, 1951.

Locke, J. Concerning civil government. In Locke, Berkeley, Hume. Chicago: Encyclopedia Britannica, 1952. Pp. 25-81.

Loomis, R. S. Arthurian tradition and Chrétien de Troyes. New York: Columbia University Press, 1949.

Lopata, H. Z. The secondary features of a primary relationship. Human Organization, 1965, 24, 116-123.

Lopez, C. Mon cher papa: Franklin and the ladies of Paris. New Haven, Conn.: Yale University Press, 1966.

Lord, E. E. Emergent Africa. In G. H. Seward & R. C. Williamson (eds.), Sex roles in changing society. New York: Random House, 1970. Pp. 44-66.

Lord, E. Queen of Sheba's heirs. Washington, D.C.: Acropolis Books, 1970.

de Lorris, G., & de Meun, J. The romance of the rose. New York: E. P. Dutton, 1962.

Lovemore, A. A letter from a father to a son on his marriage. London: E. & C. Dilly, 1778.

Löwenstern, I. A savant from Austria. In O. Handlin (ed.), This was America. Cambridge, Mass.: Harvard University Press, 1949. Pp. 179-185.

Lowie, R. H. Social organization. New York: Rinehart, 1948.

Lowrie, S. H. Dating theories and student responses. American Sociological Review, 1951, 16, 334-340.

Luckey, E. B. Marital satisfaction and congruent self-spouse concepts. Social Forces, 1960, 39, 153-157.

Luckey, E. B. Marital satisfaction and its association with congruence of perception. Marriage and Family Living, 1960, 22, 49-54.

Luckey, E. B. Numbers of years married as related to personality perception and marital satisfaction. *Journal of Marriage and the Family*, 1966, *28*, 44-48.

Luckey, E. B., & Nass, G. D. A comparison of sexual attitudes and behavior in an international sample. *Journal of Marriage and the Family*, 1970, *31*, 364-379.

Lucretius. *On the nature of things*. Chicago: Encyclopedia Britannica, 1952.

Ludovici, A. M. *Lysistrata, or woman's future and future woman*. New York: E. P. Dutton, 1925.

Lundberg, F., & Farnham, M. F. *Modern woman: The lost sex*. New York: Grosset & Dunlap, 1947.

Luther, M. *The table talk of Martin Luther*. London: George Bell & Sons, 1890.

Luther, M. *Works of Martin Luther*. Philadelphia: Muhlenberg Press, 1943, Vol. 2.

Luther, M. *Letters of spiritual counsel*. Philadelphia: Westminster Press, 1955.

Luther, M. *The sermon on the mount*. Philadelphia: Concordia, 1956.

Luther, M. *Sermons*. Philadelphia: Muhlenberg Press, 1959.

Luther, M. *The Christian in society II*. Philadelphia: Muhlenberg Press, 1962.

Luther, M. *The Christian in society I*. Philadelphia: Fortress Press, 1966.

Luther, M. *The Christian in society III*. Philadelphia: Fortress Press, 1966.

Luther, M. *Church and ministry*. Philadelphia: Fortress Press, 1966.

Lutyens, M. *Effie in Venice*. London: John Murray, 1965.

Lynd, R. S. Ideology and the Soviet family. *American Slavic and East European Review*, 1950, *9*, 268-278.

Lynd, R. S. & Lynd H. M. *Middletown*. New York: Harcourt, Brace, 1929.

Lyness, J. L., Davis, K. E., & Lipetz, M. E. Living together: An alternative to marriage. Unpublished manuscript, University of Colorado, 1971.

Lystad, R. A. *The Ashanti: A proud people*. New Brunswick, N.J.: Rutgers University Press, 1958.

McCabe, J. How Christianity has treated women. In S. D. Schmalhausen & V. F. Calverton (eds.), *Woman's coming of age*. New York: Horace Liverwright, 1931. Pp. 49-68.

McCall, A. B. The tower room. *Women's Home Companion*, September 1911, *38*, 24.

McCall, M. M. Courtship as social exchange: Some historical comparisons. In B. Farber (ed.), *Kinship and family organization*. New York: Wiley, 1966. Pp. 190-200.

McDougall, W. Marriage and the home. *The Forum*, 1928, *80*, 11-14.

Mace, D. *Does sex morality matter?* London: Rich & Cowan, 1943.

Mace, D. *Hebrew marriage*. New York: Philosophical Library, 1953.

Mace, D. The employed mother in the U.S.S.R. *Marriage and Family Living*, 1961, *23*, 330-333.

Mace, D., & Mace, V. *Marriage east and west*. New York: Doubleday, 1960.

Mace, D., & Mace, V. *The Soviet family*. Garden City, N.Y.: Doubleday, 1963.

Macfadden, B. *Marriage a lifelong honeymoon*. New York: Physical Culture Publishing Co., 1903.

McGregor, O. R. *Divorce in England: A centenary study*. London: Heinemann, 1957.

Macklin, E. D. Heterosexual cohabitation among unmarried college students. *The Family Coordinator,* 1972, *21,* 463-472.

Macklin, E. D., Jennis, W., & Meyer, D. Preliminary survey of study on heterosexual cohabitation among unmarried college students. Cornell University, 1972. Unpublished manuscript, College of Human Ecology, Cornell University, Ithaca, N.Y.

McLennan, J. F. *Studies in ancient history.* New York: Macmillan, 1896.

Madan, M. *Thelyphthora; or, a treatise on female ruin.* London: J. Dodsley, 1781.

maids complaint against the batchelors: Or an Easter-offering for young men and apprentices, The. London: J. Coniers, 1675.

Maine, H. J. S. *Ancient law.* London: Murray, 1861.

Mair, L. P. *An African people in the twentieth century.* New York: Russell & Russell, 1965.

Makletsov, A. V. Marriage and the family in Soviet Russia. *East Europe and Contemporary Russia,* 1939, *3,* 79-102.

Malthus, T. R. *An essay on the principle of population; or a view of its past and present effects on human happiness.* London: J. Johnson, 1803.

Manuel, D. F. *The government of a wife.* London: Jacob Tonson, 1697.

Manuel, F. E. *The prophets of Paris.* Cambridge, Mass.: Harvard University Press, 1962.

Maquet, J. J. *The premise of inequality in Ruanda.* London: Oxford University Press, 1961.

Maranell, G. M., Dodder, R. A., & Mitchell, D. F. Social class and premarital sexual permissiveness: a subsequent test. *Journal of Marriage and the Family,* 1970, *32,* 85-88.

Marcus, S. *The other Victorians.* New York: Basic Books, 1966.

Marcuse, J. The love affair of Comrade Wang. *New York Times Magazine,* November 8, 1964, 40-47.

Margolis, H. F., & Rubenstein, P. M. *The groupsex tapes.* New York: McKay, 1971.

Marriage in Japan takes a new tack. *New York Times,* October 22, 1970, 40.

Marriage, is it a failure? *The Spectator,* 1888, *61,* 1219-1220.

Marriage versus celibacy. *Belgravia,* 1868, *6,* 290-297.

Married College Man, A. The dislike to be waited on. *The Independent* 1909, *67,* 1301-1302.

Married Teacher, A. Should the married woman teach? *The Independent,* 1909, *67,* 361-364.

Marris, P. Individual achievement and family ties: Some international comparisons. *Journal of Marriage and the Family,* 1967, *29,* 763-772.

Marry early, down with bachelors. *The Current Digest of the Soviet Press,* 1971, *23*(15), 35-37.

Martineau, H. *Society in America.* New York: Saunders & Otley, 1837. Vol. 2.

Martines, L. *The social world of the Florentine humanists, 1390-1460.* Princeton, N.J.: Princeton University Press, 1963.

Marx, K., & Engels, F. *Manifesto of the Communist Party.* Chicago: Encyclopedia Britannica, 1952.

Massarik, F. "Saying what you feel": Reflections on personal openness in Japan. *International Understanding,* 1964-1965, *3*(1), 26-33.

Masters, W. H., & Johnson, V. E. *Human sexual response.* Boston: Little, Brown, 1966.

Masters, W. H., & Johnson, V. E. *Human sexual inadequacy.* Boston: Little, Brown, 1970.

Masuoka, E. C., Masuoka, J., & Kawamura, N. Role conflicts in the modern Japanese family. *Social Forces,* 1962, *41,* 1-6.

Mather, C. *Diary of Cotton Mather (1681-1708).* Boston: The Massachusetts Historical Society, 1912. Collections, seventh series, vol. 8.

The Matrimonial Magazine, or *Monthly Anecdotes of Love and Marriage for the Court, the City, and the Country.* Vol. 1. London: W. Nicoll, 1775.

Maurer, R. Recent trends in the Soviet family. *American Sociological Review,* 1944, *9,* 242-249.

May, G. *Social control of sex expression.* New York: William Morrow, 1931.

Mead, M. *Male and female.* New York: William Morrow, 1949.

Mead, M. Marriage in two steps. *Redbook,* July 1966, 48 ff.

Mead, M. A continuing dialogue on marriage: Why just living together won't work. *Redbook,* April 1968, 44 ff.

Meader, W. G. *Courtship in Shakespeare.* New York: King's Crown Press, 1954.

Mehnert, K. *Peking and Moscow.* New York: G. P. Putnam's Sons, 1963.

Mencken, H. L. *In defense of women.* New York: Philip Goodman, 1918.

Merydew, J. T. (ed.). *Love letters of famous men and women.* London: Remington, 1888.

Methodius. *The symposium and a treatise on chastity.* Westminster, Md.: Newman Press, 1958.

Michel, A., & Texier, G. *La condition de la française d'aujourd'hui.* Paris: Editions Gautier, 1964. Vol. 2.

Michelet, M. J. *Love.* New York: Carleton, 1863.

Middendorp, C. P., Brinkman, W., & Koomen, W. Determinants of premarital sexual permissiveness: a secondary analysis. *Journal of Marriage and the Family,* 1970, *32,* 369-379.

Middleton, R. Brother-sister and father-daughter marriage in ancient Egypt. *American Sociological Review,* 1962, *27,* 603-611.

Middleton, R., & Putney, S. Dominance in decisions in the family, race and class differences. *The American Journal of Sociology,* 1960, *65,* 605-609.

Middletown, J. *The Lugbara of Uganda.* New York: Holt, Rinehart & Winston, 1965.

Mielziner, M. *The Jewish law of marriage and divorce in ancient and modern times.* New York: Bloch, 1901.

Mill, J. S. *The subjection of women.* London: J. M. Dent, 1929.

Milton, J. *Paradise Lost.* Chicago: Encyclopedia Britannica, 1952.

Milton, J. *Complete prose works of John Milton.* New Haven, Conn.: Yale University Press, 1959. Vol. 2.

Miner, H. *The primitive city of Timbuctoo.* Princeton, N.J.: Princeton University Press, 1953.

Mironenko, Y. The evolution of Soviet family law. *Institute for the Study of the U.S.S.R.,* 1966, *13,* 33-40.

Mitchell, H. E. Social class and race as factors affecting the role of the family in thematic apperception test stories of males. Unpublished doctoral dissertation, University of Pennsylvania, 1950.

Mitchell, J. C. Marriage, matriliny, and social structure among the Yao of Southern Nyasaland. In J. Mogey (ed.), *Family and Marriage.* Leiden: E. J. Brill, 1963.

Montaigne, M. E. *The essays.* Chicago: Encyclopedia Britannica, 1952.

de Montesquieu, C. *The spirit of laws.* Chicago: Encyclopedia Britannica, 1952.

Moore, B. Thoughts on the future of the family. In M. R. Stein, A. J. Vidich, & D. M. White (eds.), *Identity and anxiety.* Glencoe, Ill.: Free Press, 1960. Pp. 391-401.

Moore, F. F. *"I forbid the banns!"* New York: Cassell, 1893.

Moralli-Daninos, A. *Histoire des relations sexuelles.* Paris: Presses Universitaires de France, 1963.

More, T. Utopia. In *Famous utopias.* New York: Tudor, 1901. Pp. 129-232.

Moreau de Saint-Méry, M. L. E. The bitter thoughts of President Moreau. In O. Handlin (ed.), *This was America.* Cambridge, Mass.: Harvard University Press, 1949. Pp. 88-103.

Morgan, E. *The descent of woman.* New York: Stein & Day, 1972.

Morgan, E. S. *The Puritan family.* Boston: Public Library, 1944.

Morgan, L. H. *Ancient society, or researches in the lives of human progress from savagery, through barbarism to civilization.* New York: Holt, 1877.

Morgenstern, J. *Rites of birth, marriage, death and kindred occasions among the Semites.* Chicago: Quadrangle Books, 1966.

Morioka, K. Changing patterns of mate selection as revealed by the two-generation research design. *Sociological Abstracts,* 1970, *18,* 834.

Morris, D. *The naked ape.* London: Corgi Books, 1968.

Morris, D. *The human zoo.* New York: Dell, 1971.

Mosely, P. E. The Russian family: Old style and new. In R. N. Anshen (ed.), *The family: Its function and destiny.* New York: Harper, 1959. Pp. 104-122.

Moynihan, D. P. *The Negro family. The case for national action.* Washington, D.C.: U.S. Department of Labor, 1965.

Mrs. Sato holds mirror to Japan. *New York Times,* January 1, 1969, 8.

Muirhead, J. *Historical introduction to the private law of Rome.* London: A. & C. Black, Ltd., 1916.

Mullahy, P. *Oedipus myth and complex.* New York: Hermitage, 1948.

Müller-Lyer, F. *The family.* New York: Alfred A. Knopf, 1931.

Münsterberg, H. *The Americans.* New York: McClure, Philips, 1904.

Murdock, G. P. *Social structure.* New York: Macmillan, 1949.

Murstein, B. I. The complementary need hypothesis in newlyweds and middle-aged married couples. *Journal of Abnormal and Social Psychology,* 1961, *63,* 194-197.

Murstein, B. I. Empirical tests of role, complementary needs, and homogamy theories of marital choice. *Journal of Marriage and the Family,* 1967, *29,* 689-696.

Murstein, B. I. Psychological determinants of marital choice. Progress Report, National Institute of Mental Health, Number 08-405-01, 1965.

Murstein, B. I. The relationship of mental health to marital choice and courtship progress. *Journal of Marriage and the Family,* 1967, *29,* 447-451.

Murstein, B. I. Marriage-role expectations of college men and women. Unpublished paper, Connecticut College, 1968.

Murstein, B. I. The sexual image in marriage throughout history. In C. Presvelou & P. de Bie (eds.), *Images and counter-images of young families*. Leuven, Belgium: International Scientific Commission on the Family, 1970. Pp. 121-132.

Murstein, B. I. Stimulus-value-role: A theory of marital choice. *Journal of Marriage and the Family*, 1970, *32*, 465-481.

Murstein, B. I. Self ideal–self discrepancy and marital choice. *Journal of Consulting and Clinical Psychology*, 1971, *37*, 47-52.

Murstein, B. I. What makes a person sexually appealing? *Sexual Behavior*, 1971, *1* (April), 75.

Murstein, B. I. Interview behavior, projective techniques, and questionnaires in the clinical assessment of marital choice. *Journal of Personality Assessment*, 1972, *36*, 462-467.

Murstein, B. I. Physical attractiveness and marital choice. *Journal of Personality and Social Psychology*, 1972, *22*, 8-12.

Murstein, B. I. Sex-drive, person perception, and marital choice. *Archives of Sexual Behavior* (in press).

Murstein, B. I. & Glaudin, V. The use of the MMPI in the determination of marital maladjustment. *Journal of Marriage and the Family*, 1968, *30*, 651-655.

Murstein, B. I., & Pryer, R. S. The concept of projection: A review. *Psychological Bulletin*, 1959, *56*, 353-374.

Murstein, B. I., & Roth, R. D. Stimulus-value-role theory, exchange theory, and marital choice. Unpublished paper, Connecticut College, 1972.

My secret life. 2 vols. New York: Grove Press, 1966.

National views on marriage. *The Saturday Review of Politics, Literature, Science and Art*, 1900, *89*, 133-134.

Neff, W. F. Through the eyes of Victorian reformers. In B. J. Stern (ed.), *The family, past and present*. New York: Appleton-Century, 1938. Pp. 162-175.

Nemy, E. Group sex: Is it "life art" or a sign that something is wrong? *New York Times*, May 10, 1971, 38.

Neubeck, G., & Schletzer, V. M. A study of extramarital relationships. *Journal of Marriage and the Family*, 1962, *24*, 279-281.

Newlyweds, young couples. *The Current Digest of the Soviet Press*, 1971, *23*(43), 17, 39.

Newman, F. X. (ed.). *The meaning of courtly love*. Albany, N.Y.: State University of New York Press, 1968.

Nichols, T. L. *Marriage*. Cincinnati, Ohio: V. Nicholson & Co., 1854.

Nimkoff, M. F. The future of the family. In M. F. Nimkoff (ed.), *Comparative family systems*. Boston: Houghton Mifflin, 1965. Pp. 357-369.

Noble, L. G. Free marriage. *Scribner's Monthly*, 1873, *6*, 658-664.

Nordhoff, C. *The communistic societies of the United States*. New York: Harper, 1875.

Novak, J. Sex, marriage, and divorce in Russia. *Saturday Evening Post*, May 14, 1960, *232*(42), 90-92.

Noyes, J. H. *History of American socialisms*. New York: Hillary House, 1961.

Noyes, H. H., & Noyes, G. W. The Oneida community experiment in stirpiculture. *Eugenics, genetics and the family*. Vol. 1: *Scientific papers of the Second International Congress of Eugenics.* Baltimore: Williams & Wilkins, 1923. Pp. 374-386.

Noyes, P. *My father's house.* New York: Farrar & Rinehart, 1937.

Nye, F. I. Child adjustment in broken and in unhappy homes. *Marriage and Family Living,* 1957, *19,* 356-361.

Ogburn, W. F. The changing functions of the family. In R. F. Winch, R. McGinnis, & H. R. Barringer (eds.), *Selected studies in marriage and the family.* New York: Holt, Rinehart & Winston, 1962. Pp. 157-163.

O'Hare, K. R. *The sorrows of Cupid.* St. Louis: The National Rip-Saw Publishing Co., 1912.

Olson, L. *Dimensions of Japan.* New York: American Universities Field Staff, Inc., 1963.

Olusanya, P. O. A note on some factors affecting the stability of marriage among the Yoruba of Western Nigeria. *Journal of Marriage and the Family,* 1970, *32,* 150-155.

Omari, T. P. Changing attitudes of students in West African society towards marriage and family relationships. *British Journal of Sociology,* 1960, *11,* 197-210.

Omari, T. P. *Marriage guidance for young Ghanaians.* London: Nelson & Sons, 1962.

Omari, T. P. Role expectation in the courtship situation in Ghana. *Social Forces,* 1963, *42,* 147-156.

O'Neill, G. C., & O'Neill, N. Patterns in group sexual activity. *Journal of Sex Research,* 1970, *6,* 101-112.

O'Neill, N., & O'Neill, G. *Open marriage: A new life style for couples.* New York: Evans, 1972.

O'Neill, W. L. *Divorce in the progressive era.* New Haven, Conn.: Yale University Press, 1967.

Only nine? *Marriage and Family Living,* 1956, *18,* 113.

original family law of the Russian Soviet republic, The. In R. A. H. Schlesinger (ed.), *Changing attitudes in Soviet Russia. The family in the U.S.S.R. Documents and readings.* London: Routledge & Kegan Paul, 1949. Pp. 33-44.

Ortega y Gassett, J. *On love.* New York: Meridian, 1957.

Orwell, G. *1984.* New York: Harcourt, Brace, 1949.

Osgood, C. E. Cross-cultural comparability in attitude measurement via multilingual semantic differentials. In M. Fishbein (ed.), *Readings in attitude theory and measurement.* New York: Wiley, 1967. Pp. 108-116.

Osmond, M. Toward monogamy: A cross-cultural study of correlates of type of marriage. *Social Forces,* 1965, *44,* 8-16.

Otite, O. Processes of family formation among the Urhobo of midwestern Nigeria. *International Journal of Sociology of the Family,* 1971, *1,* 125-136.

Ovid. *The art of love.* (Trans. C. D. Young.) New York: Horace Liverwright, 1931.

Owen, R. *The marriage system of the new moral world; with the faint outline of the present very irrational system, as developed in a course of ten lectures.* Leeds: J. Hobson, 1839.

Packard, V. *The sexual wilderness.* New York: David McKay, 1968.

Paine, T. *The writings of Tom Paine.* New York: G. P. Putnam's Sons, 1894. Vol. 1.

Painter, S. *French chivalry.* Ithaca, N.Y.: Great Seal Books, 1957.

Palson, C. Swingers and non-swingers: Conceptions of sex. *Sociological Abstracts,* 1970, *18,* 971.

Palson, C., & Palson, R. Swinging in wedlock. *Society,* 1972, *9,* 28-37.

Paris, G. Etudes sur les romans de la Table Ronde. Lancelot du Lac II. *Le Conte de la Charette. Romania,* 1883, *12,* 459-534.

Parker, R. A. *A Yankee saint.* New York: G. P. Putnam's Sons, 1935.

Parsons, T. The social structure of the family. In R. N. Anshen (ed.), *The family: Its function and destiny.* New York: Harper, 1959. Pp. 241-274.

Parsons, T. The incest taboo in relation to social structure. In R. L. Coser (ed.), *The family: Its structure and functions.* New York: St. Martin's Press, 1964. Pp. 48-70.

Parsons, T., & Bales, R. F. *Family, socialization, and interaction process.* Glencoe, Ill.: The Free Press, 1955.

Pasquier, N. Recommendations paternelles à une jeune mariée. In A. Cherel (ed.), *La famille française.* Paris: Editions Spes, 1924. Vol. 2, pp. 17-19.

Patai, R. *Sex and family in the Bible and the Middle-East.* New York: Doubleday, 1959.

Patmore, C. *Poems.* London: G. Bell & Sons, 1928.

Patmore, D. *The life and times of Coventry Patmore.* New York: Oxford University Press, 1949.

Patten, S. N. The laws of social attraction. *Popular Science Monthly,* 1908, *73,* 354-360.

Pavlova, M. Woman's lot, man's responsibility. *The Current Digest of the Soviet Press,* 1971, *23*(43), 16-17.

Pawel, E. Sex under socialism. *Commentary,* 1965, *40,* 90-95.

Pearsall, R. *The worm in the bud.* London: Macmillan, 1969.

Pellarin, C. *Lettre de Fourier au grand juge.* Paris: Dentu, Galerie D'Orleans, 1874.

Pelzel, J. Japanese kinship: A comparison. In M. Freedman (ed.), *Family and kinship in Chinese society.* Stanford, Calif.: Stanford University Press, 1970. Pp. 227-248.

Pepys, S. *The diary of Samuel Pepys.* 18 vols. New York: Macmillan, 1896.

Pepys, S. *The diary of Samuel Pepys.* 2 vols. London: I. M. Dent & Co., 1906.

Petot, P. La famille en France sous l'ancien régime. In *Sociologie comparée de la famille contemporaine.* Paris: Editions du Centre National de la Recherche Scientifique, 1955. Pp. 9-14.

Pettigrew, T. F. *A profile of the Negro-American.* Princeton, N.J.: Van Nostrand, 1964.

Pfister, G. F. Marriage among the central Basukuma. *Anthropological Quarterly,* 1962, *35,* 134-142.

Philips, A. (ed.). *Survey of African marriage and family life.* London: Oxford University Press, 1953.

Phyz, H. To the proprietors of the *American Magazine. American Magazine,* 1757, *1,* 126-128.

Pike, E. R. *Love in ancient Rome.* London: Frederick Muller, 1965.

Pike, R. Husbands and wives. *Cosmopolitan,* 1902, *32,* 611-615.

Pineo, P. Disenchantment in the later years of marriage. *Marriage and Family Living,* 1961, *23,* 3-11.

Piozzi, H. L. A letter to a young gentleman on his marriage. In *A series of letters on courtship and marriage.* Hartford: Lincoln & Gleason, 1806. Pp. 109-115.

Pitts, J. The hippies as contrameritocracy. *Dissent,* 1969, *16,* 326-337.

Pitts, J. The counter culture: Tranquilizer or revolutionary ideology? *Dissent,* 1971, *18,* 216-229.

plan to encourage large families, A. *The Current Digest of the Soviet Press* 1970, *22*(50), 24.

Plato, The dialogues of Plato (trans. B. Jowett & J. Harward.) In *Plato.* Chicago: Encyclopedia Britannica, 1952.

Plato, Lysis, or friendship. (trans. B. Jowett.) In *Plato.* Chicago: Encyclopedia Britannica, 1952. Pp. 14-25.

pleasures of a single life, or the miseries of matrimony, The. London: J. Nutt, 1701.

Plutarch. Life stories of men who shaped history. In *Plutarch's Lives of the noble Grecians and Romans.* New York: Mentor Books. (The New American Library), 1954.

Pollock, F., & Maitland, F. W. *The history of English law before the time of Edward I.* Cambridge: Cambridge University Press, 1911.

Polygamy backed at Africa parley. *New York Times,* August 3, 1969, 19.

Pond, D. A., Ryle, A., & Hamilton, M. Marriage and neurosis in a working-class population. *British Journal of Psychiatry,* 1963, *109,* 592-598.

Poulson, Z., Jr. *An essay on marriage, or the lawfulness of divorce in certain cases considered.* Philadelphia: Z. Poulson, Jr., 1788.

Powell, C. L. *English domestic relations 1487-1653.* New York: Columbia University Press, 1917.

Powell, C. L. Marriage in early New England. *New England Quarterly,* 1928, *1* 323-324.

Power, E. *Medieval people.* London: Methuen & Co., 1939.

Pravda says no to marriage bureaus. *The Current Digest of the Soviet Press,* 1971, *23*(24), 10.

Preston, A. The ideals of the bride to be. *Ladies' Home Journal,* March 1905, *22,* 26.

Preston, A. A girl's preparation for marriage. *Ladies' Home Journal,* March 1908, *25,* 22.

Preston, A. What a girl should expect of marriage. *Ladies' Home Journal,* April 1908, *25,* 30.

Price, T. African marriage. In J. K. Hadden & M. L. Borgatta (eds.), *Marriage and the family.* Itasca, Ill.: Peacock, 1969. Pp. 101-113.

Pringle, H. F. What the men of America think about women. *Ladies' Home Journal,* April 1939, *56,* 14 ff.

Proctor, S. D. Stability of the black family and the black community. In *Families of the future.* Ames, Iowa: Iowa State University Press, 1972. Pp. 104-115.

Project, A. To the proprietors of *American Magazine. American Magazine,* 1757, *1,* 125-126.

Pulszky, F. A., & Pulszky, T. The friends of Kossuth. In O. Handlin (ed.), *This was America.* Cambridge, Mass.: Harvard University Press, 1949. Pp. 232-252.

Putnam, S. The psychopathology of prostitution. In S. D. Schmalhausen & V. F. Calverton (eds.), *Woman's coming of age.* New York: Horace Liverwright, 1931. Pp. 310-339.

Quaesita, A. S. The unattractiveness of American men. *The Independent,* 1909, *67,* 1065-1067.

Queen, S. A., Habenstein, R. W., & Adams, J. B. *The family in various cultures.* Philadelphia: Lippincott, 1961.

Rabelais, F. *Gargantua and Pantagruel.* Chicago: Encyclopedia Britannica, 1952.

Rainwater, L. *And the poor get children.* Chicago: Quadrangle Books, 1960.

Rainwater, L. Some aspects of lower class sexual behavior. *The Journal of Social Issues,* 1966, *22,* 96-108.

Rainwater, L. Crucible of identity: The Negro lower-class family. In M. Barash & A. Scourby (eds.), *Marriage and the family.* New York: Random House, 1970. Pp. 215-260.

Rainwater, L., Coleman, R. P., & Handel, G. *Workingman's wife.* New York: Oceana Publications, 1959.

Ramey, J. W. Emerging patterns of behavior in marriage: Deviations or innovations? *The Journal of Sex Research,* 1972, *8,* 6-30.

Ramey, J. W. Emerging patterns of innovative behavior in marriage. *The Family Coordinator,* 1972, *29,* 435-456.

Reader, D. H. *Zulu tribe in transition.* Manchester: Manchester University Press, 1966.

Records of the governor and company of the Massachusetts Bay in New England. Vol. 1: *1628-1641.* Boston: William White, 1853.

Reiss, I. L. Toward a sociology of the heterosexual love relationship. *Marriage and Family Living,* 1960, *22,* 139-145.

Reiss, I. L. *Premarital sexual standards in America.* New York: The Free Press, 1964.

Reiss, I. L. *The social context of premarital sexual permissiveness.* New York: Holt, Rinehart & Winston, 1967.

Rensberger, B. Homosexuality linked to hormone level. *New York Times,* November 18, 1971, 30.

Rettig, S., & Pasamanick, B. Changes in moral values as a function of adult socialization. *Social Problems,* 1959, *7,* 117-125.

Rettig, S., & Pasamanick, B. Changes in moral values over three decades, 1929-1959. *Social Problems,* 1959, *6,* 320-328.

Revised principles of marriage and family legislation. *The Current Digest of the Soviet Press,* 1968, *20*(39), 14-19.

Riasanovsky, N. V. *The teaching of Charles Fourier.* Berkeley, Calif.: University of California Press, 1969.

Richardson, S. *Pamela.* 4 vols. London: William Heinemann, 1902.

Riegel, R. F. *American feminists.* Lawrence, Kan.: University of Kansas Press, 1963.

Rigby, P. *Cattle and kinship among the Gogo.* Ithaca, N.Y.: Cornell University Press, 1969.

Rimmer, R. H. *The Harrad experiment.* New York: Bantam, 1966.

Rimmer, R. H. *Proposition 31.* New York: New American Library, 1969.

Robertson, C. N. (ed.). *Oneida community: An autobiography, 1851-1876.* Syracuse, N.Y.: Syracuse University Press, 1970.

Rockwood, L. D., & Ford, M. E. N. *Youth, marriage and parenthood.* New York: Wiley, 1945.

Rodman, H. Talcott Parson's view of the changing American family. In H. Rodman (ed.), *Marriage, family, and society.* New York: Random House, 1965. Pp. 262-286.

Roe, A. Women and work. *Science,* 1966, *153,* 965-966.

Rogers, A. A. Why American marriages fail. *Atlantic Monthly,* 1907, *100,* 289-298.

Rogers, C. Interpersonal relationships: U.S.A. 2000. *Journal of Applied Behavioral Science,* 1968, *4,* 265-280.

Rogers, E. M., & Havens, A. E. Prestige rating and mate selection on a college campus. *Marriage and Family Living,* 1960, *22,* 55-59.

Rollins, B. C., & Feldman, H. Marital satisfaction over the family life cycle. *Journal of Marriage and the Family,* 1970, *32,* 20-28.

Roman marriage. In *Encyclopedia Britannica.* Chicago: Encyclopedia Britannica, 1964.

Rosenberg, M. *Eleanor of Aquitaine.* Boston: Houghton Mifflin, 1937.

Rosenthal, J. T. Marriage and the blood feud in "heroic" Europe. *British Journal of Sociology,* 1966, *17,* 133-144.

Ross, E. A. Sociological observations in inner China. *American Journal of Sociology,* 1910, *16,* 721-733.

Rossi, A. S. Women in science: Why so few? *Science,* 1965, *148,* 1196-1202.

de Rougemont, D. *Love in the Western world.* New York: Pantheon, 1956.

de Rougemont, D. The crisis of the modern couple. In R. N. Anshen (ed.), *The family: Its function and destiny.* New York: Harper, 1959. Pp. 449-462.

Rousseau, J. J. *The confessions.* London: William Glaisher, 1883.

Rousseau, J. J. *Emile,* London: J. M. Dent & Sons, 1957.

Rover, C. *Love, morals, and the feminists.* London: Routledge & Kegan Paul, 1970.

Roy, R., & Roy, D. Is monogamy outdated? *The Humanist,* 1970, *30,* 19-26.

Rubin, Z. Measurement of romantic love. *Journal of Personality and Social Psychology,* 1970, *16,* 265-273.

Ruchames, L. Race, marriage and abolition in Massachusetts. *The Journal of Negro History,* 1955, *40,* 250-273.

Ruskin, J. Letter XX (Rose gardens). In his *Complete works.* London: George Allen, 1905. Vol. 17, pp. 417-422.

Ruskin, J. Of Queen's gardens. In his *Complete works.* London: George Allen, 1905. Vol. 18, pp. 109-144.

Russia. *Time Magazine,* June 29, 1970, 23.

Russian proverbs. Mount Vernon, N.Y.: Peter Pauper Press, 1960.

Russell, B. *Marriage and morals.* New York: Bantam, 1963.

Ryan, W. Savage discovery—the Moynihan report. In R. Staples (ed.), *The black family.* Belmont, Calif., Wadsworth, 1971. Pp. 58-65.

S. L. E. Hints for young women, particularly those newly married. *The Pennsylvania Evening Herald,* June 8, 1785, No. 39.

Sacks, E. *The terrible siren.* New York: Harper, 1928.

de Sales, St. Francis. Avis pour les gens mariés. In A. Cherel (ed.), *La famille française.* Paris: Editions Spes, 1924. Vol. 2, pp. 20-36.

Saltus, E. *Historia amoris.* New York: Brentano's, 1906.

Sand, G. Letter to Alfred de Musset. In I. Schneider (ed.), *The world of love.* New York: George Braziller, 1964. Vol. 2, pp. 499-502.

Sandomirsky, V. Sex in the Soviet Union. *Russian Review,* 1951, *10,* 199-209.

Sanghui, L. Inbreeding in India. *Eugenics Quarterly,* 1966, *13,* 291-301.

Savage, H. (ed.). *The love letters of Henry VIII.* London: Allan Wingate, 1949.

Scanzoni, J. H. *The black family in modern society.* Boston: Allyn & Bacon, 1971.

Schapera, I. Bushmen hunters in the Kalahari Desert of Africa. In B. J. Stern (ed.), *The family, past and present.* New York: Appleton-Century, 1938. Pp. 27-30.

Schapera, I. *Married life in an African tribe.* New York: Sheridan House, 1941.

Scherer, W. *A history of German literature.* Oxford: Oxford University Press, 1886. Vol. 1.

Schlesinger, A., Jr. An informal history of love, U.S.A. *Saturday Evening Post,* December 31, 1966, 30-37.

Schlesinger, R. A. H. (ed.). *Changing attitudes in Soviet Russia. The family in the U.S.S.R. Documents and readings.* London: Routledge & Kegan Paul, 1949.

Schmalhausen, S. D. The war of the sexes. In S. D. Schmalhausen & V. F. Calverton (eds.), *Woman's coming of age.* New York: Horace Liverwright, 1931. Pp. 260-297.

Schmidt, G., & Sigusch, V. Sex differences in reactions to pictorial and narrative stimuli of sexual content. Paper read at the Fourth Meeting, Czecho-Slovakian Sex Research Association, Prague, June 8-9, 1972.

Schmidt, J. J. Die Huweliksluiting onder die Bantoe in die stedelike Woongebied binne die Munisipaliteit van Klerksdorpd (Marriage customs among the Bantu in the housing project in the municipality of Klerksdorp). *Sociological Abstracts,* 1963, *11,* 753.

Schopenhauer, A. Of women. In I. Schneider (ed.), *The world of love.* New York: George Braziller, 1964. Vol. 2, pp. 224-235.

Schull, W. J., & Neel, J. V. *The effects of inbreeding on Japanese children.* New York: Harper & Row, 1965.

Schulz, D. A. The role of the boyfriend in lower-class Negro life. In C. V. Willie (ed.), *The family life of black people.* Columbus, Ohio: Bobbs-Merrill, 1970. Pp. 231-243.

Schupp, C. E. An analysis of some social-psychological factors which operate in the functioning relationship of married couples who exchange mates for the purpose of sexual experience. *Dissertation Abstracts International,* November 1970, *31*(5-A), 2524.

Scott, J. F. Sororities and the husband game. *Trans-action,* 1965, *2,* 10-14.

Selehen, H. Soviet family life. *Ukrainian Quarterly,* 1949, *5,* 340-346.

Seltman, C. *Women in antiquity.* London: Thames & Hudson, 1956.

series of letters on courtship and marriage, A. Springfield, Mass.: C. Davis, 179?.

de Sévigné, M. R. *Letters of Madame de* Sévigné. 2 vols. New York: Brentano's, 1927.

Sewall, S. *Sewall papers.* Boston: Massachusetts Historical Society, 1882. Vol. 3.

Shakespeare, W. *The plays and sonnets of William Shakespeare.* 2 vols. Chicago: Encyclopedia Britannica, 1952.

Seward, R. The Colonial family in America: Toward a socio-historical restoration of its structure. *Journal of Marriage and the Family,* 1973, *35,* 58-70.

Shaw, G. B. *Collected letters of Bernard Shaw 1874-1907.* (Ed. D. H. Lawrence.) New York: Dodd, Mead, 1965.

Shelley, P. B. *Complete poetical works.* London: Oxford University Press, 1917.

Shuttleworth, F. K. A biosocial and developmental theory of male and female sexuality. *Marriage and Family Living,* 1959, *21,* 163-174.

Sigusch, V., Schmidt, G., Reinfeld, A., & Wiedemann-Sutor, I. Psychosexual stimulation: Sex differences. *Journal of Sex Research,* 1970, *6,* 10-24.

Sinclair, A. *The emancipation of the American woman.* New York: Harper & Row, 1966.

Singleton, C. S. *An essay on the Vita Nuova.* Cambridge, Mass.: Harvard University Press, 1949.

Singleton, C. S. Dante: Within courtly love and beyond. In F. X. Newman (ed.), *The meaning of courtly love.* Albany, N.Y.: State University of New York Press, 1968. Pp. 43-54.

Sir George Campbell on scientific marriage-making. *The Spectator,* 1886, *59,* 1206-1207.

Skinner, B. F. *Walden two.* New York: Macmillan, 1966.

Slater, M. K. Ecological factors in the origin of incest. *American Anthropologist,* 1959, *61,* 1042-1059.

S. L. E. Hints for young women, particularly those newly married. *Pennsylvania Evening Herald,* Wednesday, June 8, 1785. No. 39.

Slotkin, J. S. On a possible lack of incest regulations in old Iran. *American Anthropologist,* 1947, *49,* 612-615.

Smith, C. E. *Papal enforcement of some medieval marriage laws.* Baton Rouge, La.: Louisiana State University Press, 1940.

Smith, J. R., & Smith, L. G. Co-marital sex and the sexual freedom movement. *Journal of Sex Research,* 1970, *6,* 131-142.

Smith, L. B. *A Tudor tragedy.* London: Jonathan Cape, 1961.

Smith, R. Hebrew, Greco-Roman, and early Christian family patterns. In H. Becker & R. Hill (eds.), *Marriage and the family.* Boston: Heath, 1942. Pp. 59-71.

Smith, W. *Dictionary of Greek and Roman antiquities.* New York: Harper, 1873.

Smith, W. N., Jr. Rating and dating: A restudy. *Marriage and Family Living,* 1952, *14,* 312-317.

Social implications of industrialization and urbanization in Africa south of the Sahara. Lousanne, Switzerland: UNESCO, 1956.

Society and marriage. *The Nation,* 1870, *10,* 332-333.

Sofue, T. Some questions about Hsu's hypothesis: Seen through Japanese data. In F. L. K. Hsu (ed.), *Kinship and culture.* Chicago: Aldine, 1971. Pp. 284-287.

Sonnenschein, D. The ethnography of male homosexual relations. *Journal of Sex Research,* 1968, *4,* 69-83.

Sorensen, R. H. *Adolescent sexuality in contemporary America.* New York: World, 1973.

Sorokin, P. A. *Social and cultural dynamics.* Vol. 4: *Basic problems, principles and methods.* New York: American Book Co., 1941.

Sorokin, P. A. The depth of the crisis: American sex morality today. *Christianity Today,* July 4, 1960, 811-813.

Southall, A. (ed.), *Social change in modern Africa.* London: Oxford University Press, 1961.

Soviet population expert deplores the rising divorce rate. *New York Times,* September 7, 1969, 16.

Spanier, G. B., & Cole, C. L. Mate swapping: Participation, knowledge, and values in a midwestern community. Paper presented at Midwest Sociological Society, Kansas City, Mo., 1972.

Spencer, H. *Principles of sociology.* New York: D. Appleton & Co., 1912.

Spinoza, B. de *Ethics.* Chicago: Encyclopedia Britannica, 1952.

Spruill, J. C. *Women's life and work in the southern colonies.* Chapel Hill, N.C.: University of North Carolina Press, 1938.

Stafford, P. *Sexual behavior in the communist world.* New York: The Julian Press, 1967.

Stanley, H. M. Artificial selection and the marriage problem. *The Monist,* 1891, *2,* 51-55.

Statistical abstract of the United States 1971. Washington, D.C.: U.S. Bureau of the Census, 1971.

Stefaniszyn, B. *Social and ritual life of the Ambo of Northern Rhodesia.* London: Oxford University Press, 1964.

Steiner, K. The revision of the civil code of Japan: Provisions affecting the family. *Far Eastern Quarterly,* 1949, *9,* 169-184.

Stenhouse, F. *Exposé of polygamy in Utah: A lady's life among the Mormons.* New York: American News Co., 1872.

Stenton, D. M. *The English woman in history.* London: Unwin Bros., Ltd., 1957.

Stephens, W. N. *The family in cross-cultural perspective.* New York: Holt, Rinehart & Winston, 1963.

Stern, B. J. The changing status of women. In B. J. Stern (ed.), *The family, past and present.* New York: Appleton-Century, 1938. Pp. 178-185.

Stevens, E. Love and marriage—Soviet style. *New York Times Magazine,* April 26, 1964, 16 ff.

Steyn, A. F., & Rip, C. M. The changing urban Bantu family. *Journal of Marriage and the Family,* 1968, *30* 499-517.

Stinnett, N., Collins, J., & Montgomery, J. E. Marital need satisfaction of older husbands and wives. *Journal of Marriage and the Family,* 1970, *32,* 428-434.

Stone, L. Marriage among the English nobility. In R. L. Coser (ed.), *The family: its structure and functions.* New York: St. Martin's Press, 1964. Pp. 153-183.

Stone, L. *The crisis of the aristocracy (1558-1641).* London: Oxford University Press, 1965.

Stopes, M. C. *Married love.* New York: G. P. Putnam's Sons, 1931.

Strauss, M. A. The influence of sex of child and social class on instrumental and expressive family roles in a laboratory setting. *Sociology and Social Research*, 1967, *52*, 7-21.

strike of a sex, The. *The Independent*, 1909, *67*, 1323-1325.

Strong, A. L. We Soviet wives. *American Mercury*, 1934, *32*, 415-423.

suppressed book about slavery, The. New York: Carleton, 1864.

Sussman, M. B. The isolated nuclear family: Fact or fiction? *Social Problems*, 1959, *6*, 333-340.

Sutton, L., & Leshem, A. A comparative study of premarital dating behavior. Unpublished manuscript, Connecticut College, 1970.

Sverdlov, G. M. Changes in family relations in the U.S.S.R. *Transactions of the Third World Congress of Sociology*, 1956, *4*, 50-59.

Svetlov, V. Explanations of the new family policy by Soviet theorists (excerpts from *Socialist society and the family*). In R. A. H. Schlesinger (ed.), *Changing attitudes in Soviet Russia. The family in the U.S.S.R. Documents and readings.* London: Routledge & Kegan Paul, 1949. Pp. 315-342.

Swedenborg, E. *Conjugial love.* New York: Swedenborg Foundation, 1954.

Swift, J. *Gulliver's travels.* Chicago: Encyclopedia Britannica, 1952.

Swift, J. A letter to a very young lady on her marriage. In I. Schneider (ed.), *The world of love.* 2 vols. New York: George Braziller, 1964. Pp. 447-454.

Symonds, C. A pilot study of the peripheral behavior of sexual mate swappers. Unpublished master's thesis, University of California, Riverside, 1967.

Tacitus, P. C. *The annals and the histories.* Chicago: Encyclopedia Britannica, 1952.

Taeuber, I. *The population of Japan.* Princeton, N.J.: Princeton University Press, 1958.

Tanaka, K., & Sugiyama, S. Power structure of family members in urban areas of Japan. *International Understanding*, 1964-1965, *2*(1), 23-25.

Taylor, G. R. *The angel-makers.* London: Heinemann, 1958.

Technical report of the Commission on Obscenity and Pornography. Erotica and social behavior. Washington, D.C.: U.S. Government Printing Office, 1971. Vol. 8.

Tennyson, A. *Idylls of the king.* Boston: Houghton Mifflin, 1929.

Terman, L. M. *Psychological factors in marital happiness.* New York: McGraw-Hill, 1938.

Terman, L. M. Correlates of orgasm adequacy in a group of 556 women. *The Journal of Social Psychology*, 1951, *32*, 115-172.

Tertullian. *Treatises on marriage and remarriage.* Westminster, Md.: Newman Press, 1951.

Tharp, R. C. Psychological patterning in marriage. *Psychological Bulletin*, 1963, *60*, 97-117.

Theodorson, G. A. Change and traditionalism in the American family. *Journal of Social Research*, 1960, *1*, 17-28.

Theodorson, G. A. Romanticism and motivation to marry in the United States, Singapore, Burma, and India. *Social Forces*, 1965, *43*, 17-27.

Thibaut, J. W., & Kelley, H. H. *The social psychology of groups.* New York: Wiley, 1959.

Thieme, H. P. *Women of modern France.* Philadelphia: The Rittenhouse Press, 1908.

Thomas, W. I. The older and newer ideals of marriage. *The American Magazine,* 1909, *67,* 548-552.
Thomason, B. Marital sexual behaviour and total marital adjustment: A research report. In J. Himelhoch & S. F. Fava (eds.), *Sexual behavior in American society.* New York: Norton, 1955. Pp. 153-163.
Thompson, C. J. S. *Love, marriage, and romance in old London.* London: Heath, Cranton, 1936.
Thompson, F. M. Spring days in Paris. *Harper's Bazaar,* 1905, *39,* 610-612.
Thomson, P. *The Victorian heroine.* London: Oxford University Press, 1956.
Thorpe, B. (ed.), *Ancient laws and institutes of England.* 2 vols. London: G. E. Eyre & A. Spottiswoode, 1840.
Thucydides. *The history of the Peloponnesian War.* Chicago: William Benton, 1952.
Thurston, H. Mediaeval matrimony. *Dublin Review,* 1922, *171,* 44-57.
Thwing, C. W. The American family. *Living Age,* 1911, *270,* 451-458.
Timasheff, N. S. The attempt to abolish the family. In N. W. Bell & E. F. Vogel (eds.), *A modern introduction to the family.* Glencoe, Ill.: The Free Press, 1960. Pp. 55-63.
Toffler, A. *Future shock.* New York: Random House, 1970.
Tolstoy, L. *War and Peace.* Chicago: Encyclopedia Britannica, 1952.
de Toqueville, A. *Democracy in America.* New York: Alfred A. Knopf, 1945, Vol. 2.
Tortora, V. R. *The Amish folk of Pennsylvania Dutch country.* Lancaster, Pa.: Photo Arts Press, 1958.
Tout, T. F. Woman's place in the later medieval household. In B. J. Stern (ed.), *The Family: past and present.* New York: Appleton-Century, 1938. Pp. 122-127.
Trobisch, W. Attitudes of some African youth toward sex and marriage. *Practical Anthropology,* 1962, *9,* 9-14.
Trollope, F. *Domestic manners of the Americans.* New York: Alfred A. Knopf, 1949.
Troyat, H. *Tolstoy.* Garden City, N.Y.: Doubleday, 1967.
de Troyes, C. *Arthurian romances.* London: J. M. Dent & Sons, 1951.
Trumbull, J. H. (ed.), *Public records of the colony of Connecticut.* Hartford, Conn.: Brown & Parsons, 1850.
Turner, E. S. *A history of courting.* London: Michael Joseph, 1954.
Twain, M. *Roughing it.* New York: Harper & Bros., 1913.
Two hundred million Americans. Washington, D.C.: U.S. Government Printing Office, 1967.
Uchendu, V. *The Igbo of southeast Nigeria.* New York: Holt, Rinehart & Winston, 1965.
Unwilling Celibate, An. Why do not educated women marry? *The Independent,* 1909, *67,* 966-969.
Unwin, J. D. *Sex and culture.* London: Oxford University Press, 1934.
Uxorius. *Hymen.* London: I Pottinger, 1760.
Valency, M. *In praise of love.* New York: Macmillan, 1958.
Vanbrugh, J. *The provok'd wife.* London: Lawrence & Bullen, 1893.
van den Haag, E. Love or marriage? *Harper's Magazine,* May 1962, *224,* 43-47.
Van Doren, C. *Benjamin Franklin.* New York: Viking Press, 1938.

Vital statistics of the United States, 1964. Vol. 3: *Marriage and divorce.* Washington, D.C.: U.S. Department of Health, Education & Welfare, 1968.

Vogel, E. F. The go-between in a developing society: The case of the Japanese marriage arranger. *Human Organization,* 1961, *20,* 112-120.

Vogel, E. F. *Japan's new middle class: The salary man and his family in a Tokyo suburb.* Berkeley, Calif.: University of California Press, 1963.

Vogel, E. F. The Japanese family. In M. F. Nimkoff (ed.), *Comparative family systems.* Boston: Houghton Mifflin, 1965. Pp. 287-300.

Waehler, J. P. Neues sowjetisches Familienrecht. *Zeitschrift für das gesamte Familienrecht,* 1968, *11,* 557-564.

Wagatsuma, H., & De Vos, G. Attitudes towards arranged marriage in rural Japan. *Human Organization,* 1962, *21,* 187-200.

Wallace, I. *The twenty-seventh wife.* New York: Simon & Schuster, 1961.

Waller, W. The rating and dating complex. *American Sociological Review,* 1937, *2,* 727-734.

Waller, W., & Hill, R. *The family: a dynamic interpretation.* New York: Dryden, 1951.

Wallin, P. A study of orgasm as a condition of women's enjoyment of intercourse. *The Journal of Social Psychology,* 1960, *51,* 191-198.

Wallin, P., & Clark, A. L. Religiosity, sexual gratification, and marital satisfaction in the middle years of marriage. *Social Forces,* 1964, *42,* 303-309.

Waln, N. *The house of exile.* Boston: Little, Brown, 1933.

Walshe, M. O'C. *Medieval German literature.* Cambridge, Mass.: Harvard University Press, 1962.

Ward, E. *Comforts of matrimony, or love's last shift.* London: Fielding & Walker, 1780.

Ward, L. F. Our better halves. *The Forum,* 1888, *6,* 266-275.

Ward, L. F. Genius and woman's intuition. *The Forum,* 1890, *9,* 401-408.

Ward, L. F. *Pure sociology.* New York: Macmillan, 1916.

Wasserman, H. L. The absent father in Negro families: Cause or symptom? In C. V. Willie (ed.), *The family life of black people.* Columbus, Ohio: Bobbs-Merrill, 1970. Pp. 294-298.

Watkins, O. D. *Holy matrimony.* London: Rivington, Percival & Co., 1895.

Watt, I. The new woman: Samuel Richardson's Pamela. In R. L. Coser (ed.), *The family: its structure and functions.* New York: St. Martin's Press, 1964. Pp. 267-289.

Weakland, J. H. Conflicts between love and family relationships in Chinese films. Technical Report No. 2; Office of Naval Research, Contract No. N 00014-66-CO310, NR 170-703.

Webber, E. *Escape to Utopia: The communal movements in America.* New York: Hastings House, 1959.

Webster, J. B. Attitudes and policies of the Yoruba African churches towards polygamy. In C. G. Baeta (ed.), *Christianity in tropical Africa.* London: Oxford University Press, 1969. Pp. 224-248.

Weems, M. L. *Hymen's recruiting-sergeant; or the new matrimonial tat-too for old bachelors.* Hartford: Andrus & Judd, 1833.

Weigand, H. J. *Courtly love in Arthurian France and Germany.* New York: AMS Press, 1966.

Weininger, O. *Sex and character.* New York: Putnam's, 1906.

Weiss, R. S. Forms of sexual relationships: Going together, living together, and marriage. Paper presented at American Sociological Association Convention, New Orleans, 1972.

Weiss, R. S., & Samuelson, N. M. Social roles of American women: Their contribution to a sense of usefulness and importance. *Marriage and Family,* 1958, *20,* 358-366.

Wells, K. G. Why more girls do not marry. *The North American Review,* 1891, *152,* 175-181.

Wells, S. R. *Wedlock; or the right relations of the sexes.* New York: Samuel R. Wells, 1869.

Welter, B. The cult of true womanhood. *American Quarterly,* 1966, *18,* 151-174.

Werner, M. R. *Brigham Young.* New York: Harcourt, Brace & Co., 1925.

Westbrook, R. B. *Marriage and divorce.* Philadelphia: Lippincott, 1883.

Westermarck, E. *The history of human marriage.* 3 vols. London: Macmillan, 1921.

Westermarck, E. *The future of marriage in western civilization.* New York: Macmillan, 1936.

Wharton, A. H. *Colonial days and dames.* Philadelphia: J. B. Lippincott, 1895.

Wharton, E. *The custom of the country.* New York: C. Scribner's Sons, 1913.

Wharton, E. *The age of innocence.* New York: Grosset & Dunlap, 1920.

What is it that men look for? *Ladies' Home Journal,* July 1914, *31,* 4.

Whately, W. *A bride-bush: Or a wedding sermon.* London: William Iaggard for Nicholas Bourne, 1617.

White, E. M. *Woman in world history: her place in the great religions.* London: H. Jenkins, 1924.

White, W. C. Moscow morals. *Scribner's Magazine,* 1930, *88,* 277-289.

Why is single life becoming more general? *The Nation,* 1868, *6,* 190-191.

Wiegall, A. *Sappho of Lesbos: her life and times.* New York: Frederick A. Stokes, 1932.

Wilde, O. The importance of being Ernest. In M. J. Moses (ed.), *Representative British dramas.* Boston: Little, Brown, 1939. Pp. 393-427.

Wilhelm, R. The Chinese conception of marriage. In H. Keyserling (ed.), *The book of marriage.* New York: Harcourt, Brace & Co., 1926. Pp. 123-137.

Wilkinson, T. O. Family structure and industrialization in Japan. *American Sociological Review,* 1962, 27, 678-682.

Williams, M. B. Henry Fieldings's attitudes toward marriage. Unpublished doctoral dissertation, University of Alabama, 1963. In *Dissertational Abstracts,* 1964, *24,* 4204.

Williamson, K. Changes in the marriage system of the Okrika Ijo. *Africa,* 1962, *32,* 53-60.

Willie, C. V., & Weinandy, J. The structure and composition of "problem" and "stable" families in a low-income population. *Marriage and Family Living,* 1963, *25,* 439-446.

Wilson, M. *Rituals of kinship among the Nyakyusa.* London: Oxford University Press, 1957.

Wimberly, H. Self-realization and the ancestors: An analysis of two Japanese ritual procedures for achieving domestic harmony. *Anthropological Quarterly,* 1969, *42,* 38-51.

Winch, R. F. *Mate selection.* New York: Harper, 1958.

Winick, C. The beige epoch: Depolarization of sex roles in America. *The Annals of the American Academy of Political and Social Science,* 1968, *376,* 18-24.

Winston, H. Influence of genotype and infantile trauma on adult learning in the mouse. *Journal of Comparative and Physiological Psychology,* 1963, *56,* 630-635.

Winston, H. Heterosis and learning in the mouse. *Journal of Comparative and Physiological Psychology,* 1964, *57,* 279-283.

Winthrop papers. Boston: The Massachusetts Historical Society, 1889. Collections, sixth series, vol. 3.

Witherspoon, J. Necessity of equality in rank and age in the matrimonial union. In *Domestic happiness portrayed.* New York: C. Spaulding, 1831. Pp. 384-388.

Witherspoon, J. Letters on marriage: Letter 1. In B. Franklin (ed.), *Letters on courtship and marriage.* Trenton, N.J.: Daniel Fenton & James J. Wilson, 1813. Pp. 99-158.

Wolf, A. P. Childhood association, sexual attraction, and the incest taboo: A Chinese case. *American Anthropologist,* 1966, *68,* 883-898.

Wolffson, S. Explanation of the new family policy by Soviet theorists. (Extract from *Socialism and the family.*) In R. A. H. Schlesinger (ed.), *Changing attitudes in Soviet Russia. The family in the U.S.S.R. Documents and readings.* London: Routledge & Kegan Paul, 1949. Pp. 280-315.

Wollstonecraft, M. *The rights of women.* London: J. M. Dent, 1929.

Woodward, H. B. *The bold women.* New York: Farrar, Straus & Young, 1953.

Wortis, J. *Fragments of an analysis with Freud.* New York: Charter Books— Bobbs-Merrill, 1963; Simon and Schuster, 1954.

Wright, G. F. *Charles Grandison Finney.* Boston: Houghton Mifflin, 1891.

Wright, T. (ed.). *Political poems and songs relating to English history, composed during the period from the accession of Edward III to that of Richard III.* London: Longman, Green, Longman & Roberts, 1859-1861. Vol. 1, pp. 263, 266.

Wright, T. *Womankind in Western Europe.* London: Groombridge & Sons, 1869.

Wundt, W. *Elements of folk psychology: Outlines of a psychological history of the development of mankind.* London: Allen, 1916.

Wylie, P. *Generation of vipers.* New York: Farrar & Rinehart, 1942. (Now published by Holt, Rinehart and Winston, Inc.)

Xenophon. *Symposium.* London: W. Heinemann, 1922.

Xenophon. *Memorabilia and oeconomicus.* Cambridge, Mass.: Harvard University Press, 1938.

Yamane, T., & Nonoyama, H. Isolation of the nuclear family and kinship organization in Japan: A hypothetical approach to the relationships between the family and society. *Journal of Marriage and the Family,* 1967, *29,* 783-796.

Yang, C. K. *The Chinese family in the communist revolution.* Cambridge, Mass.: Massachusetts Institute of Technology Press, 1959.

Young, A. E. W. *Wife No. 19.* Hartford, Conn.: Dustin, Gilman & Co., 1875.

Young, B. Plurality of wives—the free agency of man. *Journal of Discourses,* 1856, *3,* 264-268.

Young, B. Source of true happiness—prayers, etc. *Journal of Discourses,* 1859, *6,* 39-47.

Young, B. The gifts of God—home manufactures—word of wisdom—happiness. *Journal of Discourses,* 1862, *9,* 31-40.

Young, B. Extract from a sermon delivered by Brigham Young. *Mormon Expositor,* 1875, *1,* n.p.

Young, B. *Discourses of Brigham Young.* Salt Lake City, Utah: Deseret Book Co., 1925.

Young, F. H. *The philosophy of Henry James, Sr.* New York: Bookman Associates, 1951.

Young, K. *Isn't one wife enough?* New York: Holt, 1954.

Zamiatin, E. *We.* New York: E. P. Dutton, 1952.

Zetkin, K. Excerpts from *Reminiscences of Lenin.* In R. A. H. Schlesinger (ed.), *Changing attitudes in Soviet Russia. The family in the U.S.S.R. Documents and readings.* London: Routledge & Kegan Paul, 1949. Pp. 74-79.

Zimmerman, C. C. *Family and civilization.* New York: Harper, 1947.

Zimmerman, C. C. *The family of tomorrow.* New York: Harper, 1947.

Zimmerman, C. C. The atomistic family—fact or fiction. *Journal of Comparative Family Studies,* 1970, *1,* 5-16.

Zimmerman, C. C. The future of the American family. I. The revolution. *International Journal of Sociology of the Family,* 1971, *1,* 1-9.

Zola, E. *Modern marriage.* New York: Benjamin R. Tucker, 1906.

Index

Credits